The Joan Palevsky  Imprint in Classical Literature

In honor of beloved Virgil—

"O degli altri poeti onore e lume . . ."

—Dante, *Inferno*

The publisher and the University of California Press Foundation
gratefully acknowledge the generous support of the
Joan Palevsky Imprint in Classical Literature.

City and Empire in the Age of the Successors

City and Empire in the Age of the Successors

Urbanization and Social Response in the Making of the Hellenistic Kingdoms

Ryan Boehm

UNIVERSITY OF CALIFORNIA PRESS

University of California Press, one of the most distinguished university presses in the United States, enriches lives around the world by advancing scholarship in the humanities, social sciences, and natural sciences. Its activities are supported by the UC Press Foundation and by philanthropic contributions from individuals and institutions. For more information, visit www.ucpress.edu.

University of California Press
Oakland, California

© 2018 by The Regents of the University of California

First Paperback Printing 2021

Library of Congress Cataloging-in-Publication Data

Names: Boehm, Ryan, author.
Title: City and empire in the age of the successors : urbanization and social
    response in the making of the Hellenistic kingdoms / Ryan Boehm.
 Description: Oakland, California : University of California Press, [2018] |
    Includes bibliographical references and index.
Identifier s: LCCN 2017038790 (print) | LCCN 2017041003 (ebook) |
    ISBN 9780520969223 () | ISBN 9780520296923 (cloth : alk. paper)| 9780520385719 (pbk. : alk. paper)
Subjects: LCSH: Greece—Civilization—To 146 B.C. | City-states—
    Greece—History.
Classification: LCC DF77 (ebook) | LCC DF77 .B639 2018 (print) |
    DDC938/.08—dc23
LC record available at https://lccn.loc.gov/2017038790

To my parents,
Harold and Elizabeth Boehm

CONTENTS

Acknowledgments ix
List of Abbreviations xi

Introduction 1

PART ONE. URBANIZATION AND THE IMPERIAL FRAMEWORK

1. Imperial Geographies: City, Settlement, and Ideology in the Formation of the Hellenistic Kingdoms 29

2. Urbanization and Economic Networks 89

PART TWO. CULT, POLIS, EMPIRE: THE RELIGIOUS AND SOCIAL DIMENSIONS OF SYNOIKISM

3. Civic Cults between Continuity and Change 143

4. Consensus, Community, and Discourses of Power 184

Conclusion 225

Bibliography 229
Subject Index 269
Index Locorum 285

ACKNOWLEDGMENTS

After many years of working on this project, I am greatly indebted to the many friends and colleagues who have been indispensible in bringing it to completion. This book has its origins in a University of California, Berkeley, PhD dissertation supervised by Emily Mackil. I am profoundly grateful for her intellectual guidance and friendship through the PhD and beyond. I could not have hoped for a more inspiring advisor. Erich Gruen, who first introduced me to the Hellenistic world and provided incisive commentary on the dissertation, has been an incomparable mentor and tireless advocate over the years. It is with great pleasure that I join generations of students in thanking him for the impact he has had on our lives and work. I learned a great deal about epigraphy from Nikolaos Papazarkadas, who also sat on my dissertation committee, and I have greatly benefited from his input and generosity. Mark Griffith served as an outside reader and contributed keen insights and his unrivaled knowledge of Greek. Thanks are also due to the community of faculty and students at Berkeley, from whom I have learned so much. I would like to acknowledge Dana DePietro, Nathan Arrington, Lisa Eberle, and Noah Kaye, who in particular has been a sounding board over the years on all things Hellenistic.

I am most grateful to my colleagues in the Department of Classical Studies at Tulane, which has been a stimulating and supportive environment for writing this book. In particular, Dennis Kehoe provided feedback, advice, and encouragement throughout this process. Michael Brumbaugh has been a constant interlocutor and thoughtful reader, who has sharpened my thinking on many points. Allison Emmerson read portions of the manuscript and offered valuable commentary and discussion. Liz Reyna provided unfailingly upbeat assistance on departmental matters.

Many other friends, colleagues, discussants, and readers along the way have contributed to the formulation of this book. In particular, Christof Schuler and Denver Graninger reviewed the manuscript for University of California Press and provided invaluable feedback, comments, and criticisms. I cannot thank them enough for their efforts, which have greatly improved the book. Audiences at the University of Chicago, Penn State, and the annual meeting of the American Schools of Oriental Research responded to early versions of some of the arguments in this book. I would especially like to thank Clifford Ando, Alain Bresson, and Gary Reger for their thought-provoking discussion.

The completion of this book would not have been possible without a research leave supported by the Tulane School of Liberal Arts and a Loeb Classical Library fellowship. Financial support has also come from a Lurcy grant from the Tulane School of Liberal Arts and from the Department of Classical Studies. Early research on this topic was funded by a grant from the Fulbright Foundation to study in Greece and the Aleshire Center for Greek Epigraphy at the University of California, Berkeley.

At UC Press, I am deeply indebted to my editor, Eric Schmidt, who has offered advice, guidance, and encouragement at every stage. I am most grateful to Juliana Froggatt, whose meticulous copyediting and acute queries have saved me from numerous errors and made this a much better book. Cindy Fulton shepherded the book through publication and patiently fielded all my questions. I could not have asked for a more diligent or helpful editorial team, and all of their work is greatly appreciated. Thanks are also due to Roberta Engleman for preparing the index. Elise Jakoby drafted the maps, and I am grateful for her assistance and expertise with GIS. Professor Alexandra Yerolympos generously granted me permission to reproduce an image in her collection on the cover of this book.

My family lent constant and vital encouragement along the way. I would like to thank my sister, Rebecca Carr (along with Daniel, Ian, Brendan, and Lucas), Robert and Peggy Wenning, Alecia and Bill Keen, and Darrell and Betty Bush. My parents, Harold and Elizabeth Boehm, have always supported my interests, academic and otherwise, and it is in appreciation for their love and guidance that I dedicate this book to them. Above all, my wife, Meghan Keen, has been present since the beginning of this project and been a constant source of reassurance and inspiration, and it is safe to say this book would not exist without her. For this, and much besides, I owe her a debt of gratitude I cannot hope to repay.

ABBREVIATIONS

For classical authors and works, the abbreviations used are those of The Oxford Classical Dictionary, *4th ed., edited by Simon Hornblower, Antony Spawforth, and Esther Eidinow (Oxford, 2012).*

ATL	B. D. Meritt, H. T. Wade-Gery, and M. F. MacGregor. *The Athenian Tribute Lists.* 4 vols. Cambridge, 1939–53.
BÉ	*Bulletin épigraphique.* Published annually in *Revue des études grecques.*
BMC Caria	B. Head. *A Catalogue of the Greek Coins in the British Museum: Catalogue of the Greek Coins of Caria, Cos, Rhodes, Etc.* London, 1897.
BNJ	I. Worthington, ed. *Brill's New Jacoby.* Leiden, 2006.
BNP	H. Cancik, H. Schneider, and C. F. Salazar, eds. *Brill's New Pauly: Encyclopaedia of the Ancient World.* 15 vols. Leiden, 2006.
Callim. F (Pfeiffer)	R. Pfeiffer, ed. *Callimachus.* 2 vols. Oxford, 1949–53.
CID	*Corpus des inscriptions de Delphes.* Paris, 1977–2002.
CGFPR	C. Austin. *Comicorum Graecorum fragmenta in papyris reperta.* Berlin, 1973.

Didyma II	A. Rehm. *Didyma*. Vol. 2, *Die Inschriften*. Berlin, 1958.
EKM I. *Beroia*	L. Gounaropoulou and M. B. Hatzopoulos. Ἐπιγραφές Κάτω Μακεδονίας, Τεύχος Α: Ἐπιγραφές Βέροιας. Athens, 1998.
FD	*Fouilles de Delphes*. Paris, 1902–2003.
FGrH	F. Jacoby. *Die Fragmente der griechischen Historiker*. Berlin, then Leiden, 1923–.
FHG	C. Müller. *Fragmenta Historicorum Graecorum*. 5 vols. Frankfurt, 1841–70.
Herakleides Pontikos (Wehrli)	F. Wehrli, ed. *Die Schule des Aristoteles*. Vol. 7, *Herakleides Pontikos*. 2nd ed. Basel, 1969.
I. Alexandreia Troas	M. Ricl. *The Inscriptions of Alexandreia Troas*. Bonn, 1997.
I. Assos	R. Merkelbach. *Die Inschriften von Assos*. Bonn, 1976.
IC	M. Guarducci. *Inscriptiones Creticae*. 4 vols. Rome, 1935–50.
ID	*Inscriptions de Délos*. 7 vols. Paris, 1926–72.
I. Ephesos	H. Wankel, ed. *Die Inschriften von Ephesos*. 8 vols. Bonn, 1979–84.
I. Erythrai	H. Engelmann and R. Merkelbach, eds. *Die Inschriften von Erythrai und Klazomenai*. 2 vols. Bonn, 1972–73.
IG	*Inscriptiones Graecae*. Berlin, 1873–.
IGLS IV	L. Jalabert, R. Mouterde, J.-P. Rey-Coquais, and C. Mondésert. *Inscriptions grecques et latines de la Syrie*. Vol. 4. Paris, 1955.
I. Iasos	W. Blümel. *Die Inschriften von Iasos*. 2 vols. Bonn, 1985.
I. Ilion	P. Frisch. *Die Inschriften von Ilion*. Bonn, 1975.
I. Kition	M. Yon, ed. *Kition-Bamboula V, Kition dans les textes: Testimonia littéraires et épigraphiques et Corpus des inscriptions*. Paris, 2004.
I. Laodikeia	T. Corsten. *Die Inschriften von Laodikeia am Lykos*. Vol. 1. Bonn, 1997.
I. Lindos	C. Blinkenberg. *Lindos: Fouilles et recherches*. Vol. 2, *Fouilles de l'acropole: Inscriptions*. Berlin, 1941.
I. Magnesia	O. Kern. *Die Inschriften von Magnesia am Maeander*. Berlin, 1900.

I. Mag. Sipylos	T. Ihnken. *Die Inschriften von Magnesia am Sipylos*. Bonn, 1978.
I. Mylasa	W. Blümel. *Die Inschriften von Mylasa*. 2 vols. Bonn, 1987–88.
IPArk.	G. Thür and H. Taeuber. *Prozessrechtliche Inschriften der griechischen Poleis: Arkadien*. Vienna, 1994.
I. Priene	F. Hiller von Gaertringen. *Inschriften von Priene*. Berlin, 1906.
I. Priene²	W. Blümel and R. Merkelbach, in collaboration with F. Rumscheid. *Die Inschriften von Priene*. 2 vols. Bonn, 2014.
Iscr. Cos	M. Segre. *Iscrizioni di Cos*. 2 vols. Rome, 1993.
ISE	L. Moretti. *Iscrizioni storiche ellenistiche*. 2 vols. Florence, 1967–75.
I. Smyrna	G. Petzl. *Die Inschriften von Smyrna*. 2 vols. Bonn 1982–90.
I. Stratonikeia	M. Şahin. *Die Inschriften von Stratonikeia*. Vols. 1–2. Bonn, 1981–90.
I. Tralleis	F. B. Poljakov. *Die Inschriften von Tralleis und Nysa*. Vol. 1, *Die Inschriften von Tralleis*. Bonn, 1989.
IvP	M. Fraenkel. *Die Inschriften von Pergamon*. 2 vols. Berlin, 1890–95.
LSJ⁹	H. G. Liddell, R. Scott, and H. Stuart Jones. *A Greek-English-Lexicon*. 9th ed., with a rev. supp. by P. G. W. Glare and A. A. Thompson. Oxford, 1996.
Milet I.2	C. Friedrich. "Die Inschriften." In H. Knackfuß, ed. *Milet I.2: Das Rathaus von Milet*. Berlin, 1908.
Milet I.3	G. Kawerau and A. Rehm. *Ergebnisse der Ausgrabungen und Untersuchungen seit dem Jahre 1899*. Vol. 3, *Das Delphinion in Milet*. Berlin, 1914.
ML	R. Meiggs and D. M. Lewis. *A Selection of Greek Historical Inscriptions to the End of the Fifth Century B.C.* Rev. ed. Oxford, 1988.
OGIS	W. Dittenberger. *Orientis Graeci inscriptiones selectae*. 2 vols. Leipzig, 1903–5.
PCG Kassel-Austin	R. Kassel and C. Austin, eds. *Poetae Comici Graeci*. 8 vols. Berlin, 1983–2001.

PF	R. Hallock. *Persepolis Fortification Tablets.* Chicago, 1969.
PSI	*Papiri greci e latini.* Florence, 1912–.
RC	C. B. Welles. *Royal Correspondence in the Hellenistic Period.* New Haven, 1934.
RO	P. J. Rhodes and R. Osborne. *Greek Historical Inscriptions, 404–323 BC.* Oxford, 2003.
Sardis	W. H. Buckler and M. Robinson. *Greek and Latin Inscriptions.* Leiden, 1932.
SEG	*Supplementum epigraphicum Graecum.* Leiden, then Amsterdam, then Leiden, 1923–.
SGO	R. Merkelbach and J. Stauber. *Steinepigramme aus dem griechischen Osten.* 5 vols. Munich, 1998–2004.
SNG Cop.	*Sylloge Nummorum Graecorum: The Royal Collection of Coins and Medals, Danish National Museum.* 8. vols. Copenhagen, 1942–79.
SNG von Aulock	*Sylloge Nummorum Graecorum Deutschland: Sammlung von Aulock.* Berlin, 1957–68.
SSI III	J. Gibson. *Textbook of Syrian Semitic Inscriptions.* Vol. 3, *Phoenician Inscriptions.* Oxford, 1982.
Staatsvert. III	H. Bengston and H. H. Schmitt. *Die Staatsverträge des Altertums.* Vol. 3, *Die Verträge der griechisch-römischen Welt von 338 bis 200 v.Chr.* Munich, 1969.
Syll.[3]	*Sylloge inscriptionum Graecarum.* 3rd ed. Leipzig, 1915–24.
TAM V	P. Herrmann. *Tituli Asiae Minoris.* Vol. 5, *Tituli Lydiae*, fasc. 2, *Regio septentrionalis ad Occidentem Vergens schedis ab Iosepho Keil elaboratis usus.* Vienna, 1989.
Tod	M. Tod. *A Selection of Greek Historical Inscriptions.* Vol. 2. Oxford, 1948.

Introduction

Sometime between 311 and 306 BCE, Antigonos the One-Eyed compelled the polis of Skepsis to join in the foundation of a new coastal metropolis, Antigoneia Troas, along with several other major cities of the region.¹ Situated in the rich agricultural basin of the Skamandros River, at the foot of Mount Ida in the interior of the central Troad, Skepsis was roughly sixty kilometers (thirty-seven miles) from the urban center of Antigoneia along modern routes. The city, which had identified as Ionian since its incorporation of settlers fleeing the destruction of Miletos in 494, unwillingly joined the union alongside its hated neighbor across the Skamandros, the Aiolian polis Kebren.² Antigonos's synoikism was designed to consolidate his hold on the region in the wake of the peace of 311, as the rival heirs of Alexander's empire took advantage of the cessation in hostilities to stabilize their emerging territorial kingdoms and prepare for the next round of conflict. The terms of this famous peace are most fully known from a fragmentary copy of a letter from Antigonos to Skepsis, in which he announces the settlement and professes to assent to the less palatable conditions of the agreement because he "was ambitious" (*philotimesthai*, l. 21) to secure the freedom and autonomy of the Greeks in his lifetime.³ The vaguely worded settlement was formalized through oaths requiring the Greek cities under Antigonos's control to abide by its terms. The letter

---

1. Strabo 13.1.52. For a full discussion of the synoikism, see ch. 1.
2. Political union (*sympoliteia*) with Milesian settlers: Strabo 13.1.52 (εἶτα Μιλήσιοι συνεπολιτεύθησαν αὐτοῖς καὶ δημοκρατικῶς ᾤκουν). Mutual antipathy between Kebren and Skepsis: Strabo 13.1.33. Aiolian identity of Kebren: Ephoros, *FGrH* 70 F10 (colony of Kyme); Ps.-Skylax 96.
3. *OGIS* 5 = *RC* 1.

carefully couches Antigonos's unilateral decision to agree to the treaty in the language of benefaction and agilely recasts this setback to his personal ambition (*philotimias*, l. 33) as a benevolent act of philhellenism.[4] The Skepsians responded, in a manner that would become so typical of the age, with a decree granting Antigonos cult in their city. They inscribed this decree prominently in the temple of Athena, asserting their important role in the economy of honors.[5] Antigonos's decision to incorporate the polis of Skepsis into his new port city in the Troad a short time later baldly contravened the terms of the peace and deprived the Skepsians of their autonomous existence, their corporate life, and even their name. In the aftermath of the next major conflict, the Battle of Ipsos in 301, however, the people of Skepsis managed to extricate themselves from the foundation by the permission of Lysimachos, the new master of the region, and they reconstituted their native city.[6]

Skepsis persisted as a discrete community into late antiquity, even as the new centers of the Troad surpassed it in prestige and importance. Antigoneia, refounded by Lysimachos as Alexandreia Troas, soon became a major commercial center on the coast. Ilion, reinforced with the populations of many of the small poleis and villages of the northern Troad and with its sanctuary of Athena expanded and embellished, became the major religious center and head of the regional federation (*koinon*) of the Troad. Yet the enduring civic pride and fierce particularism of Skepsis are amply manifest in the writings of the second-century antiquarian Demetrios of Skepsis, whose massive, thirty-book commentary on the catalog of the Trojans (*Iliad* 2.816–77) asserts the Homeric heritage of Skepsis and contests the claims of contemporary Ilians. The region of Skepsis, according to Demetrios, was the homeland of Dardanos, who founded Ilion, and the city itself was the royal residence of Aineias, whose descendants continued to be called "kings" of the polis even in Demetrios's time. He also denied the claims of the Ilians that their polis was the genuine site of ancient Troy. Demetrios intended his competing claim, part of both a wider discourse on Homeric heritage between the Ionian and Aiolian traditions and interpolis competition in the Troad, to undercut the cultural assertions of this "new" city of Ilion and to stake the cultural preeminence of Skepsis.[7]

---

4. For the nature of the "ambition" given up by Antigonos, see the comments of Welles (1934, 10) on *RC* 1, ll. 32–33. The reference is presumably to his desire to free the Greeks in the areas not under his control. This, of course, would have amounted to the elimination of Cassander and Ptolemy and the inheritance of the entire empire of Alexander.

5. *OGIS* 6.

6. Strabo 13.1.33, 13.1.52.

7. Strabo 13.1.26, 13.1.52. For the fragments of Demetrios's work see Gaede 1880. Notably, Hegesianax of Alexandreia Troas, a friend (*philos*) of Antiochos III, wrote a history of the Troad (*Trōika*) under the pseudonym Kephalon of Gergis (*FGrH* 45). The alias was perhaps intended to invest the work with the cultural authority of the people of Gergis, whom Herodotos (5.122.2) called "the remnant of the ancient Teucrians" (τοὺς ὑπολειφθέντας τῶν ἀρχαίων Τευκρῶν). On the competing Ionian

The case of Skepsis delineates a number of issues central to the confrontation between the Greek poleis and imperial authorities of the early Hellenistic period. Skepsis was one of dozens of polities reorganized and incorporated into larger urban structures by generals, kings, dynasts, and their agents, a phenomenon central to the formation of the Hellenistic states. The complexities of this procedure are amply attested by the relationship of Skepsis to the foundation of Antigoneia Troas: the interests of Antigonos in organizing the strategic and commercial basis of his power on the eve of his coronation; the scope of this unification, which incorporated a vast swath of the coastal and inland Troad; the unwillingness of (at least some of) its participants; the interpolis rivalry so typical of the fragmented political ecology of the Greek world; the barriers of geography and distance; the challenges of collapsing civic, religious, and ethnic identities; the issue of political autonomy; and the fragility and potential for dissolution of such unions. Critical dimensions of this encounter are also lost to us. No document as detailed as Antigonos's letter to Skepsis exists for the synoikism of Antigoneia Troas, leaving the nature of his directive and the method of its enforcement obscure. The intended effects on the pattern of settlement are undocumented: Were all the citizens of Skepsis to migrate to the new polis, or only a portion, or was the city left in place but subjected to a larger political entity? What was to be the fate of the cults of Skepsis? Would the elites of one polis be preeminent in the new city? How would the traditions of the Ionian and Aiolian cities be merged?[8] A host of other practical, economic, and social considerations critical to this process of integration are not directly attested.

By the early third century BCE, the political community of Skepsis had withstood many transformations typical of the world of the polis: a migration (*metoikisis*) of the site from the heights of Mount Ida (Palaiskepsis) down to the plain of the Skamandros;[9] refoundation and sympolity with Milesian colonists;[10] Persian

---

and Aiolian Homeric traditions and the Ionian claims to ancient Troy, see Nagy 2012, 147–217. On the Aineadai, who have often been seen as patrons of Homer, see Smith 1981, 34–43. A work of Hestiaia of Alexandreia (Troas?), cited by Demetrios of Skepsis, also discussed the location of Troy (Strabo 13.1.36).

8. In the period after Lysimachos's refoundation of the city, when Skepsis had withdrawn from the union, the preeminent role of Neandreia was particularly evident in the coinage of Alexandreia Troas, which directly imitated the emblems of its coinage: Apollo laureate on the obverse and a grazing horse on the reverse (Head 1911, 540–41; Meadows 2004). The city projected an Aiolian identity inherited from the main contributors to the synoikism. See, e.g., *FD* III 1.275, l. 1 (Αἰολεὺς ἀπὸ Ἀλεξανδ[ρείας - - -]); L. Robert 1936a, 28–31, no. 25. See also *SEG* XI 1054, l. 2 (ca. 165 BCE); Paus. 5.8.11, referring to Phaidimos, an Olympic victor of 200 BCE, as "Αἰολεὺς ἐκ πόλεως Τρῳάδος"; Helly 2006a, on a second-century decree of Larisa in Thessaly honoring two citizens of Alexandreia Troas and proclaiming the *syngeneia* of the two poleis.

9. Strabo 13.1.51.

10. See Judeich 1898 for fifth-century bronze issues of Skepsis with the legend ΣΚΑΨΙΟΝ ΝΕ(ΟΝ), possibly a reference to the refoundation of the city after the merger with Milesian colonists.

domination (when it was granted to Themistokles to furnish his bedding and clothes);[11] incorporation into a hegemonic alliance and empire (the Delian League); temporary evanescence through synoikism; and, ultimately, reemergence. The case of Skepsis draws out the complexity and resilience of the polis as a community of citizens and underscores the variety of responses to ecological, social, and imperial pressures. The coming of Macedonian domination and the emergence of the Hellenistic kingdoms brought new and profound transformations to the poleis of the Aegean world. This is particularly true of the period of intense conflict among the Successors, when the manipulations of Greek poleis like Skepsis, reorganized into larger urban agglomerations, came to play a conspicuous role in the formation of the Hellenistic states.

New and enduring cities rose from the unification of smaller poleis. But the success and frequency of this practice demand explanation. While some foundations subsequently contracted, as member communities broke away and reconstituted themselves, and still others failed entirely, the durability of the process of synoikism nevertheless stands out. Indeed, other synoikized communities expanded beyond their original conception, drawing in additional communities by the centripetal force of their success. The creation of new or drastically transformed poleis almost always built on existing communities,[12] and accordingly these cities are best understood as complex aggregates of citizen groups, cultic communities, discrete traditions, and competing interests. Viewed from this perspective, the motivations of the authorities that initiated such unions appear paradoxical. Why, given the propensity for resistance and the manifold challenges associated with overcoming the centrifugal tendencies of individual communities, would imperial authorities aspire to initiate such projects? Additionally, the consolidation of small, often weak and unwalled poleis invested them with great populations, resources, and defenses, and thus they became capable of offering resistance to the domination of the central authority. From an ideological standpoint, this policy had the added drawback of directly contradicting the rhetoric of freedom and autonomy for the Greek cities that became a cornerstone of the rivalry among the Successors, in a period when gaining the support of the Greek poleis was critical. Internally, the social stresses and competing interests intrinsic to these communities encouraged fragmentation. Yet in spite of these considerable obstacles, the process emerged as a major feature of Hellenistic rule in the first generation of kings and remained a defining phenomenon throughout the Hellenistic period.

These central issues—the relationship of urbanization to the organization of the Hellenistic states and the manner in which new communities emerged from such

11. Ath., *Deip.* 1.29f-30a.
12. See G. Cohen 1995, app., 5, for the very limited evidence for genuinely new foundations on previously uninhabited sites.

inorganic origins—are the subjects of this book. The delicate balance between centralized control and the maintenance of local autonomy is common to all imperial states. The ways that state power manifests itself in the lives of subjects, however, have often differed substantively, exposing key distinctions between imperial frameworks. In the core territories of the Aegean and western Asia Minor, areas dominated by highly organized but fragmented city-states, a conspicuous feature of the imperial policies of the Successors was the frequency of enforced synoikisms, from the merger of two independent city-states to large multipolis unions that encompassed vast territories. The result was the organization of many key regions around expanded urban centers, cities on a scale that outstripped the majority of the largest centers of the classical period, many of them, such as Ephesos or Demetrias, ringed with massive fortifications running distances as large as nine kilometers (5.6 miles), enclosing roughly 405 hectares (1,000 acres), and commanding extensive territories. Such cities became nodes anchoring further infrastructure—garrisons, ports, roads, customshouses—linking and interconnecting the vast regions that the new kingdoms aspired to embrace.

The manipulation and reorganization of communities played a central role in the structure, formation, and maintenance of the Hellenistic states, but local actors—both individuals and collectivities—reacted to, negotiated, and shaped this process in critical ways. The Hellenistic kingdoms subjected local communities to profound transformations, and in no instance is this more apparent than in the practice of synoikism. This book explores this phenomenon and argues that in such interventions, the scale and manner of the penetration of Hellenistic rule into the structure of communities, particularly Greek poleis, come into focus.[13] It reveals important dimensions of the imposition of empire at the local level, elucidates social reactions to this exercise of power, and helps to account for the durability of unions built on fragile foundations.

. . .

This book is composed of two parts, mirroring the two main questions of the study: what role did urbanization through synoikism have in structuring the imperial system of the early Hellenistic kings, and what impact did this have on the communities subjected to this process? In the first part, I examine the political, ideological, and economic interests of the Successors and how the resulting policies reshaped communities and regions under their rule. Chapter 1 presents a selective chronological narrative from 323 to circa 281, focusing on the ways in which state power became enmeshed with local communities. It documents the most important cases of synoikism and contextualizes and reconstructs the impact of synoikism on the

---

13. For a useful approach to the issue of sovereignty in the Hellenistic period as a multilayered and negotiated construct, see Davies 2002. For the economic dimensions, see Capdetrey 2006.

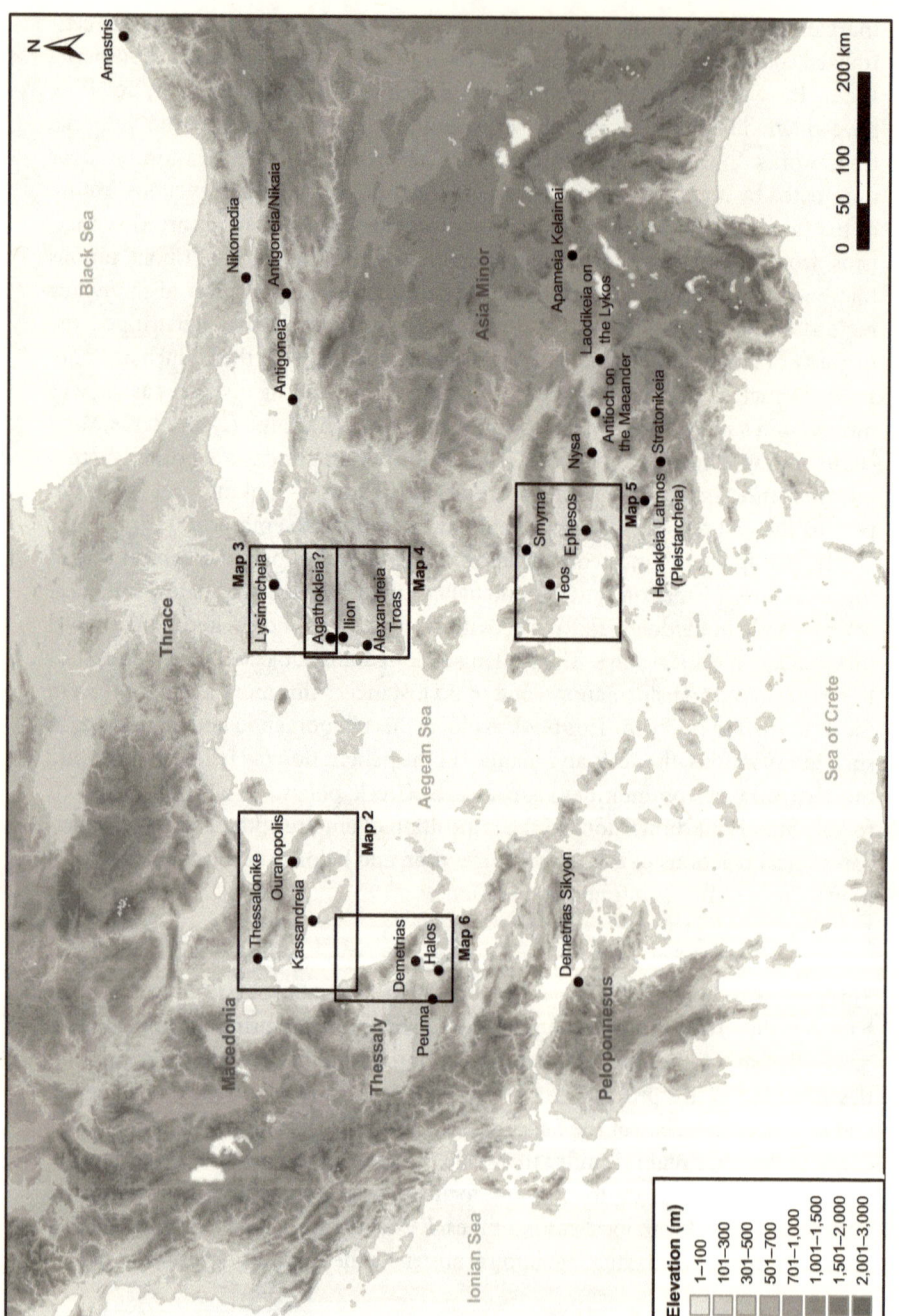

MAP 1. Regions and major sites discussed in the text.

settlement patterns and political structures of northern Greece and western Asia Minor. The focus on these regions seeks to elucidate the impact of urbanization on areas with strong polis traditions and to conceptualize the role of synoikism in structuring the early Hellenistic states (see map 1). Chronologically, this study is rooted in the early Hellenistic era, when much of the pattern of interaction between cities and the authorities of the emergent Hellenistic kingdoms developed, although it frequently ranges into later cases from the Hellenistic world and earlier instances of synoikism from the classical period. Likewise, the book follows a core set of cities (Kassandreia, Thessalonike, Herakleia Latmos, Lysimacheia, Alexandreia Troas, Ilion, Ephesos, Smyrna, and Demetrias), but the discussion is by no means limited to these sites. Chapter 2 explores the economic consequences of urbanization, examining how royal policies reshaped the productive landscape and how local communities responded to and participated in these transformations. After this largely macro-level focus on imperial structures, the second part systematically explores the internal life of the cities formed through synoikism and traces the ways in which communities negotiated the social stresses of this process to create functioning societies. Chapter 3 investigates religious activity and sites of cult and how the demographic, political, and physical ruptures of the period affected these fundamental expressions of communal self-representation and civic identity. The final chapter reconstructs the social and religious organization of the synoikized polis and the ways in which elites, communities, and the corporate body of the polis responded to the challenges of synoikism.

In the remainder of this introduction, I sketch the approach that this book adopts and the preliminary considerations that ground its investigation. First, I consider synoikism as a historical phenomenon and as a construct of modern historiography, clarifying the terminology used by ancient and modern sources and defining synoikism as a political, social, and demographic process. The importance of the Hellenistic practice, I suggest, is best understood in the wider context of the history of the eastern Mediterranean, and I analyze the ways in which centralization and state-sponsored urbanization in this period differed from previous exercises in imperial state formation. Turning to the social dimensions, the final sections explore synoikism as both a physical process and an ideological construct, exposing the problematic and contrasting impressions of synoikism provided by the literary, epigraphic, and archaeological evidence and orienting this book's interdisciplinary approach.

LANGUAGE AND PHENOMENON

This book focuses on a historical process with three main components: the emergence of new or greatly expanded urban centers populated by multiple communities (whether poleis or villages), resulting demographic and settlement shifts, and the role of outside powers (kings or dynasts) in initiating these unions. As is well known, the ancient sources, both literary and epigraphic, do not describe such political or demographic arrangements with consistency or precision.[14] In referring to the phenomenon, modern scholarship variously employs the terms *synoikismos* and *sympoliteia*, both of which the ancient sources use (though not exclusively), without consistency as to their distinction.

Synoikismos and the denominal verb *synoikizein*, literally meaning "founding/establishing a living space [for people] together," cover a wide semantic range. The original senses of these terms emphasize a physical living arrangement as well as agency. They can refer to the union of people either through wedlock or through a political arrangement. The most common, and probably the original, usage of *synoikizein* expresses the action of giving a woman to someone in marriage.[15] The verb form does not appear with a political meaning in prose before Thucydides, and in poetry its most common meaning is also that of marriage.[16] The noun *synoikismos* first appears epigraphically in the letters of Antigonos to Teos and Lebedos and in prose in Polybios.[17] Later authors commonly use both the noun and the verb in the sense of a political and physical merger of communities, but it should be stressed that they do not become technical terms. When used of cities, they can also simply mean to settle jointly, resettle, rebuild, reoccupy, or repopulate, but in each of these senses they envisage the union or reunion of people.[18] Authors also frequently employ closely related terms, such as *sympolizein*, "to unite in one city," underscoring the urbanistic dimensions of synoikism.[19] Similarly, the union of Euaimon and Orchomenos in the mid-fourth century is called *synoikia*, and Thucydides uses the noun *synoikisis* of the planned unification of Mytilene.[20] In these cases, the com-

---

14. Wörrle 2003b, 1373n49; Reger 2004, 148–49; Hansen and Nielsen 2004b; Parker 2009, 187–89; Walser 2009, 136–38; LaBuff 2016, 12–14. Compare the imprecision of our sources in describing federal structures: Mackil 2013, 4–6.

15. E.g., Hdt. 2.121.ζ.7: καὶ οἱ τὴν θυγατέρα ταύτην συνοικίσαι (and he gave his daughter to him in marriage). Used also in epigraphic documents, e.g., *I. Iasos* 4, ll. 23–25, a letter from Laodike III to Iasos ca. 196 setting up a fund for the dowries of the daughters of poor citizens and allotting money "to each of the women being married" (ἑκάσ|τηι τῶν συνοικιζομένων).

16. Cf. Pindar's description of Hegesias as the *synoikistēr* of Syracuse (*Ol.* 6, ll. 6–7), a usage derived from colonial *oikistēs/oikistēr* terminology. For the meaning of *synoikistēr*, see Foster 2013.

17. *RC* 3, ll. 79, 103; *RC* 4, l. 2; Polyb. 4.33.7 (of Messene and Megalopolis).

18. The rebuilding and repopulating of Lysimacheia after its destruction at the hands of the Thracians during the reign of Antiochos III is called a *synoikismos* (App., *Syr.* 1.4; cf. Polyb. 18.51.7–8). Similarly, in his letter to Sardeis in 213, following the siege of Achaios, Antiochos III refers to the provisioning of supplies for the rebuilding of the city as a synoikism (Gauthier 1989, 13, no. 1, l. 13). See also *BÉ* 71.251 (J. Robert and L. Robert).

19. Strabo 13.1.52: συνεπόλισε (of Skepsis). Cf. 8.3.2, where συνῳκίσθη (of Mantineia, Tegea, and Heraia) and συνεπολίσθη (of Aigion, Patrai, and Dyme) are used synonymously.

20. Euaimon and Orchomenos: *IPArk*. 15A1, ll. 2–6 (συϝοικία Εὐαι|μνίοις Ἐρχομι|νίοις ἐπὶ τοῖς ϝί|σοις καὶ τοῖς ὑμ|οίοις); see also Dušanić 1978. Mytilene: Thuc. 3.3.1.

pletion of the arrangement is emphasized over the process of foundation. Thucydides describes the synoikism of Olynthos with the verb *anoikizein*, denoting a specific geographical shift (inland), even through he uses *synoikizein* elsewhere.²¹ Alternatively, some sources refer to a synoikism elliptically, as in Herodotos's description of the foundation of Ekbatana or Strabo's account of Maussollos's refoundation of Halikarnassos.²² The phrase "to depopulate a city" (*tēn polin anastaton poiein*) is also commonly used to describe the effects on a polis of synoikism with a larger partner.²³ The term *metoikizein* (to settle [people] in another site) is another synonym for *synoikizein*, especially in cases where a city emerged on a previously uninhabited site.²⁴ This range of terminology shares a common emphasis on the site of inhabitation and the cohabitation of previously discrete population groups. Moreover, the transitive verb *synoikizen* describes agency (whether that of king, general, state, or community representatives) in effecting the union.

By contrast, *sympoliteia* and *sympoliteuein* are employed in a somewhat more restricted sense to describe a political arrangement of "shared citizenship."²⁵ These terms cover a variety of arrangements. They describe the political merger of autonomous communities into a single state—either multiple communities into a federal league²⁶ or two poleis into a single political community—and particularly the absorption of a lesser community by a greater one (so-called unequal sympolity).²⁷ These terms are also used in instances where two communities were merged by the impetus of an outside force, like the Karian towns Kildara and Thodasa, united by Antiochos III as he attempted to strengthen his position against Ptolemaic forces nearby, or Chalketor and another city, probably Iasos, united by

---

21. Olynthos: Thuc. 1.58.2; cf. Paus. 7.3.4: τῶν ἀνοικισθέντων (of the populations synoikized into Ephesos). For Thucydides's use of *synoikizein*, see Moggi 1975.

22. Ekbatana: Hdt. 1.98.3: ἠνάγκασε ἓν πόλισμα ποιήσασθαι καὶ τοῦτο περιστέλλοντας τῶν ἄλλων ἧσσον ἐπιμέλεσθαι (he compelled them to create one city and to protect it and care for the others less). Halikarnassos: Strabo 13.1.59, quoting Kallisthenes: εἰς μίαν τὴν Ἁλικαρνασσὸν συνήγαγεν (he gathered them together into a single city, Halikarnassos). Herodotos's language may reflect the fact that *synoikizein* and its cognates took on a political meaning only in the mid-fifth century, particularly in Athens, under the influence of the rhetoric surrounding the Theseus myth and the synoikism of Athens.

23. E.g., Paus. 7.3.5 (of Lebedos). For the meaning of the phrase, see Hansen and Nielsen 2004a, 123.

24. E.g., Diod. Sic. 13.75.1 (of Rhodes), 15.94.1 (of Megalopolis). See also Demand 1990, 8–9.

25. Schmitt 1994; Pascual 2007; Walser 2009.

26. For this, the so-called Bundesstaat type of *sympoliteia*, otherwise referred to as a *koinon* or *koinonia* in the sources, see Feldmann 1885; Giovannini 1971; Rzepka 2002.

27. E.g., the unions of Mylasa and Olymos (second century): *I. Mylasa* 861, ll. 3–4 ([μετὰ Μυλασέων συμ|πολι]τείαν); Miletos and Mylasa (209/8): *Milet* I.3, 146A, ll. 30–31 (ὁπόσοι δ᾽ ἂν αὐτῷ[ν] | αἱρῶνται μεθ᾽ ἡμῶν συμπολιτεύεσθαι); Miletos and Pidasa (183–164): *Milet* I.3, 149, l. 49 (εἰς τὴν συμπολιτείαν). Moggi (1976b, 65) speaks of this type of *sympoliteia* as a "simpolitia sinecistica." See also Musiolek 1981.

the same king.²⁸ These terms do not necessarily indicate that the communities were to remain physically distinct, that is, bound by a strictly political rather than a physical-political union: in the case of Euaimon and Orchomenos, the lesser party, Euaimon, persisted as a discrete settlement in some form and retained some limited local autonomy, even though the document describing the merger envisages some population movement to Orchomenos. Outside of a federal context, the use of *sympoliteia* appears to be restricted to occasions where only two cities were involved, whereas *synoikismos* frequently refers to the amalgamation of multiple communities.²⁹

As with *synoikizein* and its cognates, related terms and expressions often replace *sympoliteia* and *sympoliteuein*. In his description of a temporary union circa 392, Xenophon refers to the Corinthians' "being forced to share in the *politeia* in Argos."³⁰ The arrangement by which Mantineia absorbed Helisson as a village (*kōmē*) of the larger polis is simply called a *synthesis* (agreement).³¹ In the document that joined Latmos and Pidasa (sometime between 323 and 313), the Latmians agreed to swear individually, "I will have *politeia* [*politeusomai*] with the Pidasians," and the following line refers to "the same *politeuma*."³² Smyrna "granted *politeia*" to Magnesia under Sipylos circa 245,³³ and the agreement between the cities of Perea and Melitaia in Achaia Phthiotis in 213–212 uses similar language.³⁴ A decree from the end of the third century describes the unification of Kos and Kalymnos as the "restoration of *homopolitieia*."³⁵ Conversely, the term *sympoliteia* is employed for grants of citizenship to an individual, where the term *politeia* would be more readily expected,³⁶ and for arrangements that modern scholars would typically label *isopoliteia*, as in Polybios's description of the rela-

---

28. For Kildara and Thodasa, see *SEG* LII 1038, l. 13 (Blümel 2000; Wiemer 2001; Ma 2002, 292–94, no. 5; Dreyer 2002; LaBuff 2016, 124–29): καὶ συμπολιτεύεσθαι Κιλλαρεῖς καὶ Θ[ωδασεῖς]. For Chalketor and Iasos(?) (190s), see *I. Mylasa* 913 = *RC* 29, ll. 4–6: ἵνα συμπολειτευ|όμενος ἐπ' ἴσηι καὶ ὁμοίαι τ[ῶ]ν αὐτῶν ἡμῖν μετέ|χηι. For the identification of Chalketor and (probably) Iasos and the circumstances, see now Thibaut and Pont 2014, ch. 2, esp. 54–64; but note the reservations of van Bremen 2015.

29. Pace Rhodes 2001.

30. Xen., *Hell.* 4.4.6: πολιτείας μὲν ἀναγκαζόμενοι τῆς ἐν Ἄργει μετέχειν. For the precise nature (*isopoliteia*, *sympoliteia*, or synoikism) and date of the union, which are debated, see Griffith 1950; Kagan 1962; Hamilton 1972; Moggi 1976b, 242–50; Salmon 1984, 354–62; Whitby 1984; Bearzot 2004, ch. 2; Gray 2015, 258–62; Simonton 2017, 231–37.

31. RO 14, l. 2.

32. Wörrle 2003a, 121–22, ll. 40–42.

33. *Staatsvert.* III 492.

34. *IG* IX 2 205 = *Syll.*³ 546 B, ll. 14–15: πολιτευόντω[v] | Πηρέων μετὰ Μελιταιέων.

35. *Staatsvert.* III 545, ll. 15–16: ἀποκαταστάσει | τᾶς ὁμοπολιτείας. See also Bencivenni 2006; Habicht 2007.

36. E.g., *IG* IV² 1 59, l. 12 (Epidauros, 250–200).

tionship between Kydonia and Apollonia, two nonadjacent poleis on Krete, in 170/69.[37]

This brief survey shows the range and overlap of the terms *sympoliteia* and *synoikismos*. They have important distinctions in sense and use, but they do not adequately distinguish between phenomena or indicate the levels of nuance differentiating closely related arrangements. Accordingly, the shorthand of *synoikismos* for a political and physical unification and *sympoliteia* for only a political unification with no subsequent demographic change oversimplifies the complexity and diversity of these political and urbanistic arrangements;[38] moreover, these definitions do not map onto the ancient terminology with precision.

The degree to which settlement patterns were affected is, however, a crucial criterion for understanding types of unions and foundations. Simon Hornblower, in his illuminating discussion of the synoikisms carried out by the Hekatomnid dynast Maussollos in fourth-century Karia, develops this as the main distinction and stresses that there are essentially two types: political and physical synoikism.[39] In the former, the union entailed no change to the physical distribution of population and the existing urban centers persisted in their original form. In physical synoikism, new centers were established and old population sites frequently eliminated. Scholars have widely accepted this distinction.[40] M. Hansen and T. Nielsen, however, in their discussion of classical synoikisms, argue that there are no attested examples of "purely political" synoikism and emphasize that some degree of population movement seems to have been involved in every instance.[41] They have proposed a more detailed typology, based on settlement hierarchy,[42] but their distinctions say little about the degree to which a new or expanded settlement emerged as a consequence of synoikism or how much this affected settlement patterns and still less about the impetus for these unions.

There are important structural differences between multipolis synoikisms on the scale of Megalopolis, engineered by a committee, the projects initiated by kings, instances when a larger polis swallows up its smaller neighbor (like Mantineia and Helisson), examples such as the absorption of Pidasa into Miletos, in which Pidasa willingly entered into a union, or cases where villages gradually coalesce through shared interests and ties over a long period of time. However, creating typologies of cases based solely on these criteria does not provide significant

---

37. Polyb. 28.14.3. See also Reger 2004, 148. Polybios does, however, use *sympoliteia* in the sense of the political unification of two poleis at 18.2.4 (Byzantion and Perinthos).
38. See, e.g., Chaniotis 1996, 105n630, for such a distinction between these terms. Walser (2009, 137) also stresses the insufficiency of this contrast.
39. Hornblower 1982a, 83–84.
40. E.g., Demand 1990; Davies 1992, 28; Reger 2004, 149n19.
41. Hansen and Nielsen 2004b, 116.
42. Ibid., 117.

gains in understanding the larger issues. A further criterion, and one particularly important for this study, is the involvement of hegemonic or imperial powers in the creation of synoikized polities. Rather than envisioning the process of synoikism or *sympoliteia* as defined by two poles (political/physical), it is better conceived of as several overlapping spectrums along which various considerations can be plotted: for instance, the extent of settlement shift, the types and numbers of communities involved, the status and degree of autonomy left to the constituent groups, the level of agency of the incorporated communities in effecting the union.

This book focuses on the concentration of population in new or expanded polis centers, primarily cases in which more than two communities were joined together. For the sake of convenience, I generally use the term *synoikism* to denote the union of two or more communities, whether poleis or *kōmai*, in instances where outside powers provided the impetus for the union. This term has the advantages of preserving the sense of agency present in the Greek *synoikizein* and emphasizing the urbanistic consequences of the process. Sympolity/*sympoliteia*, by contrast, is reserved for examples where two poleis concluded an agreement to become one, regardless of the interests involved or the degree of urban change. These are nevertheless closely related phenomena, especially as *sympoliteiai* frequently resulted from the ambition of a larger neighbor to augment its position within a world of great cities by absorbing additional territory and resources or from the responses of small communities to the complex pressures of their place among competing polities and hegemonic powers.[43] The comparison of these at times overlapping and at times contrasting processes illuminates the problems and interests associated with such projects.

URBANIZATION AND IMPERIALISM: A COMPARATIVE SKETCH

By the time that Cassander undertook the first major synoikism, in 316, or Antigonos incorporated Skepsis into his new port in the Troad, the expansion or contraction of poleis as a means of extending regional hegemony or responding to imperial pressure had a long history in the Greek world. These manipulations of the Greek polis provided precedents and procedures that informed the Hellenistic practice in important ways. Nevertheless, the central role that urbanization and synoikism assumed in the formation and maintenance of the Hellenistic kingdoms characterizes a distinctive form of imperial rule and administration of subordinate communities.

---

43. For important regional studies of *sympoliteiai*, see, on Lykia, Zimmermann 1992, 123–41; on Lykia and Phokis, Schuler and Walser 2015; on Karia, Reger 2004, Schuler 2010, and LaBuff 2016.

The process of synoikism, in the form of the agglomeration of villages into a single unit, was intrinsic to the Greek conception of the polis itself, as Aristotle famously expressed at the outset of the *Politics*.[44] In some cases this does seem to have been the historical origin of many early city-states, though the details are often elusive, and Greek writers generally considered the alternative—a dispersed pattern of settlement—the exception to the norm.[45] In the late sixth and fifth centuries, a number of poleis arose through the consolidation or expansion of their territory through synoikism. Patrai formed in the late sixth or early fifth century from the synoikism of three closely linked villages, in the manner considered typical by the ancient authors, and became a substantial polis but never a major regional power.[46] Throughout the fifth century, other important poleis, such as Tegea and Mantineia, emerged by a similar process.[47] By contrast, a series of other cities greatly extended their influence and reach through more aggressive forms of expansion, far outstripping the average size of a typical Greek polis.[48] Elis, synoikized circa 471, seems to have both concentrated its population in an urban center and asserted its control over dependent (perioikic) communities in its wider territory.[49] Argos systematically conquered and absorbed its neighbors over the course of the fifth and fourth centuries, expanding its population and territory (to a maximum extent of around 1,400 square kilometers, or 541 square miles) and greatly augmenting the urban center of the polis.[50] In Sicily, tyrants significantly expanded the Syracusan state through the subjection and (partial) incorporation of neighboring poleis, along with mercenaries and other foreigners, first under Gelon and again under Dionysios I and Timoleon. Syracuse ultimately controlled a huge territory spanning about twelve thousand square kilometers (4,633 square miles) in the fourth century,[51] which represents one of the

---

44. Arist., *Pol.* 1252b.
45. Archaic synoikisms: Moggi 1991. Ancient attitudes: e.g., Thuc. 1.10.2, on the settlement of Sparta in villages.
46. Paus. 7.18.2–6; Moggi 1976b, 89–95; Petropoulos and Rizakis 1994, 203.
47. Tegea, synoikized from nine demes: Strabo 8.3.2; Paus. 8.45.1; Voyatzis 1990, 10–11. Mantineia: Strabo 8.3.2 (formed from five *dēmoi*); Diod. Sic. 15.5.4 (using the term *kōmē*; so too Ephoros, *FGrH* 70 F79); Xen., *Hell.* 5.2.7 (four *kōmai*); see also Hodkinson and Hodkinson 1981. For the supposed involvement of Themistokles in the synoikisms of Elis and Mantineia, see, e.g., Hornblower 1982a, 80; doubted by Demand 1990, 64–72.
48. According to the estimates of Hansen and Nielsen (2004c, 71), 60 percent of poleis controlled a territory of less than one hundred square kilometers (thirty-nine square miles) each and ca. 80 percent a territory of less than two hundred square kilometers (seventy-seven square miles). Only 10 percent possessed a territory of more than five hundred square kilometers (193 square miles).
49. Diod. Sic. 11.54.1 and Strabo 8.3.2, with Moggi 1976b, 57–66, and Roy 2002. Its territory spanned more than one thousand square kilometers (386 square miles): Hansen and Nielsen 2004c, 72.
50. Paus. 8.27.1, with Moggi 1974; Kritzas 1992; M. Piérart 1997; Kowalzig 2007, 161–78.
51. Hansen and Nielsen 2004c, 72.

most striking efforts to build a major regional power around the expansion of a single polis.⁵²

Consolidation and synoikism were also central to the formation of the Hellenistic monarchies, distinguishing them from their imperial forebears. An opposite approach to administering an empire is fragmentation, the principle of "divide and rule." This has clear political and military advantages. By forming larger unions, polities could more easily resist imperial hegemony. For the architects of the Athenian Empire, for example, the domination of small poleis involved the administrative headache of assessing and collecting tribute from more than two hundred states, the majority of them tiny and yielding only modest revenues.⁵³ But organizing the empire in this way had the advantage of preventing an organized coalition of opposition. To understand that this was a conscious element of the Athenian imperial system, we need look no further than the political pamphlet of the so-called Old Oligarch, which explicitly refers to the weakness of isolated island communities for whom resistance through synoikism was not an option.⁵⁴ The consolidation of cities specifically countered one of the main aims of the Athenian imperial administration: the fragmentation of regions and allegiances and the prevention of any form of viable resistance to Athenian rule. In this context, synoikism was a frequent means of resisting the Athens of the fifth century.⁵⁵ Other key Athenian instruments of empire—forced contributions to the Panathenaia, the regulation of coinage and standards, the practice of mass enslavement (*andrapodismos*), the institution of klerouchies—encouraged dependence on the imperial center. Spartan imperialism in the fourth century followed a similar logic. The Peace of Antalkidas in 387/86 specifically aimed at breaking up collectivities that might threaten Spartan preeminence, most strikingly seen in the dispersal (*dioikismos*) of Mantineia and the dismantling of the Boiotian League. As Spartan impe-

---

52. Vattuone 1994; Harris, forthcoming.

53. The Athenians did permit *synteleiai* (grouping of joint tribute payment) and restricted hegemonies over neighboring settlements, but the *synteleiai* could also be broken up and separately assessed. See Paarmann 2004; Constantakopoulou 2007, 219–22; Jensen 2010; Constantakopoulou 2013.

54. [Xen.], *Ath. Pol.* 2.2–3. This cold calculus is highly revealing of the nature of the Athenian Empire, with its explicitly economic underpinning. See also Kallet 2013.

55. When Mytilene revolted in 428/27, it resisted Athens through the synoikism of the island of Lesbos (Thuc. 3.2.3). After its defeat, the Athenians pulled down its walls, distributed the land of Lesbos to Athenian klerouchs, and took possession of its towns in the Troad (3.50.1–3). Likewise, the synoikism of the Chalkidians into Olynthos in 433/32, in the run-up to the Peloponnesian War, was orchestrated to resist Athens (1.58.2), and Thebes absorbed six communities of southern Boiotia, probably sometime between 427 and 424, as a response to growing Athenian pressure, a move that doubled its size and population (*Hell. Oxy.* 16.3, 17.3; for the controversial date, see Moggi 1976a, 197–204; Demand 1990, 82–85, which puts it at the outbreak of the Peloponnesian War; Mackil 2013, 41n93, which has it after the destruction of Plataia). In 408/7 the island of Rhodes underwent synoikism in the last phase of the Peloponnesian War (Diod. Sic. 13.75.1; Gabrielsen 2000).

rialism began to collapse, three important cities were founded or refounded through synoikism: Mantineia, Messene, and Megalopolis, the last two with the aid of Epameinondas and the Boiotians. The foundation of Megalopolis both consolidated scattered populations and provided a neutral space around which to form the new Arkadian League, which sought to neutralize the long-standing hostility between Tegea and Mantineia. Together these cities represented a powerful bulwark against future Spartan imperialism. With the rise of the second Athenian naval confederacy, we see a wider Aegean movement toward centralization, designed to counter the growing power of Athens. Maussollos, the Persian satrap of Karia (r. 377–353), consolidated his dynastic hold on the province by shifting its capital from Mylasa to the coastal city of Halikarnassos, which he expanded considerably through the synoikism of six poleis and communities.[56] The synoikism of Kos in 366/65 also belongs to this period and to this strategy, possibly initiated at the behest of Maussollos or at least with his approval.[57]

In Asia Minor, the Achaemenids found a dispersed settlement pattern conducive to their rule and typically encouraged it, as well as frequently fostering division among elites by supporting certain factions within cities. Persian control mainly eschewed direct urban development, instead mapping satrapal headquarters onto preexisting sites like Daskyleion and Sardeis and largely distributing Iranian elites to landed estates in the countryside.[58] Persian rule replicated this geographic policy in its manipulation of the social order of the empire. In effect, the elites of communities were successfully co-opted in a way that discouraged local solidarity and coordination.[59] Accordingly, elites' primary loyalties were to the Achaemenid court and were less horizontally integrated between communities, in

---

56. Strabo 13.1.59; Hornblower 1982a, 218–22.

57. Diod. Sic. 15.76.2; Strabo 14.2.19, with Moggi 1976a; Hornblower 1982, 103–4; Demand 1990, 132; Reger 2001, 171–74. Kos was allied with Maussollos and also took part in the Social War against Athens (Dem. 15.3, 15.27; Diod. Sic. 16.7.3; *Staatsvert.* III 305, with Sherwin-White 1978).

58. For an overview of Persian rule in Asia Minor, see Dusinberre 2013. See ch. 2 for further discussion. For the imperial structure of Persian rule in general, see Wiesehöfer 1996, 58–59; Khatchadourian 2016, xxx–xxxi.

59. Barjamovic 2012, 54: "Ideally they [local leaders] were appointed by their peers to act as an instrument of the community, both internally and in relation to the imperial central power. In reality both Assyrian and Persian policy pursued the familiar paradigm of *divide et impera* by actively drawing the loyalty of local leadership away from its constituency so as to penetrate and co-ordinate aspects of society to which they had only limited direct access. Multiple overlapping and intersecting sociospatial networks of power constituted society on a local level. Immersed in this multiplicity of power relations, the imperial agents sought to create a space in which to manoeuvre and play off various interest groups against each other for the benefit of imperial policy. As already argued, this may well have been the most important function of the imperial diplomacy: to act among the subjugated elites in order to create a sense of imperial unity at the expense of local social and political cohesion." Compare the modalities of Ottoman rule as described by Barkey 1994, 26–27, 40.

contrast to the dynamic interstate relations between poleis in the Hellenistic period. The implementation of dynastic rule in areas like Karia and Lykia also encouraged this segmentation.[60] By such means, the Athenian and Persian systems manipulated human geography and local agency in specific ways to support imperial rule.[61]

In important ways, the consolidation of the Macedonian state under Philip II prefigured the impact of the Hellenistic kingdoms on settlement patterns and city life in subsequent generations. Philip was celebrated, as is well known, as a great urbanizer.[62] In particular, the foundation of Philippoi in 356 provided a powerful model for the extension of Macedonian imperialism and a blueprint for royal cities.[63] Other new cities anchored Macedonian rule in neighboring regions, such as Herakleia Lynkestis in Illyria circa 358 and the numerous settlements in Thrace following the campaigns of 342–340.[64] Philip may also have refounded Gomphoi in Thessaly as another Philippopolis.[65] Such precedents undoubtedly influenced the policies of Alexander and the Successors, but differing imperatives and considerations also guided the practices of each of these periods. A conspicuous feature of Philip's rule was the development of Macedonia and its expanding borders at the expense of the rival Greek cities and neighboring tribes. Macedonian colonization played a prominent role in this project. More important, Philip's policy overwhelmingly relied on the subjection and destruction of autonomous poleis and the dispersal of populations (*dioikismos*).[66] This eliminated coordinated resistance to

---

60. Briant 1982, 199–225.

61. For continuities between the practices of Persian and Athenian imperial administrations, see Raaflaub 2009. L. Robert (1935, 488; 1951, 8–11, 34–36; 1967a, 16–19; see also J. Robert and Robert 1976) repeatedly stressed the movement from fragmentation to centralization in Asia Minor between the eras of Persian and Athenian rule and the Hellenistic period.

62. Alexander's speech to his men at Opis (Arr., *Anab.* 7.9.2–3), despite its exaggerated rhetoric, stresses this image. Cf. Just. 8.5.7, 8.6.1–2, describing the transplanting of populations throughout Philip's kingdom.

63. Philip founded Philippoi on the Thasian colony Krenides, populated in part by Macedonian settlers and in part by the remainder of the Thasian colonists and indigenous Thracian inhabitants. The city provided Philip with a bulwark against the Thracians and a major source of revenue from the rich gold mines in the area (App., *BC* 4.13.105; Strabo 7aF34; Diod. Sic. 16.3.7).

64. E.g., Philippopolis and Kabyle, in inland Thrace, grafted on to existing Thracian centers: see Hammond and Griffith 1979, 554–66; Archibald 2004, 893–95. For a discussion of the aims and impact of Macedonian urbanization in Thrace, see Nankov 2015; see also Adams 1997; Adams 2007.

65. G. Cohen 1995, 116–18.

66. For a punitive transfer of subjected people by Philip, see Polyainos, *Strat.* 4.2.12. The king moved populations "as shepherds move their flocks now to winter, now to summer pastures" (Just. 8.5.7). According to Theopompos (*FGrH* 115 F110), Philippopolis in Thrace was nicknamed Poneropolis, "City of rogues," because of the sorts of people whom Philip settled there. According to Demosthenes, he destroyed Olynthos, Methone, Apollonia, and thirty-two other poleis in Thrace (9.26), and Hypereides maintains that he expelled the inhabitants of forty poleis in the Chalkidike after the

Macedonian hegemony and allowed Philip to distribute the territory confiscated from subjected poleis to Macedonians, especially in the form of large landed estates granted to the Macedonian elite and in some cases to allied cities. Philip's legacy as a great builder of cities, accordingly, must be balanced against his reliance on settlement dispersal in his relations with the Greek world. Alexander's famous destruction of Thebes continued this tactic, and very little building can be attributed to him in Greece or Asia Minor.[67] Of course, his conquests ushered in great changes. In regions traditionally dominated by the hegemonies of large poleis, Macedonian control dramatically realigned the political landscape.[68] Likewise, in the wake of Alexander's pro-Greek pronouncements and the sudden evacuation of Persian control, the Greek communities of western Asia Minor suddenly found themselves in a very new position.[69] But Alexander's life was largely spent in conquest, and it was in the decades after his death that the greatest changes to the political geography of these core territories occurred, as the empires of the Successors took shape. The Hellenistic kingdoms, particularly those that incorporated the lands ruled by the Persian kings, maintained important aspects of the Persian imperial apparatus, inheriting, as all empires do, distinctive facets of administration and organization.[70] But the continuities between the imperial system of the Achaemenids and the Hellenistic kingdoms should not be emphasized at the

---

destruction of Olynthos in 348 (F76). Even adjusting for hyperbole, there is good reason to believe that more were involved than the three specifically named by Demosthenes (see Theopompos, *FGrH* 115 F27). Methone was destroyed in 354 (Diod. Sic. 16.31.6, 16.34.4). This policy carried over to central Greece as well, e.g., the destruction of Halos in 346 (Dem. 19.163). After the Phokians surrendered to Philip in 346, Macedonian armies destroyed their cities, numbering twenty-two (Dem. 18.36, 18.41, 19.65, 19.81, 19.141; Aischines 2.162; Paus. 10.3.2.), and forced the inhabitants to relocate to scattered villages (Diod. Sic. 16.60.2). For Demosthenes (9.22), Philip's strategy was to "chip away" at Greece until no coordinated resistance remained: καὶ καθ᾿ ἕν᾿ οὑτωσὶ περικόπτειν καὶ λωποδυτεῖν τῶν Ἑλλήνων, καὶ καταδουλοῦσθαι τὰς πόλεις ἐπιόντα (and one by one just to chip away at and despoil the cities of the Greeks and to attack and enslave them).

67. G. Cohen 1995, 420–23. An important exception is the grant of the Bottiaian polis of Kalindoia and neighboring territories to the Macedonians for resettlement as a Macedonian polis (*SEG* XXXVI 626), though here we might stress the imperative of making grants to subordinates on the eve of Alexander's Persian campaigns (Plut., *Alex.* 15). Little is known about Alexandropolis, founded by Alexander ca. 340, when he was sixteen or seventeen, in the territory of the Thracian Maidoi (Plut., *Alex.* 9.1, with G. Cohen 1995, 82). Its existence has been doubted: Fraser 1996, 26, 29–30; Archibald 2004, 892; Nankov 2015. For Alexander's "cities" in the East, see Holt 1986; Fraser 1996; G. Cohen 2006; G. Cohen 2013.

68. Gauthier (1987, 194) has called attention to the dynamic changes in regional power structures following the eclipse of the great hegemons (Athens, Sparta, Thebes) in the late fourth century.

69. Arr., *Anab.* 1.18.1–2.

70. For continuities, see, e.g., Briant 1982; Sherwin-White and Kuhrt 1993. For common institutions of control, see Ma 2009; Raaflaub 2009.

expense of identifying important structural differences in the ways that they constructed and replicated their rule.[71]

The period of the Successors was characterized by fierce interstate competition between rival kingdoms and constantly shifting borders. As a system of unrivaled imperial authority (the Achaemenids, Alexander) was replaced by competing claimants to rule and, ultimately, peer kingdoms, the development of the urban core of the kingdoms was increasingly important. This could be viewed as "structural urbanization," whose focus was not just on the selective augmentation of specific sites but also on constructing a nodal framework, linking and interconnecting cities and regions in a way that mapped out the infrastructural power of these nascent kingdoms.[72] This approach had patent benefits, of course—the marshaling of resources, the ease of administration, the simplification of diplomacy in dealing only with larger collectivities—but also dangers. It was a disruptive and difficult social process, and it created potentially powerful and dangerous entities, fortified strongholds able to resist the will of the king or even go over to a rival monarch. There was, nevertheless, a difference between what rulers sought to achieve and what was practicable. Royal power and its ambitions, I argue, introduced important structural changes to the organization of communities, but the longevity of these projects depended on the dynamics between local constituencies and actors. To understand this process, it is necessary to explore the permutations of state-fostered centralization in detail, tracing the historical circumstances of individual synoikisms and their impact on patterns of settlement.

THE PROCESS OF FOUNDATION

We do not have a complete picture of how a synoikism was achieved—the process by which kings and their agents directed populations to coalesce or the modalities by which this procedure was brokered. Our literary sources, often late, lay stress on the power and destructive force of the kings, perhaps inevitably. Most of their descriptions follow a fairly standard pattern of a city founded out of the destruction of preexisting settlements and the forced migration of their populations to the new urban center.[73] The language employed ("destroy," "raze," "lay waste," "demol-

---

71. For a useful framework for comparing imperial structures, see Barkey 2008, 9–15.

72. For "structural urbanization," see J. de Vries 1984, 12; for a critique of "urbanization" as a construct of ancient history, see Osborne 2005. Purcell (2005b) calls for greater attention to dynamic processes of urbanism (expansion, contraction, social change). These are, of course, the underlying assumptions of Horden and Purcell 2000. Vlassopoulos (2007, 195–202), building on the world-systems analysis of Immanuel Wallerstein (2004), stresses understanding the place of poleis within a larger framework, or *systèm-monde*.

73. E.g., the destructions of Kolophon (ἀνελών, Paus. 1.9.7; ἐρημωθῆναι, 7.3.4), Kardia (ἀνελών, 1.9.8), the towns (*polismata*) in Krousis and on the Thermaic Gulf (καθελών, Strabo 7a F21; cf. καθῃρέθη, Dion. Hal., *Ant. Rom.* 1.49.4–5), and Iolkos (possibly) (κατέσκαπται, Strabo 9.5.15).

ish") evokes a picture of the absolute power of the kings to transform settlement patterns by force and without the consent of the constituent parties. These descriptions conceal the degree to which settlements persisted as villages, demes, dependent poleis,[74] or fortified outposts after the synoikism and the ways in which the process was negotiated, managed, and organized.

The archaeological evidence for the synoikisms of the early Hellenistic period and their effects on patterns of settlement, though incomplete, shows no signs of systematic destruction on the scale that the sources suggest. Displacement and migration, however, are well attested, and it is perhaps inevitable that the elimination of autonomous political communities and the traumatic loss of discrete citizen identity would be translated into the trope of the destruction of a city itself, particularly by sources hostile to the kings. At face value, however, the literary sources provide a simplified and distorted picture of what was in reality a much more complex, diverse, and nuanced process. The "destruction" of a city, then, should be understood primarily as the eclipse of an autonomous unit and the transference of some or all of its population to a new site. This could also involve dismantling existing structures for building materials and carrying away movable property like windows, doors, woodwork, hearths, and other installations. The overall effect on patterns of settlement varied. There were, at times, strong continuity of inhabitation in centers now demoted to second-order status, the conversion of old sites into fortresses or other outposts, and the complete abandonment of settlements. In the aftermath of these reorganizations, many communities resisted and reconstituted themselves in some form.

Even if the kings and their agents do not seem to have resorted to violent destruction and forced deportation of populations to create their new cities, these projects may still have been deeply unpopular and depended on other forms of coercion. As we saw in the case of Skepsis, Antigonos's synoikism absorbed this community very much against its will, and it broke away as soon as the opportunity arose (as did its hostile neighbor Kebren). Numerous other communities followed suit: Lebedos broke from Teos, only to be absorbed into Ephesos,[75] but reemerged again; Kolophon secured its release after its synoikism with Ephesos;[76] Teion revolted from Amastris;[77] Pidasa broke from Latmos, reconstituted itself, and later willingly joined in sympoity with Miletos.[78] The desire for self-determination and autonomous existence was not easily overcome. Our

---

74. For dismissals of autonomy as a necessary criterion for polis status, see Hansen 1995; Vlassopoulos 2007, 191–93. For the various types of dependent poleis, see Hansen and Nielsen 2004e.
75. Paus. 1.9.7, 7.3.4–5.
76. J. Robert and Robert 1989, 77–85.
77. Strabo 12.3.10.
78. *Milet* I.3, 149; Gauthier 2001; Wörrle 2003a. See ch. 1 for detailed discussions of these cases.

sources attest to the reactions of some individuals. Phoinix of Kolophon, a choliambic poet contemporary with the synoikism of Kolophon into Ephesos (circa 294), composed a lament (*thrēnēsai*) for Lysimachos's "capture" (*halōsis*) of Kolophon, which was well known in antiquity.[79] An army of Kolophonians, along with Smyrnaeans, resisted—the only known instance of armed opposition to synoikism—but the Lysimachean forces defeated them, even if Kolophon itself does not seem to have been sacked in the manner that Phoinix's poem suggests.[80] Similarly, the great historian of the period, Hieronymos of Kardia, according to Pausanias, harbored a deep resentment of Lysimachos for the destruction of his native city, which was incorporated into Lysimacheia in 309.[81]

On the ground, however, the language and ideological presentation that shaped the negotiations between kings and cities were certainly more nuanced, and occasional epigraphic documents shed some light on these interactions. Much, it would seem, simply went unsaid. Kings wrote to communities under their control suggesting such projects, presenting these unions as beneficial arrangements, and the cities recognized the underlying command.[82] This is the overall impression of Antigonos's letters to Teos concerning its synoikism with Lebedos.[83] Throughout, Antigonos presents himself as a third party, offering advice to the embassies of each community and prefacing each injunction with the gentle phrase "we think it best" (*oiometha de dein*) or posing as an arbitrator (*epikekrikamen*, l. 60)—dealing with these cities, in other words, with what Welles describes as a "simplicity of bearing."[84] All parties recognized that force lay behind these asymmetric relationships, but equally evident in these letters is the ability of the communities to secure privileges and concessions from Antigonos, even where they ran contrary to his initial plans. Such was the power of the discourse of euergetism that defined these encounters and became such a central part of the dialogue between cities and kings.[85] Still, Antigonos overtly mentions the possibility of dismantlement (of Teos), but here again he poses as a concerned outsider, primarily interested in

---

79. Paus. 1.9.7. The description is redolent of works like Phyrnichos's infamous "Capture of Miletos" (Μιλήτου ἅλωσις, Hdt. 6.21.2) and other examples of the *halōsis* genre. For the literary tradition commemorating the fall of cities, see Bachvarova, Dutsch, and Suter 2016.

80. Paus. 7.3.4. For the archeological evidence from Kolophon, see ch. 1.

81. Paus. 1.9.8.

82. As C. Welles (1934, 135) succinctly put it, "A king would refer to his part in the matter as 'advice' (συνεβούλευσα), while the city would recognize it as an 'order' (κελεύει)" (comm. on *RC* 29, on the union of Iasos[?] and Chalketor in the 190s, probably at the hands of Antiochos III). The two documents presented as *RC* 29 in Welles's edition, however, have been shown to have no relation to each other (Crampa 1968).

83. *RC* 3-4.

84. Welles 1934, 26.

85. For a full exposition, see Ma 2002, 179-214.

securing the most advantageous site for the new city and its population and careful not to issue an absolute command.[86]

By the later Hellenistic period, royal rescripts and civic decrees increasingly document unions created by royal initiative. Their language describes the process with the typical locution of royal benefaction. An illustrative example is preserved from the foundation of Attalid Apollonis in northern Lydia during the reign of Eumenes II (197–159).[87] The agent charged with the synoikism was one of the king's brothers, whom the community honored as "founder and benefactor" for his role in bringing the king's plans to fruition. A decree of the polis of Apollonis singles out his role in "providing both [food and] money for those being synoikized, and [in addition to these, also] procuring other things related to [safety and] prosperity/happiness [*eudaimonia*], [on account of his exceeding] goodwill toward them."[88] This document illustrates the type of rhetoric employed in such contexts. Stressing the efforts of the king on behalf of the communities and his central role as founder (*ktistēs*), the decree describes the synoikism as a natural extension of the success of the kingdom. A fragmentary document from Karia, a city decree recording a royal order (likely of Antiochos III) and a subsequent resolution, reflects the ways that cities themselves replicated this discourse. From concern for the well-being of (probably) Iasos and because he "considered it a matter of greatest importance," the decree records, Antiochos wrote to its *boulē* and *dēmos* to annex Chalketor and join in sympoity with its citizens.[89] The royal interests in rewarding Iasos and shoring up the Seleukid hold on coastal Karia are, naturally, passed over, as are the aggrandizing ambitions of the larger partner in the union. Such was the presentation: the king as benefactor, interested in the prosperity and success of the cities under his command and careful to avoid the language of domination.

The importance of this form of discourse extended to the wider presentation of empire and even to its structure. In the context of the Greek poleis, it was critical for the Hellenistic dynasts to distinguish and individualize their form of kingship,

---

86. *Syll.*³ 344 = *RC* 3, l. 7: ἐὰν δὲ δεῖ κατασκάπτειν τὴν ὑπάρχουσαν πόλιν . . . (but if it is necessary to tear down the existing city . . .). Compare Thuc. 1.58.2: "Perdikkas persuaded the Chalkidians to abandon and dismantle [*katabalontas*] their poleis on the coast and settle inland at Olynthos and make it a single, strong city."

87. For the site, see G. Cohen 1995, 200–204. The community seems to have been populated in part by Macedonian military colonists and by the inhabitants of the surrounding villages.

88. *TAM* V. 2 1187, ll. 6–10: ἐπιδόντα τ[ε σῖτον καὶ] | χρήματα τοῖς συνοικισθεῖσιν, ἔ[τι δὲ αὐτοῖς καὶ] | ἄλλα περιποιήσαντα τὰ πρ[ὸς ἀσφάλειαν καὶ] | εὐδαιμονίαν ἀνήκον[τα, διὰ τὴν ὑπερφυῆ εἰς] | ἑαυτοὺς εὔνοιαν. See also the language of a Teian decree that praises Antiochos III for "the advantages through which our city reaches prosperity/happiness [*eudaimonia*]" (Herrmann 1965, 34–36, ll. 27–28 [*SEG* XLI 1003; Ma 2002, no. 17]).

89. *I. Mylasa* 913, ll. 2–6.

linking it to ideal notions and not to the autocratic image of the tyrant or the Eastern king.[90] Yet the elimination of autonomous cities and the movement of populations were patently at odds with this presentation. By the time of Xenophon and Aristotle, intervention in the organization of a civic community had become a trope typical of tyrants. Following the unification of Corinth and Argos orchestrated by anti-Spartans in 393 or 392, Xenophon described the faction in charge as "ruling as tyrants" by eliminating these cities' political and territorial distinctions.[91] Aristotle, by contrast, portrays the tyrant as marked by fear of collective action, discouraging centralized settlement and the mingling of citizens. For Aristotle, the tyrant was someone who prevented mutual acquaintance, for fear of political action, and drove citizens from the city and into scattered living arrangements.[92] According to the Aristotelian *Constitution of the Athenians*, Peisistratos encouraged a dispersed pattern of settlement and Periander did not let citizens live in the city.[93] As instruments of control, forced deportation and resettlement had a long history in Near Eastern kingship. This is particularly evident in the policies of the Neo-Assyrian kings, a pillar of whose rule was the "calculated frightfulness" of their sieges and deportations, boasted of in imperial inscriptions and represented prominently in official art.[94] More immediately, population transfers were an instrument of Achaemenid control, and literary sources attest to Greek anxieties over those undertaken or allegedly contemplated by the Persians and said to have been planned by Alexander and forestalled by his death.[95]

Two versions of encounters between kings and cities emerge from the written sources, both probably distortions: the literary trope of the king as tyrant, destroying cities and forcing their populations into new capitals, and the epigraphic image of the king as benefactor. Past approaches have attempted to resolve the apparent contradiction between the rhetoric of the Successors and their frequent interventions in the autonomous life of the Greek poleis. Writing of Antigonos's synoikism

---

90. On ideal kingship and Aristotle, see Bringmann 1993.
91. Xen., *Hell.* 4.4.6. For the nature of this union, see 000n30.
92. Arist., *Pol.* 1313b4–5, 1311a14–15.
93. Peisistratos: [Arist.], *Ath. Pol.* 16.2–5; see also Demand 1990, 46. Periander: Dilts 1971, F20.
94. "Calculated frightfulness": Olmstead 1918; deportations: Oded 1979. The next phase of Assyrian policy created massive new provincial capitals, often on the sites of former cities, which were populated with transplants from other parts of the empire. See Stern 2001, 10–13, 18–31, for the case of Palestine. For urbanization in the Jazirah, in Assyria proper, see Kühne 1994.
95. E.g., transfer of the Eretrians to the Red Sea (Hdt. 6.119.1–4; Diod. Sic. 17.119); deportation of Milesians to Susa (Hdt. 6.20.1); (supposedly voluntary) resettlement of the Branchidai in Sogdiana (Kallisthenes, *FGrH* 124 F14 = Strabo 17.1.43; Strabo 11.11.4; Curt. 7.5.28–35; Plut., *Mor.* 557b); relocation of the Paionians (Hdt. 5.15.3, 5.15.98); feared population exchange between Phoenicia and Ionia (Hdt. 6.3.1). See also Briant 2002, 505. We have already noted the contemporary view of Philip's population transfers (see 000n66). For synoikisms and population movements in the *hypomnemata* of Alexander, see Diod. Sic. 18.4.1–6, with Badian 1968 on their ultimately Perdikkan origin.

of Antigoneia in the Troad, D. Magie commented, "Whatever infraction of rights was involved, the plan may have seemed justifiable on the grounds of expediency; for a group of evidently decayed towns was replaced by a city which soon attained great commercial importance."[96] Historians have largely moved away from the legalistic framework of such an approach to a more dynamic, interactive model that stresses the role of negotiation and mutual constraint in the confrontations between kings and cities.[97] Intrinsic to Magie's "decayed towns" is the notion of the degradation and weakness of the late classical and Hellenistic poleis and the inevitability of their eclipse. Many of the communities reformed into major cities through synoikism were, of course, relatively insignificant, but the majority of poleis, small communities that rarely entered on to the international stage, nevertheless had vibrant civic lives and clung tenaciously to their traditions and autonomy.[98] Moreover, many of the cities synoikized in this period were fairly substantial places, perfectly capable of existing independently. An alternative approach to stressing the weakness of the Hellenistic polis must allow for a more complex explanation both of the role of synoikism in building the network of power and resources essential to the nascent territorial kingdoms of the Successors and of the various mechanisms by which kings and communities brokered the process of creating a unified polis in a manner that addressed the institutional complexities, varying traditions, and competing interests of its constituent groups. Such a focus exposes local dynamics of power and the ways that synoikism served to redraw the contours of political communities as part of the larger process of imperial state formation.

BECOMING A POLIS: COMMUNITY, CUSTOMS, AND ORGANIZATION

I have already alluded to the manifold institutional and social consequences of synoikism. Synoikized communities arose out of the direct application of imperial authority, but the approach I adopt here stresses how the norms of the Greek polis, the traditions of the participant communities, and ideological negotiations constrained the power of the dynasts and mediated the ways in which the synoikized poleis took shape. The interests and concerns of elites and other social actors

---

96. Magie 1950, 1:69. Magie follows the position of Heuss 1937, that the Greek cities were formally allies of the kings and thus the control of the kings did not amount to a legal encroachment on their autonomy. Bickerman 1938 thoroughly demonstrates the deficiencies of this model. Orth (1977), by contrast, stressed the repression and weakness of the Greek cities.

97. Ma 2002 fundamentally reorients this central issue, emphasizing the agency of Greek cities and the power of language to frame these interactions. The question of the formal statuses of Greek cities within the Hellenistic kingdoms remains a point of much discussion. See Ma 2002, 150–74, for a proposed typology; for an alternative, more flexible approach, see Capdetrey 2007, 191–217.

98. Gruen 1993; Ager 1998; Ma 2002.

played an important role,[99] and mechanisms other than force (whether ideological, symbolic, or ritual) shaped the formation of these communities. This encounter worked in both directions, a reciprocal exchange between king and community. At the same time, constituent parts of the new polis also brokered their new union, asserting their traditions and interests or working toward unity and consensus. There were, therefore, limits and complex dynamics that affected these projects, which should not be conceptualized as the simple result of imperial fiat or as formed on a blank slate.[100]

This book views synoikism as an evolving process, in terms of both the physical development of the city and the relations between social groups. As we saw in the case of Antigoneia/Alexandreia Troas, the union of discrete communities cut across meaningful lines distinguishing constituent members of the new polis. It is important to explain how unity and cohesiveness emerged from this diversity and competition and what the broader impact of synoikism on social organization and religious practice was. The democratic poleis created by synoikism were notionally egalitarian, but the process involved a negotiation of statuses and civic identities, and asymmetric relationships could produce winners and losers. There always was the danger that larger parties might hold greater influence in the polis, even though strategies for bridging or even obliterating the distinctions between the constituent communities of a synoikism were often put in place. Many synoikisms blurred the lines between historic ethnic groups, and where there is evidence, it would seem that a unified ethnic identity emerged from these unions, such as in Demetrias, a large-scale synoikism that combined Magnesian and Thessalian communities. In this instance, a late third-century funeral epitaph proudly calls the deceased Magnēs, a Magnesian, an unambiguous, timeless assertion of his identity, even though his polis was the result of a complex historical amalgamation of traditional ethnic divisions.[101] Particularly in Asia Minor, these projects often included indigenous, non-Greek populations or communities subordinated to a larger polis. In many cases, the precise relationship between the central polis and such population groups is unclear. Did the former royal peasants who inhabited the land directly controlled by the Persian and Hellenistic kings, the *laoi* on royal estates, enter into these communities as citizens or slaves? Should they be identified with the groups that the epigraphic sources found in many cities of Asia Minor label *paroikoi*, free but without full civic rights?[102] Did synoikism seek to expand

99. For a valuable approach to polis formation in the second century, see Savalli-Lestrade 2005.
100. Mileta's (2009) category of "Retorten-poleis" (test-tube cities), in which he places communities like Laodikeia on the Lykos ("Da die Retorten-poleis praktisch auf dem grünen Rasen entstanden waren" [85]), sidesteps some of the complexity of the genesis of such cities.
101. Moretti 1976, no. 107, ll. 6–7.
102. For discussions of this problem, see Hahn 1981; Gauthier 1987; Gauthier 1988; Wörrle 1991; Papazoglou 1997; Schuler 1998, 180–90, 202–7; Gagliardi 2009; Flinterman 2012.

cities through "concealed enfranchisement" precisely to blur lines of distinction, as has been argued for Halikarnassos or as Aristotle explicitly states of the reforms of Kleisthenes?[103]

The evidence sheds some light on these issues, but direct testimony for the modalities of forming these unions and the concerns of the communities involved is often limited. The literary sources and epigraphic record are better at elucidating the responses of civic actors to social stress and their negotiation of this changed reality. The challenges of forming a coherent civic identity and the institutions (*nomima*) and practices basic to corporate self-representation are evident in the kinds of strategies employed to bridge the social disruption of this process. Tracing the impact of synoikism on religious practice, civic rituals, social organization, and cultural identity reveals responses to the changes introduced by imperial authorities. In this manner, we can also recover the ways in which both the will of rulers and the active role of communities contributed to the construction of an imperial system.

---

103. Halikarnassos: Hornblower 1982a, 84. Reforms of Kleisthenes: Arist., *Pol.* 1275b7–8.

PART ONE

Urbanization and the Imperial Framework

1

Imperial Geographies

City, Settlement, and Ideology in the Formation of the Hellenistic Kingdoms

All ancient empires were by nature diverse patchworks of communities, institutions, and geographic zones more or less closely bound to a centralized imperial administration. Even when kings made ideological claims to universal empire (such as the Achaemenids or Alexander), a fragmented reality invariably underlay such totalizing rhetoric.[1] In no other period was the imperial landscape of the eastern Mediterranean more a loose aggregate of constantly shifting borders and alliances than in the chaotic decades after the death of Alexander. As his imperial order began to crumble, a different kind of rule, with distinct institutions and patterns of interaction, rapidly developed. While the heirs to Alexander's conquests may never have renounced the ideal of what Hieronymos of Kardia called "the whole" (*ta hola*),[2] their intense rivalries fractured the resources of the empire and made the development of regional bases of power all the more critical to competition in a multipolar world of constant warfare.[3]

In this context, all who controlled cities and population groups (*ethnē*) began to harbor hopes of kingship, as Diodoros (following Hieronymos) acutely remarked.[4] The revealing fact that this inchoate world of the Hellenistic kingdoms was deeply rooted in the support of local communities underlies this apposite observation.

---

1. For discussions of "universal empire" see Bang and Kołodziejczyk 2012.
2. E.g., Diod. Sic. 18.49.2. See Gruen 1985, 259–62. Their political situation on the ground was of course much more limited, but this did not prevent the Diadochs from leveling grand claims. See also Bang 2012; Schäfer 2014; Strootman 2014a; Strootman 2014b.
3. Kosmin (2014, 31) describes the underlying reality as the emergence of "the peer-kingdom international system."
4. Diod. Sic. 19.105.4, on the occasion of the termination of the Argead dynasty.

The surviving narrative of the wars of the Successors plays out against a complex backdrop of cities and communities, but the high-level focus on the personalities and politics of the Successors and the compression and selective interest of our extant sources often flatten the picture.[5] The vigorous struggle over the control of cities and regions, meanwhile, led to the emergence of one of the most characteristic features of relations between kings and cities in the period: the pervasive rhetoric of freedom and autonomy. This became a defining ideological battleground, one that has often led historians, ancient and modern, to attempt to parse the level of sincerity or efficacy behind such slogans.[6] If we examine this interaction from another perspective, however, one that seeks less to determine the relative value of such enunciations and instead focuses on what this struggle reveals—namely, the structural importance of cities to the creation of the Hellenistic states—we get a holistic view of the efforts of imperial authorities to organize their power through the manipulation of populations and political structures.

The staggering investment of the dynasts in urban development stands out as a major feature of the formation of the Hellenistic states. From 316/15 on, a flurry of city foundations took place across Greece, Asia Minor, and the Near East, with the greatest concentration in the first two generations of the kings. The imprint of Macedonian imperialism took a range of forms, from forts and strongholds in and out of civic territory through "military settlements" (*katoikiai*) carved out of royal land to genuine polis foundations. This scalable settlement policy radically changed the human and imperial geographies of the Hellenistic world and has rightly been seen as a defining aspect—and the most lasting contribution—of Macedonian rule. A wider outcome of the focus on urbanization was the spread of polis institutions to the less urbanized areas of the *oikoumenē*, from the peripheries of the "old" Greek world to the vast stretches of the Middle East and central Asia.

This chapter provides a selective chronological narrative of the years 323–281 and a comprehensive discussion of the central role that urbanization played in the policies of the Successors. This was the crucial period of the emergence of the Hellenistic kingdoms and the creation of many of the most important Hellenistic urban centers in Greece and western Asia Minor.[7] Concentrating on the relationship between the development of Hellenistic kingship and the structural components of territorial control, it argues that the consolidation of regions through the creation of larger urban centers was not a peripheral by-product of the policies of the Successors but a central feature of the formation of the Hellenistic states. The

---

5. Meeus 2013.

6. Gruen 1984, 134–42; Dmitriev 2011, 122–44; see also Wallace 2011. Cf. the cautionary remarks of Burstein 1986, 19.

7. For a discussion of the chronological problems of this period and a convincing revised chronology based on a synthesis of Babylonian and other documentary evidence with the narrative of Diodoros, see Boiy 2007. This chapter follows this chronology unless otherwise noted.

urbanization of these regions through large-scale synoikisms sought to reorganize and revitalize them and further integrate them into an interconnected system. This chapter also details the nature and extent of each of these expansive new urban agglomerations, describing the communities and territories they absorbed and the approximate size of the cities and their territories. Here the pressing political and strategic aims of the Hellenistic dynasts and the place of these urban centers within the wider infrastructural context of the nascent kingdoms come into view. This reconstruction also lays the groundwork for a synchronic exploration of the economic, social, and religious dimensions of the making and maintenance of these new political communities and the complex relationship between king and city visible in these processes, as well as those between the city and its constituent social groups.

"REACHING OUT FOR KINGSHIP": LOCAL COMMUNITIES AND THE STRUGGLE FOR POWER (322-316)

In September 322 BCE, the leaders of the Greek alliance sent heralds to Antipater to negotiate the terms of the cessation of the Greek revolt known as the Lamian War. When Antipater refused to make a common settlement (*koinēn sullusin*), the Greeks objected to terms that would apply to them on a city-by-city basis (*kata poleis*). Antipater and Krateros responded by besieging the cities of Thessaly. Intimidated by the assault, the majority of the Greek cities sent ambassadors and came to terms.[8] In one stroke, Antipater had dismantled the organized resistance of the Greeks and established a precedent of direct bilateral relations between the Macedonians and the Greek poleis.[9] Mopping up after the Battle of Krannon, his forces entered Athens and instituted far-reaching constitutional changes, reforms mirrored in Greek cities throughout his control.[10] Macedonian power was suddenly more present and more interventionist in the life of the polis than it had been in decades. The Corinthian League (the alliance of Greek states under the hegemony of Philip and Alexander), perhaps already obsolete, had now been fully eclipsed. No similar attempt at organizing the Greek cities of Europe, let alone Asia Minor and beyond, as a unit would be made, outside Antigonos and Demetrios's short-lived Hellenic League of 302 and the much more restricted regional leagues (*koina*) developed by the Antigonids. Direct negotiations between king and community would henceforth primarily define the structure of power relations

---

8. Diod. Sic. 18.17.6-8. Only the Aitolians and Athenians held out.
9. Bengtson 1937, 52-56, 129-32.
10. Diod. Sic. 18.18; Plut., *Phoc.* 27-28; Habicht 1997, 44.

between them. As the unrest in Greece prompted by Alexander's death subsided,[11] a much greater conflict sprang to life. After the uneasy division of the satrapies at Babylon in June 323,[12] the latent tensions among Alexander's former generals resulted in the confrontation known as the First Diadoch War (321–320). The alliances, coalitions, and unremitting violence of this conflict set the pattern for the chaotic decades to follow, and it was against this backdrop that the policies of the Successors toward cities and communities developed.

The tenuous settlement among the leading generals quickly turned to open hostilities. "Reaching out for kingship," Perdikkas broke with Antipater and accepted Olympias's offer of marriage to Alexander's sister Kleopatra, intending to use this connection to persuade the Macedonians of his legitimacy and seize the entire empire.[13] Faced with a powerful coalition, Perdikkas chose to strike Ptolemy first,[14] leaving Eumenes in Asia Minor to confront the armies of Krateros and Antipater.[15] After a disastrous attempt to cross the Nile near Memphis in the spring of 320, Perdikkas was killed by a conspiracy of his own officers.[16] That summer, at Triparadeisos in Syria, a new bargain was struck,[17] and in the fall of 319 Antipater died, having passed over his son Cassander and named Polyperchon regent and Cassander his chiliarch (second-in-command).[18] As the dust of the first major conflict among the Successors began to settle, it was clear that little had been resolved. Moreover, Cassander, intensely displeased at not inheriting his father's position, formed a new arrangement with Antigonos, Ptolemy, and Lysimachos.[19] With Polyperchon isolated in Europe, a second conflict had already been set in motion, one that would involve a more active role for the communities ruled by the rival heirs to Alexander's empire.[20]

---

11. The revolt in Greece was mirrored at the opposite end of the empire among the Greeks forced to settle in Baktria (Diod. Sic. 18.4.8, 18.7).

12. Arr., *FGrH* 156 F1 1–8; Just. 13.3–4; Curt. 10.7–10.10.

13. Diod. Sic. 18.23 (18.23.3: ὀρεγόμενος γὰρ βασιλείας); Just. 13.6.1; Arr., *FGrH* 156 F9 20–24, 26.

14. Coalition: Diod. Sic. 18.25.3–4; Just. 13.6.4–8. Ptolemy had signaled his break with Perdikkas by hijacking Alexander's funeral cortege of and bringing his body to Egypt: Arr., *FGrH* 156 F9 25, F10 1; Diod. Sic. 18.28.2–6; Paus. 1.6.3; Strabo 17.1.8.

15. Arr., *FGrH* 156 F9 26–8; Diod. Sic. 18.25.6, 18.29.1–3; Just. 13.6.10–17. Eumenes defeated and killed Krateros but failed to block the advance of Antipater: Diod. Sic. 18.29–32; Arr., *PSI* XII 1284; Plut., *Eum.* 5–8.1; Just. 13.8.3–9; Nepos, *Eum.* 3–4.

16. Arr., *FGrH* 156 F9 28; Diod. Sic. 18.33–36.5; Plut., *Eum.* 8.2.

17. Antipater assumed guardianship of the kings, Seleukos received Babylonia, Ptolemy remained in Egypt, and Antigonos became the general (*stratēgos*) of Asia, taking command of the royal forces (Arr., *FGrH* 156 F9 34–38; Diod. Sic. 18.39.5–6; Klinkott 2000, 67–74).

18. Diod. Sic. 18.48.4; Plut., *Phoc.* 31.1.

19. Diod. Sic. 18.49.1, 18.54.

20. Diodoros (18.50.1) described the death of Antipater as "the beginning of a new state of affairs and a revolution, since those in power set about pursuing their own interests" (ἀρχὴ πραγμάτων καινῶν ἐγίνετο καὶ κίνησις, τῶν ἐν ἐξουσίαις ὄντων ἰδιοπραγεῖν ἐπιβαλομένων).

This changed political reality was signaled almost immediately by a new feature of the struggle among the Successors: a rhetorical battle directed in particular at the Greek cities of Europe and Asia Minor.[21] Immediately after Antipater's death, Antigonos began to consolidate his position in Asia Minor, using the pretext of his concern for the Greek cities to eliminate his opponents.[22] With his strength and ambition manifest, the other players made ready for conflict. Polyperchon, casting about for allies, reached out to Eumenes and Olympias.[23] It was in this context that Polyperchon, in the name of Philip III, made a general announcement (*diagramma*) of amnesty to the Greek cities in the fall of 319.[24] With Antigonos and Cassander ranged against him, Polyperchon faced threats to both his legitimacy and his resources.[25] His proclamation was designed to alienate the supporters of Cassander and to counter the pro-Antipatrid oligarchies established in Greece. In reversing Antipater's interventions in the cities of Greece, the edict presented itself as a reinstitution of Philip II and Alexander's policy.[26] This was now a world where the Diadochs competed fiercely to be "masters of many *ethnē* and cities of consequence,"[27] and Polyperchon shrewdly initiated a style of propaganda that would become a major feature of the period.

The following year (318) saw the outbreak of the Second Diadoch War. Polyperchon's ideological campaign was only temporarily (and partially) successful—the

---

21. Public opinion of the Macedonian army had already played a major role in the struggles of the Successors. At Babylon, the infantry had forced the succession of Philip III and the recognition of Rhoxane's unborn child (Diod. Sic. 18.2). As long as the Argeads remained alive, personal connection to the royal family was also critical. But the passing of the old guard and the constant fracturing and reshuffling of the Macedonian army in these turbulent decades made the situation more complex. In this vacuum, mercenaries and manpower from the Greek cities rose to greater prominence.

22. In Hellespontine Phrygia, Antigonos accused the satrap Arrhidaios of attacking an allied Greek city, rebelling, and converting his satrapy into a personal domain (*dunasteia*). In Lydia, the satrap Kleitos garrisoned the cities under his control and fled to Macedonia. Antigonos stormed Ephesos and took the remainder of the cities of Ionia (Diod. Sic. 18.51–52). He then defeated the armies of Arrhidaios and Kleitos at Byzantion, securing much of western Asia Minor (18.72.2–9).

23. Eumenes: Diod. Sic. 18.57.3–4; Plut., *Eum.* 13. Olympias: Diod. Sic. 18.57.2.

24. Diod. Sic. 18.56 (derives from Hieronymos of Kardia, who probably transcribed the *diagramma* from the Macedonian royal archives).

25. In the winter of 318, Antigonos seized four ships at Ephesos carrying six hundred talents of silver from Kilikia bound for Philip III and Alexander IV (Diod. Sic. 18.52.7).

26. The *diagramma* makes no mention of democracy, freedom, or autonomy, but Polyperchon had indicated his intention of reestablishing the democracies to the Greek envoys at Pella prior to its promulgation (Diod. Sic. 18.55.4). The individual Greek cities, in turn, interpreted it in such terms in their correspondence (Diod. Sic. 18.64.3–5, 18.66.2, 18.69.3–4; Plut., *Phoc.* 34.4). See Poddighe 2013, 236–38, on the role of the Greek cities in translating the edict into civic decrees and the intentions of its original drafters in tailoring its language to the norms of Greek civic discourse for this very purpose.

27. Diod. Sic. 18.55.2.

rhetoric and the reality did not fully align.[28] By the spring of 318, when Cassander sailed into the Piraeus, many of the cities of Greece were willing to support him, and he began to find support within Macedonia itself.[29] In the fall of 317, Olympias made a dramatic reentrance into Macedonian politics, aligning herself with Polyperchon and taking control of Alexander IV and Rhoxane. The result was the execution of Philip III and Eurydike and a violent purge of the family and supporters of Cassander, but despite its initial efficacy, the alliance with Olympias proved to be the undoing of Polyperchon's cause.[30] As public opinion shifted in Macedonia, Cassander invaded in 316, capturing Olympias and Alexander IV.[31] That same winter, on a distant battlefield in Iran, another major contest was decided: Antigonos defeated and executed Eumenes and consolidated his hold over the East.[32] Possessed of vast financial resources, Antigonos marched west, now the most powerful of the Successors.

"ADMINISTERING THE AFFAIRS OF THE EMPIRE AS KING": CASSANDER'S URBAN PROJECTS (316–311)

A decade would pass before the "Jahr der Könige" (306/5)[33] made formal monarchs of erstwhile generals, but on the ground the Diadochs had already begun to define the shape of Hellenistic kingship, carving a new style of sovereignty from elements both improvised and traditional. Central to this presumptive rule were cities, essential pillars of royal legitimacy and critical nodes of resources and control. All of the Successors invested heavily in the infrastructure and urbanization of their kingdoms in this period, consolidating their power and articulating the contours of the nascent territorial kingdoms.[34] This period also saw the growing but limited

---

28. Polyperchon commanded Argos and other cities to exile or condemn the leaders of the governments installed by Antipater (Diod. Sic. 18.57.1). In Athens, a bloody elimination of those prominent in the former regime, including the illustrious Phokion, took place with the backing of Polyperchon's nearby army (Diod. Sic. 18.65–69; Plut., *Phoc.* 33–37). Similar stories probably played out in cities across Greece.

29. Diod. Sic. 18.68–72, 18.74–75.

30. Diod. Sic. 19.11.

31. Diod. Sic. 19.35–36, 19.49–52; Just. 14.6.1–12. He then had Olympias condemned by the Macedonian army and executed.

32. Diod. Sic. 19.12–35, 19.37–44; Plut., *Eum.* 13–19. In Media the satrap Peithon, locally acknowledged as king, was eliminated, and Pekeustas was removed from power in Persis (Diod. Sic. 19.46, 19.48). Antigonos then seized the treasuries in Susa and Ekbatana (Diod. Sic. 19.48.6–8, 19.56.5). In Babylon he denounced Seleukos, who fled to Ptolemy (Diod. Sic. 19.55).

33. Müller 1973.

34. Ptolemy already possessed Alexandria, now rising from Alexander's shadowy vision into reality, and with it the body of Alexander himself (Tac., *Hist.* 4.83.1, mentioning walls, temples, and religious rites; G. Cohen 2006, 355–81; Howe 2014). For its foundation myths, which stress the links between Alexander and Ptolemy, see Erskine 2013; Ogden 2013a; Ogden 2013b. Ptolemy moved the capital to Alexandria sometime before 311.

use of the title of king by the Successors in relations with non-Greek local communities under their control.[35] For the time being, however, Alexander IV still lived, and without any clear claim to legitimacy or precedent, the Successors walked a fine line between acting as kings and proclaiming themselves as such.[36]

Cassander, securely in power in Macedonia, began to surround himself with the trappings of kingship.[37] In the spring or summer of 316, he married Thessalonike, a daughter of Philip II and half sister of Alexander, securing a direct connection to the Argead line.[38] At the same time, he initiated the first major city foundation of the period of the Successors: the synoikism of Kassandreia.[39] Rounding out this royal posturing, he interred Philip III Arrhidaios, Eurydike, and her mother, Kynnane, with great ceremony at the royal cemetery at Aigai, effectively, as Diodoros remarked, "administering the affairs of the empire as king."[40] Moving south to confront Polyperchon's son Alexander in the Peloponnese, Cassander faced stiff resistance from the Aitolians at Thermopylai. On entering Boiotia, he assembled the surviving Thebans and began the restoration of the polis, which quickly gathered support from many of the cities of Greece, Asia Minor, and beyond.[41] Although the date of Thessalonike's foundation is unknown, it is highly likely that this took place in the same year, on the occasion of Cassander's marriage to the city's namesake Thessalonike.[42] At around the time, his eccentric brother Alexarchos founded the city of Ouranopolis through synoikism on the peninsula of Mount Athos, the easternmost of the Chalkidike.[43]

Within months of assuming control over Macedonia, Cassander had considerably bolstered his position. While appealing to Macedonian traditionalism, he had conspicuously embraced innovation, founding an eponymous dynastic city and symbolically and physically reversing the policies of his predecessors on the Macedonian throne.[44] His first major synoikisms fundamentally reorganized key regions under his control and set the standard for a process that would become so

---

35. The Persians offered Antigonos royal honors in 316 (Diod. Sic. 19.48.1), and Seleukos dealt with the non-Greeks as a king before assuming the diadem (Plut., *Dem.* 18.2; Bosworth 2002, 210–45).

36. Diod. Sic. 19.52.4.

37. Diod. Sic. 19.52.1; Landucci Gattinoni 2003.

38. Diod. Sic. 19.52.1; Just. 14.6.3 (mistakenly calls her the daughter of Arrhidaios); Paus. 9.7.3, 8.7.7. Earlier, it seems, Cassander had courted Kleopatra (Diod. Sic. 20.37.4). For the reputation of Philip in this period, see Errington 1976.

39. Diod. Sic. 19.52.2; *Marm. Par.* (*FGrH* 239) F B14.

40. Diod. Sic. 19.52.5: βασιλικῶς ἤδη διεξάγων τὰ κατὰ τὴν ἀρχὴν; Ath., *Deip.* 4.155a = Diyllos, *FGrH* 73 F3.

41. Restoration of Thebes: Diod. Sic. 19.61–62; *Marm. Par.* (*FGrH* 239) F B14. Support: Diod. Sic. 19.54.2; *Syll.*³ 337; Buraselis 2014.

42. For the date, see Touratsoglou 1988, 64n131.

43. Strabo 7aF35; Ath., *Deip.* 3.54; G. Cohen 1995, 105–6.

44. Touratsoglou 1996; Landucci Gattinoni 2003, 95–110.

characteristic of the Hellenistic age. With these projects, Cassander signaled his aspirations to kingship—a fact not lost on our ancient sources or his contemporaries—and the crucial role that urbanization, human mobility, and polis institutions would come to play in the development of the Hellenistic states.

Kassandreia included many features of the numerous royally directed synoikisms that followed. It was created from the territories and populations of much of the southern Chalkidike, primarily Poteidaia, Olynthos, and other communities on the peninsulas of Pallene and Sithonia, ultimately constituting the majority of the poleis of the former Chalkidian League (see map 2).[45] Kassandreia was built on the site of classical Poteidaia, a city whose fortunes had been bleak over the previous half century. In 356 Philip had compelled the Poteidaians to submit to Olynthos, giving their city and territory to the latter and subjecting them to mass enslavement and deportation (*andrapodismos*).[46] Philip destroyed Olynthos in turn in 348, and the entirety of the Chalkidike became subject to Macedonia. Cassander reassembled the surviving Poteidaians and Olynthians, some of whom had reinhabited the site of Olynthos,[47] and merged them with other communities and populations into a powerful new polity. This rich and strategically critical region had often felt the centrifugal and centripetal forces of state power, from the synoikism of Olynthos in 432 in response to Athenian imperialism and the subsequent attempts of the Athenians to break the union during the Peace of Nikias, signed in 421, to the resurgence of Olynthos as the head of the Chalkidian League in the fourth century and its defeat by Philip.[48]

Diodoros remarks that Cassander "ambitiously aided in the city's growth," adding extensive tracts of quality land to Kassandreia, which soon became one of the most important centers of the northern Aegean.[49] Its scale outstripped that of Olynthos at its height, and some seventeen poleis were included in the synoikism.[50] On the southern promontory of Pallene, Mende, the prosperous Eretrian colony famous for its wine export, and Skione became part of the civic territory of

---

45. Diod. Sic. 19.52.2-4; cf. Livy 44.11.2-3; Strabo 7aF25, 7aF27.

46. Dem. 6.20, 7.10, 23.107-8; cf. Diod. Sic. 16.8.3-5. Olynthos seems to have sent settlers to Poteidaia: Dem. 6.20, 20.60; Alexander 1963, 9; Hammond and Griffith 1979, 361.

47. Diod. Sic. 19.52.2. For the archaeological evidence of the postdestruction settlement at Olynthos and its transfer to Kassandreia, see Robinson and Graham 1938, 9-13. Olynthos was still referred to in the Hellenistic period (Hatzopoulos 1996, 1:197) and probably persisted as a *kōmē* of Kassandreia.

48. For the synoikism of Olynthos, see Moggi 1976b, 173-89. For the foundation of the Chalkidian *koinon* and its history down to Philip II, see Zahrnt 1971; Psoma 2001.

49. Diod. Sic. 19.52.2-4.

50. In addition to Poteidaia and Olynthos, these were Mende, Skione, Sane, Aphytis, Sermylia, Mekyberna, Therambos, Neapolis, Torone, Sarte, Solenas, Spartolos, Sinos, Strepsa, and Aioleion. See Hatzopoulos 1985; 1996, 1:196-99.

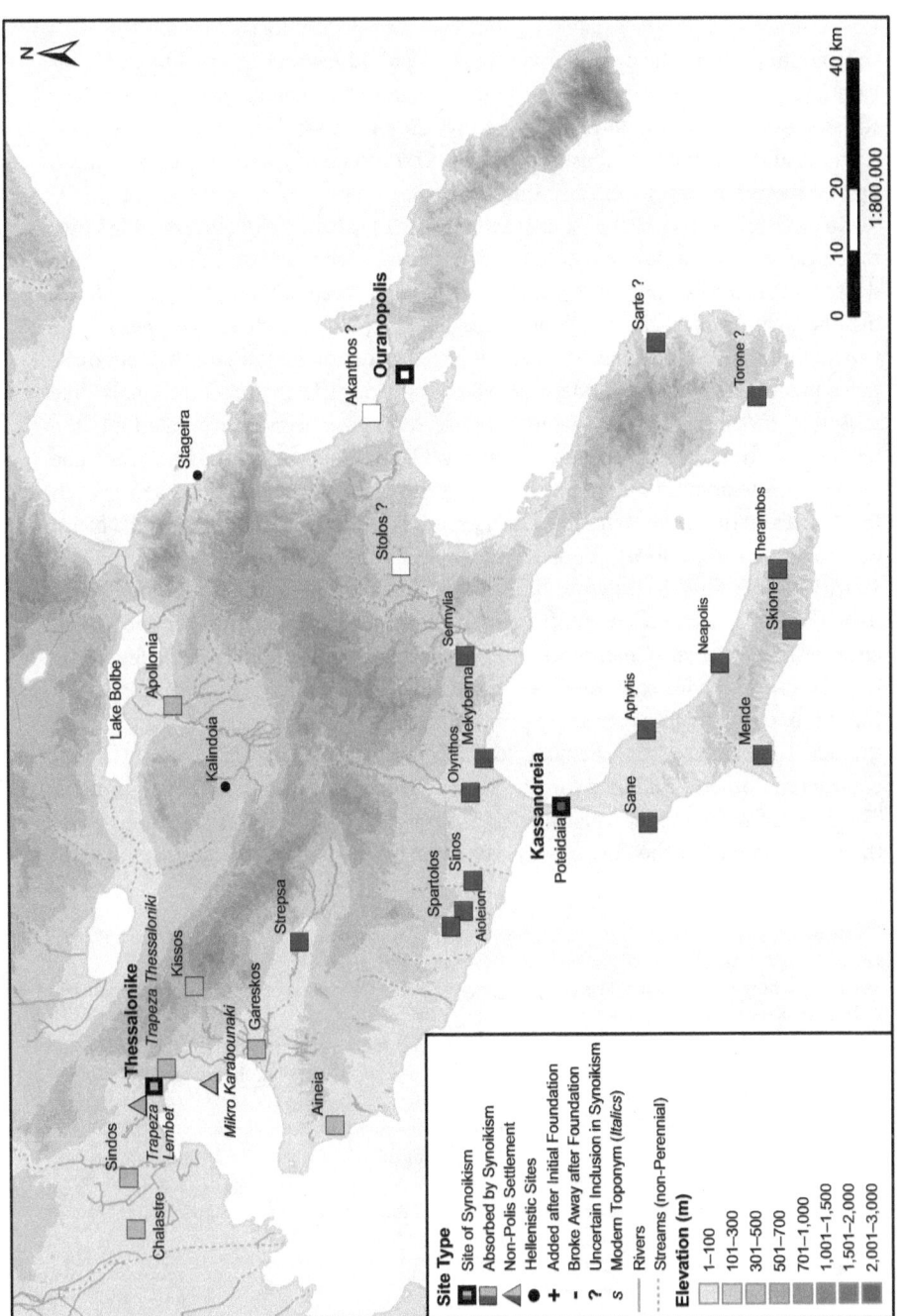

MAP 2. The Thermaic Gulf and Chalkidike.

Kassandreia, and Mende is later referred to as a seaport of Kassandreia.[51] Torone, a substantial polis on the central finger of the Chalkidike, was also included.[52] Controlling a territory of roughly one thousand square kilometers (386 square miles), Kassandreia probably extended to the borders of Cassander's foundations Thessalonike and Ouranopolis to the east and west, respectively, and to the north it ran up to Alexander's reorganized Kalindoia.

To its core of Greek and Bottiaian settlers, the flourishing city quickly added new residents, chiefly Macedonian nobles formerly in the service of the kings. Epigraphic documents record several land grants bestowed on Macedonians in the years following the synoikism.[53] The wholesale reorganization of this extensive area of the Chalkidike allowed the kings to carve out large agricultural estates for their subordinates, in one case including nonadjacent tracts stretching from the central Chalkidike to Bottike.[54] Although these estates do not seem to have been incorporated into the territory of the polis but formally lay on royal land, their owners may have become citizens of Kassandreia, and in one instance this was demonstrably the case.[55] Woven together from disparate elements, Greek, non-Greek, and Macedonian, and a blend of royal and civic authority, Kassandreia was a city for the new age.[56]

Cassander's most lasting foundation was Thessalonike, at the head of the Thermaic Gulf in Mygdonia. In contrast to Kassandreia, formed from the old Greek cities of the southern Chalkidike, the synoikism of Thessalonike centralized the populations of a comparatively less urbanized region, which was formally part of Macedonia. Owing to its strategic position and the rapid silting of Pella's outlet to the sea, Thessalonike soon became "the mother of all Macedonia"[57] and its main commercial outlet. Evidence for the form of the early Hellenistic city is limited. The original walls appear to have enclosed roughly sixty hectares (148 acres), just the northern half of the area now demarcated by the later fortifications, but only

---

51. Mendean wine: Ath., *Deip.* 11.28; Salviat 1990; Papadopoulos and Paspalas 1999. Port of Kassandreia: Livy 31.45.14 (*vicus maritimus*). Mende's tribute was assessed at five to fifteen talents (*IG* I³ 268.iii.5, 259.iii.15); typically it paid eight (*IG* I³ 262.i.7). For a description of the cities of the southern Pallene, see Meritt 1923.

52. The Athenian tribute lists record Torone as paying six to twelve talents (*IG* I³ 266.ii.28, 259. ii.15, 260.viii.10, 281.ii.17); in 447/46 it may have made two payments totaling sixteen talents (265.ii.71, 101). For the decline of the site of Torone after the synoikism, see Papadopoulos and Paspalas 1999, 173.

53. Land grant of Cassander to Chairephanes (306–298/97); ed. pr. Vokotopoulou 1997 (*SEG* XLVII 940); of Cassander to Perdikkas (305–298/97): *Syll.*³ 332 (*SEG* XXXVIII 620; Hatzopoulos 1988, 22–26, Hatzopoulos 1996, vol. 2, no. 20); of Lysimachos to Limnaios (285/84): Hatzopoulos 1988, 17–54 (*SEG* XXXVIII 619). All three of these documents likely have the same provenance, probably one of the public buildings of Kassandreia (Vokotopoulou 1997).

54. Hatzopoulos 1988, 17–54 (*SEG* XXXVIII 619).

55. Vokotopoulou 1997 (*SEG* XLVII 940).

56. For views on its status, see Vokotopoulou 1997; *BÉ* 111.269 (Hatzopoulos); Bresson 2007a, 173.

57. *Anth. Pal.* 9.428 (Antipatros).

scant traces have been explored.⁵⁸ Other, scattered remains of the Hellenistic city have also come to light, including a monumental building (perhaps the palace of the Antigonids), a bathing complex in the area of the agora, sanctuaries of Serapis and Demeter, and parts of the east and west necropoleis.⁵⁹

This region of Aegean Thrace was historically the home of the *ethnē* of the Mygdones and the Krousaians. It had been under some form of Macedonian control since at least the fifth century but was probably not fully incorporated into Macedonia until the reign of Philip II.⁶⁰ Despite its extended contact with Greek merchants and settlers, the literary sources maintain the Thracian character of this region into the fourth century.⁶¹ Archaeological and epigraphic evidence confirm the mixed cultural milieu of the cities and emporia there.⁶²

Strabo reports that Thessalonike was founded from the populations of twenty-six settlements (*polismata*) in Krousis and on the Thermaic Gulf that Cassander destroyed (*kathelōn*) and synoikized into one polis.⁶³ He specifically mentions Apollonia, Chalastre, Therme, Gareskos, Aineia, and Kissos and that Thessalonike was formerly called Therme, suggesting that the new polis was founded on or very near the site of classical Therme.⁶⁴ A number of other poleis and settlements, in particular ancient Sindos, can be added to those explicitly named by Strabo.⁶⁵

---

58. Velenis 1996; Adam-Veleni 2009b; Adam-Veleni 2011, 548–49.

59. Adam-Veleni 1989; 2011. Palace: Tasia 1996; Tasia 1997; Serapeion: Makaronas 1980; necropoleis: Romiopoulou 1989; Tsimpidou-Avloniti 1994.

60. Perdikkas II offered the land around Lake Bolbe to the Chalkidians (Thuc. 1.58.2). The Athenians subsequently took Therme in 432 but returned it to Perdikkas II shortly after (1.61.2, 2.29.6). In 368 the pretender to the Macedonian throne Pausanias held Therme (Aischines 2.27). For the incorporation of the region into Macedonia, see Hatzopoulos 1996, 1:171–74. See also Zahrnt 1971, 188–89.

61. Greek settlement: Tiverios 2008. Thracian character: Hekataios of Miletos, *FGrH* 1 F 146 (fifth century, stating that Chalastre was a Thracian polis and Therme a mixed community of Thracians and Greeks). Theopompos (*FGrH* 115 F 140, fourth century) calls Therme a Thracian city. Ps.-Skylax (66) refers to Therme as a *polis* (i.e., indigenous community). For the distinction between *polis* and *polis hellenis* in this region, see Flensted-Jensen and Hansen 1996, 151.

62. Tiverios 2008. For an overview of the prosopography of Thessalonike and the enduring attestation of Thracian names in the city from the Hellenistic into the Roman period, see Brocke 2001, 88–96.

63. Strabo 7aF21.

64. Strabo 7aF24.

65. For Sindos, see p. 41. Steph. Byz., s.v. Θεσσαλονίκη, notes that Thessalonike had once been called Halia. This may refer to the area where the city was founded (Papazoglou 1988, 195–96). Zonoras (*Hist.* 12.26) maintains that it was formerly known as Emathia. Papazoglou (1988, 196–98) suggests that this may have been the name of one of the *polismata* included in the synoikism. An inscription from Mygdonia demarcating boundaries and dating to the time of Philip II lists the ethnics of eight additional communities, most or all of which were probably included in the synoikism (Hatzopoulos 1996, vol. 2, no. 4): Eugeis?, Gedrolos?, Kallipolitai, Kisseitai, Osbaioi, Paraipioi, Prassilos, Rhamioi. In the Hellenistic period, Perdylos is attested epigraphically as a *kōmē* of Thessalonike (*IG* X 2 1 259; Hatzopoulos 1996, 1:120), and the names of several other settlements are known: Altos and Nibas (Papaconstantinou-Diamantourou 1990) and Acherdos (Nigdelis 2006, 147–49).

Despite his report that these preexisting cities were destroyed in preparation for the foundation of Thessalonike, a claim that other sources reiterate, literary texts mention the continued existence of some of them much later.[66] In his description of the Macedonian Wars, Livy mentions an attack on Aineia, which he refers to as a city (*urbs*), and it appears on a list of the Delphic *theōrodokoi* from 230–210.[67] Livy also refers to the continued existence of Apollonia, a Greek city founded by the Chalkidians near Lake Bolbe in Mygdonia, which began issuing coins again after 187 BCE.[68] Nevertheless, the synoikism seems to have greatly reduced if not in some cases entirely eliminated the major settlements of the region.

A survey of the archaeological evidence provides a more nuanced view of the effects of the foundation of Thessalonike. Aineia, said to have been established by Aineias after the fall of Troy, was a Greek polis in Krousis and the most southerly one incorporated in the synoikism. Situated at modern Nea Michaniona, where surface survey has detected pottery and architecture dating primarily to the fifth and fourth centuries, it minted an impressive silver coinage beginning in the sixth century.[69] Limited excavation has been conducted there, uncovering a cemetery of classical date.[70] The continued use of its temple of Aphrodite, however, along with its appearance on the lists of the Delphic *theōrodokoi*, suggests that it may have been a dependent polis under the control of Thessalonike. Farther north, the inland community of Kissos, at Mount Chortiatis, does not seem to have been a site of meaningful settlement after the synoikism.[71] Apollonia had been destroyed during the campaigns of Philip II, and evidently the survivors were included in the synoikism.[72]

Several Thracian or mixed Thracian-Greek communities on the northeastern shore of the Thermaic Gulf were incorporated into Thessalonike. The most important of these were the poleis of Chalastre (modern Sindos or Agios Athanasios)[73]

---

66. E.g., Dion. Hal., *Ant. Rom.* 1.49.4–5: ἐπὶ δὲ τῆς Κασάνδρου βασιλείας καθῃρέθη, ὅτε Θεσσαλονίκη πόλις ἐκτίζετο, καὶ οἱ Αἰνεᾶται σὺν ἄλλοις πολλοῖς εἰς τὴν νεόκτιστον μετῴκησαν.

67. Livy 44.10.7; cf. 40.4.9, 45.27.4, 45.30.5. *Theōrodokoi* list: Plassart 1921, 18, col. 3, l. 75 (230–210). For the list's date, see Hatzopoulos 1991; *BÉ* 107.432 (Hatzopoulos). For a discussion of whether inclusion on the list of *theōrodokoi* is evidence of polis status or implies independence, see Hansen and Nielsen 2004d.

68. Livy 45.28.8. See also Acts 17.1. Coinage: Gaebler 1926. Strabo mentions Gareskos and Chalastre (7aF36; see also Ptol. 3.12.22; Strabo 7aF20, 7aF21b, 7aF23), but he is likely following a pre-Hellenistic source (Edson 1947, 102n101). The ethnic of Kissos may be attested by an inscription after the synoikism: *SEG* XL 542, which dates to either ca. 350 or 294/93 (Hatzopoulos and Loukopoulou 1992, 123–45).

69. Zahrnt 1971, 143.

70. Tsigarida 1994.

71. Excavations have revealed the remains of domestic architecture and traces of the city's circuit wall, dating to the end of the fourth century BCE. Hammond 1972, 187; Bakalakis 1956.

72. Dem. 9.26. For the site, see Flensted-Jensen 1995, 117–21.

73. Modern Sindos: Hatzopoulos 1996, 1:107n2; Ag. Athanasios: Tiverios 1993.

and Sindos (modern Anchialos).⁷⁴ Excavations at modern Sindos have revealed a cemetery of extraordinary wealth characterized by mixed indigenous and Greek material culture (weapons, fine goldwork, imported southern Greek pottery) dating to the sixth and fifth centuries.⁷⁵ The known domestic architecture belongs exclusively to the eighth and seventh centuries, suggesting that the area of later settlement was elsewhere, possibly at Agios Athanasios,⁷⁶ but the precise fate of the community after the synoikism cannot be traced in detail. Ancient Sindos provides clearer evidence of the effects of the synoikism on this region. The settlement, inhabited since the late Bronze Age, rose to prominence in the ninth century, when the rich gold deposits of the Echedoros River began to be exploited. Recent excavations have uncovered a series of large refuse pits dating to the last quarter of the fourth century. The most instructive contained vessels that primarily date to 350–325, along with terra-cotta fragments and other small finds. The size and number of the vessels, the majority of which were produced at a local workshop, probably indicate that the pits were used for clearing out a group of adjacent households at the time of the synoikism and abandonment of the site.⁷⁷ This deposition shows the orderly preparation for abandonment and points to no forcible or violent transplantation of population. The local pottery, found here in abundance, does not extend past the last decade of the fourth century, when the workshop that produced it went out of use, eloquently demonstrating the cultural disruption of the foundation of Thessalonike. There is evidence that some limited settlement persisted at the site of ancient Sindos, in a much reduced state, but the majority of the population was incorporated into Thessalonike.⁷⁸

The synoikism most dramatically reorganized the immediate environs of Thessalonike, which formed the core of the new city. Somewhere in this area was classical Therme, the most important settlement, whose precise location and relationship to the foundation of Thessalonike are matters of long-standing debate.⁷⁹ Strabo's description strongly suggests that the two sites were either identical or at least very close to each other.⁸⁰ Some scholars have advanced this view, but others have suggested locating ancient Therme at modern Thermi, a few kilometers to the

74. Hecat., *FGrH* 1 F147 (Σινδοναῖοι· Θράικιον ἔθνος, ὡς 'Εκαταῖος ἐν Εὐρώπηι); Hdt. 7.123.3. For the excavations of the site and its chronology, see Tiverios 1993; Tiverios 1998; Tsigarida 1996; Kalliga 2004; Gimatzidis 2010.
75. Vokotopoulou 1994.
76. Tiverios 1993.
77. Kalliga 2004.
78. Gimatzidis 2010, ch. 3.
79. For an overview, see Vickers 1972; 1981: "one of the oldest problems of Macedonian topography" (327).
80. Strabo 7aF24. For the problems associated with Strabo's testimony, see Edson 1947, 101–4; Papazoglou 1988, 192–96.

southeast of Thessalonike, or on the peninsula southeast of Thessalonike now known as Mikro Karabournaki / Kalamaria, with a consensus favoring this identification.[81]

Recent excavations have greatly aided in reconstructing the settlement patterns that preceded the foundation of Thessalonike. Beneath the city and suburbs of modern Thessaloniki there is evidence for three main settlement sites in the archaic and classical periods: at Trapeza Lembet (Polichni), Trapeza Thessalonikis, and Mikro Karabournaki. Trapeza Lembet is a relatively small settlement, a large village, just to the northwest of Thessalonike. The plots explored so far in rescue excavations provide a rough impression of the site: a nucleated center surrounded by cemeteries to the east and south. Finds extend from the late sixth to the late fourth century, in general confirming the picture of abandonment at the time of the foundation and synoikism of Thessalonike. The large necropolis has tombs from the mid-fourth century BCE with extremely rich contents attesting to the wealth of the elite, similar to nearby Sindos: elaborate gold and silver jewelry and silver, bronze, and glass vessels. While the settlement shows no sign of occupation past the synoikism, the Hellenistic period saw continued use of portions of the necropolis, now probably one of the cemeteries of Thessalonike that surrounded the new city.[82]

To the east of Thessalonike, about two kilometers (one mile) from the eastern gate, is a low settlement mound, below a major Bronze Age site, at Trapeza.[83] This is the most promising candidate for ancient Therme. The city was probably a mixed community of indigenous Thracians and Greek settlers. As a major site of trade at the head of the Thermaic Gulf, it was strategically situated as an outlet for the wealth of inland Thrace. The remains from fifty or so excavation plots revealed in this area yield a fairly clear picture of the site. Ringed by cemeteries, this city with a thickly settled center was of medium size for the classical period. Several hundred burials have been excavated, providing a ceramic chronology for the habitation of the site that shows it was occupied from the early Iron Age (circa 1100 BCE) to the early Hellenistic period (as late as 300 BCE). There is good ceramic evidence for lingering use of the cemetery for several decades after the synoikism,

---

81. Therme at the site of Thessalonike: e.g., Edson 1947; Vickers 1981. Modern Thermi: A Hellenistic building with coins of Cassander and sections of an ancient cemetery with continuous burials from the archaic to the Roman period have been excavated here: Moschonissioti 1988. This site was probably included in the synoikism but not fully abandoned. Therme at Mikro Karabournaki: this view was first advanced by Rhomaios (1932; 1933; 1940), then followed by Hammond (1972, 150–51), Papazoglou (1988, 189–95), Borza (1990, 105–6), Hatzopoulos (1996, 1:107n4), and the current excavators (see p. 43n84).

82. Tzanivari and Lioutas 1993; Lioutas 1999; Lioutas 2003; Lioutas 2004; Lioutas 2010. New finds: Kotsos, Karliampas, and Karipidou 2011; *Ethnos* (newspaper), December 29, 2012; Tsimpidou-Avloniti 2105. Cemeteries of Thessalonike: Archibald 2014.

83. For the site, see Soueref 1990; 1993; 1994; 1995; 1996; 1997.

indicating that this was in all likelihood a somewhat protracted process, precisely as we have seen at Sindos and neighboring Trapeza Lembet.

On a small cape to the south, a settlement at what is now Mikro Karabournaki had significant commercial links to the Greek world. Its excavators have proposed a date in the eighth century for its establishment, and the latest horizon seems to be the fifth century, but modern activity has heavily disturbed the upper strata. The domestic architecture, which includes an example of a Thracian-style subterranean house, the burials, and local and imported pottery attest to the mixed cultural milieu of the site.[84] This was a thriving commercial center with extensive connections throughout the Aegean and the northern Balkans during the archaic and classical periods.

This clustering around the future polis suggests that prior to the foundation of Thessalonike, the pattern of settlement was characterized by several nucleated sites dispersed around the head of the Thermaic Gulf. Therme may have had its urban core at Trapeza Thessalonikis and its harbor at Mikro Karabournaki.[85] A number of smaller sites (at modern Trapeza Lembet / Polichini, Thermi, and Pylaia) were also nearby, and perhaps part of the polis of Therme.[86] The foundation of Thessalonike was in the first place a consolidation of the scattered settlements of Therme, with the secondary, and significant, addition of a number of communities and their territories from the wider region. The siting of Thessalonike just outside Therme also meant that the latter polis could be used as a base of operation for the new construction. Thessalonike drew on the populations, territories, and resources of a large swath of territory bordering the northern Thermaic Gulf and reaching as far south as Aineia. This wholesale reorganization of much of Mygdonia and the western Chalkidike probably brought the city's borders up to those of the two other major Macedonian settlements of the region: Kalindoia and Kassandreia. Farther west, the reorganization around the substantial foundation of Ouranopolis subsumed ancient Sane, along with Akanthos and the other small poleis along the southern half of the Athos Peninsula, and further redefined the settlement pattern of the Chalkidike.[87] This string of foundations established large urban centers with vast territories and considerable economic potential, cementing Macedonian control across this strategic region. Cassander soon extended this policy farther beyond the borders of Macedonia, with the refoundation of Thebes, the synoikism

84. Site: Tiverios 1987; 1990; 2008; see also Tiverios, Manakidou, and Tsiaphaki 1994; 1998; 2001; 2002; 2004; 2005; 2008; 2010. Cemetery: Pandermali and Trakosopoulou 1994; Tiverios 2008, 45–53.

85. Rhomaios 1940 suggests that its population was settled in villages (*kata kōmas*), not as an organized polis. Supported by Tiverios 2008, 26–28; rejected by Edson 1947, 103.

86. For Pylaia see Tsimpidou-Avloniti 2015.

87. The other poleis probably included Acrothooi, Dion, Kleonai, Olophyxis, and Thyssos. The circuit of Ouranopolis spanned thirty stades (ca. 5.6 kilometers, or 3.5 miles): Strabo 7F35; Papangelos 1993.

of Akarnania, and, a short time later, the foundation of Antipatreia in Illyria after he gained control of the region in 314.[88]

The reconstruction of Thebes served a dual purpose. Cassander had faced serious resistance from the Aitolians, who continued to support Polyperchon,[89] and a powerful stronghold occupying a strategic position in central Greece was a valuable asset in his bid to control all of Greece.[90] Equally important, perhaps, the reconstruction of Thebes advertised Cassander's commitment to the freedom of the Greeks and was intended to rally support throughout the Greek world and isolate his enemies, particularly Polyperchon. If Polyperchon's earlier proclamation purported to reverse the policies of Antipater and return the Greek world to the status quo under Alexander and Philip, Cassander's refoundation of Thebes signaled his willingness to go one step further and actually reverse the policies of Philip and Alexander. After its defeat at the hands of Alexander in 335, with staggering losses of around six thousand men, Thebes had been leveled and its walls pulled down. The surviving population was subjected to *andrapodismos*, with the exception of the priests, and the extensive territory of the polis was redistributed to the Boiotian allies.[91] Although the sources unanimously ascribe the decision to destroy Thebes to the council of Greek allies,[92] Alexander was surely not blind to the opportunity that lingering enmity toward the Thebans presented, and the destruction of Thebes was a powerful display of Macedonian power and a warning to other Greek poleis that might resort to arms. As Cassander's act coincided with the partial restitution of the people of Poteidaia and Olynthos, cities emblematic of the destructive power of Macedonian hegemony under Philip, its symbolism was clear in antiquity.

According to Diodoros, Cassander rebuilt Thebes "out of a desire for glory,"[93] and the poleis in Greece and Sicily aided in the resettlement because of their "pity" (*eleos*) for the fate of Thebes and the former "renown" (*doxa*) of the city. Pausanias mentions that the main supporters were Athens, which had received many of the Theban exiles, and two of the major cities of the Peloponnese, Messene and Megalopolis.[94] The identity of these cities confirms the link between the policy of Cas-

---

88. Livy 31.27.2; Polyb. 5.108.2; G. Cohen 1995, 76.

89. Diod. Sic. 19.35.2, 19.52.6–53.1.

90. At the beginning of 315, Cassander's army aided the Thebans in rebuilding their walls (Diod. Sic. 19.63.4). A Macedonian garrison remained in the city after its reconstitution (Knoepfler 2001, 12).

91. Din. 1.24; Arr., *Anab*. 1.7–9; Diod. Sic. 17.8–14; Plut., *Alex*. 11.6–12. Alexander spared the Kadmeia, the Theban citadel, where a number of its chief cults were located, along with the house of Pindar; the sacred land was not redistributed among the allies (Arr., *Anab*. 1.9.9–10). For the sanctuaries of Thebes, none of which show signs of destruction, see Symeonoglou 1985, 123–37.

92. Arr., *Anab*. 1.9.9–10; Diod. Sic. 17.14.1; Just. 11.3. See also Hurst 1989.

93. Diod. Sic. 19.54.1: φιλοδοξῆσαι βουλόμενος. Pausanias (9.7.2) ascribes Cassander's motivation to blind hatred of Alexander.

94. Paus. 9.7.1; cf. Plut., *Mor*. 814b.

sander and the ideological stakes of the reconstruction. In 316, Cassander had secured Athenian support and was contending fiercely for control of the cities of the Peloponnese with Polyperchon, whose power base was now confined to this region.[95] The reconstruction of Thebes had special resonance in the Peloponnese: in particular, the connection of the Theban general Epameinondas to the foundation of Messene and Megalopolis explains their interest in aiding in its refoundation.[96]

The effects of Cassander's refoundation of Thebes and the creation of his other capitals were also felt beyond the Peloponnese. Antigonos called for an assembly of his army at Tyre and denounced Cassander, condemning his marriage to Thessalonike, whom he claimed Cassander had wedded by force, and issuing a decree (*dogma*) demanding that he raze the cities of Kassandreia, which now housed the Olynthians, and Thebes as enemies of the Macedonians, as well as release Alexander IV and Rhoxane and submit to Antigonos as the legitimate general and guardian of the kingdom.[97] To this decree Antigonos somewhat ironically appended a clause asserting that the Greek cities should be free, autonomous, and ungarrisoned. His position underscored the fundamental significance of Cassander's foundations: they were clear steps toward not only carving out a physical empire but also asserting independence from the other Successors. While Antigonos's public gesture may have been mainly intended for the Macedonian army, his decision to issue a decree, especially one addressing the status of the Greek poleis, clearly included the Greek cities in its audience. Ptolemy, following suit, issued a similar decree.[98] Yet Antigonos's posturing ultimately fell flat. Narrow appeals to Macedonian traditionalism were no longer effective in the current political climate. The balance of Greek opinion was overwhelmingly in sympathy with Cassander on this issue, so much so that Antigonos was forced to back down.

A subscription list of donors demonstrates the continuing and widespread support for the refoundation of Thebes reported by the literary sources. This stele, displayed in Thebes sometime after 304, records the names of individuals and poleis[99] and attests to the extensive level of assistance and the protracted time

---

95. Diod. Sic. 18.74.
96. Bearzot 1997. An epigram on the base of Epameinondas's statue at Thebes credited him with the foundation of these two cities (Paus. 9.15.6). Pausanias (4.31.10) describes an iron statute of Epameinondas in the sanctuary of Asklepios at Messene, which stood beside the marble statues of the god, his sons, Apollo, the Muses, Herakles, the polis of Thebes, Tyche, and Artemis Phosphoros. See also Habicht 1998a, 43–44, fig. 8; Themelis 2000, 42–45. Messene also had a bronze statue of Epameinondas in its *hierothysion* (Paus. 4.32.1). For a discussion of Messene's commemoration of Epameinondas, see Luraghi 2008, 220, 278–79.
97. Diod. Sic. 19.61.
98. Diod. Sic. 19.62.1.
99. *IG* VII 2419 (*Syll.*³ 337; see also Holleaux 1938, 1–40; Bringmann and Steuben 1995, 130–33). For a new fragment of this inscription and a reconsideration of the old text, see Buraselis 2014. The list includes the names of the donors over a period of time, collated at a later date.

scale for executing such a project.¹⁰⁰ The now-fragmentary document preserves four entries for kings. One was probably Demetrios Poliorketes (whose name was later erased), who dedicated money for olive oil to the city from the spoils he took from the Rhodians. Philokles (Ptolemy's main representative in Greek affairs and the future king of Sidon) appears twice, dedicating large sums, and two other kings are on the list, although their names are not preserved.¹⁰¹ Greek states including Kos and (probably) Antigoneia on the Troad (both Antigonid dependencies), Eretria, Aigina, Malis, and possibly Samothrace are also named. A recently discovered fragment adds further donors from Cyprus, connected to Thebes through kinship with Athens and the Phoenician Kadmos, and Kassandreia and Pella, cities under Cassander's control.¹⁰² Appealing to sentiments of philhellenism, kinship, historical connection, and reverence for the gods of Thebes, as well as the ancient fame of the polis, Cassander's policy powerfully mobilized Greek public opinion.

Thebes, nevertheless, remained securely under Cassander's control for some time to come. Its restitution could not have been popular with all of the Boiotians, in particular the cities that had most opposed Theban hegemony earlier in the fourth century (Thespiai, Orchomenos, and Plataia) and had enthusiastically contributed to its destruction in 335 and profited from the proceeds of its former territory ever since. Diodoros remarks that Cassander (perhaps euphemistically) "persuaded" (*peisas*) the Boiotians prior to undertaking the reconstruction, pointing to the need to forestall potential objections to the revival of their former hegemon.¹⁰³ Thebes remained a base for Cassander's military operations and housed a Macedonian garrison, and it was not until three decades later, in or around 287, that it was reintegrated into the Boiotian federation (*koinon*).¹⁰⁴ In the meantime, the federation operated independently of Thebes, sending representatives to make an alliance with Antigonos in 312 and aiding the campaign of Antigonos's general Polemaios in the same year.¹⁰⁵

For the moment, Cassander's ambitious and conspicuous campaign to shore up the territories under his rule and assert his dynastic legitimacy stood out among the policies of the Diadochs. It would be answered shortly and in kind as the other

---

100. In 292 Demetrios besieged Thebes, so it must have been fully fortified by then. Plutarch remarks that it had been occupied for only ten years at the time (*Dem.* 40). Either this is imprecise or he had in mind the point at which the synoikism was completed, indicating that the city was constructed and repopulated over a period of almost thirteen years. See also Ath., *Deip.* 1.19b–c, which mentions the return of a refugee to Thebes thirty years after its destruction in 335.
101. Ll. 29–36. Knoepfler (2001, 18) suggests Pyrrhos and Lysimachos as the other two kings.
102. Buraselis 2014, 166–67.
103. Diod. Sic. 19.54.1.
104. Knoepfler 2001. The lion monument at Chaironeia was probably constructed after Thebes's reintegration into the *koinon*: Ma 2008; Mackil 2013, 97n43.
105. Alliance: Diod. Sic. 19.75.6; Polemaios's campaign in Greece: 19.77.4–7.

Successors began to invest in the urbanization of their emerging empires, but for now another round of coalition war loomed on the horizon. In the spring of 315, Ptolemy, Cassander, and Lysimachos presented Antigonos with terms in Upper Syria. He declined the ultimatum and made ready for a war on many fronts.[106] Aiming at establishing a major seaport for the coming war, Antigonos marched south to Phoenicia, where, as in 332, only Tyre offered resistance. Here he assembled his army and issued his proclamation denouncing Cassander and announcing the freedom of the Greeks.[107] In the Aegean, circa 314, Antigonos consolidated his control over the islands by bringing them into the *koinon* of the Islanders (Nesiotic League), a centralizing tactic that prefigured Antigonid policies elsewhere in the Greek world.[108] Meanwhile, the coalition against him had attracted other powerful dynasts and divided its forces to confront him on several fronts: by 315 the Third Diadoch War was under way.[109]

In Greece, Cassander entered the Peloponnese for a second time, to confront Polyperchon, Alexander, and Antigonos's lieutenant Aristodemos of Miletos. Passing through Boiotia, in what must have been a powerful piece of propaganda aimed at bolstering his commitment to "the freedom of the Greeks" he paused with his army to aid in the construction of the Thebans' walls, still rising a year after the initiation of the refoundation.[110] In the summer of 315, after little military success, Cassander made a symbolic display of his preeminece over the Peloponnese by presiding over the Nemean Games, then departed for Macedonia.[111] Isolated, Aristodemos convinced the Aitolians, ever hostile to Macedonia, to support Antigonos. Cassander responded with a strategy now typical of his rule. The Aitolians had last threatened Macedonia in 320, when Antipater had left Europe to confront Perdikkas. In his absence, the Aitolians had invaded Thessaly and convinced the Thessalians to join their cause. After defeating a Macedonian army, the Aitolians had broken off their offensive only when the Akarnanians invaded Aitolia and forced them to defend their homeland.[112] Mindful of the recent past, Cassander summoned representatives of the Akarnanian *koinon* to a common

---

106. Cassander demanded Kappadokia and Lykia; Lysimachos, Hellespontine Phrygia; Ptolemy, Syria; and Seleukos, Babylonia. Polyperchon was given the vague title "*stratēgos* of the Peloponnese." Diod. Sic. 19.57, 19.60.1.

107. Diod. Sic. 19.61.

108. Diod. Sic. 19.62.7–9, with Buraselis 1982, 41–44, 60–67. See also Constantakopoulou 2012; Meadows 2013; Buraselis 2015.

109. The kings of Cyprus joined the allied forces, along with Asandros, the satrap of Karia. See Meeus 2012.

110. Diod. Sic. 19.63.4.

111. Later that year, he convinced Alexander to defect to him. Diod. Sic. 19.64; see also Mari 2002, 192.

112. Diod. Sic.18.38.3–6. The Aitolians had invaded Akarnania and seized its harbor Oiniadai (Diod. Sic. 18.8.2–7; Plut., *Alex.* 49.14–15).

assembly on the borders of Aitolia and urged them to synoikize Akarnania by moving the populations from the scattered villages into the largest cities: Stratos, Sauria, and Agrinion.[113] Seeking to counterbalance the Aitolians, Cassander applied a policy that had already been characteristic of his efforts at building a stable kingdom in northern and central Greece. The move appears to have been effective. He left Aitolia without risking a battle, and the Aitolians were forced to turn their attention to the fortified cities of Akarnania. In the following year (313), Cassander's brother Philip based his successful assault on Aitolia in Akarnania.[114]

Meanwhile, as much of the East fell to Antigonos, Karia became a hotly contested battleground.[115] Asandros, who had received Karia at Babylon in 323 and joined Antigonos in 320, defected to the coalition in 315 and fled to Cassander in Macedonia.[116] He then returned to Karia with Cassander's trusted general Prepelaos.[117] Antigonos, leaving Demetrios in command, advanced from Syria to Kelainai in Phrygia to meet Cassander's forces.[118] After failing against Polemaios's army in 314, Asandros submitted to Antigonos, promising to cede his army and the Greek cities under his control. As quickly as he came to this arrangement, however, Asandros reconsidered his position, resuming hostilities against Antigonos and seeking aid from Ptolemy and Seleukos. With a combined offensive on land and on sea, Antigonos's generals Medios and Dokimos liberated Miletos, while Antigonos took Tralles and Kaunos and Polemaios seized Iasos, driving Asandros out of Karia by 313/12.[119]

At some point during Asandros's control of Karia, the population of its small polis of Pidasa was merged into the city of Latmos. The union is attested only by an undated decree of Latmos, one of whose stipulations reveals the hand of Asandros in initiating this project: as part of the reformed tribal allotment, Pidasians and Latmians were to be included in a new eponymous tribe called Asandris.[120] In the struggle for control of

---

113. Diod. Sic. 19.67.3-4. On the *koinon* of Akarnania in the fourth century, see Gehrke 1994-95, 42-43; Beck 1997, 31-43. For Sauria, see Freitag 1994.

114. Diod. Sic. 19.68.1, 19.74.3-6.

115. Diod. Sic. 19.57.4, 19.60.2-4.

116. For a new inscription attesting Asandros's relations with Pidasa in 321/20 and reconsideration of his rule over Karia, see Kizil et al. 2015.

117. Diod. Sic. 18.3.1, 19.62.5, 19.68.5-7.

118. Diod. Sic. 19.69; Plut., *Dem.* 5.2; App., *Syr.* 54. Tyre had capitulated in the summer of 314.

119. Diod. Sic. 19.75. A new list of *stephanēphoroi*, the annual eponymous officials of Miletos, was begun in 313/12 to mark the event, under the heading "In this year the city was made free and autonomous by Antigonos and the democracy was restored" (*Milet* I.3, 123 = *Syll.*³ 322). Dokimos's liberation of the city was commemorated by renaming the Lion Harbor "the harbor of Dokimos." He was also probably honored with burial in a heroön in Miletos's center (C. Jones 1992; Herda 2013).

120. *SEG* XLVII 1563 (Blümel 1997; Habicht 1998b; C. Jones 1999; Bencivenni 2003, 151-68; Wörrle 2003a; Saba 2007; LaBuff 2016, 81-84). Asandros's involvement probably also explains the use of the Macedonian month Dios (l. 18) and the exceptional requirement of intermarriage between the two

western Asia Minor, the synoikism of Latmos secured the route from Mylasa, Asandros's residence, to the Latmian Gulf and Miletos.[121] Textual and archaeological evidence demonstrates that Latmos was ultimately incorporated into a new, massively fortified site, Herakleia Latmos (see map 1, p. 6), five hundred meters (0.3 miles) closer to the gulf, on the slopes of Mount Latmos, and it is possible that this too happened under Asandros.[122] Later, after Ipsos, Herakleia was renamed Pleistarcheia when the region fell to Cassander's brother Pleistarchos, who briefly ruled Karia and used the city as his headquarters.[123] It was probably under his rule that the city received its massive fortification circuit running 6.5 kilometers (four miles) and the impressive network of stone roads and fortified outposts that extended on to Mount Latmos and beyond and controlled the Bafa plain.[124] The end of Pleistarchos's rule is obscure, but his subordinate Eupolemos assumed the rule of Karia by 295 and seems to have held it until circa 280.[125] Eupolemos no doubt continued to develop the city, and it was perhaps under his rule that the name reverted to Herakleia, a toponym suitable to the Macedonian traditionalism and military power advertised on his decidedly martial coinage.[126] This sequence therefore suggests that Herakleia was originally founded by either the Persian satrap Maussollos[127] or Asandros[128] or sometime between 313/12 and

---

communities. But see LaBuff 2010 and 2016, 79–87, for arguments that the impetus for the union came not from Asandros but from the communities themselves.

121. Reger 2004, 152. Mylasa as residence: SEG XXXIII 872. For the territories of Latmos and Pidasa and a description of their resources and geography, see L. Robert 1962, 504–14; W. Radt 1973–74; Wörrle 2003b.

122. For the geography, see Peschlow-Bindokat 1996b; 2005. For Latmos renamed Herakleia, see Strabo 14.1.8; Steph. Byz., s.v. Πλειστάρχεια: πόλις Καρίας, ἥ τις καὶ πρότερον καὶ ὕστερον Ἡράκλεια ὠνομάσθη (a city of Karia, which both before and after [being named Pleistarcheia] was named Herakleia).

123. For the career or Pleistarchos, see Gregory 1995.

124. For the walls of Herakleia/Pleistarcheia, see Krischen 1922 and McNicholl 1997, 75–81, which say Pleistarchos built them; Hülden 2000 argues the city was fortified under Antigonid rule. For the road network, see Peschlow-Bindokat 1996b, 51–67; 2005.

125. For Eupolemos, see Billows 1989; Descat 1998; Fabiani 2009.

126. For the coins, see Descat 1998.

127. Proposed by Hornblower 1982a, 319–23, on the basis of Ps.-Skylax's *Periplous* (99), which mentions Herakleia but not Latmos. This work has been dated to before 330 (Flensted-Jensen and Hansen 1996), suggesting that as a terminus ante quem for the foundation of Herakleia (favored also by Flensted-Jensen 2004, 1126–27; questioned by Peschlow-Bindokat 2005, 5n6). This reconstruction assumes that Herakleia and Latmos existed simultaneously for a while but does not explain why Latmos, still clearly a polis in the time of Asandros, does not appear in the *Periplous*. Moreover, as McNicholl 1997, 76, points out, Artemisia, Maussollos's wife and successor, captured Latmos (Polyainos, *Strat.* 8.53.4), which Maussollos had also captured (Polyainos, *Strat.* 7.23.2). This logically puts the foundation of Herakleia after the time of Maussollos, but it is possible that Polyainos meant Artemisia I. For a Panathenaic amphora dating between 367/66 and 341/40 dedicated by a citizen of a Herakleia, possibly Herakleia Latmos, at Labraunda, see Hellström 1965, 7–9.

128. Wörrle 2003a, 138–43.

301, when the region was under Antigonos's control.[129] The most likely date for the synoikism of Latmos and Pidasa falls in the period of Asandros's alliance with the coalition and his struggle against Antigonos (315–313/12).[130] After Alexander's siege of Halikarnassos, the political center of the Karian satrapy had reverted inland to Mylasa, as it had been prior to Maussollos's reorganization of the region. In this context, and perhaps under the influence of Cassander's policies, Asandros attempted to shore up his control of Karia in the face of Antigonos's assault, securing defensible, fortified cites commanding key routes of communication within the territories under his authority. Karia, with its multiplicity of small communities, entailed distinct challenges for imperial rule, and Maussollos had already embraced centralization as a means of building regional power structures there.[131] We will shortly see further efforts at consolidating this dispersed and contested region under Seleukid authority (Stratonikeia, Nysa, Chalketor), and in the wake of Karia's increasing urbanization, numerous communities responded to the new political landscape by entering into agreements of *sympoliteia* with one another.[132]

With Karia and much of western Asia Minor securely under Antigonid control, Antigonos attempted to cross into Europe. Breaking off his siege of Kallatis, one of the last holdouts of the revolt of the west Pontic cities, Lysimachos managed to prevent the invasion, largely because Byzantion blocked Antigonos's advance.[133] Meanwhile, Polemaios dislodged many of Cassander's garrisons in central Greece and marched on Athens.[134] Across the Mediterranean, at Gaza in the fall of 312, Ptolemy decisively defeated Demetrios and captured many of his soldiers.[135] Ptolemy then secured the cities of Phoenicia and gave an army to Seleukos, who invaded Media and recovered control of the region from Antigonos's general Nikanor.[136] Spread thin by the difficulties of fighting a war on so many fronts, Antigonos came to terms with

---

129. Blümel 1997; C. Jones 1999, 2. Rejected by Peschlow-Bindokat 2005, 5n6. Antigonos had not engaged in such projects in Asia Minor before the peace of 311, and all of the Antigonid refoundations that involved a change in site and name were given dynastic eponyms: Antigoneia or Demetrias. The toponym Herakleia, by contrast, stresses continuity with the Macedonian kings and avoids dynastic nomenclature, perhaps appropriate for a subordinate like Asandros, whose rule depended on his connections to Cassander (and Prepelaos) and Alexander.

130. *BÉ* 112.462 (Gauthier): "sans doute vers 313 ou peu avant."

131. Hornblower 1982a, 78–106.

132. Reger 2004; Schuler 2010; LaBuff 2016.

133. Diod. Sic. 19.77.5–7; Lund 1992, 33–43.

134. Thebes, still garrisoned by Cassander, in a nominal gesture of autonomy made a formal alliance with Cassander: Diod. Sic. 19.77.6. Polemaios's march on Athens: 19.77.2–78.

135. Diod. Sic. 19.80.3–85.

136. Diod. Sic. 19.86.4–5, 19.90–92. These achievements, Diodoros remarks (19.92.5), invested Seleukos with "royal majesty and a reputation worthy of rule" (βασιλικὸν ἀνάστημα καὶ δόξαν ἀξίαν ἡγεμονίας).

the coalition late in 311.[137] For the third time since the death of Alexander, the empire was divided up.[138] This settlement was a decisive moment in the development of the Hellenistic kingdoms. It sealed the termination of the Argead dynasty (Cassander immediately orchestrated the execution of Alexander IV and Rhoxane, interred with great expense at Aigai),[139] signaled that the ambiguous platform of "the freedom of the Greeks" was to be a central feature of royal policy, and marked a further step toward defining the physical shape of the territories.

Much is revealing in the responses to the peace of 311, and Diodoros's observation (drawing on Hieronymos of Kardia) that once the Argead dynasty was eliminated, "each of those controlling peoples or cities harbored royal aspirations and held the territory appointed to him as if it were a kingdom won by the spear" finds ample confirmation on the ground.[140] Between 311 and 301, the most significant efforts at reshaping the political geography of the regions controlled by the Successors took place, particularly under Antigonos. As we saw in the introduction, a short time after the announcement of the peace of 311, documented by Antigonos's letter to Skepsis, that polis was compelled to join the synoikism of Antigoneia Troas. It is perhaps an appropriately ironic accident of history that the first epigraphic evidence for the deployment of the slogan "freedom and autonomy" in this period comes from a city duly deprived of these things by the lead architect of this sloganeering, Antigonos himself. Skepsis's response, which added divine honors to the distinctions already accorded to Antigonos in the city,[141] highlights another defining element of what was to become such a familiar component of Hellenistic kingship: the cult of the ruler. This unfolding dynamic between kings and communities subsequently played out across the Greek world, a complex negotiation of sovereignty, independence, privilege, and power that underpinned the emerging kingdoms. For this period, however, the narrative of Diodoros, our main source, is far more compressed and selective. The result is that the details of this rich backdrop are often elusive.

"SEIZING A GREATER SHARE":
THE CONSOLIDATION OF POWER (311-301)

In the wake of the peace of 311, each of the Successors continued to consolidate and expand his power.[142] For Antigonos the truce was a setback, but in its immediate

137. At that point he was also campaigning against the Nabataeans (Diod. Sic. 19.94–100.3) and marching on Babylon (19.100.5–7; Plut., *Dem.* 7.2).
138. Diod. Sic. 19.105.
139. Diod. Sic. 19.105.2; Just. 15.2.5; Paus. 9.7.2.
140. Diod. Sic. 19.105.4.
141. *OGIS* 6.
142. Diod. Sic. 19.105.1–2: οὐ μὴν ἐνέμειναν γε ταῖς ὁμολογίαις ταύταις, ἀλλ' ἕκαστος αὐτῶν προφάσεις εὐλόγους ποριζόμενος πλεονεκτεῖν ἐπειρᾶτο (they did not, however, abide by

aftermath he attempted to exploit the temporary settlement. A campaign against Seleukos proved unsuccessful.[143] Forced to abandon the Far East and faced with the growing involvement of Ptolemy in the Mediterranean, Antigonos focused on consolidating his control over Asia Minor.[144] The revolts of two of his nephews, Telesphoros in the Peloponnese in 312 and Polemaios on the Hellespont in 310, showed the weakness of his far-flung operations.[145] Preying on this internal discord, Ptolemy seized Xanthos, Kaunos, and other Antigonid holdings in Asia Minor, established himself on Kos, and presented himself as the liberator of the Greek cities.[146] In 309, Polyperchon, still at large in the Peloponnese and the scapegoat of the Third Diadoch War, made one last attempt to resuscitate his old position as guardian of the kings. Summoning Alexander's illegitimate son Herakles from Pergamon, he rallied his allies and the enemies of Cassander, professing to restore Herakles to the Macedonian throne as the legitimate heir of Alexander.[147] The venture, however, was short lived. Cassander sent an embassy to Polyperchon and managed to convince him to eliminate Herakles, and thereafter Polyperchon fades from history.[148]

Amid these very unsettled conditions, the Diadochs increasingly turned to urban foundations to cement their control over regions, cities, and populations. The first of their series of important new capitals was Lysimacheia, founded in December 309 in the center of the isthmus of the Thracian Chersonese (see map 3).[149] It was sited directly between the coastal cities of Kardia (on the Melas Gulf to

---

these agreements, but each of them provided reasonable pretexts and kept attempting to seize a greater share).

143. In 309/8, Antigonos and Seleukos seem to have concluded some kind of treaty: App., *Syr.* 55; Capdetrey 2007, 25–38. By 308 Seleukos was campaigning against Chandragupta in India (Strabo 15.2.9; App., *Syr.* 55).

144. Ptolemy now held Cyprus (Diod. Sic. 20.21), and Rhodes refused to support the Antigonid offensive against him in 307, professing to have a common peace with all the kings (20.46.6).

145. Diod. Sic. 20.19.2, 20.19.5. The fate of Polemaios's rebellious forces is unknown. Ptolemy, who seems to have come to some kind of agreement with Antigonos, executed Polemaios on Kos in 309 (20.27.3; *Suda*, s.v. Δημήτριος).

146. *RC* 14 (ll. 5–6) contains a reference to Ptolemy freeing Miletos from "the harsh and oppressive tribute which certain of the kings imposed" and probably falls somewhere in this period. See also the documents, likewise undated, attesting a Ptolemaic presence in Iasos (Pugliese Carratelli 1967, 437) and Lykia (Wörrle 1977, 43). For Ptolemy as self-proclaimed liberator, see Diod. Sic. 20.27.

147. Diod. Sic. 20.20.

148. Diod. Sic. 20.28.1–3; see also Plut., *Mor., De vitioso pudore* 530c–d. Justin (15.2.1–3) says that Polyperchon was already dead at this point.

149. *Marm. Par.* (*FGrH* 239) F B19; Diod. Sic. 20.29.1; Pompon. Mela 2.24.4–6. The precise location of this major foundation was a matter of debate until the discovery of an inscription at Bolayır (Sayar 2000, 291, map 2; Sayar 2001, 103, map 1; Sayar 2007, 271; Küzler 2008, 499), where a marble shield of Philip V reading ΦΙΛΙΠΠΟΥ had previously been found (L. Robert 1955, plate 35). See now Sayar 2014; Lichtenberger, Nieswandt, and Salzmann 2015.

the north) and Paktye (to the south on the Propontic coast), in the vicinity of the elder Miltiades's foundation of Agora/Chersonesos.[150] The population derived mainly from the synoikism of the poleis of Kardia (along with its two dependent emporia Kobrys and Kypasis),[151] Paktye, and possibly Agora/Chersonesos. Pausanias reports that its foundation involved the destruction (*anelōn*) of Kardia, prompting Hieronymos's bias against Lysimachos because of the elimination of his native city, but it is clear that Kardia continued as a flourishing port and a dependent community in the territory of Lysimacheia.[152] It is likely that the civic territory extended down the Chersonese as far as the borders of Alopekonnesos and Sestos and absorbed the settlements of Krithote, Kressa, and Aigospotamoi.[153] As such, Lysimacheia controlled the northeastern half of the peninsula, including the important harbor sites and emporia along the Gulf of Melas, the rich agricultural land of the northern Chersonese, and the strategic sites along the Hellespont and the Propontic coast.[154] Little is known of the city itself. Among the surface finds are the remains of a Doric temple on its acropolis.[155] The city served as Lysimachos's royal mint and produced autonomous bronze issues, possibly with his image on

---

150. Ps.-Skylax 67. Miltiades constructed a wall between the sites of Kardia and Paktye, and presumably Agora/Chersonesos, which served as the capital of his Chersonesitan state, lay along this fortification line (Hdt. 6.36.2; Isaac 1986, 167–75). Agora/Chersonesos must have been at or very near Lysimacheia (*ATL* I 565; Kahrstedt 1954, 41–42), but it is unclear if it was still inhabited at the time of Lysimacheia's foundation. It minted coinage down to the mid-fourth century (*SNG Cop. Thrace* 824–49, suppl. 99), but little is known of the site otherwise (Isaac 1986, 159–97; Tsvetkova 2000).

151. Ps.-Skylax 67; Isaac 1986, 187.

152. Paus. 1.9.8. For a reconsideration of this supposed bias, see Lund 1992, 13–15. The literary sources continue to refer to Kardia as a distinct entity: Pliny, *HN* 4.48; Strabo 7aF52; Ptol. 3.12.2; App., *BC* 4.11.88. Either these authors were following earlier writers in their descriptions or Kardia and Paktye persisted as urban settlements and presumably ports dependent on Lysimacheia. The latter seems highly probable. Pausanias (1.10.5) speaks of Kardia and Paktye as *kōmai*. Furthermore, after the Thracians destroyed Lysimacheia in 198 (Polyb. 18.4.5–6), Antiochos III repopulated it with former inhabitants who had fled the city, presumably for nearby settlements (Livy 33.38.10–11, 33.40.6; App., *Syr.* 1); others were ransomed from the Thracians, and new settlers were added.

153. There is no evidence for the persistence of these sites past the late fourth century. Strabo (7aF56) calls Aigospotamoi a "ruined *polichnē*" (πολίχνην κατεσκαμμένην) and Krithote a "ruined *polichnion*" (πολίχνιον κατεσκαμμένον). Head (1911, 259) lists the coinage of Krithote as continuing until 281 BCE, but his justification for this date is unclear.

154. For the agricultural wealth of the Chersonese, see Isaac 1986, 158–75; see also Casson 1926, 210–11; Kahrstedt 1954. The nomenclature of the majority of the *apoikiai* founded here referred to agricultural resources—e.g., Krithote and Krithea (barley), Elaious (olives), Pteleon (timber)—and the widespread representation of Demeter on the obverse of the civic coinage of the Chersonese also points in this direction.

155. See ch. 3.

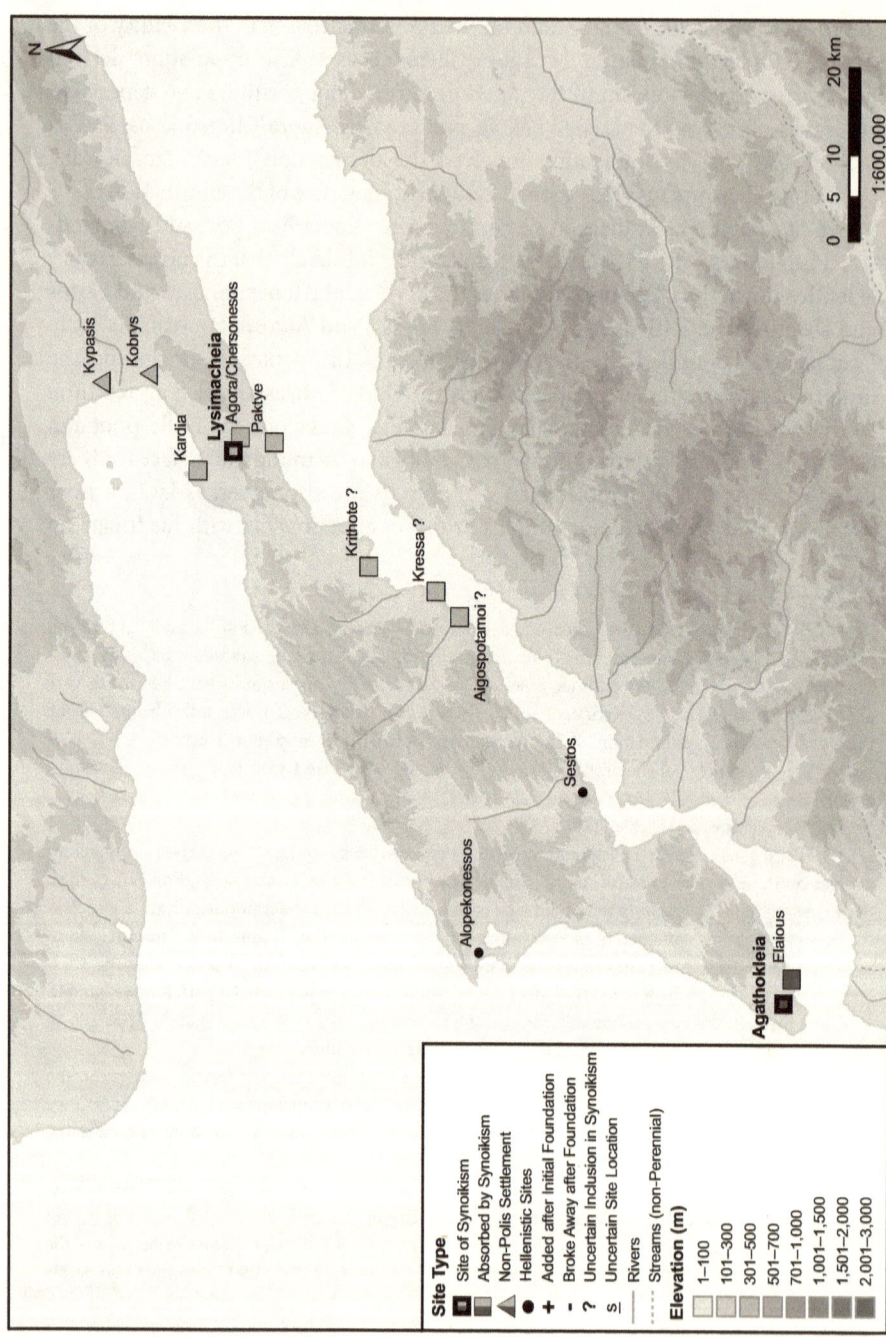

MAP 3. The Thracian Chersonese.

the obverse.¹⁵⁶ At his death, Lysimachos was buried in the city in a monument known as the Lysimacheion and accorded the honors of a hero.¹⁵⁷

Lysimacheia was intended at once to command the strategic and wealthy bridgehead between Europe and Asia and to protect Lysimachos's Thracian holdings from Antigonos.¹⁵⁸ At the same time, a powerful stronghold on the Chersonese also served to check the Thracians, with whom Lysimachos had been intermittently at war since 323.¹⁵⁹ The lack of any real authority over inland Thrace made the Greek cities an even more important commodity in defending the borders of his holdings and extending his dominion. For this reason, the cities along the western coast of the Black Sea were of particular strategic and economic value, but their united revolt against his garrisons, supported by Antigonos, revealed the fundamental weakness of Lysimachos's control in this sphere as well.¹⁶⁰ Lysimacheia was accordingly a first step to remedy this chronic problem in the changed political landscape after Ipsos. It provided a base for consolidating Lysimachos's current holdings, a strong position for controlling the Hellespont (resulting in commercial leverage over the west Pontic cities), and a jumping-off point for his ambitions in Asia Minor. As a complement, Lysimachos may have founded a city on the southern tip of the Chersonese, commanding the mouth of the Hellespont. Numismatic evidence for an Agathokleia (perhaps named in honor of Lysimachos's father) suggests that it is best located on the southern Chersonese and was a refoundation of the Attic colony Elaious, whose coinage ceased around the time of Lysimacheia's foundation and whose reverse types strongly resemble those of coins attributed to Agathokleia.¹⁶¹ If this reconstruction is correct, Lysimachos's

---

156. Lichtenberger, Nieswandt, and Salzmann 2008. The internal government of the city is poorly known but was probably overseen by a board of twelve *stratēgoi* (Hereward 1962).

157. App., *Syr.* 64.

158. Diod. Sic. 19.77.5–7. Lysimacheia played a central strategic role at many key points in the Hellenistic period: Seleukos I prepared his invasion of Europe there in 281 (App., *Syr.* 62); it served as the residence of Seleukos II (App., *Syr.* 1.4; cf. Polyb. 18.51.7–8); and Antiochos III had planned to resist the advance of Roman forces there and amassed huge stores of grain, weapons, money, siege engines, and other "resources of war" (App., *Syr.* 28). For the peninsula as a site of "connectivity," see Sayar 2014.

159. App., *Syr.* 1. Macedonian control of Thrace had collapsed under Alexander (Curt. 10.1.44). After indecisive campaigns against the Odrysian king Seuthes III, Lysimachos had come to a settlement in 323. Seuthes then built up his power in inland Thrace, founding a Hellenistic-style capital, Seuthopolis (G. Cohen 1995, 87–88). After the rebellion of the west Pontic cities in 313, Seuthes campaigned against Lysimachos, resulting in another settlement in 312 and probably a marriage alliance. Lysimachos never had more than nominal control over inland Thrace. For his campaigns against the Odrysians and Getae, see Lund 1992, 19–50.

160. Burstein 1986; Lund 1992, 37–43.

161. For the case for disassociating coinage dating to ca. 300 with the legends ΑΓΑ, ΑΓΑΘ, and ΑΓΑΘΟ from Agathopolis in Thrace, see L. Robert 1959, 172–79; 1977, 12. He further suggested that these rather belonged to an Agathokleia named for Agathokles the son of Lysimachos, a refoundation

foundations on the Chersonese controlled most of the territory of this circa nine-hundred-square-kilometer (348-square-mile) landmass.

By the spring of 308, the shifting alliances and unsettled conditions of the previous years intensified the competition among the Successors for hegemony over Greece and the Aegean. Now nominally allied with Antigonos, Ptolemy launched an unsuccessful invasion of the Peloponnese.[162] In the following year, Antigonos began an offensive aimed at controlling Greece and asserting naval supremacy over the eastern Mediterranean. The first step was Demetrios's celebrated entrance into Athens, where he was hailed as a liberator and offered divine honors,[163] followed by a major campaign against Ptolemaic-held Cyprus and a resounding victory at Cypriot Salamis in the spring of 306.[164] These achievements justified Antigonos's and Demetrios's assumptions of royal diadems and ushered in a new age of Hellenistic kings.[165] Antigonos marched against Ptolemy in Egypt in the fall of that year.[166] After this campaign ended in defection and defeat, Antigonos turned his attention to Rhodes in 305–304, aiming at dominating one of the remaining naval powers not under his control.[167]

Simultaneously, Antigonos consolidated his rule over his core territories, Asia Minor and Syria. At the same time as the Battle of Salamis, he founded a major new dynastic capital, Antigoneia, on the Orontes River, at the location of a long-standing base of operations.[168] In Asia Minor, another strategic crossroads, sometime between 311 and 306/5 Antigonos began the construction of two new regional centers, focused on Ilion and Antigoneia (later Alexandreia) Troas (see map 4). Perhaps spurred on by the revolt of Polemaios in 310 and the foundation of Lysi-

---

of Miletoupolis in Mysia (L. Robert 1960, 556n5; L. Robert 1980, 89n572; *BÉ* 82.85 [J. Robert and L. Robert]). G. Cohen (1995, 163–64) doubts this identification. Rigsby (2005) plausibly argues that Agathopolis is not a Hellenistic foundation but a Christian toponym; the coinage, following L. Robert, should be disassociated from this site and associated with an Agathokleia; the name Agathokleia more likely honors Lysimachos's father than his son, opening up the possible chronological range of its foundation date; and this city may have been on the Chersonese and possibly a refoundation of Elaious, rather than in Mysia, as Borrell (1841, 1–2) originally suggested.

162. His efforts stagnated after receiving little internal support from the cities he professedly had come to liberate, so he garrisoned Sikyon and Corinth and left the Peloponnese. For a possible explanation for Ptolemy's motivations in (briefly) abandoning Cassander for Antigonos, see Will 1964; 1984, 55.

163. Diod. Sic. 20.45–46; Plut., *Dem.* 8–14; *Suda*, s.v. Δημήτριος; Habicht 1970, 44; Mikalson 1998, 75–104.

164. Diod. Sic. 20.47–52; Just 15.2.6–9; Plut., *Dem.* 15–16; App., *Syr.* 54.

165. Gruen 1985.

166. Diod. Sic. 20.73–76; Plut., *Dem.* 19.1–2.

167. Diod. Sic. 20.81–88, 20.91–100.4; Plut., *Dem.* 21–22.

168. Diod. Sic. 20.47.5; G. Cohen 2006, 76–79.

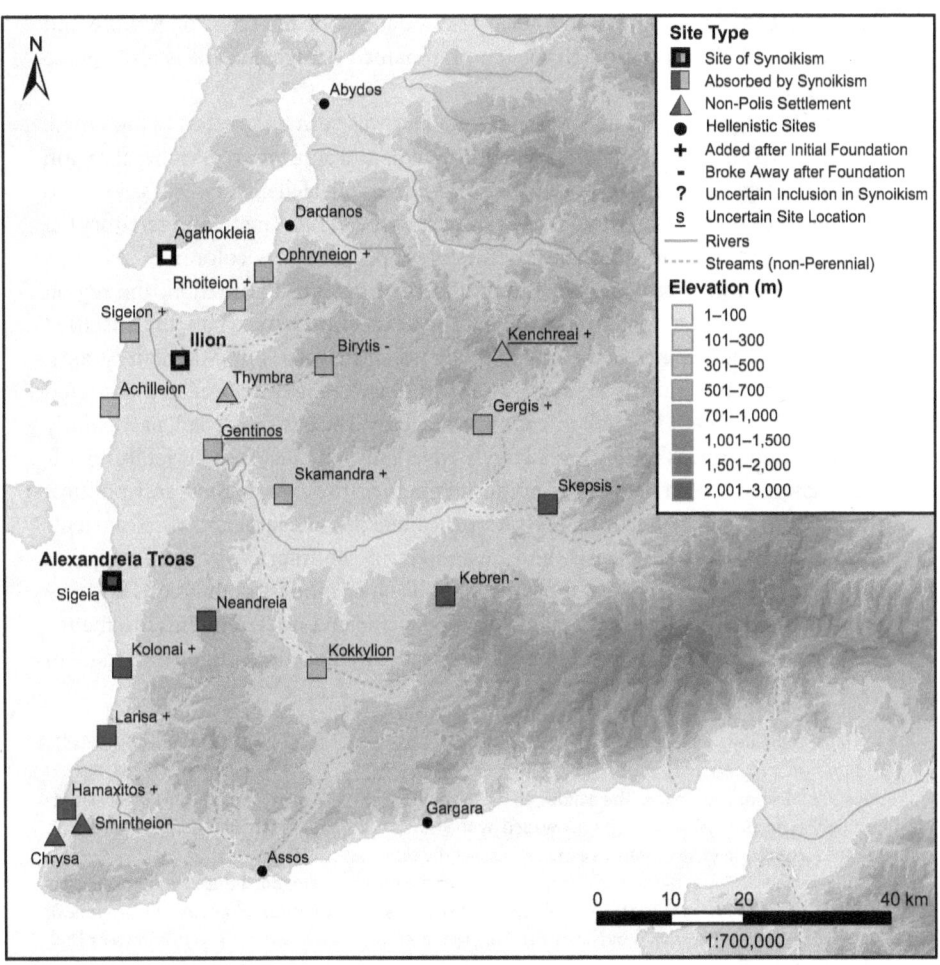

MAP 4. The Troad.

macheia in 309, a major capital poised against him across the Hellespont, Antigonos responded with an ambitious reorganization of the population and resources of the Troad. This policy was in step with his practice of consolidating and strengthening key cities and ports of western Asia Minor. We have already noted the investments that his agent Dokimos made at Miletos. Antigonos prompted the relocation and fortification of Kolophon, also between 311 and 306/5, and in the same period he developed Smyrna and promoted the well-known synoikism of

Teos and Lebedos (see map 5).[169] The refoundations of the cities of Ankore and Daskyleion in Hellespontine Phrygia, both renamed Antigoneia, likely also date to this period.[170]

The long-term impact of Antigonos's policies was perhaps greatest in the Troad. The synoikisms there transformed a fragmented and somewhat peripheral region into a strategic crossroads poised between powerful Hellenistic forces. Prior to 427, much of the coastal Troad had been part of the *peraia* (mainland territory) of Mytilene, and many of the coastal cities were originally its colonies.[171] After its detachment from Mytilene and the period of Athenian domination, the region once again fell under Persian control. For the next century and a half, the unsettled conditions that had resulted from the policies and rivalries of Athenian tyrants, Spartan generals, and the Persian satraps of Daskyleion encouraged a scattered pattern of settlement in small towns and villages.[172] The eastern Troad, particularly the area close to Daskyleion, was largely royal land, divided into agricultural villages assigned to Persian estate holders. Much of the commercial and political focus of the Troad centered on the satrapal capital and the larger, fortified agricultural cities of Kebren, Skepsis, and Neandreia in the interior. When Antigonos assumed control of this area, most of the poleis had modest populations and few were fortified. Antigonos's reorganization concentrated on two main settlements. On the western coast, he created a fortified city and harbor, Antigoneia Troas. In

---

169. Kolophon: *SEG* XIX 698 (Meritt 1935, 359–72, no. 1; Maier 1959–61, 1:223–31, no. 69). Date: L. Robert 1936b, 160. Smyrna: Paus. 7.5.1–2. Teos and Lebedos: *Syll.*³ 344 = *RC* 3–4, with Ager 1998; Pezzoli 2006; Bencivenni 2003, ch. 6. Thucydides, in his description of the Ionian War, refers to Ionia as "unfortified" (3.33.2). Miletos was certainly walled by the time of Alexander's arrival (Diod. Sic. 17.22.1–4), but the fortification of key sites was a major focus of the early Hellenistic period.

170. Ankore: Steph. Byz., s.v. Νίκαια; Strabo 12.4.7. Lysimachos refounded this city as Nikaia after Ipsos (G. Cohen 1995, 398–400). The walls spanned sixteen stadia (ca. three kilometers, or two miles). Daskyleion: Steph. Byz., s.v. Δασκύλειον (4). The location is disputed—two cities were known as Daskyleion, one the Persian satrapal capital (modern Hisartepe) and the other a Greek city on the Propontis. The latter was probably the site of Antigonos's foundation (G. Cohen 1995, 391–92). A recent survey in the Granikos valley shows a sharp change in settlement patterns in the area of satrapal Daskyleion due to the shifting political geography in the early Hellenistic period (see pp. 66–67).

171. Thuc. 3.18–49; Strabo 13.1.38. The colonies included Achilleion (Strabo 13.1.39) and Sigeion (Hdt. 5.94.1).

172. At the end of the fifth century, Ilion and Sigeion fell under the control of the dynasts of Dardanos, Zenis and Mania, clients of the Persian satrap Pharnabazos, who also controlled Skepsis, Gergis, and Kebren in the central Troad (Xen., *Hell.* 3.1.18–20). In 399, the Spartan general Derkylidas liberated Ilion and other cities of the Troad from Persian control, and in 396/95 the Spartans invaded Asia Minor under Aigisilaos and burned Daskyleion and many of the nearby estates (3.4.12–13). After the Spartan withdrawal, Persian control resumed until 362/61, when the Athenian mercenary commander Chairedemos took Kebren, Skepsis, and Ilion (Dem. 23.154). At the time of the Macedonian conquest, the Athenian general Chares held Lampsakos and Sigeion (schol. to Dem. 3.166; Arr., *Anab.* 1.12.1). See also Tenger 1999.

the northern Troad, he focused on Ilion—at the time a village dominated by neighboring Sigeion—whose ancient fame Antigonos exploited to consolidate settlement in this area and create the headquarters of the *koinon* of the Troad. Many of the more than twenty poleis that existed in the Troad in the last decade of the fourth century were incorporated into Ilion and Antigoneia Troas, concentrating much of the region's territory in their hinterlands. The wider impact of Antigonos's policy was the reorientation of the Troad's political geography, refocusing its primary economic and political networks on coastal cities and away from centers in the interior.

Ilion, despite its glorious past, had recently played little more than a minor symbolic role in the region.[173] Strabo described it as a mere village at the time of Alexander's arrival in 334, consisting of a small settlement and a "cheap" (*euteles*) temple of Athena. According to him, its *chōra* had been divided between the neighboring cities of Achilleion and Rhoiteion until the time of Kroisos, when it was refounded.[174] Whatever historical truth is behind this, it seems to preserve a record of Ilion's domination by its neighbors, which continued into the time of Alexander. Alexander famously sacrificed to Achilles and Athena here and pledged his patronage to the settlement, granting it the title of polis, ordering an improvement of the temple and other buildings, and exempting it from tribute.[175] But the restitution of the city's fortunes was in actuality left to the Successors.[176] Ilion's synoikism coincided with the creation of the *koinon* of the Troad, which centered on the temple of Athena and featured a yearly festival (*panēgyris*) and the transformation of the Iliaka into a festival on the model of the Panathenaia.[177]

Antigonos's control did not last long, and it is unclear precisely what the ascendancy of Lysimachos meant for the projects that he had initiated at Ilion. Strabo's description of Lysimachos's treatment of the city is obviously confused or marred

---

173. Xerxes had sacrificed a thousand oxen to Athena Ilias in 480 prior to his invasion of Greece (Hdt. 7.43). In the fourth century, an honorific statute of the Persian satrap Ariobarzanes was dedicated in front of the temple of Athena Ilias (Diod. Sic. 17.17.6). The Athenian tyrants Charedemos and Chares also exploited the symbolic power of this sanctuary, and, famously, the site figured largely in Alexander's presentation of his invasion of the Persian Empire (Rose 2014, 152–57).

174. Strabo 13.1.26–42. On the symbolism of building settlements from the stones of Troy, see Nagy 2012, 147–217.

175. Strabo 13.1.26. See also A. Cohen 1995.

176. Lykourgos, in an oration dating to a year after Alexander's visit (*Leoc.* 62) and surely exaggerating, refers to Ilion as "uninhabited forever" (τὸν αἰῶνα ἀοίκητος) since its destruction in the Trojan War.

177. L. Robert 1966a, 15–41; Boffo 1985, 102; G. Cohen 1995, 152–57. Foundation of the *koinon*: L. Robert 1966a, 21n2. First epigraphic evidence: *Syll.*³ 330 = *I. Ilion* 1, ca. 306/5. For a dissenting view on this date, see Verkinderen 1987, 247–69, which assigns *I. Ilion* I to the reign of Alexander; this has not met with general acceptance: see, e.g., *BÉ* 101.419 (Gauthier). For the organization of the festival at Ilion in the first century BCE, see *I. Ilion* 10, 11; see also Peuner 1926, 113–33. For the Iliaka, see Vian 1952, 246–87.

by a textual problem. He first says that after the death of Antigonos, Lysimachos devoted special attention to Ilion, building a temple and a forty-stade (roughly 7.5-kilometer, or 4.6-mile) city wall and synoikizing the surrounding "ancient poleis," which were "in a state of ruin" (*kekaōmenas*).[178] In the very next section, however, Strabo mentions that at the time of the Galatian invasion, the city was unwalled.[179] These passages clearly contradict each other, and scholars have often resolved the problem by emending the text so that in the first section Strabo is referring to Alexandreia Troas rather than Ilion.[180]

Excavation of the Hellenistic levels of Ilion has contributed decisive archaeological evidence to the discussion of this problem. On the basis of the ceramics from the foundation trench of certain sections, it is now clear that the seventeen-to-eighteen-stade (about 3.2-kilometer, or two-mile) foundation wall was not erected until the third quarter of the third century.[181] Recent research has also demonstrated that the construction of the temple of Athena Ilias began around 240–230, likely at the time of Antiochos Hierax's bid for power in the region.[182] The new evidence, in sum, shows that Strabo's description of the wall and temple of Lysimachos at Ilion must be rejected.

A mere emendation of the passage to make it refer to Alexandreia Troas (which does, in fact, have a forty-stade wall), however, does not completely resolve the problems associated with Strabo's account. He also says that at the time of his main source, Demetrios of Skepsis (first half of the second century BCE), Ilion was so depopulated that its buildings did not even have tiled roofs, and he later describes it as a "village-city" (*kōmopolis*) in the early second century. In reality, it was then experiencing a period of prosperity, with the construction of a new wall, the Athena temple and portico, and new blocks of domestic housing in the lower city.[183] Moreover, directly contradicting this testimony, roof tiles stamped with a

---

178. Strabo 13.1.26.
179. Strabo 13.1.27 (citing Hegesianax of Alexandreia Troas).
180. So Grote 1872, 300n2. Similar emendations are supported by Dörpfeld 1902, 207; Leaf 1923, 142–44; rejected by Tscherikower 1927, 17–18; L. Robert 1951, 7–8. Merkelbach (1976) proposed an emendation along these lines (not followed by Radt 2002, 560; 2008, 472) and entirely rejected the synoikism of Ilion. On this basis, Rose (2014, 168–69, esp. n. 47) sees no evidence for synoikism before the second century.
181. Tekkök 2000; Aylward and Wallrodt 2003. Blegen's excavations revealed traces of this wall, which he associated with Lysimachos (1935, 564; 1937, 594; followed by, e.g., G. Cohen 1995, 155), but this early date can no longer be sustained.
182. Rose 2003, with a review of early literature; contra Hertel (2004), who credits Lysimachos with initiating the synoikism and the construction of the temple and the city wall, though they were not finished until much later.
183. Aylward 1999; Rose 2014, 158–237. Strabo is also contradicted by Polybios (5.111.2–3), who mentions that the city withstood a siege of the Gauls in 216, and by Livy (37.37.2), who describes how the Scipios camped below its walls in 190.

monogram of the city have been found in third- and second-century contexts. Finally, excavations have also shown that the destruction caused by Fimbria in 85, at which time Strabo tells us he razed Ilion, was far less extensive than previously thought, affecting only the western part of the city and leaving the temple and much of the rest of Ilion untouched. The assembled material evidence shows the unreliability of Strabo and his informers (Demetrios and Hermesianax) for this period, and the influence on his account of the literary trope of successive destructions of Ilion. In particular, the interpolis rivalry of the Skepsian antiquarian Demetrios led him to deny that Ilion had been the site of Homeric Troy in his commentary on the Catalogue of Trojans (*Trōikos diakosmos*).[184] We should, then, be suspicious of his description of the weakness of Ilion in the Hellenistic period, and we must also revise our understanding of the roles that Ilion and the Successors played in the region at that time.

Ilion's wider political role is somewhat murkier. It is clear that Antigonos's establishment of the *koinon* transformed the city into a noteworthy religious and economic center, but it is less clear that a synoikism under Antigonos or Lysimachos accompanied it. The revision of Strabo's testimony has been seen as a reason to dismiss the commonly held notion of a synoikism of Ilion altogether and assume that here too he had Alexandreia Troas in mind.[185] There are, however, several difficulties with this view. First, Antigonos, not Lysimachos, initiated the synoikism of Antigoneia/Alexandreia Troas. Even if we assume that Strabo was referring to the subsequent refounding of that city as Alexandreia in the passage discussed above, no source mentions the incorporation of cities into Alexandreia at that time; in fact, Strabo explicitly states that Lysimachos allowed Skepsis to leave the union.[186] Moreover, his description of the cities "in a state of ruin" does not accord well with the cities he attributes to the synoikism of Antigoneia/Alexandreia (Neandreia, Kebren, and Skepsis, the most substantial poleis of the Troad at the time) and applies much more naturally to the smaller towns surrounding Ilion. Finally, Strabo explicitly refers to cities subject to Ilion.[187]

---

184. *Iliad* 2.816–77. For discussions of Demetrios of Skepsis, see Smith 1981, 34–43; Nagy 2012, 147–217.
185. Merkelbach 1976; Rose 2014, 168–69, esp. n. 47.
186. Strabo 13.1.33.
187. He discusses Achilleion in the time of Periander, then the destruction of Sigeion by the Ilians, and then remarks that "the entire coast as far as Dardanos was later subject to them, and it now is subject to them" (Strabo 13.1.39). This passage logically refers to a period between the time of Periander and the time of Demetrios of Skepsis and proceeds geographically from west to east along the northern coast of the Troad. In other words, Strabo refers to the incorporation of this area, from Achilleion to Dardanos, into Ilion. Dardanos, according to him, was so negligible (εὐκαταφρόνητον) that "the kings" kept incorporating (μετῴκιζον) it into Abydos and reconstituting it (ἀνῴκιζον) on its original site (13.1.28).

Ilion was almost certainly reinforced by the synoikism of several poleis and villages in the area, likely under Lysimachos, but the exact circumstances are obscure and effects of the reorganization and the new prominence of the city at the head of the *koinon* developed over time. It is likely that the original synoikism included the coastal settlements Achilleion[188] and Sigeion. Inland it may have included the small communities around Ilion (Ileōn Kōmē and the villages of the Simoeis valley).[189] At some point in the first half of the third century, at the time of the original synoikism or slightly later, it absorbed Kokkylion.[190] A highly fragmentary new document from Ilion attests the integration of the population of this polis and records the text of an oath sworn to Athena Ilias and displayed prominently in her sanctuary.[191] As is so often the case, not all of these cities remained in the union, and shortly after the synoikism we hear of Sigeion asserting its independence. Lysimachos took and garrisoned that city in 302 and presumably incorporated it into Ilion shortly thereafter. Strabo informs us that following this bid for independence, the people of Ilion themselves destroyed Sigeion and reincorporated it.[192] Following the Peace of Apameia in 188, Ilion absorbed Rhoiteion and Gergis, and it is likely that a fragmentary list of 231 new citizens found built into a Roman wall in Ilion is a record of the population absorbed from one of these two poleis.[193] This centripetal process continued, and by the end of the second century, Skamandra, far in the interior, was attached to Ilion by a *sympoliteia* agreement.[194] On the balance of the evidence, then, there is no reason to dismiss an early Hellenistic synoikism of

---

188. Achilleion, renowned for its cenotaph of Achilles, was a polis in the time of Herodotos (5.94) and assessed for tribute in the Delian League (*IG* I³ 71.III.137, restored), but at least by the time of Strabo's source, it had declined into a "small settlement" (*katoikia mikra*, 13.1.39), indicating both that it was likely incorporated into Ilion during the synoikism and that, though some settlement evidently continued at the site at least into the second century, it was greatly reduced. For the site (Beşik-Yassıtepe), see J. Cook 1973, 186–88; Korfmann 1988.

189. L. Robert (1951, 8n2) suggested that the synoikism ultimately included Sigeion, Achilleion, Thymbra, Glykeia, Kenchreai, the village of the Ilians, and the villages of the Simois valley; J. Cook (1973, 364–65) proposed Sigeion, Birytis, Gentinos, and the probability of Achilleion.

190. Kokkylion remains unlocated, but it was a fortified polis in the fourth century (Xen., *Hell.* 3.1.16). Pliny mentions it in a list of cities that have disappeared (*HN* 5.122).

191. Ed. pr. Rigsby 2007 (*SEG* LVII 1264).

192. Strabo 13.1.39. For a probable date of this revolt, in the first half of the third century, see L. Robert 1966b, 177.

193. Livy 38.39.10; *I. Ilion* 64 (undated) is the document enrolling new citizens—but see Catling 2004–9 for an argument that the community absorbed was an Attalid military colony. See also *I. Ilion* 80, l. 9. Rhoiteion was a substantial polis in the classical period, assessed at eight talents in 425/24 (*IG* I³ 71.III.124, 126). Its prosperity was probably due to its harbor (Thuc. 4.52, 8.101; Diod. Sic. 17.7.10). The site of Gergis/Gergitha (Karıncalı) shows no sign of inhabitation after the second century (J. Cook 1973, 347–51), and Pliny reports that it had been abandoned (*HN* 5.122).

194. *I. Ilion* 63. Presumably, at that time or sometime before, Ilion absorbed the poleis of Thymbra and Gentinos, which lay between it and Skamandra.

Ilion. It is otherwise difficult to account for the city's expansion and prosperity in the third and second centuries and its central place as the head of the *koinon*. The process of synoikism may have begun under Antigonos, when he founded the *koinon* circa 306, but there may also be some validity to Strabo's testimony, problematic as it is, that Lysimachos added to the city's territory. Sigeion, at least, fits well into such a reconstruction. The original focus seems to have been connecting Ilion to the coast. Over time, the influence of the polis spread farther into the interior, and it absorbed Gergis and Skamandra.

The nature and extent of the synoikism of Antigoneia and its refoundation and development as Alexandreia Troas under Lysimachos are also difficult to reconstruct. Antigonos founded Antigoneia Troas sometime after 311 and before 306/5 on the site of the coastal community Sigeia as a synoikism of the poleis of Kebren, Skepsis, and Neandreia.[195] As we have seen, Kebren and Skepsis were the most substantial cities of the region in the classical period, and this foundation was clearly designed to be the military and economic center of the Troad: Antigoneia Troas provided this part of Antigonos's empire with a substantial commercial center organized around a large port.[196] Sigeia, as its foundation site, must have been entirely incorporated and obliterated by Antigoneia/Alexandreia. Neandreia, though modest in the fifth century, had experienced renewed prosperity in the fourth. It had a new city wall and a newly expanded city quarter, but after the foundation of Alexandreia it shows little sign of occupation other than isolated deposits associated with cultic activity.[197] There have been no coins dating to the Hellenistic period found at the site and no other signs of systematic occupation.[198]

Antigonos's plan proved too ambitious: due to its mutual hostility with Kebren, formidable distance (more than sixty kilometers, or thirty-seven miles) from the coast, and desire for self-determination, Skepsis soon withdrew from the synoikism. Kebren remained in the union at the time of the refoundation of Alexandreia,

---

195. Strabo 13.1.33, 13.1.52. He does not mention Neandreia when discussing the initial synoikism, though he does at 13.1.47–8, referring to its incorporation into Alexandreia in his own time. But the archaeological evidence for the abandonment of the site at the end of the fourth century and the numismatic evidence from Alexandreia, which began issuing coinage with emblems borrowed from Neandreian types as early as 301/2 (Meadows 2004), confirm that it was part of the original synoikism. The foundation of Antigoneia postdated Antigonos's letter to Skepsis in 311 (*OGIS* 5 = *RC* 1; see also the introduction), when that city was still autonomous, and predated the first attestation of the *koinon* of the Troad, in 306/5. This date range is possibly supported by two other documents, the Theban donation list to which Holleaux restored "Antigoneians" in l. 16 (*IG* VII 2419 = *Syll.*³ 337) and an Eretrian decree (*IG* XII.9.210 = *Syll.*³ 348).

196. See Feuser 2009 for a detailed discussion of the harbor.

197. It was assessed at only two thousand drachmai in 425 (*IG* I³ 279, col. 2, l. 29). For the site, see Koldewey 1891; Schwertheim and Wiegartz 1994; Wiegartz 1994; Schwertheim 1994; Schulz 2000; Maischatz 2003.

198. Pohl 1994, 157–65.

but part or all of this community may have reemerged later. Its urban center has revealed no trace of occupation after the late fourth century, but textual and epigraphic evidence point to continuing activity at the site.[199] On this basis, J. Cook suggested that Kebren persisted as a small, presumably agricultural settlement, dependent on Alexandreia Troas, in the plain below the ancient citadel.[200] L. Robert, however, argued on the basis of numismatic evidence that sometime in the third century, Kebren was detached from Alexandreia and refounded, together with Birytis, as an Antioch by a Seleukid king.[201] Cook argued forcefully that these pieces of evidence do not constitute sufficient grounds to conclude that Kebren regained the status of an independent polis,[202] but Robert's thesis may be compatible with the foundation of an Antioch at the site of Birytis rather than at Kebren. Even if there was an Antioch in the Troad, it does not seem to have involved all of the territory or population of Kebren, much of which probably remained under the control of Alexandreia.

After Ipsos, Lysimachos took Antigoneia and renamed it Alexandreia Troas.[203] What all this entailed is not entirely clear, but if we take Strabo's description of Lysimachos's synoikism of Ilion, or at least elements of it, as a corrupted description of the Diadoch's building program at Alexandreia Troas,[204] it is likely to have involved more than a simple change of name and at least the construction of the forty-stade circuit wall and a temple. The walls of Alexandreia Troas have been investigated, confirming their extent and an enclosure of about four hundred hectares (988 acres).[205] In addition, two fragments of building inscriptions detail the

---

199. J. Cook 1973, 326–34, citing a series of terra-cotta votives, probably of Kybele, that date to ca. 300. The datable pottery does not extend beyond ca. 320. Supported by Akalın (2008, 8). For activity at Kebren, see *I. Assos* 4 (late third-century honorific inscription from Assos which stipulates that steles are to be set up at Kebren and Assos and mentions a festival held at Kebren); *Orac. Sibyll.* 3.343. A third-century CE inscription found near Kyzikos attests a cult of Dionysios Kebren(ios) (Hasluck 1907, 65n8).

200. J. Cook 1988, 18.

201. L. Robert 1951, 16–31, followed by G. Cohen 1995, 148–51. Robert based this theory on a rare group of coins (none found in the Troad) with an obverse or reverse of a ram's head and the head of Apollo (the traditional type of Kebren) and the legend *Antiocheōn*. The monogram BK on some of these issues and the depiction of a club (the known reverse type of Birytis) alongside the ram's head suggest that Kebren and Birytis were united in a sympolity at the time of the refoundation. Robert (1951, 33) also restored the Delphic *theōrodokoi* list to include Kebren, suggesting that the city reverted to its old name around the beginning of the second century—but see next note.

202. J. Cook (1973, 334–38; 1988) asserted that the coinage, because of its lack of provenance, could represent an Antioch anywhere, populated with people originally from Kebren and not necessarily being the revival of Kebren. Further, he disproved the restoration of Kebren to the *theōrodokoi* list by L. Robert (1951, 33) and objected that the Assos inscription (see p. 64n199) need mean only that there was a village still called Kebren, not necessarily that it was a polis.

203. Strabo 13.1.52.

204. Strabo 13.1.26. See the discussion of this passage at pp. 59–61.

205. Leaf 1923, 236–40; J. Cook 1973, 198–202.

specifications (*sungraphai*) agreed on by the building commission of the city and the contractor of public works for the construction of a city wall.[206]

By the first century BCE, according to Strabo, the coastal sties of Kolonai, Larisa, Hamaxitos, and Chrysa had been incorporated into Alexandreia.[207] They may have been part of the original synoikism, as most scholars have assumed,[208] but they were probably absorbed sometime later. Kolonai was fortified in the fourth century and seems to have evidence for occupation into the second century.[209] Larisa was a fairly substantial polis, assessed at three talents, just below Hamaxitos, in 425.[210] Cook found limited evidence for continuity of settlement at this site following the synoikism but conjectured that it had been much reduced.[211] Numismatic evidence may point to the renaming of Larisa as Ptolemais during the brief Ptolemaic control of the region (246–241), but this claim has been disputed, and Larisa once again appears under its own name on the Delphic *theōrodokoi* list of 230–210.[212] Of the cities on the southern coast ultimately synoikized into Alexandreia Troas, Hamaxitos was probably the largest and most economically powerful. The Athenians assessed it for a tribute of four talents in 425, and its coastal position and control of the salt pans at Tragasai and the renowned sanctuary of Apollo Smintheus, the great Smintheion some two kilometers (one mile) outside Hamaxitos, all contributed to its prominence.[213] Survey of the site has detected no pottery later than the fourth century.[214] Nevertheless, a decree honoring Nikomedes of Kos, a *philos* of Antigonos and Demetrios, and dating to between 311 and 306 mentions the cities of Antigoneia and Hamaxitos side by side.[215] Further, the only evidence for the control of the Smintheion by Alexandreia Troas, a decree honoring Sphodrias of Chios, is likely to date to the mid-fourth century, making it a decree of Hamaxitos rather than Alexandreia.[216] In addition, the numismatic evidence suggests that bronze issues of Hamaxitos may have persisted into the third century. All of this points to incorporation sometime in the second century, probably after 188, when Alexandreia began issuing coinage that imitated types of Hamaxitos.[217] This reconstruction is bolstered by the archeological evidence, which now demonstrates that the Smintheion was

206. *I. Alexandreia Troas* 1–2.
207. Strabo 13.1.47; *I. Alexandreia Troas* 4–8.
208. E.g., L. Robert 1951; J. Cook 1988; G. Cohen 1995, 148–51; Ricl 1997, 4–11; Akalın 2008.
209. Fortification: Xen., *Hell.* 3.1.13. Latest occupation: J. Cook 1973, 217; Akalın 2008, 14–18.
210. *IG* I³ 71.III.124, 130.
211. J. Cook 1973, 220–21. Akalın has proposed an alternative site, some six hundred meters (0.4 miles) south of Liman Tepe (1991), with evidence for settlement in the third century (2008, 18–21).
212. Numismatic evidence: L. Robert 1982, 319–31; *therodōkoi* list: Plassart 1921, 8, col. 1D, l. 19.
213. *IG* I³ 71.III.124, 129; Strabo 13.1.32.
214. J. Cook 1973, 231–35. Supported by Akalın 2008, 21–24.
215. *Iscr. Cos* ED 71g B, ll. 6, 16.
216. Hübner 1993, no. 110.
217. Bresson 2007b.

rebuilt in the mid-second century and at that time became a publication site for civic decrees of Alexandreia.[218] By then, if not earlier, Alexandreia certainly controlled Kolonai and Larisa, and Chrysa, south of the Smintheion, became the site of a fort (*phrourion*) and a small settlement in Alexandreia's territory.[219] Alexandreia thus appears to have had two main phases of development: The initial synoikism under Antigonos encompassed the coastal plain between Achaiion and Kolonai and the vast inland swath of the Skamandros valley and the neighboring highlands, subsequently diminished by the secession of Skepsis and possibly the partial withdrawal of Kebren. Then, after 188, either with the permission of Roman officials or on its own initiative, the city expanded into the rich coastal plains to the south, absorbing the cities from Kolonai to Hamaxitos.

The transformations of these urban centers, bolstered by a federation of most of the cities of the Troad, greatly altered the political and economic orientation of the region. The effects of the reorganizations under the kings are also evident at a broader level. The intensive survey of the Granikos valley in the eastern Troad adds detail to the overall picture of settlement shift that took place in the early Hellenistic period.[220] This area, inland from the Ida range, which separates the eastern and western Troad, was relatively close to the Persian (and onetime Lydian) satrapal capital Daskyleion. It is dotted with tumuli, the burial mounds of aristocratic families who served the Persian bureaucracy and farmed the land from large fortified estates.[221] Analysis of surface pottery indicates that Persian domination ushered in a period of prosperity, with intense cultivation. With the eclipse of Daskyleion as a major administrative node of the Persian Empire, the exploitation and settlement of this region shifted dramatically.[222] Whether the survey data indicate a

---

218. For the date and reconstruction of the temple, see Bingöl 1990; Özgünel 1990; Bingöl 1991; Rumscheid 1995; Özgünel 2003.

219. Strabo 13.1.32. J. Cook (1973, 234–35) identified the site at modern Göz Tepe with Chrysa, where his survey found evidence of only Hellenistic occupation. He believed that this site succeeded Hamaxitos after its abandonment. *I. Alexandreia Troas* 4, l. 7, mentions citizens (of Alexandreia) living in Chrysa.

220. For the results of the first two seasons (2004–5), see Rose, Tekkök, and Körpe 2007. For the most recent overview, see Rose 2014, chs. 7–8.

221. Rose, Tekkök, and Körpe 2007, 72–75. For the functions of the tumuli, see Arr., *Anab.* 1.13-14; Diod. Sic. 17.18–21; Plut., *Alex.* 16; Xen., *Hell.* 3.2.15.

222. Rose, Tekkök, and Körpe 2007, 106–7. Forty-one percent of the ceramic material collected in the survey dates to the late sixth through early fourth centuries. By contrast, only 5 percent of the datable artifacts belong to the Hellenistic period, most of them early Hellenistic, and the early Roman period is responsible for a meager 1 percent. Settlement in this region began to rise again only in the late Roman period (29 percent). These data are perhaps skewed by the fact that much of the focus of the 2004-5 campaigns was on the tumuli, but seventeen settlement sites were located and seem to bear out this pattern. The Persian estates did not cease to exist in the Hellenistic period, but they were largely reassigned to subordinates of the Macedonian kings and in at least some cases attached to nearby poleis: see, e.g., Aristodikides's dossier (*RC* 10–13 = *I. Ilion* 33). For estates of Laodikeia, see *RC* 18. See also ch. 2.

sharp drop in the cultivation of this region or a greater concentration of population in cities, (or both) is not fully evident.[223] In any event, they show a dramatic and apparently swift settlement change in the early Hellenistic period.[224]

As Lysimachos and Antigonos strengthened their positions against each other, the struggle for Greece continued. When the main theater of war shifted to the eastern Mediterranean, Cassander exploited the resulting vacuum to consolidate his hold on the Peloponnese and central Greece. In 304, Demetrios broke off his siege of Rhodes to direct his attentions to the recovery of Greece.[225] That fall he forced the Boiotians to rescind their alliance with Cassander and came to an agreement with the Aitolians. The next year, he set out to secure the major strongholds of the Peloponnese and eliminate the army of Prepelaos, Cassander's general in Corinth. After taking Sikyon, held by a Ptolemaic garrison, Demetrios moved the city to the fortified position around the acropolis, renamed it Demetrias, and received divine honors from its inhabitants.[226] Corinth and a number of other Peloponnesian cities soon fell.[227] In the spring of 302, Demetrios founded the short-lived Hellenic League, a conscious revival of Philip's League of Corinth. Although almost entirely passed over in silence by our literary sources, this was the first effort to reestablish a representative body aimed at dominating Greece since the Lamian War.[228] Alarmed by the growing power of Demetrios in Greece, a new coalition effort against Antigonos took shape.[229] Lysimachos and Prepelaos invaded Asia Minor. Prepelaos took Aeolis, Ephesos, and much of Ionia. Lysimachos, meanwhile, secured Hellespontine Phrygia and, advancing inland, per-

---

223. See ch. 2.

224. Özdoğan 1988; Özdoğan 1989; Özdoğan 2003; Jablonka 2004.

225. The Rhodians agreed to a nominal alliance with Antigonos in exchange for their city being left free, ungarrisoned, possessed of all its revenues, and exempt from fighting Ptolemy (Diod. Sic. 20.99.3). They promptly celebrated their success by erecting the Helios colossus in their harbor. The aid that Ptolemy, Lysimachos, and Cassander provided during the seige considerably enhanced their reputations in the Greek world, and the Rhodians sent to the oracle of Ammon for permission to honor Ptolemy as a god, subsequently dedicating a temenos called the Ptolemaion in the city, as well as honorific statues of Cassander and Lysimachos (20.100.2–4).

226. Diod. Sic. 20.102; Strabo 8.6.25; Paus. 2.7.1; Plut., *Dem.* 25.2; Thür 1995. Site: Lolos 2006; Lolos 2011, 72–73, 188–212, 329–31; Lolos and Gourley 2011.

227. Diod. Sic. 20.103. At Argos, Demetrios married Deïdameia, the sister of Pyrrhos (Plut., *Dem.* 25.1–2).

228. Plut., *Dem.* 25.3. According to Diodoros (20.46.5), Antigonos wrote to Demetrios in Athens in 307 instructing him to summon *synedroi* from the allied cities to take council in common for the affairs of Greece. Some have seen this as a first step toward the league of 302. The charter of the league is preserved in a copy from Epidauros: *IG* IV² I 68 = *Staatsvert.* III 446. See L. Robert 1946a, 15–33, for documents elucidating the role of Adeimantos of Lampsakos, the Antigonid agent and president of the league, in setting up and administering its institutions. For a general discussion, see Smarczyk 2015.

229. Diod. Sic. 20.106.1–5.

suaded Dokimos to relinquish Synnada and desert Antigonos.[230] The rapid loss of Asia Minor compelled Antigonos to march north from Antigoneia on the Orontes. Lysimachos dug in near Herakleia Pontica to await Seleukos's arrival from the upper satrapies. Antigonos likewise summoned Demetrios, and in the winter of 302/1, both sides prepared for a decisive confrontation.[231]

Antigonos's appeal reached Demetrios as he was locked in a struggle for mastery of Thessaly. In the fall of 302 Demetrios had departed Athens and landed at the port of Larisa Kremaste. Advancing north, he had converged with Cassander's forces in the open plains of Achaia Phthiotis. In the maneuvers that followed, Demetrios prevented Cassander's synoikism of Phthiotic Thebes, a strategically important polis and maritime outlet on the west coast of Achaia Phthiotis, and two otherwise unattested communities, Dion and Orchomenos.[232] The unsuccessful union was intended to brace his position against Demetrios and strengthen his hold on the cities (Pherai and Phthiotic Thebes; see map 6, p. 79) controlling the routes north toward Macedonia. Demetrios took Pherai but was forced to come to terms with Cassander to join his father. The details are unclear, but he withdrew under the cover of securing a clause protecting the freedom of the Greeks, and Thessaly fell to Cassander without a battle.[233]

Sometime during these campaigns, Demetrios probably refounded three communities (Halos, Peuma, and Narthakion) in Achaia Phthiotis and consolidated the region into a new ethnic *koinon*.[234] The details, passed over in the compressed narrative of Diodoros, are fleshed out by the archaeological material. Halos and Peuma, on the spurs of the Othrys Mountains on the southern end of the Krokian Plain, commanded the route toward Pharsalos and central Thessaly. Philip had besieged and destroyed classical Halos, a port city on the southern coast of the

---

230. Diod. Sic. 20.107. Synnada may have been an old Phrygian city (so Billows 1990, 296) reinforced by Macedonian colonization or a military settlement dating to the early Hellenistic period. Dokimos founded the nearby, eponymous Dokimeion either as an agent of Antigonos or, after his defection to Lysimachos, as a semi-independent dynast. For a discussion of the sources, see G. Cohen 1995, 295–97 (Dokimeion), 322–24 (Synnada). For Dokimos, see Kobes 1996, 77, 93–94, 101–4, 171–73, 207–19.

231. Diod. Sic. 20.108–11.

232. Diod. Sic. 20.110. For possible numismatic evidence for Dion, see Hatzopoulos and Psoma 1998. Phthiotic Thebes was itself the result of a late fourth-century synoikism of the Thessalian city Pyrasos and the Achaian polis Phylake (Herakleides Kritikos, *BNJ* 369A F3.2; Strabo 9.5.14; Ps.-Skylax 64; Stählin 1924, 170–76; Stählin 1934). Helly (2009, 341) has suggested that Cassander was responsible for the foundation of Phthiotic Thebes and not just this planned enlargement in 302. Diodoros, however, specifically mentions that it did not take part in the Lamian War along with the rest of the Achaians (18.11.1).

233. Diod. Sic. 20.112.1.

234. Since the sixth century, Achaia Phthiotis had been a perioikic dependency of the Thessalians. In the fourth century it fell under the control of the tyrant Alexander of Pherai (Westlake 1935). It was subsequently allied with Boiotian *koinon* (Diod. Sic. 15.80.6).

Pagasitic Gulf, in 346 and assigned its territory to the Pharsalians.[235] The people of Halos were absorbed into towns of Achaia Phthiotis or taken into Pharsalos or continued to live in scattered settlements around the ruins of the former city.[236] The polis had controlled an open shore suitable for beaching small ships, and its territory included a good deal of the Krokian Plain.[237] The new site of Halos, about two kilometers (one mile) farther inland, controlled the same beach but had the strategic advantage of a small acropolis.[238] The considerations here were in many ways similar to those evident in Demetrios's refoundation of Sikyon in a more advantageous (and defensible) location only one year earlier, in 303.[239] The design of New Halos, fortified with 120 towers and an innovative gate system, also seems indicative of the great besieger. Numismatic evidence too perhaps links Demetrios's army to the refoundation of the site.[240] Similar strategic imperatives appear to have motivated the refoundation of the polis at Kastro Kallithea, probably ancient Peuma, which was newly laid out in the late fourth century on an orthogonal plan and heavily fortified.[241] Narthakion, south of the Othrys Mountains on the road toward Thermopylai, was also expanded and fortified in this period.[242] The overall impression is of a wholesale Antigonid reorganization of Achaia Phthiotis, and it is highly likely that at the same time, Demetrios created an Achaian *koinon*, in keeping with the Antigonid policy elsewhere.[243]

235. Siege: Dem. 19.163. Destruction and reassignment of territory: Strabo 9.5.8; Dem. 11.1, 19.39.
236. Reinders 1988.
237. Reinders, Dijkstra, et al. 1996.
238. Reinders 1988; Reinders 1993; Reinders, Dickenson, et al. 2014. Strabo's description is explicit as to who refounded Halos, but the name is lost in a lacuna (9.5.8). Most editors restore this lacuna as συνῴ[κισαν Φαρσάλιοι] (e.g., Meineke 1877, 2:610), since Philip reassigned the former territory of Halos to Pharsalos, but συνῴ[κισε ὁ Δημήτριος] is just as possible (accepted by Radt 2008, 105). It is also unlikely that the Pharsalians would refound Halos, particularly since they enjoyed its revenues and the two had previously been enemies (Dem. 19.36).
239. Diod. Sic. 20.102–3.
240. For the gates of Halos see Reinders, Dijkstra, et al. 1996; Reinders 2005; Dickenson, Radlof, and Reinders 2006; Reinders 2006; Reinders, Dickenson, et al. 2014, 75–96. Reinders (2009, 372) adduces the following arguments: first, a late fourth-century coin hoard contains an assemblage that is uncharacteristic of other coin hoards in Thessaly (see also Reinders, Dijkstra, et al. 1996) and may reflect the progress of Demetrios's army from Rhodes to Athens, Euboia, and Achaia, where it was lost in the construction of the fortifications; second, the coins of New Halos were struck with adjusted dies, a practice that began in the Levant and is first attested in Greece following Demetrios's resuscitation of the Euboian *koinon*.
241. Tziafalias et al. 2006a; Tziafalias et al. 2006b; Haagsma et al. 2011; Surtees 2012; Surtees, Karapanou, and Haagsma 2014. Possibly because of complications stemming from its refoundation, Peuma became embroiled in a series of boundary disputes, arbitrated by judges from Kassandreia ca. 270–260 (Ager 1996, nos. 30–31).
242. Bouyia 2005; 2006.
243. Reinders 2009, 372–73; Helly 2009, 353: the *koinon* is suggested by the common monogram AX on the coinage of New Halos and Peuma. For the coinage of Peuma, see Head 1911, 304; *SNG Cop. Thessaly* 198.

"THE SUPREME STRUGGLE": THE FALL OF ANTIGONOS AND THE SHAPING OF THE HELLENISTIC KINGDOMS (301–281)

Despite their immense efforts to organize their power in Greece and Asia Minor, Demetrios and Antigonos were comprehensively defeated by the coalition forces in the summer of 301 at Ipsos in central Phrygia.[244] With Antigonos dead, Demetrios fell back on Ephesos and clung to his naval superiority in the Aegean and eastern Mediterranean, centered chiefly on Cyprus, the Cyclades, Phoenica, and the few coastal cities of Greece he still managed to control.[245] In the meantime, Lysimachos took possession of most of Asia Minor west of the Tauros Mountains, Seleukos assumed control of northern Syria, and Ptolemy, who had not appeared at Ipsos but instead invaded Koile Syria, now possessed the southern half of Syria and parts of Lykia, Pamphylia, and Pisidia.[246] Cassander had a firmer hold on Greece, and his brother Pleistarchos established a short-lived dynasty in Karia.[247] As borders shifted dramatically, the new masters of these regions sought to consolidate their emerging kingdoms, capitalizing on the fruits of their "common effort in the supreme struggle" against Antigonos.[248] In Asia Minor, as we have seen, Lysimachos quickly set about reorganizing the cities founded under Antigonid rule. Sometime in this period, probably shortly after 300, Lysimachos's former wife Amastris founded an eponymous city on the Pontic coast west of Herakleia from the synoikism of four Greek towns: Sesamos, Kytoros, Kromna, and Tieion.[249] Seleukos staked his claim to Syria, long the axis of the Antigonid kingdom, with a flurry of urban foundations—Seleukeia in Pieria, Antioch, Apameia, and Laodikeia on the Sea—that inaugurated the exceptionally prolific urbanization of the Seleukid kingdom.[250] Here, Seleukid policy fundamentally reshaped the settlement patterns of native communities, in a manner parallel to the impact of royal

---

244. Diod. Sic. 21F4b; Plut., *Dem.* 28–29.

245. Chiefly Corinth. Athens gave notice to Demetrios not to attempt to reenter the city, returned his wife, belongings, and ships, and went over to Cassander (Plut., *Dem.* 30).

246. Diod. Sic. 21.1.5; Just. 15.4; Plut., *Dem.* 28–30.1. Seleukos claimed southern Syria and was supported by the other victors at Ipsos, but Ptolemy refused to relinquish his claim to the region.

247. Plut., *Dem.* 31.4; L. Robert 1945, 55. Pleistarchos seems to have lost his kingdom after the alliance between Seleukos and Demetrios (Will 1966, 88–9).

248. Diod. Sic. 21F2: τὴν τῶν ὅλων κοινοπραγίαν.

249. Strabo 12.3.10; Memnon, *FGrH* 434 F4.9; G. Cohen 1995, 383–84. Tieion soon broke away from the foundation, probably after Amastris was murdered by her sons ca. 284. Lysimachos assumed control over the city until his death.

250. Malalas (8.199) fixes the foundation date of Seleukeia on 23 Xanthikos 300 and the foundation of Antioch a month later. For these foundations see G. Cohen 2006, 80–93, 94–101, 111–16, 126–35.

policy on the poleis of Greece and Asia Minor.[251] The aftermath of Ipsos was also characterized by shifting alliances among the remaining Successors. Now distanced from Seleukos by the dispute over Koile Syria, Ptolemy joined with Lysimachos, giving his daughter Arsinoe to the aged king and another daughter, Lysandra, to Lysimachos's son Agathokles.[252] Seleukos quickly followed suit, striking an agreement with Demetrios and wedding his young daughter Stratonike.[253]

Shortly thereafter, in 298, Cassander fell ill and died, leaving only young sons on the Macedonian throne.[254] Capitalizing on this power vacuum, Demetrios concentrated his efforts on recovering Greece. Reasserting Antigonid control over Euboia, he probably reestablished the *koinon* there in this period (297–296).[255] From Euboia, he sailed against Athens, taking it in 294.[256] His successes in Greece were counterbalanced by the loss of his eastern possessions: Lysimachos took the Ionian cities, most importantly Ephesos, Ptolemy recovered Cyprus, and Seleukos gained Kilikia.[257] But Demetrios advanced north in the fall of 294, taking advantage of the dynastic struggle between Cassander's young sons to have himself declared the king of Macedonia.[258] The next year, he took Thessaly and Boiotia and invaded Lysimachos's Thracian kingdom.[259] A new threat, however, the emergence of Pyrrhos of Epeiros, forced Demetrios to return to central Greece in 292/91 to face the combined rebellion of the Boiotians and the Aitolians, backed by the Epeirot king.[260] Meanwhile, Ptolemy dismantled the Antigonid Nesiotic League and replaced it with his own Aegean confederation[261] and by 288/87 took Tyre and Sidon. Due to growing unpopularity in Macedonia and a double invasion by its neighbors Lysimachos and Pyrrhos, Demetrios lost his army and his kingdom.[262] Falling back once more on his fleet, he sailed against the Ionian coast,

---

251. For a survey of the archaeological evidence, see Kosmin 2014, 195–99.

252. Memnon, *FGrH* 434 F4.9; Just. 15.4.23–24; Paus. 1.9.6; Plut., *Dem.* 31.5.

253. Alliance: Plut., *Dem.* 31.2, 32.1–2; *OGIS* 10. The arrangement soon fell apart: Plut., *Dem.* 33.1.

254. Diod. Sic. 21F7; Just. 16.1; Plut., *Dem.* 36–37; Plut., *Pyrrhus* 6.2–7.1; Paus. 9.7.3; Euseb., *Chron.* 231–32.

255. For the date, see Knoepfler 2015, 168, arguing against the *communis opinio* of 304. For the coinage, see W. Wallace 1956.

256. *IG* II² 646.

257. Plut., *Dem.* 35.3.

258. Plut., *Dem.* 36–37.

259. Lysimachos was locked in a desperate struggle with the Getae, who imprisoned him for a time (Diod. Sic. 19.73, 21F12; Just. 16.1.19).

260. Plut., *Dem.* 40–41.

261. Demetrios lost the Aegean islands between 291 and 287 (Merker 1970; see also Buraselis 2015).

262. Unpopularity: Plut., *Dem.* 44; *Pyrrhus* 11.4–5. Division of Macedonia: Plut., *Dem.* 44–46; Plut., *Pyrrhus* 11–12.6; Paus. 1.10.2. Ptolemy also sailed to Greece to foster a rebellion in the same year. Athens revolted against Demetrios and was lost in the spring of 287 (Plut., *Dem.* 46).

leaving his son Antigonos, probably based in the rising city of Demetrias in Magnesia, to oversee his remaining holdings in Greece.[263] Demetrios landed in Miletos but after some initial success was pushed back by Lysimachos's forces. Retreating into Seleukid-held Kilikia, he finally capitulated in 286, dying at the Seleukid court in 283.[264]

Against the tumultuous events of 294–288, two major Hellenistic centers took shape on opposite sides of the Aegean: Ephesos and Demetrias, both intimately tied to the pressing political and military needs of the period. In the opening maneuvers of the final campaign against Antigonos in 302, Cassander's general Prepelaos had taken Ephesos, leaving it "free" but depriving it of its ships.[265] When Demetrios sailed west to relieve his father, he landed at Ephesos and returned the city to its "former status"—that is, subject to the Antigonids.[266] Even after Ipsos, Ephesos remained in Antigonid hands down to 294, when Lysimachos recovered it.[267] In the intervening years, the city suffered heavily in the contest between the kings. Two honorary decrees dating to this period, one for a general of Demetrios's who worked to secure the grain supply to the city and another for a Rhodian grain dealer who sold wheat in Ephesos at a below-market price, suggest food shortages.[268] The well-known "debt law" dating to circa 299, which addresses the damage done to mortgaged estates during the "common war" against Lysimachos, further reveals the extent to which the territory of Ephesos was ravaged, and another fragmentary inscription refers to the ransoming of citizens captured in the conflict.[269]

---

263. Plutarch (*Dem.* 43–44) indicates that Demetrios was mobilizing a massive naval force to recover all of his father's empire at the time of the loss of Macedonia and suggests this was the motivation for the coalition effort against him.

264. Plut., *Dem.* 46–52.

265. There has been much discussion about whether Lysimachos instituted constitutional changes to the polis in 302, specifically if he introduced the *gerousia* and the officials known as the *epiklētoi* (whom Strabo [14.1.21] says "administered all the affairs of the city"). The *epiklētoi* are first heard of in the honorary decree for Euphronios of Akarnania (*I. Ephesos* V 1449), who aided in the negotiation of *asylia* and other privileges for the Artemision at Ephesos, making it likely that they were in fact an advisory board put in place by Lysimachos. For discussions of the *gerousia* and the question of whether Lysimachos initiated an oligarchic constitution in 302 or after the refoundation in ca. 294, see Oliver 1941, 9–20; Magie 1950, 2:855–57; Rogers 1991, 62–63; Lund 1992, 125–27; Walser 2008, 47–87; Rogers 2012, 71–83. Whether or not Lysimachos was involved, the introduction of the *gerousia* and the *epiklētoi* did not amount to the full-scale establishment of oligarchic government in Ephesos.

266. Diod. Sic. 20.111.3: ἠνάγκασε τὴν πόλιν εἰς τὴν προϋπάρχουσαν ἀποκαταστῆναι τάξιν. On this phrase, see Magie 1950, 1:89–90.

267. Plut., *Dem.* 35; Polyainos, *Strat.* 5.19; Front., *Strat.* 3.3.7. The precise date is unknown. Lund (1992, 91) favors the summer of 294.

268. *I. Ephesos* V 1452 (decree for Archestratos), 1455 = *Syll.*³ 354 (decree for Agathokles of Rhodes).

269. Debt law: *I. Ephesos* Ia 4 (*Syll.*³ 364, with the text of Walser 2008, 11–24). Date of this decree and the "common war": Walser 2008, 87–104. Ransoming of Ephesians: *I. Ephesos* V 1450, with Bielman 1994, no. 16.

As Lysimachos consolidated his control over Ionia after 294, Ephesos became a major node of his newly expanded kingdom. As we have seen, he continued the urban projects of Antigonos in the Troad, renaming and expanding Antigoneia as Alexandreia Troas, and in Hellespontine Phrygia he did the same for Antigonos's other new city, renaming it Nikaia. Lysimachos sought to anchor his hold on Ionia with a large-scale synoikism of Ephesos, far outstripping the limited reorganization of the region that Antigonos had attempted. The city had been central to the struggle for Asia Minor, and it represented the most important harbor and access point to the routes inland to Phrygia and beyond. The desire for a major capital on the scale of the centers promoted by Lysimachos on the Chersonese and in the Troad was mirrored by more immediate practical concerns. The city had suffered in the recent war, which had revealed the weaknesses of its current site, defenses, and harbor. Lysimachos's refoundation sought to remedy these problems, moving Ephesos from the low-lying floodplain around the Artemision to a more advantageous site about 1.3 kilometers (0.81 miles) distant, on the slopes between what are now Bülbüldağ and Panayırdağ, affording the city defensible heights and ready access to a deepwater harbor.[270]

The precise circumstances of the synoikism are confused by the tendentious nature of the literary sources. By 289/88, synoikized Ephesos appears in the epigraphic record under its new dynastic name, Arsinoeia.[271] References to the construction of the 8.9-kilometer-long (5.5-mile-long) wall of the Lysimachean city begin circa 290. These impressive fortifications enclosed a massive four hundred hectares (988 acres).[272] This site absorbed two existing settlements of Ephesos, the villages Koressos and Smyrna, which became quarters of the new city.[273] Strabo reports the unwillingness of the residents of Ephesos to move their city and maintains that Lysimachos blocked its drains during a heavy rainstorm to flood the city and force them to go.[274] This account certainly preserves anti-Lysimachean propaganda: by contrast, Stephanos of Byzantium, citing a contemporary epigram of

---

270. For the geography of the archaic-classical site and the alluviation of the plain, see Knibbe 1998, 93.

271. *I. Milet* I.2, 10 = *Syll.*³ 368; additional copy with slight variations: *I. Smyrna* II.1 577. The city served as a royal mint for Lysimachos. For silver issues bearing the veiled portrait of Arsinoe (obverse) and ΑΡΣΙ, stag (reverse), see Head 1911, 574. Arsinoe resided in the city until the death of Lysimachos, when she narrowly escaped the pro-Seleukid faction (Polyainos, *Strat.* 8.57). It was apparently in this context that the dynastic name was lost.

272. *I. Ephesos* IV 1441, Ia 3. See also McNicholl 1997, 103. The walls were probably unfinished when Demetrios briefly retook the city in 287 (Polyainos, *Strat.* 5.19).

273. Koressos: Karwiese 1985; Engelmann 1997; Kerschner, Kowaleck, and Steskal 2008. Smyrna: Langmann 1993.

274. Strabo 14.1.21.

Douris of Elaia, describes the inundation as a natural disaster and says it only added to Lysimachos's motivation to move the site.[275]

To supplement the population of Ephesos and fill the monumental dimensions of the new capital, Lysimachos transferred the populations of Lebedos (possibly detached from Teos) and Kolophon[276] and the coastal polis of Phygela to it (see map 5, p. 75).[277] Prepelaos had "won over" Teos and Kolophon when he first invaded in 302.[278] Still, the Kolophonians, aided by people of Smyrna, fought to resist the synoikism, and a massive tumulus on the road from Ephesos to Klaros may be the polyandrion mentioned by Pausanias of the war dead who fell in the battle with Lysimachos.[279] Pausanias also tells us that Lysimachos destroyed Kolophon and Lebedos, yet there is no archaeological evidence for this, and both cities ultimately resurfaced in one form or another.[280] Prepelaos, it seems, released Kolophon from unity with Ephesos very shortly after the synoikism and was honored as a founder with a heroön, the Prepelaion, in its territory.[281] The site of the ancient

275. Steph. Byz., s.v. "Ἔφεσος." Douris mentioned the loss of "those countless houses and the possessions of long years of wretched Ephesos" (Ἐφέσου δὲ τὰ μυρία κεῖνα ταλαίνης / αὔλια καὶ μακρῶν ἐξ ἐτέων κτέανα). However, we need not fully dispense with Strabo's claim that the Ephesians resisted the *metoikisis* of their city. Along with Koressos and Smyrna, the new city disrupted an archaic cemetery (Vetters 1978, 20; 1979).

276. Paus. 1.9.7, 7.3.4–5.

277. The weakness of Phygela in the late fourth century is perhaps evident in its isopolity agreement with Miletos: *Milet* I.3, 142 = *Staatsvert.* III 453. A Phygelan decree from the end of the fourth century records the vote of 350 citizens in the *ekklēsia* (*I. Ephesos* VII.1 3111), indicating its relatively small population. For the history of Phygela, see Charneux 1966, 198–206.

278. Diod. Sic. 20.107.5: προσηγάγετο. The fact that Lebedos is not mentioned perhaps lends support to the suggestion that Antigonos's synoikism of Teos and Lebedos had already happened. Erythrai and Klazomenai held out against Prepelaos.

279. Paus. 7.3.4 It has not been excavated, but for a description see Schuchhardt 1886.

280. Paus. 1.9.7. Pace G. Cohen 1995, 186, the American excavations of the 1920s detected no evidence for violent destruction of Kolophon (Meritt 1935; Holland 1944). Nor is there any evidence for systematic reoccupation after the synoikism, outside of some traces of continued use of the sanctuary of Mētēr Antaiē, the most important of the late fourth-century city, on the acropolis and perhaps limited reoccupation of some of the houses. Several coins of Antiochos II (Holland 1944, 94) and a fragmentary decree mentioning a tribal division *Seleuk[is]* (Meritt 1935, no. 6) were found in the Metroön. The same tribe is attested in decree set up at Klaros (J. Robert and Robert 1989, 66, col. 3.21), making it likely that this was a tribe of Notion / New Kolophon on the Sea. Eight coins of Antiochos II were also found in the vicinity of some of the acropolis houses, though not in an occupational deposit, along with a few other coins dating to the third century (Holland 1944, 143), notably a coin of Kolophon/Notion. This is consistent with epigraphic evidence that attests the presence of Kolophonians in both the harbor city (Notion / Kolophon on the Sea) and (probably on a small scale) the "ancient city" (see 000–000). For the site, see Hoepfner and Osthues 1999; Bruns-Özgan, Gassner, and Muss 2011. Notion itself was refounded and moved, perhaps sometime in the second century (Ratté and Rojas 2016). The Kolophonians minted coinage throughout the Hellenistic period, though it seems that the mint was at Notion (Milne 1951, 5–9, 63–81, nos. 101–79).

281. J. Robert and Robert 1989, 63–64, col. 1, ll. 23, 36.

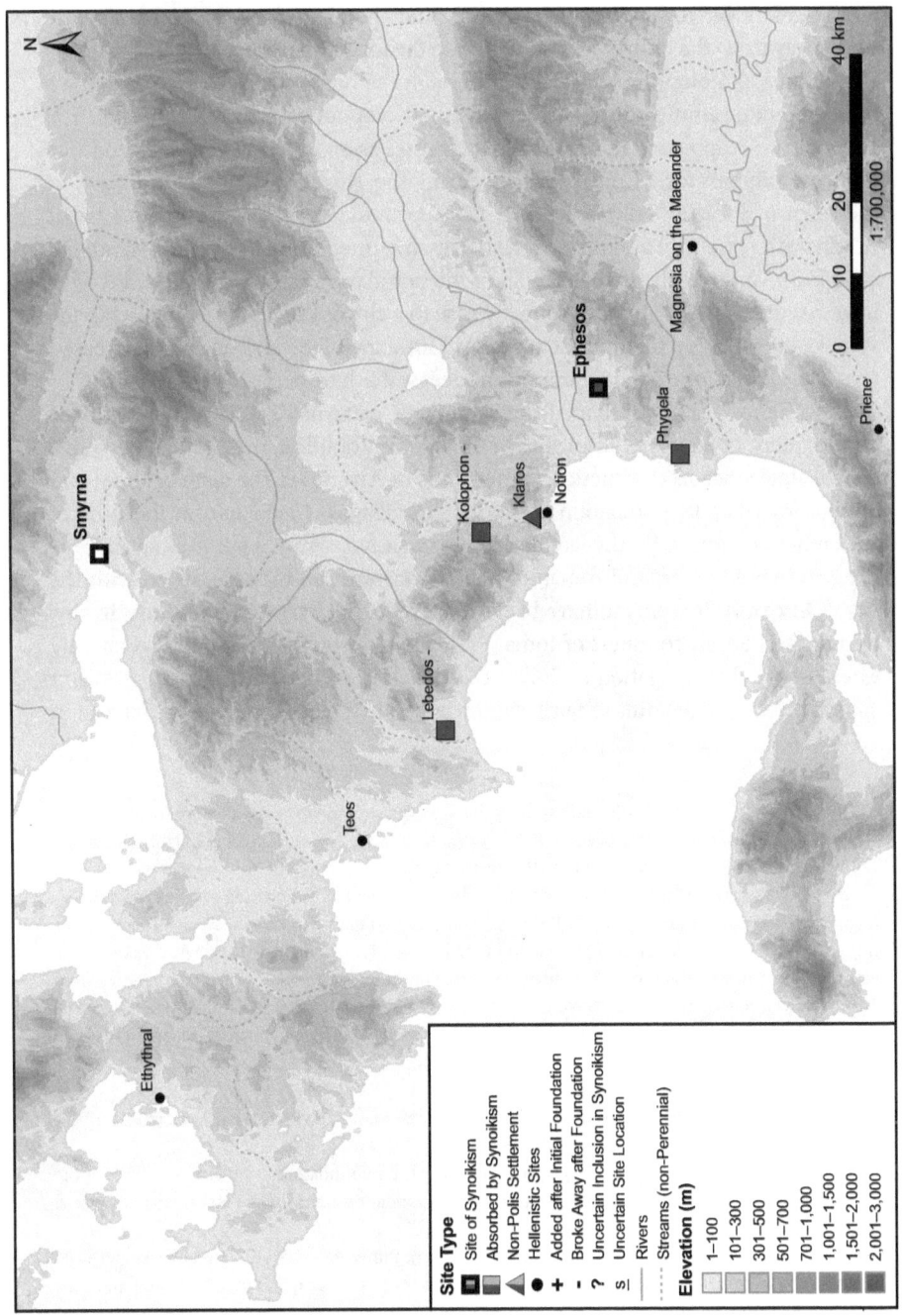

MAP 5. Ionia.

city seems never to have fully recovered, and the centrifugal processes already under way drew the bulk of its population to the former harbor site of Notion, now also known as Kolophon by the Sea. Although the two settlements persisted for a time under one ethnic, the old urban center of Kolophon was ultimately eclipsed.[282] Lebedos too reappeared in subsequent centuries as an independent polis and was named Ptolemais for a time, probably during the Third Syrian War (246–241), in the reign of Ptolemy III.[283] However, the appearance of the Lebedioi as a tribal subdivision (*chiliasty*) at Ephesos attests the early integration of its citizens into the synoikism, and it is likely that not all of the population returned to Lebedos after it was reconstituted.[284] Ephesos quickly rose to a city of the first rank following the synoikism. Strongly fortified, it possessed an expanded territory and increased population and controlled an important deepwater harbor.[285]

Lysimachos further reshaped the settlement patterns of Asia Minor with the development of Smyrna. According to the literary tradition, the city had been in a dismal state since its destruction at the hands of Alyattes in the sixth century, and Strabo describes its population as settled "in villages" (*kōmēdon*) at the time of Alexander's conquest.[286] The late literature is nearly unanimous in calling Alexander Smyrna's founder, and romantic myths grew around his association with the city.[287] In reality, it seems to have been destroyed somewhat more recently, in 545, during the Persian conquest of Ionia.[288] The sources probably also exaggerate the extent of the disaggregation of Smyrna in the classical period: archaeological and epigraphic evidence point to fairly significant activity at the site of Old Smyrna in

---

282. L. Robert 1962, 62; *I. Magnesia* 53, ll. 75–79: Κολοφώνιο[ι οἱ τὴν] | ἀρχαίαν πόλ[ιν οἰ|κ]οῦντες | Κολοφώνιοι ἀ[πὸ] | θαλάσσης. See also Polyb. 5.77.5; Livy 38.39: "Colophoniis qui in Notio habitant." The two centers were united by sympolity (Gauthier 2003).

283. *OGIS* 222 (260s) mentions Lebedos; the toponym Ptolemais designating a city between Ephesos and Teos appears in a fragment of a Delphic *theōrodokoi* list dating to ca. 230–210 (L. Robert 1946b, 512). Ptolemais is also attested by *I. Magnesia* 53, 2, ll. 79–81: Πτολεμαιεῖς οἱ | πρότερον καλού|μενοι Λεβέδιοι (late third to early second century). An inscription dating to the early second century from the Heraion in Samos records a decree of the Lebedioi, again under their original name (L. Robert 1960, 204–13). The city's name may have reverted to Lebedos after Antiochos III's reconquest of the region (Porphyry *FGrH* 260 F46).

284. Karwiese 1995, 65; Engelmann 1996.

285. On the hinterland of Ephesos in the Hellenistic period, see Davies 2011, with references; Kirbihler 2009, which proposes population estimates.

286. Strabo 14.1.37. Cf. Paus. 7.5.1–3, which describes the refoundation as more a *metoikisis* of the city to a new site. For an epigraphic reflection of the foundation myth of the Hellenistic city, see *I. Smyrna* 647.

287. Paus. 7.5.1; Aelius Aristides 20.7, 20.20, 21.4 (Keil); Pliny, *HN* 5.118. Accepted by Cadoux 1938, 95–97. Strabo (our earliest source) does not mention Alexander and is explicit that Antigonos and then Lysimachos refounded Smyrna (14.1.37).

288. Meriç and Nollé 1988.

the fourth century.[289] Its refoundation is therefore best conceived of as a reorganization of the fourth-century harbor town as a new, fortified site with a developed harbor and the consolidation of the second-order villages into a centralized polis.[290] Antigonos initiated this project, and Lysimachos continued it and renamed the site Eurydikeia.[291] Following the synoikism the city flourished, becoming a major commercial outlet and extending its influence over a greater territory in the third century. Eventually, it absorbed the Seleukid military colony attached to the city of Magnesia near Mount Sipylos in western Lydia.[292] The port became a significant harbor of coastal Asia Minor, eclipsing the many smaller cities of the seaboard that had been of greater importance in the classical period. Together with Alexandreia Troas, Miletos, and Ephesos, this newly expanded commercial center was part of a chain of advantageously situated ports that reshaped western Asia Minor.

Across the Aegean, at the same time, Demetrios Poliorketes was inaugurating a city to rival Ephesos through the synoikism of the communities on the northern and western shores of the Pagasitic Gulf and northern Magnesia (see map 6, page 79). This region provided Thessaly with an outlet to the Aegean and was a key station on the north-south land route from Macedonia through the Vale of Tempe to central and southern Greece.[293] Philip II had first sought to control this area after defeating the tyrants of Pherai. In 355/54 he had besieged and razed Methone, thus toppling the last possession of Athens that bordered his territory.[294] What remained was to set up a base of power and shore up the area against Athenian naval hegemony in the Pagasitic Gulf.[295] Philip separated the gulf's chief harbor, Pagasai, a dependency of Pherai, from Pherai, put it under direct Macedonian control, and laid claim to the profits from its harbor dues and markets.[296] It is more than likely

289. Akurgal 1983, 56–58. See also Bingöl 1976; Mellink 1985, 563; Gates 1994. Wehrli (1968, 92) thought Smyrna was already a functioning polis again in the fourth century, on the basis of a coin possibly attributable to it (Head 1911, 591–92) and an Athenian decree of 387/86 mentioning Smyrna (*Syll.*³ 136). Doubted by G. Cohen (1995, 182).

290. For the villages around Smyrna, see Bean 1955. Phlossa, the home of the Hellenistic poet Bion of Smyrna, may have been one such synoikized village (Reed 1997, 1).

291. Wall: *IG* II² 663; Cadoux 1938, 102–3; Bean 1955. Harbor: Ersoy and Alatepeli 2011. Only numismatic evidence attests its renaming as Eurydikeia: see Head 1911, 592; Cadoux 1938, 103.

292. *OGIS* 229; *Staatsvert.* III 492; *I. Mag. Sipylos* I; *I. Smyrna* 573 (ca. 241, during the Laodikeian [Third Syrian] War). The colony was probably founded by Antiochos I, who at least granted two lots (*klēroi*) to military settlers at the associated fort of Palaimagnesia. See also Rigsby 1996, 95–105; Reger 2004, 152–53.

293. Strabo 9.4.15; Polyb. 18.45.5–6: Demetrias as one of the "fetters" of Greece.

294. Diod. Sic. 16.31.6, 16.34.4. Cf. Dem. 1.22, 2.11.

295. See Westlake 1935, ch. 9.

296. Pheraian dependency: Theopompos, *FGrH* 115 F53. The control of the great Thessalian cities over the *perioikoi* may go back as far as the sixth century (Sordi 1958; Hammond and Griffith 1979, 291; Helly 1995, 131–92). By the early fourth century, a brother of Jason of Pherai was installed in Pagasai and appears to have directed its affairs on behalf of Pherai (Polyainos, *Strat.* 6.1.6). Philip besieged

that at the same time, on the eastern shore of the gulf, he created a full-scale urban foundation on the high hill overlooking the harbor now known as Goritsa, with formidable walls and massive catapult batteries.[297] This was the beginning of a dramatic redrawing of this region, which was not only strategically central but also an area of contact between Thessaly and two of her *perioikoi*, Achaia Phthiotis and Magnesia.[298]

With the defeat of the Phokians and the end of the Third Sacred War in 352, Philip was elected the head of the Thessalian *koinon*. He quickly focused on the restitution of the Thessalian tetrarchy, in what our sources brand an attempt to wrest power from individual poleis and strengthen his position.[299] In Achaia Phthiotis, which Thessaly had handed over to the Boiotian *koinon* during the Third Sacred War, Philip continued this policy of breaking up powerful entities. He destroyed Halos in 346, giving its territory to Pharsalos, and removed the polis of Echinos from the control of Thebes and reassigned it to Malis in 342, simultaneously gaining the allegiance of the polis and strengthening Macedonia against the Boiotians.[300]

Demetrios Poliorketes thus inherited a changed Thessaly in 294, which by that time had been under Macedonian control for more than fifty years. Largely reversing Philip's policies, he radically reshaped Magnesia and Achaia Phthiotis. While Philip had consolidated his power mostly through force and the reduction of cities, Demetrios focused on the foundation of urban centers as a means of control. Prior to the Battle of Ipsos, as we have seen (pp. 68–69), Demetrios had probably refounded several important cities in Achaia Phthiotis. He now employed the same strategy in eastern Thessaly and Magnesia. While he did not restore Pagasai to Pherai, he does seem to have patronized the latter city with the construction of a new temple of Ennodia and Zeus Thalios, its chief civic deities.[301] The establishment of Demetrias, a court and royal city that commanded the Pagasitic Gulf, created a major metropolis in an area of Thessaly that had always been important but not politically powerful and dramatically affected the local

---

Pagasai in 353 (Diod. Sic. 16.31.6) and later constructed forts throughout Magnesia (Dem. 1.22, 2.11). The Thessalian League asked for the return of Pagasai, but Philip is not know to have made that concession (Hammond and Griffith 1979, 292). By 346, however, he had "given back" Magnesia to the Thessalians (Dem. 6.22), seemingly an indication that this perioikic region was formally subject to the Thessalian League (with Philip as its archon) and not directly to Philip (Hammond and Griffith 1979, 540–41).

297. Bakhuizen 1992. Helly (2006b) locates Methone at Goritsa.

298. Intzesiloglou 1994.

299. Diod. Sic. 16.59.4–60.2; Dem. 9.22–27 (explicitly compares the political weakening of the poleis of Thessaly to the destruction of cities in the Chalkidike and Thrace and the *dioikismos* of Phokis). See also Westlake 1935, 196–216; Hammond and Griffith 1979, 267–95, 523–44. For the tetrads, see Helly 1995; Graninger 2011a.

300. Halos: Dem. 11.1; Strabo 9.5.8. Echinos: Dem. 9.34.

301. Béquignon 1937; Østby 1994.

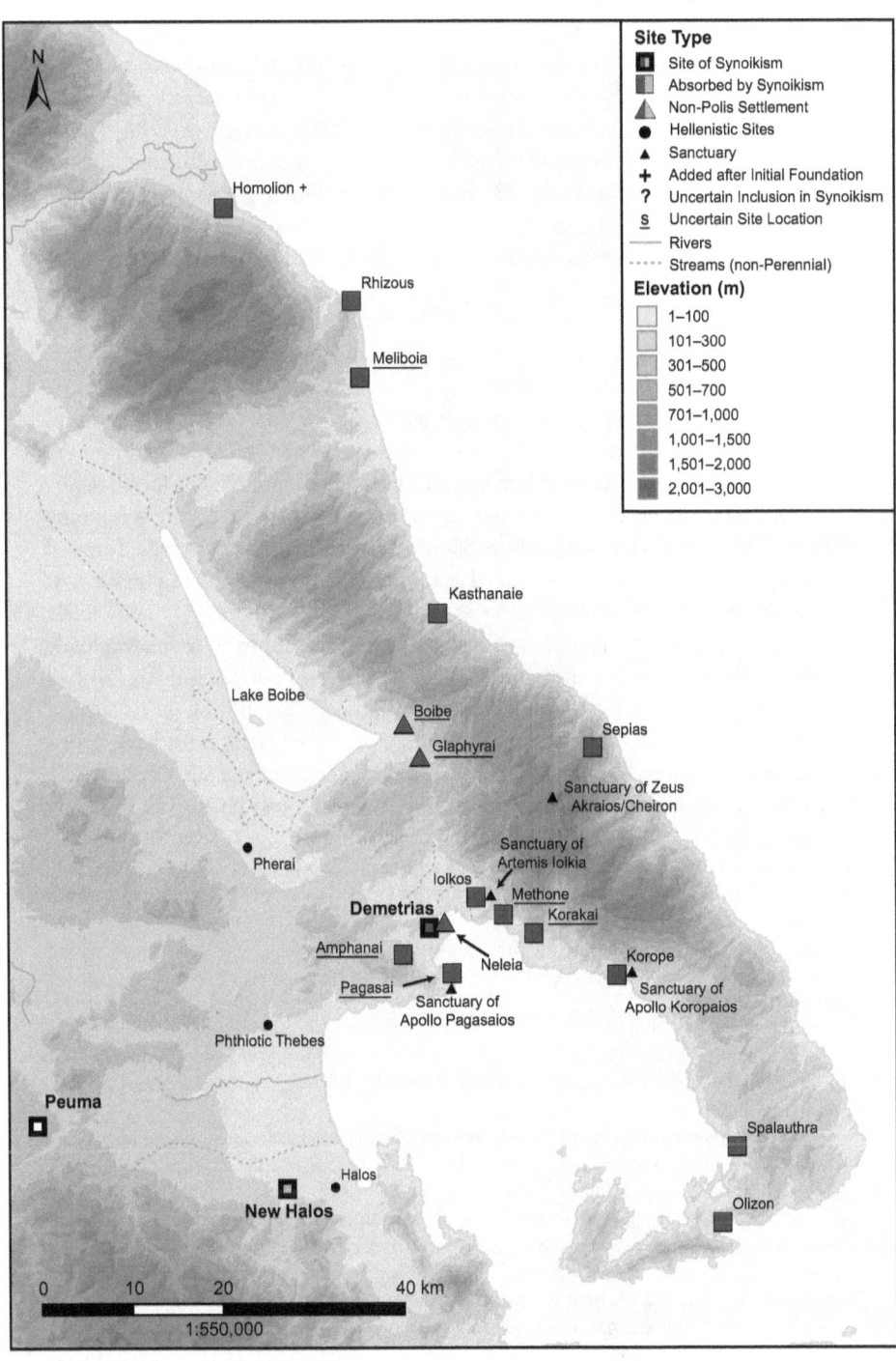

MAP 6. Magnesia and the Pagasitic Gulf.

communities and poleis, concentrating at least one-third of Magnesia's population within the city center.[302] The circuit wall ran 11.2 kilometers (seven miles) and enclosed about 439 hectares (1,085 acres).[303] Demetrias ultimately drew its population from numerous communities: Neleia, Pagasai, Ormenion, Rhizous, Sepias, Olizon, Boibe, Iolkos, Kasthanaia,[304] Amphanai, Homolion, Aiolis, Halai, Korope, Glaphyrai, Methone, and Spalauthra (map 6, p. 79).[305] Most of these were Magnesian, but Pagasai and Amphanai were in Pelasgiotis and Iolkos and the surrounding area had long been under direct Thessalian control. The synoikism was thus a dramatic political and cultural reorientation, reversing the traditional Thessalian domination of this important region and combining diverse Magnesian and Thessalian populations to form a single polity.

The structure of the synoikism and its effects on the constituent communities can be traced in some detail. The amalgamated poleis were incorporated into the social organization of Demetrias as demes or villages (*kōmai*),[306] with the erstwhile city ethnics serving as demotics. These subdivisions were afforded some autonomy in their cultic and social life and occasionally issued their own decrees. Some of the constituent communities persisted as discrete sites of settlement in their original locations (though often somewhat reduced), while others were completely abandoned in favor of the new urban center. Demetrias seems to have completely absorbed the populations of the Thessalian Pagasai and Amphanai. Pagasai had developed into the major economic center of Thessaly.[307] Building on its success and naturally eclipsing its function as the main port, Demetrias must have drawn much of its population from this polis. The evidence from the site of Soros, the most likely candidate for ancient Pagasai,[308] demonstrates that it was suddenly

---

302. See Batziou-Efstathiou and Pikoulas 2006 for evidence of royal land in the vicinity of Demetrias; Hatzopoulos 2006, 88–89, for a letter of Demetrios fixing the border of Demetrias and Pherai at a place called Iolkia.

303. Under Antigonos Gonatas, the circuit contracted to 8.2 kilometers (5.1 miles) enclosing 270 hectares (667 acres). In 88/87, during the Mithridatic Wars, the enceinte was further reduced. For the date, see Helly 1992.

304. Strabo 9.5.15, 9.5.22.

305. Amphanai: Arvanitopoulos 1929b, 126, no. 423; Homolion, Aiolis (otherwise unattested), Halai (otherwise unattested), Korope: *IG* IX 2 1109; Glaphyrai: Helly 1971, 555; Methone: *IG* IX II 1112; Spalauthra: *IG* IX 2 1111.

306. Only Strabo (9.5.15) mentions *kōmai*. See Ernst Meyer 1936; Intzesiloglou 1996; Graninger 2011b.

307. For its commercial importance, see Eduard Meyer 1909, 281–83; Westlake 1935; Ernst Meyer 1942; R. Boehm 2015.

308. Theocharis 1973, 324n90; Marzolff 1975, 46; Marzolff 1994a, 274n10; Marzolff 1994b, 59; Di Salvatore 1994, 115–16; Di Salvatore 2002, 42; Decourt, Helly, and Nielsen 2004, 691, 696; Helly 2013, 145–98; Mazarakis Ainian (2009, 273), the current excavator. This identification is disputed. Some scholars have identified Soros with Amphanai (Arvanitopoulos 1909a; Stählin 1924; Stählin, Meyer, and Heidner 1934; Milojčić 1974, 61–75; Intzesiloglou 1994, 46; Triantaphyllopoulou 2000; Batziou-Efstathiou and Triantaphyllopoulou 2009). Stählin, Meyer, and Heidner 1934 locates Pagasai at Liga-

abandoned at the time of the synoikism. From the remains, Soros appears to have been the most substantial settlement on the Pagasitic Gulf, and its position accords well with Strabo's reckoning that Pagasai was twenty stades (about four kilometers, or two and a half miles) from Iolkos and ninety (about seventeen kilometers, or ten miles) from Pherai.[309] The city was on a conical hill, ringed by an archaic acropolis wall and with fifth- or fourth-century concentric fortifications surrounding the lower town, and controlled a harbor below. Portions of the acropolis, including a monumental building that Arvanitopoulos considered the residence of the city's rulers (the tyrants of Pherai?),[310] and of the lower town, the cemetery, and an extramural temple dedicated to Apollo have been excavated.[311] No material datable to the Hellenistic period was found in any of these contexts. These findings strongly suggest that the polis was completely and suddenly deserted and its population transferred following the synoikism with Demetrias.[312] Less is know about Amphanai, whose location is subject to debate.[313]

The urban nucleus of Demetrias may also have absorbed Neleia, traditionally located on the northern edge of the city, on the promontory known as Pevkakia Magula.[314] This was the site of a prehistoric settlement, but little is known of it in the intervening period. There are some faint indications of a classical settlement and evidence for a general leveling of the mound, activity probably related to the

---

rorevma, within the southern portion of the walls of Demetrias. Intzesiloglou (1994) proposed Bourboulithra, just north of Demetrias. Some graves of classical date have been found within the walls of Demetrias, but although Batziou-Efstathiou and Triantaphyllopoulou 2012 associates them with Pagasai, this is not sufficient evidence that this city should be located at the site of Demetrias.

309. Strabo 9.5.15.

310. Arvanitopoulos 1909a; 1928, fig. 90. See also Batziou-Efstathiou and Triantaphyllopoulou 2009, 258.

311. Acropolis: Batziou-Efstathiou and Triantaphyllopoulou 2009, 258. Lower town: Milojčić 1974; Di Salvatore 1994; Batziou-Efstathiou and Triantaphyllopoulou 2009. Cemetery: Triantaphyllopoulou 2000; 2002. Sanctuary: Mazarakis Ainian 2009; 2011; 2012. For a discussion of the cult and sanctuary, see ch. 3.

312. Despite the desertion of its center, the name of this polis, whether Pagasai or Amphanai, continued as a demotic in Demetrias: see, e.g., Arvanitopoulos 1929b, 126, no. 423 (Φίλωνα Ἀλεξάνδρου Ἀμφαναιῆ); IG IX 2 1109, l. 4 (Αἰτωλίων Δημητρίου Παγασίτης).

313. Amphanai has been located at Soros, which recent scholarship favors as the site of Pagasai (see p. 80n308), and at Palio-Alikes (Marzolff 1994b, 70n6), Velanidia (Bakhuizen 1987, 323n2), or the *palaiokastro* of Sesklou (Di Salvatore 1994, 115–16, followed by Decourt, Helly, and Nielsen 2004, 691). It may have had a harbor on the southern shore of Cape Ankistri. None of these sites has evidence for occupation past the synoikism of Demetrias.

314. Strabo (9.5.15) mentions that Demetrias was founded between Neleia and Pagasai. Neleia may never have been an independent community. Baladié (1996) considers it the harbor of Iolkos, and Bakhuizen (1996) has argued that the name *Neleia* (City of Neleus) simply stood in metonymy for Iolkos. For the prehistoric site, see Theocharis 1973; Weisshaar 1989; Maran 1992; Christmann 1996. For the later remains and the Hellenistic levels, see Batziou-Efstathiou 1992.

preparation works for the laying out of Demetrias.³¹⁵ The well-fortified site at Goritsa, which was newly laid out in the fourth century and probably served as a garrison for Philip or Demetrios, was slowly depopulated following the synoikism and abandoned by 250.³¹⁶ Korakai, probably located at modern Nevestiki, appears to have been deserted soon after the foundation.³¹⁷

Many of the other little Magnesian poleis and towns persisted in some form as deme sites after the synoikism. Iolkos, on the northern shore of the Pagasitic Gulf, certainly remained a site of cult, centered on the temple of Artemis Iolkia, and maybe a small center of settlement as well.³¹⁸ Scholarly consensus places its site at Kastro/Palaia Volou, where graves dating from the sixth through fifth centuries, scattered classical and Hellenistic pottery, and scanty remains of the temple of Artemis Iolkia have been found.³¹⁹ In the reign of Antigonos Gonatas, the *dēmos* of Iolkos issued two decrees pertaining to the cultic observances of the Iolkians and the rites of Demetrias, demonstrating the corporate organization of the Iolkians within Demetrias.³²⁰

Korope, the site of a sanctuary and oracle of Apollo Koropaios, became of central importance to the religious life of Demetrias, and Apollo was refashioned into one of the main poliadic deities. The city controlled its shrine and elected an eponymous priest, and at least by the period of the Magnesian League, Apollo Koropaios was firmly incorporated as a member of the so-called Magnesian triad, along with Artemis Iolkia and Zeus Akraios.³²¹ Excavation of the site, near modern Bufa, has

---

315. Batziou-Efstathiou 2002, 9–10. If it had indeed been a polis, the demotic is not attested in Demetrias, but the cult of Aphrodite Neleia persisted after the synoikism, with a sanctuary probably on this spot (*IG* IX 2 1125; Hornung-Bertemes 2007, 79).

316. Bakhuizen 1992.

317. Wace 1906, 153–54. This could also be the site of Methone.

318. Strabo (9.5.15) reports that "Iolkos has been utterly destroyed of old" (ἡ δ᾽ Ἰωλκὸς κατέσκαπται μὲν ἐκ παλαιοῦ), but it is unclear precisely to which period he refers, though he mentions that civil discord and periods of tyranny had reduced it. The Thessalians had had long controlled Iolkos, as their offer of the site to the Athenian tyrant Hippias at the beginning of the fifth century clearly indicates (Hdt. 5.94.1). Still, the city minted coins in the fourth century (Liampi 2005).

319. For excavations at the site, see Arvanitopoulos 1910; Theocharis 1956; Theocharis 1957; Theocharis 1960; Theocharis 1961; Skafida, Tsigara, and Gkardalinou 2001–4; Skafida 2012. For identification as classical Iolkos, see Arvanitopoulos 1910; Stählin 1924, 63; Intzesiloglou 1994, 34–37; Decourt, Helly, and Nielsen 2004, 719. The site of Sesklo may have been the location of at least prehistoric Iolkos, possibly with Kastro Volou or Pefkakia serving as its port, but epigraphic evidence conclusively puts the historical center of Iolkos at Kastro Volou. For the temple of Artemis Iolkia, see ch. 3.

320. Ernst Meyer 1936; see also ch. 4. A dedicatory inscription of Hellenistic date was found there as well: *IG* IX 2 1122.

321. For whether the oracle of Korope originally belonged to the Thessalians or the Magnesians, see Papakhatzis 1960; Helly 2006b; Helly 2013, 145–98. The sanctuary is well attested epigraphically in the Hellenistic period through a *lex sacra* and a number of documents from Demetrias (*IG* IX 2 1109; Reichel 1891; Kern 1903; L. Robert 1948a, 16–28; Sokolowski 1969, nos. 83–84).

revealed the remains of the sanctuary and a settlement at the base of the small hill called Petralona.[322] The classical settlement of Korope seems to have been on the peak of Petralona, about one kilometer (0.6 miles) east of the sanctuary, where finds indicate habitation from the archaic through the early Hellenistic period. The focus of activity in the later Hellenistic-Roman period shifted to the area southwest of the sanctuary, closer to the shore. The apparent abandonment of the acropolis at Petralona may indicate either that the population moved to Demetrias or that the center of settlement moved downhill, closer to the sanctuary.

Spalauthra and Glaphyrai were two of the most peripheral of the poleis brought into the synoikism for which we have any evidence in the Hellenistic period. It suggests that such communities persisted as centers of settlement. Spalauthra, lying about three-fourths of the way down the Magnesian peninsula, at modern Chorto on the western coast,[323] is almost fifty kilometers (thirty-one miles) from the urban center of Demetrias, while Glaphyrai, in the plain north of the western spur of Pelion, on the shore of the ancient Lake Boibe, was at least thirty-three kilometers (twenty-one miles) away. The community of Boibe, also incorporated into Demetrias, probably lay somewhere in this vicinity. Three other communities listed as participating in the initial synoikism were even farther afield: the polis Olizon, on the southern end of the Magnesian peninsula,[324] Sepias, somewhere on the cape, and the polis Rhizous, on the far northeastern coast of Magnesia. Farther still, Homolion, on the western spur of Mount Ossa, evidently remained independent at the founding of the synoikism but was incorporated into Demetrias by the second century.[325]

At Glaphryai, a decree, either of the *dēmos* or of Demetrias, regulating the rites of the founders of the polis of Demetrias has been discovered near a monumental building of some kind.[326] Similar evidence comes from Spalauthra, where a decree of the *dēmos* of Spalauthra provides rare insight into an active urban center among the demes of Demetrias.[327] This document honors a certain Lysias son of Epiteles, a citizen of Demetrias and *stratēgos* of the Magnesian *koinon*, for his benefactions and attention to the interests of the Spalauthrians. The deme seems to have a number of civic institutions in place, and a further detail highlights an aspect of Spalauthra's continued existence as an urban center, as the *dēmos* also resolved to

---

322. Arvanitopoulos 1906, 123–24; Stählin 1924, 123; Bakhuizen 1996.

323. Probably on the hill of Chortokastro, where the church of Agios Nikolaos appears to be built on the foundations of an ancient temple (Sokolowski 1969, 140).

324. See Wace 1906, 148–49, for the remains of a fortification wall and possibly a small temple.

325. Independent at synoikism: Head 1911, 296. Incorporated into Demetrias: *IG* IX 2 1109. The site of Homolion, Palaiokastro Karitsa, has not been explored systematically.

326. Decree: Wilhelm 1909, 150–51 = *IG* IX 2 1099b. Monumental building: Mezières 1854, 198–99; Stählin 1924, 61. Decree of Glaphyrai rather than Demetrias: Graninger 2011b.

327. *IG* IX 2 1111.

offer Epiteles hospitality (*xenia*) whenever he visited. While these peripheral sites became demes of Demetrias, gave up their political independence, and ceased to mint coinage, they appear to have neither contributed greatly to the initial population of the synoikism nor been subject to any physical transference. Where there is evidence, it suggests that these settlements persisted as discrete urban centers, though firmly brought into the administrative and religious community of Demetrias.

The ambitious new capital Demetrias was still rising when its namesake perished.[328] As Antigonid power collapsed, Lysimachos filled the void, taking Macedonia. By 285 he held most of Asia Minor, Thrace, Macedonia, and Thessaly. Antigonos Gonatas held out, confined to Demetrias and a string of Antigonid garrisons in southern Greece. Lysimachos's ascendance, however, proved to be short lived. In 284/83 or 283/82 he put his son and heir apparent Agathokles to death at the prompting of his wife Arsinoe.[329] This move was tremendously unpopular, and the loss of the capable Agathokles and the erosion of support within his circle of friends severely undermined Lysimachos's power. In 282, Seleukos sensed the weakness of Lysimachos's hold and, prompted by Lysandra, Agathokles's widow, and her brother Ptolemy Keraunos, moved against Asia Minor. Seleukos decisively defeated Lysimachos at Kouropedion in 281, only to be assassinated as he advanced on Macedonia by Ptolemy Keraunos, who had himself proclaimed king.[330]

The death of Seleukos marks the end of the first generation of the Successors. The shape of the Hellenistic kingdoms was beginning to stabilize, but the exogenous shock of the Gallic invasion in 279 threw Macedonia and much of Greece and Asia Minor into an interregnum of chaos. In Macedonia, Ptolemy Keraunos died confronting the Gauls. In the aftermath, Antigonos Gonatas made peace with Antiochos I, defeated a large contingent of Gauls near Lysimacheia in 277, and claimed the throne in Macedonia the following year.[331] In 276, Antigonos Gonatas reclaimed Kassandreia, which had revolted and set up a tyranny following the Gallic invasion.[332] In the East, the death of Seleukos prompted a revolt of the new Seleukid foundations in Syria (the Seleukis) and the migration of the Gauls into Asia Minor.[333] By 270, Antiochos had reconquered Asia Minor and decisively defeated the Gauls after a long struggle. From this point to the death of Antiochos II in 246, Seleukid power was relatively stable in Asia Minor, and

---

328. For the development of the city under Antigonos Gonatas, see Marzolff 1976c; 1978; 1980; 1992; 1994a; 1994b; 1996a; 1999.
329. Just. 17.1.3–6; Memnon, *FGrH* 434 F5.6; Paus. 1.10.3–4.
330. Just. 17.2.2–4.
331. Just. 24–25.1–2. For the impacts of the Gallic invasion, see Nachtergael 1977; Strobel 1996.
332. Diod. Sic. 22.3–5; Just. 25.1–2.
333. Revolt in the Seleukis: *OGIS* 219 = *I. Ilion* 32. Gauls in Asia Minor: Memnon, *FGrH* 434 F11.

Seleukos's successors set about projecting the institutions of their rule over most of the area west of the Tauros Mountains.[334]

Seleukid rule in Asia Minor built on the foundations of the period of the Diadochs, maintaining and extending the urban system begun in the previous generation and linking it to the growing network of Seleukid cities that sprawled across Asia. This period, from the consolidation of Asia Minor under Antiochos I to the reign of Antiochos II, witnessed the creation of numerous Seleucid cities in western Asia Minor, especially along the inland valleys and key arteries connecting the Aegean coast to the eastern portions of the kingdom. The Maeander valley received particular attention, with the refoundation of Tralles as Seleukeia, the synoikism of the towns of Athymbra, Athymbrada, and Hydrela into Nysa,[335] the foundation of Antioch on the Maeander from two existing settlements called Symmaitheos and Kranaos,[336] and the creation of Laodikeia on the Lykos from the union of several Hellenized villages on royal land.[337] In Phrygia, at the sources of the Maeander, Apameia Kelainai was refounded and moved to a strategic crossroads.[338] Farther south, on the inland road from Tralles to Lykia, the polis of Stratonikeia was founded from the synoikism of several small Karian villages, with a contingent of Macedonians.[339] These foundations were usually smaller in scale than the massive, mostly coastal multipolis synoikisms that dominated the first generations of the Successors. This network of cities, which continued to expand during the energetic reign of Antiochos III (223–187), intersected with the dense web of *katoikiai*, places like Thyateira, Magnesia Sipylos, Toriaion, and many others, which had a quasi-civic organization and often developed into poleis in later periods. When Seleukid power in Anatolia collapsed, a dynamic new chapter of urbanization began under the Attalids after 188, which extended from the main highways and commercial arteries into isolated valleys and upland regions.[340] In this context, as Asia Minor increasingly transformed into a landscape of cities, local communities frequently asserted themselves, organizing or expanding, often through the incorporation of neighboring settlements.

---

334. For a narrative of this period, see Ma 2002, 26–43.
335. Synoikism: Strabo 14.1.46. Site: von Dienst 1913; Ratté 2008, 18–28. Hydrela seems to have been independent again and minting coins by the first century BCE (*SNG von Aulock* 3674–75).
336. Pliny, *HN* 5.108. Strabo (13.4.15) remarks on the city's sizable territory.
337. Wörrle 1975; Corsten 2007.
338. Summerer, Ivantchik, and von Kienlen 2011; 2013.
339. Şahin 1976; van Bremen 2000; Meadows 2002. Probably founded in the reign of Antiochos II (Ma 2002, 277–78).
340. Thonemann 2013b.

CONCLUSIONS

I have attempted to reconstruct the scale and impact of the urban policies of the first generations of the Hellenistic kings on the regional landscapes of the northern Aegean and western Asia Minor. Their objective was the concentration of population and resources in larger urban agglomerations, with larger regions structured around a reordered settlement hierarchy. Settlement and human mobility are by nature dynamic, and all imperial powers shape regional landscapes to some degree. But the planned urbanization and forced synoikism of crucial regions disputed by the Hellenistic kings drastically affected urban forms and population distributions, which in many cases had largely been in place for centuries. This reorganization also reversed or retooled the ways that previous empires or hegemonies had impacted and structured the lands under their control. On one level, the intensely competitive interstate context explains this imperative: in seeking to stabilize and instantiate their control over far-flung and diverse regions, the competing dynasts found it increasingly advantageous to impose coherence on their holdings. This process of state formation was a violent and messy combination of political, military, and ideological force. As the reality of the inevitable segmentation of Alexander's empire took hold, synoikism and urbanization as means of territorializing, legitimating, and administering fragmented holdings rapidly took their place as central features of Hellenistic imperialism.

On a strategic level, the concentration of resources at well-fortified nodes had a patent logic in an age of innovative siege tactics. The campaigns of Philip II against the Greek cities and of the Successors in Asia Minor and elsewhere demonstrate the ease with which large Macedonian armies could pick off small towns one by one and take a whole region. Conversely, a strategically placed and well-fortified city could halt or at least bog down a large invading force, as Byzantion did to Antigonos's army in 312. This reorganization of space also incorporated a secondary network of forts, outposts, customs stations, and military settlements that supported and projected royal interests across regions. As the web of interconnected cities and infrastructure grew, royal policy fostered urban corridors across previously dispersed landscapes. This manifestation of power naturally had profound ideological implications as the physical imprint of Hellenistic kingship became manifest in dynastic place-names and eponymous cities. These centers simultaneously served to order and intensify economic activity and the resources of the kingdom. The greater integration of the Aegean seaboard and the interior hinged on the large-scale port cities that were the particular focus of the first generations. Invested with large hinterlands and concentrated populations, these cities stood at the head of an expanded network that drew on rural production, seaborne commerce, and overland contacts. Imperial authorities mapped their political and economic apparatus onto this structure—from royal mints, palaces, and customs stations to the personnel dedicated to the collection of taxes and tribute and the machinery of royal surveillance.

Developing infrastructural power to support their kingdoms and fuel the imperial war machine were certainly priorities of the first order for the Hellenistic kings.[341] But this does not fully explain the phenomenon of early Hellenistic synoikism. These kings have traditionally been seen as caring little for the will of local communities. From this perspective, royal authorities blithely disregarded their commitment to the freedom and autonomy of the Greek cities, which they forcefully reorganized to suit their own interests, disregarding local concerns. This is largely the presentation of the literary sources, which stress the destruction of cities and the unwilling participation of many of the constituent communities. Closer inspection of the sources, literary and especially archaeological, complicates this picture. In the cases reviewed here, there is no clear instance of any violent destruction of the communities incorporated into royal foundations. In many cases the synoikized settlements persisted, demoted to dependent settlements of the centralized polis and often reduced, but nevertheless maintaining important signs of continuity. In others, the synoikism did cause large-scale depopulation, especially of the key communities close to the urban core. This undoubtedly meant considerable upheaval, engendering resentment and even resistance. But the unsatisfactory nature of the literary accounts demands a more through explanation for the process of foundation, the mechanisms by which new societies came into being, and the reasons for their often meteoric success.

The detailed account provided in this chapter shows the diversity and complexity of the effects of synoikism on patterns of settlement across the Aegean world, the extent to which these cities reshaped existing structures and the time scale on which they coalesced and, sometimes, disintegrated. These cities materialized through imperial will, and coercive force, whether physical or ideological, certainly played a role in their genesis. But in contrast to many imperial exempla, the aspiration of the kings in creating them was not solely the control and extraction of resources but rather the encouragement of flourishing, autonomous (in the sense of self-regulating) centers that would support the construction and maintenance of large territorial states. It is important to account for the role that these conspicuous urban entities played in the economic and symbolic orders of the kingdoms and to understand how such cities negotiated the extreme disruption of synoikism to create functioning, unified political communities. This was an evolving process, which ran in tandem with the development of these cities and played out over generations. Yet the essential governmental mechanisms of the polis seem

---

341. For a discussion of "infrastructural power" in the context of ancient states, see Ando 2017b.

to have materialized extraordinarily quickly, with cities issuing decrees, minting coinage, and developing central expressions of shared citizenship soon after their creation. The basic urban form (walls, public buildings, temples) also often took shape at an impressive pace. The ways in which civic actors, royal representatives, and the kings themselves interacted within this space and the consequences, both intended and unintended, for the social fabric of these cities are the subjects of the following chapters.

2

Urbanization and Economic Networks

According to Pausanias, Lysimachos consigned Lebedos to the synoikism of Ephesos not because Lebedos lacked sufficient resources or population to exist independently but "in order that the *synteleia* [joint contribution] for Ephesos might become great."[1] Ephesos itself indeed became great, rising from its position of relative economic parity with the cities of Ionia and Aiolis in the previous centuries[2] to the foremost entrepôt of Asia Minor.[3] Pausanias's language points to the economic priority underlying the Lysimachos's project: the *synteleia* that he envisioned comprised population, land, produce, natural resources, livestock, tax revenue, and customs and harbor dues, all of which the new union bolstered. On a

---

1. Paus. 7.3.5: Λεβεδίοις δὲ ἐποίησε μὲν Λυσίμαχος ἀνάστατον τὴν πόλιν, ἵνα δὴ συντέλεια ἐς μέγεθος τῇ Ἐφέσῳ γένοιτο· χώρα δέ σφισιν ἔς τε τὰ λοιπά ἐστιν εὐδαίμων καὶ λουτρὰ παρέχεται θερμὰ πλεῖστα τῶν ἐπὶ θαλάσσῃ καὶ ἥδιστα. For the advantageous location of Lebedos, see Hdt. 1.142. Pausanias's use of *synteleia* in this context echoes descriptions of federal leagues. Translations of this passage often (unsuitably) render *synteleia* as "population," e.g., W. Jones 1933. In the Hellenistic period, *synteleia* typically denoted a union of cities and was mostly confined to descriptions of larger entities like the Achaian or Boiotian *koina* (e.g., Polyb. 5.94.1; Paus. 7.15.2–3; Diod. Sic. 15.38.4; Hdt. 6.108.5: τελέειν) but not synoikisms of this kind. For the terms *synteleia* and *syntelein* in the context of fourth-century Boiotia and the hegemony of Thebes, see Bakhuizen 1994, which proposes a translation of "contribution" (of taxes or soldiers) while emphasizing that this is not a technical term. Hornblower (1991–2008, 2:252), commenting on Thuc. 4.76.3, notes the term's sense of financial obligations of smaller communities to larger ones.

2. In the Athenian tribute lists, Ephesos is assessed at between six and seven and half talents (*IG* I³ 260.vi.13, 267.v.17). Kyme, by contrast, paid twelve talents at its highest assessment, while Teos paid six and Miletos five (Meiggs 1972, 538–61). Knibbe (1998, 97) speaks of Ephesos's "komethaften Aufstieg" in the Hellenistic period. See also Davies 2011.

3. Strabo 12.8.15.

much more specific level of fiscal intervention, Athenaios tells us that when Cassander synoikized Kassandreia in 316, he commissioned the great sculptor Lysippos to devise a new ceramic container (*keramos*) "because of the great export of Mendean wine from the city."[4] In addition to promoting the reputation of the future king, this vessel was evidently intended to enhance the distribution and status of this already famous vintage, a valuable commodity swallowed up by the new polis of Kassandreia.[5] Cassander was "very ambitious for the city's growth," and to this end he invested Kassandreia with great resources in the form of land and population and did not overlook the commercial potential of his new harbor city.[6] In each of these cases, on a general and surprisingly direct level, we see the interest that Lysimachos and Cassander took in using the opportunity of a synoikism to shape the economies of the subject cities of their empires.

The kings and dynasts of the early Hellenistic era intervened intensively in the organization of the Greek city-states, with profound economic consequences. Large urban centers were, of course, valuable repositories of resources and manpower, and the anecdotes above could be interpreted as attempts at simply amassing resources and pursuing predatory taxation. But as the notion that the Hellenistic kingdoms, along with other ancient states, were primarily predatory—that is, organized to extract the maximum revenue with little or no regard for wider social and economic repercussions—has begun to be questioned, more room has opened up for understanding policies that provided mutual benefit for central powers and subordinate communities.[7] Likewise, increased scholarly attention has recently

---

4. Ath., *Deip.* 11.28: Λύσιππον τὸν ἀνδριαντοποιόν φασι Κασάνδρῳ χαριζόμενον, ὅτε συνῴκισε τὴν Κασάνδρειαν, φιλοδοξοῦντι καὶ βουλομένῳ ἴδιόν τινα εὑρέσθαι κέραμον διὰ τὸ πολὺν ἐξάγεσθαι τὸν Μενδαῖον οἶνον ἐκ τῆς πόλεως, φιλοτιμηθῆναι καὶ πολλὰ καὶ παντοδαπὰ γένη παραθέμενον κεραμίων ἐξ ἑκάστου ἀποπλασάμενον ἴδιον ποιῆσαι πλάσμα.

5. This vessel is usually identified with the amphora shape produced in Mende and in the southern Chalkidike more widely, now securely identified with the so-called Parmeniskos group (Salviat 1990; Badoud 2013; see also pp. 36–39). Lawall (2004), pointing to the surrounding context of the Athenaios passage (see previous note) and parallels with other honorific cups named for Hellenistic kings, suggests that the vessel may rather have been a sympotic cup. The wealth of Mende in the classical period, derived largely from its export of wine, is evident from the Athenian tribute lists, where it is assessed at up to fifteen talents (*IG* I³ 259.iii.15), though it usually paid eight (*IG* I³ 262.i.7).

6. Diod. Sic. 19.52.3.

7. Hellenistic kingdoms as predatory states: Finley 1985, 154–65; Kressig 1978 (for the Seleukid kingdom, which he viewed as an "oriental" state). The most fully developed models are the "predatory state" of Barzel (1989; 2002), which seeks to extract the largest amount of resources at the expense of the rest of society, and the "stationary predatory state" of Dixit (2004), which guards its ability to collect revenues by making concessions to political and social elites at the expense of the other levels of society. Kehoe (2013) has recently argued that neither model is compatible with the fiscal policies of the Roman Empire, and the same conclusion is probably valid for the Hellenistic kingdoms. For the economic benefits of the Seleukid kingdom see Descat 2004, 573; Schuler 2004; more generally, Chankowski and

focused on the role of state power in shaping economic activity and of the state itself as an economic actor.[8] The difficulties associated with applying state power across vast kingdoms with uneven levels of urbanization, infrastructure, and productivity confronted each of the Successors, and the instruments of imperial control instituted by this first generation of dynasts established the structures of the Hellenistic states that would broadly define subsequent centuries. Though in large part keeping many of the preexisting fiscal regimes, administrative units, and policies in place, in a fashion typical of ancient empires, the Successors preferred to restructure urban settlement through synoikism and regions through federations of cities (*koina*), two of the most direct interventions in the sovereignty, organization, administration, and finance of constituent parts of the Hellenistic states. The focus on urban development and urbanization emerged as a key and defining aspect of Macedonian imperialism, and the economic effects of these processes elucidate the nature, goals, and impact of Hellenistic rule.[9] Yet the economic dimension of urbanization has often been subordinated to political or military priorities and rarely been considered systematically.[10]

This chapter investigates two principal strands of the encounter between kings and subject populations: first, the role of state power in shaping and organizing economic activity through the concentration of population, land, and resources in larger urban centers; and second, the ways in which communities and individuals adapted and responded to such interventions. Lysimachos and Cassander, in attributing great resources to Ephesos and Kassandreia, envisioned the emergence of these centers as major commercial entities, nodal points for wider regions. The

---

Duyrat 2004; see also Gabrielsen 2011, esp. 216–18. For recent approaches to the Ptolemaic kingdom, see Manning 2003; Manning 2010; Monson 2012.

8. For the political economy of the Greek polis: Eich 2006; Bissa 2009. For the *koinon*: Mackil 2013, ch. 5. For the Seleukid kingdom: Chankowski and Duyrat 2004. Lo Cascio 2007 treats the Roman state as an economic actor.

9. Cf. Reger 2007. These issues have received more attention from economic historians of the Roman world: for Pleket (2003) and Hanson (2011; 2016), for example, the incorporation of Asia Minor into the Roman Empire considerably stimulated the urbanization of the region and had concomitant effects on the economy.

10. Demand 1990, 166–68, concludes that synoikism and *metoikisis* never took place for economic reasons in the classical world. For criticism, see Mackil 2004, 496. For the purpose of Seleukid foundations see G. Cohen 1978; van der Spek 1993; van der Spek 2000, esp. 35. G. Cohen 1995, 64–65, briefly considers the economic importance of the Hellenistic foundations. Gauthier (1987, 196) gestures toward the importance of economic interests, particularly the crucial intersection between institutions and the economy. Aperghis (2001; 2004; 2005), concerned with the tax structure of the Seleukid Empire, is unique in proposing a model for the economic role of urban foundations (see pp. 103–4). Thonemann (2013b) is prepared to see explicitly economic interests at work in the later Attalids' promotion of "military settlements" (*katoikiai*) to polis status.

first section of this chapter examines the impact of synoikism at the level of the civic economy, isolating both the challenges of building, organizing, and sustaining a metropolis formed from a collectivity of social groups and the advantages of expanding one polity at the expense of others and of consolidating discrete civic fiscal regimes into a single entity. The reorganization of space at the city level in turn fostered a network of cities at the regional scale and had important repercussions for both the civic and royal economies. The next section argues that the expansion of key urban nodes intersected with royal interest in simplifying and controlling the patchwork of fiscal regimes by redefining the relationship between the Greek cities and the royal land under the direct control of the king. I suggest that here too we see a strategy of putting more land under the control of the sophisticated bureaucracies of poleis in an attempt to strengthen the network, a short-term concession of revenue from high direct taxation and of direct administrative control for the sake of longer-term infrastructure development. This understanding of royal interest and intervention leads to an investigation of the impact of imperial structures on the overall economy of the cities, how urban networks affected regional economies, trade, markets, and patterns of exchange. First, the *koina* established through royal intervention, I suggest, formed a logical extension of the kings' interest in synoikism, by centralizing political and economic activity within a wider regional framework. These regional leagues extended the reach of shared institutions (such as *ateleia*, exemption from taxation), sometimes created common coinages, and facilitated economic exchange, access to resources, and joint economic ventures. Second, the profound manipulation of political and human geography, including the development of harbors and commercial routes, realigned and otherwise adjusted patterns of exchange. I survey aspects of this complex reorientation through a reconstruction of the movement of goods, primarily from the evidence of amphorae. The chapter concludes by assessing the economic impact of urbanization and considering the potential of using urbanization as a proxy for economic growth.

THE CIVIC ECONOMY, LOCAL AUTONOMY, AND ROYAL INTERVENTION

The unification of independent communities faced several initial difficulties: the consequences of redistributing public and private property, the high up-front costs of funding the most substantial building projects, the incorporation of new citizens and new elites into a new civic body, and the merging of discrete systems of civic finance, taxation, debts, legal codes, liturgies, and economic privileges into a single, functioning polis. For instance, for most of the large multipolis synoikisms, the basic city elements—walls, public buildings, housing, streets, roads—were conceived on a grand scale and newly constructed. The outlay would have been massive. A number of documents provide fragmentary evidence of these new political entities grappling with these very problems and show their machinery reacting to the wide-ranging economic consequences of royally directed synoikism. While the best epigraphically attested cases, like the proposed synoikism of Teos and Lebedos, provide illuminating details of the ramifications of merging the civic finances of independent poleis, we can only guess at the huge expenses involved in the larger multipolis synoikisms like Kassandreia, Thessalonike, Alexandreia Troas, or Demetrias.

One striking feature of the letters of Antigonos to Teos and Lebedos is the complete absence of any prescription for defense or security, concerns to which historians usually attribute the motivation for the urban projects of the Successors. Of course, these may have underlain many of the objectives of these documents, but practical, legal, institutional, and economic concerns dominate, displaying the complexity of the royal authority's economic planning and the circumspection of both the king and local actors in these matters. Details of civic finance from the *sympoliteia* agreements in the later Hellenistic period amplify the import of these issues, similarly revealing the financial complexity of such mergers, albeit with different circumstances.[11] Defense and consolidation were certainly goals of this centralization, but infrastructure, access to the sea (where possible), and commercial revitalization of cities were of chief interest: the tremendous cost and effort of the construction of the new city and circuit wall of Kolophon, initiated by Antigonos between 311 and 306, did not prevent Lysimachos from incorporating its population into Ephesos.

Building a New City: Burdens and Opportunities

The city and its elites took on a large share of the burden of constructing the urban center and infrastructure. While there is illuminating evidence for the direct role that the kings played in the minutiae of planning synoikisms (particularly in the case of Antigonos's proposed merger of Teos and Lebedos), there is much less for royal financial support: the monarchs may have made contributions in the form of manpower, materials, or benefaction, but the overall execution remained securely within the ambit of civic finance and governance.[12]

A fragmentary inscription from Ephesos dating to circa 290 records the notice of the lease of public land (*[gēn d]ēm[osi]an*, 1.2) adjacent to the line of the new city

---

11. E.g., the *sympoliteiai* of Smyrna and Magnesia under Sipylos (*OGIS* 229 [*I. Smyrna* 573; *I. Mag. Sipylos* 1]); of Medea and Stiris (*IG* IX 1 32 = *Syll.*³ 647); and of Miletos and Pidasa (*Milet* I.3, 149, with Migeotte 2001); also the incorporation of the fortress Kyrbissos into Teos (J. Robert and Robert 1976, with Sokolowski 1980 and Chankowski 2007, 310–11).

12. For a comprehensive treatment of the financing of public buildings in Hellenistic Asia Minor, see Meier 2012.

wall, which was then being constructed for Lysimachos's refoundation.[13] This document provides illuminating details concerning the issues of private property arising from the synoikism and the role of the state in repurposing and redistributing land and property within civic territory. The land in question originally belonged to "the sons of Kleitophon" but had been purchased by the polis at the time of the synoikism for the construction of the city wall. The city then leased out portions of this swath of public land to its citizens, with the exception of a six-meter-wide (twenty-foot-wide) stretch along the sea, which was to be used for the construction of a road, and some amount of space left empty as an easement on either side of the wall and its towers. The inscription, a summary of a longer lease agreement, was publicly disclosed and conspicuously displayed on a lighter-colored block of the so-called Tower of Paul, part of the southwestern circuit running along the top of Mount Preon (now Bülbüldağ), the area of the parcel in question. The slopes of this hill were likely cultivated before the foundation of the Hellenistic city and were close to the village of Smyrna, which was leveled to make way for the expanded polis. This area southeast of the Tetragonos Agora and near the harbor became the heart of Hellenistic Ephesos, and private owners like the sons of Kleitophon had to make way for the construction of the new public buildings, walls, and roads. A much more fragmentary decree found near the harbor reports legal problems, probably also involving landownership, associated with the foundation of the West Agora, the likely political center of the Hellenistic city.[14] The evidence from Ephesos thus provides valuable insight into the legal and financial difficulties that communities faced in laying out their new cities; property rights were at issue, and legal disputes undoubtedly arose with frequency. Moreover, the polis had to meet these challenges while still recovering from the "common war" against Lysimachos, when its territory had been severely ravaged, leaving private holdings and lease agreements in shambles.[15]

Financing public building projects presented further challenges. Greek cities often found it difficult to do this with their ordinary revenues, even under normal circumstances.[16] The Ephesian evidence provides no testimony for how the walls were paid for, apart from a decree praising a foreigner, Athenis son of Apollodoros of Kyzikos, for his help (presumably monetary) in their construction.[17] From Kolophon, however, from the period before its incorporation into Ephesos (311–306), we possess a series of inscriptions originally published in the sanctuary of Mētēr

13. *I. Ephesos* Ia 3 = Maier 1959–61, vol. 1, no. 71.
14. *I. Ephesos* IV 1381.
15. *I. Ephesos* Ia 4 = *Syll.*³ 364, with the comprehensive discussion of Walser 2008.
16. On the finances of Greek cities see Migeotte 2014.
17. *I. Ephesos* IV 1441 = Maier 1959–61, vol. 1, no. 72. It is possible that Athenis was in the service of Lysimachos, but he may have been just a wealthy metic who donated money for the construction (so Magie 1950, 1:888).

Antaiē detailing the financial arrangements for the construction of a new city center. This was not properly a synoikism, but Antigonos, sometime before his coronation, was clearly the impetus for this relocation and new fortification. In this instance, which gives us a clearer picture of the workings of the city, the burden fell largely on the polis and its elites. The *dēmos* of Kolophon passed a resolution appointing a board of ten men to oversee the construction of the new city center, including the planning of the walls.[18] This commission was to select an architect, decide his salary, and raise money by means of a public subscription from citizens, metics, and foreigners. It was also responsible for laying out the roads and building lots, planning for their sale or lease, and setting aside space for workshops, the agora, and "other public buildings." A lengthy list of names follows, of whom the majority were Kolophonians or metics, though a number of the big spenders were foreigners, including two Macedonians.[19] A second inscription provides a more detailed balance sheet.[20] In addition to the subscription, the city arranged for a series of measures to repay money advanced to it. The polis arranged to repay its loans with the income from a wide variety of public revenues—including taxes from fisheries, pasture lands, and horse rearing and funds derived from mortgaged property. Citizens agreed not to charge interest on the mortgaged properties but were given usufruct until the loans were repaid (ll. 85–87). Such were the mechanisms of the polis for raising considerable sums of money for the building project initiated by Antigonos, all while still having to make payments to the royal treasury (*ta basilika*, l. 34).

From Alexandreia Troas, the fragmentary yet detailed text of an agreement (*sungraphē*) between the building commission and the contractors for the construction of a new circuit wall shows the machinery of the newly synoikized polis organizing a major building project.[21] This document is the outcome of precisely the sort of planning with which the ten commissioners (*sungrapheis*) from Kolophon were charged. The agreement spells out the minutiae of the wall's construction—design, dimensions, materials, and methods—in extraordinary detail: the level of precision of the polis and its officials is noteworthy. Alexandreia Troas, newly synoikized from a group of disparate communities, appears to have

---

18. Ed. pr. Meritt 1935, 359–72, no. 1 (Wilhelm 1939, no. 1; SEG XIX 698; Maier 1959–61, vol. 1, no. 69; Migeotte 1984, no. 69; Meier 2012, 362–68 [before 307/6]). See also La Genière 1994.

19. For the prosopography, see L. Robert 1936b. See Descat 2010 on the meaning of ἀργυρίου συμμαχικοῦ in l. 153 (silver Alexander coins of Miletos—the name refers to membership in the Karian League). In total, the amount raised in the surviving lines was 3,400 gold staters and 245,000–360,000 drachmai.

20. Ed. pr. Meritt 1935, 372–77, no. 2 (Wilhelm 1939, no. 2; SEG XIX 699; Maier 1959–61, vol. 1, no. 70; Migeotte 1984, no. 87; Meier 2012, 369–73). This may be from between 306 and 302 (on the basis of the reference to *ta basilika*, l. 34), but an earlier date cannot be excluded.

21. *I. Alexandreia Troas* 1–2.

been fully up and running in a remarkably short time. In contrast to Ephesos, which probably retained a greater sense of continuity, relying on a core set of existing civic elites, this was in many ways a community starting *a novo*. It would be interesting to know who emerged as the leading civic officials in this situation, especially because it is striking that a new community of such ambitious scale managed to negotiate the strain of such a problematic transition. The very flexibility and sophistication that polis institutions demonstrated here were what made the urban core of the Hellenistic kingdoms such a valuable asset.

Civic infrastructure was a challenging component of synoikism, but the finances, property, and status of individual citizens, especially elites, presented even more thorny financial issues. Once again, the letters of Antigonos concerning the merger of Teos and Lebedos provide important details of the economic concerns of a king and reflect the pressures to which communities were subject.[22] When these letters were written, the details of the projected synoikism were not fully decided. The unification was to take one of three possible forms: either the polis of Teos would remain in its location, the people of Lebedos would be absorbed into it (*RC* 3, ll. 5–7; *RC* 4.9), and one-third of the existing houses of Teos would be provided to the people of Lebedos while new housing was constructed; Teos would be completely torn down after a new city was constructed, but in the meantime half of its old houses would be left standing, one-third of which would go to the people of Lebedos and two-thirds to the people of Teos (*RC* 3, ll. 7–9; presumably the excess population would be encamped at the new site, working on the city); or a portion of Teos would be left in its location but partially redesigned, and the Teans and the Lebedians would live there until new houses were constructed (ll. 9–14). The costs of the second and third scenarios would clearly be substantial, as they would involve the construction of not only the largest number of houses, meaning the greatest import of timber, bricks, and costly roof tiles,[23] but also a completely or partially new circuit wall, new public buildings, and potentially new harbor works. Moving Teos farther down the peninsula (option 2) seems to have been the preference of Antigonos, who surely saw the proposed location as the most strategically and commercially advantageous. The options may indicate behind-the-scenes negotiations with envoys of Teos and Lebedos, who may have been resistant to a more momentous reconfiguration, but the agencies of their communities are only partially visible in the document. In addition to the building expenses, the cost of feeding the city during this period of disruption would have

22. *RC* 3–4 (*Syll.*³ 344; *SEG* IV 618; Migeotte 1984, no. 86). This synoikism is generally assumed never to have been completed, although Ager 1998 makes the case that it was, associating *SEG* II 579 = J. Robert and Robert 1976, 175–87, the enrollment of new citizens in Teos ca. 300 (against the *communis opinio*), with the synoikism.

23. *RC* 3. The roofs were to be supplied to the Lebedians over four years. It is unclear whether royal funds or public revenue was to pay for them.

been challenging. Wrangling over the importation of grain (ll. 72–94) highlights the centrality of this issue.

The institutional and financial stability of the new polis depended on successfully merging the elites of the constituent cities and dealing with their expected contributions. Antigonos's letter stipulates that those who had performed the *chorēgia*, the trierarchy, or any other liturgy in either city would not be expected to perform the same liturgy in the new city, and the Lebedians, as the party subject to the greatest burden, would be exempt from liturgies for three years if the city was formed at Teos. Another provision offered exemption from liturgies to anyone who would move out to the peninsula and required those whose houses were not demolished to assume the duty (*RC* 3, ll. 70–72). Here Antigonos seems to have provided an incentive to move to a more commercially favorable, although yet undeveloped, location. Likewise, rights of proxeny, citizenship, tax exemption, and so forth were to shift from Lebedos to Teos (ll. 21–24). We may imagine difficulties with the merging of elites, but greater and more immediate problems were financing the building works and the strain caused by that outlay. The second letter of Antigonos is almost entirely concerned with this point. It stresses that completing the physical merger of the cities as soon as possible is his main interest, but the nature of Greek civic finance made impossible the quick raising of funds from a city's limited public revenues. Antigonos therefore ordered the "wealthiest" six hundred Teans to immediately pay the Lebedians one-fourth of the value of their former houses, established by arbitrators from Kos, to be repaid within a year from the city's revenues (*RC* 4, ll. 8–11). The burden on the city, especially on its elite, is impressive. One would of course like to know how individuals reacted to these propositions. In the short term, the elite would have had to front a considerable amount of money, but perhaps there were perceived opportunities to be had after the synoikism was complete. Two additional documents dealing with the integration of new citizens and territories into Teos shed further light on the kinds of financial considerations that went into such unions. A late fourth-century document found in the village of Olamiş, to the north-northeast of Teos, provides detailed stipulations for enrolling the new citizens of an unknown community (possibly Lebedos) absorbed into Teos.[24] These citizens were exempted from liturgies and a wide range of civic taxes for four years. Later Teos incorporated the small, fortified community of Kyrbissos on the borders of its territory, and a detailed decree of the polis records the specifics of the administration and funding of this outpost and the payment of its commander (*phrourarchos*) and his troops.[25]

---

24. Ed. pr. Judeich 1891, 291–95, no. 7 (*SEG* II 579; J. Robert and Robert 1976, 175–87). See also Chandezon 2003, 53; Migeotte 2014, 236–37. For the possible relationship between this document and the synoikism of Teos and Lebedos, see Ager 1998.

25. J. Robert and Robert 1976. For the location of Kyrbissos, see Korparal 2013.

A document from Herakleia Latmos records similar concerns in the Karian satrap Asandros's enforced union of the poleis of Latmos and Pidasa in the late fourth century.[26] The inscription records a number of measures for incorporating the Pidasians into Latmos, among them provisions for their housing in Latmos and the remarkable requirement that for six years, all Pidasian marriages should be with Latmians and vice versa, part of an effort to efface any distinction of identity between the two poleis.[27] The civic finances of the two cities were to be united, with nothing belonging solely to either, and the Pidasians provided with housing for one year and allowed to build on the public land of Latmos. This stands decidedly in contrast to the kinds of sympoity agreements that preserved discrete civic identities among the constituent cities, even to the extent of outlining provisos for economic matters should either city leave the union.[28] The synoikism was perhaps not fully realized, and Pidasa later reemerged; Latmos was moved and refounded as Herakleia and again refounded and renamed by Pleistarchos in the 290s.[29] The network of well-built stone roads extending from Herakleia/Pleistarcheia on to and around Mount Latmos and connecting the town to the Bafa plain and the rich territory of the Maeander valley probably dates to this period.[30] Pidasa was finally absorbed into Miletos in the 180s but remained a site of settlement for the Pidasians who chose to stay there, and Miletos dispatched officials to see to its defenses and establish a permanent military outpost for it.[31] Expanded infrastructure was also needed as these two cities became one: a clause in their *sympoliteia* agreement provided for the construction of a road to connect the urban center of Miletos to the land of the former territory of Pidasa, ensuring their economic linkage. For the Pidasians who moved to Miletos, this enabled continued access to their old fields, farmsteads, and so on, and it granted the former Pidasians use of the harbor of

---

26. Ed. pr. Blümel 1997 (C. Jones 1999; *BÉ* 112.462 [Gauthier]; *SEG* XLVII 1563; Wörrle 2003a, 121–43; LaBuff 2016, 81–87). See also Bencivenni 2003, 151–68; Reger 2004, 152–54.

27. Stressed by *BÉ* 112.462 (Gauthier); Reger 2004, 152–54. For the housing provisions, see Saba 2007. LaBuff (2010; 2016, 86), however, has suggested that the agreement uniting these poleis did not necessarily envisage the full incorporation of Pidasa but rather sought to "incentivize" its people's move to Latmos.

28. E.g., the union of Melitaia and Pereia: *IG* IX 1² 1.188 (*Syll.*³ 546b; Ager 1996, no. 56); *IG* IX 2 205, a fragmentary copy from Delphi. See also Migeotte 1984, 31. The document records the decision of three judges from Kalydon appointed by the Aitolian League to arbitrate the details and disputes involved in the sympoity of Melitaia and Pereia. Pereia was to become a deme of Melitaia, the finances of the cities were to be merged, and the Pereians were to use the same laws as Melitaia. Pereia, the junior partner, was given the option to leave the union, so the Kalydonian judges provided a precise demarcation of the boundaries of each city and prevented Melitaia from selling the common land for its own advantage.

29. G. Cohen 1995, 261–63.

30. Peschlow-Bindokat 1996b, 43–48.

31. *Milet* I.3 149§4 (Gauthier 2001; LaBuff 2016, 93–103).

Miletos, surely one of the factors that prompted the Pidasians to enter into the agreement.

The costs of these synoikisms would have been considerable. So what of the economic benefits? Modernization of the civic infrastructure would certainly have been a boon: for example, city walls suited to third-century siege methods, modern houses and street networks, enlarged civic architecture, new harbor facilities. From the king's perspective, synoikism would potentially solve a number of problems endemic to fourth-century poleis (debt, backlogs of court cases, etc.). But while the Hellenistic kings surely had a hand in these projects, the tendency of modern scholarship to refer to, for example, the "Lysimachean" wall of Ephesos obscures the fact that these building projects were executed largely under civic oversight and at least in part with civic funds.[32] Royal exemptions from taxation and tribute could help, and kings might facilitate access to raw materials, craftsmen, or other specialists, but these resources were still channeled through and embedded in civic finance. The "coercive fund-raising" involved in constructing the walls and infrastructure of a new polis undoubtedly strained the communities tasked with shouldering this burden.[33] But one result was the investing of these expanded and centralized cities with advantages from siting and infrastructure to expanded territory and population. The agglomeration of numerous communities, including their elites, also created a critical mass of those able to perform liturgical functions and thus fund some of the projects that went into the making of the polis.

Synoikism, Transaction Costs, and the Legal Framework

A further advantage of synoikism seems to have been its potential to cut down on friction between neighboring states that perennially squabbled over borders and territory. In the immediate aftermath of Alexander's conquests, it was necessary to delineate what land belonged to the poleis of Asia Minor and what belonged directly to the king. We see this concern in Alexander's well-known letter to Priene, a new charter of status and territorial limits inscribed prominently on the façade of the city's main temple.[34] But in addition to clarifying the lines between royal and civic land, the Hellenistic kings became embroiled in the messy world of interstate disputes and border wars, which they were frequently called upon to arbitrate.[35] Lysimachos's frustration with the falsified claims of the envoys of Priene

---

32. Magie (1950, 1:76) argued that the Ephesians contributed much of the funding for their wall. McNicholl (1997, 103) is somewhat ambivalent on the sources of funding.

33. The phrase is McNicholl's (1997, 72).

34. *I. Priene* 1 = *I. Priene*² 1, with Thonemann 2013a; see also 000–00.

35. Chaniotis 2005, 129–37, with comments on the economic dimension of these disputes. See also Ma 2000. For arbitration, see Ager 1996; 2013.

is palpable in his letter adjudicating its long-standing territorial dispute with Samos.[36] The Persians had encountered this same administrative difficulty of checking the often fractious and destructive relations between neighboring Greek city states, and in 493 Artaphernes had found it expedient to compel the cities of Ionia to arbitrate among themselves rather than resolve disputes by war, effectively unifying them and preventing them from settling their scores through violence. Herodotos makes it clear that this was part of a larger reassessment of the Ionian tribute, measured thereafter by the productive capacity of each polis.[37] In the same vein, disputes over territory and situations that required arbitration frequently preceded sympolity agreements between two independent poleis, for instance Miletos and Myous.[38] The sources rarely speak directly to this issue, but many synoikisms were the product of traditionally antagonistic or at least highly competitive states. Strabo offers one such description, noting that Kebren and Skepsis were "always hostile to each other and at war" before Antigonos synoikized them into Antigoneia/Alexandreia Troas.[39] In this case, the synoikism did not go completely as planned, and Skepsis regained its independence in the power vacuum following the defeat of Antigonos, although Kebren did not.

On legal and institutional levels, synoikism would potentially have addressed a number of problems endemic to fourth-century poleis. In Antigonos's letter to Teos and Lebedos, his initial *diagramma* instructs them to resolve both all of their personal lawsuits within two years and their disputes with each other, subject to the arbitration of Mytilene if necessary (*RC* 3, l. 30). Further, the public debts of Lebedos were to be taken over by Teos and paid for with common funds (ll. 18–20). Antigonos was clearly frustrated by the backlog of cases in both cities, which had led to a standstill, making their successful resolution in court impossible and leading to a situation where interest compounded indefinitely on debts whose contracts were in dispute. He proposed a simple solution: if debtors paid willingly,

---

36. *RC* 7 (*OGIS* 13; Ager 1996, no. 26). Despite Lysimachos's definitive ruling, this remained a live issue until Rome finally resolved it in 135 BCE (*Syll.*³ 688).

37. Hdt. 6.42.1–2. Artaphernes may have imposed this arbitration through the existing institutions of the Ionian *koinon*. Herodotos comments that it was "very beneficial" (χρήσιμα κάρτα) for the Ionians. See also Tod 113, for the ability of the Ionian *koinon* to judge disputes around 390.

38. For Miletos and Myous's arbitration, see *Syll.*³ 134 = RO 16 (ca. 391–388); *sympoliteia, I. Milet* 1.3, 33E (234/33); physical synoikism, Strabo 14.1.10 and Paus. 7.2.11, which give differing accounts of the circumstances. The *chorion* of Myous was handed over to the Magnesians by Philip V in 201 (Polyb. 16.24.9) and became the source of dispute between Magnesia and Miletos in the second century (*Syll.*³ 588). For a discussion of the factors that let to Miletos's absorption of Myous, see Mackil 2004, 494–97. Compare the small polis of Melitaia in Achaia Phthiotis, whose border disputes underwent arbitration numerous times in the third century: in 270–260 (Ager 1996, nos. 30, 32), 214/13 (Ager 1996, no. 55), and 213/12 (Ager 1996, no. 56), when the arbitrators organized a sympolity agreement between it and Pereia (see p. 98n28).

39. Strabo 13.1.33.

their debt would not exceed twice its original value, but if it proved necessary to go to court, they would be liable to pay three times the value of the original debt. The synoikism was accordingly an opportunity to clear the court dockets, eliminate both civic and private disputes and debts, and resolve the friction between these two neighboring states, as well as to make headway in eliminating the public debt of the future synoikized Teos.

This merger also involved the adoption of a new civic law code. Here too the final decision was the result of negotiations among the representatives of both cities and Antigonos, all of whom had competing interests.[40] Antigonos called for the appointment of a board of three men (their city of origin is not specified) to codify the laws for the new community. Any citizen could propose a new law, and the *dēmos* would vote on each proposal. If disagreement arose, Antigonos instructed the cities to refer the matter to him, at which point either he or another city would arbitrate. The full code was ultimately subject to royal approval, and Antigonos specifically mentioned his interest in punishing any codifiers who might introduce an unsuitable law. In the meantime, the synoikism was to use an existing law code, but while Teos preferred to use its own, Lebedos wished to adopt one from a third-party city. Antigonos decided in favor of Lebedos, and both cities agreed to use the laws of Kos, itself the product of a synoikism and respected for its laws.[41] Antigonos's judgment in this matter had several aims. One was to eliminate a source of distinction between the two communities, uniting them under a shared set of laws and avoiding a situation where laws could be written to the benefit of individuals from a particular city. A second was to create a law code on the model of other successful states which would ensure that the new city was governed well and in keeping with royal interests. Further, where regions were incorporated into *koina*, their cities participated in large economic and administrative networks, widening the reach of shared institutions and even coinage. These cities maintained the ability to grant economic privileges in their territory—immunity from taxes (*ateleia*),[42] the right to own property (*enktisis*), and the right to free entry into civic land exempt from customs dues ([*eis*]*aphixis*)—and the *koina* could dispense similar honors across the wider region.

Markets, Monetization, and the Royal Economy

From the perspective of the royal authorities, the Greek cities were only one part of the complex fiscal patchwork that composed their kingdoms. Although not alone in this, the city-states represented sophisticated and highly monetized markets for agricultural products amassed by the kings. For one thing, they required

---

40. *RC* 3, ll. 43–65, with Bencivenni 2003, ch. 6.
41. *RC* 3, ll. 58–66. For the laws of Kos, see Sherwin-White 1978, ch. 5.
42. Bresson 1993, 138–49; Rubinstein 2009.

large amounts of grain and other commodities to feed their populations, and many resorted to imports to fulfill their needs, particularly in difficult times.[43] In Achaemenid and Hellenistic times, kings recognized the importance of cities as consumers of in-kind surpluses.[44] This is evident in the letters of Antigonos to Teos and Lebedos, which clearly underscore his interest in managing the relationship between these cities and the tributary land directly under his control. In the first letter, he indicates his initial unwillingness to allow them to set aside fourteen hundred staters from the civic revenues as a fund from which a private individuals could borrow, against security, for the importation of grain, with additional funds for the period when the synoikism was taking place.[45] The king claimed this was because he wished to keep the cities that were under his control free of debts and because there was plentiful royal land (*phorologoumenēs chōras*) nearby from which grain could be imported. This has been met with almost universal suspicion as the predatory economic policy of a king seeking to profit off a monopoly on grain importation, and indeed Antigonos seemed at pains to assure the cities that there was no private advantage for him in the arrangement.[46] While his concerns for eliminating public and private debt may have been genuine and the system that he proposed might have offered Teos and Lebedos a more stable source of grain imports, the benefits of this system to the king are manifest. The unwillingness of the citizens of Teos and Lebedos to accept such an intervention in their finances attests the strong desire of the Greek cities to be the masters of their own revenues as much as possible, and their ability to gain an exemption from the king's policy attests one way in which special fiscal privilege mapped onto the negotiation of sovereignty.[47] Although it ran counter to his interests, Antigonos acceded to their request and granted this privilege. As a final stipulation, the letter required all imports and exports of grain to be declared in Teos's agora (*RC* 3, ll. 94–101). This injunction was evidently intended to ensure the payment of the relevant taxes, both civic and royal.

43. See, e.g., the honorary decrees of Ephesos praising Archestratos, one of Demetrios's generals (*I. Ephesos* V 1452), and Agathokles of Rhodes (*I. Ephesos* V 1455 = *Syll.*³ 354) for their aid in supplying the city with grain during the war against Lysimachos.
44. Briant 1994; de Callataÿ 2004.
45. *RC* 3, ll. 72–94.
46. *RC* 3, ll. 86–87.
47. Gabrielsen (2011) has pointed to a further dimension of this negotiation, stressing the room for independent action by Teos and, specifically, one individual merchant. The city, with the permission of the king, set up a fund for the purchase of grain—exempt from its *phoros* assessment—which it passed to a private citizen. This citizen would thus have had credit and a monopoly. Gabrielsen sees this as a prime example of the power of cities to retain control over their finances and extract concessions from kings, even when they were contrary to the royal interest. On fiscal exemptions and sovereignty, see Capdetrey 2006; 2007, 418–22.

This encounter sheds light on the overlapping economic interests of king and communities in the synoikism of two old Greek poleis. The emerging city was to be a robust harbor town occupying a strategic site on the Ionian coast, one poised to capitalize on seaborne commerce and the resources of an expanded *chōra* well know for its productivity. Antigonos's stake in securing a market for the agricultural surpluses from royal land such as this elucidates the important role that cities played in the conversion of in-kind commodities into cash. The immense wealth of the Hellenistic kings came from a variety of sources, such as tribute in cash (the *phoros* or *syntaxis* collected from cities and customs stations, and the tax, assessed in silver, on highly perishable crops from villages and estates), but the vast majority of it derived from resources in kind.[48] The kings had only limited use of these stockpiles, and after satisfying their own needs and redistributing portions to dependents and other beneficiaries, they seem to have preferred to convert what remained into money. Cities certainly played an important role in this facet of the royal economy, alongside indigenous towns and villages, temple-states, and the periodic markets associated with religious festivals. The interest of kings in reinforcing, expanding, and refounding Greek poleis through synoikism or similar processes, however, stresses their particular place in the royal economy. Phrygian Kelainai and Toriaion, for example, were already important market towns that served this purpose in Achaemenid times.[49] Both of them, notably, were converted into Greek-style poleis. This focus on development and intensification points to one of the central roles of the royal authority as a regulator of the economy, but the precise way that civic economies intersected with the royal economy has been subject to considerable debate.[50]

The most robust model, proposed by G. Aperghis, essentially argues that the prime motivation for city building in the Seleukid Empire was not defense and control but economic stimulus.[51] New cities were a means of promoting the agricultural exploitation of underutilized regions such as northern Syria (where foundations were particularly thick on the ground), but more important, they served the very specific purpose of providing a market where raw materials were converted into silver coin, which then could flow into the coffers of the royal treasury. Proposing rough estimates for the population of the Seleukid Empire and the amount of tribute it collected per year, Aperghis has suggested a direct correlation between the coinage supply and the needs of the state. The Seleukid state, on this

---

48. E.g., the tribute from the estate of the Macedonian landowner Krateuas (*Syll.*³ 302, with Thonemann 2009; see also pp. 108–9). This kind of mixed-*phoros* regime was also common to the Achaemenids. For the use of the terms *phoros* and *syntaxis* in the Hellenistic period, see Schuler 2007.

49. Toriaion: Xen., *Anab.* 1.2.14. See pp. 135–36 for Apameia Kelainai.

50. For models of the royal economy, see Bickerman 1938; Rostovtzeff 1941, 1:440–71; Descat 2003; Aperghis 2004; Chankowski and Duyrat 2004; Capdetrey 2007, 395–436.

51. Aperghis 2001; 2004, esp. 2; 2005.

model, required cash to pay its personnel and maintain its army, and here the cities provided an essential service in receiving agricultural and other products from the countryside and paying for them in cash, which then flowed to the royal treasury in the form of tribute from peasants. Seleukid minting can thus be correlated to the needs of this cycle, "topping up" the coinage as pieces fell out of circulation.[52] Aperghis characterizes the importance of new cities as perpetuating this system, minimizing the significance of revenue derived directly from them in the form of tribute or other taxes. This provocative picture of a highly monetized, structured (and decidedly modernist) royal economy, including the role of cities and city foundations in it, has been shown to underestimate the importance of in-kind tribute and taxes.[53] Scholars have also been skeptical of Aperghis's view of the level of monetization in the royal economy, which in turn casts doubt on his model. In the case of the Seleukid kingdom, the west was already urbanized enough that the silver already in circulation in the early third century largely sufficed, so Seleukid mints added little, despite the swift pace of urbanization in that period.[54] Cities were certainly markets for products from royal land, as the case of Teos and Lebedos demonstrates, but Aperghis's unitary model flattens their complex and multifaceted role within the Hellenistic kingdoms and minimizes their importance as valuable repositories of manpower and institutional complexity (useful to the strategic and ideological interests of the king). Cities contributed revenues derived from tribute and a wide variety of indirect taxes on the movement and sale of goods. They remained zones of high monetization in the patchwork of the royal economy and privileged spaces that negotiated their status and sovereignty largely through fiscal exemptions.[55] We should accordingly take a wider view of the significance of urbanization to the economies of both cities and kingdoms. In the Aegean and western Asia Minor, the existing framework of cities, towns, temples, and villages functioned perfectly well for the Achaemenid tributary system, and these zones were already highly monetized before the Hellenistic period. The logic of urbanization, therefore, has less to do with the pressing needs of royal authorities to extract payments in silver and far more to do with the overall function of cities as useful and fiscally accessible nodes of resources, manpower, communication, and revenue intensification. The relationship between the cities and royal land elucidates this view, alongside the changes to the system of land tenure initiated in the Hellenistic period, the subject of the next section.

---

52. Aperghis 2004, ch. 11 ("topping up": 236, 261, 300).
53. Bringmann 2001; de Callatäy 2004; Houghton 2004; Schuler 2004; Bringmann 2005; Mileta 2008.
54. Houghton 2004; de Callatäy 2005.
55. Cities as highly monetized: Bresson 2005; fiscal privileges and sovereignty: Capdetrey 2006.

KINGDOM, CITY, AND LAND

A fundamental change brought on by the Macedonian conquest of western Asia Minor was the restructuring of the fiscal status of land and systems of land tenure. The Achaemenid kings, in theory if not fully in practice, laid claim to the entirety of their realm as their personal patrimony. Alexander, by contrast, announced a new order by clearly distinguishing between poleis and civic land on the one hand and the *chōra* on the other.[56] To the cities he granted a privileged fiscal status, exemption from the direct taxation of land and property, whereas the *chōra* became the direct possession of the king and subject to tribute. This dichotomy is made plain in Alexander's letter to Priene, which elucidates a process that must have taken place throughout the newly conquered lands: the king delineated the boundaries of the Greek city and its harbor (Naulochon) and claimed the indigenous settlements that lay outside as royal land.[57] The sharp demarcation between these two zones is important because they had differing institutions, statuses, and fiscal responsibilities.

This section investigates the intersection between the restructuring of both of these zones (civic and royal) through the reorganization and synoikism of many of the cities of Asia Minor and the northern Aegean and the reassignment of royal land to individuals, cities, and other collectivities. I argue that these policies were interrelated in several important ways: through a general preference for urban centers that dramatically changed patterns of settlement, through a willingness to alienate royal land to civic territories, and through the granting of large estates to individuals who were increasingly part of, or at least closely associated with, the civic territory of these poleis. Such policies, which attached large tracts of land to densely inhabited urban centers and introduced large new landholders to civic bodies, had important consequences for the cities' finances and patterns of landholding. This of course brought new opportunities and sources of income for the poleis, which could tax the land and expect liturgies and other benefits from their extraordinary new citizens. At the same time, however, the king served his own interests, rewarding his close associates with land and fiscal privileges and further developing the markets, infrastructure, and resources that linked the *chōra* to the institutions of the Greek polis. Further, royal functionaries could be embedded within the framework of the cities, and the royal treasury would continue to

---

56. Mileta 2002; Mileta 2008, 20–35; Thonemann 2009; Thonemann 2011b, 242–51; Bresson 2016, 110–17. Despite this bipolar distinction, the *chōra* had a range of components and statuses, e.g., organized temple states and *ethnē* with special privileges, military settlements (*katoikiai*) given exemptions, and landed estates granted in usufruct to high-ranking officials.

57. *I. Priene* 1 = *I. Priene*² 1, with Sherwin-White 1985 and Thonemann 2013a. Pace Mileta 2002, 159–60, there is no evidence that this reassessment deprived Priene of civic territory (see Sherwin-White 1985, 83).

benefit from their contributions there (*phoros/syntaxis*), albeit at a lower rate than if they were assessed on royal land.

The details of this evolving system, however, are not entirely straightforward. The documentation for fiscal privileges and land grants dating to the early Hellenistic period has provoked a vigorous debate about the status of these landholdings, the rights of their possessors, and their relationship to prior Macedonian or Achaemenid practice.[58] Consequently, this has important repercussions for the issue of the relative continuity or discontinuity between the Hellenistic and Persian administrative systems. It has become increasingly clear that institutions of the Hellenistic kingdoms owed much to Macedonian precedents, but the extent to which aspects of Achaemenid land tenure policy may have influenced Macedonian practice in Asia, at least in the transitional period under Alexander, is a more difficult question.[59] I argue that the Hellenistic land tenure regime, a patchwork of classifications and statuses, departed from the Achaemenid system in crucial respects, even though certain procedures bore a strong resemblance to the Achaemenid tributary system. It was chiefly the increasing practice of devolving royal land to cities and other collectivities that played the largest role in transforming the patterns of settlement and economic interaction in western Asia Minor.

In the Macedonian kingdom of Philip, Alexander, and their predecessors, the kings rewarded their associates and beneficiaries with several types of grants: estates from royal land or revenues from villages, harbors, and other kinds of settlements outside cities.[60] These could be for usufruct alone or heritable possessions, but both types of concession formally remained classified as royal land. The kings could also confer, either alone or in conjunction with other benefactions, fiscal immunity from taxes (*ateleia*) on imports and exports. Such grants are attested as early as the reign of Amyntas III, in the context of the timber trade, and Alexander famously conferred *ateleia*, among other privileges, on the families of his soldiers who died on campaign.[61] Finally, the kings could give land to settlers of new cities founded on conquered territory, which formally became civic land. Two docu-

---

58. Papazoglou 1997; Schuler 1998; Boffo 2001; Mileta 2002; Mileta 2008; Capdetrey 2007, 135–66; Bresson 2016, 110–17.

59. Macedonian precedents: Hatzopoulos 1996; 2006. Achaemenid precedents: Briant 2006. Thonemann 2009 interprets the conveyance of the estate of Krateuas to Aristomenes (*Syll.*³ 302, from 326/25 or 325/24; see pp. 108–9) in this way.

60. Philip II gave Apollonides of Kardia the right of usufruct of all the land north of Agora on the Thracian Chersonese (Dem. 7.39). Plutarch provides a clear description of Alexander's financial situation on the eve of his invasion of Asia (*Alex.* 15.3–4): The king assigned a farm or village or the revenues from a settlement or harbor to each of his companions, all taken from royal lands. This supposedly prompted Perdikkas to ask what Alexander had left for himself, to which the latter replied, "My hopes."

61. Amyntas III: Borza 1987. Philip II granted fiscal immunity to Hippokles, which Antigonos Gonatas renewed (*SEG* XLVII 893). Alexander's *ateleia* grants: Arr., *Anab.* 1.16.5 (after Granikos), 7.10.4 (reported at Opis).

ments elucidate the details of this kind of arrangement during Alexander's reign. The first records his decisions given (probably) in the winter of 335/34 to ambassadors from Philippoi, which Philip II had created from the failed Thasian colony Krenides on land taken from the Thracians.[62] Alexander authorized Philotas and Lennatos, the famous companions, to define a boundary between Philippoi and the neighboring Thracian tribes in one contested area, clearly demarcating the distinction between civic territory and the *chōra* inhabited by the Thracians (ll. 18-20). This letter also confirmed that the people of Philippoi were allowed to cultivate another tract of land (ll. 23-25), a privilege originally granted by Philip. Here the reference is to royal land, which would be subject to tribute, unlike civic land. Disputes brought about by the lack of clear boundaries, possibly due to land reclamation work carried out in the 340s,[63] presumably prompted the need for the restatement of this right. Thus, in this document three types of land are apparent: civic land (Philippoi), royal land inhabited by an indigenous population group (the Thracians), and royal land granted in usufruct (to the citizens of Philippoi).

In the second document, also from 335/34, Alexander "gave" (*edōke*) the Bottian polis Kalindoia and the territory of three neighboring towns that were probably poleis in the fifth century, Thamiskos, Kamakai, and Tripoiai, to the Macedonians.[64] This region had been conquered in the reign of Philip, circa 357/56, and incorporated into the Macedonian kingdom after the dissolution of the Chalkidian League in 348.[65] Parts of the former territory of these cities were then granted to estate holders or reorganized into new poleis like Kalindoia and, ultimately, Kassandreia. The refoundation of Kalindoia probably amounted to a synoikism of the populations of the four settlements and the introduction of new Macedonian colonists, much in the same way that Philippoi had been formed. The Macedonians were either granted land individually by Alexander at the time of the refoundation of Kalindoia or later admitted as a group of colonists and assigned lots by the officials of the polis.[66]

A document from the reign of Cassander (306-298) sheds further light on the terms of land grants dating to the reigns of Philip and Alexander from confiscated civic territory of Chalkidian poleis. It was originally set up on a public building in

---

62. Ed. pr. Vatin 1984 (Missitzis 1985; *SEG* XXXIV 664; Hammond 1988; Badian 1989; Hatzopoulos 1996, vol. 2, no. 6). Badian 1989, 67, questions the date.

63. Theophr., *Caus. pl.* 5.14.5-6.

64. Ed. pr. Vokotopoulou 1986 (*SEG* XXXVI 626; Hatzopoulos 1996, vol. 2, no. 62). For the geography and history of the region, see Flensted-Jensen 1995.

65. Ed. pr. Vokotopoulou 1990 (*SEG* XL 542; Hatzopoulos and Loukopoulou 1992, 123-45; Hatzopoulos 1996, vol. 2, no. 4), a boundary settlement from prior to 348 in the reign of Philip II delimiting the territories of the conquered cities in the region of Kalindoia.

66. Individual grants: Vokotopoulou 1986; Errington 1998. Grant to Macedonians as a whole: Hammond 1988; Hatzopoulos and Loukopoulou 1992, 110-17.

Kassandreia along with several other inscriptions recording the fiscal privileges of estate holders in the region and is dated by the eponymous priest of the city.[67] In it Cassander confirms the claim of Perdikkas the son of Koinos (the famous companion of Alexander) to four nonadjacent parcels of land. Two of these Perdikkas's grandfather Polemokrates had obtained by lot (e|klērouchēsen, ll. 7–8) in the reign of Philip; Perdikkas's father received the third from Philip; and Perdikkas bought the fourth from another estate holder, Ptolemaios, who had received it from Alexander. Cassander declared that Perdikkas owned these pieces of land, on the same terms as those of the original grantees, namely "as a patrimonial possession, both they and their descendants being entitled to possess, alienate, and sell them" (ll. 10–15).[68] In addition to these estates, Cassander awarded *ateleia* to Perdikkas and his descendants on imports and exports of the things for personal use on his property.

Such is the sum of the evidence for royal grants of land and fiscal privileges in Europe under Philip and Alexander. The picture is mostly clear. The kings regularly disposed of various kinds of land and revenues from the royal territory to reward their subordinates and develop their kingdom. This ranged from temporary grants of usufruct of revenues from land, harbor taxes, and so on, through heritable gifts of estates that could be alienated and sold to the reorganization of royal land into civic territory. Kings also regularly conferred *ateleia* on individuals. Much of the evidence comes from the period of the expansion of the Macedonian state under Philip and Alexander, in particular the subjection of the Chalkidike and much of Thrace, the "new lands." The conquest of Asia under Alexander and the passage of this territory into the successor states raises the question of how these same issues of land tenure were managed in these regions in the time of Alexander and the Successors and the degree to which Macedonian or Achaemenid practice prevailed or innovations were introduced. The evidence has generated much debate on these points. I argue below that the Macedonian penchant for promoting cities and granting estates as patrimonial possessions had a significant impact on land tenure policy in Asia and that in the early Hellenistic kingdoms, Macedonian policy diverged in important ways from Achaemenid practice, marking an institutional development that had wide-ranging economic effects.

A key source in this discussion is the well-known document pertaining to the estate of the otherwise unattested Krateuas in Lydia, the only example of a land grant in Asia from the reign of Alexander.[69] This inscription has been interpreted as evidence of strong administrative continuity with Persian practice during Alexander's lifetime. It is dated both by Alexander's eleventh regnal year (326/25 or

---

67. *Syll.*³ 332 (*SEG* XXXVIII 620; Hatzopoulos 1988, 22–26; Hatzopoulos 1996, vol. 2, no. 20).

68. ἔδ[ω]||κεν ἐμ πατρικοῖς καὶ αὐτ|οῖς καὶ ἐκγόνοις κυρίοι|ς οὖσι κεκτῆσθαι καὶ | ἀλλάσσεσθαι καὶ ἀ|ποδόσθαι. See also ll. 19–24.

69. *Syll.*³ 302 (Thonemann 2009, 371).

325/24) and eponymously by the satrap Menandros (ll. 4–6), in purely Achaemenid fashion,[70] though also by the eponymous prytane of the nearby polis of Gambreion (ll. 6–7).[71] This document records the transfer of an estate (or part of an estate) from Krateuas, to whom Alexander had originally granted it, to a third party, Aristomenes. The parcel consisted of a plot of arable land measuring 170 *kyproi* of seed (circa seventeen hectares, or forty-two acres) with several buildings, a garden (*kēpos*), and a nursery for vines (*phuton*, l. 11) probably planted by Krateuas. Aristomenes was to settle on (*epoikisai*, l. 10) the land—that is, construct a house there and work the land—and would henceforth be responsible for tribute in kind on the arable part (at a rate of one-tenth or one-twelfth of the harvest) and tribute (*phoros*) of one gold stater per annum, levied on the garden (ll. 11–18). Unlike the estates of Perdikkas, this land was given to Krateuas not as a patrimonial possession but merely in usufruct—and he in turn sublet it to Aristomenes. It remained subject to the king and classified as royal, and it was liable to tribute in kind and in coin, just as under the Achaemenid system. What is additionally salient about this document is the precise relationship of the land to the nearby polis of Gambreion. The dating of the document by the eponymous prytane has been taken to indicate that the land lay in the civic territory of that polis,[72] which would contradict the usual understanding of a bipolar division between royal and civic territory. It is more likely, however, that the lease was simply recorded at Gambreion because that was the nearest appropriate urban center where it could be displayed and the lands in question bordered the civic territory of that polis.[73]

This form of grant is mirrored in the troubled estate (*oikos*) of Mnesimachos in Lydia, conferred by Antigonos sometime in the late fourth century and attested by a lengthy inscription from the temple of Artemis at Sardeis.[74] It consisted of villages (*kōmai*) and land allotments (*klēroi*), each of which were assessed for an annual tribute (*phoros*) in gold staters. The rates listed in the document, as R. Descat has shown, appear to correspond to the conversion of an original one-twelfth assessment of the theoretical cash value of the estate in Persian darics to Macedonian

70. Thonemann 2009, 373.
71. Compare the formulae of *I. Mylasa* 21 (*SEG* XIII 488), a land grant of Philip Arrhidaios to Hermaios(?), dated by the regnal year of Philip III and the satrap Asandros and registered in Mylasa ca. 317. This grant, however, was made *en patrikois* (l. 10), if the supplement is correct. Hermaios in turn dedicated the land, on which he founded a sanctuary of Herakles and Hermes, to Mylasa's palaistra and gymnasion (to which this plot provided water).
72. Rigsby 1989.
73. Tarn 1950, 221–22. This would make Gambreion parallel to Kassandreia in the documents discussed at pp. 107–8 and 111–12.
74. Ed. pr. Buckler and Robinson 1912, no. 1 (1932, no. 1). For discussions and various interpretations of this text, see Atkinson 1972; Debord 1982, 244–51; Descat 1985; Billows 1995, 111–45; Dignas 2002, 70–73, 279–87; Thonemann 2009, 386–89.

gold staters, meaning that the estate and its method of taxation were taken over directly from the Achaemenid system.⁷⁵ Mnesimachos had sublet the *klēroi* on emphyteutic lease (contingent on the lessee working and improving the land) to two individuals, Pytheos and Adrastos, and mortgaged the rest to the temple of Artemis at Sardeis, but he was still officially the leaseholder, and the king could still reclaim the estate, a possibility accounted for in the document. The agreement was not a sale: Mnesimachos was tied to the estate, which he could not sell or alienate. In sum, the two documents describing the estates of Krateuas and Mnesimachos, both dating to the late fourth century, record a type of grant that was not given to the beneficiary as personal patrimony and was not necessarily heritable. Such conditions were applied to certain grants in Macedonia under Philip and Alexander (see pp. 106–8) and were standard in Achaemenid Asia Minor.⁷⁶ Two types of grants predominated in Macedonian practice: estates given *en patrikois*, which were heritable, could be alienated, bought, and sold, and did not require reconfirmation when a new king came to the throne, and grants with a more temporary and contingent right of usufruct, which did not necessarily pass from father to son.⁷⁷ Both formally remained royal land, and there is no reason to think they could not exist side by side. The estates of Krateuas and Mnesimachos therefore do not provide clear evidence for Alexander privileging Achaemenid systems of land tenure in Asia Minor over traditional Macedonian procedures, outside the convenience of maintaining the method of dating and registration and the preexisting assessment of the tribute from the prior administration.

Hellenistic practice in both Europe and Asia Minor, however, certainly followed Macedonian traditions and departed from the Achaemenid system. But here too, grants with various statuses and responsibilities continued to coexist. In this sense, the process of attributing various cities, towns, and lands to a synoikism bears a strong resemblance to the foundation of cities like Kalindoia and Philippoi, except that unlike these poleis, the synoikisms were created not exclusively from conquered land but from formally allied communities. A major new trend, however, was the Hellenistic kings' willingness to alienate land to large urban foundations, in an effort to harness existing viable and revenue-producing structures. This was done in various ways: the unification of several poleis, which may also have entailed adding additional land to the resulting city; the synoikism of villages, towns, and temple land, which had the effect of reclassifying royal land as civic territory; the sale or gift of land to a city; the promotion of a rural settlement

---

75. Descat 1985.
76. See Thonemann 2009, 368–69, 380, for a discussion of the Achaemenid evidence.
77. Criscuolo 2011; Bresson 2016, 110–17. The distinction, therefore, is identical to that of lands given as a *klērouchia* (heritable, alienable) and lands given *en doreai* in Ptolemaic Egypt. For recent discussions of the status of klerouchs in Ptolemaic Egypt, see Monson 2012, 6–79, 88–90, 94–95; Fischer-Bouvet 2014, 210–37.

(*katoikia*) to the status of polis or the absorption by a polis of such a settlement; or the granting of an estate to a subordinate with the further right of attaching the land to a polis.

We have already seen examples of the first two in the Chalkidike and Thrace. For many of the other synoikisms of the Successors, we simply do not know whether parcels of royal land were attributed to the new city, but this would perhaps not be surprising. A possible exception is the case of Kassandreia. Two documents from the reign of Cassander, the grant to Perdikkas (see pp. 106–8) and a grant of *ateleia* to a certain Chairephanes from the same year,[78] have been taken as evidence for the changing status of estates formerly on royal land but included in the civic territory of Kassandreia after its foundation in 316. They are from the same architectural context, a public building in Kassandreia where a third document, a land grant from Lysimachos to Limnaios dating to 285/84, was also displayed.[79] The two land grants conveyed parcels to powerful friends of the king as patrimonial possessions (*en patrikois*). In both cases they were confiscated territory of former Chalkidian poleis and in particular appear to have been on the edges of those places, bordering the hilly regions of the central Chalkidike.[80] But unlike those of Perdikkas, whose earlier grant required reconfirmation, the estate of Limnaios was newly bestowed by Lysimachos sometime after he became the king of Macedonia. The terms of ownership for both of these grants, then, remained consistent from the time of Philip to the reign of Lysimachos. All told, Limnaios's estate consisted of 2,480 plethra (223 hectares, or 551 acres), on roughly the same order as other large estates granted to beneficiaries of the kings in Asia Minor (see pp. 112–14).

The most difficult question is the relationship of these grants to the city of Kassandreia. Most scholars have assumed that these lands became part of its civic territory because the synoikism of the city in 316 should have incorporated the land of most of the poleis of this part of the Chalkidike. In addition, Kassandreia's interest in these grants is suggested by the facts that the inscriptions are dated by one of its eponymous officials, that the decrees were displayed at a public building there, and that one of the beneficiaries, Chairephanes the son of Aischylos, is further designated by his tribe (or *genos*), Hippotadeis, making him (at least) a citizen of Kassandreia. On this reading, the foundation of the city between the original grants of Philip and Alexander and the reign of Cassander necessitated

---

78. Ed. pr. Vokotopoulou 1997 (*SEG* XLVII 940). For the identification of this Chairephanes with the wealthy contractor who was involved with a major land reclamation project in Euboia, see Bresson 2016, 115, 165–66 (discussing *IG* XII 9 191).

79. Hatzopoulos 1988 (*SEG* XXXVIII 619). For the architectural context, see Vokotopoulou 1997, 48–49.

80. Hatzopoulos 1988, 36–43.

the confirmation that Perdikkas was the rightful owner of lands that had since been reclassified as civic territory.[81] Such a reconstruction, however, presents several major difficulties, as A. Bresson has shown. The grant to Perdikkas was confirmed some ten years after the foundation of Kassandreia, calling into question the assumption that a change in the status of the land prompted this. Similarly, Lysimachos made his grant to Limnaios some thirty years after synoikism, and if this was in fact civic land, the king should have had no role in assigning it.[82] Some other vicissitude prompted Cassander's confirmation, then, some dispute concerning the land or perhaps the new conferral of *ateleia*.[83] These grants were accordingly set up in Kassandreia because it was the nearest suitable location to display the documents and because the lands bordered the territory of the polis, which naturally would have made it necessary to clearly delineate their owners and statuses for fiscal purposes (just as with Gambreion and the adjacent estate of Krateuas). Cassander and Lysimachos, therefore, conferred *ateleia* not on estates in civic territory but on landholders who were or may have been citizens of the city but also held estates on adjacent royal land. Moreover, there is no need to assume that all the land of the Chalkidike was assigned to one of the synoikisms in the region. There is evidence for tracts of royal land elsewhere in European regions under Macedonian control, namely in the vicinity of Demetrias.[84]

In addition to making this form of grant, kings regularly alienated large tracts of royal land to estate holders, who were allowed to incorporate it into the civic territory of a polis. This appears to have been particularly common in Seleukid Asia Minor, but probably not limited to it, and had important consequences for the relationship between royal and civic land. The well-known dossier detailing Antiochos I Soter's conferral of land on Aristodikides of Assos circa 275 (*RC* 10–13) illustrates a shift in the granting of parcels to subordinates in the Hellenistic period and underscores the basic connection of the process to a wider program of urbanization.[85] These three letters of Antiochos to Meleager the *stratēgos* of the Hellespontine satrapy, forwarded to the city of Ilion and preceded by a cover letter from Meleager explaining the contents and providing instructions for the city, record three stages of a land grant to Aristodikides, a *philos* of the king (*RC* 11, l. 12). The first document assigns two thousand plethra (180 hectares, or 445 acres) of cultivable land (*gē ergasimos*, *RC* 10, l. 3) from the royal territory bordering the polis of Gergis or Skepsis, to be attached (*prosorisai*) to only Ilion or Skepsis (ll. 6–8) fol-

---

81. Hatzopoulos 1988, 43–49; Vokotopoulou 1997; *BÉ* 111.269 (Hatzopoulos); Thonemann 2009.
82. Bresson 2007a, 173–75, with *BÉ* 121.340 (Hatzopoulos); Bresson 2016, 110–17. It should be noted, however, that all of this assumes a rather static view of the synoikism as an event rather than as an evolving process. Nevertheless, these objections are convincing.
83. Criscuolo 2011.
84. Batziou-Efstathiou and Pikoulas 2006.
85. *RC* 10–13 = *I. Ilion* 33, with Bencivenni 2004. See also Papazoglou 1997, T1.

lowing the transfer of ownership. Presumably after some lapse of time or change of circumstance, Aristodikides again met with the king, who agreed to his request for an otherwise unknown *chorion* called Petra,[86] fifteen hundred plethra (135 hectares, or 334 acres) of cultivable land belonging to that place, and another two thousand plethra (*RC* 11). The second letter also gave Aristodikides the right to attach all of this land to any city in the territory controlled by Antiochos and in alliance with him, presumably a significant detail that increased Aristodikides's bargaining power for honors and exemptions from cities competing for the land. In the interval between the second and third letters, he again had an audience with the king, informing him that Petra had already been assigned to someone else (in fact, the Seleukid naval commander Athenaios) and asking for the same amount of land elsewhere, plus another two thousand plethra. Antiochos again assented to the request, ordering that Meleager make this grant from the royal land and allowing Aristodikides to attach it to any city in alliance with the king (*RC* 12). All told, Aristodikides was given either eight thousand or six thousand plethra (720 or 540 hectares, or 1,779 or 1,334 acres),[87] which Meleagar's cover letter indicates that Aristodikides had decided to attach to Ilion "because of the sanctuary of Athena and his goodwill toward the Ilians" (*RC* 13, ll. 10–11), even though many other cities had approached him and given him crowns (ll. 6–7). Meleager closed by adding that Aristodikides was to inform the Ilians of the privileges he expected them to vote him and advised them to do so (ll. 15–17).

The connection of these grants to the poleis of the Troad and the urbanization of this region is instructive. The earmarked royal land bordered the territories of Gergis and Skepsis, both of which lay in the central Troad, but in the original allocation, Antiochos indicates that it should be attached to only Ilion or Skepsis—and not Gergis or Rhoteion or any of the other poleis in the region—after being given to Aristodikides. This clause is significant, and Antiochos's later amendment allowing Aristodikides to attach his land to any city in alliance with the Seleukids should be interpreted as a meaningful expansion of privilege in accordance with the overall better terms of the subsequent grants. Antigonos had used Ilion as a regional focal point (see pp. 58–63), and in this dossier we see the mechanisms of that process continuing. Antiochos clearly viewed it as in his interest to increase the largest poleis in the Troad rather than allow the land to be attached to any polis, in full accordance with the Successors' general policy of elevating some

---

86. It was evidently not a village but some sort of fortified settlement. Descat (1985) suggests that it may have been what is called a *baris* in other documents, e.g., *RC* 18, detailing a similar grant of land. Or perhaps it was a fortified estate (*tursis*) of the type common in the Achaemenid era and confiscated from an Achaemenid or Antigonid landlord.

87. Depending on whether the two thousand plethra in *RC* 11 and 12 were separate grants or repetitions of the same grant. Aperghis (2004, 101–2) estimates the size of the estate at 5,500 plethra (3,500 if there is repetition). Followed by Bresson 2016, 112.

cities at the expense of others. Eventually, Attalos I transferred at least some of the citizens of Gergis to a new settlement,[88] and following 188 BCE the city's eclipse finally resulted in its incorporation into Ilion. In his grant to Aristodikides, Antiochos left room for the poleis to bid for the land to be attached to them, preserving some autonomous action for them and clearly benefiting the landholder.

This form of grant is closely paralleled in the case of the Seleukid officer Larichos whom Priene honored in a series of three decrees circa 275–270.[89] The polis responded to Larichos's benefactions (attaching his estate to the city and perhaps other services) with numerous civic privileges (compare the scenario envisaged by Meleagar in his letter to the Ilians), including freedom from taxation on his person and "whatever he imports or exports to his own *oikos*" (A., ll. 6–7) and "on the flocks and slaves on his private property and in the city" (B., ll. 24–26). Antiochos II's 254/53 divorce settlement has a further instance of alienating royal land to cities: a royal estate near Kyzikos and Zeleia, with its land, house, village, and inhabitants, was sold to his former queen Laodike, who was allowed to chose the city to which it would then be attached.[90] In each of these cases a preference for dealing with larger collectivities and a willingness to cede the assessment of tribute to larger administrative units is apparent.

In addition to granting the privilege of attaching formerly royal estates to civic territories within their kingdoms, kings might divest themselves of land by selling or gifting it to cities. Antiochos I sold to the small Aiolian polis of Pitane a large tract "in the plain," the Kaikos valley, for 380 talents.[91] Its ownership was thereafter subject to a long-standing dispute between Pitane and Mytilene, which claimed this land as part of its mainland territory (*peraia*). Sometime between 150 and 133 the matter was submitted to arbitration by Pergamene judges, who decided in favor of Pitane, and decrees of the three states were set up on a stele in Pergamon. According to the documents produced by the citizens of Pitane, Antiochos had granted them "[for all] time the indisputable and agreed [right of full ownership of the land]."[92] Philetairos, the ruler of Pergamon, had partially subsidized the original purchase with a number of talents (perhaps forty; ll. 44–45). The reason for the sale is not elucidated by the document, but it is best understood in the context of Seleukid consolidation of Asia Minor, which saw a considerable investment in the foundation and strengthening of cities within the empire.

---

88. Livy 38.39.10. Attalos moved them to a village called Gergitha, near the sources of the Kaikos, after "destroying" (ἐξελών) the polis (Strabo 13.1.70).

89. *I. Priene* 18 = *I. Priene*² 29–31, with Gauthier 1980.

90. *Didyma* II 492 A–C = *RC* 19–20. The land was required to stay attached to the city if Laodike sold it.

91. *IvP* I 245 C, l. 42 (*OGIS* 335; Ager 1996, no. 146).

92. *IvP* I 245 C, ll. 51–52: [τὴν κυρεία]ν δὲ καὶ τὴ[ν εἰς | τὸν πάντα χρό]νον, τὴν ἀναμφισβήτητον καὶ ὁμολογουμέ[νην . . .]

A comparable case comes from Miletos, to which Ptolemy II granted a large piece of land as a reward for remaining loyal to his house. The gift is known from a decree of Miletos dating to circa 262/61 that quotes an early letter of Ptolemy's recalling past benefactions.[93] The grant, as C. Welles suggested, was probably royal land that had been seized from Antiochos and bordered the *chōra* of Miletos.[94] Its size is unknown but must have been considerable: a major donation intended to secure both continued loyalty during the troubled time of the Chremonidean War and the well-being of the city, which had already suffered considerably during the wars of the Successors. This investment in the polis may be compared to those made by the Antigonids (viz. the harbor of Dokimos), but here Ptolemy aimed at expanding the city's agricultural basis rather than enhancing its urban fabric. These cases of Pitane and Miletos demonstrate the willingness of monarchs to devolve royal land directly to poleis when it was expedient for their wider purposes.[95] These grants of course have qualitative differences (one a sale, the other a benefaction), but both were intended to reward and support allied cities.

The inland cities of western Asia Minor founded through synoikism in the early third century, particularly under the first Seleukid kings, also benefited from such decisions. As we have seen, the majority of the urban projects undertaken by the first generation of the Successors concentrated on coastal sites or major crossroads, for obvious strategic and economic purposes. But in the third and second centuries they increasingly focused on inland valleys (e.g., the Maeander) and other arteries that linked the less urbanized interior of Anatolia to the urban systems of western Asia Minor. Such foundations, in contrast to the large multipolis synoikisms of the coast, were meant to unite existing village communities or promote second-order sites, such as military settlements (*katoikiai*), to polis status.[96] Kings assigned royal villages, formerly royal estates, and other lands occupied by nonpolis communities to such new cities. The clearest instance of this policy, which must have been applied frequently across Asia Minor, was in the foundation of Laodikeia on the Lykos by Antiochos II in the 250s, on a strategic site in the valley of the Lykos, a tributary of the Maeander River. A long inscription from 267 elucidates the region's earlier settlement pattern.[97] The city was formed from the synoikism of several indigenous villages, including Kiddiou Kome and Baba Kome, along with the inhabitants of a fortified settlement or manor house called

---

93. *I. Milet* I.3 39, ll. 3, 29–32 (*RC* 14 provides only the royal letter). See also. *I. Milet* I.3 123, ll. 38–40 = *Syll.*³ 322.

94. Welles 1934, 76 (comm. on *RC* 14).

95. This continued throughout the Hellenistic period. See, for example, the grant of a piece of land to Mylasa (and introduction of new settlers?) attested in a letter probably from the Seleukid official Olympiarchos to the city (*I. Mylasa* 22, ll. 2–4, ca. 230–225).

96. For the rural, not strategic, nature of these settlements, see L. Robert 1948, 20n5.

97. Wörrle 1975 = *I. Laodikeia* 1. See also Corsten 2007.

Neon Teichos (New castle), probably established by the major landholder in the area, Achaios, a relative of the Seleukid kings and a grandfather of the Achaios who later revolted against Antiochos III. There is also evidence for a contingent of Ionian settlers in Laodikeia.[98] Prior to the city's foundation, the land and the villages belonged to the estate granted to Achaios by the Seleukid king Antiochos II. Kiddiou Kome and Neon Teichos already had a degree of Greek political organization by 267: each held assemblies, and both joined together to issue a decree honoring Lachares and Banabelos, the managers of Achaios's estate, and initiating sacrifices to them and Achaios for their aid in ransoming villagers taken by invading Galatians.[99] The associated sanctuaries of Zeus at Baba Kome and Apollo at Kiddiou Kome, the prominent cult centers around which the villages were organized, served as appropriate places for publishing this decree. What is salient for our purposes is the way in which these settlements and cult centers, already part of an estate, contributed to the formation of the new city: Achaios's presumably vast local holdings were reorganized from a private grant of royal land into an autonomous urban unit. Such a process, of course, required kings to remove large amounts of land from their personal domains, but they could potentially reap the benefits of collecting tribute from the cities so created. A medium city like Stratonikeia, along with the small city of Kaunos, for example, yielded 120 talents in annual tribute to the Rhodians in the second century.[100]

Royal land, villages, and estates given to subordinates must have formed the core of many other foundations, and these exceptional landowners often became important and powerful citizens once they were integrated into these new poleis. One of Laodikeia's citizens, Hieron, who by Strabo's time had dedicated several civic monuments and amassed a fortune of two thousand talents, which he left to the city, probably owed his wealth to an exceptionally large agricultural estate.[101] Other great landholders emerge in our sources by the late Hellenistic period in similar cities founded in the same way, such as the family of Chairemon of Nysa, who supplied the Roman army at Apameia during the Mithridatic Wars and whose son Pythodoros was reputedly also worth two thousand talents.[102] On a parallel but administratively distinct level from poleis founded through the synoikism of villages on royal land, second-order settlements on royal land could also benefit from

---

98. L. Robert 1936a, 126, citing the Ionian city tribe Ias (*I. Laodikeia* 2, ll. 16–17) and use of the Ionian month name Antiocheon (*I. Laodikeia* 85, ll. 16–17) there.

99. *BÉ* 89.667 (J. Robert and L. Robert) suggests that Banabelos (whose name is Semitic) was a descendant of a family charged with the administration of an estate in the region in the Persian period. Achaios's estate was thus essentially a direct outgrowth of a Persian domain.

100. Polyb. 30.31.6–7.

101. Strabo 12.8.16. Laodikeia's rise as a major center of wool production in the later Hellenistic period may help explain this extreme wealth. For this industry, see Thonemann 2011b, 187–90.

102. Chairemon: *Syll.*³ 741; Pythodoros: Strabo 14.1.42. On the family, see Thonemann 2011b, 205–18.

land grants or sales. These collectivities, though formally subject to the king, had a specific organization and status within the *chōra*. For example, the inhabitants of Kardakon Kome, a struggling Seleukid *katoikia* near Telmessos, received permission from its new master, Eumenes II, to retain a piece of land that had devolved to him after the Treaty of Apameia but that they had purchased on credit from the local dynast Ptolemaios.[103] In addition to granting other fiscal exemptions, Eumenes also remitted the remaining sum owed by the Kardakoi. Similarly, the royal land distributor (*geōdotēs*) of Eumenes II gave territory to Apollinoucharax, a Seleukid or Attalid *katoikia* in central Lydia, to shore up its faltering community after a war had ravaged it.[104] Such a settlement could also become a polis through a royal grant, as the letters of Eumenes II to Toriaion detail.[105]

The policies of the Hellenistic kings changed two important features of landholding under the tributary system of the Achaemenids. The first was the fundamental distinction between civic and royal territory. The second was the expansion of rights of ownership to include hereditary estates and the alienation of royal land to cities (either directly, through synoikism, sale, or gift, or indirectly, through grants to subordinates with the right of attachment to a polis). Continuities, of course, remained: many estates were given with the right of usufruct alone, taxes continued to be collected in kind and in cash (the mixed-*phoros* regime of the Achaemenids), and state officials still directly administered dependent peasants and indigenous populations on royal land.

What emerges from the evidence for Hellenistic land tenure regimes is a patchwork of varying statuses and fiscal responsibilities. What was the impact of this system? The various options open to a king provided a flexible framework for how to dispose of land, from temporary grants of usufruct through heritable estates to full alienation of land to cities. On an institutional level, the extension of land grants on heritable conditions gave wider latitude for stable rights of ownership and preserved the superior position of the king. In this sense, grants of this type bore a strong similarity to the category of private land (*idioktētos gē*) in Ptolemaic Egypt, except that there only a small proportion of land fell into this category.[106] Conceptualizing land tenure in this way, as a degree of rights on a spectrum from temporary grants of usufruct to full alienation of land, has the advantage of nuancing the old question of whether real private property existed outside civic territory.[107] Perhaps the most important result of this system was the concentration of substantially

103. Segre 1938, 190–207.
104. Herrmann and Malay 2007, 49–58, no. 32, with Thonemann 2011a.
105. Ed. pr. Jonnes and Ricl 1997 (*SEG* XLVII 1745), with Schuler 1999.
106. For this classification, see Monson 2012, 78–79.
107. For the view that private property existed only in civic territory, see Papazoglou 1997, 100–112, and Aperghis 2004, 87–113, with references to earlier literature. For criticism of this position, see Schuler 1998, 159–94; Schuler 2004, 514–19; Mileta 2002, 157–75; Mileta 2008.

more land in the hands of cities than in the Achaemenid era,[108] especially large cities reorganized through synoikism and situated at major ports or along key commercial arteries. As a corollary to this process, within such cities these policies also contributed to the creation of large estates held by great landowners.

Archaeological evidence sheds further light on shifts in settlement and exploitation in and other effects of the transition from the Achaemenid to the Hellenistic period. The Achaemenid Empire's presence and impact were probably most evident in the rural landscape. The Achaemenids never embraced a policy of extensive colonization or urban restructuring: systematic investigation of settlement in Asia Minor has demonstrated the relatively low numbers of Iranian personnel involved in the government of the satrapies,[109] and Achaemenid control was usually mapped onto the administrative centers of its predecessors, such as Lydian Sardeis or Daskyleion. These satrapal capitals display a certain degree of Persian elite culture at the highest levels, particularly in luxury goods. Above all, to reward their followers and enable the exploitation of royal land, the Achaemenids granted Iranian or local elites large rural estates that centered on a fortified manor (*tyrsis*) and often encompassed several villages.[110]

The effects of the Macedonian conquests on Achaemenid patterns of land tenure and settlement in Asia Minor are reflected at the broadest level in the data from recent intensive survey projects. The surface pottery in the Granikos valley, near Daskyleion, indicates dense settlement centered around rural estates in the period of Persian domination, with the land intensively cultivated. By contrast, there is a sharp decline in surface finds from the Hellenistic period, a pattern that continues into the Roman period.[111] Alexander's conquests naturally would have resulted in the vacancy of these estates, making vast amounts of land available for redistribution.[112] The sharp drop in surface pottery indicates that either cultivation

---

108. Thonemann 2009, 375n47, however, adduces the fifth-century gift in perpetuity of a Persian king of Dor and Joppa to the king of Sidon as an example of attributing royal land to cities in Achaemenid times (*SSI* III, no. 28). However, such a transfer to a client king is surely on a different order and cannot be taken as indicative of general policies for the landholding of private individuals within the Achaemenid Empire.

109. For detailed studies of the satrapies, see Sekunda 1985 (Lydia); Sekunda 1988 (Hellespontine Phrygia); Sekunda 1991 (Karia, Lykia, and Greater Phrygia); Hornblower 1982a (Karia); Keen 1998 (Lykia). On Iranian personnel, see L. Robert 1963; Briant 2006. For an overall model of Achaemenid government in Asia Minor, see Dusinberre 2013.

110. E.g., the estates of the Persians Asidates and Itamenes in the Kaikos valley near Pergamon (Xen., *Anab.* 7.8.9–23); the estates of the Greek exiles Gongylos of Eretria and Demaratos the Spartan (Xen., *Hell.* 3.1.6). Xenophon's description of Daskyleion (*Hell.* 4.1.15–16) is a good example of the relationship of a satrapal capital to the surrounding estates. See also Schuler 1998, 66–69.

111. Rose, Tekkök, and Körpe 2007, 106–7.

112. Compare the description of Laodike's estate granted in this region (*OGIS* 225 [*Didyma* II 492 A–C; *RC* 18–20]), which mentions that a section of the Persian "royal road" in this area had already

of this land did decline dramatically, as the region around Daskyleion decreased in importance, or settlement became more nucleated, concentrated in urban centers rather than scattered among small estates and villages. A similar pattern is visible in Lydia, where there is evidence for almost complete abandonment of the rural settlements of the Persian period in favor of the growing urban sites clustered along the major routes of communication.[113] In this case, cultivation of the land does not seem to have declined: the survey evidence primarily seems to reflect a shift toward more nucleated settlement. Both of these regions were closely connected to major centers of Persian administration and personnel. In these instances, a dramatically altered political geography and changing relationship between city and countryside are readily apparent. By contrast, other intensive surveys in Asia Minor have shown a growth in rural sites and land exploitation. The *chōra* of Miletos, a major recipient of royal benefaction in the early Hellenistic period, saw an increase of rural sites at that time, indicating increased exploitation of the countryside.[114] Here the survey evidence corresponds well with the picture of an ascendant Miletos with a flourishing urban nucleus. Surveys of parts of Lykia and the Rhodian Peraia in Karia likewise reveal increases in rural settlement and perhaps population.[115] Overall, the body of archaeological evidence for the countryside of western Asia Minor gives the impression of growth, in sharp contrast to the decline visible in intensive survey of parts of southern Greece.[116] This accords well with the evidence for the increase in city sizes and, in some regions, numbers in the northern Aegean and western Asia Minor, as well as the reorienting of trade routes and markets away from Athens and its allies and toward new networks (see pp. 127–32).

From a regional perspective, increased urbanization and the concentration of more land in cities, coupled with evidence for changing patterns of rural habitation and exploitation, attest the impact of the Hellenistic kingdoms on land tenure. But what of the effects on individual cities? The policies of the Hellenistic monarchs both added large estates that outstripped even the largest preexisting landholdings to civic territory and integrated powerful new elites into the citizen communities of many poleis.[117] Whether this had a positive or negative effect on these communities is largely a question of how one views the political culture of the

---

been plowed up and its course was no longer visible. This was evidently part of the inland route leading to Daskyleion, which was no longer used. For the geography and road system, see Hasluck 1910, 127.

113. Roosevelt 2006; Roosevelt, 2009, chs. 5 and 7; Roosevelt and Luke 2012.
114. Lohmann 2004.
115. Lykia: Kolb and Thomsen 2004; Karia: Debord and Varinlioğlu 2001.
116. Alcock 1993. See also Bresson 2016, 56–64, for a survey of recent work.
117. Recent excavations have identified several agricultural complexes in Macedonia that date to the late fourth century and correspond to the scale of agricultural production suggested by the large estates attested in the epigraphic sources (Adam-Veleni 2009a; Bresson 2016, 151–52).

Hellenistic polis.[118] Interpreted teleologically, the introduction of powerful new elites into the democratic life of the cities could be viewed as the beginning of the movement away from the egalitarian ideal of the polis and toward a system dominated by a privileged and hereditary group of benefactors, and thus the shift from the Greek to the Roman city.[119] With a strict focus on the contemporary ramifications of this development, however, it is less clear that such individuals upset the balance of political power in the democracies of the East in the first centuries of the Hellenistic era or that they did not have a positive effect in representing their adoptive cities before higher authorities or aiding their development through benefactions.[120] The expansion of their agricultural base was surely also a benefit for these communities.[121]

KOINA, REGIONAL CONSOLIDATION, AND ECONOMIC INTERDEPENDENCE

The foregoing sections have argued that population, land, and other resources were localized in specific poleis through the process of synoikism, as part of a conscious development of large-scale cities. An important corollary was the consolidation of regions and the mapping out of networks through the creation of regional or ethnic leagues. These *koina* played important religious and political roles, but they also had significant implications for polis economies, regional patterns of exchange, and the interactions among kings, cities, and regions. The early Hellenistic period saw the creation or revival of a number of major *koina*: the *koinon* of Athena Ilias, the Ionian Koinon, the *koinon* of the Islanders, almost certainly a *koinon* of the cities of Achaia Phthiotis, and possibly an Aiolian Koinon. All of these were organized by the Antigonids, either Antigonos himself or his son Demetrios, but they were sustained and supported by the kings who later inherited control over these regions. Typically oriented around a shared cultic center (e.g., the Panionion or the sanctuary of Athena at Ilion), the *koina* provided a

---

118. Thonemann (2011a, 242–51) argues that it led to a destabilization of traditional patterns of land tenure, pointing to both the policies of the kings and the increasing willingness of poleis to allow buyers to snatch up land to create large estates. But his binary opposition between the democratic *klēros* and the great latifundial estates obscures to a certain extent the facts that more large landholdings would inevitably have concentrated in the hands of the wealthy without the introduction of new landowners (though not on the scale attested in the Hellenistic land grants) and that partible inheritance would often have fragmented *klēroi* over time.

119. Quass 1993.

120. Gauthier 1985; Mann and Schloz 2011.

121. It is unlikely that many cities had more than a few such exceptional estates attached to them, which would have amounted to only a small percentage of the overall civic territory, especially in the case of the large synoikized centers.

venue for common participation in the management of a shared sanctuary and the celebration of sacrifices, other rituals, and choral and athletic contests. These activities were "generators of value,"[122] but of even more direct economic significance was the role of *koina* in extending shared markets, other institutions, and cooperation across a large territory. Councils (*synedria*) composed of representatives from the member states administered them, and elected magistrates oversaw certain aspects of their activity, such as *agoranomoi* (supervisors of the market of the festivals and collectors of revenue), *agonothetai* (officials in charge of public games), gymnasiarchs, secretaries, and treasurers. The *synedria* could raise contributions from the member states for the maintenance of the sanctuaries and festivals, fine offending states, collect revenues from transactions at the vibrant periodic markets associated with the sanctuaries, in some cases issue their own coinage, and grant fiscal privileges across the civic territories encompassed by the *koina*. It should be stressed that there were important institutional differences among these *koina* (insofar as they are known), and they by no means functioned in precisely the same ways in each region. Nevertheless, general conclusions can be drawn about the economic impacts of their activities and their structural relationship to urbanization in the early Hellenistic period.

The *koinon* of Athena Ilias is well attested in the documentary sources, and the rich archaeological and epigraphic evidence associated with the synoikism of Ilion makes exploring the intersection between these two particularly fruitful. Antigonos established this *koinon* in or before 306/5 as part of the wider development of the Troad through the foundation of Antigoneia and the reinforcement of Ilion.[123] It consisted of at least twelve cities at its height, at the end of the third century, when its reach extended into the Propontis and beyond.[124]

The *koinon*'s role in contributing to Ilion's development and providing an institutional framework for regional cooperation is evident from its first attestation in the documentary record, in a series of decrees in honor of a certain Malousios, a wealthy citizen of Gargara, who represented his polis on the *synedrion*.[125] These decrees attest to the *koinon*'s extensive building activity in its early years, financed in part by Malousios, who extended an interest-free credit line of 3,500 gold staters to subsidize the construction of the theater of Ilion, associated buildings, and an embassy, plus the purchase of sacrificial animals (D, ll. 39–40). He contributed a further 1,450 staters for the erection of the theater's stage building (*skēnē*) and associated costs (E, l. 28). Ilion saw a great deal of construction in this period, to

---

122. Chankowski 2011.
123. *I. Ilion* 1 (*Syll.*³ 330; L. Robert 1966a, 19–23; Meier 2012, 323–26). See p. 59n177 for further bibliography.
124. Magie 1950, 1:869–70; L. Robert 1966a, 18–20.
125. *I. Ilion* 1.

which the Athenaion, the *koinon*'s headquarters, built within the temenos of Athena, also belongs.¹²⁶

Malousios also provided funds for embassies to Antigonos on behalf of the cities of the *koinon*, once to discuss their "freedom and autonomy" (E, ll. 24–25). This stock phrase is so generic that the embassy's business could have been almost anything, but one of the issues must have been the negotiation of tribute, exemptions, and privileges. Here the king's interests in initiating and supporting the *koinon* are apparent: simplifying the administration of the area and possibly routing some taxation through a corporate body while centralizing resources and manpower. From the perspective of the cities, the unity of most of the Troad held the promise of greater bargaining power with the king. It may even have been the case that the league charter had provisions for mutual aid in times of war.¹²⁷

In return for his benefactions, Malousios was voted honorary crowns in the gymnastic contests worth one thousand drachmai and granted *ateleia* for both himself and his descendants on goods bought and sold throughout the cities of the *koinon*, surely an important benefit to this probably wealthy landowner (F, ll. 16–18).¹²⁸ Such commercial privileges helped to draw the private wealth of individuals into the institutional framework of the *koinon*.

Malousios's activities are paralleled by those of honorees of the *koinon* of Athena Ilias in later periods: for instance, Kydimos of Abydos, who served as a gymnasiarch at the Panathenaia in the late third century and subsidized the cost of the gymnasium's oil.¹²⁹ Still more instructive is a third-century decree in honor of an *agoranomos* from Parion.¹³⁰ Parion lay on the Propontis outside the Troad, but by the third century it had become a member of the *koinon*, demonstrating the league's vitality.¹³¹ The document praises a citizen elected to be one of the *agoranomoi* for the market of the *koinon* at the great Panathenaia, who distinguished himself by securing the grain supply for the festival at the cheapest rate, seeing to the other things that needed to be purchased (l. 14), and providing a doctor to care for the sick at the festival (ll. 15–17).

---

126. For an overview, see Aslan and Rose 2013, 18–23; Rose 2014, 175–93. The temple and city walls date to the later third century (Rose 2003; see also ch. 1).
127. *I. Ilion* 18, l. 7 (ca. 300), an account of financial contributions to the *koinon*. Polybios (5.111.2–4) mentions that ca. 216, Alexandreia Troas sent a force of four thousand soldiers to relieve Ilion during a siege by the Gauls.
128. The source of Malousios's wealth and influence is not certain. Rostovtzeff (1941, 1:151) assumed he must have been a retired officer of one of the Diadochs, but there is no evidence for such a royal connection besides the level of his wealth.
129. *I. Ilion* 2.
130. *I. Ilion* 3.
131. The inclusion seems to have been preceded by ties to Skepsis, with whom Parion had an agreement of *isopoliteia* (*BÉ* 85.371 [L. Robert]).

Such documents underscore the economic realities of the *koinon*.[132] The periodic market associated with the festival (*panēgyris*) was an important point of exchange, especially for high-cost items like slaves and livestock, and the common market, ultimately served by a common coinage and policed by shared officials, integrated and complemented the economic lives of the individual poleis.[133] Sales taxes and market entry fees were sources of revenue for the *koinon*.[134] The temple of Athena, the repository of the *koinon*'s wealth, operated as a banking center, providing loans for the region and profiting from the interest. The commercial importance of the fair and market associated with the Panathenaia gave rise to the striking of coins on the Attic standard in the name of Athena Ilias alone in the second century.[135] They served as both a standard of exchange for activities related to the *koinon* and its festivals and a common currency for other economic activity in the Troad.[136]

By the end of the third century, the *koinon* had extended its reach to include cities as distant as Myrleia in Hellespontine Phrygia and Kalchedon on the Bosporos, as attested by a list of debts owed to the sanctuary of Athena.[137] This wide catchment is perhaps explained in part by the fact that the political importance of Ilion (and indeed of the *koinon* itself) was always secondary to its religious and economic significance. We can also see the link between the synoikism of the city of Ilion and the establishment of the *koinon* as the means of setting up a dual mechanism of centralization of land and resources and forging a common identity in the region. The evidence for Ilion's commercial network, elucidated by the recent publication of the transport amphorae found in the lower city (see pp. 131–32), attests to markedly increased prosperity in the city, coinciding with the period of the *koinon*'s

---

132. Stressed by L. Robert 1966a, 38.
133. Strabo (10.5.4) described the *panēgyris* of Delos as "a kind of commercial affair" (ἥ τε πανήγυρις ἐμπορικόν τι πρᾶγμά ἐστι). For the economic dimension of periodic markets, see Chandezon 2000; for *panēgyreis* in Asia Minor, Dignas 2002, 167–68. The *lex sacra* of Andania (*Syll.*³ 736 = Sokolowski 1969, no. 65, with Gawlinski 2012) preserves some illuminating economic prescripts (esp. l. 110, on not charging for space). An Attalid royal letter grants the *katoikoi* Apollo Tarsenos freedom from the tax on livestock at the *panēgyris* (Feyel 1940). *IGLS* IV 4028, ll. 37–39, records a first-century BCE tax emption on the sale of slaves at the *panēgyris* of Zeus at Baitokaike in Syria. Pausanias (10.32.15), describing the *panēgyris* of Isis at Tithorea, mentions the sale of slaves, animals, clothing, gold, and silver. For periodic markets in the Roman Empire, see de Ligt 1993; Frayn 1993. For fascinating ethnographic comparisons of the economic role of regional religious festivals in modern Greece, see Forbes 2007, ch. 9.
134. See *IG* IX 1² 583 for the handling of sales tax in the *koinon* of Akarnania.
135. L. Robert 1966a, 22–46; Psoma 2009; Ellis Evans 2016.
136. On the economic importance of the "cooperative coinages" issued by *koina* in archaic and classical Greece, see Mackil and van Alfen 2006.
137. *I. Ilion* 5. By 77 BCE they had apparently left the *koinon* (10). A decree of the *koinon* honoring the gymnasiarch Antikles of Lampsakos, dating to the last quarter of the third century, now adds greater depth to the scale of its activity in this period. See Özhan and Tombul 2003 (*SEG* LIII 1373), with *BÉ* 117.267 (Gauthier); Habicht 2004. For the date, see Ma 2007.

greatest activity (late third century). This time also saw the swiftest pace of construction in Ilion—the city wall, temple of Athena, and propylon were all finished then—which is also visible in the domestic contexts of the lower city.

Similar institutional developments can be detected in the less-well-attested *koina* established in the early Hellenistic age. There was a resurgence of the Ionian *koinon*, now relocated to its original home at Melie after having been in Ephesos for some time.[138] The activity of this *koinon* is difficult to trace in this period, but the archaeological and documentary evidence points to the same basic profile that we saw at Ilion: collective building at the sanctuary site and the organization of the members' contributions to the sanctuary and festival.[139] This *koinon* too honored and interacted with kings and their agents and dispensed commercial privileges within the region.[140] This latter activity is most clearly elucidated by an honorary decree of the *koinon* dating to circa 289/88 that grants *atelia* in the cities of Ionia to Hippostratos the son of Hippodemos of Miletos, the *stratēgos* of Ionia and agent of Lysimachos, and his descendants.[141] Taken together, these *koina* organized much of the coast of western Asia Minor and the regions most intensively reshaped by the Successors into leagues that integrated their member cities.

A series of coins that bear the monogram AX and were found at Halos, Peuma, Larisa Kremaste, and some of the other poleis of Achaia Phthiotis points to the existence of a *koinon* in this region, almost certainly established by Demetrios Poliorketes. Achaia Phthiotis was served by the other major port on the Pagasitic Gulf besides Demetrias, Phthiotic Thebes, the result of the late fourth-century synoikism of Phylake and Pyrasos. These two outlets for the riches of Thessaly were to an extent complementary: one had organized the resources of the gulf through a large-scale synoikism (Demetrias), and the other unified the (new and old) cities of Achaia Phthiotis and channeled their surpluses to the harbor of Phthiotic Thebes.

The Antigonids also grouped the Kykladic Islands into a federal league (the League of the Islanders, or Nesiotic League), circa 314.[142] This *koinon* centered on

---

138. Diod. Sic. 15.49; Thuc. 1.104.3, with Hornblower 1982b. The earliest attestations of this *koinon* are *I. Priene* 139 = *I. Priene*² 398, a decree allowing the Lebedians to erect a statue in the Panionion; *I. Erythrai* 16, a fragmentary decree of Klazomenai, the Ionians, and the Aiolians; Hommel, Kleiner, and Müller-Wiener 1967, 45–63, a law regulating the contributions of member states to the Panionia.

139. Lohmann 2004.

140. *OGIS* 222 = *I. Erythrai und Klazomenai* 504. It is likely that a *koinon* of the Aiolian cities also came into being in this period (see *I. Erythrai und Klazomenai* 16), but the evidentiary basis is too slim to draw any conclusions. See Billows 1990, 219–20.

141. *Syll.*³ 368 (*I. Smyrna* II.1 577; *I. Milet* I.2 10), from shortly before or in 289/88.

142. Diod. Sic. 19.62.9, with Buraselis 1982, 41–44, 60–67. Diodoros uses the term συμμαχία for this alliance; the phrase τὸ κοινὸν τῶν νησιωτῶν first appears in *IG* XI 4.1036.2—a decree dealing with the festival in honor of Demetrios, which was to be held in the same manner as those already celebrated for Antigonos—whose dating is controversial. See Buraselis 1982, 67–75, and Buraselis 2015, arguing

Delos, now removed from Athenian control, and particularly the sanctuary of Apollo, where the *synedrion* met and religious festivals for Antigonos and Demetrios were held. Internally, the league oversaw common religious festivals, issued honorary decrees, and collected financial contributions from the member states or imposed penalties if a member polis failed to pay.[143] Externally, it served as the main point of interaction between the islands and the representatives of the Antigonids. After 307, it was probably administered by a *nēsiarchos* who was appointed by Antigonos, resided on Delos, represented the Antigonids, and collected the annual tribute from the *synedrion*. The league may also have served as a mechanism for recruiting soldiers from the islands to serve in the Antigonid armies, but the evidence for this is limited.[144] It has often been suggested that the documentary evidence from the early years of the *koinon* indicates a heavy burden of taxation imposed by the Antigonids, but this case may be overstated.[145] The operations of the league become clearer after circa 288, in the period of Ptolemaic control. It seems that the Ptolemies left much of the apparatus of the Antigonid league in place while introducing some changes.[146] Documentary sources flesh out the functions of the *nesiarchos* at this time, which included calling the *synedrion* into session, adjudicating disputes between member poleis, and issuing orders to military officials.[147] Decrees of the *synedrion* demonstrate that it had the ability to confer citizenship and *proxenia* on honorands throughout the cities of the *koinon*.[148] Above the nesiarch, the Ptolemies appointed Philokles the king of the Sidonians, whose authority extended to regions beyond the Kyklades. A financial officer (*oikonomos*) was also evidently installed within this hierarchy, incorporating the islands more fully into the Ptolemaic administration.[149] The league remained the

---

for 307, when Demetrios recovered the islands after the revolt of Antigonos's nephew Polemaios; see also Billows, 1990, 220–25; Constantakopoulou 2012. Meadows 2013 suggests that the *koinon* was founded under Ptolemy II (rejected by Buraselis 2015, 361).

143. *IG* XI 4 1036, XII 7 506.

144. Geagan 1968, no. 1, an inscription from Nemea listing *pezoi* (infantry) from a number of the Kykladic Islands. This was evidentially in the context of Polemaios's operations in the Peloponnese in 312 (see p. 52). Constantakopoulou (2012, 53) suggests that this should not necessarily be viewed as a burden imposed on the islanders but rather as a mutually beneficial system for recruiting mercenaries.

145. Migeotte 1984, 156, and Reger 1994, 37–38, claim that many of the loans taken out by poleis in the early third-century Kyklades were used for the payment of taxes to the new monarchs. Chankowski (2008, 328–39), however, has questioned whether these loans can be taken as direct evidence for harsh Antigonid imposts and suggests that some may have been the lingering results of Athenian domination.

146. E.g., the reduction of *syntaxis* (*IG* XII 7 13).

147. *IG* VII 7 506, ll. 2–4 = *Syll*³ 390 (convening the *synedrion*); *IG* XII 5 1065 (settling disputes); *IG* XII 5 1004, l. 2 (commanding military officers).

148. *IG* XI 4 1038, 1040.

149. *IG* XII supl. 169, l. 4, with Bagnall 1976, 146–47.

main mechanism by which the islanders interacted with the king, as a decree of the *synedrion* agreeing to their participation in the festivals in honor of Ptolemy I and arranging to send sacred ambassadors (*theōroi*) to Alexandria eloquently attests.[150]

The *koinon* shaped the Kyklades into an administrative unit whose political and economic network was focused on Delos. Although these islands had always formed a natural region, throughout much of the fifth and fourth centuries the Kykladic economy, particularly that of Delos, was intertwined with foreign powers. The advent of Macedonian hegemony and the creation of the *koinon* effectively severed the Kyklades from the rest of the Aegean.[151] G. Reger has traced the regional economy of Delos in this period in detail, providing insight into the effects of this political realignment on the prices of commodities in the temple accounts of Delian Apollo. With the Kyklades separated from Athenian control and turned in on themselves, their economy was largely confined to local networks of exchange.[152] High prices on key commodities marked the first quarter of the third century, reflecting political instability. Prices began to stabilize in the 290s, and the evidence points to a phase of growth beginning in the last decades of that century.[153]

All of these federations had similar purposes. The kings encouraged the grouping of allied cities into a regional framework, united by cultic associations and political interests. This simplified administration and, in some cases, organized the collection of tribute. At a regional level, *koina* shaped patterns of exchange, organized political activity, and projected common institutions. Variations are also evident. The Nesiotic League transformed the Kyklades into a largely self-sufficient unit. The *koinon* of Athena Ilias, in the Troad, promoted a greater integration of city and hinterland, fostered connections between cities, and complemented the concentration of resources into two major commercial centers, Alexandreia Troas and Ilion. This fostered growth in both the regional economy and long-distance trade, as we will see in the next section. In each case, the policies of outside hegemons exerted tremendous influence, both intended and unintended, on cities and regions through the reorganization of settlement and the realignment of the networks with which they interacted.[154] These interventions had broad repercussions for the networks of exchange across the Aegean world.

---

150. *IG* XII 7 506.
151. Reger 1994, 253; Constantakopoulou 2007, ch. 3.
152. Reger 1994, 252–53.
153. Reger (1994, 257–64) suggests that the greatest prosperity corresponded to the time of Kykladic independence (ca. 230–167).
154. Purcell 2005a, 216.

PATTERNS OF INTERREGIONAL TRADE

The rise of the Hellenistic kingdoms spelled the eclipse of Athens as the dominant Aegean commercial center and prompted a rebalancing and reorganization of the trade networks clustered around it. New hubs of commerce arose from this disequilibrium, from independent centers such as Rhodes that were advantageously situated and vigorously asserted themselves on the international stage to the cities that the kings developed as major nodes in their nascent empires.[155] The foundation and expansion of poleis contributed to the transformation of regions into interconnected networks of cities. This section explores the consequences of synoikism and changing political geography on trade and markets in the Aegean. The transformation entailed two major components. First, the development of large port cities and the urbanization of important overland routes of commerce and communication connected the interior base of agricultural and natural resources to the sea and allowed the ascendance of urban centers poised to profit from their place along the network. Second, patterns of trade realigned as new centers fueled new markets.

Harbors, Seaborne Commerce, and Routes of Trade

The most important component of this program of urbanization was the development of ports, connecting regions and their hinterlands to wider networks of commerce and mobility and matching trade routes to new markets. A conspicuous feature of early Hellenistic synoikisms was the concentration of populations and resources on coastal outlets, including the movement of cities from inland settlements to the sea. The simultaneous enlargement of the polis territory ensured that the interior agricultural base would not be separated from the new maritime center. The greater integration of the Aegean and the interior, particularly of Asia Minor, was an important consequence.

The expansion of the Macedonian kingdom in the fourth century had already brought profound changes to this region. Pella, a major consumer but also a producer and site of much industry, expanded at the expense of many Greek commercial cities. Methone, the major port of the southern Thermaic Gulf, was destroyed and depopulated in 355/54, and some or all of its population—which surely included many skilled craftsmen, judging from the extensive archaeological evidence for craft production—may have been moved to Pella to augment its

---

155. Purcell 2005a, 209: "It is not appropriate to use the language of determinism about the development of communities in the zones favoured in the geography of connectivity. The place did not somehow spontaneously generate the entrepôt: Bacchid Corinth, post-synoecism Rhodes, Delos after 166 were in suitable places, but their response to the advantages was the result of the political choices of elites, inside or outside the community."

population and industry.[156] The Macedonians also eliminated Torone and Poteidaia, along with many other cities of the Chalkidike. The early Hellenistic period saw the reversal of this trend, with the foundation of major port cities at Thessalonike and Kassandreia, poised to capitalize on the vibrant north Aegean trade networks.[157]

The development of Demetrias closely connected the Pagasitic Gulf to the commerce of the northern Aegean. The city's site was naturally advantageous. In the classical period, Pagasai, the port of Pherai and main center replaced by Demetrias,[158] had a substantial trade in grain, slaves, and meat and served as the most important outlet for the agricultural wealth of Thessaly.[159] Demetrias was designed both to capitalize on this strategic location and to draw on this commercially important region. Philip II's removal of Pagasai from Pheraian control and the subsequent consolidation of the Pagasitic Gulf under Demetrios realigned its western shore away from Thessaly and toward Magnesia. Magnesia, in turn, became a direct dependency of Macedonia.[160]

The commerce and connections of the Pagasitic Gulf were traditionally oriented predominantly southward. The literary evidence for Pagasai suggests this trend in broad outline, indicating significant commercial contacts with Attica, central Greece, and the Peloponnese.[161] If, as has been plausibly suggested, the site of Soros is to be identified with ancient Pagasai,[162] the imported ceramic materials recovered from the excavations in its temple of Apollo, cemetery, and citadel also bear out this general picture.[163] The trend appears to have altered substantially following the foundation of Demetrias. The amphora fragments and amphora stamps from the extensive excavations of the Antigonid palace found in securely dated construction fills and

---

156. As recently suggested by Bessios, Papadopoulos, and Morris (2016). Helly (2006b), by contrast, has argued that Methone was reconstituted at Goritsa, across from the future Demetrias.

157. For a synthetic treatment of the economies of the north Aegean, see Archibald 2013.

158. Theopompos, *FGrH* 115 F53.

159. In 377, during the tyranny of Jason, the Thebans bought ten talents' worth of grain from Pagasai after the Spartans ravaged two successive harvests (Xen., *Hell.* 5.4.56; see also Ephippos, fr. 1 [*PCG* Kassel-Austin]). Alexander of Pherai exported grain, slaves (Ar., *Plut.* 521; Hermippos, fr. 63.19 [*PCG* Kassel-Austin]), and meat (Plut., *Mor.* 193d–e).

160. See pp. 77–78 for references.

161. For the literary evidence, see n159 above. Two fourth-century proxeny decrees (Peek 1934, 56–57, nos. 14–15, with the discussion of Graninger 2009, 122–24) perhaps originally published in the sanctuary of Ennodia at Pherai, where a number of similar decrees (*SEG* XXIII 415–32) were found, also suggest commercial connections with central Greece. The first is a decree of the Pheraioi honoring individuals from Opous with *proxenia*, *asylia*, and *ateleia*, and the second a decree of the Petthaloi (Thessalians) conferring the same honors on an individual from Chalkis.

162. See ch. 1 for a discussion of the evidence.

163. Milojčić 1974; Triantaphyllopoulou 2000; Triantaphyllopoulou 2002; Batziou-Efstathiou and Triantaphyllopoulou 2009; Mazarakis Ainian 2009; Vitos and Panagou 2009.

foundation trenches (dating from between the foundation of the city, circa 294, and the construction of the building, circa 220–200) provide important insights into the economic contacts of the city in the period of firm Antigonid control. This material shows a distinctly northward orientation, with the overwhelming majority of the amphorae originating from Thasos, Kassandreia (the so-called Parmeniskos group), and Rhodes and a far lesser proportion from the Black Sea and the Aegean Islands.[164] By contrast, nearly contemporary deposits from the fills of the Middle Stoa in the Athenian Agora (beginning of the second century) show a distinctly different priority of trade contacts, with 59 percent of the amphorae coming from Rhodes and only 4 percent from Thasos and 0.3 percent from the Parmeniskos group.[165] The coins from the fills of the palace in Demetrias support the same picture of its orientation in this period, indicating limited contact with southern Greece and the Aegean. Most conspicuous is the almost complete lack of evidence of trade with the important port of Histiaia on Euboia, which was a traditional point of interaction with the Pagasitic Gulf and also in Antigonid hands in the third century.[166] There is likewise little evidence for connections between Demetrias and Phthiotic Thebes, the other major port on the Pagasitic Gulf, which does show extensive trade with Histiaia.[167] Analysis of the fineware from the same fills in the palace at Demetrias has revealed illuminating patterns. From the foundation of the city to the 280s, large amounts of Attic West Slope pottery were imported. After only a decade or so, Demetrias began local production of fineware in this style, possibly spurred on by the migration of Athenian potters to the city.[168] Less is known about the degree to which this pottery was exported, but by the second half of the third century the scale of production seems to have increased, with more carelessly executed and simplified forms, as well as local innovations in shape and decoration.[169] The evidence points to Demetrias's emergence as a major site of craft production in its own right.[170]

164. Furtwängler 1992; 2003. The subsequent Greek excavations from the palace, Pefkakia, the Thesmophorion, and several other areas of the city closely mirror these distributions (Batziou-Efstathiou 2009). For the origin of the Parmeniskos group in Kassandreia and the southern Chalkidike, see Garlan 2004; Badoud 2013.

165. Grace 1985.

166. Only two coins of Histaia have been found at Demetrias (Furtwängler 1992, 369); at Goritsa, notably, many were recovered (Bakhuizen 1992). L. Robert (1951, 178) referred to Histaia as "le relais indispensable de Démétrias, c'est comme l'avant-port de la Thessalie." See also Picard 1979, 269.

167. Furtwängler 1992, 369; Picard 1979, 320. The grave stelai from the cemetery of Phthiotic Thebes display a prosopography of distinctly international character and extensive southern contacts (Stählin 1924, 173). Phthiotic Thebes and Halos operated in close connection in this period (Freitag 2006; Helly 2009). Halos also has clear connections with Euboia: Reinders 1997; 2004; 2009.

168. Athenian craftsmen may also have been active in the production of the numerous painted grave stelai from Demetrias (von Graeve 1979; von Graeve 1984; Wolters 1979).

169. Furtwängler 1990b; Seilheimer 2013.

170. See Zimmer 2003 for the evidence for bronze working and lamp production.

The patterns are suggestive. Over the course of the third century, the predominant contacts of the northern Pagasitic Gulf shifted northward, away from the region's traditional connections to central and southern Greece. Precisely why this was so is less clear. Macedonian domination may have played a role, but the emergence of major centers like Kassandreia and Thessalonike in the northern Aegean, along with the increasing reach of Rhodes and the networks of the eastern Mediterranean, may provide a better explanation.[171] The north Aegean trade axis intersected with the most prominent trade route of the Hellenistic period, the north-south passage along the coast of Egypt, the Levant, and Asia Minor. Integration into this network ushered in a period of considerable renewal for many of the cities of western Asia Minor.[172] The fifth and fourth centuries had been a period of turbulence and decline for much of this region: over the course of the fifth century, for instance, Ionia swung from Persian control through independence to membership in the Athenian Empire before returning to Persian dependence.[173]

Recent work on amphora assemblages excavated from securely datable contexts in the Tetragonos Agora at Ephesos have shed light on the city's economic fortunes in the fifth through third centuries. Analysis of all the fragments of imported amphorae, both stamped and unstamped, has yielded a picture of contracted trading networks from the 490s to the end of the fifth century, mostly in the central eastern Aegean. In the late fourth century, however, the sources and quantity of imports increased dramatically, with the appearance of a large number of north Aegean amphorae.[174] The amphorae recovered at other Ionian and Karian sites,

---

171. Furtwängler (1992, 367) has suggested that the more limited range of imports apparent at Demetrias as compared to a site like Pella (Makaronas 1960) reflects a more closed trading policy, directed by the Antigonid kings and royal agents in the city. Still, commercial connections between garrisoned cities are attested: for ties between Antigonid Corinth and Athens, see James 2010. Less is know about the period when Demetrias was a free city and the center of the *koinon* of the Magnesians and whether its trade patterns shifted in the absence of Macedonian control. The prosopography of Demetrias's grave stelai dating from between the city's foundation and 88/87 (Arvanitopoulos 1909b; Arvanitopoulos 1928; see Helly 1992 for the date) indicates that it had large numbers of northern Greeks and Macedonians, as well as a significant amount of people of Levantine origin (Arvanitopoulos 1909b, nos. 80, 151; Arvanitopoulos 1949, no. 257; Arvanitopoulos 1952, nos. 322, 347, 349; with Masson 1969).

172. Bresson and Descat 2001; Billows 2007.

173. The material decline of the coastal cities of Asia Minor in the fifth and early fourth centuries, particularly those of Ionia, has long been controversial. Roebuck (1959, 131–38) thought it was due to a loss of overseas markets following the Persian conquest. J. Cook's (1961) main argument was that their economies were crippled by having to pay tribute to Athens as maritime cities while most of their arable land was subject to taxation as the Persian king's land. Subsequent scholars have been skeptical of this view (Murray 1988; Dandamaev 1989); Osborne (1999) critiqued Cook's thesis and the overall premise of equating the lack of monumental architecture with the decline of Ionia by noting that a reduction in building does not necessarily correlate with economic conditions. In a series of studies, Balcer (1984; 1985; 1988; 1991) has pointed to the Athenian Empire as the main driver of Ionia's decline.

174. Lawall 2005.

such as Klazomenai, Didyma, Miletos, and Halikarnassos, mirror this history in broad outline.[175] An identifiable pattern has emerged on the western coast of Ionia: the ports were increasingly integrated into the trade network of the north Aegean, broadening the range and scale of their commercial contacts.

At Ilion, recent data show a similar pattern. Excavations of a stratified sequence of terrace fills south of the acropolis and below the acropolis wall have yielded rich finds of transport amphorae. The nature of deposition suggests that the assemblages found there are likely refuse from use on the acropolis, cleared out and deposited as fill. As such, they are good indices of the commercial and ritual activity on the acropolis. The number of imported transport amphorae from the mid- to-late sixth century in these deposits is relatively low, and although imports are in evidence, they were overwhelmingly from a limited, nearby region, especially Lesbos. However, locally produced storage jars are well represented, indicating an agricultural surplus and a market for the export of agricultural products, and the forms of the local transport amphorae from this period imitate Lesbian amphorae, emphasizing the restricted and regional yet healthy character of the economy. Incorporation into the Lydian and Persian Empires was the key factor for this period of economic vitality, as their wider networks provided a consumer base for Ilion's agricultural products. As at Ephesos, the fifth century was a period of steep decline in the production of local storage jars and in imported amphorae. After Persian withdrawal from this area in 478, Mytilene dominated Ilion until 428, when Athens exerted its control, until circa 410. There are no amphora fragments that date to the first three-quarters of the fifth century and very few that date to the last quarter of the fifth. This gap agrees with a general lack of fifth-century material across the site. Recovery began only at the very end of the century, but by the middle of the fourth century, local storage jars were being produced in fairly high numbers again and the range of imports had expanded substantially, indicating broader contacts and an increasing role for the Troad as a mediator between the Aegean and the interior of Asia Minor.[176] By this time, the Troad was again paying tribute to Persian satraps, one factor, along with the requisitioning of supplies from the region, in the increase in transport amphorae. But the city's reincorporation into the Persian network also brought commercial benefits, and evidence from fourth-century Ilion (fineware imports, architecture, ritual activity in the sanctuary of Athena, etc.) paints a picture of prosperity for at least a segment of the city's population.[177]

---

175. Lawall 2005, 253n722; Klazomenai: Y. Ersoy 1993; Didyma: Schattner 2007; Halikarnassos: W. Radt 1970.

176. Lawall 2002.

177. Contemporary ritual deposits provide important evidence of substantial external patronage of the sanctuary of Athena Ilias: Berlin 1999.

In the Hellenistic period this prosperity reached its peak. By the late third century, exactly contemporaneous with the construction of the circuit wall and the temple of Athena, the quantity and range of imported amphorae in deposits from the lower city of Ilion (the domestic area) increase dramatically. The transport amphorae from the Hellenistic levels near the acropolis have not yet been published, so no direct comparison with the material from the fourth century can be made. However, in the area of domestic housing built in the Hellenistic period, stratified deposits have provided important new evidence for the commercial connections of the Hellenistic city. This was an important expansion of the city, probably due to an increase in population. The site was a quarry in the late fourth and early third centuries; therefore, evidence for the early Hellenistic period is skewed by the fact that it was still a work area and not a place of habitation, significantly reducing the number of amphorae that would otherwise be present.[178] Nevertheless, there is evidence here, paralleled in the city center, for an expansion of the types of amphorae imported in the early-to-mid-Hellenistic phase, with specimens from as far afield as the southeast Aegean and Chios.

This picture of economic vitality, especially when taken alongside the epigraphic evidence related to the activity of the *koinon*, attests the transformation of the city in the early third century. We see the widest range of imports and of locally produced amphora types in the period from 225 to 130, following this domestic area's major construction phase. Amphorae produced in Ilion began to appear in Assos then, and amphorae stamped in Ilion at that time have been found at Pergamon and numerous sites along the west and north coasts of the Black Sea.[179] Imports to Ilion span the Aegean: northern Greek, Lesbian, Chian, southern Aegean, Koan, Rhodian, and Chersonesan amphorae are all represented.[180] Both exports and imports expanded dramatically in the region of Ilion in the late third century. While early third-century evidence for the city's economic life is largely lacking, all indications of prosperity later in that century are linked to processes put in motion in the later fourth century: the synoikism of Ilion and the establishment of the city as a regional power at the head of the *koinon* and the site of a Panhellenic sanctuary.

This outline of the maritime commercial contacts of cities reorganized by synoikism is necessarily broad, but the evidence sheds some light on the impact of such urbanization on local, regional, and transregional economies. The emergence of large commercial centers and the patterns of Macedonian control affected the scale and direction of commerce. New markets emerged, and new regional hubs of exchange formed a wider network.

178. Lawall 1999, 187–88.
179. Lawall 1999, 216.
180. Lawall 1999, 199–213.

Roads, Overland Commerce, and Connectivity

In addition to the investment in urban ports, the urbanization of key arteries of the interior brought significant changes to flows of people and goods and patterns of commercial exchange. The economic effects can especially be observed in Asia Minor, where the political unification of the Aegean and the interior of Anatolia and the development of urban infrastructure fostered the connection of the ports on the western coast to the interior of Asia Minor and beyond.

New or expanded coastal cities along most of the fertile river valleys of western Asia Minor, part of greatly enlarged territories, stood at the head of this network. To take just a few examples, Antigoneia/Alexandreia Troas, in its original incarnation, controlled territory as far away as Skepsis, extending its reach from the coast into the plain of the Skamandros. Pergamon came to control most of the Kaikos valley, serviced by its maritime outlet, Elaia.[181] Smyrna developed into a major port and extended its reach into the Hermos valley. Ephesos drew on a large part of the Kaystros valley and was the terminus of much of the commerce of the Maeander valley. Each of these nodes had a place on both the prominent route extending north-south along the coast of Asia Minor and a road linking it to inland sites like Sardeis.[182] Many of these roads were of course ancient, but the projection of imperial authority over the political landscape of these regions shifted the direction and intensity of economic exchange. In particular, the extensive urbanization and changing political geography of the Hellenistic era had profound effects.

In many respects, this system built on centuries of Achaemenid rule and patterns of movement through the Persian Empire. The famous royal road linking Sardeis to Susa, with its highly developed infrastructure and personnel, was the most sophisticated network of overland communications and transportation in the classical period.[183] Near cities, these roads were particularly well developed and substantial.[184] The so-called travel-ration texts of the Persepolis Fortification Tablets provide insight into the activities of numerous individuals, both private and official, who served a variety of functions along this network, from messengers, hired laborers, goods and money transporters, pilgrims, and "caravan leaders" to

---

181. Pirson 2004; Pirson et al. 2015.

182. For an example of royal (probably Attalid) oversight of the road system from Ephesos to Sardeis, see French 1997, with Thonemann 2003, 95–96.

183. The fundamental treatments of the Persian road system are Briant 1991; Briant 2012; Debord 1995; Graf 1996; French 1998, with some comment on its economic implications.

184. A section of the royal road dating to the Seleukid era has been excavated near Pasargadae (Stronach 1978). In the Seleukid period, inscribed milestones began to mark the royal road system (Stronach 1978, 159–61; Callieri 1995, 65–73, 75–77). The "royal road" at Gordion described by Young (1956, 266; 1963, 348–50) is actually a section of the Roman road (Marston 2012, 378n4). Kosmin 2014, 166–69, has evocative maps illustrating the relative frequency with which the royal court moved along certain arteries.

Persian administrative officials called "road controllers," "express messengers," and "traveling companions."[185] Greek and Roman sources further elucidate the details of a highly developed postal and message system, with relay points, riders and horses stationed at intervals, and the use of fire, mirrors, and other devices for communication over shorter distances.[186] Although the bulk of our attestations for the use of these roads is official and military (exacting tribute; moving officials, information, and troops), this network must have encouraged private commerce, a supposition that meshes well with recent work on the economic benefits of the Persian imperial framework.[187]

This organization of imperial space, with key places connected along royal routes, had an important impact on cities. The contours of this process can be closely traced far in the interior of Asia Minor, at Gordion, the capital of the Phrygian kingdom from circa 900 to 540. While the Persian conquest ushered in great political changes, including the demotion of this city to a provincial town, the size of Gordion's urban settlement remained relatively stable throughout the Persian period.[188] Still, the nature of the settlement shifted. Many of the public buildings of the Middle Phrygian period fell out of use and were dismantled, and the public area was given over to industry.[189] A new focus of administrative life emerged, probably the seat of local Persian government.[190] Achaemenid rule also integrated Gordion into the Persian imperial road network, most importantly the royal road but also overland routes north to the Hellespont. These built on preexisting routes, but the emergence of satrapal centers like Daskyleion in Hellespontine Phrygia would have significantly increased their traffic and infrastructure. The advent of Persian rule corresponded with a sharp rise in imported Greek fineware at Gordion, much of which probably arrived through Hellespontine trade networks.[191] Analysis of Greek transport amphorae has revealed distinct economic patterns in these years. Between this period and 480, after the development of the Persian road system and after the Achaemenid Empire established greater control over Aegean exporters, contacts between Gordion and the Aegean expanded substan-

185. "Road controllers" (*datimara*): PFa 30; "express messengers" (*pirradaziš*): PF 1285; "traveling companions" (*barrišdama*): PF 1363, 1409, 1572. Herodotos (7.239.3) mentions "road watchmen" (ὁδοφύλακες).

186. Relay posts: Diod. Sic. 19.17.6. Relay riders: Hdt. 8.98. Fire signals: Hdt. 9.3.1.

187. For the general argument for the benefits of Persian rule, highlighting the positive economic consequences of Persian military campaigns and military supply, see Briant 1982, 175–226; 1991; 2002, 388–471.

188. Voigt and Young 1999, 191.

189. Voigt and Young 1999, 220–23; Voigt 2002, 194; 2011, 1086–87; Kealhofer 2005.

190. Burke 2013.

191. K. De Vries 1990; De Vries 1996; De Vries 2005; Lynch and Matter 2013.

tially.[192] The range of imports at Gordion bears much similarity to the picture at other Achaemenid sites in Asia Minor,[193] suggesting that the increase in long-distance trade at this site had a definite link to Persian infrastructure and political control.[194] These patterns changed only with the large-scale changes in political geography and imperial authority of the third century, as the Seleukids lost control of central Phrygia after the Gallic invasion. With the retreat of Seleukid authority, a southern axis, the so-called common road (*koinē odos*),[195] displaced the royal road. This route, already in existence in the Achaemenid period and increasingly important in the fourth century, extended from Ephesos through the Maeander valley, up to Apameia Kelainai, and beyond to Mesopotamia and became the main artery of communication and transport. Gordion remained a settlement, but cut off from the major commercial network and probably also from Hellespontine Phrygia, it declined in size and importance and its imports fell away suddenly.[196]

The development of the common road in the Hellenistic period involved its integration with a dense web of cities and *katoikiai*. Some of these built on Achaemenid towns and commercial centers along the Persian road, such as the Phrygian Kelainai, refounded by Antiochos I, and Toriaion, which received a military colony under the Seleukids and developed into a full-fledged polis under the Attalid king Eumenes II.[197] Others, like Dokimeion, founded by Antigonos's general Dokimos in the late fourth century near the native village of Synnada, organized local populations and Macedonian soldiers into new settlements on strategic sites. The Seleukids framed the eastern part of the route, toward Syria and Mesopotamia, with a series of settlements: Laodikeia Katakekaumene, Toriaion, Philomelion, perhaps south Phrygian Metropolis, Apameia Kelainai, Lysias, Blaundos, and Antiocheia by Pisidia. In the west, the Maeander valley also saw investment in refounded and synoikized cities: Seleukeia Tralleis, Nysa, Antioch on the Maeander, and Laodikeia on the Lykos.[198]

The economic impact of inland Asia Minor's development was clear by the early Roman period. In Strabo's time, the reach of the "*emporion* of Ephesos" had penetrated as far as Kappadokia, where it redirected toward itself the export of a

---

192. Chian and Lesbian amphorae appear at Gordion in large numbers, along with significant imports from Samos and Miletos and a very small number from northern Greece. Voigt et al. 1997, 21–22; Lawall 2010; Lawall 2012.

193. Voigt et al. 1997, 20–21.

194. There is a correspondingly high level of luxury items in ivory, stone, etc., from this period in Gordion.

195. Strabo 14.2.29.

196. Stewart 2010; Lawall 2012; Marston 2012.

197. Apameia Kelainai: see p. 136. Toriaion: Jonnes and Ricl 1997; BÉ 112.509 (Gauthier); Schuler 1999; SEG XLVII 1745.

198. For the growth of the cities of the Maeander valley, see Ratté 2008, 18–28.

particularly fine ruddle (*miltos*), or red ocher, which merchants (*emporoi*) from Sinope had formerly channeled to their harbor.[199] This corresponds to other well-attested commodities that moved along this route to the Aegean. Marble from the Synnada quarries was brought to the Maeander valley and transported along the river and then overland to Ephesos. Slaves from central Anatolia were also channeled along this route, along with wool and cloth.[200] By the Roman period at least, owing to its strategic position at the confluence of the Marsyas and Maeander Rivers and at the crossroads between Phrygia and Pamphylia and between Lydia and Ionia, Apameia Kelainai had developed into the largest *emporion* in Asia Minor after Ephesos.[201] Antiochos I founded the Hellenistic city through the forced transfer of the native inhabitants of the nearby hilltop settlement Kelainai, which had been an important administrative center under the Achaemenids, the location of a fortified palace and a *paradeisos* (enclosed park) and where Antigonos had resided as the satrap of Phrygia.[202] By the time of Antiochos's foundation, there is already evidence for a substantial Greco-Macedonian contingent at Apameia: this urbanization carried out by Antiochos, as was so often the case, was probably begun by Antigonos.[203] The refoundation of Kelainai as Apameia Kelainai in the fertile plain below and the insertion of this polis into an elaborate network of connectivity transformed it from a fortified satrapal capital and market town into a thriving commercial center. The simultaneous expansion of both Ephesos and Apameia and the interdependent foundation of all the cities along the common road show the importance of this network in the economic development of Hellenistic Asia Minor, and the clear planning of the city foundations in Anatolia's interior underscores the complexity of royal economic behavior and its dependence on cities and urbanization.[204]

CONCLUSIONS: URBANIZATION, PROXIES, AND THE QUESTION OF GROWTH

This chapter has stressed the important role of synoikism in creating urban nodes with expanded resources and integrating cities into wide regional networks of

---

199. Strabo 12.2.10.

200. Marble: Strabo 12.8.14; slaves: *I. Ephesos* Ia 13 ii.18 (tax on slaves at Ephesos), with Gschnitzer 1989. For the route from the Maeander to Ephesos and the cooperative role of cities in its upkeep under the Romans, see J. Robert and Robert 1983, 30–31.

201. Strabo 12.8.15.

202. Xen., *Anab.* 1.2.7–8; J. Robert and Robert 1983, 47–53, 101–18; L. Robert 1963, 348–49. For new research on the site, see Summerer, Ivantchik, and von Kienlen 2011; 2013. For the *emporion* in the Roman period, see Thonemann 2011b, 99–129.

203. Billows 1990, 296.

204. Cf. Lolos 2009, on the Via Egnatia.

mobility and exchange. Also crucial in the early Hellenistic period was the development of infrastructure and regional trade networks that sought to intensify the connections between the Aegean and the interiors of northern Greece and Asia Minor. Synoikism constituted an effective response to the fragmentation of the landscape that characterized these regions in the classical period, reducing the risks and transaction costs of long-distance trade, facilitating the movement of materials and labor, and creating new markets. Documented increases in the volume of trade and the differentiation of the sources of imports trace the concrete economic results of some of these processes in the archaeological record. Urbanization has also been investigated as part of a larger process of regional integration and interdependence. *Koina* emerged as an important tactic in creating broad links between communities and forging shared infrastructure and institutions, such as coinage, loans and other banking practices, fiscal privileges, religious centers, and mechanisms of common defense. In the realm of trade and commerce, royal intervention radically reshaped the volume and flow of goods, with the emergence of new ports, routes, and urban networks.

The key place of urbanization in Macedonian imperialism underscores its importance as a structural framework for approaching central aspects of the Hellenistic economy.[205] Even without a major expansion of population numbers, urbanization and a shift to larger cities can entail a wide variety of economic consequences and challenges with the potential to restructure regional patterns of exchange.[206] The exact correspondence between urbanization and economic growth is somewhat equivocal, and in principle the former can carry both stimuli and hindrances to economic development. Increased urban settlement has attendant risks, such as the challenges of supplying cities, the inherent nature of cities as population sinks (due to decreased life expectancy there), and strain on the productive capacity of the hinterland. Yet these very problems also have the potential to yield technological advancements, expanded infrastructure, increased networks of mobility and connectivity of goods and manpower, the development of

---

205. Ancient empires were at their basis fiscal entities, and their mechanisms of control and patterns of interaction with subject communities were largely mapped out in this sphere. In particular, the Athenians practiced a brand of imperialism that rested primarily on extraction of revenues and not on territorial annexation (Purcell 2005a, 225–26). For the Athenian Empire, see Kallet 2013. On the structural similarities between the Athenian and Persian systems, see Raaflaub 2009. For a comparative approach to "tributary empires," see Bang and Bayly 2011.

206. Scheidel 2007, 81: "Urbanization may be envisaged as the outcome of any one of four processes: the concentration of a previously dispersed non-agrarian population of rentiers, craftsmen, traders, and even farmers in cities, without concurrent changes in population density or productivity; increasing population density at constant per capita output, creating a larger cumulative surplus that sustains larger, urban, settlements for the non-agrarian population; increasing per capita output at constant population levels, expanding the relative share of the non-agrarian sector and encouraging urban residence; and, finally, concurrent increases in population and productivity."

complexity and flexibility in social and economic institutions, craft and trade differentiation, and expanded markets. Cities can also be means of alleviating the pressures of population in the countryside and of promoting agricultural efficiency to accommodate increasing demand. Just as the influential Weberian view of the "consumer city" has become considerably more nuanced, leading to an understanding of the ancient city as embodying both parasitical and productive tendencies that are neither mutually excusive nor separable, the relationship between urbanization and economic performance also requires reassessment.[207] Most important in this period, in the context of an overarching imperial power structure, developed urban centers were key stations in a large network—of taxation, trade, mobilization of resources, and exploitation—that had significant benefits (along with obvious detriments) which carried over to nonstate economic activity.

Synoikism primarily involved the consolidation of land, population, and resources around an urban center. This seems to have yielded a larger total urban population, in some cases augmented by an influx of new settlers (especially Macedonians), but for the most part the process unified existing populations.[208] These cities still relied primarily on the agricultural hinterland to sustain them, but port cities, a particular focus of the early synoikisms, could rely more on trade and capitalize on the opportunity to export some of the surplus drawn from the countryside. The extension of a city's *chōra* through the attachment of landed estates of kings' beneficiaries may also have contributed to both the produce needed to feed the city and its fiscal revenue. In addition, the relationship between urban markets and royal land would have allowed cities to sustain populations larger than their land's carrying capacity, through imports of grain and oil. Archaeological surveys have begun to shed some light on overall trends in this period, revealing signs of growth and more intensive agricultural exploitation in the north Aegean and western Asia Minor.

With these considerations in mind, the question of the relationship between urbanization and economic growth comes into sharper focus. Recent studies have offered an optimistic appraisal, viewing changes in settlement patterns and the sizes of urban centers and populations as promising proxies for economic growth.[209] As

---

207. See Scheidel 2007, 82–85, for an overview. The debate over the "producer" vs. the "consumer" model of the ancient city includes Parkins 1997; Erdkamp 2001; Mattingly and Salmon 2001; Hansen 2004; Vlassopoulos 2007, 123–41; Morley 2011.

208. Scheidel 2007, 74–80. Current scholarship on ancient demography rightly cautions against lending credence to claims of population growth without very good evidence, especially considering the limits on secular growth in ancient societies.

209. For recent arguments for sustained economic growth in the Greek world from the late archaic through the early Hellenistic period, see Ober 2010; Ober 2014; Ober 2015; Bresson 2016. For urbanization as a proxy of economic growth, see Wilson 2009; Wilson 2011; Wilson 2014; Lo Cascio 2009; Morley 2011.

we have seen, the largely dispersed settlements, from villages to "agro-towns," in the regions affected by synoikism were consolidated into cities that exceeded the average size of those in the classical period. While precision is not possible here, the net result was certainly a greater percentage of the population residing in urban centers, with an implied increase in per capita efficiency.[210] The large degree of building might lend some support as an additional proxy. We have seen the tremendous outlay in the construction of walls, houses, public architecture, palaces, and other infrastructure.[211] The overall logic of this policy of urbanization and centralization, enacted on several overlapping levels, suggests the effects of state power in promoting the intensification of economic activity through synoikism.

---

210. Wilson 2011.

211. As Davies (2005) has shown, Hellenistic palaces were potentially important economic entities, as major building projects, consumers, employers, and potentially redistributive agents. For detailed treatments of Hellenistic palaces, see Hoepfner and Brands 1996; Marzolff 1996a; I. Nielsen 1999.

PART TWO

Cult, Polis, Empire

The Religious and Social Dimensions of Synoikism

3

Civic Cults between Continuity and Change

In the Greek world, the foundation or refoundation of a city was conceived of as a ritual act. In the case of a city assembled through synoikism, the reconfiguration of the physical and political landscape had complex repercussions for the relationships between its communities (new and old) and their gods. The effects of synoikism on patterns of settlement threatened ancient configurations of cultic activity intimately tied to place and landscape. Furthermore, in societies where politics and religion were inextricably linked, citizen identity was intimately bound up with participation in cults and communal rituals, and conversely, political power was cloaked in and often constituted by religion and ritual. The creation of a city through synoikism, particularly one drawing on multiple poleis, had the potential to disrupt the order of traditional sacrifices and rites; the personnel, infrastructure, and finances of cults; priesthoods; sacrificial calendars; the prerogatives of subpolis associations like *genē* and phratries; the affiliation of citizens in civic tribes and their subdivisions; and a host of other facets of religious life. On each of these levels of civic religion, the foundational act of synoikism faced the challenge of integrating diverse traditions, cults, and communities into a single city.

The acute pressures of synoikism prompted reactions in the realm of religion and ritual—new cults were introduced, ritual changes were enacted, and at times rites fell into abeyance. Negotiating this rupture in the traditional order, involving a range of social actors, necessitated a variety of strategies for accommodating change and innovation while preserving a sense of continuity. Normative interventions in the cultic and ritual life of these new cities, whether by kings or the communities themselves, sought to address the underlying tension of synoikism and to create a stable religious underpinning for the new foundation. Such attempts at assuring permanence and continuity are particularly striking in surviving inscriptions. In addition, the manipulation or introduction of civic cults and rituals could conceal or bridge periods of political stress or discord and forge a collective sense of belonging in the new polis.[1]

But this aspect of religion and ritual—their ability to serve as cohesive, consensus-building forces within communities—was counterbalanced by their potential to play a subversive role, marking out distinctiveness and division.[2] The disruption of cults or innovations in religious and ritual practice could foster tensions between central authorities (whether royal or civic) and the diverse social groups that composed the new polis. In many of the synoikisms of the early Hellenistic period, as we have seen, continuing attachment to communal ties and physical location prompted synoikized communities to break away from royal foundations, calling attention to the fact that religion can equally play a role in resistance to centralized authority. Conceptualizing religion in this way reveals the complex negotiation of authority and agency between various civic constituencies and kings in the formation of these new communities. Building on the theoretical perspectives that rituals often reflect tensions within a community and that innovations and adjustments reveal potential resolutions to social crisis, mapping the reactions of communities in the sphere of religious activity elucidates processes of dialogue, negotiation, and social response that are rarely visible in the literary sources.[3] Here the question of agency becomes particularly pressing. Where we can see elements of central planning that attempted to order a new society around shared cults or sought to obviate the pressures of synoikism, it is often difficult to identify the hand behind them. Royal intervention, often with the cooperation of local elites or royal agents (garrison commanders, *philoi* of the kings, or local *epistatai*), sometimes stands out clearly, but in many cases it is not possible to determine whether the impetus came from a king, royal representative, governing elite, or section of the community.

This chapter addresses the degree to which the cults of synoikized communities experienced continuity, disruption, and adaptation. The transference and incorporation of established civic cults into a centralized state are of foremost importance in understanding the process of royal polis foundation. Examining the polities eliminated and created by the urban projects of the kings, I map the religious landscapes of these regions—including sanctuaries and sacred places—before and after synoikism, highlighting instances of continuity and discontinuity and considering

1. For discussions of ritual adaptation or innovation, see Stavrianopoulou 2006; 2011.
2. Kertzer 1988; Lukes 1975. See also Levy 1990, ch. 7.
3. For a discussion of ritual's role in constructing communities, see Bell 1992; 1997. For the application of this approach to the Greek *koinon*, see Kowalzig 2007, ch. 7; Mackil 2013, ch. 4. For the role of cult in the expansion of Argos, see Kowalzig 2007, ch. 3. On ritual and communication, see Stavrianopoulou 2006. For an exploration of the emotional dimensions of ritual, see Chaniotis 2011.

how and why particular cults survived or died out and what this meant for the kinds of communities that emerged. I then investigate the ways in which certain cults become focal points of the new communities. The evidence has important indications of how traditional cultic and religious identities intersected with innovation, demonstrating how the religious organization of the synoikized polis reveals an effort to promote a unified cultic identity around shared sanctuaries. Likewise, the ways in which the sacred topography of the *chōra* (and the old polis centers within it) was incorporated or respected rather than effaced open up a nuanced understanding of how cults were transferred and shared in the synoikized city. Finally, I explore the extent to which synoikism affected participation in cults beyond the polis, such as those of federations like *koina* and amphiktyonies.

ASSERTIONS OF CONTINUITY

> And this is a fitting arrangement for these matters: there should be twelve villages [*kōmai*], one in the middle of each of the twelve districts; and in each village it is first necessary to set aside sanctuaries and an agora for the gods and the demigods attending to the gods; and if any indigenous [*entopoi*] deities of the Magnesians or shrines of other ancient gods have been preserved in memory, we should pay them the same worship as did the men of old; and in each village we should found temples to Hestia and Zeus and Athena, and whatever other deity is the founder [*archēgos*] of the district concerned.[4]

This section of Plato's *Laws* points to several issues bearing on the study of religion in newly founded or significantly reorganized Greek urban centers. The interlocutors, concerned with establishing ideal, rational guidelines for a new foundation, the polis Magnesia, orient an agora and temples at the center of each of twelve districts, each of which was to be organized around a member of the Olympian pantheon. In each *kōmē*, temples of Hestia, Zeus, and Athena replicated the sanctuary of these deities on the city's acropolis and connected the individual villages to the polis center.[5] Yet the indigenous cults, whose sanctity depended on their local significance and connection to the landscape, could not be abrogated, even in this ideal scenario. The dramatic setting of the *Laws* underscores the significance of this detail: in creating this city in speech over the course of a pilgrimage to the cave of Idean Zeus, the interlocutors reenact the myth of Minos's descent into the cave where Zeus was reared to receive the laws of Knossos. The dialogue self-consciously

---

4. Pl., *Leges* 8.848c–d: τάξις δὲ ἥδε πρέπει τοῖς τοιούτοις. δώδεκα κώμας εἶναι χρή, κατὰ μέσον τὸ δωδεκατημόριον ἕκαστον μίαν, ἐν τῇ κώμῃ δὲ ἑκάστῃ πρῶτον μὲν ἱερὰ καὶ ἀγορὰν ἐξῃρῆσθαι θεῶν τε καὶ τῶν ἑπομένων θεοῖς δαιμόνων, εἴτε τινὲς ἔντοποι Μαγνήτων εἴτ' ἄλλων ἱδρύματα παλαιῶν μνήμῃ διασεσωμένων εἰσίν, τούτοις ἀποδιδόντας τὰς τῶν πάλαι τιμὰς ἀνθρώπων, Ἑστίας δὲ καὶ Διὸς Ἀθηνᾶς τε, καὶ ὃς ἂν ἀρχηγὸς ᾖ τῶν ἄλλων τοῦ δωδεκάτου ἑκάστου μέρους, ἱερὰ πανταχοῦ ἱδρύσασθαι.

5. Pl., *Leges* 5.745b–e.

places itself against a background of Greek thinking about the divine origin of law and the fundamental connection between the identity of a polis and the indigenous deities and heroes that inhabit it. In the new city, then, cult would function as both a repository of tradition and a means of structuring social change.

The assurance of cultic continuity was, as Thucydides famously related, a widely held expectation of the Greeks even in contexts of warfare and territorial conquest. As one state conquered or assumed hegemony over another, it was responsible for tending the cults "in whatever way is customary and in whatever way [it is] able."[6] This, according to Thucydides, was the response of the Athenians to Boiotian displeasure with the occupation of the sanctuary of Apollo at Delion in 424, specifically their horror at the Athenians' drawing sacred water for profane use and the impiety of men engaging in behavior unsuitable to a sanctuary. The Boiotians, of course, saw things quite differently, and for them the desecration of Delion amounted to almost a violation of the rules of engagement. The practical reality, however, of the complex process of negotiating traditional religious identities and tending local cults in the wake of imperial expansion was another matter. This focus on the maintenance of cultic practice elides the fact that military conquest more often than not brought considerable change to the religious life of conquered communities, as the cynical response of Thucydides's Athenian ambassadors to the Boiotians reveals. In the case of the Athenian Empire, as R. Parker has demonstrated, the changes evident in the cults at the organizational level—in the new sets of priesthoods, in religious calendars, and in their very emphasis—were far more extensive than broad statements of continuity would suggest.[7]

Consideration for continuity across political disruption was frequently asserted, but it is important to look past such guarantees, however interesting as ideological declarations about the intrinsic relationship between political and religious iden-

---

6. Thuc. 4.98.2: τὸν δὲ νόμον τοῖς Ἕλλησιν εἶναι, ὧν ἂν ᾖ τὸ κράτος τῆς γῆς ἑκάστης ἥν τε πλέονος ἥν τε βραχυτέρας, τούτων καὶ τὰ ἱερὰ αἰεὶ γίγνεσθαι, τρόποις θεραπευόμενα οἷς ἂν πρὸς τοῖς εἰωθόσι καὶ δύνωνται (the custom of the Greeks is that whoever has control over any territory, whether greater or smaller, always has possession of the sanctuaries, which are tended in whatever way is customary and in whatever way they are able). For the effects of subjection and dependency on religious practice, see Parker 2009.

7. Where we have evidence for the impact of Athenian imperialism on regional cults, the veneer of continuity often masked profound change. At Lemnos, Aigina, and Samos, for example, the Athenians carefully tended the cults over a long period, but it was clearly Athenian personnel in charge of the inventories and a distinctly Athenian mode of management (Parker 1994; see also Cargill 1995, 201–2, for the tendency of Athenian klerouchs to administer local cults; for a comprehensive discussion of the intersection of politics and religion in the Delian League, see Smarczyk 1990). At Delos, Athenian domination of the sanctuary of Apollo prompted the Delians to appeal to Philip (Parker 1996, 222–25), while at Oropos, Athenian expansion entailed wholesale expulsion of the local population, and although the worship of Amphiaraos was maintained assiduously, it was treated essentially as an Athenian cult (Parker 1996, 148–51; Mikalson 1998, 208–41).

tity, and into the realities of the changes they can often occlude. This section explores this issue in detail, determining to what degree we can trace religious continuity, discontinuity, and innovation across the process of synoikism. This exercise will lay the groundwork for addressing more difficult questions of how the components of religious and civic identity—sanctuaries, sacrifices, rites, rituals, priesthoods, and worshiping groups—adapted to or were shaped by the process of synoikism.

The official governmental bodies of poleis that emerged from synoikism often responded directly to cultic issues stemming from the realities of political and urban union. Here epigraphic documents provide some explicit testimony. Decrees express the concern of new communities for the continued tending of the cults of the absorbed poleis and stress a commitment to maintain the ancestral rites of the synoikized communities. The details of an early third-century decree of Ephesos elucidating the situation of the cults and religious festivals of Phygela, a small polis included in Lysimachos's expansion of Ephesos, are typical. The document honors a certain Melanthios, a royal officer and citizen of Karian Theangela, for his protection of the land and inhabitants of Phygela and his aid in tending its cults:

> ἔ[δοξ]εν [τῆι βουλ]ῆι καὶ τῶι δήμωι· Φιλαίνετος εἶπεν· ἐπειδὴ Μελάνθιος
> ὑπὸ τοῦ βασιλέως κατασταθεὶς ἐπὶ τῆς φυλακῆς τῆς ἐμ Φυγέλοις
> πᾶσαν εὔνοιαγ καὶ προθυμίαμ παρεχόμενος διατελεῖ καὶ τὰ περὶ
> τὴμ φυλακὴν τοῦ χωρίου καὶ τῶμ πολιτῶν τῶν ἐμ Φυγέλοις κατοι-
> κ[ού]ντων τὴν ἐπιμέλειαμ ποιούμενος καὶ τῶν νεωποιῶν τῶν ἀπο-   5
> στελλομένων ὑπὸ τῆς πόλεως ἐπὶ τὰς θυσίας τὰς ἐμ Φυγέλοις μετὰ πά-
> σης εὐνοίας καὶ προθυμίας χρήσιμός ἐστιν, καὶ περὶ τούτων οἱ νεωποῖαι
> προγραψάμενοι διελέχθησαν τῆ βουλῆι καὶ ἐξήγγειλαν τὴν εὔνοιαν
> καὶ προθυμίαν τὴμ Μελανθίου·

> Resolved by the *boulē* and *dēmos*. Philainetos moved: Since Melanthios, after he was appointed by the king to the garrison in Phygela, was continually exhibiting every good will and zeal and saw to matters concerning both the defense of the *chōrion* and the citizens [of Ephesos] living in Phygela and is useful to the temple administrators [*neōpoiai*] appointed by the polis for the sacrifices in Phygela according to every good will and zeal, and writing concerning these things the *neōpoiai* conveyed them to the *boulē* and proclaimed the good will and zeal of Melanthios...[8]

This document provides important information about the measures taken to incorporate the traditional cults (and former citizens) of Phygela into the religious life of Ephesos. The king mentioned in line 2 must be Lysimachos, who stationed Melanthios in Phygela, the location of a royal garrison. There were clearly still people living in Phygela, though the settlement appears to have been reduced to a

---

8. *I. Ephesos* IV 1408, ll. 1–9; L. Robert 1967b.

fortified outpost of the city. This document makes it clear that the people living there were citizens of Ephesos and that Phygela no longer had any civic or religious infrastructure of its own. The *neōpoiai* charged with conducting the sacrifices in Phygela were envoys of Ephesos, dispatched there to perform this ritual. We know from Strabo that there was a renowned sanctuary of Artemis Mounychia in Phygela,[9] and its continued importance is attested in the second century, when it was a refuge for slaves and citizens fleeing marauding pirates.[10] Melanthios, a royal officer, had clearly taken an interest in facilitating the observance of Phygela's religious traditions, and it was the *neōpoiai* themselves who recommended him for the honors voted by the *boulē* of Ephesos. Whether Melanthios's actions reflect a royal policy enjoined by Lysimachos is difficult to say, but this is not unlikely, given the king's involvement in other sacred matters in the city. The document also does not elucidate the fate of the lesser cults of Phygela or the attitudes of its former citizens. Major sanctuaries stood a much better chance than minor ones of being included in the religious life of a new city. On the one hand, this decree affirms the continuity of religious observance across the synoikism and the concern of all parties—the Ephesians, the former Phygelians who remained in Phygela, and the king and his officers—to maintain the religious life of an absorbed polis. But on the other hand, it may simply gloss over what was in fact a period of great disruption for the many minor cults of Phygela, and it tells us little about what the loss of an autonomous religious life meant to the citizens of the former polis.

Another expression of what the restructuring of a city could mean for the sacred identity of a community comes from an important inscription from Kolophon. The document, dating to between 311 and 306, reveals the hand of Antigonos in initiating a project to fortify the city and unify its old settlement (*palaia polis*) with a planned new polis center higher up on the acropolis, whose layout it details.[11] Of greatest significance for our purposes are the stipulated religious observances, to be completed before the works began:

ὅπως ὁ δῆμος φαίνηται, ἐπειδὴ παρέδωκεν αὐτῶι Ἀλέξανδρος ὁ βασιλεὺς
τὴν ἐλευθερίαν καὶ Ἀντίγονος, κατὰ πάντα τρόπον φιλοτιμούμενος δια-
φυλάττειν τὴν τῶμ προγόνων δόξαν, ἀγαθῆι τύχηι καὶ ἐπὶ σωτηρίαι παντὸς
τοῦ δήμου τοῦ Κολοφωνίων ἐψηφίσθαι τῶι δήμωι τὴμ παλαιὰμ πόλιν ἣν τῶν
θεῶν παραδόντων τοῖς προγόνοις ἡμῶν κτίσαντες ἐκεῖνοι καὶ ναοὺς καὶ   10
βωμοὺς ἱδρυσάμενοι παρὰ πᾶσι τοῖς Ἕλλησιν ἦσαν ἔνδοξοι σ[υ]ντειχίσαι

---

9. Strabo 14.1.20: εἶτα Πύγελα πολίχνιον, ἱερὸν ἔχον Ἀρτέμιδος Μουνυχίας, ἵδρυμα Ἀγαμέμνονος, οἰκούμενον ὑπὸ μέρους τῶν ἐκείνου λαῶν (next is Phygela, a small town, which has a temple of Artemis Mounychia, a foundation of Agamemnon and inhabited by a portion of his men). L. Robert (1967b) assumed that this temple was the main concern of the *neōpoiai*.

10. *IG* XII 3 1286; Bielman 1994, no. 51.

11. Ed. pr. Meritt 1935, 359–72, no. 1 (*SEG* XIX 698; Maier 1959–61, 1:223–31, no. 69; Meier 2012, 362–68). For the date, see L. Robert 1936b, 160.

πρὸς τὴν ὑπάρχουσαν· ἵνα δὲ συντελῆται κατὰ τάχος τὸμ μὲν ἱερέα τοῦ
Ἀπόλλωνος καὶ τοὺς ἄλλους ἱερεῖς καὶ τὰς ἱερέας καὶ τὸμ πρύτανιν [με]τὰ
τῆς βουλῆς καὶ τῶν ἀποδειχθέντων ἐν τῶιδε τῶι ψηφίσματι καταβάντας
εἰς τὴμ παλαιὰν ἀγορὰν τῆι τετράδι ἱσταμένου τοῦ εἰσιόντος μηνὸς [ἐπὶ]   15
τοὺς βωμοὺς τῶν θεῶν οὓς ἡμῖν οἱ πρόγονοι κατέλιπον εὔξασθαι τῶι Διὶ τῶι
Σωτῆρι καὶ τῶι Ποσειδῶνι τῶι Ἀσφαλείωι καὶ τῶι Ἀπόλλωνι τῶι Κλαρίωι καὶ
τῆι Μητρὶ τῆι Ἀνταίηι καὶ τῆι Ἀθηνᾶι τῆι Πολιάδι καὶ τοῖς ἄλλοις θεοῖς
πᾶσι καὶ πάσαις καὶ τοῖς ἥρωσιν οἵ κατέχουσιν ἡμῶν τήν τε πόλιν καὶ τὴν
χώραν ἐπιτελῶγ γενομένων τῶν ἀγαθῶν πρόσοδον ποιήσεσθαι καὶ θυσίαν   20
καθότι ἂν τῶι δήμωι δόξηι·

In order that the *dēmos* seem ambitious to maintain the glory of its ancestors in every way, when King Alexander and Antigonos granted freedom to it, with good fortune, and for the salvation of the whole *dēmos* of the Kolophonians, be it resolved by the *dēmos* to enclose in a common wall with the present city the ancient city, which, when it had been bestowed by the gods to our ancestors, they founded and established temples and altars and were held in esteem with all the Greeks. In order that it may be accomplished as quickly as possible, the priest of Apollo and the other priests and priestesses and the prytanis with the *boulē* and those appointed in this decree will go down to the old agora on the fourth day of the coming month to the altars of the gods that our ancestors handed down to us and will vow to Zeus Sōtēr and Poseidon Asphaleios, and Apollo Klarios, and Meter Antaiē, and Athena Polias, and all the other gods and goddesses, as well as all the heroes who occupy our city and land, that, when all our blessings have been completed, they will make a solemn procession and sacrifice however it seems best to the *dēmos*.

These prescriptions are perhaps the fullest documented expression of religious concerns involved in moving a settlement. Here the *dēmos* of the Kolophonians characterizes the *palaia polis* as a gift of the gods to their ancestors and ties the importance of the cults to a wide Panhellenism integral to the fame and identity of the city. In reality, Kolophon's fortunes had been in steep decline over the preceding centuries, and the fourth century was the beginning of its recovery. The creation of the new polis center required, for the Kolophonians, symbolic unification with the *palaia polis* through procession, sacrifice, and due attention to the traditional cults. Although the *palaia polis* has not been securely identified, it was probably just down the hill from the new center on the acropolis and in no way outside the dimensions of the polis, especially since a single wall was to include both settlements. This document thus highlights a fundamental facet of Greek religion: the deep connection of deities and heroes to physical spaces, including sanctuaries, and the symbolism invested in locales, structures, and rituals. The obvious disruption that the relocation of the civic center posed to the religious life of the Kolophonians clearly raised significant concerns for the *dēmos*. As a community, they vowed continuity in cult practice to their gods. Nothing, we might imagine, would have prepared them for the much more significant challenge to their civic and religious identity that arose with Lysimachos's synoikism a decade or so later. Pausanias records a battle between Lysimachos's forces and the Kolophonians, notably augmented by some troops from Smyrna, and mentions that the grave of the Kolophonians who died in this confrontation was still visible in his day on the road from their city to Klaros.[12] Indeed, once the Kolophonians were released from this union, the temple of the mother goddess Meter Antaië, the publication site of this inscription and their central civic sanctuary, certainly saw renewed use, even as the main center of urban settlement shifted to the coastal site of Notion.[13]

THE SITES OF CULT: TRACKING MAINTENANCE, ABANDONMENT, AND ADAPTATION

Epigraphic statements such as those discussed above reveal anxiety over the consequences of political unions for religious matters. They assert a commitment to continuity, promising to incorporate ancestral deities into the new community, to maintain their shrines, and to observe their rites, and they suggest that religion will be a common bond rather than a point of division.[14] How did this operate on the ground? This section explores these issues in detail, focusing on several of the epigraphically and archaeologically best-documented regions (Magnesia/Thessaly, the Thermaic Gulf, and the Troad) and tracing the degree of religious continuity, discontinuity, and innovation across the process of synoikism. It demonstrates the significant efforts made to transfer, maintain, and accommodate cults and traditions but also stresses the disruption, abandonment, and upheaval involved in the formation of a new polis.

---

12. Paus. 7.3.4; see also 1.9.7.
13. Meritt 1935, 380–81, no. 4 (attests a tribe named for Seleukos). See ch. 1 for further details.
14. Concerns over cultic matters are frequently found in sympolity agreements, particularly when a larger community absorbed a smaller partner. A variety of arrangements is attested, often with the individual communities maintaining discrete religious identities. When Helisson became a constituent *kōmē* of Mantineia (390s?), the two resolved that the people of Helisson would be Mantineians "on like and equal terms" (Thür and Taeuber 1994, no. 9 = RO 14). In the specifics that follow this phrase, religious matters come first, and the agreement stipulates that the *kōmē* will contribute a *thearos* to the city, sacrifices will be made at Helisson, and religious delegations will be received "in accordance with tradition." In the union of Latmos and Pidasa (323–313/12), envisioned as a physical merger of the two communities, the Pidasians were explicitly to "share in all the hiera," but the decree states nothing about the cults of Pidasa (Blümel 1997 [SEG XLVII 1563; Wörrle 2003a; LaBuff 2016, 81–87]). The later *sympoliteia* agreement (188/87 or 187/86?) between Miletos and Pidasa (*Milet* 1.3 149) has the same silence about the cults of the lesser partner. But in second-century Achaia Phthiotis, the agreement between Melitaia and Pereia included a clause that the senior partner, Melitaia, would tend and fund the common hiera in Pereia (*Syll.*³ 546b; *IG* IX 1² 1 188). In Phokis, Stiris and Medeon agreed (second century) that a *hierotamias* would be appointed from the Medeonians, receive funds, and make the traditional sacrifices in Medeon with the archons of Stiris (*Syll.*³ 647; *IG* IX 1 32).

Demetrias and the Pagasitic Gulf

The Pagasitic Gulf was a region celebrated in myth.[15] Centered on Mount Pelion, the home of the centaur Cheiron, it figured largely in the cycle of Apollo and Kyknos, Peleus and Thetis, Pelias and Jason, and the expedition of the Argonauts. As we have seen (pp. 77–84), the foundation of Demetrias substantially altered the settlement pattern of the Pagasitic Gulf, whose traditional borders were redrawn in such a way that its western shore and the Thessalian poleis Pagasai and Amphanai became part of Magnesia. The new urban center drew from the populations of the communities involved in the synoikism to a greater or lesser extent, to the point of completely absorbing the nearest ones. Ultimately, Magnesia's principal cults (those of Artemis Iolkia, Apollo of Korope, and Zeus Akraios on Pelion) took on a special prominence in Demetrias, but it is unclear if this was consciously at the expense of the cults of Thessalian origin, particularly from the beginning of the synoikism.[16] Despite these lacunae, the evidence for the city's religious life is rich, and it presents an overall picture of dynamic change and adaption in the cultic life of the region resulting from the synoikism. I will first examine the effects of the synoikism on the cults of the individual communities merged into Demetrias before reconstructing the intersection of religious traditions and the religious life of the city as a whole.[17]

The Thessalian polis Pagasai, the most significant settlement and chief port of the Pagasitic Gulf, played a central role in the mythology of the region. The Hesiodic *Shield of Herakles* mentions a "sacred grove and altar of Apollo Pagasaios," and Herakleides Pontikos (fourth century) reports the tradition that Trophonios established the cult of Apollo there.[18] It is also in this area that most sources locate

---

15. For discussions of Thessalian myth, see Philippson 1944; Mili 2015, 165–97.

16. The cults of Demetrias are epigraphically best attested in the second century, after the creation of the Magnesian League, and it is difficult to determine whether they underwent significant changes following the end of Macedonian rule and the creation of the Magnesian League. However, as we will see, many of the central features of the city's cultic life (e.g., the cult of the *archēgetai* and *ktistai*; the importance of Zeus Akraios, Cheiron, and Artemis Iolkia) can be dated to the third century, suggesting that many of its religious adaptations happened at the time of the synoikism.

17. For an overview of the cults of Demetrias, see Stählin, Meyer, and Heidner 1934, 187–94; Ernst Meyer 1936; Hornung-Bertemes 2007, 78–94; Kravaritou 2011; Kravaritou 2016; Mili 2015, 165–68, 197–212.

18. Hes., *Sc.* 70: ἄλσος καὶ βωμὸς Ἀπόλλωνος Παγασαίου; Heraclides Pontikos F137a (Wehrli): Πάγασος πόλις τῆς Θετταλίας, τόπος ὠνομασμένος παρὰ τὸ ἐκεῖ τὴν Ἀργὼ πεπῆχθαι. Ἡρακλείδης δὲ ὁ Ποντικὸς ἐν τῷ περὶ χρηστηρίων τὸν ἐν Παγασαῖς Ἀπόλλωνα ὑπὸ Τροφωνίου ἱδρῦσθαί φησι (Pagasos, polis of Thessaly, a place named from the *Argo* having been constructed there. And Herakleides Pontikos says in his *On Oracles* that the cult of Apollo in Pagasai was established by Trophonios). This has frequently been taken to mean that the cult of Apollo Pagasaios had an oracular component (e.g., by Arvanitopoulos [1928, 76], who even suggested that the oracle was transferred from Pagasai to Korope sometime in the archaic period). But the passage specifically mentions only that "Apollo" was established at Pagasai and says nothing about an oracle.

the mythical King Kyknos, the "cleaver of strangers" (*xenodaiktas*), who waylaid pilgrims traveling on the sacred road to Delphi and used his victims' skulls to decorate the temple of his father, Ares.[19] Pagasai also came to be associated with the construction of the *Argo*, the event that by some accounts gave the site its name, and the Argonauts were supposed to have founded a sanctuary to Apollo Aktios or Embasios along the shore there before their departure.[20] The literary sources clearly connect the sanctuary with the axis of amphiktyonic Apolline worship extending from Delphi into Thessaly, but they do not fully elucidate the nature of the cult.[21] The presence of Apollo Pagasaios on the coinage of Pagasai reflects his position as its main poliadic deity.[22]

The modern site of Soros has been plausibly suggested as the site of ancient Pagasai (see pp. 80–81), and the discovery of an important sanctuary of Apollo there bolsters this association. This city did not survive synoikism, and the archaic extramural sanctuary, likely that of Apollo Pagasaios, also went out of use at the time of the synoikism, or shortly after. The material assemblage found within it indicates an important sanctuary of regional significance.[23] The plan of the tem-

---

19. Hes., *Sc.* 57–138, 318–480; Hyg., *Fab.* 31; Apollod., *Bib. Epit.* 2.7.7; Diod. Sic. 4.37.4. See also Ernst Meyer 1942. Eur., *HF* 389–93, associates Kyknos with Amphanai. See Janko 1986 for the various versions of the myth.

20. Construction of the *Argo*: Strabo 9.5.15, which says it sailed from Iolkos. Pin., *Pyth.* 4.185–88, does not mention Pagasai. Hyginos (*Poet. astr.* 2.37) anachronistically makes the point of departure Demetrias (ascribing this to Pindar), but synoikized cities commonly inherited and advertised the cultural claims of the cities they absorbed (see ch. 4). Similarly, Apollonios of Rhodes (1.238) refers to Παγασαὶ Μαγνήτιδες (Magnesian Pagasai), despite the fact that Pagasai had been a Thessalian city. Sanctuary of Apollo Embasios/Aktios: Ap. Rhod. 1.359, 1.403, schol. to 1.407; Callim. F18 (Pfeiffer); Hyg., *Poet. astr.* 2.37; see also Arvanitopoulos 1928, 77. Apollonios Rhodios (1.411–12, with schol.) makes Jason call on Apollo as "lord, dwelling in Pagasai and the city of Aisōnis, named for my father" (ἄναξ, Παγασάς τε πόλιν τ' Αἰσωνίδα ναίων, / ἡμετέροιο τοκῆος ἐπώνυμον). Aisōn (Pherecydes, *FGrH* 3 F103b; Pindar F273; Steph. Byz. 54.16, which says it was in the vicinity of Iolkos) was probably another name for Iolkos rather than an independent polis (Stählin 1924, 62–64; Bakhuizen 1996, 92–93). Apollo Aisōnios is attested in several inscriptions from Gonnoi from the fourth through second centuries (Kontogiannis 2003 = *SEG* LIII 530–31; Tziafalias 1984 = *SEG* XXXV 570–71; cf. *IG* IX 2 1098).

21. Mili (2015, 165–66) associates the cult with seafaring, trade, travel, and the protection of sailors and characterizes it as "open." But while Pagasai was closely connected to the voyage of the *Argo* and flourished as a major commercial port, there is no clear evidence that the cult was oriented toward foreigners or even allowed them to participate, as Mili rightly notes. The epithets Embasios and Aktios specifically related to the voyage of the *Argo* and the altars that the Argonauts set up on the shore, and by extension seafaring in general, but these associations with Apollo, marked by distinct *epiklēseis*, perhaps should not be used to characterize the emphasis of the cult as a whole.

22. Liampi 2005.

23. Milojčić 1974; Mazarakis Ainian 2009; Mazarakis Ainian 2011; Mazarakis Ainian 2012; Vitos and Panagou 2009; Vitos and Panagou 2012. Mazarakis Ainian (2011, 168) suggests that such an important temple was unlikely to have been abandoned except under exceptional circumstances and considers the possibility that the earthquake attested ca. 265 at Halos in Achaia Phthiotis was responsible for

ple is a naos with a wooden, axial colonnade running down the center. A stone hearth (*eschara*) was uncovered between the fourth and fifth column bases. Along the east, south, and west walls of the cella ran a low bench, which must have accommodated dining, and there is a side door in the long wall of the cella opening toward the north.[24] The original naos dates to the late sixth century, and its form closely parallels the Oikos of the Naxians at Delos, also dedicated to Apollo.[25] The character of the pottery (exclusively decorated fineware), the faunal remains, and the architectural form all strongly indicate that ritual banqueting took place within.[26] In a later phase, a small pronaos was added to the temple's eastern end of the temple. It was here that the first excavations uncovered most of the important finds, deliberately deposited in a heap just below the floor level. These include a votive relief, three sculptures of young boys, seven statue bases (two of which were inscribed), fragments of inscribed *kioniskoi*, and large fragments of a Panathenaic amphora dating to 336/35.[27] Two adjacent rooms, also later additions, flank the southern wall of the temple. Their undisturbed levels were sealed by stones and Lakonian tiles from the temple's superstructure, indicating that these finds date to the period before the temple went out of use.[28] Below the layer of roof collapse was a thick fill with a large number of ceramic vessels.[29] The chronological range of this material extends from the late archaic to the late classical period and is firmly in line with the dating of the grave goods from the necropolis at Soros.[30] These finds bolster the evidence for dining uncovered within the temple and suggest that it served as a *hestiatorion*, a cult building where communal feasting took place.[31]

---

its desertion. There is no evidence, however, that the earthquake affected the region around the northern Pagasitic Gulf, and a simpler explanation is that the sanctuary went out of use with the synoikism.

24. At some point the width of the bench was doubled, from 0.45 to 0.98 meters (1.5 to 3.2 feet).
25. Courbin 1980.
26. Pottery and small finds: Vitos and Panagou 2009; 2012. Figurines have also been found: Leventi 2012.
27. Mazarakis Ainian 2009, 275. For all of the sanctuaries where Panathenaic amphorae have been found, see Tiverios 2000.
28. The terra-cotta superstructure had sculptural decorations (a leafy anthemion, a spear-bearing horseman) dating to the late archaic or early classical period.
29. The material consists mostly of cooking pots and storage jars, as well as miniature vessels, lamps, fragments of standing female terra-cotta figurines of late classical to early Hellenistic date, several bronze and glass pieces of jewelry, and other small finds. The character of the small finds—votives, cooking and domestic ware—points to the storage of dedications from the temple in these rooms and almost certainly to the preparation and/or storage of food for ritual dining in the temple.
30. Mazarakis Ainian 2009, 276.
31. These structures seem to have replaced private households as sites of ritual dining, where this commonly occurred from the Iron Age to the Late Geometric period, and with the rise of the polis this activity moved into a public edifice. See Sinn 2004, 38–46. Besides at Delos (the Oikos of the Naxians), such sanctuaries survive into the Hellenistic period at Naxos (Yria), Andros (Hypsile), and Thasos. To the northwest of the temple at Pagasai, a small, square "oikos" dating to the late archaic or classical

Epigraphic and iconographic evidence securely attests to the worship of Apollo at the sanctuary and provides further details of the cult's character. An archaic inscribed *kioniskos* was dedicated by a female worshiper to Apollo,[32] and a fourth-century statue base records the dedication of a certain Philokrates to Apollo, made on behalf of Euktēmon and Hippokratēs, presumably his sons.[33] A votive relief found in the same deposit depicts a youthful divine figure wearing a himation alongside a smaller, clearly mortal female worshiper. The god holds his right arm, bent at the elbow, above his head and touches a single braid on the center of his head with his fingers (an ephebic characteristic). The youthful iconography suggests either Asklepios or Apollo, but the latter, probably with a kourotrophic aspect, is to be preferred on the basis of the epigraphic evidence.[34] This helps explain the dedication probably made by a father on behalf of his sons.

How do we account for the demise of this important sanctuary after the foundation of Demetrias? There is no evidence that the cult was transferred or incorporated into that city, as happened with many others of the synoikized poleis.[35] This may be a simple absence of evidence, but in any event it is striking that a sanctuary of this importance was completely abandoned (which was not the case for other cult sites around the Pagasitic Gulf), and its cult certainly did not play a major role in the religious life of Demetrias, even if it did live on in some form. The reason for this may lie in the character of the cult. First, the oracular significance of the cult of Apollo Koropaios, which became central to the polis life of Demetrias, may have overshadowed the significance of this somewhat strange cult of the god.[36] Second, the healing/kourotrophic function of the cult of Apollo at Soros may have been subsumed by the more customary healing cult of Asklepios attested at Demetrias[37] or the "descendants" of Cheiron in Demetrias, who had a healing function in the polis, or been viewed as competitive with the poliadic cult and ritual centered on Zeus Akraios and Cheiron that focused on integrating the elite

---

period has been identified. This may have been the original cult building, later converted into a treasury (Mazarakis Ainian 2012).

32. According to A. Intzesiloglou, this inscription, now in the Athanasakeion Archaeological Museum of Volos, reads Ποτίχα μ' ἀνέθεκε Ἀπ[- - -] (reported in Mazarakis Ainian 2009, 273n33), and not Ποτιδάνι ἀνέθεκε Ἀπ[- - -], as Milojčić (1974, 74) originally published it, apparently incorrectly.

33. Milojčić 1974, 74: Φιλοκράτης | ὑπὲρ Εὐκτήμονος καὶ Ἱπποκράτους | Ἀπόλλωνι. Dated to the fourth century by C. Habicht.

34. Leventi (2009, 296–302) argues that the Apollo worshiped at Soros had a healing and kourotrophic function, an interpretation that accords well with the sculptures of young boys found in the pronaos and Philokrates's dedication. Further, dedications of this sort were paralleled in the worship of Apollo on Cyprus and the cult of Eshmun/Apollo at Sidon. As a major Aegean port, Soros may well have been in a position to be influenced by these traditions. See also Bobou 2015, 70–71.

35. See pp. 115–56, 175–77.

36. The cult of Apollo Koropaios and its oracle are discussed at p. 157.

37. Chourmouzides 1969.

youth of Demetrias.³⁸ Finally, we must consider the significance of ritual dining to the sanctuary. Temples that functioned as *hestiatoria* are relatively rare in the classical period, and it may be that the cult depended on the participation of the civic elite of Pagasai and that, with their eclipse and incorporation into the wider state identity of Demetrias, the cult's significance could not be sustained. If so, this is one case in which the decline of a cult may have been closely tied to the new position of the elites of a synoikized polis and the greater priority of integration.

But if this cult of Apollo seems to have declined or died out as a result of the synoikism, other cults of the constituent communities were accommodated in the religious life of Demetrias. Amphanai and Pagasai, among other poleis, were fully incorporated into the city but lived on as urban demes, with some of their cults. A second-century inscription from Demetrias, for example, records the dedication of a marble *naiskos* by a woman named Dunatis to Artemis of Pagasai: "Dunatis Meanthiou Artemidi Pagasitidi nebeusa[sa]."³⁹ The enigmatic participle *nebeusasa*, likely from *nebeuō* (νεβεύω = νεϝεύω in the Thessalian dialect), "to be young," has been convincingly interpreted as referring to a sacred initiatory race, a rite of passage performed by an age class of young women.⁴⁰ This intriguing document raises questions that confront the limits of the evidence. It is apparent that this cult of Artemis was transferred from Pagasai to Demetrias, but who were its participants? Did it incorporate the (elite) young women of Demetrias as a whole or a more restricted group of citizens from Pagasai, now incorporated into the city as a unit and holding fast to their traditional customs and rituals? Was the Thessalian origin of this cult within the Magnesian sphere of Demetrias significant? Other cults in Demetrias were also marked by their community of origin, most prominently that of Artemis Iolkia. But a cult of Neleia also persisted in Demetrias, as evidenced by a second-century dedication of a certain Antiphanta, who had been the priestess of Aphrodite Neleia.⁴¹ Neleia, probably to be located on the promontory of

38. *FHG* II 254–64 FF2.8, 2.12 = *BNJ* 369A FF2.8, 2.12. See ch. 4 for further discussion.
39. *IG* IX 2 1123 = *SEG* XLIV 456.
40. Hatzopoulos (1994) connects the term to a gloss of Hesychios (s.v. νέαι: ἀγωνισάμεναι γυναῖκες τὸν ἱερὸν δρόμον) and rejects the traditional association of the verb with νεβρός (fawn), which would make this a rite of passage analogous to that of the "bears" of Brauron. He groups this text with (mainly third-century) Thessalian dedications of women to Artemis Throsia that he believes refer to the life stages of young women, from the completion of their maturation (τελέουμα) through their participation in a sacred race (νεβεύω) to their "ransom" (λύτρον), marking the transition from virginity to marriage. See also Graninger 2007, which is skeptical of Hatzopoulos's reconstruction, and the remarks of *BÉ* 121.297 (Decourt and Helly). Goukowsky (2009, 149–69) recently suggested that the term refers to a bathing ritual. Rejected by *BÉ* 123.359 (Decourt and Helly), which favors Hatzopoulos's view.
41. *IG* IX 2 1125: Ἀντιφάντα | Πόλκου(?) | [ἱ]ερητεύσασα | Ἀφροδίτηι | Νηλείαι. Kravaritou (2011, 123) refers to this inscription as evidence of a reintroduction in the later second century of the traditional cults of the communities that preceded the synoikism. But the dedication to Artemis of Pagasai is closely comparable to other third-century dedications throughout Thessaly, and the absence of evidence for these cults in the third century may not be meaningful.

Pefkakia Magoula, was within the limits of the new city, and the cult probably persisted in that spot.[42]

There is abundant evidence for such maintenance of traditional cults in their original locations. In these cases, however, the synoikism brought important changes. On the northern shore of the Pagasitic Gulf, Iolkos persisted as a discrete settlement to some extent after the foundation of Demetrias, and a number of sources attest the continuing observance of its cults in their traditional precincts. Strabo mentions a festival: "and this continuous coastline is also called Iolkos: and here also they held the Pyliac *panēgyris*."[43] The sacred road from Delphi to Tempe ran through this region, and it was perhaps here that the Magnesians observed a local festival for Apollo in connection with their role in the Delphic-Anthelic amphiktyony. As intriguing as Strabo's report is, it becomes even more salient when coupled with an early Hellenistic inscription from Iolkos (discussed in detail in the next chapter) that may shed further light on how this festival fared following the synoikism of Demetrias and may elucidate the dynamics and social actors at work in its preservation. Ernst Meyer rightly pointed to the possible relationship of this *panēgyris* to the agones that a decree of the *dēmos* of the Iolkians mentions Antigonos Gonatas (r. 277–239) reinstituting, alongside sacrifices he made to Apollo, Leto, Artemis, and the other gods and heroes of Iolkos.[44] The remains of the temple of Artemis Iolkia of classical date have been identified,[45] with evidence

---

42. Hornung-Bertemes, 2007, 79. Bakhuizen 1996 suggests that Neleia may have been the harbor of Iolkos or perhaps another name for Iolkos itself.

43. Strabo 9.5.15: καλεῖται δὲ καὶ συνεχὴς αἰγιαλὸς Ἰωλκός· ἐνταῦθα δὲ καὶ τὴν Πυλαϊκὴν πανήγυριν συνετέλουν. Πυλαϊκήν, "Pyliac" (referring to the meetings of the Delphic-Anthelic amphiktyony at the temple of Demeter in Thermopylai), has been viewed as making little sense in this context or this location. Accordingly, it has been emended to Πελαϊκήν (Groskurd 1831 and H. Jones 1927, ad loc.), that is "Peliac," referring to a festival in honor of Pelias, the mythical king of Iolkos whose funeral games are celebrated in myth and art (Roller 1981). Meyer questioned this on the basis that the funeral games of Pelias are always referred to as a onetime celebration (Stählin, Meyer, and Heidner 1934, 184). Radt (2004, 134), retains Πυλαϊκήν. The importance of Apollo to the amphiktyons and to the region may explain a local iteration of this festival. Strabo 9.3.7 describes the Πυλαία in detail, and we need not assume the text is corrupt there. A scholiast commenting on a fragment of an unknown Greek tragedy (*CGFPR* 238 9–10) glosses Πυλαϊκή as ἡ ἐν ταῖς Πύλαις καὶ Ἀ[μφικτύο]]σι γεγομένη. This seems to suggest that "Pyliac" designated a festival held not just at Thermopylai but also in the various amphiktyonic states.

44. Stählin, Meyer, and Heidner 1934, 184; Ernst Meyer 1936. The Magnesians no longer sent *hieromnēmones* to the amphiktyony after the Aitolian reorganization in 279 (Flacelière 1937; Scholten 2000). If Meyer's association of this inscription with the text of Strabo is correct, it is tempting to connect the decline of the agones at Iolkos with the Magnesians' removal from the amphiktyonic council and the turmoil of the synoikism.

45. Arvanitopoulos 1908; see also Stählin 1916. Arvanitopoulos (1909a) located poros fragments of triglyphs, metopes, and Doric capitals used as spolia in a house on the east side of the acropolis of Iolkos. For new research on the site, see Skafida 2012.

for continued activity and local personnel in the Hellenistic period.⁴⁶ But the importance of Iolkos and its cults was no longer limited to the site itself. In Demetrias, the cult of Artemis Iolkia took on a central role. A new sanctuary to the goddess was constructed in the center of the polis, which Artemis represented on its official seal and coinage.⁴⁷

On the northwestern shore of the Pagasitic Gulf, the polis Korope and its sanctuary of Apollo Koropaios, an oracular shrine of regional significance, were also incorporated into the foundation of Demetrias. Unlike that of Apollo Pagasaios, this cult attained central importance in the religious life of Magnesia after the synoikism of Demetrias. The sanctuary is well attested epigraphically in the later Hellenistic period, in a *lex sacra* dealing with the proper protocols for consulting the oracle and regulations for the maintenance of the shrine, and in a number of documents from Demetrias.⁴⁸ Although the classical settlement of Korope seems to have been abandoned or at least shifted to the immediate area of the sanctuary, the sanctuary flourished under the administration of the officials of Demetrias, where its priest was appointed.⁴⁹ The cult was fully incorporated into the pantheon of Demetrias, and revenue from the sale of skins from the sacrificial victims at the sanctuary in Korope partially financed the central priesthood of Zeus Akraios.⁵⁰ Like Artemis Iolkia, for whom a subsidiary precinct was built in Demetrias, Apollo Koropaios and Zeus Akraios may have had small sanctuaries in the city.⁵¹

In a similar way, the cults of Pelion became focal points of the religious life of the polis, both incorporated into Demetrias and rooted in their original location. The mythology of Cheiron dominated the leafy mountain in the archaic and classical periods, and he received cult in a small cave near the summit. In the period after the synoikism, the cult of Zeus Akraios, worshiped on the peak of Pelion, is also well attested. The excavations of the site, conducted briefly in 1911, revealed a temenos surrounded by an oval peribolos wall, accessed on the north by a monumental gateway.⁵² A north-south wall or small stoa divided the precinct into two halves. On the western side, where the level ground gives way to a steep rock face, was a small cave of Cheiron, evidently hewn into the side of the cliff. Two small buildings are to the east of the cave, an apsidal structure (which may be modern)

---

46. Ernst Meyer 1936; *IG* IX 2 1122 (second century): Διογένης [- - -]| τὴν ἑαυτοῦ γ[υναῖκα - - -] | Μενάνδρου ἱε[ρητεύσασαν] |Ἀρτέμιδι Ἰ[ωλκίαι] (Diogenes ... [on behalf of his] his wife [name], daughter of Menander, after she served as priestess, [dedicated this] to Artemis Iolkia).

47. Sanctuary: Marzolff 1976a. Seal and coinage: Franke 1967; Furtwängler and Kron 1978; Furtwängler and Kron 1983.

48. *IG* IX 2 1109 (Reichel 1891; Kern 1903; L. Robert 1948, 16–28; Sokolowski 1969, nos. 83–84).

49. Papakhatzis 1960.

50. *IG* IX 2 1100a, with Sokolowski 1969, 171–72, no. 85 (*SEG* XXV 687).

51. Helly 1971, 544–48.

52. Arvanitopoulos 1911; see also Arvanitopoulos 1938; Philippson 1944, 147–50.

and a small mud-brick temple. In the western portion of the temenos are two buildings side by side. The larger one, a rectangular temple made of large drafted stone blocks and a tiled roof, stands on the highest elevation and is the best-constructed building on the site. This is likely the temple of Zeus Akraios. A. Arvanitopoulos reported several fragments of marble votive stelai, miniature cups, black-glazed pottery (particularly skyphoi of the fifth and fourth centuries), kylikes of the fourth and third centuries, a fourth-century coin of Chalkis, six buried amphorae containing ash, the iron points and butts of spears, a small votive spear, and several figurines, including one of an eagle, all in the vicinity of Cheiron's cave. Exploration of the area around the putative temple of Zeus Akraios was limited, and no finds were reported there. Arvanitopoulos's dates are imprecise, but the cult of Cheiron goes back to at least the fifth century, centered on the cave and the modest building in the western half of the precinct. The division of this "double cult" and the distinct difference in the quality and scale of the construction of the cult buildings may suggest that the cult of Zeus was a latecomer, and this pairing and the monumentalization of the temenos probably date to the period after the foundation of Demetrias. This would certainly be in line with the literary sources, all of which focus on Pelion as the abode of Cheiron and make no mention of Zeus Akraios prior to the synoikism, but unfortunately, clear chronological markers are lacking. It may well be that the cult of Zeus Akraios, its associated rituals, and its prominent priesthood were all innovations resulting from the synoikism rather than elaborations of a traditional Magnesian cult. In any event, this cult certainly rose to prominence with the foundation of Demetrias.

More-distant Magnesian communities persisted to some degree as nucleated settlements. Though dependent on Demetrias, they seem to have functioned somewhat as rural demes of Athens, and the demotics appear in decrees of Demetrias in the time of the Magnesian *koinon*. Spalauthra and Glaphyrai are two of the most peripheral of the communities brought into the synoikism for which we have any evidence in the Hellenistic period. Both may have issued decrees,[53] like Iolkos, and they had their own local administrative and cultic apparatus. Nevertheless, they were firmly brought into the political and religious community of Demetrias, participated in its main cults and priesthoods, and received decrees of the city concerning centralized state cults, which were distributed to and displayed in the rural demes.[54]

In addition to the manipulation of preexisting civic cults, there is important evidence for the creation of cults in Demetrias, some closely associated with Macedonian authority and others that may have been products of the multicultural milieu of this cosmopolitan city. Royal authority as an agent of religious change is

---

53. E.g., *IG* IX 2 1111, a decree of Spalauthra (ca. 130–126).
54. *IG* IX 2 1099b.

most plainly seen in the development of the cult of the *archēgetai* and *ktistai*, the board of heroes comprising the founders of the constituent poleis and the Antigonid kings.⁵⁵ This is a clear case of Macedonian involvement in shaping the religious identity of the polis, blending innovation with continuity as a means of uniting the ancestral founders of the composite communities and tying them to the cult of Demetrias's Macedonian founder. But how far was this viewed as an intrusion?⁵⁶ A further piece of evidence for the level of royal orchestration in the cultic life of the city comes from a new inscription found south of the *proskenion* of its theater, which attests a sanctuary of Herakles and cultic officials called the *kunēgoi* (huntsmen) of Herakles.⁵⁷ The document records a letter from Philip V to Antipatros, the local magistrate (*epistatēs*) of Demetrias, concerning the dress of the *kunēgoi*.⁵⁸ The cult and its officials are also attested in inscriptions from Macedonia, particularly in a series of letters from Demetrios II to the *epistatēs* of Beroia, and elsewhere in Thessaly.⁵⁹ Philip's letter clearly applies to all of the sanctuaries of Herakles Kynagidas in the cities under Antigonid control (*hierois*, l. 15) and regulates the minutiae of this cult. It instructs the *kunēgoi* to change their *petasoi* (hats) and chlamydes, which had been colorful (*chrōmatinou[s]*), to a mute shade of gray black (*pellous*), according to the account (*historia*) that the king conveyed to his cities.⁶⁰ M. Hatzopoulos has interpreted these officials as members of the Macedonian court, royal ephebes who were charged with protecting royal forests and leading the royal hunts and presumably also functioned as a kind of elite paramilitary

55. See ch. 4 for a full discussion of the cult.
56. This cult may have built on traditions of shared lineage between Macedonia and Magnesia, which go at least as far back as Hesiod (in F7 West, the mythical eponymoi Magnēs and Macedōn, sons of Zeus and Thyia, are brothers). The shared tradition of the *karpaia*, a mimetic dance that enacts the theft of cattle and was performed by the Magnesians and the Ainianes (Xen., *Anab.* 6.1.7–8), called an ὄρχησις Μακεδονική by Hesychios (s.v. καρπαία), is perhaps evidence for this convergence. Both the Magnesians and the Macedonians, according to Hegesandros (Ath., *Deip.* 13.31), celebrated a festival called the Hetaireidia in honor of Zeus Hetaireios. But the Magnesian tradition referred to the *hetaireia* of Jason and the Argonauts, while the festival in Macedon centered on the kings and their companions. The two may have nothing to do with each other (so Nilsson 1906, 34). For the connections between Macedonia and Thessaly more broadly, see Graninger 2010.
57. Ed. pr. Intzesiloglou 2006. A second document, *IG* IX 2 359a ('Ηρακλέου[ς]), though in secondary deposition, was found nearby, so it is likely that the sanctuary of Herakles Kynagides was in this area.
58. For the nature of the *epistatēs* (a local citizen magistrate rather than a royal overseer), see Hatzopoulos 1996, 1:372–423.
59. Beroia: *SEG* XLIII 379 (Hatzopoulos 1994, 102–4; Hatzopoulos 1996, vol. 2, no. 8; *EKM I. Beroia* 3). Thessalian attestations: *SEG* XLVII 686 (a third-century epitaph from Atrax): Πολύ[χ]αρμος κυναγός; Intzesiloglou 2006, 71n10, which refers to evidence for the cult in Perrhaibia. The institution is also attested at an Attalid *katoikia* in Lydia (Herrmann and Malay 2007, no. 32; *SEG* LVII 1150) and in Ptolemaic Kition (*I. Kition* 2015 [*OGIS* 20; *SEG* LIX 1612]).
60. Κατὰ | τὴν ἱστορίαν ἥν ὁ βα|σιλεὺς εἰσηγεῖται πε|ρὶ τοῦ πράγματος (ll. 8–11).

force in Macedonian cities. After that service, they could be elected as priests of Herakles Kynagides.[61] This group of aristocrats therefore had close ties to the cult of Herakles in Demetrias and to the Macedonian royal house. But it is unclear who participated in the cult—whether it was limited to Macedonians or also incorporated elite citizens of Demetrias. In other words, did it demarcate a Macedonian class within the cities of Thessaly or integrate the aristocrats of the allied cities into the structure of the Macedonian kingdom? M. Mili has recently pointed to the fact that the epitaph of Polycharmos from Atrax, who served as a *kunēgos*, suggests that the deceased was a local citizen, perhaps indicating that the cult was open to Thessalian notables.[62]

Other cults attested in Demetrias are probably best explained as results of the emergence of the city as a significant entrepôt of the Hellenistic world. This major port, commercial center, and royal seat attracted an influx of metics, traders, and craftsmen. Macedonians, Athenian potters and stoneworkers, and Levantine sailors, along with numerous other foreigners, are well attested in the city, and these constituencies all certainly had an impact on its cults.[63] A third-century decree of the *astynomoi* (city wardens) of Demetrias commanded the replacement of a stele in the sanctuary of Pluto and Demeter by the *exēgētēs*, a magistrate overseeing religious matters, whose existence may suggest the concern of this complex and pluralistic polis for regulating its cultic life.[64] Also in the third century, a sanctuary of the Mother of the Gods is attested in the eastern part of the city.[65] By the second century, the priest of Sarapis was a prominent civic official and the Serapeion a site for the publication of civic decrees.[66] Outside the city walls, near the south cemetery, was a sanctuary of a goddess usually identified by her worshipers as Pasikrata but in one instance as Ennodia.[67] Its cult, like that of Ennodia elsewhere in Thessaly, seems to have been primarily connected to the concerns of women, kourotrophy, and liminal spaces. The sanctuary was long lived, with numerous inscriptions and evidence for dedications ranging from the third century BCE to the third century CE. M. Mili has suggested that the association of Pasikrata, a deity known from other parts of the Greek world, with the typically Thessalian Ennodia might

---

61. Hatzopoulos 1994, 102–11. See also Pleket's commentary on *SEG* XLIII 382.
62. Mili 2015, 205.
63. Athenians: see ch. 2. Phoenicians: Masson 1969. Egyptians: Arvanitopoulos 1909b, 248–52, no. 52; Stamatopoulou 2008.
64. Arvanitopoulos 1929a, 32, no. 420. For the sanctuary, see Arvanitopoulos 1915; Batziou-Efstathiou 2010, 179–88.
65. Batziou-Efstathiou 1996, 22–24; 2002, 31–32, with references.
66. Priesthood: *IG* IX 2 1107b, 1133. Publication of decrees: *IG* IX 2 1101; Arvanitopoulos 1929a, 32, no. 420.
67. For the sanctuary, see Arvanitopoulos 1912; Arvanitopoulos 1915; Papakhatzis 1958, 53, fig. 2; Stamatopoulou 2014.

reflect a blending of Thessalian customs with foreign influence.⁶⁸ In this way, the cult seems to have accommodated a variety of practices, united by the common interests of the worshiping groups. Of the numerous inscriptions found at the sanctuary of Pasikrata, one is dedicated specifically to Ennodia, with the possibly significant epithet *patroa* (ancestral).⁶⁹ Does this mark out the veneration of the goddess in her "traditional," Thessalian form or tell us anything about the practices of Thessalian communities absorbed into Demetrias?⁷⁰ Or does it simply attest Ennodia's popularity throughout northern Greece?

What is clear is the complex intermingling of continuity and change brought on by the foundation of Demetrias. The most dramatic effects are visible from the beginning of the synoikism: the decline of prominent cults like that of Apollo Pagasaios and the abrupt break in ritual activity at Soros, and the emergence of a coherent, centralized set of civic cults. These, such as the cults of the *archēgetai* and *ktistai*, of Artemis Iolkia, and of Apollo Koropaios, blended tradition with innovation, and it is clear that even in continuity these rites were subject to profound change. As I argue in the next chapter, many of these transformations aimed at the integration of discrete populations but also left room for diversity and differentiation. Kings, civic magistrates, and local representatives of demes are all evident as agents in this process, alongside the more passive forces of demographic change and cultural contact. Similar dynamics can be traced in the geneses of other communities that emerged through synoikism.

Thessalonike and the Thermaic Gulf

The synoikism of Thessalonike encompassed many of the communities on the northern and eastern shores of the Thermaic Gulf. Some of the most distant cities and towns, such as Aineia, persisted as discrete sites of settlement but now dependent on Thessalonike. In the case of Aineia, it is certain that the cults of Aphrodite and Aineias continued to be observed in their original locations past the synoikism.⁷¹ The nucleated settlements that ringed the site of the future polis, by contrast, were systematically evacuated over the course of a decade or so to populate Thessalonike, and there is no evidence for the maintenance of any of their cults in their original locations after the synoikism. At the site of Trapeza Thessalonikis,

---

68. Mili 2015, 207, 273–74.
69. *IG* IX 2 358: Ἐννοδίαι | Πατρ<ώ>ᾳ.
70. For Ennodia see Chrysostomou (1994; 1998, 85–100), who views the expansion of Pherai as the cause of the spread of her cult (1998, 100). Morgan (2003, 139–40) has similarly suggested that the worship of Ennodia was limited to Pherai before the late sixth century. See, however, the remarks of Graninger (2009, 114–20), who charges the tyrants of Pherai with fostering the claim that the Ennodia cult originated there. For the epithet Patrios/Patroos as a means of defining social groups through (real or fictitious) cultic traditions, see Höfer 1992; Aly 1949.
71. Livy 40.4.9–10. See ch. 4 for further discussion.

for instance, just to the northeast of ancient Thessalonike, the excavation of a well-preserved complex has revealed a private cult devoted to the Kyrbantes (Korybantes). A room dedicated to a ritual function within the complex contained fragments of lamps, imported tableware, and a wine pitcher, a stone *loutron* (bathing tub), and a kantharos bearing a dedicatory inscription: "Hadista [Doric for *Hediste*] to the Kyrbantes."[72] The ceramic date of the assemblage is the second half of the fourth century—in other words, the time of the last generation of habitation at the site. The Kyrbantes were deities of ultimately Phrygian origin who attended the orgiastic dances of the Great Mother Kybele. They also had a long tradition in Thracian religion and attended the birth of Dionysos.[73] Theirs was a mystery cult, and Hadista's dedication, in association with the lamps and other ceramic material, points to nighttime rites of initiation.[74] If the Greek name of the dedicant is any indication of her ethnicity, it may suggest Greek devotion to Thracian gods in such mixed communities. While this site went out of use with the synoikism, late sources attest to the popularity of the Kyrbantes within Thessalonike.[75]

An indigenous Thracian cult may be indicated by the sacral character of a large structure excavated on a neighboring plot. Only two rooms of this building were investigated. In one, a square structure bearing traces of fire was uncovered, along with two mud-brick sacrificial hearths. Burned pottery, charred deer bones and antlers, and a large knife were found on one of the two hearths. Deer sacrifice is usually connected with Artemis, and in Thrace her counterpart Bendis had the same association.[76]

At the northeast end of Trapeza Thessalonikis, a rectangular structure has a circular reservoir in its center that drained into a sloped covered water conduit. The building also contained stone-lined tubs, large storage vessels, and pits with traces of sacrificial offerings and ritual dedications. The pottery dates its latest use to the second half of the fourth century. These findings are indicative of a small sanctuary that hosted rites of purification and perhaps divination.[77] Precise parallels to its architectural form are difficult to find, but there are numerous examples of reading prophecies in the movement of water (including in cults from Asia Minor), and it

---

72. Soueref 1990; Voutiras 1996: Ἀδίστα Κύρβασι.

73. Burkert 1993.

74. For the rituals associated with the Kyrbantes, see Bremmer 2014, 48–53. Plutarch describes the rites of Dionysos performed by Macedonian women as imitating the "excessive and superstitious" ceremonies of the Edonian and Thracian women around Mount Haimos (*Alex.* 2.7-8).

75. Firm. Mat., *Err. prof. rel.* 11: "Hic est Cabirus cui Thessalonicenses quondam cruento cruentis manibus supplicabant." Cf. Clem. Al., *Protr.* 2.19.

76. Soueref 1990. See Bremmer 2001 for deer sacrifice.

77. The excavators labeled it the "sanctuary of the waters" and proposed no identification (Soueref 1990).

may be that the reservoir and channel were used for this practice.⁷⁸ Thracian oracles are almost all associated with Dionysos, and the bathing tubs, reservoir, and water channel fit well with his aspect as the god who presides over purification, release, and revelation.⁷⁹ The composite picture from these small buildings in Trapeza Thessalonikis points to the prominent place that mystery cults and rites of initiation held in the community and perhaps indicates the important role that Dionysos played for its mixed Thracian and Greek population. None of the domestic or cultic contexts shows any sign of use after the synoikism, revealing the extent to which this foundation displaced populations and disrupted the cults of these settlements, but as we have seen, many of their traditions found expression within the new polis.

Thessalonike's urban nucleus does not appear to have been founded directly on a major prior settlement, but at least one important site of cult was within its limits, with evidence for ritual activity dating as far back as the Iron Age.⁸⁰ While the precise location and identity of this cult cannot be determined, it points to the significance of this site before the foundation of the Hellenistic city. Adding to this picture is the impressive late archaic Ionic temple of Thasian marble whose architectural members (column capitals and bases, a sima fragment, and a fragment of an Ionic frieze) have turned up throughout Thessalonike since the early twentieth century. The foundations of this temple, first excavated in 1936 but hastily covered over and subsequently lost, have recently been relocated and reexamined.⁸¹ The temple is in "the area of the sanctuaries," along with a third-century Serapeion and a putative center of imperial cult in the Roman period.⁸² Prior to the new

---

78. L. Robert 1939; F. Boehm 1914. In the Roman period, a priest and *hydroskopos* of Dionysos is attested in Thessalonike (*IG* X 2 1 503), pointing to the connection between the worship of Dionysos and the practice of divination through water in the region. This priesthood and ritual are also attested at Beroia (L. Robert 1939).

79. E.g., Hdt. 7.111. See also Iliev 2011.

80. Per Tiverios 1990, on the basis of an unprovenanced pre-Hellenistic ceramic assemblage that probably originates from a ritual or votive deposit somewhere within the future site of Thessalonike. The material, dating from the Iron Age to the fourth century, was stored in the Panayia Acheiropoietos church, in the western part of the city, and may have been excavated at a site nearby. From the Roman period, inscriptions from this area attest the worship of Dionysos, and an inscribed *bomiskos* dedicated to him was discovered just to the west of the church, apparently in situ (Edson 1948, 158–60). Another candidate is the church of Ayios Demetrios, in the northern section of the city, where the records of excavations in the 1950s report ceramic material from the fifth and fourth centuries, which was subsequently lost (Tiverios 1990). Finally, it is possible that the material came from the early excavations in the area of the late archaic temple discussed in the rest of this paragraph.

81. Tasia, Lola, and Peltekis 2000; Schmidt-Dounas 2004; Karadedos 2008. See also Tiverios 2008, 27, 30.

82. Sarapeion: Makaronas 1980. Imperial cult: Vokotopoulou 1995, nos. 1065 (Augustus), 2467–68 (Claudius and Tiberius), 1527–29 (Hadrian), 1528 (fragment of a male togate figure), 1526 (probably Roma); Tasia, Lola, and Peltekis 2000 (life-size statue of Zeus Aigiochos from the reign of Hadrian, first-century CE cuirassed torso of an emperor).

excavation, G. Bakalakis assembled the *disiecta membra* of this temple, which he associated with Dionysos on the basis of an archaic marble phallus originating from the same area and a late antique source that mentions a temple of Dionysos named Phallos in this part of the city, where the Greeks carried out "unseemly rites of the Phalloi." He further argued for the identification of the site of Therme with Thessalonike on this evidence.[83] It has always been evident, however, that the temple in its present form was rebuilt in the early Roman period. The new excavations have shown that the stylobates up to the plinth bases of the columns were constructed in the Roman period, and Roman mason marks on archaic capitals and pieces of entablature indicate that the superstructure was reerected in the same era. E. Voutiras, on this basis, has suggested that the temple originally stood in Aineia, where sources mention a temple of Aphrodite, and was relocated to Thessalonike in the time of Augustus to celebrate his family's descent from Aineias and to serve as the locus of imperial cult, on the model of the "wandering temples" transferred to Athens by the Romans.[84]

Archaic peripteral temples of these dimensions and level of embellishment are extremely rare in Macedonia and the northern Aegean.[85] The identification of this temple's original location would accordingly shed important light on the significance of where it was established. Voutiras's association of the sanctuary with Aphrodite hinges on the theory that it was transferred from Aineia, which, while ingenious, is pure conjecture.[86] It is far simpler to suppose that the temple was rebuilt in the early imperial period from the remains of a temple from the immediate area or somewhere else in Thessalonike. There is evidence, as we have seen, for preexisting cultic activity on the future site of Thessalonike; furthermore, the recent excavations of the temple's foundations show that they cut into an earlier limestone building and incorporate part of the superstructure of an archaic building.[87] The marble phallus, if it can be associated with the temple, points strongly in favor of identifying this sanctuary with Dionysos, which is attractive given his

---

83. Bakalakis (1953; 1963; 1983) identified the sanctuary with the worship of Dionysos Thermaios, reinterpreting Therme's name as deriving not from the presence of thermal springs but from the "internal fire" of Bacchic worship, originating in an indigenous Thraco-Phrygian cult later associated with Dionysos. See also Zahrnt 1971, 247; Höfer 1934.

84. Voutiras 1999. The concentration of imperial portraits found in the area suggests imperial cult. Four inscriptions attest the cult of Aphrodite in Thessalonike: *IG* X 2 1 61 (181/82 CE), 299 (second century CE), 965 (third century BCE); *SEG* XLII 625 (90/91 CE). For Aphrodite at Aineia, see Dion. Hal., *Ant. Rom.* 1.49.4–5.

85. Schmidt-Dounas 2004. The temple of Herakles on Thasos and the Parthenos temple in Neapolis are the only comparable monuments.

86. Accepted by Schmidt-Dounas 2004 and Karadedos 2008, without justification.

87. Tasia, Lola, and Peltekis 2000, 240.

importance in Thrace.[88] Dedications of the polis and its officials, as well as numerous inscriptions from the Roman period, highlight the centrality of his cult in Thessalonike's civic religion. There was also a tribe of the city named for the god.[89]

The distribution of settlements in the area and fragmentary evidence from Thessalonike suggest that the site of its foundation lay outside one of the urban agglomerations that surrounded the future city. If this reconstruction is correct, it may shed light on the reason for founding Thessalonike here. As a location of ancient cult and possibly a significant temple, it may have had regional significance.[90] An important sanctuary such as this, centrally located and accessible to the numerous communities that surrounded the Thermaic Gulf, would have provided a clear link between the traditional cultic identities of these settlements and the new polis. As such, it was a powerful symbolic center around which to build the core of the city.

Alexandreia Troas and the Western Troad

Alexandreia Troas was founded on a relatively insignificant site of prior settlement and drew its main populations from the more important communities of the inland Troad: Neandreia, Kebren, and (initially) Skepsis. Neandreia was clearly of special significance to the new polis: its types were the basis of Alexandreia's coinage, and its cults and traditions were central to Alexandreia's identity.[91] Neandreia had a prominent cult of Apollo, with an elaborate temple in the heart of the city dating back to the sixth century.[92] It is likely that the temple Lysimachos built in Alexandreia was intended to house this deity, who was transferred from Neandreia and set up as the central poliadic deity.[93] The foundations of a six-by-eleven-column peripteral Doric temple are preserved in Alexandreia, oriented, at variance to the city grid, toward the acropolis of Neandreia. Several factors point to its early date (probably contemporaneous with the synoikism): the use of the Doric order, the material (a shelly limestone), and the modest dimensions (14.11 by 27.4 meters, or 46.29 by 89.9 feet).[94]

---

88. If Bakalakis's thesis is correct, the sanctuary's location near the water may hold cultic significance. For the connection of Dionysos to water, particularly seashores, see Sourvinou-Inwood 2005, ch. 6; Faraone 2013.

89. Hellenistic dedication of polis: Hatzopoulos 1996, vol. 2, no. 72; Roman dedications: Edson 1948; tribe: *IG* X 2 1 185.

90. Tiverios 1990.

91. For the coinage, see Meadows 2004.

92. Koldewey 1891; Wiegartz 1994.

93. Strabo 13.1.26. See also ch. 1.

94. Pohl 1999, 85–93.

In Neandreia, despite its clear abandonment except as an outpost of Alexandreia, there is evidence of cultic continuity beyond the synoikism. Deposits associated with ritual activity are conspicuous as the only material that dates to after the synoikism.[95] Recent excavations near the city wall have revealed an offering pit containing stratified deposits of miniature *hydria*, kernoi, and female terra-cotta figurines dating as early as the seventh and as late as the second half of the third century. The assemblage points in all likelihood to a votive pit for Demeter, which must have been associated with an undiscovered Demeter sanctuary in the immediate vicinity. The dates of the material are surprising, pointing to unbroken activity until almost a century after the synoikism.[96] The present state of exploration precludes a definitive statement on whether any cultic activity persisted at the Apollo temple in Neandreia, but the fact that the temple in Alexandreia visually engaged the sanctuary in Neandreia may suggest that the latter remained significant to the new polis after the synoikism.

The important polis of Hamaxitos was also eventually incorporated into Alexandreia Troas (probably after 188). At that time, the temple of Apollo Smintheus, an extraurban sanctuary of Hamaxitos located at modern Gülpınar, near ancient Chrysa, became a religious centerpiece of Alexandreia. The cult of Apollo, with his distinctively Troadic epithet Smintheus, was of importance throughout the Troad, mentioned already by Homer, and had associated games called the Sminthia.[97] In the second century, the sanctuary, which by then served as an *epiphanestatos topos* for the publication of decrees of Alexandreia,[98] was completely rebuilt on a grander scale.[99] After its absorption into Alexandreia, Hamaxitos declined, and the settlement that persisted shifted to Chrysa, which probably served as a base for temple staff, other cultic personnel, and visitors. Alexandreia's use of the Smintheion as a central sanctuary underscores the way in which temples could extend and maintain regional influence, as the synoikized polis absorbed more communities and integrated them into its collective religious life.

SANCTUARIES AND CENTRAL PLACES

Sanctuaries and civic cults provided a focus for corporate religious expression, centralized rituals, and individual participation. They delineated the contours of the new political and cultic communities created through royal intervention and provided a venue for showcasing a unified face to the community. The effort to

---

95. Schwertheim 1999; Pohl 1994.
96. Filges and Matern 1996; Filges and Posselt 1999.
97. *Il.* 1.37–39; games: *I. Ilion* 125.
98. Ricl 1997.
99. Bingöl 1990; Bingöl 1991; Özgünel 1990; Özgünel 2003; Rumscheid 1995.

manipulate existing cults or even invent new ones signals the priority of fostering *communitas*,[100] yet it is also evident that there was no attempt at a central projection of religious unity that would monopolize religious expression in the synoikized polis or efface the diversity of cults and their worshiping communities. This section discusses several cases of investment in preexisting sanctuaries and cults or the "invention" of new cults, which, it argues, grounded the nascent political community in symbols of a cohesive identity. This process, I suggest, formed a communal basis for citizen integration; shared observance, rituals, and priesthoods; and a level of centralized religious expression. (The next chapter explores elements of the religious life of the unified polis that, by contrast, accommodated differentiation, preserved tradition, or even asserted distinctions.)

Such priorities can be identified in many other cases of foundation through synoikism. Ilion, for example, received a substantial increase in territory and population in the late fourth or early third century, and as the religious center of the Troad and the seat of the *koinon* of Athena Ilias (created by Antigonos between 310 and 306) it was invested with powerful new symbolic significance. While the construction of the new temple and the fortification of the city were protracted events, the synoikism of Ilion and the creation of the *koinon* substantially altered the city's trajectory.[101] This was aided, to a large extent, by the reputation of the cult of Athena and the Homeric heritage of the region, and the sanctuary formed the core for the expansion of the settlement and the basis for the subordination of neighboring communities.

The evidence from the sanctuary points to the cult's prominence in the region, despite the near-total insignificance of the polis in the classical period. Our knowledge of the temple's ritual life between the sixth century and Alexander's arrival is slight, but recent excavations have shed important light on its "dark age" in the fifth and fourth centuries. There are few literary references to Ilion or the sanctuary in this period, and the scarce contemporary testimony that does exist gives the

---

100. For the concept of *communitas*, see Turner 1969; 1974. He viewed ritual as having the ability to defuse social conflict and articulate the shared values of social groups through the presentation of unified symbolism.

101. Rose (2003) has argued that the new date of the temple and fortification wall (see p. 60), coupled with the well-known inscription against tyranny (*I. Ilion* 25), demonstrates that Lysimachos neglected Ilion, which may have had a hostile relationship with him. However, this interpretation seems unlikely. As ch. 1 suggests, Lysimachos probably added Sigeion and perhaps Kokkylion to Ilion, augmenting its power. It would hardly have been in his interest to weaken Ilion, which was the head of the *koinon* and whose symbolic power was too valuable a commodity to squander. It is more likely that with two other bases of power—Lysimacheia, across the Hellespont, and Alexandreia Troas to the south—Lysimachos felt that an extensive fortification wall at Ilion was unnecessary. He did construct a temple (of Apollo?) in Alexandreia Troas and an Asklepeion in the vicinity of the Heptaporos in the central Troad (Strabo 13.1.44; new inscription: Körpe and Körpe 2005; for the location, see Cortieu 2013).

impression that Ilion was not a major population center then.[102] In the sanctuary of Athena Ilias, there are no finds from this period, although it was clearly in operation.[103] Likewise, in the so-called West Sanctuary, a sacred complex with multiple altars and a temple, there are numerous finds from the late seventh through sixth centuries but no traces of cult from the fifth or fourth century, and the religious structures appear to have fallen out of use during that time.[104] Only scant finds have been located in the upper city, in the northeastern end of the agora below the later bouleuterion, but these date no later than the early classical period. In the lower city, there is no evidence for occupation in the classical period.[105] An important new ritual deposit found below the acropolis helps to nuance this picture. The preponderance of table vessels and the other artifacts (numerous loom weights, lamps, and graffiti) in the deposit strongly suggest a ritual context, and it is probable that this debris was originally cleared out from the sanctuary of Athena Ilias above and deposited as fill in the area below the acropolis wall in the late fourth century, during the building projects associated with the new *koinon*. The dates of the vessels, coins, and lamps in the deposit demonstrate a consistent dedicatory record beginning circa 380–375 and continuing throughout the fourth century.[106] There is a distinct spike in the ritual activity at Ilion in the mid-fourth century, which demands explanation. A. Berlin has suggested that this rise was associated with the activity of two rogue Athenian generals who sought to consolidate power in the Troad and legitimate their authority. In 360 the Athenian Charidemos seized Ilion, Kebren, and Skepsis. The strategic function of the last two in this period is obvious, but Ilion could have held only symbolic power. Likewise, after another Athenian, Chares, seized control of Sigeion in 355 and held it until Alexander's arrival, there is again evidence for renewed cultic activity in Ilion.[107] This deposit indicates a close connection between these political ambitions and the renewal of ritual activity at the sanctuary and is a clear precursor of the kind of activity that took place at Ilion in the Hellenistic period. Ilion was one of the weakest settlements in the region at the time of the synoikism, with other poleis having absorbed its territory, but its symbolic weight, its connection to the Greek past, made it a valuable possession for legitimating power. It was here that the relics of the Trojan War had been on display since the archaic period, and Alexander's enthusiastic

---

102. Lycurgos, *Leoc.* 62; Thompson (1963, 3): "virtually stagnant in the fifth and fourth centuries B.C."

103. Polyb. 12.5.7; Strabo 13.1.40. See also the Lokrian maiden inscription *IG* IX 1² 3 706; *SEG* XXX 511.

104. Berlin 2002, 133. See also Rose 1993, 98–105; Rose 1994, 76–86; Rose 1995, 82–97; Rose 1996; Rose 1997, 76–92; Aslan and Rose 2013; Rose 2013, ch. 7.

105. Berlin 2002, 133. See also Rose 1999, 40; Berlin 1999, 74, 144.

106. Berlin 2002, 133–35. See also Wallrodt 2002.

107. Berlin 2002, 145–47.

manipulation of the Homeric past on reaching Ilion set the mold for his successors.[108] The principal religious celebration of the *koinon* was the Panathenaic festival, which included games, musical competitions, and recitations of the *Iliad* against the backdrop of the very monuments and tombs of the Trojan War. The temenos and terrace were enlarged in this period, and the Athenaion was constructed to house the meetings of the *koinon*'s council.[109] While Ilion never emerged as one of the great population centers of the Hellenistic world, it served as a religious and political center for the entire Troad, whose diplomatic, economic, and cultic life it played an important role in directing. Ilion is thus a striking example of the symbolic power of cult in ordering a synoikism around shared ties to a central sanctuary.

Another strategy was to build a polis around several existing cults, which would shape the development of the city and in turn be altered by the rise of a new political center. Stratonikeia, founded in the reign of Antiochos II from a number of Karian poleis and villages, most importantly Hierakome, Koranza, Koliorga, Koraia, and Lobolda, which became demes of the new city, incorporated several of their principal cults into the presentation of its religious identity.[110] The site selected for the urban center of the polis seems to have been Hierakome (Sacred village), largely because this was the location of the sanctuary of Zeus Chrysaoreus, a cult of pan-Karian significance and the meeting place of the Chrysaoric League.[111] While this cult grounded the core of the polis, two others that now fell in the territory of Stratonikeia were also privileged: the cults of Hekate at Lagina and Zeus Karios at Panamara were developed and embellished into central civic cults, and in time their sites hosted annual festivals and processions that linked the urban center to the *chōra*.[112]

The dynamic visible at Stratonikeia may be fruitfully compared to the role of preexisting sanctuaries as kernels of organization and unity in nonpolis settlements that were elevated to the status of poleis in many parts of the Hellenistic world. In the early third century, the future site of Laodikeia on the Lykos (founded by Antiochos II in the 250s on a strategic point in Phrygia commanding the Lykos valley) lay within a vast estate of Achaios (the elder), a relative of the Seleukid kings. A lengthy document dating to 267 describes two indigenous villages of the region, Baba Kome, with its associated temple of Zeus, and Kiddiou Kome, with its

---

108. Arr., *Anab.* 1.11.7–8; Diod. Sic. 17.17.6–7, 18.1, cf. 18.4.1–6; Plut., *Alex.* 15.7–8. Heroic cults of Achilles and Patroklos centered on nearby tumuli (Strabo 13.1.32).

109. Aslan and Rose 2013, 15–26; Rose 2014, chs. 8–9. For the *koinon*'s political and economic dimensions, see chs. 1–2.

110. Strabo 14.2.25. For the organization and religious life of the city, see van Bremen 2000; 2004.

111. For the identification of the site of Hierakome, see Şahin 1976, 1–15.

112. Williamson 2012.

temple of Apollo.[113] A fortified settlement called Neon Teichos (New castle) housed the local commander (*epimelētēs*), Helenos, and some of the local population and appears to have included Baba Kome as a dependency. The document records a resolution of the inhabitants of Neon Teichos and Kiddiou Kome that followed a meeting of the assembly (*ekklēsia*) of the two villages. It uses the language of Greek civic decrees to praise two managers of Achaios's estate, Banabelos and Lachares, for their help during the recent war against the Gauls and the ransom of villagers who had been taken prisoner. It also honors these two and Achaios for their benefactions, with, among other things, the establishment of an annual sacrifice of an ox to Achaios ("the lord of the region and savior") at the temple of Zeus and two rams to Banabelos and Lachares at the temple of Apollo. Copies of the decree were set up in both sanctuaries, which served as places of public disclosure for Neon Teichos and Kiddiou Kome. After the foundation of Laodikeia, these indigenous gods were identified with Zeus and Apollo and elevated to the main poliadic deities of the new city, eventually appearing on its coinage. In this way, cults of the villages formed the basis of the common religious identity of the new polis, blending the traditions of two previously distinct communities and introducing new settlers to them—but even before that point the sanctuaries of these gods provided venues for coordinated action, civic organization, and public assembly and disclosure, preconditions for becoming a polis.

The investment in central cults and sanctuaries to promote the unified religious identity of new communities was complemented by a perhaps more distinctive development: the emergence of cults that were essentially "invented traditions."[114] The most celebrated iteration of this solution in the classical period comes from Rhodes, where the synoikism of the island placed a new divine figurehead, Halios (Helios), at the helm of the unified state. The god had not been prominent in cult anywhere on the island prior to the synoikism, despite his importance to myth, but Halios was the perfect symbol for a pan-Rhodian polity, as the progenitor of divinities after whom the poleis merged into Rhodes were named.[115] If this was innovation, however, the effort to craft a unifying mythology seems to have taken into account an existing, if modest, sanctuary of Halios at the future site of Rhodes town as a physical symbol of island identity.[116] Such cults are also evident in other synoikized states. Kos produced a cult of Aphrodite Pandamos (Pandēmos), "Aphrodite of the whole people," while Megalopolis situated new cults of Zeus Philios, "Zeus who promotes friendship," and Zeus Sōter, "Zeus the savior," in the heart of its

---

113. Wörrle 1975; *I. Laodikeia* 1; *SEG* XLVII 1739; see also *BÉ* 88.667 (J. Robert and L. Robert); Corsten 2007. For a discussion of these villages, see Schuler 1998, 187–89.

114. Hobsbawm 1983.

115. Pindar, *Ol.* 7.73–75; Diod. Sic. 5.56.3–6; Zenon, *FGrH* 523 F1; cf. Homer, *Il.* 2.656, 2.662; Strabo 14.2.6.

116. Van Gelder 1900, 291–92. The identification is insecure. See also Parker 2009, 207.

civic center.¹¹⁷ In the cities of the early Hellenistic world, Sōter cults had particular resonance, linking the success of the poleis to the protection and power of their divine founders.¹¹⁸ They also had the advantage of precedents, as in Megalopolis. The use of such shared emblems of cultic participation in fostering unity underscores the extent to which these cities were not artificial, ex nihilo creations or simply products of imperial will. The process of synoikism at times took into account the locations of major sanctuaries, which to some extent shaped the terms of such foundations, and demarcating poliadic cults that could act as focal points for the community always required due attention.¹¹⁹

REPLICATING THE SACRED LANDSCAPE

Communities emerging from synoikism, as we have seen, sought to create a coherent assemblage of state cults and central sanctuaries to establish a kind of symbolic foundation for the polis. If this process expressed a sense of unity for the new citizen community, it also had the potential to select or elevate particular cults to a more prominent position. Additionally, while this effort centered the diverse groups included in the foundation (and in many cases still dispersed in dependent settlements) on the urban core, it could also undermine unity by effacing connections to the original sites of cult.

One means of negotiating this challenge to traditional religious identities was to partially transfer the cult to the new urban center or establish a subsidiary branch there, ritually translated into the city but maintaining a conscious sense of connection and subordination to the original site of cult. This produced a double that directly originated but was also deliberately distinguished from its prototype. Ancient terminology encapsulates this distinction and the relationship of the subsidiary to the original, designating such cults and their associated rites as *aphidrymata* (literally, "things set up from another place").¹²⁰ The practice most commonly

---

117. Aphrodite Pandamos: Paul 2013, 79–91, 285–87; Zeus Philios: Paus. 8.31.4; sanctuary of Zeus Sōter at Megalopolis: Lauter-Bufe 2009. For the Pandēmos cult, Athens, as so often, seems to have had the prototype. According to Pausanias, Theseus established a cult of Aphrodite Pandēmos in an effort to foster social harmony there (1.22.3; see also Pl., *Symp.* 180C–185C; Xen., *Symp.* 8.9; schol. to Soph., *OC* 10; Pirenne-Delforge 1988). Other sources credit Solon with the construction of the sanctuary of Aphrodite Pandēmos in the agora (Harp., s.v. "Aphrodite Pandēmos"; *Suda*, s.v. "Aphrodite Pandēmos"; Ath. *Deip.* 13.569). The goddess conspicuously received cult at other cities that had undergone synoikism: Thebes and Megalopolis (Paus. 8.32.2, 9.16.3).

118. E.g., the cult of Artemis Soteria at Ephesos (Rogers 2012; see also ch. 4).

119. Voyatzis 1999.

120. Brunel (1953) has demonstrated that ἀφίδρυμα, far from serving simply as another synonym for a statue or image of a god or more specifically a copy of a cult image (pace *LSJ*⁹, s.v. ἀφίδρυμα), was linked to an object taken from a sanctuary to set up a subsidiary cult somewhere else. He even argued that the *aphidruma* was the "remains of the sacrifice." L. Robert (1965) suggested that an *aphidruma*

took place during the period of Greek expansion overseas, when a cult was translated from one political community to another, or in other contexts where the identity of the worshiping community was inextricably linked to original site of cult. This was, then, a means of adapting cults to sociopolitical realities, providing a sense of continuity and connection across migrations, other movements, and political changes, but historical examples also demonstrate that it could be contentious. The creation of a subsidiary branch took the cult outside the strict control of its original worshiping group; hence, it threatened the cult's exclusivity.[121] In the context of synoikism, this strategy was employed in the opposite direction, allowing for the maintenance of connections to original communities and cults of the constituent settlements, now reduced to second-order sites or fully incorporated into a centralized political community. As a corollary, in some sacred architecture or cultic precincts, there is evidence of conscious archaism, diminution, or even visual engagement with the primary site, seeking to connect to but not rival it. In effect, these cults were essentially doubles of the preexisting cults of the incorporated territories. These doublets represent one of the prevailing strategies for maintaining a sense of tradition and continuity across such breaks and an effort to resolve the tension between the primacy of the original worshiping community and the participation of the whole *dēmos* of the synoikized polis. But they were not the only one. This delicate balancing of old and new stood alongside the abandonment of traditional sites of cult, the neglect of temples, the creation of new cults and rites, and the forced relocation of cults and their sacred objects.

Versions of the doubling solution can be identified in many classical poleis where the unity of the state was an issue. In Attica, the relationships of the demes to the urban center of Athens were cemented with cultic ties of subsidiary urban sanctuaries in Athens that mirrored major ones in demes:[122] for instance, the sanctuaries of Artemis Brauronia and the city Eleusinion. In addition, Athens held a yearly festival of unity, the Synoikia, to celebrate and reinforce the original synoik-

---

was a wooden statue; Gras (1987), that it was a "temple model." Malkin (1991) has shown that the term refers to any sacred object that is used to set up a subsidiary cult and thus can be just about anything, but what it is *not* is a copy of the cult statue. See also Anguissola 2006a; 2006b.

121. The locus classicus is the transference of the cult of Poseidon Helikonios from Achaia to Ionia. The external pressure of war motivated this transplant from Mount Mykale to a location near Ephesos (Diod. Sic. 15.49.1–2), and the requirement of the *aphidruma* from Helike (the original site of the cult) necessitated appealing to an ancestral claim at two levels of state actors. At the polis level, Helike jealously asserted its exclusive claim to the cult: Poseidon Helikonios belonged to it alone and was a cultic identity it was not willing to share. For the *koinon*, however, more inclined to inclusive political policies, brokering interstate bonds based on cult with the Ionians was clearly a desirable outcome. The friction that this episode created is evident: the polis Boura joined Helike in resisting the decision of the *koinon*, and it was only with Helike's destruction in 373 that the situation was resolved (Herakleides Pontikos F46a [Wehrli]). See also Malkin 1991; Mackil 2013, 194–98.

122. Osborne 1985, 154–77; Anderson 2003, ch. 8.

ism of Theseus, during which sacrifice was made on the Acropolis.[123] Similarly, after the synoikism of the island of Kos in 366/65, the cult of Apollo Dalios (Delios) was replicated in the new city center, but the original, preeminent site of cult at Astypalaia (now the deme of Isthmos) was also maintained.[124] But Megalopolis is the prototype of a megacity on the scale of the Hellenistic foundations that incorporated a large number of polities from poleis to villages.[125] There, a centralized authority, a board of ten *oikistai* representing both the powerful Arkadian poleis that planned the synoikism and the communities that were synoikized, took steps to maintain the ancestral cults and create a religious life in the urban center that blended many of the traditions of Arkadia.[126]

Arkadia, with its rugged topography, was defined by its dispersed pattern of settlement, its multiplicity of sanctuaries, and its fragmented identities, all of which presented formidable challenges to urbanizing and uniting. The archaeological evidence for the religious life of the communities absorbed into Megalopolis points to a conscious effort to both maintain the continuity of their cults and fashion a link between these cults and the urban core of the polis.[127] In the case of communities that the synoikism wholly depopulated, the polis often maintained the sanctuaries after the settlement had decayed into ruin, as at Basilis in Parrhasia, where Pausanias tells us the cult of Demeter Eleusinia could be observed in the second century, and at Akakesion, where Hermes Akakesios was still worshiped and whose cult statute could still be seen in Pausanias's day.[128] Communities that served as outposts for Megalopolis, like the distant Gortys, witnessed an increase

---

123. For the Synoikia, which predated the reforms of Kleisthenes, see Parker 1996, 112–13; Parker 2005, 207, 480–81; Robertson 1992; Anderson 2003, 143–45. On the role of mythology in the synoikism of Athens, see Gouschin 1999. For the sacrifice, see *IG* I³ 244, face c1, ll. 16–20, ritual calendar of the deme Skambonidai (ca. 475–450).

124. Sokolowski 1969, no. 156B; *IG* XI 2 287B, l. 45. See also Paul 2013, 63–67, 190–209.

125. Megalopolis was founded either after Leuktra, in 371/70, or after the Tearless Battle, in 368/67, as a measure to strengthen Arkadia against the Lakedaimonians. For the sources for the synoikism see Moggi 1976b, 293–325; Demand 1990, 111–18; Jost 1973. For the date see Hornblower 1990, 71–77; T. Nielsen 2004, 520–21, which resolves the conflict between those provided by Pausanias and Diodoros by suggesting that Pausanias describes the decision to go forward with the synoikism, which came later, while Diodoros describes the actual event, which took place in 368/67 (see next note).

126. There were two *oikistai* each from Mantineia, Tegea, Kleitor, the Mainalians, and the Parrhasians (Paus. 8.27.2). The extent of the synoikism is unclear; Pausanias (8.27.3–6) claims that it was to incorporate thirty-nine poleis, including some belonging to formerly Spartan perioikic communities, but that the scale was reduced after some rebelled. Diodoros (15.72.4), however, mentions only twenty *kōmai* from the Mainalians and the Parrhasians, and it may be that Pausanias was projecting a later expansion of the territory of Megalopolis into the period of its foundation.

127. Preliminary results from archaeological survey in some areas of the *chōra* of Megalopolis have demonstrated that nucleated settlement continued in the countryside after the synoikism, but the scale was reduced overall: Roy, Lloyd, and Owens 1988; cf. Sourvinou-Inwood 1990.

128. Paus. 8.29.5, 8.36.10.

in the prosperity of their sanctuaries after the synoikism, which can be detected archaeologically; likewise, the sanctuary of the Great God at Theisoa and the suburban temple of Methydrion at Petrovouni also prospered following the synoikism, demonstrating the scale of the polis's material investment in the religious life of its countryside.[129] Indeed, the only known religious site to be abandoned because of the synoikism is the sanctuary of Pan at Berkela, but this may be explained at least in part by its extremely peripheral location.[130]

In the city, the other side of this integration was even more visible, in the form of the doubles of many of these cults. The most conspicuous and central example was the major Parrhasian sanctuary of Zeus Lykaios, who was worshiped on the very top of Mount Lykaion on an ash altar demarcated by a temenos flanked by monumental golden eagles.[131] This became one of the chief cults of Megalopolis, and there was significant investment in its lower sanctuary in the Kato Kanos valley, pointing to an expansion in the attendance at the festival and games of the Lykaia in this period. Back in Megalopolis, Pausanias tells us, there was a stone peribolos demarcating the inner sanctuary (*abaton*) of Zeus Lykaios, which contained altars, two tables, two eagles, and a marble statue of Pan Sinoeis. As at Lykaion, Zeus was here worshiped alongside Pan,[132] and this sanctuary exactly replicates the one there, with the *abaton* corresponding to that on Mount Lykaion, the altar replacing the ash altar, and the eagles mirroring those on the sacred way to the mountain.[133] Likewise, in the agora of Megalopolis there was a temple of Hermes Akakesios, mirroring that at the *kōmē* of Akakesion, and a copy of the cult statue was made for the urban cult, while the rural sanctuary kept the original. Animals sacrificed in the center of the city in the precinct of Apollo Parrhasios were conveyed in a procession out to the original temple, where the ritual was completed.[134] In only one instance in the synoikism was a cult actually transferred: following the rebellion of Trapezous, Megalopolis brought its xoana (cult statutes) to the city, thus effacing the cult and the identity of Trapezous, a harsh and drastic act. This demonstrates the power of the treatment of cults and its importance to state actors wishing to exert influence on a broad region.[135]

---

129. Jost 1986; 1996.
130. Jost 1994, 226.
131. For the site, see now Romano and Voyatzis 2014; Romano and Voyatzis 2015; cf. Romano 1997; Romano 2005.
132. The civic coinage of Megalopolis after 360 bore the image of Pan on the obverse and Zeus Lykaios on the reverse (Head 1911, 445; Jost 1994, 227).
133. Paus. 8.30.2–3.
134. Paus. 8.38.8.
135. Cf. the case of Kyzikos and Prokonessos (Dem. 50.5; Paus. 8.46.4, with Moggi 1976b, 341–44): In 362/61 the Kyzikians defeated the Prokonessians in battle and, in an attempt to compel them to live at Kyzikos as *synoikoi*, transferred the agalma of Meter Dindymene, a quasi-chryselphantine statue (made

Still, the harmonious picture created by the careful tending of the cults of southern Arkadia of course obscures the fact that to a large extent the synoikism of Megalopolis was executed by force. After agreeing to the union, many of the communities that were absorbed found life in the new city difficult and attempted to return to their original settlements shortly afterward.[136] As Diodoros describes the conflict, these communities enlisted the aid of the Mantineans and the Elians against Megalopolis, while the great city was compelled to recall the Theban forces to check the rebellion.[137] In the end, the city was reconstituted through force of arms, reminding us of both the limits of the bonds created by these kinds of adaptations in the realm of cult and the fact that strong attachments to ancestral cults and traditions could run counter to the project of unity.

In the great cities of the early Hellenistic period, the clearest evidence for the replication of sanctuaries of the constituent communities in the polis center comes from Demetrias. As we have seen, the cult of Artemis Iolkia, a deity who appears on the coinage of the city and whose urban sanctuary was used as a privileged site for displaying city decrees, emerged as a particularly important civic cult following the synoikism. A temple of Artemis Iolkia remained in use at the site of ancient Iolkos.[138] In Demetrias, a diminutive temple of Artemis Iolkia, in the middle of the "sacred agora," as it is referred to in the epigraphic texts, became a central monument of the polis.[139] The sacred agora, which was flanked by stoas, was in the middle of the urban plan, its width precisely that of one insula, with the massive palace of the Antigonid kings lying immediately to the north, luxuriously embellished in its interior and projecting royal power. These two structures, located in the heart of the city, seem to have been planned as the symbolic centerpiece of the new settlement, and the palace communicates directly with the agora on its northern side. Farther to the west, looming over this sector from the highest and most visible point in the city, is a massive monument that is likely the sanctuary of the *archēgetai*

---

with hippopotamus teeth instead of ivory), to Kyzikos. Incidentally, there is evidence that Prokonessos later resurfaced as a separate community (Dem. 18.302), a fact perhaps suggestive of the fragility of unions achieved exclusively through force.

136. Most of the Arkadian communities willingly joined the foundation, motivated by their hatred of the Spartans, but several had second thoughts. The inhabitants of Trapezous were ultimately compelled to flee the Peloponnese en masse, while Trikolonoi was compelled to join Megalopolis after resisting, but Lykosoura was allowed to remain a dependent polis out of respect for its sanctuary of Demeter (Paus. 8.27.3–5).

137. Diod. Sic. 15.94.1.

138. See pp. 156–57 for a discussion of the evidence.

139. Dedicated to Artemis Iolkia: Arvanitopoulos 1908, 211; 1928, 92n1, on epigraphic grounds. Supported by Stählin, Meyer, and Heidner 1934. Arvanitopoulos found scant remains of the superstructure. Subsequently explored by German excavations (Marzolff 1976a, 47–58). Sacred agora: e.g., *IG* IX 2 1105.I.

and *ktistai*, a new cult that incorporated the mythical founders and heroes of the synoikized cities and the new founders of Demetrias.

The contrast between the importance of the temple of Artemis Iolkia and its modest size (only 8.75 by 15.25 meters, or 28.7 by 50.03 feet) is immediately arresting. Its precise plan cannot be determined with accuracy, but the most likely reconstruction is a six-by-ten-column peripteral Doric or Ionic temple. This would make it the smallest peripteral temple in mainland Greece. The foundations and foundation courses were made of limestone, while the superstructure appears to have been of mud brick and wood. There is some evidence for marble revetment, but fragments are few.[140] The temple is thus also conspicuous for its modest expense. It does not appear to have been a particularly lavish monument, especially compared to the adjacent palace or the sanctuary of the *archēgetai* and *ktistai*. The small size is most closely comparable to that of the temple of Zeus Sosipolis, where a similar relationship and situation may have been at work: it too was built in the center of a newly laid out agora after its polis (Magnesia on the Maeander) underwent a *metoikisis*.[141]

With its modest dimensions and symbolic siting, the new temple of Artemis Iolkia did not seek to replace the ancient sanctuary or its connection to the site and history of Iolkos, but it still brought the goddess into the civic core and created a direct link between the incorporated center of Iolkos and the city of Demetrias. A decree from the reign of Antigonos Gonatas attests continued concern for the cults of Iolkos, and it seems clear that from the very beginning of Demetrias, its founders conceived of Artemis Iolkia as one of the city's main poliadic divinities.[142] Her cult held special symbolic significance for this new center of Magnesia: as the main divinity of the celebrated site of Iolkos and with connections to seafaring and specifically the voyage of the *Argo*, Artemis was an obvious choice for a unifying symbol for a new naval and commercial headquarters of the Antigonid kings, and Demetrios Poliorketes's coinage and personal iconography echoed these references.[143] The temenos and agora served as privileged places for the publication of civic decrees, reinforcing the roles of the goddess as the protector of the city and the official emblem of the civic body, as on the coinage and seals of Demetrias.[144] Paired with the palace to the north, the temenos of Artemis Iolkia balanced royal power with civic authority.[145]

140. Marzolff 1976a, 47–58.
141. See K. Humann 1904, plates 2–3.
142. Ernst Meyer 1936. See the discussion of the text at pp. 190–93.
143. See Mørkholm 1991, 77–80 for Demetrios's coinage.
144. For the civic emblems and iconography of Demetrias, see Franke 1967; Furtwängler and Kron 1978; Furtwängler and Kron 1983.
145. See Lauter 1987 for the suggestion that the proximity of the palace and the sanctuary in Demetrias served to incorporate the king's residence, usually on the outskirts of a city or on a fortified acropolis, into the civic fabric of the community.

Rounding out this picture, as we have seen, was the continued maintenance of the sanctuaries of Zeus Akraios / Cheiron on Mount Pelion and of Apollo Koropaios at Korope, the latter under the administration of Demetrias and tended by a priest appointed by the polis. Although it is not definitive, the evidence strongly implies that there was a sanctuary of Zeus Akraios in Demetrias,[146] and because the polis assumed tight control over the administration of the sanctuary of Apollo, it is probable that this was doubled in the city center as well.[147] The priest of Zeus Akraios, worshiped on the peak of Mount Pelion, held the most important civic office in Demetrias and served as the eponymous official in civic decrees. He also oversaw the annual procession of the city's young elites, possibly from the city sanctuary of Zeus, up to the peak of Pelion, where sacrifice took place.[148] This peak was directly engaged by the orientation of the sanctuary of the *archēgetai* and *ktistai* on "hill 84," linking the cult of founders, assembled from the various demes of the city, to the region's most prominent geographical feature, the central civic cult of Zeus Akraios, and the ritual initiation of the city's youth. Simultaneously, it associated the power of the Antigonid kings with that of the king of the gods. Marble architectural members from this sanctuary also connect it closely with traditions of elaborate monumental funerary architecture from Asia Minor, lavish projections of royal power that contrast with the modest, traditional temple lying at the heart of the agora just below.[149] What emerges is a complex assemblage of religious symbols fully integrated into the urban landscape and connected to the original sites of cult. Intertwined with and inseparable from these were the apparatus and representatives of the new civic community—public archive, priests and other officials, citizen elite—and the holders of royal power.

The relationship of the earliest temple in Alexandreia Troas to the urban and rural topography of the polis suggests that a similar dynamic may have been at work there. As we have seen (p. 165), the remains of a Doric temple in the southeastern part is the most likely candidate for the temple that Lysimachos built in the city. It was probably intended to house the cult of Apollo of Neandreia, who was transferred and set up as the poliadic deity of the new foundation. The siting supports this proposition: the temple was built with an almost exact east-west orientation, conspicuously off the grid of the rest of the city, so its front directly faces the acropolis of Neandreia, to which it has a clear line of sight.[150] The excavators have pointed to the suitability of the Doric order for an ancient cult set up in a new foundation, and this "conservative" element lends weight to the association of the

146. Helly 1971, 544–48.
147. *IG* IX 2 1110; cf. Sokolowski 1969, 171–72, no. 85.
148. *FHG* II 254–64 F2.8 = *BNJ* 369A F2.8. See ch. 4 for a discussion of this ritual.
149. Marzolff 1996b.
150. Pohl 1999, 85–93.

temple with the cult of Apollo of Neandreia. In the early years of the city, Neandreia and the cult of Apollo were clearly of special significance to Alexandreia, which based its coinage on the types traditional to Neandreia and its identity on the cults and traditions of that polis, particularly before the absorption of Hamaxitos and the Smintheion in the second century (see pp. 65–66, 166).[151]

The new city Herakleia Latmos likewise strikingly incorporated the central cults and traditions of the former polis of Latmos and towering mountain of Latmos. The temple of Athena Latmia was transferred to or duplicated on a high ridge in the center of the city, overlooking the agora. The orientation of this small temple breaks from the axial regularity of the rest of the city plan, and the view from its doorway precisely frames the highest peak of Mount Latmos.[152] This summit had been the focus of cult since prehistoric times, as a number of Chalcolithic petroglyphs attest. The ancient Anatolian cult associated with the mountaintop and an indigenous weather god was later assimilated into a cult of Zeus Akraios observed by the citizens of Herakleia and likely patronized by one of its Macedonian rulers.[153] The sanctity of this mountain and its traditions can be traced in several other cults of Herakleia. The mythology of Endymion was intimately tied to Latmos from an early period, and sources tell us he was worshiped in a cave somewhere on its slopes.[154] A small hero shrine dedicated to him has been identified in the agora of Latmos, and his cult was certainly transferred to Herakleia, in whose southern part he was worshiped in a small apsidal temple. This temple too breaks from the city's orthogonal grid and is oriented toward the sacred mountain. Its façade conforms to a regular prostyle plan, but the rear wall is composed of curved ashlar connecting two large boulders.[155] The effect is an architectural re-creation of a kind of cave, harking back to the original site of cult in a mountain cave. A fragment of a lyric hymn from the third century composed for the central civic festival of Athena Latmia refers to Endymion as "the founder of the demos," demonstrating how the traditions of the region formed the basis of the new city's cultic identity.[156]

These instances of "architectural conservatism" reflect the ways in which the needs of individual communities interfaced with royal hegemony and political change. They distinctly contrast with the experimental styles of temple building that dominated the second half of the third century and later, which are notable for their focus on dramatic monumentality and the conscious avoidance of the Doric order.[157] Other cases from the late fourth and early third centuries appear to mirror

---

151. Pohl 1999; Schwertheim and Wiegartz 1994; Schwertheim and Wiegartz 1996.
152. Krischen 1922; Peschlow-Bindokat 1996a.
153. Peschlow-Bindokat 1996b. See also pp. 219–20.
154. Strabo 14.1.8; Paus. 5.1.5.
155. Krischen 1922; Peschlow-Bindokat 1996a.
156. *SGO* 1.23.1, l. 6.
157. See, e.g., the views expressed by the great Hellenistic architect Hermogenes (Vitr., *De arch.* 3.2.6).

these architectural priorities that have more to do with stressing continuity with the past than underscoring change.[158]

Such reflections of the concerns of a political community in its public architecture and cultic observances have been well documented elsewhere. The hero cults that emerged at the Bronze Age tombs in the late classical and Hellenistic periods and the "enigmatic" Bronze Age–style tholos tomb on Samothrace actually built in the Hellenistic period are iterations of this phenomenon.[159] The Pnyx, the site of the meetings of the assembly of Athens, offers another case. It was monumentalized in the late fourth century, in the time of Lykourgos or just before, with a project including a massive retaining wall constructed at the base of the hill. This wall was deliberately built with massive polygonal stones—almost cyclopean in size—to hearken back to and create a sense of continuity with old Athens, perhaps even archaizing to a degree that would reference the original, Kleisthenic reforms in a place so emblematic of the values of the democracy.[160] But the masonry is, in a sense, timeless; it is both archaic in style and prehistoric in scale, and it is the resulting effect that invests it with such powerful symbolic import for another period of transition: that of Lykourgos and his reforms, when the institutional and religious restructuring of Athens triggered this retrospective spirit. The consequence is a smoothing over of change, a deliberate appeal to continuity, invested in and expressed through subtle yet compelling architectural detail.

This architectural traditionalism seems to have been designed expressly to convey a sense of legitimacy to the political reshuffling of these regions under the kings. As central symbols of the civic community and repositories of social memory, the major sanctuaries were particularly effective in creating links between the old civic order and the new and are conspicuous examples of how cultural symbols can be translated into monumental architecture. These monuments were embedded in the wide social fabric of the synoikized community, providing centralized sanctuaries while not effacing, in many cases, the original sites of cult in the *chōra*. Through the symbolic siting of new sanctuaries, including their visual engagement

---

158. E.g., the late fourth-century Doric temple at Pherai. Demetrios seized Pherai and expelled Cassander's garrison in 302 (Diod. Sic. 20.110.6). Pherai had suffered from the loss of Pagasai and its other possessions (see pp. 77–80). Given its waning fortunes, it is likely that Demetrios had a hand in the construction of a new temple there ca. 300, dedicated to Zeus Thalios or Ennodia—the central divinities of the polis. There are architectural similarities between the temple at Pherai and the temple of Artemis Iolkia in Demetrias, suggesting a connection between the craftsmen or architects of these two sanctuaries (Marzolff 1994a). The temple at Pherai too has strikingly disjunctive architectural details, both respecting the form of its archaic predecessor and combining Periklean prototypes with new innovations (Béquignon 1937; Østby 1994, 140). Although the details are sketchy, a similar Doric temple may be in evidence at Lysimacheia (Lichtenberger, Nieswandt, and Salzmann 2015).

159. Tomb cult: Alcock 1991; Samothracian tholos: Alcock 1997.

160. Travlos 1971, s.v. "Pnyx." See also Mitchel 1970; for the issue of the date, Camp 2000, 45–46.

with significant landmarks of the *chōra,* and the ritual maintenance of preexisting shrines, communities asserted a new identity rooted in local traditions.

RELIGIOUS NETWORKS

Of all religious activity, Macedonian intervention most directly shaped that grounded in the polis, but the political effects of synoikism—depriving communities of polis status and creating new cities across traditional regional and ethnic boundaries— also had wide repercussions for the participation of communities in amphiktyonies, *koina,* and other forms of interpolis religious networking, like sending and receiving sacred ambassadors (*theōria*). Involvement in Panhellenic festivals and regional cults constituted another important level of religious identity beyond the polis and was also mediated by political communities.[161] This religious interaction was a prime venue for displaying and reinforcing the place of a city within the wider Greek world.

We can see the immediate consequences of synoikism in disrupting or restructuring these activities. As a Macedonian dependency, Magnesia no longer sent representatives to Delphi after the reorganization of the amphiktyony in 279, and the synoikism of Demetrias, which brought Thessalian communities into Magnesia, severed them from the amphiktyony as well.[162] Antigonos's directives for the synoikism of Teos and Lebedos in 303, which surely contained other religious prescriptions at the beginning of the first preserved letter, stipulate that a Lebedian representative be sent to the Panionion and "perform all the common ceremonies for an equal period of time and set up his tent and celebrate the *panēgyris* with those sent by you and be called a Teian."[163] Thus, the polis of Lebedos was deprived of discrete representation within the Ionian *koinon,* though Antigonos was careful to reserve a place for a Lebedian *theōros* in this prestigious, albeit inferior, office within the new city.[164] The importance of these relationships to the wider religious celebrations of the Greek world is underscored by the fact that some communities retained the right to send or receive sacred missions (*theōriai*) after being absorbed into a synoikism:[165]

---

161. Sourvinou-Inwood 1990, 20.

162. After the reorganization of 279: Flacelière 1937; Scholten 2000. After Magnesia was freed from Macedonian control in 196 and reconstituted under the Magnesian *koinon,* it was once again represented at Delphi (Stählin, Meyer, and Heidner 1934, 195–205), and the elites of Demetrias participated.

163. *RC* 3, ll. 2–4: [πράττειν πάντα τὰ κο] ινὰ τὸν ἴσον χρόνον, σκηνοῦν δὲ τοῦτον καὶ πανηγυράζειν μετὰ τῶν παρ' [ὑμῶν ἀπεσταλμέ]|νων καὶ καλεῖσθαι Τηΐον.

164. Ager 1998.

165. Per the agreement they struck in the early fourth century, Helisson was to become a *kōmē* of the polis of Mantineia but remain a discrete community (RO 15, ll. 8–9). As such, it would contribute one *thearos* to Mantineia, along with the other *kōmai* from which Mantineia had been synoikized, and it retained the right to receive *theōroi* from other parts of the Greek world. For the relationship between *theōrodokoi* and polis status, see Hansen and Nielsen 2004d; Rutherford 2013, 217–22.

although they had been politically subordinated to another polis, they still retained some aspects of their communal cultic identity. Such seems to have been the case with Aineia, even after it was amalgamated into Thessalonike.[166] Likewise, after their synoikism into Ephesos, Lebedos and Kolophon still appear to have been represented in some independent form in the Ionian *koinon*, presumably as dependencies of Arsinoeia/Ephesos.[167]

The revival of a polis through synoikism could also result in the addition of a community to a *koinon*. Despite proving its Ionian credentials to the satisfaction of the other cities of Ionia, Smyrna may not have been admitted to the Panionion before its destruction in 585; it finally joined the *koinon* after its synoikism.[168] It was in fact Lysimachos and Arsinoe's direct intervention that finally secured Smyrna's acceptance into the league, centuries after its initial application.[169] More broadly, Macedonian investment in the cities of Ionia breathed new life into the *koinon* and the festival of the Panionia, and from the late fourth century the activity of this theoric network is well attested epigraphically and archaeologically. The league issued honorary decrees for important officials like Hippostratos the son of Hippodemos of Miletos, the *stratēgos* of Ionia and agent of Lysimachos, granted important privileges like *ateleia* within the *koinon*, and had a role in arbitrating interstate conflicts.[170] It also, as we have seen, oversaw the periodic market at the festival, issued sacred laws regulating the participation of the communities in the Panionia, and imposed penalties on member poleis that failed to make sacrificial contributions (see p. 124).[171] Aside from filling these practical roles, the

---

166. Aineia, perhaps a dependent polis of Thessalonike in the third century, appears on the lists of the Delphic *theōrodokoi* (Plassart 1921, 18 col. III, l. 75 [230–210]). An extreme case seems to be that of Kos, where after the synoikism, the former polis of Astypalaia (the tribe and city of Isthmos within Kos) was the only Koan community with the right to send its own *theōria* (Rutherford 2013, 221n42, with refs.). Moreover, Kalymnos, after the *homopoliteia* with Kos in the late third century, sent a *theōria* to Delos in the 140s, possibly under the supervision of Kos (*ID* 1432, Bb, col. 2, ll. 9–10; Rutherford 2013, 221).

167. *I. Smyrna* II.1 577, a copy of a decree of the Ionian League referring to Ephesos as Arsinoeia (*Syll.*³ 368; *Milet* I.2 10 [289/88]). See also Ager 1998.

168. According to Herodotos (1.149.1–150.2), a group of exiles from Kolophon drove the original Aiolian settlers out of Smyrna. Thereafter, Smyrna attempted to join the Ionian League, but there is no secure evidence for its admission before the Hellenistic period (Rubenstein 2004, 1054). After its destruction, Smyrna did not have a role in the Panionion, aside from the possible right of Kolophon to cast a vote on its behalf in the event of a tie (schol. to Pl., *Tht.* 153C). The first evidence for Smyrna as a fully fledged member dates to the reign of Lysimachos (*I. Smyrna* II.1 577 [ca. 289/88], cf. 575.15–19 [mid-third century?]).

169. Vitr., *De arch*. 4.1.4.

170. *I. Milet* I.2 10 = *Syll.*³ 368; copies with slight variations: *I. Smyrna* II.1 577; *SEG* LVI 999 (from Chios).

171. Ed. pr. Hommel, Kleiner, and Müller-Wiener 1967, 45–63; cf. Sokolowski 1970, 114–15, but see the reservations of *BÉ* 84.582 (J. Robert and L. Robert). For the significance of *theōria* and choral performance to the communities participating in the Panionia, see Kowalzig 2005, 45–56.

resuscitated league reasserted a common Ionian social and religious identity that had flagged during the preceding century.[172] The rituals performed at the Panionia, which included a common sacrifice to Zeus Boulaios and the other associated gods and required the participation of representatives and contributions from the member cities, articulated a stable social order.

The upswing of the Ionian League was not the only effect of Macedonian rule—such leagues bound wide regions in shared political, economic, and religious communities. Beginning with its creation circa 306/5 under Antigonos, for instance, the *koinon* of Athena Ilias centered the whole Troad on the common worship of this goddess.[173] It included the synoikized poleis Ilion and Alexandreia Troas, and its catchment extended to the most significant cities of the Propontis, Parion and Lampsakos, in part because of its limited political importance and because it was not organized along ethnic lines. Like the Ionian League, this *koinon* was a venue for coordinated diplomatic and economic activity and other forms of institutional interdependence. But it also rooted this diverse group of communities in the celebration of an ancient cult and provided a focal point for collective ritual action across a turbulent period. In a similar way, the Nesiotic League, set up by Antigonos and Demetrios around 314, served to organize the Kyklades islanders and bound them together in a common cultic association. This *koinon* centered on Delos and its sanctuary of Apollo, where religious festivals for Antigonos and, beginning in 307, Demetrios were held.[174] As this shows, there were also religious advantages afforded to the kings in these relationships, as the leagues provided regional venues for embedding their cults and authority into networks of poleis and an existing culture of interpolis theoric activity.[175]

CONCLUSIONS

The evidence surveyed in this chapter demonstrates the degree to which the cultic life of communities subjected to the political and social manipulations of the Hellenistic kings experienced disruption, adaptation, and other alteration. Some sanctuaries appear to have been entirely abandoned at the moment of synoikism,

---

172. The Panionia was relocated from Melie to Ephesos sometime in the fifth or early fourth century (Hornblower 1982b favors a date of 440/39, when Miletos and Samos fought over Priene). It returned to Melie, a site in the territory of Priene, sometime in the mid-to-late fourth century, probably at the same time as the refoundation of Priene.

173. See *I. Ilion* 1–18 for inscriptions of the *koinon* and the organization of the *panēgyris*.

174. *IG* XI 4 1036.

175. See *OGIS* 219 = *I. Ilion* 32, ll. 35–38, for the impressive honors voted by Ilion to Antiochos I, including a gilt equestrian statue of the king displayed prominently in the sanctuary of Athena Ilias and the announcement of these honors at the Panathenaia before all the representatives of the *koinon*. This added to sacrifices made to the king by the city and by individuals at household altars.

with no identifiable continuation or transference of their cults, while others were assiduously maintained in their original location decades or even centuries after their associated poleis were depopulated or abandoned. Thus, the ability of worshiping groups to maintain their cults was highly contingent on the political and social realities of the new communities of which they became a part. This complex social dynamic and the strong attachment of communities to their cults, traditions, and sacred spaces led to a number of accommodations brokered by the combined political community, its elites, and, at times, the kings themselves. These strategies attempted to mitigate the disruption caused by massive political and demographic mergers while simultaneously crafting a unified cultic identity for the emergent polity. Central state sanctuaries were some of the most convenient spaces to be communal focal points, as their cults provided an organizing principle around which the political community could crystallize. The competing interests and traditions of these communities, with their diversity of cults and attachment to the original sites of worship, are also evident in these foundations. The process of duplicating or replicating the cults of constituent communities inside the new city allowed for a delicate balance of tradition and innovation. The new political center co-opted and administered these cults, without replacing their original sites. A degree of autonomy was also given to subpolis entities like demes, which could still have a role in administering aspects of their cults and even enter directly into dialogue with the royal authority. Such strategies elucidate the degree to which consensus and negotiation contributed to the making of these polities, helping us to reconstruct a process with dimensions beyond the power and force of the kings and their agents.

4

Consensus, Community, and Discourses of Power

The survey of the religious consequences of synoikism presented in the previous chapter focuses on the structural dimensions of the encounter between Macedonian imperialism and the religious life of poleis. This evidence reveals important aspects of religious adaptation and other changes stemming from synoikism but tells us less about what role religion played in forming and structuring these communities. In other words, if we move beyond describing changes in religious observance to looking for ways in which cults and rituals defined these new societies and delineated contours of belonging and identity, we can identify elements of this process that reveal a negotiation of power among king, city, and individuals. The complexities of local traditions meant that religion and cult had important roles in determining the framework of Hellenistic city foundations. These cities were not blank canvases ready for the application of a new order; rather, they imposed certain limitations on the power of the monarchs and reserved a space for collectivities to exert their own agency. Thus, religion was neither a simple instrument of empire that served to create cohesion in a city nor an exclusively conservative force that fostered separatism or resistance. I suggest that the strategic employment of ritual and symbolism to bridge the discontinuity of population movement, settlement shift, and political change was a powerful mechanism, shaped by king and community alike, in the building of new cities.

Viewing the evidence from this perspective, we can identify aspects of a discourse, with elements of consensus alongside strands of particularism. What emerges is a picture of the synoikized polis as a tessellation of various interests and agencies. The artificial origins of such societies meant that for their members, religion was not a shared cultural inheritance or an unchanging set of traditions but an assemblage of cults and practices that were in part handed down and in part newly articulated by political authorities both civic and royal. This chapter highlights thematic features of this discourse to unravel how the constituent groups and interests that made up these new polities defined themselves and how myth, ritual, and symbolism could be employed to broker compromises between them.

I begin with a discussion of how the synoikized polis conceived of and accommodated traditional founders and embedded the figure of the king in its cultic identity. I next explore the ways in which cities were organized and how they blended different political communities and ethnicities. The administration of central cults, particularly those with preeminent priesthoods, posed a challenge for the integration of civic elites. The following section examines which citizens had a share in participating in and administering cults. I finish the chapter with a consideration of the roles of the kings and the communities in promoting or reconfiguring certain cults, introducing new civic rituals, and initiating other strategies for fostering unity and overcoming division or tension. Although kings instituted important ritual changes and became embedded in the religious fabric of the poleis under their control, this is not to say religion was reduced to a hollow gesture—the religious rites, traditions, and concerns of communities were complex local considerations around which kings and royal agents had to operate. In this sense religion was a limiting factor, but it also provided a space of negotiation for kings and cities to articulate their relative positions and define the shape of the new political community.

THE PROBLEM OF ORIGINS: CITY FOUNDERS AND FOUNDATION MYTHS

Political disruption and social stress often prompted communities to reflect on their origins.[1] As a group of citizens defined by shared myths of foundation, ancestry, and descent, the polis depended on a coherent understanding of its beginning. The celebration of the cult of the founder was a central ritual that grounded the community in its past and articulated its identity as a political unity, reinforcing its origins at each moment of sacrifice. Synoikism shook this foundation by eliminating individual poleis and merging formerly distinct groups into a single society. These constituent communities all had traditions about their founders and celebrated their heroic cults. Accordingly, building a new political community in the synoikism necessitated making choices about founders:

---

1. See Malkin 1987, 261–66, on the role of the colonial experience in prompting the invention of founder cults in the older Greek cities. For comparative discussions of foundation myths as reflective of social discourse, see Mac Sweeny 2015.

privileging the origins of one community over another, accommodating a plural board of *oikistai* (founders), or finding another balance. A further vector complicated this situation: the very real role of the Hellenistic kings as city founders. The evidence reveals a range of strategies employed to construct a narrative about the origins of a new city, revealing the distinctive priorities of such communities.

The circumstances of each foundation varied and inevitably produced different arrangements. But whether the new city was built around the augmented core of an existing settlement, was composed of villages or poleis, or bore a dynastic name, its creation constituted a ritual act and the inauguration of a new era or layer of foundation. A decree of the *synedroi* of the Ephesian gerousia (council of elders) in the reign of Commodus, for example, refers to "former [times] during the foundation of the polis," still looking back on the Lysimachean synoikism of the city as a watershed moment long after it had lost its dynastic *epiklēsis,* Arsinoeia.[2] Similarly, in 104 CE, the wealthy Ephesian (and Roman eques) Gaius Vibius Salutaris made a lavish dedication that included thirty-one statues, in silver and gold, which were to be used in a procession from the Artemision to the theater and back. Along with representations of the emperors and Rome were personifications of the *boulē* and *dēmos,* the tribes, and the city of Ephesos and, notably, a portrait of Lysimachos as its founder.[3] The procession, as G. Rogers has demonstrated, conducted the citizen community through a "map of foundations," as the participants moved from the sanctuary of Artemis to the newest quarter of the city (the "upper city," founded in the Roman period) and down to the Hellenistic Lysimachean city, then progressed to the Koressian Gate and the sites associated with the earliest Ionian foundation, associated with the hero Androkles. The procession moved backward through the layers of foundation and linked the Roman present to the various stages of the city's past.[4] In a similar way, the monumental mausoleum at Belevi, regardless of whom it was intended for (probably Antigonos I), was sited conspicuously next to the archaic heroön of Pixodaros, the discoverer of the

---

2. *I. Ephesos* Ia 26.1–6. See pp. 220–21 for further discussion.

3. Several inscriptions attest G. Vibius Salutarius's benefactions. The great bequest (*I. Ephesos* Ia 27, with Rogers 1991; see also Elsner 2007, 229–31) was preceded by a smaller dedication including three silver statues, of Artemis Ephesia, Lysimachos, and Salutaris's tribe, Tēioi (*I. Ephesos* Ia 29). Whether the cult of Lysimachos fell into abeyance after the Seleukid take-over of Ephesos (so Habicht 1970, 41) and was resurrected only in the Roman period with the gerousia (Oliver 1941, 55), which is attested for the first time since Lysimachos then, is unclear. However, the key points are the long memory of the founder and the political dimensions of his foundation of the city. For an early Hellenistic marble portrait of Lysimachos from Ephesos, see Atalay and Turkoglou 1972.

4. Rogers 1991, chs. 3–4.

marble quarries of Ephesos, who received yearly sacrifice from that city's civic magistrate.[5]

To take another example, when Antigonos simply moved the city of Kolophon to a new site circa 311–306, the physical and conceptual disjuncture between the "ancient city" (*palaia polis*), founded by the Kolophonians' ancestors and bestowed by the gods, and the new city center had to be ritually addressed, as a surviving inscription makes clear. The Kolophonians quite literally secured their enduring connection with a wall encircling both settlements and established ritual processions to connect the two.[6] The concern for maintaining an association with the city of their founders and ancestors (*progonoi*, repeatedly stressed: ll. 10, 16) is conspicuous in this document.[7] A little more than a decade later, when Lysimachos forced them into the synoikism of Ephesos, the Kolophonians fought bravely, if in vain, to preserve their independence. Later still, Lysimachos's general Prepelaos secured their release from the union (see pp. 74–76). They commemorated this by conferring heroic honors on him as a new founder of the city, including constructing a sanctuary for him (the Prepelaion), which was still an active site of cult after 133.[8]

That the identity of the founder of a jointly settled polis could be a highly contentious issue is demonstrated by the case of Thourioi. The city was established in 444/43 on the site of Sybaris by a Panhellenic contingent led by the Athenians Xenokritos and Lampon, to whom Diodoros refers as the *ktistai*.[9] Earlier, in 445/44, Sybaris had been reinforced by Athenian and Peloponnesian settlers, but the city soon fell into *stasis* (civil discord) after the Sybarites assigned themselves the highest civic offices and the best land and reserved precedence for their wives at civic sacrifices.[10] The other colonists addressed this imbalance by slaughtering most of the Sybarites. Some ten years after the foundation of Thourioi, in 434, *stasis* again broke out, as Athens and several cities of the Peloponnese claimed to be Thourioi's metropolis and the city's leading citizens competed for the honor of being regarded

---

5. The mausoleum is sixteen kilometers (ten miles) north of Ephesos and was constructed sometime between 310 and 270 (Ruggendorfer 2016). The original excavators suggested that it was commissioned by Lysimachos and was intended to serve as his burial site or cenotaph, or at least the burial site of some closely affiliated royal dignitary (Praschniker et al. 1979; cf. Lund 1992, 177). (Lysimachos, of course, was buried in Lysimacheia, in the heroön know as the Lysimacheion [App., *Syr.* 64]). They further suggested that this monument might have been completed later by the Seleukids and served as the burial chamber of Antiochos II. In a recent reexamination, Ruggendorfer (2016, 169–82) convincingly argues for associating the heroön with Antigonos Monophthalmos.

6. Meritt 1935, 359–72, no. 1.

7. For the complex foundation myths of Kolophon and their political dimensions, see Mac Sweeny 2013, 104–37.

8. J. Robert and Robert 1989, 63, col. 1, l. 23, with the commentary at 77–85.

9. Diod. Sic. 12.10.4. Plutarch (*Mor.* 812d) mentions only Lampon. Elsewhere a board of ten *manteis* is specified (schol. to Ar., *Nub.* 332; *Suda*, s.v. Θυριομάντεις). See further Rutter 1973. For *ktistēs* as synonymous with *oikistēs* in the Hellenistic period, see Leschhorn 1984, 333–36.

10. Diod. Sic. 12.11.1.

as the oikist.[11] When the citizens of Thourioi sent a delegation to Delphi to determine their oikist's identity, Apollo replied that he should be considered its founder, and this compromise resolved the *stasis*.[12]

How, then, did communities emerging from synoikism grapple with the issue of their origins? The evidence points to conscious efforts by leaders of new poleis to address this problem at the time of foundation. One option was to privilege one community above the others. Such seems to have been the case at Nysa, founded by Antiochos I from three small settlements sometime after 281. The oikist of the leading community, Strabo reports, became the founder of the new polis: "They give the account that three brothers, Athymbros, Athymbrados, and Hydrelos, having come from Lakedaimon, founded their own eponymous cities. But later, when the populations declined, Nysa was synoikized from them. And now the Nysaeans consider Athymbros their founder [*archēgetēs*]."[13] The exclusivity of this selection stands out. The Athymbrians controlled the famous sanctuary of Pluto and Korē and the cave of Charon, which became the cultic focal points of Nysa, and the elevated status of their founder in the synoikism (which also included Ionian settlers) seems to be confirmed by their continued prominence in the sanctuary's priesthoods.[14] At Antioch on the Maeander, founded by Antiochos I from the synoikism of Symmaithos and Kranaos, coins of the imperial period variously vaunt Antiochos and the eponymous Kranaos as the city's founder.[15]

The elites of some foundations seem to have asserted primacy on the basis of their descent from the founders,[16] but as we saw in the case of Thourioi, an asymmetrical arrangement among the citizens of a new community could easily lead to violence and dissolution. That might be why the majority of the early Hellenistic synoikisms, by contrast, had a strong inclusive emphasis. This is particularly evident in the large multipolis synoikisms of the late fourth and early third centuries.

11. Diod. Sic. 12.35.3.
12. Diod. Sic. 12.35.3. See also Malkin 1987, 254–55; Leschhorn 1984, 128–39.
13. Strabo 14.1.46: Ἱστοροῦσι δὲ τρεῖς ἀδελφούς, Ἄθυμβρόν τε καὶ Ἀθύμβραδον καὶ Ὕδρηλον, ἐλθόντας ἐκ Λακεδαίμονος τὰς ἐπωνύμους ἑαυτῶν κτίσαι πόλεις, λειπανδρῆσαι δ' ὕστερον, ἐξ ἐκείνων δὲ συνοικισθῆναι τὴν Νῦσαν· καὶ νῦν Ἄθυμβρον ἀρχηγέτην νομίζουσιν οἱ Νυσαεῖς. The reverse of coins from Nysa from the reign of Marcus Aurelius depict the hero Athymbros and contain the legend ΑΘΥΜΒΡΟΣ ΝΥΣΑΕΩΝ (von Dienst 1913, 81, no. 78). For the semantic range of *archēgetēs*, see Leschhorn 1984, 180–85; Malkin 1987, 241–50.
14. For a discussion of the priests of the Plutonion, see pp. 208–9.
15. Pliny, *HN* 5.108; Steph. Byz., s.v. Ἀντιόχεια. Kranaos as founder: *SNG* 2421; L. Robert 1958. Antiochos as founder: *BMC Caria* 23, no. 59.
16. At Aphrodisias, a group of "first citizens" descended from the "founders of the *dēmos*" is prominent in several inscriptions (Chaniotis 2004, 381–83; Chaniotis 2009; cf. Savalli-Lestrade 2005; Ratté 2008). At Hierapolis in Phrygia, which developed from the core of a Seleukid *katoikia*, some individuals advertised their descent (real or otherwise) from the original settlers by adding the ethnic Μακεδών *vel sim.* to their names (Humann et al. 1898, nos. 153, 255, 339a).

The architects of these cities widely seized the opportunity to build consensus around a centralized cult of the mythical founders of the constituent communities, coupled with the historical founder (the king himself), perhaps one of the most straightforward ways to assert unity. The long tradition of synoikism in the Greek world provided ready models. The foundation of Rhodes elevated Halios to the status of the first founder of the polis of the Rhodians, but this arrangement also left room for the eponymous founders of the original constituent poleis.[17] Inscriptions attest to the concern for inclusiveness. A treaty between Hierapytna and Rhodes from the beginning of the second century, for example, required that "the sacrificers [*hierothytai*] [of Hierapytna] pray to Halios and to Rhodos and to all the other gods and goddesses, and to the *archēgetai*, and to the heroes, as many as occupy the polis and the *chōra* of the Rhodians."[18] In this vein, the religious calendar of Kos set up after the synoikism of 366 in a corporate sanctuary of the Twelve Gods in Kos town, the new capital, took a similarly comprehensive approach to state sacrifices.[19] At Athens, the reforms of Kleisthenes, including the creation of the *eponymoi* for the ten tribes (selected from a list of one hundred names submitted to the Delphic oracle), and the elevation of Theseus achieved a similar centralization while leaving the old phratries, *genē*, and priesthoods intact.[20] Inclusive strategies such as these had the potential and the intent to obviate or even heal civil discord.[21]

17. Diod. Sic. 5.56.4; see also p. 170. A similar arrangement may have been struck at Mykonos, synoikized in the late third century, where a cult of the *archēgetēs* was created to promote an islandwide identity (*Syll.*³ 1024 = Sokolowski 1969, no. 96, with Reger 2001 and Constantakopoulou 2005).

18. *IC* III.3. 3A, ll. 2–5 = *Syll.*³ 581. This treaty likely followed the conclusion of a war between Rhodes, which clearly held the superior position, and Cretan cities (including Hierapytna).

19. *IG* XII 4.1 278 (*Syll.*³ 1025; Sokolowski 1969, no. 151; RO 62; Paul 2013, 382–83). The first preserved lines of this inscription have sometimes been restored (as in, e.g., RO 62 A, ll. 1–2) to stipulate that the Koans were to "pray to the gods brought into the other tribes just as to the other gods" ([- - - κα]ὶ εὔχο[ν]τ[αι] τοῖς ἐσαγμένοις ἐς ἄλλ[α]|[ς] φυλὰς [θ]ε[οῖ]ς καθάπερ τοῖς ἄλλ[οι]ς θεοῖς), but the editors of *IG* XII print only stray letters followed by καθάπερ τοὺς ἄλλ[ο]υς θεοὺς.

20. [Arist.], *Ath. Pol.* 21.6. On religious change and continuity after the Kleisthenic reforms, see Kearns 1985; Parker 1996, 102–21.

21. An illustrative example of this dimension, albeit in somewhat different circumstances, was the creation of the board of γενέτορες (mythical *oikistai* or *archēgetai*) of the city of Nakona in Sicily in the early third century after a period of strife in the polis. This religious reform was coupled with the institution of social groups called ἀδελφοὶ αἱρετοί, which were made up of five citizens each, determined by lot and excluding relatives. Thirty of these groups included two former political opponents and three other individuals. They apparently had no practical role in the city other than to build consensus and reconcile the citizens, who were required to participate in an annual festival in them, at which time the civic magistrates (*archai*) sacrificed to the *genetores* and to Homonoia (*SEG* XXX 119 = Lupu 2009, no. 26; see also Dössel 2003, 235–47; Eich 2004; Gray 2015, ch. 1). The Koan cult of Homonoia may have resulted from a *stasis* that led to the synoikism in 366: *IG* XII 4.1 280a–c = Sokolowski 1969, no. 169, l. 4 (cult calendar of the deme Isthmiotai [early second century]); see also Sherwin-White 1978, 329–30; Paul 2013, 145–50.

The most detailed case of this kind of accommodation can be found at Demetrias. From its inception, this foundation had a common cult of multiple city founders, focused on a shrine in the polis center, extending out into the former polis centers, now demes of Demetrias, and attested by several fragmentary inscriptions. The first example, an opisthographic stele from the vicinity of ancient Iolkos, recorded two important decrees of the *dēmos* of the Iolkians. The stone was broken down the center, preserving only about half of the document on each side. Ernst Meyer's text, though heavily supplemented, nevertheless provides the general sense of the resolutions:[22]

A

ἔδοξεν τῶι δήμωι τῶι Ἰωλκ[ίων - - - εἶπεν· ἐπειδὴ ὁ βα]-
σιλεὺς Ἀντίγονος ἔν τε τ[ῶι πρόσθεν χρόνωι ἀεὶ φανερὸς ἦν]
διαφυλάσσων τήν τε πρὸς τ[ὸν δῆμον προαίρεσιν καὶ τὴν πρὸς]
τοὺς αὐτοῦ προγόνους ε[ὐσέβειαν καὶ ἐπιμέλειαν ποιούμε]-
νος καὶ κοινῆι τῆς πόλεως [καὶ κατ' ἰδίαν τοῦ δήμου τοῦ Ἰωλ]-   5
κίων καὶ ἀναμιμνησκόμε[νος τούτων ἐνέτυχε τῶι δήμωι]
τοὺς ἀγῶνας ὁρμώμεν[ος συντελεῖν καθάπερ ὁ πατὴρ αὐ]-
τοῦ Δημήτριος θύσας [τὰς πατρίας θυσίας τῆι Ἀρτέμιδι]
καὶ τῆι Λητοῖ καὶ τῶι Ἀπόλλ[ωνι καὶ τοῖς ἄλλοις θεοῖς καὶ ἥ]-
ρωσι τοῖς κατέχουσι τὸν [δῆμον τῶν Ἰωλκίων ἔπαυσεν ἃ δια]-   10
[τ]ετέλεκεν κακὰ [πάσχων ὁ δῆμος - - - - - - - - - -]

The *dēmos* of the Iolk[ians resolved. - - - proposed: since Ki]ng Antigonos [was always conspicuous in former times in] maintaining [goodwill toward the people and reverence] for his ancestors and [taking care] both for the city in general [and in particular for the *dēmos* of Iol]kos and being mindful [of these things, he met with the *dēmos*], because he was eager [to celebrate] the *agones*, [just like his father,] Demetrios. Having made [the ancestral sacrifices for Artemis] and Leto and Apoll[o and the other gods and h]eroes who dwell among the [*dēmos* of the Iolkians, he stopped the things] which [the *dēmos* had] continually [suffered ...]

B

[- - - εἶπεν· ἔδοξεν τοῖς Ἰωλκί]οις· ἐπειδὴ τὰ μὲν κοινὰ
[τῶν ἀρχηγετῶν καὶ κτιστῶν ἱερὰ[23]] βραχέα ἐστίν, θυσίαι δὲ
[ἄλλαι οὐκέτι ποιοῦνται, κατ]ὰ τὰ πάτρια θύειν τὸν
[δῆμον τὸν Ἰωλκίων τοῖς ἀρχη]γέταις καὶ κτίσταις
[τοῦ δήμου[24], ὅπως μηδέν τι ἐκε]ῖθεν μήνισμα γίνηται   5
[τῆι πόλει ὀλιγωρουμένων τῶ]ν ἡρώων, ἀλλὰ ὑγιαίνον-

---

22. Ernst Meyer 1936; ed. pr. Arvanitopoulos 1929d, no. 425 (photos and squeezes); see also supplements of Béquignon 1935, 74–77. The stone is now lost.
23. Béquignon 1935, 75: χρήματα?
24. Béquignon 1935, 75: τῆς πολέως, referring to Demetrias rather than Iolkos.

[τες οἵ τε πολῖται καὶ οἱ ξένοι οἱ σ]υνοικοῦντες μετ' αὐτῶν
[τὸ λοιπὸν οἷοί τε ὦσιν τήν τε π]όλιν καὶ τὴν χώραν ἐπὶ τὸ
[βέλτιον συναύξειν τὰ δίκαια ποιοῦντες το]ῖς θεοῖ[ς]
[καὶ τοῖς ἥρωσιν - - -]   10

[- - - proposed: the Iolkians resolved]: since the common [rites of the *archēgetai* and *ktistai* are] infrequent and the [other] sacrifices [are no longer being performed, that the *dēmos* of the Iolkians], in accordance with the ancestral customs, sacrifice to the *archēgetai* and *ktistai* [of the *dēmos*, so that] there may be no wrath [in the city] because the heroes [are being slighted], but [both the citizens and the foreigners] living together with them, being sound in religious matters, [may be able in the future to join in increasing] the city and the land [for the better, by doing what is proper for the] gods [and the heroes . . .]

These resolutions, of course, do not explicitly identify the *archēgetai* and *ktistai* or indicate that the Macedonian kings were honored alongside the gods and heroes as founders. There can, however, be little doubt that this was the case, based on the documentation from other poleis (particularly the honors that Sikyon bestowed on Demetrios as its founder)[25] and Demetrios's clear role as the founder of Demetrias.[26] Further, Plutarch describes Antigonos Gonatas's theatrical conveyance of Demetrios's ashes to Demetrias for burial, possibly in the very sanctuary of the founders.[27] A similar cult building for Cassander in the heart of his eponymous foundation Kassandreia bolsters this interpretation.[28]

Despite their fragmentary state, these documents powerfully demonstrate the negotiation of religious authority between civic communities and king in the synoikized polis. Side A records an honorific decree for Antigonos Gonatas, praising him for caring for both Demetrias generally and specifically the *dēmos* of Iolkos. Its context seems to have been some period of political or economic difficulty (*kaka* [*paschōn ho dēmos*], l. 11) that had afflicted the Iolkians and disrupted the observance of some of their deme's rites. Antigonos put a stop to the trouble and restored the sacrifices to Artemis, Apollo, and Leto, the chief deities of Iolkos, and to all the Iolkian deities and heroes that inhabited the land of the *dēmos*. While Antigonos is honored for these actions, the initiative may have originated with the Iolkians, who here appeal to the privileges given to them to safeguard their cultic identity by Antigonos's father, Demetrios. Side B, however, may better reflect the interests of the king or at least the corporate religious life of Demetrias. It seems that along with the rites of the Iolkian cults, the *koina hiera* for the cult of the *archēgetai* and *ktistai* were infrequent and some of the sacrifices were no longer

---

25. Diod. Sic. 20.103.2.
26. For parallels, see Leschhorn 1984; Habicht 1970.
27. Plut., *Dem.* 53.3.
28. *SEG* XII 373, l. 15. For the eponymous priest of Cassander, see *Syll.*³ 332.

being observed. This decree explicitly raises concern for the wrath (*mēnisma*, l. 5, a hapax) that might result from the neglect of the heroes of Iolkos, perhaps drawing a causal connection between the cessation of observance of these rites and the recent evils the demos had suffered. Either way, the integrity and well-being of the polis and *chōra*, the document stresses, are dependent on the dutiful performance of these rites. Likewise, the king's status as the patron of the traditional cults of Iolkos and his investment in his own cult as founder were inextricable from the maintenance of local rites.

These decrees established a dialogue between the *dēmos* of the Iolkians and the king alone, in contrast to documents of the polis that spoke for all of the demes together. Their focus on the cults of Iolkos shows the power of such communities to continue to negotiate their local rites within the larger framework of a corporate cultic identity. The relationship between the centralized polis and its constituent communities allowed the demes to maintain clear, distinct cultic identities and to use the language of shared cultic bonds to appeal for concrete benefaction and aid from the central authority. Iolkos, in turn, was of symbolic importance to the origin of Demetrias. The cult of Artemis Iolkia, as we have seen (pp. 156–57, 175–77), was duplicated in the center of the agora, the images of Artemis and a ship's prow appeared on the civic coinage and were closely connected to the iconography of Demetrios Poliorketes himself, and Iolkos's heroic pedigree was of clear interest to the Macedonian kings. In this regard, it is possible that Iolkos held something of a privileged place in this kind of discourse. Still, continuity blends with change here as the maintenance of the innovative cult of the city's *archēgetai* and *ktistai* is couched in terms of a return to the ancestral customs of one of its communities (B, l. 3).

Another document attests a central sanctuary of the *archēgetai* and *ktistai*, administered by officials of Demetrias. The archons, officeholders, and financial officer (*ho epi tēs dioikēsōs*) of the polis oversaw religious ceremonies consisting of the sacrifice of an ox and ritual feasting, presided over by multiple priests perhaps corresponding to representatives of the *archēgetai* of the demes.[29] A monumental structure on the high hill 84 is a likely candidate for this sanctuary.[30] It consists of a large (37.5-by-150-meter, or 123-by-492-foot) rectangular platform on one of the most prominent hills of the city, overlooking the theater, the commercial agora, the harbor, and one of the main routes in, and is centrally located in the city plan. Moreover, there is a clear symbolic importance to the orientation of the sanctuary, sited in line above the royal palace and directly facing the peak of Mount Pelion. In

---

29. Kravaritou 2013, 260, notes that *hiereis* in a context such as this is a hapax for Thessaly, indicating the particular importance of the ceremony.

30. Arvanitopoulos (1928, 96) first excavated this structure and tentatively identified it as a sanctuary of Dionysos. For reinvestigations by German excavators, see Marzolff 1987; 1996b.

the center of the platform was a rectangular monument, 16.08 by 10.72 meters (52.76 by 35.17 feet), of uncertain plan. There is an underground cavity that was built into the platform below the monument, interpreted as either a bothros (offering pit) or a burial chamber. Nearby, F. Stählin found a number of fine architectural fragments of Parian marble, probably originating from the monument, including two sculptural fragments of, respectively, a lion and a deer, decorative motifs that also appear on monumental funerary architecture in Asia Minor.[31] It seems clear that the monument was never completed, though this does not necessarily mean that it was never in use: at least one (fragmentary) inscription was set up there, and a coin and some Hellenistic plainware have been recovered from the site.[32] The positioning and significant similarities to other known mausolea make it likely that this was the sanctuary of the *archēgetai* and *ktistai* and the tomb-heroön of Demetrios Poliorketes.

If this identification is correct, this must be where the document regulating the religious ceremonies for the cult of the *archēgetai* and *ktistai* mentioned above was to be published. The text provides helpful insights into the character of the cult, decreeing:

ἐπιμελεῖσθαι τοὺς ἄρχοντας [.]ΑΙΤ[......]
ΝΟΜΟ[....] τὸ δὲ ἀνά]λωμα τὸ [εἰς] τὸν βοῦ[ν]
[δ]ιδόναι τὸ[ν] τ[αμ]ίαν [ἀεὶ] τὸν ἐπὶ τῆ[ς διοι]-
[κ]ή[σ]ε[ως] ὄντα. [τῆς δὲ λ]ο[ιπ]ῆς θυσίας ἐ[πι]-
[μελεῖ]σθαι τούς τε ἱερεῖς καὶ τοὺς ἐν τοῖς   25
[ἀ]ρχείοις ὄντας. τὴν δὲ ἐπιμέλειαν τῆ[ς]
ἑστιάσεως ποιεῖσθαι τοὺς ἄρχοντας·
[ἵ]να δὲ τούτων συντελουμένων ἦι ὑπό-
μνημα τῆι πόλει τῆς πρὸς τοὺς ἀρχηγέ[έ]-
τα[ς] καὶ κτίστας εὐσεβείας, ἀναγράψαι   30
τόδε τὸ ψήφισ[μα τοὺς ἄρχο]ντας εἰς στή-
λην λιθίνη[ν καὶ ἀναστῆσαι ἐν τῶι ἱερ]ῶι
τῶν ἀρχηγ[ετῶν. *vacat*]

Let the archons see to it that . . . let the treasurer in charge of administration on that occasion [always] provide the expense for the ox . . . and let the priests and those holding office take care of the rest of the sacrifice, and let the archons take care of the feast. In order that, since these things are being carried out, there be a record for the polis of the piety toward the *archēgetai* and *ktistai*, let the archons publish this present decree on a stone stele [and set it up in the sanctuary] of the *archēgetai*. . . .[33]

---

31. Marzolff 1987; 1996b, plate 21.
32. Marzolff 1987, 26–35.
33. Wilhelm 1909, 150–51 (slightly improved text of *IG* IX 2 1099b).

This document was found not in Demetrias but in the modern village of Kanalia near Lake Boibe (Karla), the site of ancient Glaphyrai or Boibe, one of the northernmost demes of Demetrias and some twenty kilometers (twelve miles) from its city center.³⁴ Nearby is the putative site of the acropolis of the former polis, where early travelers described the remains of a monumental building.³⁵ The findspot admits three possible scenarios: either this was a *pierre errante* that found its way from its original site of publication in Demetrias to Kanalia;³⁶ multiple copies of this decree of Demetrias were made and disseminated to all of the demes; or it was a decree of the deme itself.³⁷ M. Mezières, before this inscription was known, thought that the remains were those of the heroön of the hero-founder of Boibe (the eponymous Boibos), and Stählin, accepting this hypothesis, suggested that the decree is a copy disseminated from Demetrias and set up in the sanctuary of the local hero, where sacrifices took place on the same day as the centralized rites of the *archēgetai* and *ktistai*.³⁸ The importance of the officials named in the decree points to the fact that this ritual was a centerpiece of the religious life of Demetrias. Taken with the decrees from Iolkos, this document demonstrates the degree to which a corporate cult of hero-founders could be used as an instrument of unity, emanating from a central shrine in the polis center, including all of the *archēgetai* of the traditional communities, and placing the kings alongside them.

Though less well understood, similar arrangements appear to have been common in the multipolis synoikisms of the early Hellenistic kings. A decree of Kassandreia, dating to 242, confirming the *asylia* of the sanctuary of Asklepios on Kos, and accepting an invitation to participate in the Asklepieia (in response to requests of Koan *theōroi*), resolves that "the treasurer give hospitality to the [*theōroi*] when they are present, in accordance with the customary arrangement, and invite them also to the *archēgeteion*."³⁹ This was evidently a prominent public building dedicated to the cult of the founder(s), likely the combined founders of Poteidaia, Olynthos, Mende, and the other Chalkidian cities in the synoikism, along with the Macedonian kings.⁴⁰ This sanctuary would have served as the civic and sacral

---

34. Wace 1906, 162.
35. Mezières 1854, 198–99; see also Leake 1835, 4:430; Georgiades 1894, 130; Stählin 1924, 61.
36. Rejected by Stählin (1929, 208).
37. Graninger (2011b) argues that the disclosure formula suggests that this is a decree of Glaphyrai, like the resolutions of Iolkos (pp. 190–92). Cf. Kravaritou 2013, 262–67, with no firm conclusion.
38. Mezières 1854, 198–99; Stählin 1929, 208.
39. *SEG* XII 373, ll. 14–15: δοῦναι δὲ τὸν ταμίαν τοῖς παραγεγενημένοις ξένιον τὸ διάταγμα τὸ | ἐκ τοῦ νόμου · καλέσαι δὲ αὐτοὺς καὶ εἰς τὸ ἀρχηγέτειον.
40. So *BÉ* 66.152 (J. Robert and L. Robert); Alexander 1963, 131. Elsewhere we hear of *heroa* dedicated specifically to the cult of the king, such as the Lysimacheion at Lysimacheia (App., *Syr.* 64) or the Nikatoreion at Seleukeia Pieria (App., *Syr.* 63). Cf. Leschhorn 1984, 252–57; Habicht 1970, 140n12.

center of Kassandreia, much like the prytaneion in other Greek poleis.[41] The dating formulae at the head of a series of documents from a public building in Kassandreia also indicates that the city had an eponymous priest of the cult of the combined founders at the time of its foundation.[42]

There is no direct evidence for a centralized cult of the founder(s) in Thessalonike, but there may be some indication of how the synoikism accommodated the oikist cults of its original communities. Livy, following Polybios, relates the story of how Theoxena and her husband Poris, called "by far the leading man of the gens of the Aineians [gentis Aenianum]"[43] but evidently a citizen of Thessalonike, attempted to escape the wrath of King Philip V in the late 180s. In describing their flight, Livy records the following: "They set out from Thessalonike to Aineia to an appointed sacrifice that they [the Aineians] make every year to Aineias, their founder, with elaborate ceremony. Having spent a day there in the ritual feasts, when all were asleep, at about the third watch they went aboard a ship made ready in advance by Poris, as if to return to Thessalonike, but their intention was to cross over into Euboia."[44] (Poris's ruse ultimately failed, and he and Theoxena committed suicide as the king's agents closed in.) This passage is highly suggestive of the relationship between Aineia and Thessalonike and the role of the cult of Aineias. As we have seen, the literary sources indicate that Aineia was incorporated into Thessalonike at the time of Cassander's synoikism in 316/15, yet several sources attest the persistence of a settlement of some kind at the site of Aineia.[45] It seems that this

41. Alexander 1963, 131. In the same inscription, the Koan *theōroi* are indeed invited to the prytaneion at Philippoi (l. 51).

42. *Syll.*³ 332, l. 1: ἐφ' ἱερέως Κυδία (land grant of Kassander to Perdikkas); Vokotopoulou 1997 = *SEG* XLVII 940, l. 1: ἐπὶ Κυδία (grant of *ateleia* from Kassander to Chairephanes). Findspot: Vokotopoulou 1997, 40–44. See also Habicht 1970, 140; Alexander 1963, 128. An honorary decree likely from Kassandreia, dated by an eponymous priest (ἐφ' ἱερέως Ἄρχωνος), is attested ca. 250–200 (*SEG* XXXVII 558 [Robinson 1938, 55–56, no. 8; Hatzopoulos 1988, 26–28]). Two honorary decrees from the final years of the reign of Antigonos Gonatas are also dated by an eponymous priest (Εφ' ἱερέως Ἀντιλέ|οντος; see Hatzopoulos 1990, 136–48 = *SEG* XXXIX 595–96). Hatzopoulos (Hatzopoulos 1988, 21–29) argues that the eponymous priesthood of Kassandreia was transferred from the priest of all the founders to the priest of Lysimachos (on the basis of *Syll.*³ 380, ll. 1–2: ἐφ' ἱερέως τοῦ Λυσιμάχου | Τιμησίου) and finally to the priest of Asklepios, in conformity with other cities of Macedonia.

43. Livy 40.4.4. There is a textual issue here. *Aenianum* should refer to the Ainianes, a people of central Greece who inhabited the Sperchios valley, but clearly the polis of Aineia in the Chalkidike is meant. See Briscoe 2008, 419–22.

44. Livy 40.4.9–10: "proficiscuntur ab Thessalonica Aeneam ad statum sacrificium, quod Aeneae conditori cum magna caerimonia quotannis faciunt. Ibi die per sollemnes epulas consumpto navem praeparatam a Poride sopitis omnibus de tertia vigilia conscendunt tamquam redituri Thessalonicam: sed traicere in Euboeam erat propositum."

45. Synoikism: Dion. Hal., *Ant. Rom.* 1.49.4–5; Strabo 7F21, 7F24. For the archaeological evidence, see ch. 1. In addition to this passage, Livy mentions Aineia at 44.10.7, 44.32.8, and 45.30.4, all in the context of the Third Macedonian War. It is also attested on the *theōrodokoi* list: Plassart 1921, 18, col. 3, l. 75 (230–210).

polis, while reduced by the synoikism, still functioned as a semi-independent community (its harbor in particular may have remained significant), though subordinate to Thessalonike. Nevertheless, the cult of its founder, the illustrious Aineias, and the associated cult of Aphrodite continued to be central to the Aineians, whether living in Aineia or Thessalonike.[46] This festival in celebration of the original *ktistēs*, possibly held at the tomb of Aineias or the temple of Aphrodite, marks the clear importance of incorporating the founder-heroes of the constituent communities into the religious life of Thessalonike. The ritual feast symbolically bound the protective gods of Aineia to the city and reenacted the union of this community with the others in the synoikism of Thessalonike.[47]

Heroic cult for city founders had undergone a long evolution by the Hellenistic period, extending from the often shadowy figures of the archaic age to more recent historical founders, like Hagnon and Brasidas at Amphipolis. Even eponymous foundations were hardly a novelty by that time.[48] The extension of the heroic cult of the oikist to the Hellenistic dynasts was therefore natural and well suited to its dynamism and flexibility. While this was a distinctive and significant phenomenon, it is important not to lay undue stress on its novelty. Sikyon serves as a convenient example. The mythical founder was the eponymous Sikyon, who replaced the earlier toponym Aigiale/Aigialeia and its founder, Aigialeus.[49] The Sikyonians had no problem according heroic honors as a second founder to Euphron, the "tyrant" who orchestrated a democratic coup there and was hailed as the *archēgetēs* at his death in 366 and buried in the city's agora.[50] Demetrios Poliorketes accordingly fit quite comfortably into the layers of foundation when he moved the polis center to a more defensible site in 302, thus earning divine honors: the Sikyonians renamed their polis Demetrias and voted to celebrate yearly sacrifices, festivals, and games for him and accord him "the other honors" due to a founder.[51] Later, Aratos of Sikyon was declared an *oikistēs* and *sōter* of the polis and buried in its new agora.[52] Indeed, many of the poleis refounded in the Hellenistic period had

---

46. According to Dion. Hal., *Ant. Rom.* 1.49.1, Hegesianax of Alexandreia Troas (a.k.a. Kephalon of Gergis), in his history of the Troad, claimed that Aineias founded Aineia (*FGrH* 45 F7), as did Hegesippos of Mekyberna in the Chalkidike in his history of the Pallene (*FGrH* 391 F5). There was certainly a tomb of Anchises in the area of Aineia: Steph. Byz., s.v. Ἀίνεια; Konon, *FGrH* 26 F1 46; schol. on Lycoph. 1236. See also Erskine 2001, 93–98.

47. See the Roman-period funerary stele from Thessalonike of a fish seller who was a member of an association dedicated to the hero Aineias (Nigdelis 2006, 206–11, no. 15 = *SEG* LVI 766).

48. See Malkin 1985 for the precedents for eponymous foundations before Phillip II.

49. Hes., *Cat.* 73; Paus. 2.6.5, 2.5.6. See also Strabo 8.6.25.

50. Xen., *Hell.* 7.3.4–12.

51. Diod. Sic. 20.102.2–3.

52. Plut., *Aratus* 53.2–4; Paus. 2.9.4. See also Leschhorn 1984, 178–79.

already experienced the interventionist hand of powerful hegemons in the previous centuries. Following the celebrated cases of Themistokles, Miltiades, Hagnon, Brasidas, and Thibron, a number of communities granted heroic honors to tyrants and other powerful leaders in the fourth century.[53]

The flexible attitute toward oikists allowed conceptual space for multiple layers of foundation, plural founders, and the incorporation of the founders of absorbed communities. This meant that the presentation of the foundation of these cities entailed choices.[54] Such malleability also had the potential to open room for contesting the honors associated with certain founders as a mode of reinvention or resistance. In other words, these honors depended on the political will of the constituent communities to celebrate them. As Diodoros famously noted, time nullified the honors accorded to Demetrios at Sikyon.[55] Dynastic names of cities were often lost, particularly where they were applied to ancient communities with long traditions (e.g., Ephesos, Smyrna, Sikyon), but many others survived to the end of their history (e.g., Demetrias, Thessalonike, Kassandreia). Some communities produced alternative narratives that effectively eclipsed their historic founders. Smyrna shook off its *epiklesis* Eurydikeia and claimed to have been reconstituted by Alexander rather than Antigonos or Lysimachos.[56] The romantic story of Alexander's inspired dream outside the temple of the Nemeseis on the slopes of Mount Pagos which led him to refound Smyrna commands little credence, but it does point to a conscious choice by the Smyrnaeans to recast the account of their city's foundation. Herakleia Latmos reverted to that name after the death of Pleistarchos and celebrated Endymion, who was worshiped in a cave on Latmos and in the city, as its founder.[57] Antigonos founded an Antigoneia from a settlement originally known as Angkore; Lysmiachos refounded it as Nikaia, after his wife. Rival traditions that removed the historical founders from the narrative later arose, however. There were claims that Herakles or Dionysos founded the city and that Dionysos

---

53. See, e.g., Boehm 2015 for the transfer of the heroic cult of the tyrant Alexander of Pherai from Pagasai to Demetrias.

54. For the evolution of foundation myths in Greek and Roman Asia Minor, see Strubbe 1984; Weiss 1984.

55. Diod. Sic. 20.102.3. The name Demetrias seems to have fallen out of use just months after the city's refoundation in 302 (*Staatsvert.* III.445; for the date see Lolos 2011, 72–73). (Of course, Diodoros, and presumably the Sikyonians, had hardly forgotten Demetrios's role in its refoundation.) But note the long life in antiquarian circles at least of the toponym Demetrias, which, as G. Cohen points out (1995, 128), the Byzantine historian Nikephoros Gregoras was still using to refer to Sikyon in the fourteenth century (*Hist. Byz.* 4.9).

56. Paus. 7.5.1–3; Aristides, *Orat.* 20.5, 20.7, 20.20, 21.4, 21.20; Pliny, *HN* 5.118. Cadoux 1938, 94–97, however, is sanguine that there is a core of truth to the tradition that Alexander refounded Smyrna.

57. *SGO* 1.23.1, l. 6 (lyric hymn for the festival of Athena Latmia). Worship of Endymion: Strabo 14.1.8; Paus. 5.1.5; Peschlow-Bindokat 1996b, 29–43.

named it after the nymph Nikaia.[58] Alternative traditions connected its origins directly to Macedonian veterans of Alexander's campaigns, and Alexander himself appears on some Nikaian coins of the imperial period.[59]

In presenting their civic identity, communities in synoikisms made choices based on the history available to them. The political dimensions of such decisions are evident, but if the malleability afforded by this practice could lead to the rejection or elision of founders, it could also uniquely accomodate change. This flexibility frequently ensured the long remembrance of founders who were deeply, and ritually, embedded in the communities they had formed. We can clearly recover the agency of constituent communitites in their founder cults, even when the Hellenistic kings began to use these powerful tools for asserting the unity of a community to their own ends.

SOCIAL ORGANIZATION, COMMUNAL CUSTOMS, AND ETHNICITY

In redrawing political boundaries, imperial states had far-reaching impacts on social organization and ethnic identity. They amalgamated communities across traditional lines and divided social groups with common ties.[60] The new borders could have purposeful effects and unintended results. A famous example of the former is seen in Rome's partitioning of Macedonia into four districts (*merides*) at the conclusion of the Third Macedonian War in 168 BCE, with juridical rights like intermarriage and political and economic activity forbidden across these artificial lines.[61] The intent, under the familiar pretext of securing "the freedom of the Greeks," was to divide the Macedonian ethnos to ensure that it would never again be able to threaten Rome through coordinated action; notably, however, this policy sparked resistance and rebellion and was ultimately rescinded. The impact of Macedonian policy in the early Hellenistic period, however, largely moved in the opposite direction: synoikism cut across political, ethnic, and cultural lines to amalgamate distinct populations into a single political community. The process

---

58. Herakles as *ktistēs*: Waddington, Babelon, and Reinach 1908, vol. 1, nos. 56–58, 108; Dio. Chrys. 39.8. Dionysos as *ktistēs*: Waddington, Babelon, and Reinach 1908, vol. 1, nos. 44, 54–55, 219. Dionysos and Nikaia as *ktistai*: Waddington et al. 1908, vol. 1, no. 819; See also L. Robert 1977, 11–15.

59. Memnon (*FGrH* 434 F41) claims that veterans from Nikai in Lokris founded Nikaia. Steph. Byz., s.v. Νικαία, says that it was a colony of Bottiaia; Tscherikower (1927, 47) considered it possible that the Bottiaians mentioned by Stephanos were veterans of Antigonos's army. Coins displaying Alexander: Head 1911, 517.

60. For general observations on the impact of empire on ethnicity, see Derks and Roymans 2009. For one example, a detailed treatment of early Roman Batavia, see Roymans 2004.

61. Livy 45.29.

obliterated traditional touchstones of social identity, principally through the elimination of the city ethnic (ethnikon), but also at times blurred higher levels of cultural and ethnic identity, grouping populations across macroethnic divisions such as Aeolians/Ionians (as at Antigoneia Troas) or Thessalians/Magnesians (Demetrias) or even broader ethnic and cultural divisions, such as Greek/Macedonian/Thracian (Thessalonike, Kassandreia) or Greek/Anatolian (the cities of inland Asia Minor). At the same time, a number of ethnic leagues were formed or revived in this period, as direct initiatives of the kings. Synoikism necessitated the integration of diverse traditions and interests, creation of new systems of social organization (tribes, demes, other civic subdivisions), establishment of institutions (*nomima*) of the polis (calendars, months, coinage, cults, etc.), and addressing of potential sources of conflict between interest groups. Imperial reorganization was thus one of the many dynamic forces that shaped social groupings and ethnic constructs in the early Hellenistic period.[62] Much as we saw in the negotiation of foundation traditions and narratives (previous section), the evidence shows a flexible approach to creating the political basis of new cities, with both centralized efforts by royal officials and long-standing local traditions and interests playing their part.

Tribal reform, which reorganized people and vectors of belonging, was a typical means of introducing social and political change in the Greek world. The synoikism of Argos, for example, incorporated populations of the Argive plain through a redefinition of the city's tribes:[63] at that point, probably in the middle of the fifth century, the three existing Dorian tribes were augmented by a fourth.[64] Athens, the prototype of the synoikized polis, managed its civic integration and democratic reform by finding a balance between the maintenance of markers of local belonging and political unity. Kleisthenes's reforms specifically did not make physical residence a requirement for enrollment in a deme, and the cross-cutting civic subdivisions of *phylē* and *trittys* further disassociated civic identity from location. This system, in other words, was designed to reduce conflict based on local associations and allegiances.[65] Rhodes enacted wholesale tribal reform after its synoikism, retaining its three old poleis (Ialysos, Kameiros, and Lindos) as territorial *phylai* but subdividing them into a number of territorial demes on the mainland and in the *peraia*.[66] Thus, the state maintained territorial divisions and measures of local

---

62. For the ways in which Greek ethnic identity could be adjusted to respond to new social circumstances, see Hall 1997; 2002. For important methodological comments, see Morgan 2009; see also Malkin 2001.
63. Moggi 1974; M. Piérart 2000.
64. Ephoros, *FGrH* 70 F15; *IG* IV 487–88 (late fourth or early third century) = *SEG* XI 293.
65. See Anderson 2003 for a detailed treatment of the integration of Attica in the fifth century.
66. N. Jones 1987, 243–53; Papachristodoulou 1999.

autonomy even as it unified around the new capital city, the polis of Rhodos, and a centralized priesthood of Halios. This eponymous priesthood was held in rotation by each of the three groupings of demes (which corresponded to the three tribes, Ialysia, Kameiris, Lindia) for three-year periods.[67] Not everything promoted unity, though: alongside this shared highest office, the state hosted festivals at which the tribes competed in a series of athletic, poetic, and musical contests.[68] At Kos, synoikized in 366/65, the traditional three Dorian tribes were introduced as the fundamental divisions of the state, further subdivided into *chiliastyes* (or *enatai*). Cutting across these divisions were the demes, some of which were old poleis (for instance, Isthmiotai was the former Astypalaia). Local non-Dorian tribes also persisted in the demes. Two concurrent tribal systems in one polis is unlikely, so the Dorian one was probably introduced with the synoikism on an islandwide scale, accounting for the presence of both this schema and some holdovers.[69] All of these synoikisms saw the application of similar strategies that responded to local conditions. Nevertheless, tensions between centralized political power and local autonomy still surfaced. At Kos, Astypalaia in particular seems to have expressed resentment at the union.[70]

The natural strains of political unification and social redefinition were exacerbated in situations where broad cultural or ethnic divisions separated the constituent parts of the state. In the case of Thourioi, as we have seen (pp. 187–88), the ethnic diversity of this joint foundation soon sparked stasis and disagreement over the identification of the colony's founder: the former Sybarites, who had originally inhabited the area, held on to the best civic offices, religious honors, and land for themselves, at the expense of the city's other participants. The Sybarites were ultimately put to death, and in the aftermath of this civil discord, unity was achieved by drafting a new constitution and other laws, as well as reassigning land and space for housing within the *asty* on egalitarian principles. Division was still the rule, however, as four broad avenues (*plateiai*) running its length and three running its width partitioned the city,[71] in which each citizen group was assigned to a quarter and tribe, broadly based on origin (Achaian, Amphiktyonian, Arkadian, Athenian, Boiotian, Dorian, Eleian, Euboian, Ionian, or Islander).[72] Thourioi was an extreme case, but across all these instances of synoikism and joint foundation we can detect the common issue of balancing unity with autonomy and innovation with tradition. Territorial continuity was one approach: in such schemes, the syn-

---

67. Badoud 2015, 137–99.
68. Pugliese Carratelli 1953.
69. Sherwin-White 1978, 153–74; N. Jones 1987, 236–42.
70. Sherwin-White 1978, ch. 4.
71. The avenues were, significantly, named after divinities: Herakleia, Aphrodisia, Olympias, Dionysias, Heroa, Thuria, and Thurina (Diod Sic. 12.10.7).
72. Diod. Sic. 12.11.

oikized state had an overarching political structure but civic subdivisions preserved a degree of the original organization.

In the large synoikisms of the Hellenistic age too, centralized innovation blended with tradition to create the institutions of the polis, which were intended to broker the competing interests and identities of these multiethnic polities. The most basic necessity was the organization of the citizen body and the integration of the constituent communities. In Ephesos (and similar places), where an existing large polis formed the core of the union, the institutions of that city inevitably dominated, and the product was less an amalgamation of institutions of various constituencies than an integration of the populations of the other cities (Kolophon, Lebedos, Phygela). Ephesos's expansion had the added advantage of drawing exclusively on other Ionian communities, with common traditions and a history of cooperation (though also competition) in the Ionian League. Still, Kolophon and Lebedos ultimately broke from the synoikism—Kolophon soon after and Lebedos a good deal later, probably in the aftermath of the Ptolemaic conquest of southern Ionia during the Third Syrian War (246–241), when it was renamed Ptolemais (see pp. 74–76). But it is likely that some of the citizens of Kolophon remained in Ephesos, and even more probable that numerous Lebedians, who were blended with the Ephesian citizen body after several generations, did not leave. It seems that the Lebedians were originally incorporated into Ephesos all together, as a tribal subdivision (*chiliasty,* "group of a thousand") named Lebedioi.[73] Still, because new citizens were assigned to tribe and *chiliasty* by lot, even if the Lebedians initially formed a single subdivision, the boundaries with others could blur over time. It may rather have been that the Lebedioi *chiliasty* simply commemorated the incorporation of these people, much as the tribe Tēioi recalled the mythical settlement of citizens from Teos, and it remained part of the organization of Ephesos even after Lebedos was refounded as Ptolemais and reemerged as Lebedos still later. The integration of Ephesos was difficult, and as we will see below (pp. 220–21), a ritual celebration focusing on civic unity seems to have been developed in response.

The blending of numerous communities in the more diverse synoikisms required fundamental change, but even in these situations, certain communal traditions were inherited. In Kassandreia, for example, the epigraphic sources preserve the names of two divisions of the citizen body: *Hippotadeis* (a *genos* or a deme), derived from the Herakleid Hippotes, the father of Aletes the founder of Corinth, and *Hippolyteus,* referring to Hipplytos the son of Theseus, also

---

73. Engelmann 1996. This arrangement parallels the new, apparently territorial subdivision (the *pentekostys*) of Argos in the fourth century, which was added to the civic body's tribe-phratry structure after the absorption of the polis Kleonai (*SEG* XXX 355, l. 3 [330–300]).

connected to the Doric Peloponnese, especially Troezen.[74] Corinth was the metropolis of Poteidaia, the polis on which Kassandreia was founded and from which a substantial portion of its population came. In Thessalonike, we know of four tribes: Antigonis, Asklepias, Gnaïas, and Dionysias.[75] Gnaïas is of Roman date,[76] but the other three seem to reflect the city's organization at the time of Antigonos Gonatas (r. 277–239).[77] Antigonis, of course, commemorates the Antigonid house, specifically Antigonos Gonatas. Asklepias reflects the importance of Asklepios to the cities of Macedonia, while Dionysias points to the centrality of that deity, whose cult, as we have seen, was of long-standing significance to the region before becoming a state cult of Thessalonike.

Within certain synoikisms, some large constituent communities seem to have maintained a kind of discrete existence, as part of the social organization or as dependent poleis. As we have seen (pp. 195–96), Livy could still refer to a citizen of Thessalonike in the reign of Philip V who originated from the constituent community of Aineia as belonging to "the gens of the Aineians."[78] The best example of the organization of a synoikized polis incorporating but preserving local identities and (to some degree) territorial divisions is Demetrias, which was composed of demes or villages (*kōmai*) corresponding to the original poleis and whose decrees include these old ethnika as demotics.[79] Some of these poleis, as we saw in chapter 1, were abandoned and had their populations entirely absorbed by the city, in particular Thessalian Pagasai and Amphanai. Others, however, persisted as discrete sites within the *chōra* of Demetrias, though there was certainly population movement to the center of the polis from them as well. At least two of these demes issued decrees on their own.[80] Thus, a strong degree of territorial continuity and autonomy persisted alongside unification. When the Magnesian League was created, after the region's liberation from Macedonian rule, it subsumed the organizational scheme of Demetrias.[81] For example, the same individual, Menandros son of Nikon, a *stratēgos* of the Magnesian League, appears with the ethnikon Demetrieus in a decree of the *koinon* and simply with the *dēmotikon*

---

74. Hippotadeis: *SEG* XLVII 940; Hippolyteus: *SEG* XXIX 600. Hippolyteus may also have been connected to the cult of Poseidon in Poteideia, later a central cult of Kassandreia (Ernst Meyer 1965).

75. N. Jones 1987, 267–68.

76. *IG* X 2 1 278. Brocke (2001, 160) has argued convincingly that this tribe was named for Cn. Egnatius, the proconsul responsible for the construction of the Via Egnatia, rather than for Pompey, as suggested by Touratsoglou (1988, 6n9).

77. Edson 1948; Brocke 2001, 159–60.

78. Livy 40.4.4.

79. E.g., Pagasitēs, Iolkios, Aioleus, Spalauthreus, Koropaios, Homolieus (*IG* IX 2 1109), Amphanaios (Arvanitopoulos 1929b, no. 423).

80. Iolkos (Ernst Meyer 1936) and Spalauthra (*IG* IX 2 1111). See ch. 1.

81. For the chronology of the inscriptions of Demetrias and the Magnesian League, see Stählin 1929; for observations on the league's organization, Intzesiloglou 1996.

Koropaios in a decree of the city.[82] The ethnic Demetrieus never appears in civic decrees (and rarely in funeral epitaphs), which either mark citizens by their demotic or do not give them any designation beyond name. Yet there is no other Magnesian city ethnic in the (extant) federal decrees. *Magnēs* (Magnesian), however, does appear as an overarching designation in several *koinon* decrees and even in private dedications before the league's creation.[83] Demetrias, therefore, despite its complicated history as an amalgamation of Thessalian and Magnesian communities, seems to have advertised a single ethnic identity. There were levels of belonging, however, and its citizens could identify themselves by their demotic, by their city ethnic, or more broadly as Magnesians.[84]

Stratonikeia in Karia, a Seleukid foundation that synoikized a number of Karian villages along with a Macedonian contingent, was organized in a similar way. It was divided into tribes, about which little is known, subdivided into demes that corresponded to the old Karian villages, and in some cases further divided into *koina*, which coincided with smaller units that predated the synoikism.[85] This had the advantage of preserving levels of distinction and local prerogatives within the state. The alternative was to attempt to extinguish any previous distinctions between citizens. In this vein, when the Karian satrap Asandros merged the communities of Latmos and Pidasa into the new polis Herakleia, he introduced an eponymous tribe, Asandris, in which both Latmians and Pidasians were to be enrolled, and the document describing the union mandated exclusive intermarriage between these two groups for six years, specifically to eliminate the distinctions between them.[86] It is instructive, of course, that this unification failed: the Pidasians ultimately withdrew and reconstituted themselves.

Ethnic leagues, as we have seen, like synoikisms, emerged as a direct consequence of Macedonian policy. In many cases they were simply the revival, with some innovation, of a formerly existing federation (the Ionian League, the Euboian League). Others were entirely novel. A particularly notable example is the *koinon* of Achaia Phthiotis, almost certainly created by Demetrios Poliorketes at the time of his refoundations of Halos and Peuma. This league built on the elevation of these cities to more substantial and defensible entities, seemingly part of an

---

82. *IG* IX 2 1103, l. 110.

83. *IG* IX 2 1104, l. 36, 1103, l. 1; Arvanitopoulos 1949, 90, no. 270 (294–168): Μουσὶς Φιλιάρχου | Γομφίτις | Πρωτεσίλαος | Πρωτίωνος Μάγνης; Moretti 1976, 90, no. 270, ll. 6–7 (see next note).

84. In one case, a citizen of Demetrias also identified himself as a Magnesian before the creation of the Magnesian League (Moretti 1976, no. 107, ll. 6–7): Μάγνης δὲ δόμος καὶ πατρὶς ἔπολβος | ἡ Δημητριέων (Magnesia my home and my prosperous *patris* Demetrias).

85. Şahin 1976; N. Jones 1987, 335–36; van Bremen 2000. The *asty* also had a military organization, based on residence in the *amphoda* (wards): *I. Stratonikeia* 1004.

86. *SEG* XLVII 1563 (Blümel 1997; C. Jones 1999; Wörrle 2003a; LaBuff 2016, 79–84). See also pp. 48–50.

Antigonid strategy to construct a permanent home for the Achaian *ethnos*, now free from centuries of Thessalian rule.[87] At the same time, however, although the synoikism of much of Magnesia into Demetrias increased the region's prestige and created a powerful Magnesian city free of its historical Thessalian domination, Macedonian rule spelled the demise of Magnesia's independent role in the Amphiktyonic League after its reorganization in 279, and no ethnic league of Magnesians was created until after the period of Macedonian suzerainty. In the Troad, in the other major league created by the kings, the *koinon* of Athena Ilias, a different strategy can perhaps be detected. This *koinon* centered on the shared cult of Athena, not ethnicity, and incorporated the largely Aiolian populations of the Troad but also Ionian cities like Skepsis and Ionian cities of the Propontis like Parion and Lampsakos.

Social organization was of course of primary importance, but other institutions, traditions, and cultural markers also played significant roles in defining the contours of new civic identity. The synoikized poleis frequently inherited or assumed *nomima* from their constituent communities. The evidence is particularly rich in the realm of cult (as the previous chapter shows), but there are also indications of a variety of other adaptations. Coinage, the most widely disseminated badge of civic identity, became a prime medium for carrying the traditions of the incorporated communities into the synoikized polis. Alexandreia Troas, for example, used the civic emblems of Neandreia, perhaps the most significant contributor to the union, on obverses (Apollo) and reverses (grazing horse) soon after its foundation by Lysimachos.[88] Later, in all likelihood after 188, when Hamaxitos and the sanctuary of Apollo Smintheus were incorporated into the city, it issued a series of coin types taken from those of Hamaxitos. Alexandreia thus incorporated and advertised the traditions of this newly acquired and prestigious community and its cult, in addition to using the sanctuary of Apollo as the primary location for displaying civic decrees.[89] In the same way, the coinage of Demetrias directly imitated that of the incorporated city Iolkos, making iconographic reference to the cult of Artemis Iolkia (goddess on the obverse), one of the most significant of the region, and the myth of Jason and the voyage of the *Argo* (ship's prow on the reverse).[90] The reverse image doubled as a reflection of Antigonid naval hegemony and victory at sea, reinforced by royal issues of Demetrios displaying the goddess Nike alighting on a ship's prow.[91] Later authors even shifted the mythological setting of the construction and departure of the *Argo* from Iolkos/Pagasai to Demetrias, and it should come as no sur-

87. Chykerda, Haagsma, and Surtees 2015; Surtees, Karapanou, and Haagsma 2014. See Hall 2015 for a discussion of ethnicity and federalism.
88. Meadows 2004.
89. Coin types: Head 1911, 540–41; chronology: Meadows 2004.
90. Coinage of Iolkos: Liampi 2005; of Demetrias: Mørkholm 1991, 77–80.
91. Franke 1967; Furtwängler and Kron 1978; Furtwängler and Kron 1983; Mørkholm 1991, 77–80.

prise that the city actively absorbed and proclaimed this heritage.[92] Another particularly remarkable example of inherited traditions comes from Amastris in Paphlagonia, synoikized from the cities of Teion, Kromna, Kytoros, and Sesamos circa 302. Kromna, which was on a river called Meles, apparently claimed to be the birthplace of the "Meles-born" Homer,[93] appropriating the title of the more famous, homonymous river near Smyrna. By the imperial period, the coinage of Amastris was prominently advertising this inherited distinction, with Homer on the obverse and the river god Meles on the reverse.[94] But influence could work in the opposite direction as well. Teion, which revolted and reconstituted itself almost immediately, nevertheless retained traces of the tribal organization of Amastris, *nomima* that were relics of the temporary union.[95]

Yet alongside these markers of tradition and continuity were numerous innovations and signs of the direct application of royal authority. The naming of tribes after monarchs, for example, was a common commemorative strategy in cities under Macedonian rule (e.g., Latmos under Asandros), refounded or not, and signaled a clear integration of royal presence into civic norms.[96] Also instructive are the commonalities in the *nomima* of a number of communities founded by the kings. For example, the civic calendars of Kassandreia, Demetrias, and Philippoi all demonstrate that their months were eponymous with the twelve gods, and these cities had councils of *nomopylakes* and *stratēgoi*, as well as eponymous priesthoods of the oikists.[97] It has been suggested that this evidence indicates that the founders of these cities were influenced by Platonic thought in approaching the creation of civic constitutions and organization.[98] Naming the months after the Olympian pantheon, for example, would be analogous to naming the tribes after these twelve gods, as the *Laws* prescribes.[99] Tribes and other divisions in these cities were also named after gods and heroes (as we saw in the case of Kassandreia), conforming with Plato's model, and the Platonic prototype of the royal burials at Aigai

92. Hyg., *Poet. astr.* 2.37. See also ch. 3.
93. *Certamen Homeri et Hesiodi*, l. 28.
94. Head 1911, 505–6.
95. N. Jones 1987, 271.
96. Latmos: *SEG* XLVII 1563. The impetus typically came from a city's desire to honor the monarchs, e.g., the addition of one tribe each for Antigonos and Demetrios at Athens (Plut., *Dem.* 10.2–4). In the Seleukid period, cities in Asia Minor (e.g., Smyrna) frequently renamed months or tribes after the royal family (Gauthier 1985; Price 1984, 25–40).
97. Kassandreia: Athenaion, Demetrion (Hatzopoulos 1996, vol. 2, nos. 21, 44); Demetrias: Athenaion, Areios, Artemision, Demetrion, Seios, Hermaion, Hestios, Hephaistion, Poseideon (*BÉ* 86.77 [J. Robert and L. Robert]; Knoepfler 1989); Philippoi: Aphrodision, Hermaion, Hephaistion (Hatzopoulos 1993, 320–22).
98. Piérart 1974, 122–208, 236–46, 321–23; Hatzopoulos 1996, 1:158–60, referring to an unpublished paper by C. Habicht.
99. Pl., *Leges* 8.828.

(Vergina) has also been stressed.[100] Whether these innovations can be traced directly back to Plato is perhaps debatable, but they more convincingly reflect a background of political thought on the ideal form of a city. On a more general level, the organizational potential of religion in royal foundations was clearly a consideration of the Hellenistic kings. While refoundation represented a chance to rationalize a city and to integrate royal cults into the civic origins, it also posed a vast problem for negotiating the traditional cults and identities of the constituent populations.

Unity and coherence were undoubtedly aims of the dynamic blend of tradition and innovation in the architecture of the synoikized polis. Strategies for integrating the constituent communities clearly sought a balance that would diffuse or even preclude sources of potential conflict. In many cases they seem to have succeeded. But we have also seen poleis that broke away from these unions, and markers of division like community of origin or cultic affiliation were certainly powerful drivers of this kind of separatism. As much as sources of discord could be stifled, they often still smoldered below the surface. For instance, the kind of disorder that could stem from the reshuffling of political and social equilibria stands out in an evocative inscription from Demetrias describing conflict in the Magnesian *koinon* in the mid-second century:

```
[- - -]Ọ[- - - - - - - - - -]
[Ἀ]φροδισιῶνος ιη΄. στρα[τηγοῦντος - - - μη]-
νὸς Ἀφροδισιῶνος δεκάτηι Ἀλκ[ίμ]α[χ]ο[ς - - -],
Ἀντίπατρος Εὐθυδήμου, Ἀρίσταρχος Σωΐδου, Ἀριστο-
κράτης Ἀριστάρχου, Θεόφιλος Θεοφίλου, Μενέστρατος        5
Μενεστράτου Δημητριεῖς εἶπαν· ἐπεὶ Δημήτριος Αἰ-
τωλίωνος Δημητριεὺς γενόμενος κοινὸς στρατηγὸς
[ἐ]ζήτησεν ἔν τε τοῖς ἄλλ[οι]ς τὴν ἀρίστην κατάστασιν
[τῶ]ι ἔθνει περιποιῆσαι ἐ[πιστρ]έ[ψ]ας τοὺς ἐπιτηδευομ[έ]-
[νο]υς τὰ χείριστα, καὶ διαφο[ρᾶς οὔ]σης π[ρ]ὸς αὐτοὺς Μά-        10
γνησιν ἐκ πλείονος χρόνου πάντων ἀναγκαιότατον ἡγ[ή]-
σάμενος εἶναι τὸ ε[ἰ]ς [τὸ πέ]ρας ἀγαγεῖν ταύτην ε[ἰ [σενεγ]-
κάμενος ψήφισμα παραίτιος ἐγένετο τοῦ λ[αβεῖν λύ]-
σιν τὴν διαφορὰν καὶ εἰς ὁμόνοιαν καταστ[ῆναι τὰς πόλεις],
τῆι τε λοιπῆι ἀναστροφῆι κα[ὶ ἑα]υτ[οῦ ἄξιος ἐγένετο καὶ τῶν]        15
ἐνχειρισάντων αὐτῶι τὴν ἀρ[χήν· δεδόχθαι τοῖς συνέδροις]
ἐπαινέσαι τε Δη[μ]ή[τριον Αἰτωλίωνος Δημητριῆ ἐπὶ τῆι]
[ε]ὐνοίαι τ[ῆι - - - - - - - - - -]
```

[. . .] Eighteenth of Aphrodisas. In the generalship of [. . .], on the tenth of the month of Aphrodisias, Alk[im]acho[s . . .] Antipatros son of Euthydemos, Aristarchos son of Soidos, Aristokrates son of Aristarchos, Theophilos son of Theophilos, and

---

100. Platonic burial of examiners: Pl., *Leges* 12.947d–e; royal burial at Vergina: Andronicos 1984, 65–66, 229–32.

Menestratos son of Menestratos, citizens of Demetrias, proposed: Since Demetrios son of Aitolion, of Demetrias, general of the *koinon*, sought, among others, to secure the best settlement for the ethnos, correcting those pursuing the worst, and since the Magnesians had a disagreement among themselves for a long time, he considered it the most necessary thing of all to bring it to an end, and by proposing a vote, he was in part responsible for finding a solution to the conflict and restoring [the cities] to concord [*homonoia*], and since in other aspects of his life [he was worthy] both of himself and of those holding office with him: [resolved by the *synedroi*] to praise De[m]e[trios son of Aitolion of Demetrias for his g]oodwill toward [. . .].[101]

The details can only be extrapolated from this text. As we saw above, the Magnesian League was dominated by its most powerful polis, Demetrias, which encompassed most of the region's population and territory and seems to have monopolized the *koinon*'s offices and honors. Synoikism created an imbalance, often giving one polis overwhelming weight within a federal league, like Thebes in the *koinon* of the Boiotians. The nature of the unrest described by this decree is unknown, but certain cities of Magnesia seem to have agitated against the dominance of Demetrias. Perhaps a few decades later (121–117), there may be evidence for the creation of a splinter Magnesian *koinon*: a certain Parmeniskos son of Amyntas, from the northern Magnesian polis Homolion, is designated "a Magnesian from Thessaly" on a list of the Delphic *hieromnēmones*, appearing in the place where the Perrhaibians, from Thessaly, were normally listed.[102] In all of the later lists, by contrast, the Perrhaibians reemerge in their normal place, and the only Magnesian representatives are called "Magnesians from Demetrias."[103] Homolion, however, a short time after the document that includes Parmeniskos, appears as the demotic of a priest of Zeus Akraios, the highest civic office of the polis, in a decree of Demetrias.[104] Among others, the grandson of Demetrios son of Aitolion (the individual honored for healing the discord in the league during the mid-second century) is mentioned as a *stratēgos* of the Magnesian League.[105] Many questions remain, but it seems clear that Homolion, which avoided the initial synoikism and remained independent throughout the third century and perhaps much of the second, was ultimately absorbed into Demetrias. This polis, one of the most significant of Magnesia before the synoikism,[106] was probably involved in the unrest described in the document

---

101. *IG* IX 2 1100a (ca. 140?; see Stählin 1929, 210–11).
102. *CID* 4 117, ll. 9–10 (*IG* II² 1134, l. 14; Kip 1910, 107–8; Daux 1936, 346; Lefèvre 1998, 90).
103. *CID* 4 119E.
104. *IG* IX 2 1109, ll. 1–2 (ca. 100).
105. For a stemma of the family, see Stählin 1929.
106. Independence: for the third-century coinage of Homolion, see *SNG Cop. Thessaly* 70–73. Significance: Homolion regularly provided the Amphiktyonic League with one of the Magnesian *hieromnēmones* (*CID* 2 32, l. 48 [late fourth century], 74, l. 40 [337/36]; Lefèvre 1998, 89). Korakai, Methone, or Olizon, all included in the synoikism of Demetrias, provided the others.

from the Magnesian League and possibly even sent an independent representative to Delphi for a time. In any case, the mid-second century witnessed significant stress in the Magnesian *koinon* as a result of Demetrias's power, and this decree shows the integrative and disintegrative forces at work. Homolion and perhaps other cities of Magnesia were brought into the synoikism in the second century, after the initial foundation, by either coercive absorption or the brokerage of some kind of agreement. A citizen of Homolion, Krinon son of Parmenion, held a prominent position in Demetrias soon after its absorption in to the city, attesting to the flexibility of the institutions of the synoikized polis to incorporate new constituencies.[107] This series of documents powerfully demonstrates such communities' efforts toward unity and the potential pitfalls and separatism they faced. Civic and ethnic discourse remained central in the assertion and balancing of the claims of the diverse constituencies that made up these poleis.

CULTIC OFFICIALS AND SACRIFICIAL CALENDARS

As we have seen, the incorporation of existing cults and sanctuaries was a central component of asserting the identity of a new foundation while preserving continuity with the past. If cults and sanctuaries formed a base of civic expression, however, the integration of cults (and the communities that celebrated and administered them) had a wide variety of practical concerns, such as the appointment of priests and other cultic officials, the performance of sacrifice, and the codification of sacrificial calendars. Beyond these logistical challenges, the perhaps more important issue of how local rites and priesthoods would be incorporated into the city, shared (or not) with the other citizens, and integrated into the wider religious identity of the polis had far-reaching social and political repercussions. As central cults were elevated and even invented to represent the synoikized polis, competition among elites for the tenure of priesthoods took on a new dimension. To what extent did this promote a sense of solidarity or tendencies toward separatism? How did local actors and the central polis administration negotiate this obstacle? Did certain groups have special religious prerogatives within the city? The evidence points to arrangements sensitively tailored to local circumstances, but one common thread is a concern to reach some kind of equilibrium that both accommodated particular claims, ancestral ties, or local prerogatives and allowed for a shared platform in the religious sphere where elites from the various communities assembled by the synoikism could all participate in the distinctions of central priesthoods.

In some cases, we can see elite families holding on to chief priesthoods across a synoikism. At Nysa, founded after 281 by Antiochos I, one such family occupied a

---

107. *IG* IX 2 1109.

preeminent position at the famous sanctuary of Pluto and Korē. In 281, in the unsettled aftermath of the Battle of Koroupedion, Athymbra, the principal community that later contributed to Nysa's foundation, sought important privileges for its Plutonion from the Seleukid official Sopatos now that the region was under Seleukid control. A certain Artemidoros was one of the three envoys who negotiated the resulting arrangement.[108] The synoikism of Nysa followed sometime after, and several generations later, in the second century, another Artemidoros, almost certainly a member of the same family, confirmed the Plutonion's traditional privileges with an unknown king.[109] On that occasion, however, Artemidoros represented the *boulē* and *dēmos* of Nysa, and the sanctuary had become the city's central poliadic cult. Centuries later, still another Artemidoros reconfirmed the sanctuary's privileges with the Roman proconsul Cnaeus Cornelius Lentulus Auger, in 1 BCE.[110] Likewise, a probable descendant of another priest, Iatrokles, in the delegation that the Athymbrians sent to the Seleukids in 281 appears on Delos in the late third or second century. This individual, also named Iatrokles, interestingly identifying himself by the sole ethnic *Athynbrianos* even after the synoikism, made a dedication to the Delian cults of Pluto and Korē, Artemis, Hermes, and Anoubis.[111] What emerges is the dramatic continuity of priestly families of Athymbra in the administration of the Plutonion, spanning centuries and the foundation of Nysa, but also the dominance of a narrow elite comprising individuals from the main community that formed the core of the new city. A similar arrangement can be identified in Stratonikeia, founded in the reign of Antiochos II primarily from Karian villages and poleis that became demes of the new city. One of the absorbed communities, the Panamareis, maintained a prerogative in the administration of the regionally important sanctuary, at Panamara, of Zeus Karios, which they had controlled before the synoikism: they asserted themselves as a *koinon* within the polis (Stratonikeia)–deme (unknown)–subdeme unit (Panamareis) structure and furnished most of the priests of Zeus Karios, although this position had become an office of the polis.[112] Despite losing their autonomy, the Panamareis retained important aspects of their corporate religious identity, which invested this community with significance in the civic body.

108. *RC* 9, l. 3 (a letter of Seleukos I and Antiochos I to an official granting *hikesia*, *asylia*, and *ateleia* to the Plutonion).
109. *RC* 64, l. 2.
110. *Syll.*³ 781.
111. *IG* XI 4 1235.
112. *SEG* XLV 1556, with van Bremen 2000 and van Bremen 2004. For a review of the evidence for priests of Stratonikeia, see now Williamson 2013. The Panamareis identified themselves in inscriptions of Stratonikeia as a *koinon*, a term common in Karia, which indicates a community or number of communities organized into a *dēmos* and having a decision-making apparatus (van Bremen 2000, 391).

A relatively extensive prosopography exists for the priests of Zeus Akraios, the most important civic cult of Demetrias. All of it, however, comes from after the creation of the Magnesian *koinon* in 167, and it is not entirely clear that the structure of the priesthood then was the same in the third century. The cult's importance in the city's earlier history and Demetrias's apparent domination of the Magnesian League, however, argue for the development of the *koinon* not changing the constitution of Demetrias. The priest of Zeus Akraios served as the eponymous official for all the civic decrees of Demetrias and was regularly the first of all the civic officials listed in decrees of the *koinon*.[113] It is evident from the fairly numerous civic decrees and Delphic lists of *hieromnēmones* from the second century that a relatively narrow group of elite families controlled this priesthood, most of the high civic offices of Demetrias, and the federal offices of the Magnesian League, which citizens of Demetrias entirely filled. To take just one example, a decree of the *koinon* honoring Hermogenes son of Hadymos, a citizen of Demetrias and the secretary of the *koinon*'s council, also names Hadaios the priest of Zeus Akraios, known to have been his brother.[114] Thebagenes son of Apollonios, mentioned in the decree as one of its proposers before the federal assembly (l. 8), is later attested as the civic priest of Zeus.[115] In another family, the two sons of Epiteles, Zoilos and Lysias, both distinguished themselves with high-profile civic and federal offices: Zoilos was a general of the Magnesian League and a judge in an arbitration in Perrhaibia,[116] while Lysias also served as a general of the *koinon* and held the priesthood of Zeus Akraios.[117]

This priesthood, then, stood at the top of the *cursus* of civic offices in Demetrias and was central to the careers of its citizens who served in the Magnesian League. The city's religious life focused on this central cult that united the mythology of Pelion with the new community, and its priesthood became the prime civic magistracy that ordered competition among elite families and bound their young men together in a yearly sacrifice and rite of passage. This ritual, discussed in the next section, consisted of a procession of the most distinguished youths of the city, chosen by the priest of Zeus, to the sanctuaries of Zeus and Cheiron on the peak of Pelion.[118] While the priesthood was confined to a narrow aristocracy, it does not appear to have been claimed exclusively by a privileged subdivision of this community. In one case, the priest of Zeus originated from Homolion, a community apparently absorbed into Demetrias sometime after the initial synoikism, and other holders of high civic and federal offices, from the sorts of elite families from

---

113. E.g., *IG* IX 2 1108, l. 6; IX 2 1109, ll. 1, 58, 70; V 2 367, l. 30.
114. *IG* IX 2 1103, l. 7. For the chronology, see Stählin 1929.
115. *IG* IX 2 1105II, l. 2.
116. *Stratēgos*: *IG* V 2 367; judge: *IG* IX 2 1106.
117. *Stratēgos*: *IG* IX 2 1111, ll. 1–3; priest: *IG* IX 2 1108, l. 6.
118. Herakleides Kritikos, *FHG* II 254–64F2.8 = *BNJ* 369AF2.8.

which the priests of Zeus were drawn, bear a wide range of demotics in the extant texts.[119] In contrast to Nysa, then, we can see how the priesthood of Zeus in Demetrias served as a means not of privileging one community's control over a central cult and sanctuary but of uniting the synoikized city's elites.

A somewhat different dynamic can be identified among the priests of Rhodes, a model for the synoikisms of the Hellenistic period, after its unification in 408/7.[120] The rich evidence, with its uniquely detailed prosopographical information, permits a reconstruction of the stemmata of priests and their families in the classical and Hellenistic periods in a way that is not possible elsewhere. Two characteristics of Rhodes's religious life stand out: strict adherence to traditionalism, which was guarded by the original poleis that maintained exclusive prerogatives in the realm of cults and priesthoods, and the creation of a venue that allowed for elite competition and coalescence at an islandwide level (discussed in the next paragraph). A wide variety of evidence points to the jealously guarded exclusivity of the local cults. The old poleis of Ialysos, Kameiros, and Lindos maintained control over their territories, administration, and cults even after becoming territorial *phylai* of synoikized Rhodes. The cult of Athana Lindia is the best documented. Although it was of islandwide significance before the synoikism, its priesthood was restricted to members of the *phylē* Lindia afterward. The list of these priests began in 406/5, soon after the synoikism, a clear sign that the new political reality prompted the Lindians to consolidate their control over this office.[121] The cult of Athana Lindia, along with the other central cults of the original poleis, was not duplicated in the new polis of Rhodos, in contrast to many cases of synoikism, and it remained prominent throughout the classical and Hellenistic periods. The remarkable exclusivity of its priesthood was matched by efforts to permeate the strict barriers set by the Lindians. The most visible method was adoption, which is extremely common throughout the lists of the priests of Athana. This pattern demonstrates the ability of elites from other tribes to use formal channels to get around the obstacles of this separatism and highlights the desirability for elites of making alliances across the subdivisions of the Rhodian state.[122] Yet the other side of this coin, also visible in the priestly lists, was the use of adoption to monopolize the office and limit it to a relatively small circle of elite families. The impediments also seem to have been challenged in other ways. An important document from the late fourth century

---

119. Krinon son of Parmenion, with the demotic Homolieus, is attested as the priest of Zeus Akraios (*IG* IX 2 1109, ll. 1–2) and as a mover of a decree (*IG* IX 2 1105 III, l. 3). Citizens of Demetrias regularly have a demotic in civic decrees. In, e.g., *IG* IX 2 1109, ll. 2–8, most of the demotics of the poleis included in the synoikism are represented among the civic officials.

120. Gabrielsen (2000) favors a slightly earlier date for this synoikism, with signs of federal cooperation preceding it; see also Badoud 2015, 337.

121. *I. Lindos* 1, with Blinkenberg 1941, 90–98.

122. Gabrielsen 1997, 112–20, app. 1.

preserves a resolution of the councilors (*mastroi*) and the people of Lindos in honor of individuals who "ensured that the election at Lindos of priests and sacrificers [*hierothytai*] and overseers of sacred rites [*hieropoioi*] and others appointed over common affairs are made from among the Lindians as is prescribed in the laws, and that the hiera at Lindos are not shared with those who did not hold them previously ..."[123] This came almost a century after the synoikism, and while it stresses the desire to protect the exclusivity of the cultic life of Lindos, it also indicates that this had been violated.

Alongside the demarcations of the religious prerogatives of discrete parts of the polis, there was room at Rhodes for an islandwide venue of cultic participation. Many of the Rhodian priests whose careers are visible in the evidence followed a specific *cursus honorum* through the tenure of priesthoods, first grounded in their local communities but culminating in that of Halios (Helios), the central deity of the Rhodian pantheon after the synoikism.[124] The synoikism of a new city for the island and a symbolic heart of pan-Rhodian belonging, focalized by the expressly built sanctuary of Halios, created a unified priestly group identity.[125] The intentional manipulation of mythology to elevate this cult—which, although of little ritual significance before the synoikism, became the chief one of the island—bridged and united the aristocracies of the three old poleis as its priesthood became the "stage that was shared by all three local aristocracies," accommodating cooperation and competition.[126] Moreover, as N. Badoud has traced in detail, the Rhodian calendar had two different but interrelated years (eponymous, a remnant of the presynoikism calendar, and civic, introduced with the synoikism), a complex system that included a three-year term for each community.[127] Rhodes was highly experimental in restructuring its local cults, creating a structure that was innovative and conservative at the same time, preserving a sense of stability while uniting formerly autonomous communities into a single new state.

The polis of Kos was synoikized in a similar manner, but its religious life demonstrates some unique features in the binding together of constituted communi-

---

123. *IG* XII 1 761 = *Syll.*³ 340, ll. 38–42: συνδιαφυλάξαντες Λινδίοις ὅπως | ταὶ αἱρέσιες γίνωνται ἐν Λίνδωι τῶν ἱερέων κ[αὶ] ἱεροθυτᾶν κα[ὶ] | ἱεροποιῶν καὶ τῶν ἄλλων τῶν ἐπὶ τὰ κοινὰ τασσομέν[ω]ν ἐξ | αὐτῶν Λινδίων καθ' ἅ καὶ ἐν τοῖς νόμοις γέγραπται κα[ὶ μ]ὴ μετέ|χωντι τῶν ἐν Λίνδωι ἱερῶν οἵ μὴ καὶ πρότερον μετεῖχον. After the sympoliteia of Olymos and Mylasa in Karia (late third century), Olymos remained a discrete entity, even though it was fully incorporated into Mylasa. Its main civic cults of Apollo and Artemis continued to flourish, and their priesthoods evidently remained under the control of families from Olymos (*I. Mylasa* 861, with Reger 2004, 164–68; LaBuff 2016, 108–12).

124. Morricone 1949–51. The earliest list of the priests of Halios begins immediately after the synoikism in 408/7, as Badoud (2015, ch. 8) has shown convincingly, pace Gabrielsen (2000, 187, 202n49), who attempted to downdate it to 358.

125. Dignas 2003, 50. For a rich discussion of Halios after the synoikism, see Kowalzig 2007, 239–66.

126. Dignas 2003, 49.

127. Badoud 2015, ch. 1, with table on 140.

ties. The city was formed in 366/65 on or near Kos Meropis, which was joined with the much larger Astypalaia (and perhaps other unattested communities). The foundation entailed a large-scale transfer of population to the new site, the majority of which came from Astypalaia, the island's most important polis. The synoikism also involved the reorientation of cults, priesthoods, and other facets of religious life, despite the fact that many cults of Astypalaia, which continued on as a center of population and a deme of the city (Isthmiotai), remained rooted in their original location.[128] It appears that the cults represented in the center of the new city of Kos did not replace but rather replicated and duplicated the original rituals and sanctuaries. This seems to have been the case for Apollo Delios, as well as Zeus Poleius and Demeter.[129] The original cults continued to be tended in their demes, and there is ample evidence of extremely active locally administered cults, for instance that of Apollo and Herakles in Halasarna.[130] However, the reverse also happened: the cult of Aphrodite Pandamos (Of the whole *dēmos*), whose epithet and lack of attestation before the synoikism suggest an innovation meant to foster a unified Koan identity, was celebrated on the same day by both the city and the demes.[131] This was likely a case of the city exporting the cult to the demes rather than vice versa. The cult of Asklepios, perhaps grafted on to a preexisting Apollo cult, also gained significant focus after the synoikism, culminating in the construction of a monumental complex in the early third century.[132] This process of unification ultimately necessitated the drafting of a new sacrificial calendar at the polis level, set up in the sanctuary of the new Twelve Gods in Kos town.[133] This calendar, which dates to the mid-third century, along with a contemporary document regulating the terms of office of the priest of Zeus Poleius and dealing with the cult of Apollo Dalios (Delios), clearly reflects postsynoikism efforts to integrate the chief cults of the formerly independent poleis into the new urban center. Fragments of deme calendars are also extant and demonstrate attention to local rites and efforts to synchronize sacrifices with the polis center.[134] Priesthoods too were shared, more freely than in Rhodes, for example, throughout the island. The usual Koan practice was to auction them off to the highest bidder, and most were open to all Koans above a minimum age. Yet some were still limited to specific subdivisions of the tribes, like the priesthood of the important cult of Zeus

128. Strabo 14.2.19.
129. *IG* XII 4.1 276 (Sokolowski 1969, no. 151A; RO 62A).
130. Kokkoru-Aleura 2004, 27–82.
131. Paul 2013, 79–90; Parker 2002, 152–56; Parker 2009, 204. A cult of *homonoia* was also introduced, to which Koan magistrates were particularly connected (see 000n21).
132. Sherwin-White 1978, 334–39; Paul 2013, 167–89.
133. *IG* XII 4.1 276 (Sokolowski 1969, no. 151A; RO 62A).
134. Sokolowski 1969, no. 169 = *IG* XII 4.1 280a–c, cult calendar of the deme Isthmiotai (early second century). See also Sherwin-White 1978, 329–30.

Poleius.[135] In addition, it is likely that the three Dorian tribes into which the island was divided were newly imposed with the synoikism. The overall result was a relatively open system that respected the ancient orientation of the original cults and fostered the construction of an islandwide identity.

Priesthoods offer a rare insight into the careers and roles of individuals in the framework of the synoikized polis. The accommodations we have identified within this realm complimented the concomitant effort to identify and promote key cults and central sanctuaries that would assert and reinforce the sacred identity of the unified political community. Prominent priesthoods became a way for eminent citizens to participate in a hierarchy of civic honors that encouraged both competition and unity. In the majority of cases, we have seen that such offices were shared across the constituent communities of the synoikized polis. This arrangement could coexist with continued exclusivity for certain cults, for which certain sections of the citizen community maintained their traditional prerogatives of administration or participation. Thus, the contours of inclusion and exclusion were carefully delineated through a process of negotiation and compromise that is highly revealing of the limits of shared religion in the making of new political communities.

DEFINING THE COMMUNITY: RITUAL, MYTH, AND CIVIC IDENTITY

We have seen the role that orienting synoikized poleis around major divinities, their sanctuaries, and their cults played in creating a unified religious identity. In connecting the urban center to the *chōra*, the siting and duplication of these sanctuaries directed the attention of their communities to the social reality of belonging to a new society. Such strategies maintained continuity with the past for individual communities, allowed room for their original political identities in the synoikized city, and articulated a cohesive identity from a diverse amalgamation of social groups and their cults. This picture of accommodation and innovation provides a rich if somewhat static view of the range of possible social responses to the profound changes in the cultic landscape. Civic rituals and myths were part of these reactions, reflecting and addressing the tensions of synoikism. Ritual became a formalized method of communication that embraced the constituent communities of the polis, the unified polis, and the royal authorities. This kind of action had

---

135. Sherwin-White 1978, 155–56. She wondered (293) if the new calendar might have fostered unity by cutting down on the number of priesthoods restricted to hereditary *genē* but noted that the lack of evidence prevents any conclusion.

the power to reconfigure potentially divisive attachments and realign them into a structure that underpinned rather than undercut the new political order.[136]

The role of ritual in forging such bonds can be traced throughout instances of synoikism in the archaic, classical, and Hellenistic worlds. At Patrai, the tradition of a problematic sexual union (referring to the tensions involved in the synoikism) offers a celebrated case. There Komaitho, the priestess of Artemis Triklaria ("Of the three divisions," whose cult was shared by the villages that would make up Patrai), fell in love with Melanippos. When their marriage was forbidden, the couple resorted to using the sanctuary of Artemis for their assignations, angering the virgin goddess. Famine and disease resulted, and the oracle at Delphi ordered the sacrifice of the offending pair and the annual sacrifice of the most beautiful unwed young man and woman of the community to Artemis Triklaria. This oracle thus explained an earlier prophecy that foretold the arrival of "a foreign king bringing a foreign god" that would end the sacrifice to Artemis Triklaria. Eurypylos, a Greek hero wandering around in a state of madness since his return from the Trojan War, arrived in Aroë, the future site of Patrai, carrying a chest containing an image of Dionysos. He had got the chest in Troy and lost his sanity upon opening it and beholding the image. He consulted Delphi and received a prophecy that he would recover his sanity when he found a people conducting a strange sacrifice and both settled the chest and made a home for himself there. Appearing just as the human sacrifice to Artemis was about to commence, Eurypylos instituted the cult of Dionysos Aisymnetes (Corrector), simultaneously recovering his sanity and putting an end to this annual sacrifice.[137]

The historical ritual involved the symbolic re-creation of these mythical events and a procession that reenacted the process of Patrai's synoikism. During the

---

136. For the potential of religion to play a divisive role in the community, see Kertzer 1988. See Bell 1992; 1997 for discussions of the role of ritual and "ritualization" in effecting political power. In his study of the Nepalese city Bhaktapur, R. Levy (1990, 1997; see also Jameson 1997) powerfully demonstrates the complex and competitive levels of a city that developed from the urbanization of smaller communities. He delineates how the space of the archaic city hosts coexisting symbolic systems: what he terms "embedded" symbolism, derived from timeless, natural features or occurrences, and "marked" symbolism, of that which is specifically set apart and "sacralized." Levy describes the multivalent way that communal religion can be exploited as an organizational resource in the ancient city. This highlights both the fact that forms of religious expression are inherently competitive and interactive and the attendant challenge of integration as smaller political units coalesce into a complex polity. It is precisely such a multifaceted relationship among religion, social identity, politics, and imperial structures that defined the process of accommodating change and tradition across the upheavals of synoikism in the early Hellenistic period. For a nuanced treatment of religion and urbanization in ancient Mexico, see Carballo 2016.

137. Paus. 7.19.1–9, with Bonnechere 1994, 63–76. The river flowing past the sanctuary was then renamed from Ameilichos ("implacable, relentless") to Meilichos ("mild, gentle").

festival of Dionysos, youths from Patrai processed to the rural sanctuary of Artemis Triklaria adorned with garlands of grain. After placing these before the goddess, they bathed in the Meilichos River, put garlands of ivy on their heads, and processed back to the sanctuary of Dionysos Aisymnetes in the urban center of Patrai, between the agora and the sea.[138] This ritual at once initiated the city's youth and emphasized the purification of the polis from the terrible rites of Artemis Triklaria. As part of the ceremony, three images of Dionysos were brought into his sanctuary, one for each of the *dēmoi* of Patrai and named after them,[139] symbolically linking the countryside and the urban center.[140] The ritual thus maintained the unique identities of the original settlements while reenacting their unification through the procession of the youths across the territory of Patrai to emphasize the political unity of the polis through the common bond of cult.[141] The hero Eurypylos was also included in this festival, receiving yearly sacrifice as the founding hero (*ktistēs*) of Patrai at a tomb significantly positioned between the temple and altar of Artemis. The details of this myth and the historical ritual elegantly bear out the potential crisis of the union of Patrai and the capacity of religious innovation to resolve political problems. In this one example, a number of the strands of ritual concern emerge: anxiety about political union, reflected in the metaphor of marriage; the maintenance of differentiation alongside unity; the employment of new cults; and the binding of the city and the country through ritual processions, common cults, and central sanctuaries.

In the early Hellenistic kingdoms, similar innovations addressed the profound changes that synoikism initiated. The most detailed is the incorporation of the myths and cults of Mount Pelion into the polis of Demetrias. The cult of Zeus on the peak, as we have seen, became an important civic cult.[142] The third-century historian Herakleides Kritikos[143] described the following ritual, observed every year:

Ἐπ' ἄκρας δὲ τῆς τοῦ ὄρους κορυφῆς σπήλαιόν ἐστι τὸ καλούμενον Χειρώνιον καὶ Διὸς ἀκραίου ἱερόν, ἐφ' ὃ κατὰ κυνὸς ἀνατολὴν κατὰ τὸ ἀκμαιότατον καῦμα ἀναβαίνουσι τῶν πολιτῶν οἱ ἐπιφανέστατοι καὶ ταῖς ἡλικίαις ἀκμάζοντες, ἐπιλεχθέντες ἐπὶ τοῦ ἱερέως, ἐνεζωσμένοι κώδια τρίποκα καινά· τοιοῦτον συμβαίνει ἐπὶ τοῦ ὄρους τὸ ψῦχος εἶναι.

On the peak of the summit of the mountain is the cave named for Cheiron and the sanctuary of Zeus Akraios, to which, at the rising of the Dog Star, when the heat of

138. Paus. 7.20.1–2.
139. Paus. 7.21.6.
140. Nilsson 1906, 294–97; Massenzio 1968; Mackil 2013, 217–20.
141. Polignac 1995, 68–71.
142. For the remains of the sanctuary of Zeus and Cheiron on Pelion see ch. 3. For Zeus Akraios in general, see A. Cook 1925, 871–72.
143. Fl. ca. 294–220 BCE. See Arenz 2006.

the day is at its height, the citizens of Demetrias who are the most distinguished and in the prime of their life ascend, chosen by the priest and girded with new, triple-thick sheepskins; such is the cold on the mountain.[144]

This is one of the clearest examples of a civic ritual responding to the social pressures of a synoikism, and it is particularly valuable since it is closely dated to the early years of the foundation and was described by a contemporary witness. Its primary concern was to initiate and bind together the young elites of the city. We have seen the preeminent position of the priest of Zeus Akraios in the city, and it was he, an emblem of state cult and high civic office, who selected the participants. The association of this ritual with the wise centaur Cheiron underscores this point. Although closely tied to a life in nature and linked to the rustic science of herbology, Cheiron is most important as a figure who initiated young heroes into their cultural tradition: Herakles, Achilles, Jason, and Asklepios all came of age under his tutelage. The procession from the city to the top of Pelion on the hottest day of the summer linked the citizens of the polis to the most significant topographical feature in the *chōra*. The centrifugal movement away from the city conducted the citizens along a route that must have passed the citadel of Iolkos and the sanctuary of Artemis before ascending the mountain.[145] From the summit, the view embraced all of the territory included in the synoikism. The contrast between the heat of the day and the cold of the mountain signaled a transformation, and the richness of the sacrifice was heightened by the symbolism of the initiates' clothing themselves in the skins of the freshly sacrificed animals. Here again the participants took on a firsthand connection to the landscape, identifying with the livestock that it supported.[146] The ritual took place at the height of summer, when the rising of Sirius was thought to threaten drought and pestilence, and we can identify "weather magic" in it, calling on Zeus to bring rain and cooling winds.[147] Similar rituals, like that on Keos, where the men of military age assembled under arms at the mountaintop sanctuary of Zeus at night to await the first rising of the Dog Star and to conduct sacrifices,[148] also reveal a concern for civic solidarity. The high summer,

---

144. *FHG* II 254–64 F2.8 = *BNJ* 369A F2.8.
145. See F. Graf 1996 for the significance of centripetal vs. centrifugal processions.
146. Burkert (1983) emphasized the aspect of purification of the guilt of sacrifice, the *Umschuldskömodie* made famous by Mueli (1946). Buxton (1994, 93–94) focused on the rural orientation of the ritual, arguing that it evoked a return to a pastoral life of transhumance. These approaches neglect the cult's historical context and the level of innovation. A. Cook (1940, 31–32) viewed the sheepskin as imitating the "fleecy vapours" of the clouds. See also Bonnechere 1994, 147.
147. See Burkert 1983, 109–14, with references.
148. The ritual was connected with the rustic deity Aristaios (who is associated with sheep and hunting and has been presumed to represent the aristoi). In myth, he brought the Arkadian priests descended from Lykaon to Keos to end a drought by erecting an altar to Zeus Ikmaios and Sirius. See Schachter 1994, 107.

when the hardest work of the agricultural year was over and the citizen body had the most time to spare, was a fitting time to reflect on the unity of the polis and the bond between city and country, and indeed at this very time the festival of unity, the Synoikia, took place at Athens, as well as the festival of all Athenians, the Panathenaia.[149]

Cheiron, so emblematic of Pelion and the indigenous traditions of Magnesia, was closely associated with Zeus Akraios in cult and ritual in Demetrias. The Magnesians made offerings of herbs and other plants to Cheiron, one of the first medical practitioners, and his image appeared on the reverse of the coinage of the Magnesian League, paired here too with Zeus, on the obverse.[150] His significance extended to securing the health and well-being of the polis, and hence the start of the dog days of summer was an appropriate time to sacrifice to this centaur. His centrality to the city is further elaborated by a fragment from Herakleides describing a kinship group that preserved Cheiron's healing arts:

> Ταύτην δὲ τὴν δύναμιν ἐν τῶν πολιτῶν οἶδεν γένος· ὃ δὴ λέγεται Χείρωνος ἀπόγονον εἶναι. παραδίδωσι δὲ καὶ δείκνυσι πατὴρ υἱῷ, καὶ οὕτως ἡ δύναμις φυλάσσεται, ὡς οὐδεὶς ἄλλος οἶδε τῶν πολιτῶν· οὐχ ὅσιον δὲ τοὺς ἐπισταμένους τὰ φάρμακα μισθοῦ τοῖς κάμνουσι βοηθεῖν ἀλλὰ προῖκα. τὸ μὲν οὖν Πήλιον καὶ τὴν Δημητριάδα συμβέβηκε τοιαύτην εἶναι.

> One *genos* of the citizens of Demetrias, which is in fact said to be descended from Cheiron, understands this power. This knowledge is revealed and handed down from father to son, and thus the power is guarded, as no one else among the citizens knows it; it is sacrilegious for those possessing the drugs to aid the sick for pay; they must do it for free. This is what Pelion and the region of Demetrias are like.[151]

Here the distinctive capacity of religion to promote unity while preserving difference stands out: the *genos* descended from Cheiron claimed a prerogative and special status within the city, but this was based on their knowledge, which was put to use for the common good. This testimony likely explains the Roman-period dedication of a priest of Zeus Akraios with a curious additional name: "Aurelios Teimasitheos | Kentaurios, priest, | [dedicated this] to Zeus Akraios."[152] *Kentaurios* must be a title,[153]

---

149. Parker 2005, 207: "In particular it is noticeable that the only three festivals for which good numbers of celebrants climbed to the acropolis itself—the *Dipolieia, Synoikia, Panathenaea*—are all bunched in this period. High summer, it seems, was less the time when harvesters relaxed after their labours than when Attica looked inwards to its centre, a time of civic consciousness."

150. Plut., *Quaest. conv.* 3.1.3 (Mor. 647a1); coins: Head 1911, 255–56.

151. *FHG* II 254–264 F2.12 = *BNJ* 369A F2.12.

152. Wilhelm 1890; *IG* IX 2 1128: Αὐρ(ήλιος) Τειμασίθεος | Κενταύριος ὁ ἱερ[ε]|ὺς τῷ Ἀκραίῳ Δι[ί].

153. Kentauros appears very rarely as personal name, but compare the surname Kentaurianos, found in only two inscriptions: Πό(πλιον) Κλαύδιον Με|νητιανὸν Κεν|ταυριανὸν (a priest of Helios;

surely in this context indicating the *genos* that was said to have perpetuated the healing secrets of Cheiron in Demetrias, which survived into the Roman period. The close link here between the priesthood of Zeus Akraios and Cheiron, mirrored by the material remains of the joint sanctuary on the peak of Pelion, is also noteworthy.

The ritual innovations at Demetrias, particularly surrounding the cult of Zeus Akraios, which were introduced or given new emphasis after the synoikism, focused the new community on the priority of solidarity but also built on the foundations of ancient traditions and local cults. We have already seen another ritual that emanated from the center of Demetrias and embraced all of its demes: the sacrifice to the *archēgetai* and *ktistai* (pp. 190–94). This ritual expressed clear concerns for the well-being and prosperity of the city, which it presented as inseparable from the observance of the traditional honors of the local gods and heroes of the composite demes. If the reconstruction offered above is correct, copies of the decree issued by Demetrias regulating the festival of the *archēgetai* and *ktistai* were disseminated to all the demes. The priorities of this ritual correspond to those of the summer ritual described by Herakleides, but here the royal founder stands at the center. The visual engagement of the sanctuary of the founders with the peak of Mount Pelion further connected these two rituals, linking the seat of Antigonid kingship in the polis to the domain of the king of the gods on the mountaintop.

Suggestively, another cult of Zeus Akraios is now known from another early Hellenistic royal foundation, Herakleia Latmos / Pleistarcheia. This city, as we have seen, was the synoikism of two Karian poleis, Latmos and Pidasa, initiated by Asandros sometime between 323 and 312. The region then fell to Antigonos, who held it until the Battle of Ipsos, and then Pleistarchos, Cassander's brother, established a short-lived dynasty in the early 290s, which ultimately passed to his lieutenant Eupolemos.[154] It was under one of these dynasts that the city was moved from the site of Latmos to Herakleia, fortified, and developed into the capital of Karia. In addition to impressive walls, the city had well-built stone roads that extended into the Latmos massif.[155] At its summit was an altar of Zeus Akraios. A temple to the deity lay in a nearby valley, securely attributed by an early Hellenistic dedicatory inscription on its architrave.[156] The antae of this small temple carry sculpted reliefs of a Macedonian shield and a Chalkidian helmet, emblems of Macedonian authority that also appear on the bronze coinage

---

I. Tralleis 134); Πο(πλίου) Κλ(αυδίου) Μενίππο[υ Κ]ενταυριανοῦ | υἱοῦ (*I. Tralleis* 67). L. Robert (1969, 650–52) wondered if there was a Thessalian influence in the Maeander valley via Magnesia on the Meander.

154. See p. 49 for a discussion of the sources.
155. For a description of the system and illustrations, see Peschlow-Bindokat 1996b, 51–67.
156. Peschlow-Bindokat 1996a, 224: Διὶ Ἀκραίωι [- - -]ργος Διονυσίου ΓΛ[- - -].

of Cassander/Pleistarchos and Eupolemos struck in Karia and suggest the close association between the foundation of the Hellenistic city and the embellishment of this sanctuary.[157] The cult was probably ancient, rooted in an Anatolian mountain god like the cult at nearby Labraunda and later assimilated to Zeus.[158] One of the stone roads that wind up the mountain from Herakleia/Pleistarcheia, passing fountains and rest points, in all likelihood was a sacred way that linked the city to the mountaintop and the cult of Zeus. A Christian source describes a sacred stone, supposedly the bedrock of the summit itself, which was the seat of a powerful weather god. This was a destination of pilgrims in pre-Christian times, according to this text, and was almost certainly part of an ancient ritual.[159] This testimony, joined with the physical remains on Latmos, suggests that the cult of Zeus Akraios became an important ritual focus of the reorganized polis of Herakleia/Pleistarcheia. The most likely candidate to have developed the city and extended the sophisticated road network and ritual way is Pleistarchos or Eupolemos. The civic procession to the sanctuary of Zeus Akraios bears striking similarity to the ritual observance known from Demetrias. Here Latmos, the major landmark of the region, centered the community much as Pelion did for Demetrias.

The innovations at Demetrias and Herakleia/Pleistarcheia can be compared to a striking example of ritual change initiated by Lysimachos at Ephesos. A fragmentary decree of the *synedrion* of that city's gerousia dating to the reign of Commodus offers a retrospective look at the refoundation of the polis under the Greek king and the reorganization of an important ritual observed by the Ephesians for centuries to follow:

ἀγαθῇ τύχῃ.
[περὶ ὧν - - -¹³⁻¹⁵- - - εἰσφέρει· ἐν μὲν τοῖς ἄν]ωθεν ὑπὸ τὸν οἰκισμὸν τῆς πόλεως
    [χρόνοις Λυσίμαχον τὸν βασιλέα, κύριον]
[γεγονότα τῶν τῆς πόλεως πραγμάτων, τὰ μὲν ἄλλα] πάντα περί τε μυστηρίων καὶ
    θυσιῶν [καὶ περὶ τοῦ συνεδρίου ἡμῶν ἄριστα δια]-
[κεκοσμηκέναι πάσῃ εὐσεβείᾳ τε καὶ φιλαγα]θίᾳ, ἰδρυσάμενον δὲ καὶ νεὼ καὶ ἄγαλμα
    Σωτείρ[ας - - - διατετα]-
[χέναι τοὺς] μετέχοντας τοῦ συ[νεδρίου πάν]τας ἐκ τῶν κοινῶν τῆς γερουσίας
    χρημάτων ἕκ[αστον - - - λαβόντας εὐωχεῖν καὶ]   5
[θύειν] τῇ θεῷ·

With good fortune.
[Concerning the things which ... proposes: In] former [times] during the foundation of the polis, [King Lysimachos, once he had acquired supreme authority over the

---

157. Valassiadis 2005.
158. For the origins of the cult at Labraunda, see Karlsson 2013.
159. *Vita S. Pauli Iunioris in Monte Latro* 18.

affairs of the polis, set in the best order] all the [other] things concerning the mysteries and the sacrifices and [concerning our *synedrion*, with all piety and benevolence], and after he dedicated the temple and the cult statue of the Savior [Artemis, he made arrangements] for all those who were members of the *sy*[*nhedrion*], each [to take] from the common funds of the gerousia, [and to feast and to sacrifice] to the goddess.[160]

This document reveals that Lysimachos, at the time of the refoundation of Ephesos as Arsinoeia, established a cult of Artemis Soteria, "the Savior," in the mountain groves of Ortygia and reconfigured the ritual activities and mysteries associated with the goddess's birth. His arrangements included the consecration of a temple and a shift in both the emphasis of the festival and the civic authorities who administered it. Strabo describes the rites associated with the sanctuary, and a series of inscriptions of imperial date attest the administration and personnel of the mysteries.[161] Their location was the reputed site where Leto gave birth to Apollo and Artemis, with the assistance of the nurse Ortygia, before bathing herself in the river Kenchrios.[162] Nearby, on Mount Solmessos, the armed youths know as Kouretes frightened off Hera with the clattering of their weapons and their war dance. Strabo notes that there were several temples in the sanctuary, including the adyton where the birth was reputed to have taken place, some containing ancient wooden cult statues (xoana) and others works of the famous Skopas of Paros. The site was of clear importance before the time of Lysimachos and, significantly, lay on the border with the incorporated polis of Phygela, but what this document shows is a ritual change initiated by the monarch after his refoundation of the city. In Strabo's day, there was an annual festival (*panēgyris*) at the site, at which the *neoi* of the city competed with one another in the splendor of their banquets and the association of the Kouretes held symposia and "mystic sacrifices."[163] The reorganization of the rites built on ancient traditions but achieved novel results: the establishment of a Savior cult, associated with Lysimachos and the foundation of the polis as well as Artemis, symbolically bound the polis center and the expanded *chōra*[164] and augmented the power of the Ephesian gerousia at the expense of the priests of the Artemision. With a complex intertwining of old and new, Lysimachos and the gerousia of Ephesos instituted important ritual changes that endured into the fourth century CE.

---

160. *I. Ephesos* Ia 26. For a detailed discussion of this inscription and these mysteries, see Rogers 2012, esp. chs. 1–3. Clinton (2014) questioned Rogers's claim that the *mysteria* were associated with the Soteria cult and argued that they should instead be located at the Artemision.
161. Strabo 14.1.20.
162. For the location, see Rogers 2012, 36–27. For an alternative theory, see Scherrer 2001, 81n139.
163. Strabo 14.1.20.
164. Rogers 2012, 80–81.

CONCLUSIONS: RELIGION, POWER, AND CONSENSUS

Over the course of this and the previous chapter, I have explored aspects of Hellenistic kingship and imperialism that became deeply embedded within the religious and social fabric of the Greek polis. Studies of Greek religion and Hellenistic kingship have tended to focus on well-attested phenomena like ruler cult (for obvious reasons) and royal patronage of sanctuaries and cults or the thorny problem of long-term changes in religious practice and personal belief ushered in by the new political realities of the era.[165] Building on the insights of these approaches, these chapters have reconstructed a wide picture of the ways that local populations responded to and participated in the manipulations of the religious life and social organization of the polis brought on by Macedonian imperialism. Ruler cult, in the first generations after Alexander largely a spontaneous response of Greek poleis, built on existing traditions to recognize the extraordinary position of the Hellenistic dynasts. This phenomenon has rightly been seen as one of the most revealing features of the negotiation of power between local communities and royal authorities and of the ways that rulers became embedded in the institutions of the polis.[166] I have suggested that examination of the widespread phenomenon of early Hellenistic synoikism reveals a complex web of interaction among individuals, communities, and royal powers that shows the role of religion and ritual in mitigating and organizing the most direct intervention of the kings in the world of the polis. In the first generation we can see a wide variety of strategies beyond ruler cult for negotiating this new world of royal authority, but I have also stressed that kings and individuals alike could resort to the long traditions of synoikism in the Greek world for models of how to accommodate change and build consensus within a dramatically altered political order.

It is clear that the articulation of a religious identity was central to building a royal city and effecting and legitimizing the kings' political dominance. There was, accordingly, a distinct limit to what kings could do with religion, including the extent to which they could consolidate their control around a coherent ritual authority. Demetrios Poliorketes's residence in Athens, for instance, was fraught with the challenge of integrating a king with very real power into a democratic

---

165. E.g., Potter 2003; Chaniotis 2003; Mikalson 1998. Walbank's (1984) discussion of monarchy and religion identifies four main aspects of this interaction: the association of ruling dynasties with certain deities (e.g., the Seleukids and Apollo), particular rulers' assimilation to or identification with gods, ruler cult promoted by cities, and fully fledged dynastic cult. Kindt (2009; 2012) uses the Hellenistic polis as a pillar of her multifaceted critique of the utility of the "polis religion" model developed by Sourvinou-Inwood (1988; 1990) and others (e.g., Cole 1994; Burkert 1995). For a recent defense of this model's usefulness, see Scheid 2016. See also Harrison 2015.

166. From a vast bibliography, see Habicht 1970; Price 1985; Walbank 1984; Chaniotis 2003. For the Ptolemies: Koenen 1993. For the Seleukids: Ma 2002, 219–26; Sartre 2006. For the Antigonids: Mari 2008.

polis. The communication between them was primarily brokered through religious honors, most strikingly demonstrated in the Athenians' decision to treat the king as an oracle.[167] The flexibility of the economy of these honors made them a potent means of negotiation, yet the religious strategies that Demetrios employed in Athens ultimately brought him as much resentment and rejection as political advantage.

We have seen striking instances of rupture in cultic observance alongside dramatic attempts to maintain a sense of cultic continuity, calling attention to the fundamentally disruptive nature of synoikism and the necessity of addressing its inherent social pressures. Cities, kings, and elites went to great lengths to assert a shared identity while allowing for mechanisms that preserved the distinctiveness of constituent groups. A wide variety of traditions, cults, and practices were incorporated into the new city, and, as I have argued, the religious identity of the synoikized polis was built with a careful orchestration of central sanctuaries, rituals, and religious symbols as well as a sensitive incorporation of the preexisting sacred landscape, local particularities, and traditional prerogatives. Inclusiveness—whose emphasis we have traced in the realms of founder cult, priesthoods, and civic cult—was a primary tool for forging a new urban order from the chaos of population transfer and the obliteration of lines between formerly discrete polities. While many of these unions proved exceptionally durable, there are also many examples of disintegration, whether partial or whole. Religion and cult played an important role in this too. We have seen cases of competition—instances in which certain cults were privileged over others or traditional attachments led to the dissolution of unity. The power of religion and ritual to underscore difference and heighten the tensions between social groups certainly contributed to the frequent examples of resistance to synoikism.

From the polis to the *koinon*, shared cultic ties and religious activity—from common sanctuaries to integrative rituals—played an important role in the formation of states.[168] The emergence of many poleis, *koina*, and synoikized states in the Greek world was often the result of common bonds and interactions that spanned centuries. Thus preexisting cultic communities could become politicized over time. The early Hellenistic synoikisms, by contrast, started from a primarily political motivation: the merger of smaller states and other entities under the direction of an external ruler. In such instances, new cities were forced to come together suddenly, composed of parts that might not have had close ties or even cordial relations before. The role that religion and ritual played in forming and maintaining the body politic was no less critical here than in cases of states that coalesced from drawn-out relations between communities. In many respects, kings and

---

167. Plut., *Dem.* 13; Kuhn 2006.
168. E.g., Mackil 2013, ch. 4, for the Greek *koinon*.

cities appealed to deep traditions in Greek poleis of negotiating the challenges that political transformations presented to religious life and social structures. Religious symbolism and ritual activity were employed to sacralize the new political community in a way that sought to mask the profound changes at hand and forge the common bonds within the nascent polis that would be intrinsic to its success.

Conclusion

This book has explored the ways in which the formation of a new civic community enmeshed royal authority in a complex web of social relations, religious structures, polis institutions, and civic expectations. At the same time and no less importantly, the imprint of Hellenistic imperialism profoundly shaped communities reorganized and transformed by this encounter. This book began by exploring the local repercussions of a famous episode in the political history of the Hellenistic period: Antigonos, his objectives temporarily thwarted, reluctantly assenting to the peace of 311. This truce was, of course, a major turning point in the development of the Hellenistic kingdoms. In his celebrated letter to Skepsis, Antigonos reframed the narrative of the peace by presenting his motives in terms of his *philotimia* (ambition) on behalf of the freedom of the Greeks, even as he admitted that his wider ambitions had been frustrated.[1] The ancient sources often cite the cardinal civic virtues of *philotimia* and the closely related *philodoxia* as the kings' motivations for founding cities in this period.[2] The notion of individual outlay and achievement harnessed for the collective good of the community was a fundamental means of accommodating and democratizing personal ambition. No doubt this language reflected the kings' ideological presentation of their profound interference in the organization of subject communities, but it also reveals the extent to which the

---

1. *OGIS* 5, ll. 21 (φιλοτιμεῖσθαι), 33 (φιλοτιμίας).
2. E.g., Thebes: Diod. Sic. 19.54 (φιλοδοξῆσαι); Kassandreia: Diod. Sic. 19.52.3 (συμφιλοτιμηθέντος); Ath., *Deip.* 11.28 (φιλοδοξοῦντι, φιλοτιμηθῆναι). On *philotimia* as a civic virtue, see Whitehead 1983; Ferrucci 2013.

ambitions of the Successors, particularly when they collided with the world of the polis, were restricted by influential normative values.

The desire for recognition, the city as *ergon*, was powerful, but it does not fully explain the phenomenon of early Hellenistic synoikism. The dynastic capital (a name city, *Residenzstadt*, imperial symbol, and much besides) projected legitimacy and ideological assertions. It instantiated imperial pronouncements and reified claims to kingship. Cassander began to administer Macedonia "as king" in 316/15,[3] the same year when he founded Kassandreia and Thessalonike and married the Argead Thessalonike, though this was long before he claimed the royal title. Antigonos and Demetrios, the first of the Successors to formally accept this title, did so in the context of two great achievements: the victory over Ptolemy at Cypriot Salamis and the foundation of Antigoneia in Syria. Both of these supported their coronation, which initiated a new age of kings, drawing on deep traditions that associated kingship with extraordinary accomplishments and foundational acts.[4]

Yet the style of rule that developed in the first generations of the Hellenistic kings was also improvisatory and fluid, highly adaptive to the unique circumstances in which it arose. In the fragmented and competitive context of the early Hellenistic period, the support of local communities and the organization of power into coherent territorial kingdoms was increasingly important as the practical reality of universal rule faded. At the same time, the political and strategic imperatives facing the Successors also do not fully explain their propensity for synoikism, and such considerations tell us still less about the development of these cities. Ancient poleis that were perfectly defensible and possessed of significant productive territory and population were nonetheless attributed to these unions; likewise, synoikized cities, now invested with formidable walls and resources, later revolted from or resisted their overlords. From a political or military perspective, then, synoikism potentially presented as many drawbacks as opportunities.

This book has attempted to move beyond a static or unitary view of Hellenistic city foundations, instead stressing the complex political, economic, and religious dimensions of synoikism. The result is an investigation of the process of creating new political communities that explores how both ruler and subject shaped their genesis. Accordingly, the phenomenon of synoikism is best understood within the context of both the particular political ecology and life cycle of the polis and the period of imperial state formation that gave rise to the Hellenistic kingdoms.

I have stressed the distinctive place that urbanization held in the overall structure of these kingdoms. Once Cassander embraced the practice in 316, it soon became an imperial instrument of all the other Successors, as well as subsequent generations of Hellenistic kings. There is a surprising level of uniformity: kings

3. Diod. Sic. 19.52.5.
4. Gruen 1985.

and local dynasts ruling kingdoms and empires of vastly different scales engaged in this practice. The process radically redefined the organization of the territories under Hellenistic rule and was an important legacy of this period.[5] As I have argued, the Successors' preference for organizing their power around large urban units, links in a wide chain of infrastructure and authority, contributed to the distinctive architecture of the Hellenistic states. The kings could draw on a deep tradition of how states and empires organized their power with respect to subject communities: the cities of the Sicilian tyrants, the capitals of the Persians, the synoikisms of Maussollos, and, most important, the foundations of Philip and Alexander, whose legacy loomed over the Successors. There were important differences, however, from what had come before, and the continuities with past precedents do not fully account for synoikism's central place in the empires of the Hellenistic kings.

This book has examined the role of urbanization from two perspectives. One focuses on the structure of Hellenistic empire—how the reorganization of communities ordered, articulated, and maintained these nascent kingdoms. I have attempted to show how widespread the practice of synoikism was and how profoundly it shaped the regional and productive landscapes of the Hellenistic kingdoms. One result of this phenomenon was that royal power became deeply embedded in the culture of the polis. This had the advantage of enabling kings to harness the sophisticated political structure and institutions of the polis, but it also meant that they had to rely on the cooperation and support of local communities. In contrast to the impression given by many of the literary sources, physical violence seems to have rarely, if ever, played a role in forming cities by synoikism. The coercive power of the king certainly lay in the background of these transformations, and the extent to which synoikism did symbolic violence to civic communities, stripping them of their autonomy, physically uprooting their citizens, and threatening the traditional markers of their identities, should not be underestimated. But the kings seem to have preferred mechanisms beyond force to broker this arrangement and transform cities in ways that had the potential to be mutually beneficial. Faced with the new reality, these communities exploited the constraints under which the kings operated. At times this meant that they could reassert themselves as autonomous political units, freeing themselves from these unions at moments of imperial weakness or when territories changed hands. Such cases of disunion, nevertheless, are in the minority; still more rare were instances of actual resistance. Many of the large-scale synoikisms were remarkably successful ventures.

This observation is at the center of the second main focus of this book. I have attempted to explain how such foundations came to flourish under circumstances of profound social stress. In approaching this question, I have underscored the

---

5. Roman officials later transformed the less urbanized areas of the eastern provinces through synoikism and metoikism. See Ando 2012; 2017a.

wide variety of obstacles these projects faced, from the cost and scale of building a new community to the accommodation of diverse citizen groups, discrete cultural and religious traditions, different civic customs, distinct ethnic identities, and conflicting interests. While serious considerations of defense, control, productivity, and prestige motivated the Hellenistic kings to interfere with existing patterns of urban settlement, the creation of these foundations was far from one-sided. The formation of a united political community was an immense challenge, and the agency of the constituent groups in dictating the terms of these mergers deserves emphasis. I have described and explored the process of forming a new city as the result of a drawn-out series of social tensions, negotiations, and communal and individual actions. Approaching synoikism in this way recovers an important chapter in the history of the polis and elucidates a central form of interaction between subject and ruler.[6]

What emerges is the extent to which the interests and agencies of civic communities, individuals, and kings were intimately intertwined throughout this process. The parameters of this exchange gave cities distinctive geneses, forms, and institutions. At the same time, they were fundamentally Greek poleis, built on the foundations of the diverse citizen groups that constituted them. The practice of synoikism reveals the flexibility and resilience of polis institutions, the very traits that made them so valuable to the Hellenistic kings. The proliferation of the polis was one of the great legacies of the age. But it is essential to not lose sight of the complex ways in which poleis formed. Royal authority played a defining role in articulating urban space and organizing political communities, but the participation of local actors had fundamental repercussions for the shape of Hellenistic rule. The same is true for the wider Hellenistic *oikoumenē*, particularly in regions with no prior history of polis institutions. In such contexts, a similarly complex, if distinctive, process of polis formation no doubt played out, but in these cases the nature of the sources makes the dynamic somewhat more difficult to trace. In Greece and western Asia Minor, by contrast, the organized and articulate poleis, with their fierce independence, local particularism, and epigraphic habit, have left a telling if fragmentary record. A delicate balance between royal authority and local concerns characterized imperial state formation in the early Hellenistic period. This model blended tradition with innovation to form a distinctive kind of empire.

---

6. See Tilly 2005 for the complex role of networks of trust in the relationship between ruler and subject.

BIBLIOGRAPHY

The abbreviations used for modern scholarly journals are those of L'annee philologique, except for the following:

AAA	Αρχαιολογικά Ανάλεκτα εξ Αθηνών
ΑΔ	Ἀρχαιολογικὸν Δελτίον
AE	Ἀρχαιολογικὴ Ἐφημερίς
ΑΕΜΘ	Αρχαιολογικό Έργο στη Μακεδονία και στη Θράκη
ΑΕΘΣΕ	Αρχαιολογικό Έργο Θεσσαλίας και Στερεάς Ελλάδας
Ark. Derg.	Arkeoloji dergisi
AST	Araştırma Sonuçları Toplantısı
Πρακτικά	Πρακτικὰ τῆς ἐν Ἀθήναις Ἀρχαιολογικῆς Ἑταιρείας

Adam-Veleni, P. 1989. "Ελληνιστικά στοιχεία από ανασκαφές στη Θεσσαλονίκη." ΑΕΜΘ 3: 227–40.

———. 2009a. "Farmhouses in Macedonia: The Beginnings of Feudalism?" In *20 Χρόνια το Αρχαιολογικό Έργο στη Μακεδονία και στη Θράκη*, edited by P. Adam-Veleni and K. Tzanavari, 1–17. Thessaloniki.

———. 2009b. *Macedonia-Thessaloniki*. Athens.

———. 2011. "Thessalonike." In *Brill's Companion to Ancient Macedonia*, edited by R. Lane-Fox, 545–62. Brill.

Adams, W. 1997. "Philip II and the Thracian Frontier." In *Thrace ancienne*, 81–87. Komotini.

———. 2007. "'Symmiktous Katoikisas' and the City Foundations of the Thracian Frontier." In *Thrace in the Graeco-Roman World*, edited by A. Iakovidou, 3–12. Athens.

Ager, S. 1996. *Interstate Arbitrations in the Greek World, 337–90 B.C.* Berkeley.

———. 1998. "Civic Identity in the Hellenistic World: The Case of Lebedos." *GRBS* 39: 5–21.

———. 2013. "Interstate Governance: Arbitration and Peacekeeping." In *A Companion to Ancient Greek Government*, edited by H. Beck, 497–511. Malden, MA.
Akalın, A. 1991. "Larisa und der Liman-Tepe in der Troas." In *Studien zum antiken Kleinasien: F. K. Dörner zum 80. Geburtstag gewidmet*, 63–68. Bonn.
———. 2008. "Der hellenistische Synoikismos in der Troas." *Studien zum antiken Kleinasien* 6: 1–38.
Akurgal, E. 1983. *Alt-Smyrna I.* Ankara.
Alcock, S. 1991. "Tomb Cult and the Post-classical Polis." *AJA* 95: 447–67.
———. 1993. *Graecia Capta: The Landscapes of Roman Greece.* Cambridge.
———. 1997. "The Heroic Past in a Hellenistic Present." In *Hellenistic Constructs*, edited by P. Cartledge, P. Garnsey, and E. Gruen, 20–34. Berkeley.
Alexander, J. 1963. *Potidaea: Its History and Remains.* Athens.
Aly, W. 1949. "Patroioi Theoi." *RE* 18, no. 4: 2254–62.
Anderson, G. 2003. *The Athenian Experiment: Building an Imagined Political Community in Ancient Attica, 508–490 BC.* Ann Arbor.
Ando, C. 2012. "The Roman City in the Roman Period." In *Rome, the City and Its Empire in Perspective*, edited by S. Benoist, 109–24. Leiden.
———. 2017a. "The Ambitions of Government: Territoriality and Infrastructural Power in Ancient Rome." In *Ancient States and Infrastructural Power*, edited by C. Ando and S. Richardson, 115–48. Philadelphia.
———. 2017b. "Introduction: States and State Power in Antiquity." In *Ancient States and Infrastructural Power*, edited by C. Ando and S. Richardson, 1–16. Philadelphia.
Andronicos, M. 1984. *Vergina: The Royal Tombs and the Ancient City.* Athens.
Anguissola. 2006a. "Note on Aphidruma 1: Statues and Their Function." *CQ* 56, no. 2: 641–43.
———. 2006b. "Note on Aphidruma 2: Strabo on the Transfer of Cults." *CQ* 56, no. 2: 643–46.
Aperghis, G. 2001. "Population—Production—Taxation—Coinage: A Model for the Seleucid Economy." In *Hellenistic Economies*, edited by Z. Archibald, J. Davies, V. Gabrielsen, and G. Oliver, 69–102. London.
———. 2004. *The Seleukid Royal Economy: The Finances and Financial Administration of the Seleukid Empire.* Cambridge.
———. 2005. "City Building and the Seleukid Royal Economy." In *Making, Moving and Managing: The New World of Ancient Economies, 323–31 BC*, edited by Z. Archibald, J. Davies, and V. Gabrielsen, 27–44. Oxford.
Archibald, Z. 2004. "Inland Thrace." In *An Inventory of Archaic and Classical Poleis*, edited by M. Hansen and T. Nielsen, 885–99. Oxford.
———. 2013. *Ancient Economies of the Northern Aegean: Fifth to First Centuries BC.* Oxford.
———. 2014. "Macedonia and Thrace: Iron Age to Post-Roman Urban Centres." *AR* 60: 88–105.
Arenz, A. 2006. *Herakleides Kritikos "Über die Städte in Hellas."* Munich.
Arvanitopoulos, A. 1906. "Ἀνασκαφαί ἐν Θεσσαλίᾳ." Πρακτικά: 123–30.
———. 1908. "Ἀνακαφαί καὶ ἔρευναι ἐν Σικυῶνι καὶ Θεσσσαλίᾳ." Πρακτικά: 145–223.
———. 1909a. "Ἀνασκαφαί καὶ ἔρευναι ἐν Ἀμφαναίς." Πρακτικά: 162–79.
———. 1909b. Θεσσαλικά Μνημεῖα: Κατάλογος τῶν ἐν τῶι Ἀθανασακείῳ Μουσείῳ Βόλου Ἀρχαιοτήτων. Athens.
———. 1910. "Ἐν Ἰωκλῷ." Πρακτικά: 168–72.

———. 1911. "Ἐπὶ τῆς κορυφῆς τοῦ Πηλίου." *Πρακτικά*: 305–15.
———. 1912. "Ἀνακαφαί καὶ ἔρευναι ἐν Θεσσαλίᾳ." *Πρακτικά*: 154–234.
———. 1915. "Ναὸς Πλούτωνος, Δήμητρος καὶ Κόρης." *Πρακτικά*: 191–92.
———. 1928. *Γραπταί στῆλαι Δημητριάδος*-Παγασῶν. Athens.
———. 1929a. "Θεσσαλικαὶ ἐπιγραφαί." *Πόλεμων* 1, no. 1: 27–38.
———. 1929b. "Θεσσαλικαὶ ἐπιγραφαί." *Πόλεμων* 1, no. 2: 119–28.
———. 1929c. "Θεσσαλικαὶ ἐπιγραφαί." *Πόλεμων* 1, no. 3: 201–26.
———. 1929d. "Θεσσαλικαὶ ἐπιγραφαί." *Πόλεμων* 1, no. 4: 227–53.
———. 1938. "Pelion." *RE* 19: 339–41.
———. 1949. "Θεσσαλικαὶ ἐπιγραφαί." *Πόλεμων* 4, no. 2: 81–92.
———. 1952. "Θεσσαλικαὶ ἐπιγραφαί." *Πόλεμων* 5, no. 1: 1–58.
Aslan, C., and C. B. Rose. 2013. "City and Citadel at Troy from the Late Bronze Age through the Roman Period." In *Cities and Citadels in Turkey*, edited by S. Redford and N. Ergin, 7–38. Walpole, MA.
Atalay, E., and S. Turkoglou. 1972. "Ein frühhellenistischer Porträtkopf des Lysimachos aus Ephesos." *JÖAI* 50, *Beiblatt*: 123–50.
Atkinson, K. 1972. "A Hellenistic Land-Conveyance: The Estate of Mnesimachus in the Plain of Sardis." *Historia* 21: 45–74.
Aylward, W. 1999. "Studies in Hellenistic Ilion: The Houses in the Lower City." *Studia Troica* 9: 159–87.
———. 2005. "The Portico and Propylaia of the Sanctuary of Athena Ilias at Ilion." *Studia Troica* 15: 127–75.
Aylward, W., and J. Wallrodt. 2003. "The Other Walls of Troia: A Revised Trace for Ilion's Hellenistic Fortifications." *Studia Troica* 13: 89–113.
Bachvarova, M., D. Dutsch, and A. Suter, eds. 2016. *The Fall of Cities in the Mediterranean: Commemoration in Literature, Folk-Song, and Liturgy*. Cambridge.
Badian, E. 1968. "A King's Notebooks." *HSCP* 72: 183–204.
———. 1989. "History from 'Square Brackets.'" *ZPE* 79: 59–70.
Badoud, N. 2013. "Timbres amphoriques de Mendée et de Cassandreia." In *PATABS III: Production and Trade of Amphorae in the Black Sea*, edited by L. Buzoianu, P. Dupont, and V. Lungu, 89–103. Constanța.
———. 2015. *Le temps de Rhodes: Une chronologie des inscriptions de la cité fondée sur l'étude de ses institutions*. Munich.
Bagnall, R. 1976. *The Administration of the Ptolemaic Possessions outside Egypt*. Leiden.
Bakalakis, G. 1953. "Θερμαῖος." *AE* 22–23: 221–29.
———. 1956. "Κισσός." *Μακεδονικά* 3: 353–62.
———. 1963. "Therme-Thessaloniki." *Antike Kunst: Beiheft* 1: 30–34.
———. 1983. "Ἱερὸ Διονύσου καὶ φαλλικά δρώμενα στην Θεσσαλονίκη." *Ἀρχαία Μακεδονία* 3: 31–43.
Bakhuizen, S. 1987. "Magnesia unter makedonischer Suzeränität." In *Demetrias 5*, edited by S. Bakhuizen, F. Gschnitzer, P. Marzolff, and C. Habicht, 319–38. Bonn.
———, ed. 1992. *A Greek City of the Fourth Century B.C. by the Goritsa Team*. Rome.
———. 1994. "Thebes and Boeotia in the Fourth Century B.C." *Phoenix* 48, no. 4: 307–30.
———. 1996. "Neleia, a Contribution to a Debate." *Orbis Terrarum* 2: 85–120.
Baladié, R., ed. and trans. 1996. *Géographie: 6, Livre IX*. Paris.

Balcer, J. 1984. *Sparda by the Bitter Sea: Imperial Interaction in Western Anatolia.* Chico.
———. 1985. "Fifth Century B.C. Ionia: A Frontier Redefined." *REA* 87: 31–42.
———. 1988. "Ionia and Sparda under the Achaemenid Empire." In *Le tribut dans l'empire perse,* edited by P. Briant and C. Heerschmidt, 2–24. Paris.
———. 1991. "The East Greeks under Persian Rule: A Reassessment." In *Achaemenid History VI,* edited by H. Sancisi-Weerdenburg and A. Kuhrt, 57–65. Leiden.
Bang, P. 2012. "Between Aśoka and Antiochos." In *Universal Empire: A Comparative Approach to Imperial Culture and Representation in Eurasian History,* edited by P. Bang and D. Kołodziejczyk, 60–75. Cambridge.
Bang, P., and C. Bayly. 2011. *Tributary Empires in Global History.* New York.
Bang, P., and D. Kołodziejczyk, eds. 2012. *Universal Empire: A Comparative Approach to Imperial Culture and Representation in Eurasian History.* Cambridge.
Barjamovic, G. 2012. "Propaganda and Practice in Assyrian and Persian Imperial Culture." In *Universal Empire: A Comparative Approach to Imperial Culture and Representation in Eurasian History,* edited by P. Bang and D. Kołodziejczyk, 43–59. Cambridge.
Barkey, K. 1994. *Bandits and Bureaucrats: The Ottoman Route to State Centralization.* Ithaca, NY.
———. 2008. *Empire of Difference: The Ottomans in Comparative Perspective.* Cambridge.
Barzel, Y. 1989. *Economic Analysis of Property Rights.* Cambridge.
———. 2002. *A Theory of the State: Economic Rights, Legal Rights, and the Scope of the State.* Cambridge.
Batziou-Efstathiou, A. 1992. "Νεότερες ανασκαφικές έρευνες στην ευρύτερη περιοχή της Μαγούλας 'Πευκάκια.'" In *Διεθνές Συνέδριο για την Αρχαία Θεσσαλία,* edited by E. Kypraiou, 279–85. Athens.
———. 1996. "Δημητριάδα." In *Αρχαία Δημητριάδα,* edited by E. Kontaxi, 11–43. Volos.
———. 2002. *Demetrias.* Athens.
———. 2009. "Το εμπόριο οίνου στη Δημητριάδα." *Οἶνον ἱστορῶ* 8: 55–94.
———. 2010. "Λατρείες Δήμητρας και Κόρης στη Δημητριάδα." In *Ιερά και λατρείες της Δήμητρας στον αρχαίο Ελληνικό κόσμο,* edited by I. Leventi and X. Mitsopoulou, 179–99. Volos.
Batziou-Efstathiou, A., and Y. Pikoulas. 2006. "A *Senatus Consultum* from Demetrias." In *Inscriptions and History of Thessaly: New Evidence (Festschrift for C. Habicht),* edited by Y. Pikoulas, 79–89. Volos.
Batziou-Efstathiou, A., and P. Triantaphyllopoulou. 2009. "Επιφανειακές και ανασκαφικές έρευνες στο 'Σωρό.'" *ΑΕΘΣΕ* 2: 257–67.
———. 2012. "Από τα νεκροταφεία της αρχαίας Δημητριάδος-Παγασών." *ΑΔ* 58–64: 211–324.
Bean, G. 1955. "The Defences of Hellenistic Smyrna: B. Epitaphs at Alabanda." *Jahrbuch für kleinasiatische Forschung* 3: 43–55.
Bearzot, C. 1997. "Cassandro e la ricostrusione di Tebe." In *Recent Developments in the History and Archaeology of Central Greece,* edited by J. Bintliff, 265–76. Oxford.
———. 2004. *Federalismo e autonomia nelle elleniche di Senofonte.* Milan.
Beck, H. 1997. *Polis und Koinon.* Stuttgart.
Bell, C. 1992. *Ritual Theory, Ritual Practice.* Oxford.
———. 1997. *Ritual: Perspectives and Dimensions.* Oxford.
Bellinger, A. 1961. *Troy: The Coins.* Princeton.

Bencivenni, A. 2003. *Progetti di riforme costituzionali nelle epigrafi grece dei secoli IV–II a.C.* Bologna.

———. 2004. "Aristodikides di Asso, Antioco I e la scelta di Ilio." *Simbolos* 4: 159–85.

———. 2006. "I Tolemei e l'homopoliteia di Cos e Calimna." *Simbolos* 5: 7–29.

Bengtson, H. 1937. *Die Strategie in der hellenistischen Zeit.* Vol. 1. Munich.

Béquignon, Y. 1935. "Études Thessaliennes VII." *BCH* 59: 36–77.

———. 1937. *Recherches Archéologiques à Phères de Thessalie.* Paris.

Berlin, A. 1999. "Studies in Hellenistic Ilion: The Lower City—Stratified Assemblages and Chronology." *Studia Troica* 9: 73–159.

———. 2002. "Ilion before Alexander: A Fourth Century Ritual Deposit." *Studia Troica* 12: 131–67.

Bessios, M., J. Papadopoulos, and S. Morris. 2016. "Ancient Methone Archaeological Project." Paper presented at the Archaeological Institute of America Annual Meeting, San Francisco, January 8.

Bickerman, E. 1938. *Institutions de Séleucides.* Paris.

Bielman, A. 1994. *Retour à la liberté.* Athens.

Billows, R. 1989. "Anatolian Dynasts: The Case of the Macedonian Eupolemos in Karia." *CA* 8, no. 2: 173–205.

———. 1990. *Antigonos the One-Eyed and the Creation of the Hellenistic State.* Berkeley.

———. 1995. *Kings and Colonists: Aspects of Macedonian Imperialism.* Leiden.

———. 2003. "Cities." In *A Companion to the Hellenistic World*, edited by A. Erskine, 196–215. Oxford.

———. 2007. "Rebirth of a Region: Ionia in the Early Hellenistic Period." In *Regionalism in Hellenistic and Roman Asia Minor*, edited by H. Elton and G. Reger, 33–43. Bordeaux.

Bingöl, O. 1976. "Die Dachziegel von Bayraklı." *Anadolu* 20: 63–81.

———. 1990. "Der Oberbau des Smintheion in der Troas." In *Hermogenes und die hochhellenistische Architektur*, edited by W. Hoepfner and E.-L. Schwandner, 45–50. Mainz.

———. 1991. "Die Problematischen Bauglieder des Smintheion." *RA* 1: 115–28.

Bissa, E. 2009. *Governmental Intervention in Foreign Trade in Archaic and Classical Greece.* Leiden.

Blegen, Carl. 1935. "Excavations at Troy, 1935." *AJA* 39: 550–87.

———. 1937. "Excavations at Troy, 1937." *AJA* 41: 553–97.

Blinkenberg, C. 1941. *Lindos: Fouilles et recherches, 1902–1914*, vol. 2, *Les inscriptions.* Århus.

Blümel, W. 1997. "Vertrag zwischen Latmos und Pidasa." *EA* 29: 136–42.

———. 2000. "Rhodisches Dekret in Bargylia." *EA* 32: 94–96.

Bobou, O. 2015. *Children in the Hellenistic World.* Oxford.

Boehm, F. 1914. "Hydromanteia." *RE* 9: 79–86.

Boehm, R. 2015. "Alexander, 'Whose Courage Was Great': Cult, Power, and Commemoration in Classical and Hellenistic Thessaly." *CA* 34, no. 2: 209–51.

Boffo, L. 1985. *I re ellenistici e i centri religiosi dell'Asia Minore.* Florence.

———. 2001. "Lo statuto di terre, insediamente e persone nell'Anatolia ellenistica." *Dike* 4: 233–55.

Boiy, T. 2007. *Between High and Low: A Chronology of the Early Hellenistic Period.* Frankfurt am Main.

Bonnechere, P. 1994. *Le sacrifice humain en Grèce ancienne.* Athens.
Borrell, H. 1841. "Unedited Autonomous and Imperial Greek Coins." *NC* 4: 1–11.
Borza, E. 1987. "Timber and Politics in the Ancient World: Macedon and the Greeks." *Proceedings of the American Philosophical Society* 131: 32–52.
———. 1990. *In the Shadow of Olympus.* Princeton.
Bosworth, A. B. 2002. *The Legacy of Alexander: Politics, Warfare and Propaganda under the Successors.* Oxford.
Bouyia, P. 2005. "Insights into Narthakion of Phthiotic Achaia in Hellenistic Times." *NumAntCl* 34: 119–38.
———. 2006. "Αρχαιολογικές μαρτυρίες από τον οικισμό και τη νεκρόπολη του Ναρθακίου παρά το Λιμογάρι Φθιώτιδος." *ΑΕΘΣΕ* 1: 927–44.
Bremmer, J. 2001. "Sacrificing a Child in Ancient Greece: The Case of Iphigeneia." In *The Sacrifice of Isaac,* edited by E. Noort and E. J. C. Tigchelaar, 21–43. Leiden.
———. 2014. *Initiation into the Mysteries of the Ancient World.* Berlin.
Bresson, A. 1993. "Les cités grecs et leurs *emporia*." In *L'emporion,* edited by A. Bresson and P. Rouillard, 163–226. Paris.
———. 2005. "Coinage and Money Supply in the Hellenistic Age." In *Making, Moving and Managing: The New World of Ancient Economies, 323–31 BC,* edited by Z. Archibald, J. Davies, and V. Gabrielsen, 44–72. Oxford.
———. 2007a. *L'économie de la Grèce des cités (fin VIe-Ier siècle a.C.).* Vol. 1. Paris.
———. 2007b. "Hamaxitos en Troade." In *Espaces et pouvoirs dans l'antqiuité de l'Anatolie à la Gaule,* edited by J. Dalaison, 139–58. Grenoble.
———. 2016. *The Making of the Ancient Greek Economy.* Translated by S. Rendall. Princeton.
Bresson, A., and R. Descat, eds. 2001. *Les cités d'Asie mineure occidentale au IIe siècle a.C.* Bordeaux.
Briant, P. 1973. *Antigone le Borgne.* Paris.
———. 1982. *Rois, tributs et paysans.* Paris.
———. 1991. "De Sardes à Suse." In *Achaemenid History VI,* edited by H. Sancisi-Weerdenburg and A. Kuhrt, 67–82. Leiden.
———. 1994. "Prélèvements tributaires et échanges en Asie Mineure achéménide et hellénistique." In *Les échanges dans l'antiquité,* edited by J. Andreau, P. Briant, and R. Descat, 69–82. Saint-Bertrand-de-Comminges.
———. 2002. *From Cyrus to Alexander.* Translated by P. Daniels. Winona Lake, IN.
———. 2006. "L'Asie mineure en transition." In *La transition entre l'empire achéménide et les royaumes hellénistiques (vers 350–300 av. J.-C.),* edited by P. Briant and F. Joannès, 309–51. Paris.
———. 2012. "From the Indus to the Mediterranean: The Administrative Organization and Logistics of the Great Roads of the Achaemenid Empire." In *Highways, Byways, and Road Systems in the Pre-modern World,* edited by J. Bodel, S. Alcock, and R. Talbert, 185–201. Malden, MA.
Bringmann, K. 1993. "The King as Benefactor: Some Remarks on Ideal Kingship in the Age of Hellenism." In *Images and Ideologies: Self-Definition in the Hellenistic World,* edited by A. Bulloch, E. Gruen, A. Long, and A. Stewart, 7–24. Berkeley.

———. 2001. "Grain, Timber, and Money: Hellenistic Kings, Finance, Buildings and Foundations in Greek Cities." In *Hellenistic Economies*, edited by Z. Archibald, J. Davies, V. Gabrielsen, and G. Oliver, 205–14. London.

———. 2005. "Königliche Ökonomie im Spiegel des Euergetismus der Seleukiden." *Klio* 87: 102–15.

Bringmann, K., and H. von Steuben. 1995. *Schenkungen hellenistischer Herrscher an griechische Städte und Heiligtümer*. Vol. 1. Berlin.

Briscoe, J. 2008. *A Commentary on Livy, Books 38–40*. Oxford.

Brocke, C. vom. 2001. *Thessaloniki: Stadt des Kassander und Gemeinde des Paulus*. Tübingen.

Brunel, J. 1953. "À propos des transferts de cultes: Un sens méconnu du mot ἀφίδρυμα." *RPh* 27: 21–33.

Bruns-Özgan, C., V. Gassner, and U. Muss. 2011. "Kolophon: Neue Untersuchungen zur Topographie der Stadt." *Anatolia Antiqua* 19: 199–239.

Buckler, W., and D. Robinson. 1912. "Greek Inscriptions from Sardes I." *AJA* 16: 11–82.

———. 1932. *Sardis*, vol. 7, pt. 1, *Greek and Latin Inscriptions*. Leiden.

Buraselis, K. 1982. *Das hellenistische Makedonien und die Ägäis*. Munich.

———. 2014. "Contributions to Rebuilding Thebes: The Old and a New Fragment of *IG* VII 2419 = *Sylloge*³ 337." *ZPE* 188: 159–80.

———. 2015. "Federalism and the Sea: The *Koina* of the Aegean Islands." In *Federalism in Greek Antiquity*, edited by H. Beck and P. Funke, 358–76. Cambridge.

Burke, B. 2013. "The Rebuilt Citadel of Gordion: Building A and the Mosiac Building Complex." In *The Archaeology of Phrygian Gordian, Royal City of Midas*, edited by C. B. Rose, 203–18. Philadelphia.

Burkert, W. 1983. *Homo Necans: The Anthropology of Ancient Greek Sacrificial Ritual and Myth*. Translated by P. Bing. Berkeley.

———. 1993. "Bacchic *Teletai* in the Hellenistic Age." In *Masks of Dionysos*, edited by R. Carpenter and C. Farone, 259–75. Ithaca, NY.

———. 1995. "Greek Poleis and Civic Cults: Some Further Thoughts." In *Studies in the Ancient Greek Polis*, edited by M. Hansen and K. Raaflaub, 201–10. Stuttgart.

Burstein, S. 1986. "Lysimachus and the Cities: The Early Years." *AncW* 14: 19–24.

Buxton, R. 1994. *Imaginary Greece: The Contexts of Mythology*. Cambridge.

Cadoux, C. 1938. *Ancient Smyrna*. Oxford.

Callieri, P. 1995. "Une borne routière grecque de la région de Persépolis." *CRAI* 139: 65–95.

Camp, J. 2000. "Walls and the Polis." In *Polis and Politics*, edited by P. Flensted-Jensen, T. Nielsen, and L. Rubenstein, 41–59. Copenhagen.

Capdetrey, L. 2006. "Économie royale et communautés locales dans le royaume Séleucide: Entre négotiation et imposition." In *Approaches de l'économie hellénistique*, edited by R. Descat, 359–86. Saint-Bertrand-de-Comminges.

———. 2007. *Le pouvoir séleucide: Territoire, administration, finances d'un royaume hellénistique (312–129 avant J.-C.)*. Rennes.

Carballo, D. 2016. *Urbanization and Religion in Ancient Central Mexico*. Oxford.

Cargill, J. 1995. *The Athenian Settlements of the Fourth Century BC*. Leiden.

Casson, S. 1926. *Macedonia, Thrace and Illyria*. London.

Catling, R. 2004–9. "Attalid Troops at Thermon: A Reappraisal of *IG* IX 1² (1) 60." *Horos* 17–21: 397–439.

Chandezon, C. 2000. "Foires et panégyries dans le monde grec classique et hellénistique." *REG* 113: 70–100.

———. 2003. *L'élevage en Grèce*. Paris.

Chaniotis, A. 1996. *Die Verträge zwischen kretischen Poleis in der hellenistischen Zeit*. Stuttgart.

———. 2003. "The Divinity of the Hellenistic Rulers." In *A Companion to the Hellenistic World*, edited by A. Erskine, 431–45. Oxford.

———. 2004. "New Inscriptions from Aphrodisias (1995–2001)." *AJA* 108: 377–416.

———. 2005. *War in the Hellenistic World: A Social and Cultural History*. Malden, MA.

———. 2009. "Myths and Contexts in Aphrodisias." In *Antike Mythen*, edited by U. Dill and C. Walde, 313–38. Berlin.

———. 2011. "Emotional Community through Ritual: Initiates, Citizens, and Pilgrims as Emotional Communities in the Greek World." In *Ritual Dynamics in the Ancient Mediterranean*, edited by A. Chaniotis, 263–90. Stuttgart.

Chankowski, V. 2007. "Les catégories du vocabulaire de la fiscalité dans les cités grecques." In *Vocabulaire et expression de l'économie dans le monde antique*, edited by J. Andreau and V. Chankowski, 299–331. Pessac.

———. 2008. *Athènes et Délos à l'époque classique*. Athens.

———. 2011. "Divine Financiers: Cults as Consumers and Generators of Value." In *The Economies of Hellenistic Societies, Third to First Centuries BC*, edited by Z. Archibald, J. Davies, and V. Gabrielsen, 161. Oxford.

Chankowski, V., and F. Duyrat, eds. 2004. *Le roi et l'économie: Autonomies locales et structures royales dans l'économie de l'empire Séleucide*. Paris.

Charneux, P. 1966. "Liste argienne de théarodoques." *BCH* 90: 156–229.

Chourmouzides, G. 1969. "Γλαφυραί." *ΑΔ* 23, no. 2: 269.

Christmann, E. 1996. *Die deutschen Ausgrabungen auf der Pevkakia-Magula in Thessalian*, vol. 2, *Die frühe Bronzezeit*. Bonn.

Chrysostomou, P. 1994. "Εν(ν)οδία, Ενοδία Εκάτη, Εκάτη Ενοδία." In *Θεσσαλία: Δεκαπέντε χρόνια αρχαιολογικής έρευνας, 1975–1990*, 339–46. Athens.

———. 1998. *Η Θεσσαλική Θεά Εν(ν)οδία ή Φεραία Θεά*. Athens.

Chykerda, M., M. Haagsma, and L. Surtees. 2015. "Ethnic Constructs from Inside and Out: External Policy and the Ethnos of Achaia Phthiotis." Paper presented at the "Greek Ethnos States: Internal Mechanics, External Relations" conference, Delphi, May 25.

Clinton, K. 2014. "Mysteria at Ephesos." *ZPE* 191: 117–28.

Cohen, A. 1995. "Alexander and Achilles—Macedonians and 'Mycenaeans.'" In *The Ages of Homer: A Tribute to E. T. Vermeule*, edited by J. Carter and S. Morris, 483–505. Austin.

Cohen, G. 1978. *The Seleucid Colonies*. Wiesbaden.

———. 1995. *The Hellenistic Settlements in Europe, the Islands, and Asia Minor*. Berkeley.

———. 2006. *The Hellenistic Settlements in Syria, the Red Sea Basin, and North Africa*. Berkeley.

———. 2013. *The Hellenistic Settlements in the East from Armenia and Mesopotamia to Bactria and India*. Berkeley.

Cole, S. 1994. "Civic Cult and Civic Identity." In *Sources for the Ancient Greek City-State*, edited by M. Hansen, 292–395. Copenhagen.

Constantakopoulou, C. 2005. "Proud to Be an Islander: Island Identity in Multi-polis Islands in the Classical and Hellenistic Aegean." *MHR* 20 1: 1–34.
———. 2007. *The Dance of the Islands: Insularity, Networks, the Athenian Empire and the Aegean World*. Oxford.
———. 2012. "Identity and Resistance: The Islanders' League, the Aegean Islands and the Hellenistic Kings." *MHR* 27: 49–70.
———. 2013. "Tribute, the Athenian Empire and Small States/Communities in the Aegean." In *Handels- und Finanzgebaren in der Ägäis im 5. Jh. v. Chr.*, edited by A. Slawisch, 25–42. Istanbul.
Cook, A. 1925. *Zeus: A Study in Ancient Religion*, vol. 2, pt. 2, *Zeus God of the Dark Sky: Thunder and Lightening*. Cambridge.
———. 1940. *Zeus: A Study in Ancient Religion*, vol. 3, pt. 1, *Zeus God of the Dark Sky: Earthquakes, Clouds, Wind, Dew, Rain, Meteorites*. Cambridge.
Cook, J. 1961. "The Problem of Classical Ionia." *PCPS* 7: 9–18.
———. 1973. *The Troad*. Oxford.
———. 1988. "Cities in and around the Troad." *ABSA* 83: 7–19.
Corsten, T. 2007. "The Foundation of Laodikeia on the Lykos: An Example of Hellenistic City Foundation." In *Regionalism in Hellenistic and Roman Asia Minor*, edited by H. Elton and G. Reger, 131–36. Bordeaux.
Cortieu, G. 2013. "La localisation de l'Asklépieion de Lysimaque (Troade)." In *L'Anatolie des peuples, des cités et des cultures*, edited by B. Hadrien and G. Labarre, vol. 1, 97–106. Besançon.
Courbin, P. 1980. *L'oikos des Naxiens*. Paris.
Crampa, J. 1968. "Some Remarks on Welles, *Royal Correspondence*, 29." *Opuscula Atheniensia* 8: 171–78.
Criscuolo, L. 2011. "La formula *en patrikois* nelle iscrizioni di Cassandrea." *Chiron* 41: 461–85.
Dandamaev, M. 1989. *A Political History of the Achaemenid Empire*. Translated by W. Vogelsang. Leiden.
Daux, G. 1936. *Delphes au IIe et au Ier siècle: Depuis l'abaissement de l'Etolie jusqu'à la paix romaine 191–31 av. J.-C.* Paris.
Davies, J. 1992. "Greece after the Persian Wars." In *The Cambridge Ancient History*, 2nd ed., vol. 5, *The Fifth Century B.C.*, edited by D. Lewis, J. Boardman, J. Davies, and M. Ostwald, 15–33. Cambridge.
———. 2002. "The Interpenetration of Hellenistic Sovereignties." In *The Hellenistic World: New Perspectives*, edited by D. Ogden, 1–21. London.
———. 2005. "The Economic Consequences of Hellenistic Palaces." In *Making, Moving and Managing: The New World of Ancient Economies, 323–31 BC*, edited by Z. Archibald, J. Davies, and V. Gabrielsen, 117–35. Oxford.
———. 2011. "The Well-Balanced Polis: Ephesos." In *The Economies of Hellenistic Societies, Third to First Centuries BC*, edited by Z. Archibald, J. Davies, and V. Gabrielsen, 177–206. Oxford.
Debord, P. 1982. *Aspects sociaux et économiques de la vie religieuse dans l'Anatolie grécoromaine*. Leiden.
———. 1995. "Les routes royales en Asie minore occidentale." *Pallas* 43: 89–97.

Debord, P., and E. Varinlioğlu, eds. 2001. *Les hautes terres de Carie*. Bordeaux.
de Callataÿ, F. 2004. "La richesse de rois séleucides et le problème de la taxation en nature." In *Le roi et l'économie: Autonomies locales et structures royales dans l'économie de l'empire Séleucide*, edited by V. Chankowski and F. Duyrat, 23–47. Paris.
———. 2005. "A Quantitative Survey of Hellenistic Coinages: Recent Achievements." In *Making, Moving and Managing: The New World of Ancient Economies, 323–31 BC*, edited by Z. Archibald, J. Davies, and V. Gabrielsen, 73–91. Oxford.
Decourt, J., B. Helly, and T. Nielsen. 2004. "Thessalia and Adjacent Regions." In *An Inventory of Archaic and Classical Poleis*, edited by M. Hansen and T. Nielsen, 676–731. Oxford.
de Ligt, L. 1993. *Fairs and Markets in the Roman Empire*. Amsterdam.
Demand, N. 1990. *Urban Relocation in Archaic and Classical Greece*. Norman, OK.
Derks, T., and N. Roymans. 2009. Introduction to *Ethnic Constructs in Antiquity*, edited by T. Derks and N. Roymans, 1–10. Amsterdam.
Descat, R. 1985. "Mnésimachos, Hérodote et le système tributaire achéménide." *REA* 87: 99–102.
———. 1998. "La carrière d'Eupolemos, stratège macèdonien en Asie Mineure." *REA* 100: 167–90.
———. 2003. "Qu'est-ce que l'économie royale ?" *Pallas* 62: 149–68.
———. 2004. Conclusion to *Le roi et l'économie: Autonomies locales et structures royales dans l'économie de l'empire Séleucide*, edited by V. Chankowski and F. Duyrat, 571–76. Paris.
———. 2010. "*Argyrion symmachikon* et l'histoire de la Carie à la fin du IVe siècle a.C." In *Hellenistic Karia*, edited by R. van Bremen and J.-M. Carbon, 133–44. Talence.
de Vries, J. 1984. *European Urbanization, 1500–1800*. Cambridge, MA.
De Vries, K. 1990. "The Gordion Excavation Seasons of 1969–1973 and Subsequent Research." *AJA* 94: 371–406.
———. 1996. "The Attic Pottery from Gordion." In *Athenian Potters and Painters*, vol. 1, edited by J. Oakley, W. Coulson, and O. Palagia, 447–55. Oxford.
———. 2005. "Greek Pottery and Gordion Chronology." In *The Archaeology of Midas and the Phrygians*, edited by L. Kealhofer, 36–55. Philadelphia.
Dickenson, C., L. Radlof, and H. Reinders. 2006. "The Southeast Gate of the Hellenistic City of New Halos." *Pharos* 13: 77–92.
Dignas, B. 2002. *Economy of the Sacred in Hellenistic and Roman Asia Minor*. Oxford.
———. 2003. "Rhodian Priests after the Synoecism." *AncSoc* 33: 35–51.
Dilts, M, ed. and trans. 1971. *Heraclidis Lembi Excerpta Politiarum*. Durham, NC.
Dinsmore, W. 1940. "The Temple of Ares at Athens." *Hesperia* 9, no. 1: 1–52.
Di Salvatore, M. 1994. "Ricerche sul territorio di Pherai: Insediamenti, difese, cie e confini." In Θεσσαλία: Δεκαπέντε χρόνια αρχαιολογικής έρευνας, 1975–1990, 93–124. Athens.
———. 2002. "La storia proiettata sul territorio: Il caso della città greca di Pherai." In *Sviluppi recenti nella ricerca antichistica*, edited by V. De Angelis, 25–53. Milan.
Dixit, A. 2004. *Lawlessness and Economics: Alternative Modes of Governance*. Cambridge.
Dmitriev, S. 2011. *The Greek Slogan of Freedom and Early Roman Politics in Greece*. Oxford.
Dörpfeld, W. 1902. *Troja und Ilion*. Athens.
Dössel, A. 2003. *Die Beilegung innerstaatlicher Konflikte in den griechischen Poleis vom 5.–3. Jahrhundert v. Chr.* Frankfurt am Main.

Dreyer, B. 2002. "Der 'Raubsvertrag' des Jahres 203/02 v. Chr." *EA* 34: 119-38.
Dušanić, S. 1978. "Notes épigraphiques sur l'histoire arcadienne du IVe siècle." *BCH* 102, no. 1: 333-58.
Dusinberre, E. 2013. *Empire, Authority, and Autonomy in Achaemenid Anatolia*. Cambridge.
Edson, C. 1947. "Notes on the Thracian Phoros." *CP* 42, no. 2: 88-105.
———. 1948. "Cults of Thessalonica (Macedonica III)." *HTR* 41, no. 3: 153-204.
Eich, A. 2004. "Probleme der staatlichen Einheit in der griechischen Antike." *ZPE* 149: 83-102.
———. 2006. *Die politische Ökonomie des antiken Griechenland*. Cologne.
Ellis Evans, A. 2016. "The Koinon of Athena Ilias and Its Coinage." *AJN* 28: 105-58.
Elsner, J. 2007. *Roman Eyes: Visuality and Subjectivity in Art and Text*. Princeton.
Emiliov, J. 2015. "Celts." In *A Companion to Ancient Thrace*, edited by J. Valeva, E. Nankov, and D. Graninger, 366-81. Malden, MA.
Engelmann, H. 1996. "Phylen und Chiliasten von Ephesos." *ZPE* 113: 94-100.
———. 1997. "Der Koressos, ein Ephesisches Stadtviertel." *ZPE* 115: 131-35.
Erdkamp, P. 2001. "Beyond the Limits of the Consumer City: A Model of the Urban and Rural Economy in the Roman World." *Historia* 50: 332-56.
Errington, R. 1976. "Alexander in the Hellenistic World." *Entretiens sur l'antiquité classique de la Fondation Hardt* 22: 137-79.
———. 1998. "Neue epigraphische Belege für Makedonien zur Zeit Alexanders des Grossen." In *Alexander der Große*, edited by W. Will, 77-90. Bonn.
Erskine, A. 2001. *Troy between Greece and Rome: Local Tradition and Imperial Power*. Oxford.
———. 2013. "Founding Alexandria in the Alexandrian Imagination." In *Belonging and Isolation in the Hellenistic World*, edited by S. Ager and R. Faber, 169-83. Toronto.
Ersoy, A., and S. Alatepeli. 2011. "Der Hafen von Smyrna," *MDAI(I)* 61: 105-15.
Ersoy, Y. 1993. "Clazomenae: The Archaic Settlement." PhD diss., Bryn Mawr College.
Fabiani, R. 2009. "Eupolemos Potalou o Eupolemos Simalou? Un nuovo documento da Iasos." *EA* 42: 61-77.
Faraone, C. 2013. "Gender Differentiation and Role Models in the Worship of Dionysus: The Thracian and Thessalian Pattern." In *Redefining Dionysus*, edited by A. Bernabé, A. Jiménez, M. Herrero, and R. Martín, 120-43. Berlin.
Feldmann, W. 1885. "Analecta Epigraphica ad Historiam Synoecismorum et Sympolitiarum Graecorum." Inaug.-Diss., University of Strasbourg.
Ferrucci, S. 2013. "L'ambigua virtù: Φιλοτιμία nell'Atene degli oratori." In *Parole in movimento: Linguaggio politico e lessico storiografico nel mondo ellenistico*, edited by M. Mari and J. Thornton, 123-35. Pisa.
Feuser, S. 2009. *Der Hafen von Alexandria Troas*. Bonn.
Feyel, M. 1940. "La fête d'Apollon Tarsenos." *REA* 42, no. 1: 137-41.
Filges, A., and P. Matern. 1996. "Eine Opfergrube der Demeter in Neandria." In *Die Troas: Neue Forschungen zu Neandria und Alexandria Troas II*, edited by E. Schwertheim and Hans Wiegartz, 43-86. Bonn.
Filges, A., and E. Posselt. 1999. "Hellenistische Keramik." In *Die Troas: Neue Forschungen III*, edited by E. Schwertheim, 139-57. Bonn.
Finley, M. 1985. *The Ancient Economy*. London.

Fischer-Bouvet, C. 2014. *Army and Society in Ptolemaic Egypt*. Cambridge.
Flacelière, R. 1937. *Les Aitoliens à Delphes*. Paris.
Flensted-Jensen, P. 1995. "The Bottiaians and Their Poleis." In *Studies in the Ancient Greek Polis*, edited by M. Hansen and K. Raaflaub, 103–32. Stuttgart.
———. 2004. "Karia." In *An Inventory of Archaic and Classical Poleis*, edited by M. Hansen and T. Nielsen, 1108–37. Oxford.
Flendsted-Jensen, P., and M. Hansen. 1996. "Pseudo-Skylax' Use of the Term *Polis*." In *More Studies in the Greek Polis*, edited by M. Hansen and K. Raaflaub, 137–68. Stuttgart.
Flinterman, J. 2012. "Pannucome Revisited: Lines 11–13 of the Laodice Inscription Again." *ZPE* 181: 79–87.
Forbes, H. 2007. *Meaning and Identity in a Greek Landscape*. Cambridge.
Foster, M. 2013. "Hagesias as *Sunoikistêr*: Seercraft and Colonial Ideology in Pindar's Sixth Olympian Ode." *CA* 32, no. 2: 283–321.
Franke, P. 1967. "Ἄρτεμις Ἰολκία." *AA* 1: 62–64.
Fraser, P. 1996. *The Cities of Alexander the Great*. Oxford.
Frayn, J. 1993. *Markets and Fairs in Roman Italy*. Oxford.
Freitag, K. 1994. "Oiniadai als Hafenstadt: Einige historischtopographische Überlegungen." *Klio* 76: 212–38.
———. 2006. "Ein Schiedsvertrag zwischen Halos und Thebai aus Delphi." In *Kult-Politik-Ethnos*, edited by K. Freitag, P. Funke, and M. Haake, 211–37. Stuttgart.
French, D. 1997. "Pre- and Early Roman Roads of Asia Minor: A Hellenistic Stadion-Stone from Ephesus." *Ark. Derg.* 5: 189–96.
———. 1998. "Pre- and Early-Roman Roads of Asia Minor: The Persian Royal Road." *Iran* 36: 15–43.
Furtwängler, A. 1990a. "Demetrias: Eine makedonische Gründung im Netz hellenistischer Handels- und Geldpolitik." Habilitation diss., Saarland University, Saarbrücken.
———. 1990b. "Demetrias, ein Produktionsort 'attischer' Keramik?" In *Β' Επιστημονική Συνάντηση για την Ελληνιστική Κεραμική*, 9–53. Rhodes.
———. 1992. "Zur Handelsausrichtung der Stadt Demetrias im Lichte neuerer Grabungsergebnisse." In *Διεθνές Συνέδριο για την Αρχαία Θεσσαλία*, edited by E. Kypraiou, 366–69. Athens.
———. 2003. "Amphorenfunde in Demetrias." In G. Zimmer, *Demetrias 6*, edited by A. Furtwängler and G. Zimmer, 113–57. Würzburg.
Furtwängler, A., and U. Kron. 1978. "Das Siegel der Stadt Demetrias." *MDAI(A)* 93: 133–60.
———. 1983. "Demetrios Poliorketes, Demetrias und die Magneten." In *Αρχαία Μακεδονία* 3: 147–68.
Gabrielsen, V. 1997. *The Naval Aristocracy of Hellenistic Rhodes*. Århus.
———. 2000. "The Synoikized Polis of Rhodes." In *Polis and Politics*, edited by P. Flensted-Jensen, T. Nielsen, and L. Rubenstein, 177–205. Copenhagen.
———. 2011. "Profitable Partnerships: Monopolies, Traders, Kings, and Cities." In *The Economies of Hellenistic Societies, Third to First Centuries BC*, edited by Z. Archibald, J. Davies, and V. Gabrielsen, 216–50. Oxford.
Gaebler, H. 1926. "Zur Münzkunde Makedoniens VIII: Das mygdonische Apollonia." *ZfN* 36: 133–99.

Gaede, R. 1880. *Demetrii Scepsii quae supersunt*. Diss., University of Greifswald.
Gagliardi, L. 2009. "I 'paroikoi' delle città dell'Asia Minore in età ellenistica e nella prima età Romana." *Dike* 12–13: 303–22.
Garlan, Y. 2004. "Η προέλευση της 'ομάδας Παρμενίσκου' από τη Μένδη." In *AEMΘ* 18: 141–48.
Gates, M. 1994. "Archaeology in Turkey." *AJA* 98: 249–78.
Gauthier, P. 1980. "Les honneurs de l'officier séleucide Larichos à Priène." *JS* 1, no. 1: 35–50.
———. 1985. *Les cités grecques et leurs bienfaiteurs*. Athens.
———. 1987. "Grandes et petites cites: Hegemonie et autarcie." *Opus* 6–8: 187–202.
———. 1988. "Meteques, perieques et paroikoi: Bilan et points d'interrogation." In *L'etranger dans le monde grec*, edited by R. Lonis, 23–46. Nancy.
———. 1989. *Nouvelles inscriptions de Sardes II*. Geneva.
———. 2001. "Les Pidaséens entrent en sympolitie avec les Milésiens: La procédure et les modalités institutionnelles." In *Les cités d'Asie mineure occidentale au IIe siècle a.C.*, edited by A. Bresson and R. Descat, 117–27. Bordeaux.
———. 2003. "Le décret de Colophon l'ancienne en l'honneur du Thessalien Asandros et la sympolitie entre les deux Colophon." *JS* 1, no. 1: 61–100.
Gawlinski, L. 2012. *The Sacred Law of Andania: A New Text with Commentary*. Berlin.
Geagan, D. 1968. "Inscriptions from Nemea." *Hesperia* 37: 381–85.
Gehrke, H.-J. 1994–95. "Die kulturelle und politische Entwicklung Akarnaniens vom 6. bis zum 4. Jahrhundert v. Chr." *Geographia Antiqua* 3–4: 41–48.
Georgiades, N. 1894. *Θεσσαλία*. 2nd ed. Volos.
Gimatzidis, S. 2010. *Die Stadt Sindos*. Rahden, North Rhine–Westphalia.
Giovannini, A. 1971. *Untersuchungen über die Natur und die Anfänge der bundesstaatlichen Sympolitie in Griechenland*. Göttingen.
Goukowsky, P. 2009. *Études de philologie et d'histoire ancienne*, vol. 1, *Macedonica varia*. Nancy.
Gouščhin, V. 1999. "Athenian Synoikism of the Fifth Century B.C., or Two Stories of Theseus." *Greece and Rome* 46, no. 2: 168–87.
Grace, V. 1985. "The Middle Stoa Dated by Amphora Stamps." *Hesperia* 54: 1–54.
Graf, D. 1996. "The Persian Royal Road System." In *Achaemenid History VIII: Continuity and Change*, edited by A. Kuhrt, M. Root, and H. Sancisi-Weerdenburg, 167–89. Leiden.
Graf, F. 1996. "'Pompai' in Greece: Some Considerations about Space and Ritual in the Greek Polis." In *The Role of Religion in the Early Greek Polis*, edited by R. Hägg, 55–65. Jonsered, Sweden.
Graninger, D. 2007. "Studies in the Cult of Artemis Throsia." *ZPE* 162: 151–64.
———. 2009. "Apollo, Ennodia, and Fourth-Century Thessaly." *Kernos* 22: 109–24.
———. 2010. "Macedonia and Thessaly." In *A Companion to Ancient Macedonia*, edited by I. Worthington and J. Roisman, 306–25. Malden, MA.
———. 2011a. *Cult and Koinon in Hellenistic Thessaly*. Brill.
———. 2011b. "*IG* IX.2 1099B and the Komai of Demetrias." *ZPE* 177: 119–22.
Gras, M. 1987. "Le temple de Diane sur l'Aventin." *REA* 99: 47–61.
Gray, D. 2015. *Stasis and Stability: Exile, the Polis, and Political Thought, c. 404–146 BC*. Oxford.

Gregory, A. 1995. "A Makedonian *Dynastés*: Evidence for the Life and Career of P. Antipatrou." *Historia* 44: 11–28.
Griffith, G. 1950. "The Union of Corinth and Argos (392–386 B.C.)." *Historia* 1, no. 2: 236–56.
Groskurd, G., trans. 1831. *Strabons Erdbeschreibung*. Vol. 2. Berlin.
Grote, G. 1872. *A History of Greece*. Vol. 1. London.
Gruen, E. 1984. *The Hellenistic World and the Coming of Rome*. Berkeley.
———. 1985. "The Coronation of the Diadochoi." In *The Craft of the Ancient Historian: Essays in Honor of Chester G. Starr*, edited by J. Eadie and J. Ober, 253–71. Lanham, MD.
———. 1993. "The Polis in the Hellenistic World." In *Nomodeiktes: Greek Studies in Honor of Martin Ostwald*, edited by R. Rosen and J. Farrell, 339–54. Ann Arbor.
Gschnitzer, F. 1989. "Beurkundungsgebühren im römischen Kaiserreich. zu *Inschr. Eph.* Ia 13." In *Symposion 1985*, edited by G. Thür, 389–403. Cologne.
Haagsma, M., S. Karapanou, T. Harvey, and L. Surtees. 2011. "A New City and Its Agora: Results from the Hellenic-Canadian Archaeological Work at the Kastro Kallithea in Thessaly, Greece." In *Η αγορά στη Μεσόγειο από τους ομηρικούς εως τους ρωμαϊκούς χρόνους*, edited by A. Giannikouri, 197–207. Athens.
Habicht, C. 1970. *Gottmenschentum und die griechische Städte*. 2nd ed. Munich.
———. 1997. *Athens from Alexander to Antony*. Cambridge, MA.
———. 1998a. *Pausanias' Guide to Ancient Greece*. Berkeley.
———. 1998b. "Zum Vertrag zwischen Latmos und Pidasa." *EA* 30: 9–10.
———. 2004. "Ein neuer Gymasiarch am Fest der Athena Ilias." *EA* 37: 91–94.
———. 2007. "Neues zur hellenistischen Geschichte von Kos." *Chiron* 37: 123–52.
Hahn, I. 1981. "Periöken und Periökenbesitz in Lykien." *Klio* 63: 51–61.
Hall, J. 1997. *Ethnic Identity in Greek Antiquity*. Cambridge.
———. 2002. *Hellenicity: Between Ethnicity and Culture*. Chicago.
———. 2015. "Federalism and Ethnicity." In *Federalism in Greek Antiquity*, edited by H. Beck and P. Funck, 30–48. Cambridge.
Hamilton, C. 1972. "The Politics of Revolution in Corinth, 395–386 B.C." *Historia* 21, no. 1: 21–37.
Hammond, N. 1972. *A History of Macedonia*. Vol. 1. Oxford.
———. 1988. "The King and the Land in the Macedonian Kingdom." *CQ* 38, no. 2: 382–91.
Hammond, N., and G. Griffith. 1979. *A History of Macedonia*. Vol. 2. Oxford.
Hansen, M. 1995. "The Autonomous City-State: Ancient Fact or Modern Fiction?" In *Studies in the Ancient Greek Polis*, edited by M. Hansen and K. Raaflaub, 21–43. Stuttgart.
———. 2004. "The Concept of the Consumption City Applied to the Greek Polis." In *Once Again: Studies in the Ancient Greek Polis*, edited by T. Nielsen, 9–47. Stuttgart.
Hansen, M., and T. Nielsen. 2004a. "Destruction and Disappearance of *Poleis*." In *An Inventory of Archaic and Classical Poleis*, edited by M. Hansen and T. Nielsen, 120–23. Oxford.
———. 2004b. "The Emergence of *Poleis* by *Synoikismos*." In *An Inventory of Archaic and Classical Poleis*, edited by M. Hansen and T. Nielsen, 115–19. Oxford.
———. 2004c. "Territory and Size of Territory." In *An Inventory of Archaic and Classical Poleis*, edited by M. Hansen and T. Nielsen, 70–73. Oxford.
———. 2004d. "*Theorodokoi* as Evidence for *Polis* Identity." In *An Inventory of Archaic and Classical Poleis*, edited by M. Hansen and T. Nielsen, 103–6. Oxford.

———. 2004e. "A Typology of Dependent *Poleis.*" In *An Inventory of Archaic and Classical Poleis*, edited by M. Hansen and T. Nielsen, 87–94. Oxford.

Hanson, J. 2011. "The Urban System of Roman Asia Minor and Wider Urban Connectivity." In *Settlement, Urbanization and Population*, edited by A. Bowman and A. Wilson, 229–75. Oxford.

———. 2016. *An Urban Geography of the Roman World, 100 BC to AD 300*. Oxford.

Harris, J. Forthcoming. "Continuity through Rupture: Space, Time, and Politics in the Mass Migrations of Dionysius the Elder." In *La question de l'espace au IVe siècle av J.-C.: Continuités, ruptures, reprises*, edited by S. Montel and A. Pollini. Besançon.

Harrison, T. 2015. "Review Article: Beyond the *Polis*? New Approaches to Greek Religion." *JHS* 135: 165–80.

Hasluck, F. 1907. "Inscriptions from the Cyzicus Region, 1906." *JHS* 27: 61–67.

———. 1910. *Cyzicus*. Cambridge.

Hatzopoulos, M. 1985. "Strepsa." In *Two Studies in Ancient Macedonian Topography*, edited by M. Hatzopoulos and L. Loukopoulou, 21–60. Athens.

———. 1988. *Une donation du roi Lysimaque*. Athens.

———. 1990. *Poikila*. Athens.

———. 1991. "Un prêtre d'Amphipolis dans la grande liste des théarodoques de Delphes," *BCH* 115: 345–47.

———. 1993. "Décret pour un bienfaiteur de la cité de Philippes." *BCH* 117: 315–26.

———. 1994. *Cultes et rites de passage en Macédoine*. Athens.

———. 1996. *Macedonian Institutions under the Kings*. 2 vols. Paris.

———. 2006. *La Macédoine*. Paris.

Hatzopoulos, M., and L. Loukopoulou. 1992. *Recherches sur les marches orientales des Téménides*. Athens.

Hatzopoulos, M., and S. Psoma. 1998. "Cités de Grèce septentrionale portant le nom de Dion." *Tekmeria* 4: 1–12.

Head, B. 1911. *Historia Numorum*. 2nd ed. Oxford.

Hellström, P. 1965. *Labraunda: Swedish Excavations and Researches*, vol. 2, pt. 1, *Pottery of Classical and Later Date, Terracotta Lamps and Glass*. Lund.

Helly, B. 1971. "Décrets de Démétrias pour les juges étrangers." *BCH* 95: 543–59.

———. 1992. "Stèles funéraires de Démétrias: Recherches sur la chronologie des remparts et des nécropoles méridionales de la ville." In Διεθνές Συνέδριο για την Αρχαία Θεσσαλία, edited by E. Kypraiou, 349–66. Athens.

———. 1995. *L'état thessalien: Aleuas le Roux, les tétrades et les tagoi*. Lyon.

———. 2006a. "Décret de Larisa pour Bombos, fils d'Alkaios, et pour Leukios, fils de Nikasias, citoyens d'Alexandrie de Troade (ca 150 av. J.-C.)." *Chiron* 36: 171–203.

———. 2006b. "Un nom antique pour Goritsa?" *ΑΕΘΣΕ* 1: 145–69.

———. 2009. "La Thessalie au 3e siècle av. J-C." *ΑΕΘΣΕ* 2: 339–65.

———. 2013. *Géographie et histoire des Magnètes de Thessalie*. Vol. 1. Sainte-Colombe-sur-Gand.

Herda, A. 2013. "Burying a Sage: The Heroon of Thales in the Agora of Miletos." In *Le mort dans la ville: Pratiques, contextes et impacts des inhumations intra-muros en Anatolie, du début de l'âge du bronze à l'époque romaine*, edited by O. Henry, 67–122. Istanbul.

Hereward, D. 1962. "Inscriptions from the Khersonese." *ABSA* 57: 176–85.
Herrmann, P. 1965. "Antiochos der Grosse und Teos." *Anadolu* 9: 29–159.
Herrmann, P., and H. Malay. 2007. *New Documents from Lydia*. Vienna.
Hertel, D. 2004. "Zum Heiligtum der Athena Ilias von Troia IX und zur frühhellenistischen Stadtanlage von Ilion." *AA* 1: 177–205.
Heuss, A. 1937. *Stadt und Herrscher des hellenismus*. Leipzig.
Hobsbawm, E. 1983. "Introduction: Inventing Traditions." In *The Invention of Tradition*, edited by E. Hobsbawm and T. Ranger, 1–14. Cambridge.
Hodkinson, S., and H. Hodkinson. 1981. "Mantineia and the Mantinike: Settlement and Society in a Greek Polis." *ABSA* 76: 239–96.
Hoepfner, W., and G. Brands, eds. 1996. *Basileia*. Mainz.
Hoepfner, W., and E.-W. Osthues, 1999. "Kolophon." In *Geschichte des Wohnens*, edited by W. Hoepfner, vol. 1, 280–91. Stuttgart.
Höfer, O. 1934. "Thermaios." *RE* 5: 2389.
———. 1992. "Patrioi Theoi." In *Ausführliches Lexikon der griechischen und römischen Mythologie*, edited by W. Roscher, vol. 3, pt. 2, 1684–90. Hildesheim.
Holden, B. 1964. *The Metopes of the Temple of Athena at Ilion*. Northampton.
Holland, L. 1944. "Colophon." *Hesperia* 13, no. 2: 91–171.
Holleaux, M. 1938. *Études d'epigraphie et d'histoire grecques*. Vol. 1. Paris.
Holt, F. 1986. "Alexander's Settlements in Central Asia." Αρχαία Μακεδονία 4: 315–23.
Hommel, P., G. Kleiner, and W. Müller-Wiener. 1967. *Panionion und Melie*. Berlin.
Horden, P., and N. Purcell. 2000. *The Corrupting Sea: A Study of Mediterranean History*. Malden, MA.
Hornblower, S. 1982a. *Mausolos*. Oxford.
———. 1982b. "Thucydides, the Panionian Festival, and the Ephesia (III 104)." *Historia* 31: 241–45.
———. 1990. "When Was Megalopolis Founded?" *ABSA* 85: 71–77.
———. 1991–2008. *A Commentary on Thucydides*. 3 vols. Oxford.
Hornung-Bertemes, K. 2007. *Demetrias 7: Terrakotten aus Demetrias*. Würzburg.
Houghton, A. 2004. "Seleucid Coinages and Monetary Policy of the 2nd C. B.C." In *Le roi et l'économie: Autonomies locales et structures royales dans l'économie de l'empire Séleucide*, edited by V. Chankowski and F. Duyrat, 49–79. Paris.
Howe, T. 2014. "Founding Alexandria: Alexander the Great and the Politics of Memory." In *Alexander in Africa*, edited by P. Bosman, 72–91. Pretoria.
Hübner, A., ed. 1993. *Repertorium der griechischen Rechtsinschriften*, fasc. 1, *Troas—Mysien*. Munich.
Hülden, O. 2000. "Pleistarchos und die Befestigungsanlagen von Herakleia am Latmos." *Klio* 82: 382–408.
Humann, C., C. Cichorius, W. Judeich, and F. Winter, eds. 1898. *Altertümer von Hierapolis*. Berlin.
Humann, K. 1904. *Magnesia am Mäander*. Berlin.
Hurst, A. 1989. "La prise de Thèbes par Alexandre selon Arrien." In *Boiotika: Vorträge vom 5. internationalen Böotien-Kolloquium zu Ehren von Professor Dr. Siegfried Lauffer*, edited by H. Beister and J. Buckler, 183–92. Munich.
Iliev, J. 2013. "Oracles of Dionysos in Ancient Thrace." *Haemus* 2: 61–70.

Intzesiloglou, B. 1994. "Ιστορική τοπογραφία της περιοχής του κόλπου του Βόλου." In *Θεσσαλία: Δεκαπέντε χρόνια αρχαιολογικής έρευνας, 1975–1990*, 31–56. Athens.
———. 1996. "Ο συνοικισμός και η πολιτκή οργάνωση της Δημητριάδας και του Κοινού των Μαγνήτων κατά την ελληνιστική περίοδο." In *Αρχαία Δημητριάδα*, edited by E. Kontaxi, 91–111. Volos.
———. 2006. "The Inscription of the *Kynegoi* from Demetrias." In *Inscriptions and History of Thessaly: New Evidence (Festschrift for C. Habicht)*, edited by Y. Pikoulas, 66–77. Volos.
Isaac, B. 1986. *The Greek Settlements in Thrace until the Macedonian Conquest*. Leiden.
Jablonka, P. 2004. "Vorbericht zum archäologischen Survey im Stadtgebiet von Troia." *Studia Troica* 15: 27–34.
James, S. 2010. "Hellenistic Deposits from the Panayia Field, Corinth." PhD diss., University of Texas, Austin.
Jameson, M. 1997. "Sacred Space and the City: Greece and Bhaktapur." *International Journal of Hindu Studies* 1, no. 3: 485–99.
Janko, R. 1986. "The *Shield of Heracles* and the Legend of Cycnus." *CQ* 36: 38–59.
Jensen, S. 2010. "Rethinking Athenian Imperialism: Sub-hegemony in the Delian League." PhD diss., Rutgers University.
Jones, C. P. 1992. "Hellenistic History in Chariton of Aphrodisias." *Chiron* 22: 91–102.
———. 1999. "The Union of Latmos and Pidasa." *EA* 30: 1–7.
Jones, H., trans. 1927. *Geography of Strabo*. Vol. 4. Cambridge, MA.
Jones, N. 1987. *Public Organization in Ancient Greece*. Philadelphia.
Jones, W., trans. 1933. *Pausanias: Description of Greece*. Vol. 3. Cambridge, MA.
Jonnes, L., and M. Ricl. 1997. "A New Royal Inscription from Phrygia Paroreios: Eumenes II Grants Tyriaion the Status of a *Polis*." *EA* 29: 1–30.
Jost, M. 1973. "Pausanias en Mégalopolitide." *REA* 75: 241–67.
———. 1986. "Villages de l'Arcadie antique." *Ktema* 11: 146–58.
———. 1994. "The Distribution of Sanctuaries in Civic Space in Arkadia." In *Placing the Gods*, edited by S. Alcock and R. Osborne, 217–30. Oxford.
———. 1996. "Les cultes dans une ville nouvelle d'Arcadie au IVème siècle: Megalopolis." In *Le IVe siècle av. J.-C.: Approches historiographiques*, edited by P. Carlier, 103–9. Paris.
Judeich, W. 1891. "Inschriften aus Ionien." *MDAI(A)* 16: 285–99.
———. 1898. "Nordwestlichen Kleinasien." In *Beiträge zur alten geschichte und Geographie*, 225–40. Berlin.
Kagan, D. 1962. "Corinthian Politics and the Revolution of 392 B.C." *Historia* 11: 447–57.
Kahrstedt, U. 1932. "Synoikismos." *RE*, 2nd ser., vol. 4, no. 2, 1435–45.
———. 1954. *Beiträge zur Thrakischen Chersones*. Baden-Baden.
Kallet, L. 2013. "The Origins of the Athenian Economic *Arche*." *JHS* 133: 1–18.
Kalliga, K. 2004. "Anchialos-Sindos Double Trapeza, Pit C: Observations on the Painted and Black-Glazed Pottery of Local Fourth-Century BC Workshops." *ABSA* 99: 291–313.
Karadedos, G. 2008. "Ο 'περιπλανώμενος' υστεραρχαϊκός ναός της Θεσσαλονίκης." In *ΑΕΜΘ* 20: 319–32.
Karliampas, G., G. Bouzara, and S. Chatzitoulouis. 2009. "Ανασκαφικές έρευνας στην τράπεζα της Πολίχνης κατά το 2009." *ΑΕΜΘ* 23: 237–46.
Karlsson, L. 2013. "The Sanctuary of the Weather God of Heaven at Karian Labraunda." In *Perspectives on Ancient Greece*, edited by A.-L. Schallin, 173–89. Stockholm.

Karwiese, S. 1985. "Koressos: Ein fast vergessener Stadtteil von Ephesos." In *Pro Arte Antiqua: Festschrift für Hedwig Kenner*, edited by W. Alzinger and G. Neeb, vol. 2, 214–25. Vienna.

———. 1995. *Groß ist die Artemis von Ephesos*. Vienna.

Kealhofer, L. 2005. "Settlement and Land Use: The Gordion Regional Survey." In *The Archaeology of Midas and the Phrygians*, edited by L. Kealhofer, 137–48. Philadelphia.

Kearns, E. 1985. "Change and Continuity in Religious Structures after Cleisthenes." In *Crux: Essays Presented to G. E. M. de Ste. Croix on His 75th Birthday*, edited by P. Cartledge and F. Harvey, 189–207. Exeter.

Keen, A. 1998. *Dynastic Lycia*. Leiden.

Kehoe, D. 2013. "The State and Production in the Roman Agrarian Economy." In *The Roman Agricultural Economy: Organization, Investment, and Production*, edited by A. Bowman and A. Wilson, 33–53. Oxford.

Kern, O. 1903. *Zum Orakel des Apollon Koropaios*. Berlin.

Kerschner, M., I. Kowalleck, and M. Steskal. 2008. *Archäologische Forschungen zur Siedlungsgeschichte von Ephesos in geometrischer, archaischer und klassischer Zeit: Grabungsbefunde und Keramikfunde aus dem Bereich von Koressos*. Vienna.

Kertzer, D. 1988. *Ritual, Politics, and Power*. New Haven.

Khatchadourian, L. 2016. *Imperial Matter: Ancient Persia and the Archaeology of Empires*. Berkeley.

Kindt, J. 2009. "Polis Religion: A Critical Appreciation." *Kernos* 22: 1–21.

———. 2012. *Rethinking Greek Religion*. Cambridge.

Kip, G. 1910. *Thessalische Studien*. Halle.

Kirbihler, F. 2009. "Territoire civique et population d'Ephèse (Ve siècle av. J.-C.–IIIe siècle apr. J.-C.)." In *L'Asie mineure dans l'Antiquité*, edited by H. Bru, F. Kirbihler, and S. Lebreton, 301–33. Rennes.

Kizil, A., P. Brun, L. Capdetrey, R. Descat, P. Fröhlich, and K. Konuck. 2015. "Pidasa et Asandros: Une nouvelle inscription (321/0)." *REA* 117, no. 2: 371–409.

Klinkott, H. 2000. *Die Satrapienregister der Alexander- und Diadochenzeit*. Stuttgart.

Knibbe, D. 1998. *Ephesos-Ephesus*. Frankfurt am Main.

Knoepfler, D. 1989. "Le calendrier des Chalcidiens de Thrace." *JS* 1, no. 2: 23–58.

———. 2001. "La réintégration de Thèbes dans le koinon béotien après son relèvement par Cassandre; ou, Les suprises de la chronologie épigraphique." In *Recherches récentes sur le monde hellénistique en l'honneur de Pierre Ducrey*, edited by R. Frei-Stolba and K. Gex, 11–26. Bern.

———. 2015. "The Euboian League—an 'Irregular' Koinon?" In *Federalism in Greek Antiquity*, edited by H. Beck and P. Funck, 158–78. Cambridge.

Kobes, J. 1996. *Kleine Könige: Untersuchungen zu den Lokaldynasten im hellenistischen Kleinasien (323–188 v. Chr.)*. Sankt Katharinen, Rhineland-Palatinate.

Koenen, L. 1993. "The Ptolemaic King as a Religious Figure." In *Images and Ideologies: Self-Definition in the Hellenistic World*, edited by A. Bulloch, E. Gruen, A. Long, and A. Stewart, 25–115. Berkeley.

Kokkoru-Aleura, G. 2004. *Επιγραφές απο την αρχαία Αλάσαρνα*. Athens.

Kolb, F., and A. Thomsen. 2004. "Forschungen zu Zentralorte und Chora auf dem Gebiet von Kyaneai (Zentrallykien)." In *Chora und Polis*, edited by F. Kolb, 1–42. Munich.

Koldewey, R. 1891. *Neandria*. Berlin.
Kontogiannis, A. 2003. "Ἀπόλλωνι Αἰσωνίῳ: αναθηματικές επιγραφές από τους Γόννους." In *Τὸ Ἔργο τῶν Ἐφορειῶν Ἀρχαιοτήτων καὶ Νεωτέρων Μνημείων τοῦ ΥΠΠΟ στὴ Θεσσαλία καὶ τὴν εὐρύτερη περιοχή της (1990–1998)*, 125–43. Volos.
Korfmann, M. 1988. "Beşik-Tepe: Vorbericht über die Ergebnisse der Grabungen von 1985 und 1986." *AA* 1, no. 3: 391–98.
Korparal, E. 2013. "Teos and Kyrbissos." *Olba* 21: 45–70.
Körpe, R., and F. Körpe. 2005. "A New Inscription of Asklepios from the Troad." *Studia Troica* 15: 205–8.
Kosmin, P. 2014. *The Land of the Elephant Kings: Space, Territory, and Ideology in the Seleucid Empire*. Cambridge, MA.
Kotsos, S., G. Karliampas, and E. Karipidou. 2011. "Ανασκαφή στο δυτικό νεκροταφείο της τράπεζας της Πολίχνης." *ΑΕΜΘ* 25: 255–60.
Kowalzig, B. 2005. "Mapping out *Communitas*: Performances of *Theōria* in Their Sacred and Political Contexts." In *Pilgrimage in Graeco-Roman and Early Christian Antiquity*, edited by J. Elsner and I. Rutherford, 41–72. Oxford.
———. 2007. *Singing for the Gods: Performances of Myth and Ritual in Archaic and Classical Greece*. Oxford.
Kravaritou, S. 2011. "Synoecism and Religious Interface in Demetrias (Thessaly)." *Kernos* 24: 111–35.
———. 2013. "Thessalian Perceptions of Ruler Cult: *Archegetai* and *Ktistai* from Demetrias." In *Epigraphical Approaches to the Post-classical Polis*, edited by N. Papazarkadas and P. Martzavou, 255–75. Oxford.
———. 2016. "Sacred Space and the Politics of Multiculturalism in Demetrias (Thessaly)." In *Hellenistic Sanctuaries: Between Greece and Rome*, edited by M. Melfi and O. Bobou, 128–51. Oxford.
Kressig, H. 1978. *Wirtschaft und Gesellschaft im Seleukidenreich*. Berlin.
Krischen, F. 1922. *Die Befestigungen von Herakleia am Latmos*. Berlin.
Kritzas, C. 1992. "Aspects de la vie politique et économique d'Argos au Ve siècle avant J.-C." In *Polydipsion Argos*, edited by C. Piérart, 231–40. Paris.
Kuhn, A. 2006. "Ritual Change during the Reign of Demetrius Poliorcetes." In *Ritual and Communication in the Graeco-Roman World*, edited by E. Stavrianopoulou, 265–81. Liège.
Kühne, H. 1994. "The Urbanization of the Assyrian Provinces." In *Nuove fondazioni nel vicino oriente antico: Realtà e ideologia:*, edited by S. Mazzoni, 55–84. Pisa.
Küzler, A. 2008. *Tabula imperii Byzantini 12: Ostthrakien (Eurōpē)*. Vienna.
LaBuff, J. 2010. "The Union of Latmos and Pidasa Reconsidered." *EA* 43: 115–24.
———. 2016. *Polis Expansion and Elite Power in Hellenistic Karia*. Lanham, MD.
La Genière, J. de. 1994. "Quelques réflexions à propos des murailles de Colophon." *REA* 96: 137–41.
Landucci Gattinoni, F. 2003. *L'arte del potere: Vita e opere di Cassandro di Macedonia*. Stuttgart.
Langmann, G. 1993. "Smyrna gefunden." In *Die epigraphische und altertumskundliche Erforschung Kleinasiens*, edited by G. Dobesch and G. Rehrenböck, 283–87. Vienna.
Lauter, H. 1987. "Les éléments de la *regia* hellénistique." In *Le système palatial en Orient, en Grèce et à Rome*, edited by E. Lévy, 345–55. Leiden.

Lauter-Bufe, H. 2009. *Das Heiligtum des Zeus Soter in Megalopolis*. Mainz.
Lawall, M. 1999. "Studies in Hellenistic Ilion: Transport Amphoras from the Lower City." *Studia Troica* 9: 187–224.
———. 2002. "Ilion before Alexander: Amphoras and Economic Archaeology." *Studia Troica* 12: 197–244.
———. 2003. "'In the Sanctuary of the Samothracian Gods': Myth, Politics, and Mystery Cult at Ilion." In *Greek Mysteries*, edited by M. Cosmopoulos, 79–111. New York.
———. 2004. "Nothing to Do with Mendaian Amphoras? Athenaeus 11.784C." In *"Daimonopylai": Essays in Classics and the Classical Tradition Presented to Edmund G. Berry*, edited by R. Egan and M. Joyal, 241–49. Winnipeg.
———. 2005. "Amphoras and Economic History." In *Die Tetragonos Agora in Ephesos*, edited by P. Scherrer and E. Trinkl, vol. 1, 253–55. Vienna.
———. 2010. "Pontic, Aegean and Levantine Amphoras at Gordion." In *PATABS I: Production and Trade of Amphorae in the Black Sea*, edited by D. Kassab Tezgör and N. Inaishvili, 159–65. Istanbul.
———. 2012. "Pontic Inhabitants at Gordion? Pots, People, and Plans of Houses at Middle Phrygian through Early Hellenistic Gordion." In *The Archaeology of Phrygian Gordian, Royal City of Midas*, edited by C. B. Rose, 219–24. Philadelphia.
Leaf, W., ed. and trans. 1923. *Strabo on the Troad*. Cambridge.
Leake, W. 1835. *Travels in Northern Greece*. 4 vols. London.
Lefèvre, F. 1998. *L'Amphictionie pyléo-delphique: Histoire et institutions*. Paris.
Leschhorn, W. 1984. *Gründer der Stadt*. Stuttgart.
Leventi, I. 2009. "Τα γλυπτά αναθήματα από το ιερό στη θέση Σωρός και η συμβολή τους στην ταύτιση της λατρευόμενης θεότητας." *ΑΕΘΣΕ* 2: 295–308.
———. 2012. "Τα πήλινα ειδώλια από το ιερό του Απόλλωνος στη θέση Σωρός Μαγνησίας." *ΑΕΘΣΕ* 3: 299–313.
Levy, R. 1990. *Mesocosm: Hinduism and the Organization of a Traditional Newar City in Nepal*. Berkeley.
———. 1997. "The Power of Space in a Traditional Hindu City." *International Journal of Hindu Studies* 1, no. 1: 55–71.
Liampi, K. 2005. "Iolkos and Pagasai: Two New Thessalian Mints." *NC* 165: 23–40.
Lichtenberger, A., H. Nieswandt, and D. Salzmann. 2008. "Ein Porträt des Lysimachos?" In *Vom Euphrat bis zum Bosporus: Festschrift Elmar Schwertheim*, edited by E. Winter, 391–407. Bonn.
———. 2015. "Die hellenistische Residenzstadt Lysimacheia: Feldforschungen in der Zentralsiedlung und der Chora." In *Urbane Strukturen und bürgerliche Identität im Hellenismus*, edited by A. Matthaei and M. Zimmerman, 163–92. Heidelberg.
Lioutas, A. 1999. "Σταυρούπολι." *ΑΔ* 49, pt. 2, no. 2: 444.
———. 2003. "Πολίχνη-Σταυρούπολι." *ΑΔ* 52, pt. 2, no. 2: 640–42.
———. 2004. "Πολίχνη-Σταυρούπολι." *ΑΔ* 53, pt. 2, no. 2: 575.
———. 2010. "Πολίχνη" *ΑΔ* 55, pt. 2, no. 2: 683.
Lo Cascio, E. 2007. "The Early Roman Empire: The State and the Economy." In *The Cambridge Economic History of the Greco-Roman World*, edited by W. Scheidel, I. Morris, and R. Saller, 619–50. Cambridge.

———. 2009. "Urbanization as a Proxy of Demographic and Economic Growth." In *Quantifying the Roman Economy*, edited by A. Bowman and A. Wilson, 87–107. Oxford.
Lohmann, H. 2004. "Milet und die Milesia: Eine antike Grossstadt und ihr Umland im Wandel der Zeiten." In *Chora und Polis*, edited by F. Kolb, 325–60. Munich.
———. 2005. "Melia, das Panionion und der Kult des Poseidon Helikonios." In *Neue Forschungen zu Ionien*, edited by E. Schwertheim, 57–91. Bonn.
Lolos, Y. 2006. "Δημητριάς στην Θεσσαλία και την Πελοπόννησο." *ΑΕΘΣΕ* 1: 171–83.
———. 2009. "Via Egnatia after Egnatius: Imperial Policy and Inter-regional Contacts." In *Greek and Roman Networks in the Mediterranean*, edited by I. Malkin, C. Constantakopoulou, and K. Panagopoulou, 264–84. London.
———. 2011. *Land of Sikyon*. Princeton.
Lolos, Y., and B. Gourley. 2011. "The Town Planning of Hellenistic Sikyon." *AA* 1, no. 1: 87–140.
Lukes, S. 1975. "Political Ritual and Social Integration." *Sociology* 9, no. 2: 289–308.
Lund, H. 1992. *Lysimachus: A Study in Hellenistic Kingship*. New York.
Lupu, E. 2009. *Greek Sacred Law: A Collection of New Documents (NGSL)*. 2nd ed. Leiden.
Luraghi, N. 2008. *The Ancient Messenians: Constructions of Ethnicity and Memory*. Cambridge.
Lynch, K., and S. Matter. 2013. "The Trade in Athenian Figured Pottery and the Effects of Connectivity." In *Athenian Potters and Painters*, vol. 3, edited by J. Oakley, 107–15. Oxford.
Ma, J. 2000. "Fighting Poleis of the Hellenistic World." In *War and Violence in Ancient Greece*, edited by H. van Wees, 337–76. London.
———. 2002. *Antiochos III and the Cities of Western Asia Minor*. Paperback ed. Oxford.
———. 2007. "Dating the New Decree of the Confederation of Athena Ilias." *EA* 40: 55–57.
———. 2008. "Chaironea 338: Topographies of Commemoration." *JHS* 128: 72–91.
———. 2009. "Empire: Statuses and Realities." In *Interpreting the Athenian Empire*, edited by J. Ma, N. Papazarkadas, and R. Parker, 125–48. London.
Mackil, E. 2004. "Wandering Cities: Alternatives to Collapse in the Greek Polis." *AJA* 108: 403–516.
———. 2013. *Creating a Common Polity: Religion, Economy, and Politics in the Making of the Greek Koinon*. Berkeley.
Mackil, E., and P. van Alfen. 2006. "Cooperative Coinages." In *Agoranomia*, edited by P. van Alfen, 201–46. New York.
Mac Sweeny, N. 2013. *Foundation Myths and Politics in Ancient Ionia*. Cambridge.
———, ed. 2015. *Foundation Myths in Ancient Societies: Dialogues and Discourses*. Philadelphia.
Magie, D. 1950. *Roman Rule in Asia Minor*. 2 vols. Princeton.
Maier, F. 1959–61. *Griechische Mauerbauinschriften*. 2 vols. Heidelberg.
Maischatz, T. 2003. *Neandreia: Untersuchungen zur Bebauung und Stadtentwicklung*. Bonn.
Makaronas, C. 1960. "Ἀνασκαφαὶ Πέλλας 1957–1960." *ΑΔ* 16: 72–83.
———. 1980. "Ἀνασκαφή παρά το Σαραπείον." *Μακεδονικά* 1: 464–65.
Malkin, I. 1985. "What's in a Name? The Eponymous Founders of Greek Colonies." *Athenaeum* 63: 114–30.
———. 1987. *Religion and Colonization in Ancient Greece*. Leiden.

———. 1991. "What Is an 'Aphidruma'?" *CA* 10, no. 1: 77–96.
———, ed. 2001. *Ancient Perceptions of Greek Ethnicity.* Cambridge, MA.
Mann, C., and P. Schloz, eds. 2011. *"Demokratie" im Hellenismus: Von der Herrschaft des Volkes zur Herrschaft der Honoratioren?* Berlin.
Manning, J. 2003. *Land and Power in Ptolemaic Egypt.* Cambridge.
———. 2010. *The Last Pharaohs: Egypt under the Ptolemies, 305–30 BC.* Princeton.
Maran, J. 1992. *Die deutschen Ausgrabungen auf der Pevkakia-Magula in Thessalien,* vol. 3, *Die mittlere Bronzezeit.* 2 pts. Bonn.
Mari, M. 2002. *Al di là dell'Olimpo.* Athens.
———. 2008. "The Ruler Cult in Macedonia." *Studi ellenistici* 20: 220–68.
Marston, J. 2012. "Agricultural Strategies and Political Economy in Ancient Anatolia." *AJA* 116, no. 2: 377–403.
Marzolff, P. 1975. "Demetrias, Elemente einer hellenistischen Hauptstadt." *Architectura* 5: 43–60.
———. 1976a. "Untersuchungen auf der 'heiligen Agora.'" In *Demetrias 1,* edited by V. Milojčić and D. Theocharis, 47–58. Bonn.
———. 1976b. "Untersuchungen auf Höhe 33 ('Anaktoron'-Hügel)." In *Demetrias 1,* edited by V. Milojčić and D. Theocharis, 17–45. Bonn.
———. 1976c. "Zur Stadtanlage von Demetrias." In *Demetrias 1,* edited by V. Milojčić and D. Theocharis, 5–16. Bonn.
———. 1978. "Bürgerliches und herrscherliches Wohnen im hellenistischen Demetrias." In *Wohnungsbau im Altertum,* 129–44. Berlin.
———. 1980. *Demetrias 3: Demetrias und seine Halbinsel.* Bonn.
———. 1987. "Die Bauten auf Höhe 84 ('Heroon'-Höhe)." In *Demetrias 5,* edited by S. Bakhuizen, F. Gschnitzer, P. Marzolff, and C. Habicht, 1–47. Bonn.
———. 1992. "Zur Stadtbaugeschichte von Demetrias." In *Διεθνές συνέδριο για την αρχαία Θεσσαλία,* edited by E. Kypraiou, 337–48. Athens.
———. 1994a. "Antike Städtebau und Architektur in Thessalien." In *Θεσσαλία: Δεκαπέντε χρόνια αρχαιολογικής έρευνας, 1975–1990,* 255–76. Athens.
———. 1994b. "Développement urbanistique de Démétrias." In *Θεσσαλία: Δεκαπέντε χρόνια αρχαιολογικής έρευνας, 1975–1990,* 57–70. Athens.
———. 1996a. "Der Palast von Demetrias." In *Basileia,* edited by W. Hoepfner and G. Brands, 148–63. Mainz.
———. 1996b. "Ein Stuck Kleinasien in Europa?" In *Fremede Zeiten,* edited by F. Blakolmer, 105–23. Vienna.
———. 1996c. "Η πολεοδομική εξέλιξη και τα κυριότερα αρχιτεκτονικά έργα της περιοχής της Δημητριάδας." In *Αρχαία Δημητριάδα,* edited by E. Kontaxi, 47–73. Volos.
———. 1999. "Zentrum und Peripherie im Wandel der Besiedlungsstruktur an der Bucht von Iolkos." In *Stadt und Umland,* edited by E. Schwandner and K. Rheidt, 168–85. Mainz.
Massenzio, M. 1968. "La festa di Artemis Triclaria e Dionysos Aisymnetes a Patrai." *Studi e materiali di storia delle religioni* 39: 101–32.
Masson, O. 1969. "Recherches sur les Phéniciens dans le monde hellénistique." *BCH* 93, no. 2: 679–700.
Mattingly, D., and J. Salmon. 2001. *Economies beyond Agriculture in the Classical World.* London.

Mazarakis Ainian, A. 2009. "Ανασκαφή ιερού των αρχαϊκών-κλασσικών χρόνων στη θέση 'Σωρός' (2004-2005)." *ΑΕΘΣΕ* 2: 269-95.

———. 2011. "Το ιερό του Απόλλωνος στο Σωρό." In *Ταξιδεύοντας στην κλασική Ελλάδα*, edited by P. Valavanis, 143-70. Athens.

———. 2012. "Ανασκαφικές έρευνες στο ιερό του Απόλλωνος στο Σωρό (2006-2008)." *ΑΕΘΣΕ* 3: 287-308.

Mazzucchi, R. 2008. "Mileto e la sympoliteia con Miunte." *Studi ellenistici* 20: 387-407.

McNicholl, A. 1997. *Hellenistic Fortifications from the Aegean to the Euphrates*. Oxford.

Meadows, A. 2002. "Stratonikeia in Caria: The Hellenisitic City and Its Coinage." *NC* 162: 79-134.

———. 2004. "The Earliest Coinage of Alexandria Troas." *NC* 164: 47-70.

———. 2013. "The Ptolemaic League of Islanders." In *The Ptolemies, the Sea and the Nile: Studies in Waterborne Power*, edited by K. Buraselis, M. Stefanou, and D. Thompson, 19-38. Cambridge.

Meeus, A. 2012. "Diodorus and the Chronology of the Third Diadoch War." *Phoenix* 66: 74-96.

———. 2013. "What We Do Not Know about the Age of the Diadochi: The Methodological Consequences of the Gaps in the Evidence." In *After Alexander: The Time of the Diadochi (323-281 BC)*, edited by V. Alonso Troncoso and E. Anson, 84-98. Oxford.

Meier, L. 2012. *Die Finanzierung öffentlicher Bauten in der hellenistischen Polis*. Mainz.

Meiggs, R. 1972. *The Athenian Empire*. Oxford.

Meineke, A., ed. 1877. *Strabonis Geographica*. 3 vols. Leipzig.

Mellink, M. 1985. "Archaeology in Anatolia." *AJA* 89: 545-67.

Meriç, R., and J. Nollé. 1988. "Eine archaische Inschrift aus dem Gebiet von Smyrna." *Chiron* 18: 225-32.

Meritt, B. 1923. "Scione, Mende, and Torone." *AJA* 27: 447-60.

———. 1935. "Inscriptions of Colophon." *AJP* 56, no. 4: 358-97.

Merkelbach, R. 1976. "Strabon XIII 1, 26 (Ilion und Alexandreia Troas)." *ZPE* 23: 241-42.

Merker, I. 1970. "The Ptolemaic Officials and the League of the Islanders." *Historia* 19: 141-60.

Meyer, Eduard. 1909. *Theopomps Hellenika mit einer Beilage über die Rede an die Larisaeer und die Verfassung Thessaliens*. Halle.

Meyer, Ernst. 1936. "Eine Inschrift von Jolkos." *RhM* 85: 367-76.

———. 1942. "Pagasai 1, Thessalische Stadt." *RE* 18, no. 2: 2287-90, 2297-309.

———. 1965. "Poteidaia." *RE*, supplement 10: 616-39.

Mezières, M. 1854. *Mémoire sur le Pélion et l'Ossa: Archives des missions scientifiques*. Vol. 3. Paris.

Migeotte, L. 1984. *L'emprunt public dans les cités grecques*. Paris.

———. 2001. "Le traité entre Milet et Pidasa (*Delphinion* 149): Les clauses financières." In *Les cités d'Asie Mineure occidentale au IIe siècle a.C.*, edited by A. Bresson and R. Descat, 129-35. Bordeaux.

———. 2014. *Les finances des cités grecques: Aux périodes classique et hellénistique*. Paris.

Mikalson, J. 1998. *Religion in Hellenistic Athens*. Berkeley.

Mileta, C. 2002. "The King and His Land: Some Remarks on the Royal Area (*Basilikê Chôra*) of Hellenistic Asia Minor." In *The Hellenistic World: New Perspectives*, edited by D. Ogden, 151-76. London.

———. 2008. *Der König und sein Land*. Berlin.
———. 2009. "Überlegungen zum Charakter und zur Entwicklung der neuen Poleis im hellenistischen Kleinasien." In *Stadtbilder im Hellenismus*, edited by A. Matthei and M. Zimmerman, 70–89. Berlin.
Mili, M. 2015. *Religion and Society in Ancient Thessaly*. Oxford.
Miller, M. 2011. "Town and Country in the Satrapies of Western Asia Minor: The Archaeology of Empire." In *Kelainai-Apameia Kibotos: Stadtentwicklung im Anatolischen Kontext*, edited by L. Summerer, A. Ivantchik, and A. von Kienlen, 319–44. Bordeaux.
Milne, J. 1951. *Kolophon and Its Coinage: A Study*. New York.
Milojčić, V. 1974. "Bericht über die deutschen archäologischen Ausgrabungen in Thessalien 1973." *AAA* 7: 65–75.
Missitzis, L. 1985. "A Royal Decree of Alexander the Great on the Lands of Philippi." *AncW* 12: 3–14.
Mitchel, F. 1970. *Lykourgan Athens*. Cincinnati.
Moggi, M. 1974. "I sinecismi e le annessioni territoriali di Argo nel V secolo a.C." *ASNP* 4: 1249–63.
———. 1975. "Συνοικίζειν in Tucidide." *ASNP* 5: 915–24.
———. 1976a. "Il sinecismo di Tebe e la costituzione federale della Beozia nel V sec. a.C." *CS* 13: 193–206.
———. 1976b. *I sinecismi interstatali greci*. Pisa.
———. 1991. "Sinecismi arcaici del Peloponneso." In *La transizione dal Miceneo all'alto arcaismo*, edited by M. Domenico, 155–65. Rome.
Monson, A. 2012. *From the Ptolemies to the Romans*. Cambridge.
Morley, N. 2011. "Cities and Economic Development in the Roman Empire." In *Settlement, Urbanization and Population*, edited by A. Bowman and A. Wilson, 143–60. Oxford.
Moretti, L. 1976. *Iscrizioni storiche ellenistiche*. Vol. 2. Florence.
Morgan, C. 2003. *Early Greek States beyond the Polis*. Cambridge.
———. 2009. "Ethnic Expression in the Early Iron Age and Early Archaic Greek Mainland: Where Should We Be Looking?" In *Ethnic Constructs in Antiquity*, edited by T. Derks and N. Roymans, 11–36. Amsterdam.
Mørkholm, O. 1991. *Early Hellenistic Coinage*. Cambridge.
Morricone, L. 1949–51. "I sacerdoti di Halios: Frammento di catalogo rinvenuto a Rodi." *ASAA* 11–13: 351–80.
Moschonissioti, S. 1988. "Θέρμη—Σίνδος." *ΑΕΜΘ* 2: 283–95.
Mueli, K. 1946. *Griechische Opferbräuche*. Basel.
Müller, O. 1973. *Antigonos Monophthalmos und das "Jahr der Könige."* Bonn.
Murray, O. 1988. "The Ionian Revolt." In *The Cambridge Ancient History*, 2nd ed., vol. 4, *Persia, Greece and the Western Mediterranean c. 525 to 479 B.C.*, edited by J. Boardman, D. Lewis, N. Hammond, and M. Ostwald, 461–90. Cambridge.
Musiolek, P. 1981. "Zum Begriff und zur Bedeutung des Synoikismos." *Klio* 63, no. 1: 207–13.
Nachtergael, G. 1977. *Les Galates en Grèce et les Sôtéria de Delphes*. Brussels.
Nagy, G. 2012. *Homer the Preclassic*. Berkeley.
Nankov, E. 2015. "Urbanization." In *A Companion to Ancient Thrace*, edited by J. Valeva, E. Nankov, and D. Graninger, 399–411. Malden, MA.
Nielsen, I. 1999. *Hellenistic Palaces: Tradition and Renewal*. Århus.

Nielsen, T. 2004. "Arkadia." In *An Inventory of Archaic and Classical Poleis*, edited by M. Hansen and T. Nielsen, 505–39. Oxford.
Nigdelis, P. 2006. *Epigraphika Thessalonikeia*. Thessaloniki.
Nilsson, M. 1906. *Greichische Feste von religiöser Bedeutung*. Leipzig.
Ober, J. 2010. "Wealthy Hellas." *TAPA* 140: 241–86.
———. 2014. "Greek Economic Performance, 800–300 BCE: A Comparison Case." In *Quantifying the Greco-Roman Economy and Beyond*, edited by F. de Callatäy, 103–22. Bari.
———. 2015. *The Rise and Fall of Classical Greece*. Princeton.
Oded, B. 1979. *Mass Deportations and Deportees in the Neo-Assyrian Empire*. Wiesbaden.
Ogden, D. 2013a. "The Alexandrian Foundation Myth: Alexander, Ptolemy, the *Agathoi Daimones*, and the *Argolaoi*." In *After Alexander: The Time of the Diadochi (323–281 BC)*, edited by V. Alonso Troncoso and E. Anson, 241–53. Oxford.
———. 2013b. "The Birth Myths of Ptolemy Soter." In *Belonging and Isolation in the Hellenstic World*, edited by S. Ager and R. Faber, 184–98. Toronto.
Oliver, J. 1941. *The Sacred Gerusia*. Baltimore.
Olmstead, A. 1918. "The Calculated Frightfulness of Ashur Nasir Apal." *JAOS* 38: 209–63.
Orth, W. 1977. *Königlicher Machtanspruch und städtische Freiheit*. Munich.
Osborne, R. 1985. *Demos: The Discovery of Classical Attica*. Cambridge.
———. 1999. "Archaeology and the Athenian Empire." *TAPA* 129: 319–32.
———. 2005. "Urban Sprawl: What Is Urbanization and Why Does It Matter?" In *Mediterranean Urbanization, 800–600 BC*, edited by R. Osborne and B. Cunliffe, 1–16. Oxford.
Østby, E. 1994. "A Reconsideration of the Classical Temple at Pherai." In *Θεσσαλία: Δεκαπέντε χρόνια αρχαιολογικής έρευνας, 1975–1990*, 139–42. Athens.
Özdoğan, M. 1988. "1987 Yili Edirne ve Balıkesir Illeri Yüzey Araştırması." *AST* 6: 571–90.
———. 1989. "Yili Trakya ve Marmara Bölgesi Araştırmaları." *AST* 7: 443–57.
———. 2003. "The Black Sea, the Sea of Marmara and Bronze Age Archaeology—an Archaeological Predicament." In *Troy and the Troad*, edited by G. Wagner, E. Pernicka, and H. Uerpmann, 105–20. Berlin.
Özgünel, C. 1990. "Das Fundament des Smintheion." In *Hermogenes und die hochhellenistische Architektur*, edited by W. Hoepfner and L. Schwandner, 35–44. Mainz.
———. 2003. "Das Heiligtum des Apollon Smintheus und die 'Ilias.'" *Studia Troica* 13: 261–91.
Özhan, T., and M. Tombul. 2003. "A New Hellenistic Decree of το κοινὸν τῶν πόλεων from Ilion." *EA* 36: 109–13.
Paarmann, B. 2004. "Geographically Grouped Ethnics in the Athenian Tribute Lists." In *Once Again: Studies in the Ancient Greek Polis*, edited by T. Nielsen, 77–109. Stuttgart.
Pandermali, E., and E. Trakosopoulou. 1994. "Καραμπουρνάκι 1994." *ΑΕΜΘ* 8: 203–15.
Papachristodoulou, I. 1999. "The Rhodian Demes within the Framework of the Function of the Rhodian State." In *Hellenistic Rhodes*, edited by V. Gabrielsen, 27–44. Århus.
Papaconstantinou-Diamantourou, D. 1990. " Χώρα Θεσσαλονίκης." In *Μνήμη Δ. Λαζαρίδη: Πόλις και χώρα στην αρχαία Μακεδονία και Θράκη*, 99–107. Thessaloniki.
Papadopoulos, J., and S. Paspalas. 1999. "Mendaian as Chalkidian Wine." *Hesperia* 68: 161–88.
Papakhatzis, N. 1958. "Η Πασικράτα της Δημητριάδας." *Θεσσαλικά* 1: 50–65.
———. 1960. "Η Κορόπη και το ιερό του Απόλλωνα." *Θεσσαλικά* 3: 3–24.
Papangelos, I. 1993. "Ουρανοπόλεως τοπογραφικά." *Αρχαία Μακεδονία* 5, no. 2: 1155–73.

Papazoglou, F. 1988. *Les villes de Macédoine à l'époque romaine.* Paris.
———. 1997. *Laoi et paroikoi.* Belgrade.
Parker, R. 1994. "Athenian Religion Abroad." In *Ritual, Finance, Politics*, edited by R. Osborne and S. Hornblower, 339–46. Oxford.
———. 1996. *Athenian Religion: A History.* Oxford.
———. 2002. "The Cult of Aphrodite Pandamos and Pontia on Cos." In *Kykeon: Studies in Honour of H. S. Versnel*, edited by H. Horstmanshoff, H. Singor, F. van Straten, and J. Strubbe, 143–60. Leiden.
———. 2005. *Polytheism and Society at Athens.* Oxford.
———. 2009. "Subjection, Synoecism and Religious Life." In *The Politics of Ethnicity and the Crisis of the Peloponnesian League*, edited by P. Funke and N. Luraghi, 183–214. Cambridge, MA.
Parkins, H. 1997. *Roman Urbanism: Beyond the Consumer City.* New York.
Pascual, J. 2007. "La sympoliteia griega en las épocas clásica y helenística." *Gerión* 25, no. 1: 167–86.
Paul, S. 2013. *Cultes et sanctuaires de l'île de Cos.* Liège.
Peek, W. 1934. "Griechische Inschriften." *MDAI(A)* 59: 35–80.
Peschlow-Bindokat, A. 1996a. "Der Kult des anatolischen Regen- und Wettergottes auf dem Gipfel des Latmos und das Heiligtum des Zeus Akraios im Tal von Dikilitas." *MDAI(I)* 46: 217–25.
———. 1996b. *Der Latmos: Eine unbekannte Gebirgslandschaft an der Türkischen Westküste.* Mainz.
———. 2005. *Feldforschungen im Latmos: Die Karische Stadt Latmos.* Berlin.
———. 2009. "The Gods of Latmos: Cults and Rituals at the Holy Mountain from Prehistoric to Byzantine Times." In *Sacred Landscapes in Anatolia and Neighboring Regions*, edited by C. Gates, J. Morin, and T. Zimmerman, 55–62. Oxford.
Petropoulos, M., and A. Rizakis. 1994. "Settlement Patterns and Landscape in the Coastal Area of Patras: Preliminary Report." *JRA* 7: 183–207.
Peuner, E. 1926. "Die *Panegyris* der Athena Ilias." *Hermes* 61: 113–33.
Pezzoli, F. 2006. "Il progetto di sinecismo fra Teo e Lebedo (306–302 a.C.)." In *Le vie della storia*, edited by F. Bertenelli and M. Donati, 367–75. Rome.
Philippson, P. 1944. *Thessalische Mythologie.* Zurich.
Picard, O. 1979. *Chalcis et la confédération eubéenne.* Paris.
Piérart, C. 1974. *Platon et la cité grecque.* Brussels.
Piérart, M. 1997. "L'attitude d'Argos à l'égard des autres cités d'Argolid." In *The Polis as an Urban Centre and a Political Community*, edited by M. Hansen, 321–51. Copenhagen.
———. 2000. "Argos: Une autre Démocratie." In *Polis and Politics*, edited by P. Flensted-Jensen, T. Nielsen, and L. Rubenstein, 297–314. Copenhagen.
Pirenne-Delforge, V. 1988. "Épithètes cultuelles et interprétation philosophique: À propos d'Aphrodite Ourania et Pandémos à Athènes." *AC* 57: 142–57.
Pirson, F. 2004. "Elaia: Der maritime Satellit Pergamons." *MDAI(I)* 54: 197–213.
Pirson, F., G. Ates, M. Bartz, H. Brückner, S. Feuser, U. Mania, L. Meier, and M. Seeliger. 2015. "Elaia: Eine aiolische Polis im Dienste der hellenistischen Residenzstadt Pergamon?" In *Urbane Strukturen und bürgerliche Identität im Hellenismus*, edited by A. Matthei and M. Zimmerman, 22–55. Heidelberg.

Plassart, A. 1921. "Inscriptions de Delphes: La liste des Théorodoques." *BCH* 45: 1–85.
Pleket, H. 2003. "Economy and Urbanization: Was There an Impact of Empire in Asia Minor?" In *Stadt und Stadtentwicklung in Kleinasien*, edited by E. Schwertheim and E. Winter, 85–95. Bonn.
Poddighe, E. 2013. "Propaganda Strategies and Political Documents: Philip III's Diagramma and the Greeks in 319." In *After Alexander: The Time of the Diadochi (323–281 BC)*, edited by V. Alonso Troncoso and E. Anson, 225–40. Oxford.
Pohl, D. 1994. "Münzen und andere Metallfunde." In *Neue Forschungen zu Neandria und Alexandria Troas*, edited by E. Schwertheim and H. Wiegartz, 157–74. Bonn.
———. 1999. "Der dorische Tempel von Alexandreia Troas." In *Die Troas: Neue Forschungen III*, edited by E. Schwertheim, 85–95. Bonn.
Polignac, F. 1995. *Cults, Territory, and the Origins of the Greek City-State*. Chicago.
Potter, D. 2003. "Hellenistic Religion." In *A Companion to the Hellenistic World*, edited by A. Erskine, 407–30. Oxford.
Praschniker, C., M. Theuer, W. Alzinger, and R. Fleischer, eds. 1979. *Das Mausoleum von Belevi*. Vienna.
Price, S. 1984. *Rituals and Power: The Roman Imperial Cult in Asia Minor*. Cambridge.
Psoma, S. 2001. *Olynthe et les Chalcidiens de Thrace*. Stuttgart.
———. 2009. "Profitable Networks: Coinages, *Panegyreis*, and Dionysiac Artists." In *Greek and Roman Networks in the Mediterranean*, edited by I. Malkin, C. Constantakopoulou, and K. Panagopoulou, 230–48. London.
Pugliese Carratelli, G. 1953. "Sui damoi e le phylai di Rodi." *SCO* 2: 69–78.
———. 1967. "Supplemento epigrafico di Iasos." *Annuario*, n.s., vols. 29–30: 437–86.
Purcell, N. 2005a. "The Ancient Mediterranean: A View from the Customs House." In *Rethinking the Mediterranean*, edited by W. Harris, 200–232. Oxford.
———. 2005b. "Statics and Dynamics: Ancient Mediterranean Urbanism." In *Mediterranean Urbanization, 800–600 BC*, edited by R. Osborne and B. Cunliffe, 249–72. Oxford.
Quass, F. 1993. *Die Honoratiorenschicht in den Städten des griechischen Ostens*. Stuttgart.
Raaflaub, K. 2009. "Learning from the Enemy." In *Interpreting the Athenian Empire*, edited by J. Ma, N. Papazarkadas, and R. Parker, 89–124. Oxford.
Radt, S., ed. and trans. 2002. *Strabons Geographika*, vol. 1, *Buch I–IV*. Göttingen.
———, ed. and trans. 2004. *Strabons Geographika*, vol. 3, *Buch IX–XIII*. Göttingen.
———, ed. and trans. 2008. *Strabons Geographika*, vol. 7, *Buch IX–XIII: Kommentar*. Göttingen.
Radt, W. 1970. *Siedlungen und Bauten auf der Halbinsel von Halikarnassos*. Tübingen.
———. 1973–74. "Pidasa bei Milet." *MDAI(I)* 23–24: 169–74.
Ratté, C. 2008. "The Founding of Aphrodisias." In *Aphrodisias Papers*, edited by C. Ratté and R. Smith, vol. 4, 7–36. Portsmouth, RI.
Ratté, C., and F. Rojas. 2016. "Archaeological Research at Notion." Paper presented at the Archaeological Institute of America Annual Meeting, San Francisco, January 7.
Reed, J., ed. and trans. 1997. *Bion of Smyrna: The Fragments and the Adonis*. Cambridge.
Reger, G. 1994. *Regionalism and Change in the Economy of Independent Delos, 314–167 B.C.* Berkeley.
———. 2001. "The Mykonian Synoikismos." *REA* 103: 157–81.

———. 2004. "*Sympoliteiai* in Hellenistic Asia Minor." In *The Greco-Roman East: Politics, Culture, Society*, edited by S. Colvin, 145–80. Cambridge.

———. 2007. "Hellenistic Greece and Western Asia Minor." In *The Cambridge Economic History of the Greco-Roman World*, edited by W. Scheidel, I. Morris, and R. Saller, 460–83. Cambridge.

Reichel, A. 1891. *Der Bundesstaat der Magneten und das Orakel des Apollōn Koropaios*. Prague.

Reinders, H. 1988. *New Halos: A Hellenistic Town in Thessalia, Greece*. Utrecht.

———. 1993. "Η τοποθεσία της Άλου." *Αχαιοφθιωτικά* 1: 49–59.

———. 1997. "Τα νομίσματα της Άλου." *Αχαιοφθιωτικά* 2: 105–20.

———. 2004. "Coinage and Coin Circulation in New Halos." In *Το νόμισμα στο Θεσσαλικό χώρο*, 185–206. Volos.

———. 2005. "De Opgraving van de Zuidoostpoort van Nieuw Halos (Griekenland) in Het Olympisch Jaar 2004." *Paleo-Aktueel* 16: 84–88.

———. 2006. "Enceinte, Gates and Communication Lines of New Halos: A Reconstruction." *ΑΕΘΣΕ* 1: 137–43.

———. 2009. "The Hellenistic City of New Halos: A Creation of Demetrios Poliorketes?" *ΑΕΘΣΕ* 2: 369–79.

Reinders, H., C. Dickenson, K. Kondoyianni, B. Lee, Z. Malakasioti, A. Meiwaard, E. Nikolaou, et al. 2014. *The City of New Halos and Its Southeast Gate*. Groningen.

Reinders, H., Y. Dijkstra, V. Rondiri, S. Tuinstra, and Z. Malakasioti. 1996. "The Southeast Gate of New Halos." *Pharos* 4: 121–38.

Rhodes, P. 2001. "Sympoliteia." In *Der Neue Pauly*, edited by H. Canick and H. Schneider, vol. 11, 1138. Stuttgart.

Rhomaios, K. 1932. "Ἀνασκαφὴ ἐν Θέρμῳ." *Πρακτικά* 86: 61–70.

———. 1933. "Ἀνασκαφη ἐν Θέρμῳ." *Πρακτικά* 87: 55–56.

———. 1940. "Πού έκειτο η παλαιά Θέρμη." *Μακεδονικά* 1: 1–7.

Ricl, M., ed. 1997. *The Inscriptions of Alexandreia Troas*. Bonn.

Rigsby, K. 1989. "Two Inscriptions from Mysia." *Hermes* 117, no. 2: 246–50.

———. 1996. *Asylia: Territorial Inviolability in the Hellenistic World*. Berkeley.

———. 2005. "Agathopolis and Doulopolis." *EA* 38: 109–15.

———. 2007. "A New Greek Inscription from Troia." *Studia Troica* 17: 43–45.

Robert, J., and L. Robert. 1976. "Une inscription grecque de Téos en Ionie: L'union de Téos et de Kyrbissos." *JS* 1: 153–235.

———. 1983. *Fouilles d'Amyzon en Carie*. Vol. 1. Paris.

———. 1989. *Claros I: Décrets hellénistiques*. Paris.

Robert, L. 1935. "Inscriptions de Lesbos et de Samos." *BCH* 59: 471–88.

———. 1936a. *Collection Froehner*, vol. 1, *Inscriptions grecques*. Paris.

———. 1936b. "Études d'épigraphie grecque: XLVI, Décret de Kolophon." *RPh* 10: 158–68.

———. 1939. "Hellenica." *RPh* 13: 128–31.

———. 1945. *Le sanctuaire de Sinuri près de Mylasa*, vol. 1, *Les inscriptions grecques*. Paris.

———. 1946a. *Hellenica: Recueil d'épigraphie, de numismatique et d'antiquités grecques*. Vol. 2. Paris.

———. 1946b. "Villes de Carie et d'Ionie dans la liste des Théorodoques de Delphes." *BCH* 70: 506–23.

———. 1948. *Hellenica: Recueil d'épigraphie, de numismatique et d'antiquités grecques.* Vol. 6. Paris.
———. 1951. *Études de numismatique grecque.* Paris.
———. 1955. *Hellenica: Recueil d'épigraphie, de numismatique et d'antiquités grecques.* Vol. 10. Paris.
———. 1958. "Sur des types de monnaies impériales d'Asie Mineure." In *Centennial Publication of the American Numismatic Society,* edited by H. Ingholt, 577–84. New York.
———. 1959. "Les inscriptions grecques de Bulgarie." *RPh* 33: 165–236.
———. 1960. *Hellenica: Recueil d'épigraphie, de numismatique et d'antiquités grecques.* Vols. 11–12. Paris.
———. 1962. *Villes d'Asie mineure.* Paris.
———. 1963. *Noms indigènes dans l'Asie-mineure gréco-romaine.* Paris.
———. 1965. *Hellenica: Recueil d'épigraphie, de numismatique et d'antiquités grecques.* Vol. 13. Paris.
———. 1966a. *Monnaies antiques en Troade.* Paris.
———. 1966b. "Sur un décret d'Ilion et sur un papyrus concernant des cultes royaux." In *Essays in Honor of C. Bradford Welles,* edited by R. Fink, 175–211. New Haven.
———. 1967a. *Monnaies grecques: Types, légendes, magistrats monétaires et géographie.* Geneva.
———. 1967b. "Sur des inscriptions d'Éphèse: Fêtes, athlètes, empereurs, épigrammes." *RPh* 41: 7–84.
———, ed. 1969. *Opera minora selecta: Épigraphie et antiquités grecques.* Vol. 1. Amsterdam.
———. 1977. "La titulature de Nicée et de Nicomédie: La gloire et la haine." *HSCP* 81: 1–39.
———. 1980. *À travers l'Asie mineure.* Athens.
———. 1982. "Documents d'Asie mineure." *BCH* 106: 309–78.
Robertson, N. 1992. *Festivals and Legends: The Formation of Greek Cities in the Light of Public Ritual.* Toronto.
Robinson, D. M. 1938. "Inscriptions from Macedonia." *TAPA* 69: 43–76.
Robinson, D. M., and J. W. Graham. 1938. *Excavations at Olynthus,* pt. 8, *The Hellenic House.* Baltimore.
Roebuck, C. 1959. *Ionian Trade and Colonization.* New York.
Rogers, G. 1991. *The Sacred Identity of Ephesos: Foundation Myths of a Roman City.* London.
———. 2001. "The Foundation of Arsioneia." *Mediterraneo Antico* 4: 587–630.
———. 2012. *The Mysteries of Artemis of Ephesos: Cult, Polis, and Change in the Graeco-Roman World.* New Haven.
Roller, L. 1981. "Funeral Games in Greek Art." *AJA* 85, no. 2: 107–19.
Romano, D. 1997. "Topographical and Architectual Survey of the Sanctuary of Zeus on Mt. Lykaion, Arcadia." *AJA* 101: 374.
———. 2005. "A New Topographical and Architectural Survey of The Sanctuary of Zeus at Mt. Lykaion." In *Ancient Arcadia,* edited by E. Østby, 381–96. Athens.
Romano, D., and M. Voyatzis. 2014. "Mt. Lykaion Excavation and Survey Project, Part 1: The Upper Sanctuary." *Hesperia* 83, no. 4: 569–652.
———. 2015. "Mt. Lykaion Excavation and Survey Project, Part 2: The Lower Sanctuary." *Hesperia* 84, no. 2: 207–76.

Romiopoulou, K. 1989. "Κλειστά ταφικά σύνολα υστεροκλασσικών χρόνων από τη Θεσσαλονίκη." In *Φίλια έπη εις Γεώργιον Μυλωνάν δια τα 60 έτη του ανασκαφικού του έργου*, 194–218. Athens.

Roosevelt, C. 2006. "Tumulus Survey and Museum Research in Lydia, Western Turkey: Determining Lydian- and Persian-Period Settlement Patterns." *Journal of Field Archaeology* 31, no. 1: 61–76.

———. 2009. *The Archaeology of Lydia: From Gyges to Alexander*. Cambridge.

Roosevelt, C., and C. Luke. 2012. "The Central Lydia Archaeological Survey: 2011." *AST* 30: 238–54.

Rose, C. B. 1993. "The 1992 Post–Bronze Age Excavations at Troia." *Studia Troica* 3: 97–116.

———. 1994. "The 1993 Post–Bronze Age Research and Excavations at Troia." *Studia Troica* 4: 75–104.

———. 1995. "The 1994 Post–Bronze Age Research and Excavations at Troia." *Studia Troica* 5: 81–105.

———. 1996. "The 1995 Post–Bronze Age Research and Excavations at Troia." *Studia Troica* 6: 97–101.

———. 1997. "The 1996 Post–Bronze Age Research and Excavations at Troia." *Studia Troica* 7: 73–110.

———. 1999. "The 1998 Post–Bronze Age Excavations at Troia." *Studia Troica* 9: 35–71.

———. 2003. "The Temple of Athena at Ilion." *Studia Troica* 13: 27–89.

———. 2014. *The Archaeology of Greek and Roman Troy*. Cambridge.

Rose, C. B., B. Tekkök, and R. Körpe. 2007. "Granicus River Valley Survey Project, 2004–2005." *Studia Troica* 17: 65–150.

Rostovtzeff, M. 1941. *The Social and Economic History of the Hellenistic World*. 3 vols. Oxford.

Roy, J. 2002. "The Synoikism of Elis." In *Even More Studies in the Ancient Greek Polis*, edited by Thomas Heine Nielsen, 249–64. Stuttgart.

Roy, J., J. Lloyd, and E. Owens. 1988. "Tribe and Polis in the Chora at Megalopolis: Changes in Settlement Pattern in Relation to Synoikism." In *Πρακτικά του XII Διεθνούς Συνεδρίου Κλασικής Αρχαιολογίας*, 179–82. Athens.

Roymans, N. 2004. *Ethnic Identity and Imperial Power: The Batavians in the Early Roman Empire*. Amsterdam.

Rubinstein, L. 2004. "Ionia." In *An Inventory of Archaic and Classical Poleis*, edited by M. Hansen and T. Nielsen, 1053–107. Oxford.

———. 2009. "Ἀτέλεια Grants and Their Enforcement in the Classical and Early Hellenistic Periods." In *Greek History and Epigraphy*, edited by L. Mitchell and L. Rubinstein, 115–43. Swansea.

Ruggendorfer, P. 2016. *Das Mausoleum von Belevi*. Vienna.

Rumscheid, F. 1995. "Die Ornamentik des Apollon-Smintheus-Tempels in der Troas." *MDAI(I)* 45: 25–55.

Rutherford, I. 2013. *State Pilgrims and Sacred Observers in Ancient Greece: A Study of Theôriâ and Theôroi*. Cambridge.

Rzepka, J. 2002. "*Ethnos, Koinon, Sympoliteia*, and Greek Federal States." In *Εὐεργεσίας Χάριν*, edited by T. Derda, J. Urbanik, and M. Weçowski, 225–47. Warsaw.

Rutter, N. 1973. "Diodorus and the Foundation of Thurii." *Historia* 22:155–76.

Saba, S. 2007. "Temporary and Permanent Housing for New Citizens." *EA* 40: 125–34.
Şahin, M. 1976. *The Political and Religious Structure in the Territory of Stratonikeia in Caria*. Ankara.
Salmon, J. 1984. *Wealthy Corinth*. Oxford.
Salviat, F. 1990. "Vignes et cins anciens de Maronée à Mendè." In *Μνήμη Δ. Λαζαρίδη: Πόλις και χώρα στην αρχαία Μακεδονία και Θράκη*, 457–76. Thessaloniki.
Sartre, M. 2006. "Religion und Herrschaft: Das Seleukidenreich." *Saeculum* 57: 163–90.
Savalli-Lestrade, I. 2005. "Devenir une cité: Poleis nouvelles et aspirations civiques en Asie mineure à la basse époque hellénistique." In *Citoyenneté et participation à la basse époque hellénistique*, edited by P. Fröhlich and C. Müller, 9–37. Geneva.
Sayar, M. 2000. "Doğu Trakya'da Epigrafi ve Tarih-Coğrafya Araştırmaları 1999." *AST* 18, no. 1: 289–300.
———. 2001. "Doğu Trakya'da Epigrafi ve Tarih-Coğrafya Araştırmaları 2000." *AST* 19, no. 2: 99–110.
———. 2007. "Doğu Trakya'da Yüzey Araştırmaları 2006." *AST* 25, no. 2: 269–71.
———. 2014. "Lysimacheia: Eine hellenistische Hauptstadt zwischen zwei Kontinenten und zwei Meeren—Ein Ort der Interkonnektivität." In *Interconnectivity in the Mediterranean and Pontic World during the Hellenistic and Roman Periods*, edited by V. Cojocaru, A. Coşkun, and M. Dana, 363–82. Cluj-Napoca.
Schachter, A. 1994. *The Cults of Boeotia*. Vol. 3. London.
Schäfer, C. 2014. "Die Diadochenstaaten: 'Imperium' oder doch konkurrierende Territorialstaaten?" In *Imperien und Reiche in der Weltgeschichte*, edited by M. Gehler and R. Rollinger, vol. 1, 387–400. Wiesbaden.
Schattner, T. 2007. *Didyma*. Vol. 3. Mainz.
Scheid, J. 2016. *The Gods, the State, and the Individual: Reflections on Civic Religion in Rome*. Translated by C. Ando. Philadelphia.
Scheidel, W. 2007. "Demography." In *The Cambridge Economic History of the Greco-Roman World*, edited by W. Scheidel, I. Morris, and R. Saller, 38–86. Cambridge.
Scherrer, P. 2001. "The Historical Topography of Ephesos." In *Urbanism in Western Asia Minor*, edited by D. Parrish, 57–87. Portsmouth, RI.
Schliemann, H. 1884. *Troja*. Leipzig.
Schmidt-Dounas, B. 2004. "Frühe Peripteraltempel in Nordgriechenland." *MDAI(A)* 119: 107–45.
Schmitt, H. 1994. "Überlegungen zur Sympolitie." In *Symposion 1993: Vorträge zur griechischen und hellenistischen Rechtsgeschichte*, edited by G. Thür, 35–44. Cologne.
Scholten, J. 2000. *The Politics of Plunder: The Aitolians and Their Koinon in the Early Hellenistic Era, 279–217 B.C.* Berkeley.
Schuchhardt, C. 1886. "Kolophon, Notion und Klaros." *AM* 11: 398–434.
Schuler, C. 1998. *Ländliche Siedlungen und Gemeinden im hellenistischen und römishcen Kleinasien*. Munich.
———. 1999. "Kolonisten und einheimische in einer Attalidischen Polisgründung." *ZPE* 128: 124–32.
———. 2004. "Landwirtschaft und königliche Verwaltung im hellenistischen Kleinasien." In *Le roi et l'économie: Autonomies locales et structures royales dans l'économie de l'empire Séleucide*, edited by V. Chankowski and F. Duyrat, 509–43. Paris.

———. 2007. "Tribute und Steuern im hellenistischen Kleinasien." In *Geschenke und Steuern, Zölle und Tribute: Antike Abgabenformen in Anspruch und Wirklichkeit*, edited by H. Klinkott, S. Kubisch, and R. Müller-Wollermann, 371–405. Leiden.

———. 2010. "Sympolitien in Lykien und Karien." In *Hellenistic Karia*, edited by R. van Bremen and J.-M. Carbon, 393–413. Talence.

Schuler, C., and A. Walser. 2015. "Sympolitien und Synoikismen: Gesellschaftliche und urbanistische Implikationen von Konzentrationsprozessen in hellenistischer Zeit." In *Urbane Strukturen und bürgerliche Identität im Hellenismus*, edited by A. Matthaei and M. Zimmerman, 350–60. Heidelberg.

Schulz, A. 2000. *Die Stadtmauern von Neandreia in der Troas*. Bonn.

Schwertheim, E. 1994. "Die Inschriften." In *Neue Forschungen zu Neandria und Alexandria Troas*, edited by E. Schwertheim and H. Wiegartz, 39–49. Bonn.

———, ed. *Die Troas Neve Forschungen III*. Bonn.

Schwertheim, E., and H. Wiegartz, eds. 1994. *Neue Forschungen zu Neandria und Alexandria Troas*. Bonn.

———, eds. 1996. *Die Troas: Neue Forschungen zu Neandria und Alexandria Troas II*. Bonn.

Segre, M. 1938. "Iscrizioni di Licia: I. Tolomeo di Telmesso." *Clara Rhodos* 9: 181–208.

Seilheimer, H. 2013. "Attische und attisierende Gefäß- und Verzierungstypen aus Demetrias." In *Networks in the Hellenistic World*, edited by N. Fenn and C. Römer-Strehl, 93–103. Oxford.

Sekunda, N. 1985. "Achaemenid colonization in Lydia." *REA* 87: 7–30.

———. 1988. "Persian Settlement in Hellespontine Phrygia." In *Achaemenid History III*, edited by H. Sancisi-Weerdenburg and A. Kuhrt, 175–96. Leiden.

———. 1991. "Achaemenid Settlement in Caria, Lycia and Greater Phrygia." In *Achaemenid History VI*, edited by H. Sancisi-Weerdenburg and A. Kuhrt, 83–143, Leiden.

Sherwin-White, S. 1978. *Ancient Cos*. Göttingen.

———. 1985. "Ancient Archives: The Edict of Alexander to Priene, a Reappraisal." *JHS* 105: 69–89.

Sherwin-White, S., and A. Kuhrt. 1993. *From Samarkand to Sardis: A New Approach to the Seleucid Empire*. London.

Simonton, M. 2017. *Classical Greek Oligarchy: A Political History*. Princeton.

Sinn, U. 2004. "Hestiatorion." *Thesaurus Cultus et Rituum Antiquorum* 4: 38–46.

Skafida, E. 2012. "Το Κάστρο: Παλαιά Βόλου κατά τους Ρωμαϊκούς Χρόνους." *ΑΕΘΣΕ* 3: 365–72.

Skafida, E., M. Tsigara, and G. Gkardalinou. 2001–4. "Παλαιά Βόλου: Ανασκαφικές έρευνας στο διατηρητέο Κυλινδρόμυλο Λούλη." *ΑΔ* 56–59, no. 2: 510–15.

Smarczyk, B. 1990. *Untersuchungen zu Religionspolitik und politischen Propoganda Athens im Delisch-Attischen Seebund*. Cologne.

———. 2015. "The Hellenic Leagues of Late Classical and Hellenistic Times and Their Place in the History of Greek Federalism." In *Federalism in Greek Antiquity*, edited by H. Beck and P. Funck, 452–70. Cambridge.

Smith, P. 1981. "Aineiadai as Patrons of Iliad XX and the Homeric Hymn to Aphrodite." *HSCP* 85: 17–58.

Sokolowski, F. 1969. *Lois sacrées des cités grecques*. Paris.

———. 1970. "Règlement relatif à la célébration des Panionia." *BCH* 94, no. 1: 109–12.

———. 1980. "On the Decree of Teos concerning the Appointment of the φρούραρχος for Kyrbissos." *ZPE* 38: 103–6.
Sordi, M. 1958. *La lega Tessala fino ad Alessandro Magno.* Rome.
Soueref, K. 1990. "Λατρευτικά στοιχεία απο το προκασσανδρειό πόλισμα στην Τούμπα Θεσσαλονίκης." *AAA* 223–28: 31–46.
———. 1993. "Τούμπα Θεσσαλονίκης 1993: Το ανασκαφικό έργο στην τράπεζα." *ΑΕΜΘ* 7: 87–301.
———. 1994. "Τούμπα Θεσσαλονίκης 1994: Ανασκαφή στην τράπεζα, το νεκροταφείο και τη γύρω περιοχή." *ΑΕΜΘ* 8: 189–96.
———. 1995. "Τούμπα Θεσσαλονίκης: Ανασκαφές στην τράπεζα και το νεκροταφείο." *ΑΕΜΘ* 9: 267–76.
———. 1996. "Τούμπα Θεσσαλονίκης 1985–1996: Το ανασκαφικό έργο στην τράπεζα και το νεκροταφείο." *ΑΕΜΘ* 10: 389–406.
———. 1997. "Τούμπα Θεσσαλονίκης 1997: Ανασκαφή ανατολικά της Τράπεζας και στο αρχαίο νεκροταφείο." *ΑΕΜΘ* 11: 337–41.
Sourvinou-Inwood, C. 1988. "Further Aspects of Polis Religion." *Annali dell' instituto universitario orientale di Napoli* 10: 259–74.
———. 1990. "What Is Polis Religion?" In *The Greek City from Homer to Alexander,* edited by O. Murrary and S. Price, 295–322. Oxford.
———. 2005. *Hylas, the Nymphs, Dionysos and Others: Myth, Ritual, Ethnicity.* Stockholm.
Stählin, F. 1916. "Iolkos." *RE* 9: 1850–55.
———. 1924. *Das hellenische Thessalien.* Stuttgart.
———. 1929. "Zur Chronologie und Erklärung der Inschriften von Magnesia und Demetrias." *AM* 54: 201–26.
———. 1934. "Thebai." *RE* 5: 1582–93.
Stählin, F., E. Meyer, and A. Heidner. 1934. *Pagasai und Demetrias.* Berlin.
Stamatopoulou, M. 2008. "Ouaphres Horou, an Egyptian Priest of Isis from Demetrias." In *Essays in Classical Archaeology for Eleni Hatzivassiliou, 1977–2007,* edited by D. C. Kurtz, C. Meyer, D. Sauders, A. Tsingarida, and N. Harris, 249–57. Oxford.
———. 2014. "The Pasikrata Sanctuary at Demetrias and the Alleged Funerary Sanctuaries of Thessaly: A Re-appraisal." *Kernos* 27: 201–49.
Stavrianopoulou, E. 2006. "Normative Interventions in Greek Rituals: Strategies for Justification and Legitimation." In *Ritual and Communication in the Graeco-Roman World,* edited by E. Stavrianopoulou, 131–49. Liège.
———. 2011. "'Promises of Continuity': The Role of Tradition in the Forming of Rituals in Ancient Greece." In *Ritual Dynamics in the Ancient Mediterranean,* edited by A. Chaniotis, 85–104. Stuttgart.
Stern, E. 2001. *Archaeology of the Land of the Bible,* vol. 2, *The Assyrian, Babylonian, and Persian Periods (732–332 B.C.E.).* New Haven.
Stewart, S. 2010. "Gordion after the Knot: Hellenistic Pottery and Culture." PhD diss., University of Cincinnati.
Strobel, K. 1996. *Die Galater.* Vol. 1. Berlin.
Stronach, D. 1978. *Pasargadae.* Oxford.
Strootman, R. 2014a. "Hellenistic Imperialism and the Ideal of World Unity." In *The City in the Classical and Post-classical World,* edited by C. Rapp and H. Drake, 38–61. Cambridge.

———. 2014b. "'Men to Whose Rapacity Neither Sea nor Mountain Sets a Limit'—the Aims of the Diadochs." In *The Age of the Successors and the Creation of the Hellenistic Kingdoms (323–276 B.C.)*, edited by H. Hauben and A. Meeus, 307–22. Leuven.

Strubbe, J. 1984. "Gründer kleinasiatischer Städte: Fiktion und Realität." *AS* 15–17: 253–304.

Summerer, L., A. Ivantchik, and A. von Kienlen, eds. 2011. *Kelainai-Apameia Kibotos: Stadtentwicklung im Anatolischen Kontext*. Bordeaux.

———. 2013. "Kelainai: A Phrygian City between East and West." In *L'Anatolie des peuples, des cités et des cultures*, edited by B. Hadrien and G. Labarre, vol. 2, 221–30. Besançon.

Surtees, L. 2012. "On the Surface of a Thessalian City: The Urban Survey of Kastro Kallithea, Greece." PhD diss., Bryn Mawr College.

Surtees, L., S. Karapanou, and M. Haagsma. 2014. "Exploring Kastro Kallithea on the Surface." In *Meditations on the Diversity of the Built Environment in the Aegean Basin and Beyond*, edited by D. Rupp and J. Tomlinson, 431–52. Athens.

Symeonoglou, S. 1985. *The Topography of Thebes from the Bronze Age to Modern Times*. Princeton.

Tarn, W. W. 1950. *Alexander the Great: Sources and Studies*. Vol. 2. Cambridge.

Tasia, A. 1996. "Η σωστική ανασκαφή της ΙΣΤ' Εφορίας στην Πλατεία Διοικητηρίου." *ΑΕΜΘ* 7: 329–41.

———. 1997. "Διοικητήριο '97." *ΑΕΜΘ* 11: 417–18.

Tasia, A., Z. Lola, and O. Peltekis. 2000. "Θεσσαλονίκη—ο υστεροαρχαικός Ναός." *ΑΕΜΘ* 14: 227–46.

Tekkök, B. 2000. "The City Wall of Ilion: New Evidence for Dating." *Studia Troica* 10: 85–97.

Tenger, B. 1999. "Zur Geographie und Geschichte der Troas." In *Die Troas: Neue Forschungen III*, edited by E. Schwertheim, 103–81. Bonn.

Themelis, P. 2000. *Ήρωες και ήρωα στη Μεσσήνη*. Athens.

Theocharis, D. 1956. "Ανασκαφαί Ιωλκού." *Πρακτικά*: 119–30.

———. 1957. "Ανασκαφαί Ιωλκού." *Πρακτικά*: 54–69.

———. 1960. "Ανασκαφαί Ιωλκού." *Πρακτικά*: 49–59.

———. 1961. "Ανασκαφαί Ιωλκού." *Πρακτικά*: 45–54.

———. 1973. *Νεολιθική Ελλάς*. Athens.

Thibaut, B., and A.-V. Pont. 2014. *Chalkètôr en Carie*. Paris.

Thompson, D. B. 1963. *Troy: The Terracotta Figurines of the Hellenistic Period*. Princeton.

Thonemann, P. 2003. "Hellenistic Inscriptions from Lydia." *EA* 36: 95–108.

———. 2009. "Estates and the Land in Early Hellenistic Asia Minor: The Estate of Krateuas." *Chiron* 39: 363–93.

———. 2011a. "Eumenes II and Apollonioucharax." *Gephyra* 8: 19–30.

———. 2011b. *The Maeander Valley*. Cambridge.

———. 2013a. "Alexander, Priene and Naulochon." In *Epigraphical Approaches to the Post-classical Polis*, edited by P. Martzavou and N. Papazarkadas, 23–36. Oxford.

———. 2013b. "The Attalid State, 188–133 BC." In *Attalid Asia Minor: Money, International Relations, and the State*, edited by P. Thonemann, 1–47. Oxford.

Thür, G. 1995. "Zu den Hintergründen des Rechtswährungsvertrags zwischen Stymphalos und Demetrias." In *Rom und der griechische Osten*, edited by C. Schubert, K. Brodersen, and U. Huttner, 267–72. Stuttgart.

Thür, G., and H. Taeuber. 1994. *Prozessrechtliche Inschriften der griechischen Poleis: Arkadien (IPArk)*. Vienna.
Tilly, C. 2005. *Trust and Rule*. Cambridge.
Tiverios, M. 1987. "Όστρακα από το Καραμπουρνάκι." *ΑΕΜΘ* 1: 247-60.
———. 1990. "Από τα απομεινάρια ενός προελλενιστικού ιερού 'περί Θερμαίον Κόλπον.'" *Μνήμη Δ. Λαζαρίδη: Πόλις και χώρα στην αρχαία Μακεδονία και Θράκη*, 71-80. Thessaloníki.
———. 1993. "Εισαγμένη κεραμική από τη Διπλή Τράπεζα της Αγχιάλου κοντά στη σημερινή Σίνδο." *Παρνασσός* 35: 553-60.
———. 1998. "The Ancient Settlements in the Anchialos-Sindos Double Trapeza: Seven Years (1990-1996) of Archaeological Research." *Euboica: L'Eubea e la presenza euboica in Calcidica e in Occidente*, edited by M. Bats and B. D'Agostino, 243-53. Naples.
———. 2000. *Μακεδόνες και Παναθήναια*. Thessaloniki.
———. 2008. "Greek Colonisation of the Northern Aegean." In *Greek Colonisation*, edited by G. Tsetskhladze, vol. 2, 1-154. Leiden.
Tiverios, M., E. Manakidou, and D. Tsiaphaki. 1994. "Ανασκαφικές έρευνες στο Καραμπουρνάκι κατά το 1994: ο αρχαίος οικισμός." *ΑΕΜΘ* 8: 197-202.
———. 1998. "Ανασκαφικές έρευνες στο Καραμπουρνάκι κατά το 1998: Ο αρχαίος οικισμός." *ΑΕΜΘ* 12: 221-30.
———. 2001. "Ανασκαφικές έρευνες στο Καραμπουρνάκι κατά το 2001: Ο αρχαίος οικισμός." *ΑΕΜΘ* 15: 255-62.
———. 2002. "Ανασκαφικές έρευνες στο Καραμπουρνάκι κατά το 2002: Ο αρχαίος οικισμός." *ΑΕΜΘ* 16: 257-66.
———. 2004. "Ανασκαφικές έρευνες στο Καραμπουρνάκι κατά το 2004: Ο αρχαίος οικισμός." *ΑΕΜΘ* 18: 337-44.
———. 2005. "Ανασκαφικές έρευνες στο Καραμπουρνάκι κατά το 2005: Ο αρχαίος οικισμός." *ΑΕΜΘ* 19: 187-95.
———. 2008. "Ανασκαφικές έρευνες στο Καραμπουρνάκι κατά το 2008: Ο αρχαίος οικισμός." *ΑΕΜΘ* 22: 329-34.
———. 2010. "Ανασκαφικές έρευνες στο Καραμπουρνάκι κατά το 2010: συνοψίζοντας τα πρόφατα αρχαιολογικά δεδομένα." *ΑΕΜΘ* 24: 359-64.
Touratsoglou, I. 1988. *Die Münzstätte von Thessaloniki in der römischen Kaiserzeit (32/31 v. Chr. bis 268 n. Chr.)*. Berlin.
———. 1996. "Die Baupolitik Kassanders." In *Basileia*, edited by W. Hoepfner and G. Brands, 177-81. Mainz.
Travlos, J. 1971. *A Pictorial Dictionary of Athens*. Athens.
Triantaphyllopoulou, P. 2000."Νεκροταφείο των Αμφανών. In *Ελληνιστική κεραμίκη από τη Θεσσαλία*, edited by E. Kypraiou, 60-69. Volos.
———. 2002. "Αμφανές: Αρχαιολογικά δεδομένα—πρόταση ανάδειξης." In *Μνημεία της Μαγνησίας: Μνημεία της Μαγνησίας. Πρακτικά συνεδρίου ανάδειξη του διαχρονικού μνημειακού πλούτου του Βόλου και της ευρύτερης περιοχής*, 134-39. Volos.
Tscherikower, V. 1927. *Die hellenistischen Städtegründungen von Alexander dem grossen bis auf die Römerzeit*. Leipzig.
Tsigarida, E. 1994. "Ανασκαφική έρευνα στην αρχαία Αίνεια." *ΑΕΜΘ* 8: 217-22.

———. 1996. "Ανασκαφική έρευνα στην περιόχη της αρχαίας Σίνης-Ουρανόπολης." *ΑΕΜΘ* 10a: 333–46.
Tsimpidou-Avloniti, M. 1994. "Σύνολα κεραμικής από το ελληνιστικό νεκροταφείο της Θεσσαλονίκης." In *Γ' Συνάντηση για την Ελληνιστική Κεραμική*, 80–89. Athens.
———. 2015. "Πυλαία 2001–2010: Ανασκαφικές ψηφίδες από μια 'άγνωστη' περιοχή." *ΑΕΜΘ* 24: 375–84.
Tsvetkova, J. 2000. "Siedlungen und Siedlungssystem auf der Thrakischen Chersonesos in der vorrömischen Zeit." *Thrakia* 13: 431–62.
Turner, V. 1969. *The Ritual Process: Structure and Anti-structure*. London.
———. 1974. *Dramas, Fields, and Metaphors: Symbolic Action in Human Society*. Ithaca, NY.
Tzanivari, K., and A. Lioutas. 1993. "Λεμπέτ." *ΑΕΜΘ* 7: 265–73.
Tziafalias, A. 1984. "Ανέκδοτες θεσσαλικές επιγραφές." *Θεσσαλικό Ημερολόγιο* 7: 193–236.
Tziafalias, A., S. Karapanou, M. Haagsma, and S. Gouglas. 2006a. "Preliminary Results of the Urban Survey Project at Kastro Kallithea, Achaia Phthiotis." *ΑΕΘΣΕ* 2: 217–29.
———. 2006b. "Scratching the Surface: A Preliminary Report on the 2004 and 2005 Seasons from the Urban Survey Project at Kastro Kallithea ('Peuma'), Thessaly." *Mouseion* 6, no. 2: 91–135.
Valassiadis, C. 2005. "A Contribution to Cassander's Bronze Coinage." In *Actas del XIII Congreso Internacional de Numismática, Madrid 2003*, edited by C. Alfaro, C. Marcos, and P. Otero, 405–13. Madrid.
van Bremen, R. 2000. "The Demes and Phylai of Stratonikeia in Karia." *Chiron* 30: 389–401.
———. 2004. "Leon Son of Chrysaor and the Religious Identity of Stratonikeia in Caria." In *The Greco-Roman East: Politics, Culture, Society*, edited by S. Colvin, 207–44. Cambridge.
———. 2015. Review of Thibaut Boulay and Anne-Valérie Pont, *Chalkètôr en Carie*. *Sehepunkte* 15, no. 12: www.sehepunkte.de/2015/12/27334.html.
van der Spek, R. 1993. "New Evidence on Seleucid Land Policy." In *De Agricultura: In Memoriam Pieter Willem De Neeve (1945–1990)*, edited by H. Sancisi-Weerdenburg, R. van der Spek, H. Teitler, and H. Wallinga, 61–77. Amsterdam.
———. 2000. "The Seleucid State and the Economy." In *Production and Public Powers in Classical Antiquity*, edited by E. Lo Cascio and D. Rathbone, 27–36. Cambridge.
van Gelder, H. 1900. *Geschichte der alten Rhodier*. Haag.
Vatin, C. 1984. "Lettre adressée à la cité de Philippes par ses ambassadeurs auprès d'Alexandre, I." In *Πρακτικά τοῦ η' διεθνοῦς συνεδρίου ἑλληνικῆς καὶ λατινικῆς ἐπιγραφικῆς, Ἀθήνα, 3–9 ὀκτωβρίου 1982*, vol. 1, 259–70. Athens.
Vattuone, R. 1994. "*Metoikesis:* Trapianti di popolazioni nella Sicilia greca fra VI e IV sec. a.C." In *Emigrazione e immigrazione nel mondo antico*, edited by M. Sordi, 81–112. Milan.
Velenis, G. 1996. "Πολεοδομικά Θεσσαλονίκης." *ΑΕΜΘ* 10b: 491–99.
Verkinderen, F. 1987. "The Honorary Decree for Malousios of Gargara and the κοινόν of Athena Ilias." *Tyche* 2: 247–69.
Vetters, H. 1978. "Recent Archaeological Research in Turkey." *Anatolian Studies* 28: 9–37.
———. 1979. "Ephesos: Vorläufiger Grabungsbericht 1978." *AAWW* 116: 123–44.
Vian, F. 1952. *La guerre des Géants: Le mythe avant l'époque hellénistique*. Paris.
Vickers, M. 1972. "Hellenistic Thessaloniki." *JHS* 92: 156–70.

---. 1981. "Therme and Thessaloniki." In *Ancient Macedonian Studies in Honor of Charles F. Edson,* edited by H. Dell, 327–33. Thessaloniki.
Vitos, G., and M. Panagou. 2009. "Η κεραμική από το ιερό του Απόλλωνος στο Σωρό: προκαταρκτική μελέτη." *ΑΕΘΣΕ* 2: 309–28.
---. 2012. "Μικρά ερεύματα από το ιερό του Απόλλωνος στο Σωρό: προκαταρκτική μελέτη." *ΑΕΘΣΕ* 3: 315–30.
Vitti, M. 1996. *Η πολεοδομική εξέλιξη της Θεσσαλονίκης.* Athens.
Vlassopoulos, K. 2007. *Unthinking the Greek Polis.* Oxford.
Voigt, M. 2002. "Gordion: The Rise and Fall of and Iron Age Capital." In *Across the Anatolian Plateau,* edited by D. Hopkins, 187–96. Boston.
---. 2011. "Gordion: The Changing Political and Economic Roles of a First Millennium City." In *The Oxford Handbook of Ancient Anatolia (10,000–323 B.C.E.),* edited by S. Steadman and G. McMahon, 1069–94. Oxford.
Voigt, M., K. De Vries, R. Henrickson, M. Lawall, B. Marsh, A. Gürsan-Salzman, and T. Cuyler Young Jr. 1997. "Fieldwork at Gordion, 1993–1995." *Anatolica* 23: 1–59.
Voigt, M., and R. Young. 1999. "From Phrygian Capital to Achaemenid Entrepot: Middle and Late Phrygian Gordion." *IrAnt* 34: 191–241.
Vokotopoulou, I. 1986. "Ἡ ἐπιγραφή τῶν Καλινδοίων." *Αρχαία Μακεδονία* 4: 87–114.
---. 1990. "Νέα τοπογραφικά στοιχεία για τή χώρα των Χαλκιδέων." In *Μνήμη Δ. Λαζαρίδη: Πόλις και χώρα στην αρχαία Μακεδονία και Θράκη,* 109–44. Thessaloniki.
---, ed. 1994. *Macedonians: The Northern Greeks and the Era of Alexander the Great.* Athens.
---. 1995. *Οδηγός Αρχαιολογικού Μουσείου Θεσσαλονίκης.* Thessaloniki.
---. 1997. "Ο Κάσσανδρος, η Κασσάνδρεια και η Θεσσαλονίκη." In *Μνήμη Μανόλη Ανδρόνικου,* 39–50. Thessaloniki.
von Dienst, W., ed. 1913. *Nysa ad Maeandrum.* Berlin.
von Graeve, V. 1979. "Zum Zeugniswert der bemalten Grabstelen von Demetrias für die griechische Malerei." In *La Thessalie,* edited by B. Helly, 111–37. Lyon.
---. 1984. "Le stele di Demetriade." *DArch,* 3rd ser., vol. 2: 59, 145–47.
Voutiras, E. 1996. "Un culte domestique des Corybantes." *Kernos* 9: 243–56.
---. 1999. "Η λατρεία της Αφροδίτης στην περιοχή του Θερμαίου Κόλπου." In *ΣΤ΄ Διεθνές Συμπόσιο για την Αρχαία Μακεδονία,* vol. 2, 1329–41.
Voyatzis, M. 1990. *The Early Sanctuary of Athena Alea at Tegea and Other Archaic Sanctuaries in Arcadia.* Göteborg.
---. 1999. "The Role of Temple Building in Consolidating Arkadian Communities." In *Defining Ancient Arkadia,* edited by T. Nielsen and J. Roy, 130–68. Copenhagen.
Wace, A. 1906. "The Topography of Pelion and Magnesia." *JHS* 26: 143–68.
Waddington, W., E. Babelon, and T. Reinach. 1908. *Recueil général des monnaies grecques d'Asie mineure.* Paris.
Walbank, F. 1984. "Monarchies and Monarchic Ideas." In *The Cambridge Ancient History,* 2nd ed., vol. 7, pt. 1, *The Hellenistic World,* edited by F. Walbank, A. Astin, M. Frederiksen, and R. Ogilvie, 62–100. Cambridge.
Wallace, S. 2011. "The Politics of Freedom: Kings and Cities in the Early Hellenistic Period, 323–229 BC." PhD diss., University of Edinburgh.

Wallace, W. 1956. *The Euboian League and Its Coinage*. New York.
Wallerstein, I. 2004. *World-Systems Analysis: An Introduction*. Durham, NC.
Wallrodt, S. 2002. "Ritual Activity in Late Classical Ilion: The Evidence from a Fourth Century B.C. Deposit of Loomweights and Spindlewhorls." *Studia Troica* 12: 179–97.
Walser, A. 2008. *Bauern und Zinsnehmer: Politik, Recht, und Wirtshaft im frühellenistischer Ephesos*. Munich.
———. 2009. "Sympolitien und Siedlungsentwicklung: Gesellschaftliche und urbanistische Implikationen von Konzentrationsprozessen in hellenistischer Zeit." In *Urbane Strukturen und bürgerliche Identität im Hellenismus*, edited by A. Matthaei and M. Zimmerman, 135–55. Berlin.
Weber, H. 1965. "Myus: Grabung 1964." *MDAI(I)* 15: 43–64.
Wehrli, C. 1968. *Antigone et Démétrios*. Geneva.
Weiss, P. 1984. "Lebendiger Mythos: Gründerheroen und städtische Gründungstraditionen im griechisch-römischen Osten." *WJA* 10: 179–208.
Weisshaar, H.-J. 1989. *Die Deutschen Ausgrabungen auf der Pevkakia-Magula in Thessalien*, vol. 1, *Das späte Neolithikum und das Chalkolithikum*. Bonn.
Welles, C. 1934. *Royal Correspondence in the Hellenistic Period*. New Haven.
Westlake, H. 1935. *Thessaly in the Fourth Century B.C.* London.
Whitby, M. 1984. "The Union of Corinth and Argos: A Reconsideration." *Historia* 33, no. 3: 295–308.
Whitehead, D. 1983. "Competitive Outlay and Community Profit: Φιλοτιμία in Democratic Athens." *C&M* 34: 55–74.
Wiegartz, H. 1994. "Äolische Kapitelle: Neufunde 1992 und ihr Verhältnis zu den bekannten Stücken." In *Neue Forschungen zu Neandria und Alexandria Troas*, edited by E. Schwertheim and H. Wiegartz, 117–33. Bonn.
Wiemer, H. 2001. "Karien am Vorabend des 2. Makedonischen Krieges." *EA* 33: 1–14.
Wiesehöfer, J. 1996. *Ancient Persia from 550 BC to 650 AD*. London.
Wilhelm, A. 1890. "Inschriften aus Thessalien." *MDAI(A)* 15: 283–317.
———. 1909. *Beiträge zur griechischen Inschriftenkunde*. Vienna.
———. 1939. "Athen und Kolophon." In *Anatolian Studies Presented to William Hepburn Buckler*, edited by W. Calder and J. Keil, 345–68. Manchester.
Will, E. 1964. "Ophellas, Ptolémée, Cassandre et la chronologie." *REA* 66: 320–33.
———. 1966. *Histoire politique du monde hellénistique*. Vol. 1. Nancy.
———. 1984. "The Succession to Alexander." In *The Cambridge Ancient History*, 2nd ed., vol. 7, pt. 1, *The Hellenistic World*, edited by F. Walbank, A. Astin, M. Frederiksen, and R. Ogilvie, 23–61. Cambridge.
Williamson, C. 2012. "Sanctuaries as Turning Points in Territorial Formation: Lagina, Panamara and the Development of Stratonikeia." In *Manifestationen von Macht und Hierarchien in Stadtraum und Landschaft*, edited by F. Pirson and M. Bachmann, 113–50. Istanbul.
———. 2013. "Civic Producers at Stratonikeia: The Priesthoods of Hekate at Lagina and Zeus at Panamara." In *Cities and Priests*, edited by M. Horster and A. Klöckner, 209–45. Berlin.
Wilson, A. 2009. "Indicators for Roman Economic Growth: A Response to Walter Scheidel." *JRA* 22: 71–82.

———. 2011. "City Sizes and Urbanization in the Roman Empire." In *Settlement, Urbanization and Population*, edited by A. Bowman and A. Wilson, 161–95. Oxford.

———. 2014. "Quantifying Roman Economic Performance by Means of Proxies: Pitfalls and Potentials." In *Quantifying the Greco-Roman Economy and Beyond*, edited by F. de Callataÿ, 147–67. Bari.

Wolters, C. 1979. "Recherches sur les stèles funéraires hellénistiques de Thessalie." In *La Thessalie*, edited by B. Helly, 81–110. Lyon.

Wörrle, M. 1975. "Antiochos I., Achaios der ältere und die Galater: Eine neue Inschrift in Denizli." *Chiron* 5: 59–87.

———. 1977. "Epigraphische Forschungen zur Geschichte Lykiens I." *Chiron* 7: 43–66.

———. 1991. "Epigraphische Forschungen zur Geschichte Lykiens IV." *Chiron* 21: 203–39.

———. 2003a. "Inschriften von Herakleia am Latmos III: Der Synoikismos der Latmioi mit den Pidaseis." *Chiron* 33: 121–43.

———. 2003b. "Pidasa du Grion et Héraclée du Latmos: Deux cités sans avenir." *CRAI* 4: 1361–79.

Young, R. 1956. "The Campaign of 1955 at Gordion: Preliminary Report." *AJA* 60, no. 3: 249–66.

———. 1963. "Gordion on the Royal Road." *PAPhS* 107, no. 4: 348–64.

Zahrnt, M. 1971. *Olynth und die Chalkidier*. Munich.

Zimmer, G. 2003. "Hellenistische Bronzegusswerkstatten in Demetrias." In *Demetrias 6*, 11–68. Würzburg.

Zimmermann, M. 1992. *Untersuchungen zur historischen Landeskunde Zentrallykiens*. Bonn.

SUBJECT INDEX

Page references in italics refer to maps.

Achaemenids: communication system of, 134; control over Aegean exporters, 134; imperialism of, 15–16; land tenure under, 105, 106, 109, 118–19; overland communications of, 133–35; population transfers of, 22; satrapal capitals of, 118, 119; taxation system of, 110; transition from, 118, 119; tributary system of, 104, 117

Achaia Phthiotis, 68; Achaion ethnos of, 203; Antigonid reorganization of, 69; cult in, 150n; under Demetrios Poliorketes, 78; *koinon* of, 120, 124

Achaios (landowner): land grant to, 116; sacrifice to, 170

Achilleion: in Delian League, 62n; in synoikism of Ilion, 62

Adeimantos of Lampsakos, 67n

Aegean: agricultural exploitation of, 138; archaic temples of, 164; centralization in, 15; city-states of, 5; connections with Asia Minor, 137; economies of, 128n; exchange networks of, 126; integration of, 86; political unification of, 133; trade routes of, 130

Agathokleia, numismatic evidence for, 55

Agathokles, execution of, 84

Ager, S., 96n

agonothetai (games officials), 121

agoranomoi (market officials), 121; of Athena Ilias, 122

Aigai (Vergina), royal burials at, 205–6

Aineia, 43; cultic identity of, 161, 181; cult of Aphrodite at, 196; in Delphic *theōrodokoi* lists, 181n; *ktistēs of*, 196; in Thessalonike synoikism, 40, 195–96, 202

Aineias, cult of, 195–96

Ainian, Mazarakis, 152n

Aiolian League, 120, 124n

Akalin, A., 65n

Akarnanian *koinon*, Cassander and, 47–48

Alexander (son of Polyperchon), 35, 227

Alexander IV of Macedon, 34, 35, 45; execution of, 51

Alexander of Pherai, 68

Alexander the Great: *ateleia* under, 106; colonization under, 16; death of, 32; fiscal immunity under, 106n; funeral cortege of, 32n; at Ilion, 59, 168–69; land policies of, 106–7, 108–9, 110; letter to Priene, 99, 105; on Nikaian coins, 198; refounding of Smyrna, 197; population transfers planned by, 22–23

Alexandreia Troas, 2; aid to Ilion, 122n; in Athena Ilias *koinon*, 182; building commission of, 95; civic identity of, 165; coinage of, 3n, 63n, 65; cultic life of, 165–66; cult of Apollo

270 SUBJECT INDEX

Alexandreia Troas *(continued)*
in Neandreia, 177–78; Doric temple of, 165, 166, 177–78; emblems of Neandreia in, 204; excavation of, 64–65; incorporation of traditions, 204; public building construction in, 95–96; refoundation of, 63, 64; site of, 165; synoikism of, 65, 165. *See also* Antigoneia Troas

Alexandropolis, founding of, 17n

Alexarchos (brother of Cassander), 35

Alyattes, destruction of Syria, 76

Amastris, revolt of Teion from, 19; foundation of, 70; inherited traditions of, 205

Amastris (wife of Lysimachos), 70

Ammon, oracle of, 67n

Amphanai, 81; location of, 80n308; cults of, 155; in Magnesia, 151

Amphiktyonic League, 204; Magnesian *hieromnēmones* of, 207n

amphorae: evidence of commerce, 92, 127–32; Ionian, 130–31; Panathenaic, 153; of Parmeniskos group, 129

Amyntas III of Macedon, *ateleia* under, 106

Anatolia: links to urban systems, 115; Seleukid power in, 85

Andania, *lex sacra* of, 123n

Androkles, foundation of Ephesos, 186

Antigonas Gonatas: burial of Demetrios, 191; control of Demetrias, 80n, 84; cult under, 156; honorific decree for, 191; organization of Thessalonike, 202; peace with Antiochos I, 84

Antigoneia Troas: date of foundation, 63n; early name of, 197; formation of, 1–2, 3, 12, 56–59, 61, 226; refoundation as Alexandreia Troas, 63; Skepsis in, 1–2, 3, 12, 63, 64, 133; synoikism of, 3, 51, 63–64. *See also* Alexandreia Troas

Antigonids: collapse of, 84; control of Karia, 50; *koina* of, 120–21; Nesiotic League of, 124–26; trade policy of, 130n

Antigonos the One-Eyed: 72; ambition of, 2; conflict with Asandros, 48, 50; conflict with Cassander, 45, 47; conflict with Lysimachos, 50, 55, 67; conflict with Ptolemy, 56; conflict with Seleukos, 50, 52; control of Asia Minor, 52; death of, 70; defeat of Eumenes, 34; economic policies of, 102; exiles under, 34n; fall of, 70; following Alexander's death, 33; formation of Antigoneia Troas, 1–2, 3, 12, 56–59, 61; land grants from, 109–10; letters to communities, 1, 8, 20–21, 51, 63n, 96, 97, 100, 102, 225; loss of Asia Minor, 68; offensive of 307, 56; and peace of 311, 51, 225; philhellenism of, 2; refoundation of Ilion, 59; refoundation of Smyrna, 77; relocation of Kolophon, 95, 148; reorganization of Troad, 57–59; royal honors for, 35n; strategic interests of, 3; synoikism of Teos-Lebedos, 100–101, 102; synoikisms of, 19, 22–23; treaty with Seleukos, 52n

Antiochos III:

Antiochos I Soter: foundations of, 188; Ilion's honoring of, 182n; land grant from, 112, 114; sale of land, 114; Asia Minor under, 85; peace with Antigonas Gonatas, 84; urbanization under, 113–14, 136

Antiochos II: burial chamber of, 187n; death of, 84; divorce of, 114; foundation of Laodikeia, 115–16; founding of Stratonikeia, 169; land grant to Achaios, 116

Antiochos III: resistance to Rome, 55n158, synoikisms of, 9–10, 21; urbanization under, 85

Antiochos Hierax, 60

Antipater: death of, 32; siege of Thessaly, 31

Apameia Kelainai, 70, 85, 103n49, 135; *emporion* of, 136

Aperghis, G., 91n, 103–4

Aphrodisias, founders' descendants at, 188n

Aphrodite: cult at Aineia, 196; cult in Thessalonike, 164n

Aphrodite Neleia, cult of, 155–56

Aphrodite Pandēmos, cult of, 170, 171n, 213

Apollinoucharax, land grant to, 117

Apollo: Anthelic festival, 156; cult at Neandreia, 165, 177–78; oracle for Thourioi, 188; sanctuary at Athens, 146; sanctuary at Kiddiou Kome, 116, 169–70

Apollo Aisōnios (Gonnoi), 152n

Apollo Aktios, sanctuary at Pagasai, 151

Apollo Delios, cult in Kos, 173, 213

Apollo Koropaios, 161; centrality to Demetrias, 154; oracle of, 82; sacrifice to, 156?; temple at Korope, 157–58, 177

Apollonios of Rhodes, on Pagasai, 152n

Apollo Pagasaios sanctuary, 161; demise of, 154–55; epigraphic evidence of, 154; *hestiatorion* of, 153; material assemblage of, 152–53

Apollo Parrhasios, cult at Megalopolis, 174

Apollo Smintheus, sanctuary of (Hamaxitos), 65–66, 166, 178, 204

archēgetai, cult of: association with Pelion, 177; of Demetrias, 159, 161, 175–76, 191–94, 219

SUBJECT INDEX   271

architecture: funerary, 177, 193; sacred, 172; of synoikisms, 206; traditionalism in, 178–80. *See also* sanctuaries
Argead dynasty, termination of, 29n, 51
Argo myth: of Pagasai, 151, 152; in symbolism of Demetrias, 204–5
Argos, synoikism of, 13, 199
Aristaios (deity), 217n
Aristodikides of Assos, land grant to, 112–14
Aristomenes, land grant to, 109
Aristotle: *Politics*, 13; on rule of tyrants, 22
Arkadia, cults of, 175
Arsinoe II, 73n, 84; intervention in Smyrna, 181
Arsinoeia. *See* Ephesos
Artaphernes, territorial disputes under, 100
Artemidoros (priest), in Nysa, 209
Artemis: deer sacrifice to, 162; sanctuary at Patrai, 215–16
Artemis Brauronia, sanctuaries of, 172
Artemis Iolkia, 161; on coinage, 204; cult at Demetrias, 155–57, 175–76, 192, 217; temple of, 82, 156–57, 175, 176
Artemis Mounychia, sanctuary at Phygela, 148
Artemis of Pagasai, 155
Artemis Pandamos, cult at Kos, 170–71
Artemis Soteria, cult at Ephesos, 221
Arvanitopoulos, A., 81, 156n; excavation of Demetrias, 192n; on temple of Zeus Akraios, 158
Asandros (Karian satrap): conflict with Antigonos, 48, 50; control of Karia, 48, 49, 50; Herakleia under, 49, 203; Latmos/Pidasa union under, 98, 219
Asia Minor: agricultural exploitation of, 138; under Alexander, 17; centralization in, 16n; city-states of, 5; coastal cities of, 133; connections with Aegean, 137; consolidation under Antiochos I, 85; decline of coastal cities, 130n; funerary architecture of, 177, 193; inland development of, 135–36; Lysimachos's invasion of, 67–68, 70; non-Greek population of, 24; *paroikoi* of, 24; Persian rule in, 15–16; ports of, 77; rural development of, 119; Seleukid power in, 84–85, 114; Successors' struggle over, 49; synoikisms of, 115; urban infrastructure of, 133
Asklepios, cults of, 154, 202, 213
Astypalaia: cults of, 213; in synoikism of Kos, 200, 213
ateleia (taxation immunity), 106; grants of, 108; Successors' conferral of, 112

Athana Lindia, cult of, 211
Athena: temple at Ilion, 167–68
Athena Ilias *koinon*, 120, 121–24; *agoranomoi* of, 122; building activity of, 121, 168; cities of, 122–23; coinage of, 123; contribution to Ilion's development, 121; cult of Athena in, 167, 204; economy of, 122, 123; embassies to Antigonos, 122; financial contributions to, 122; honorees of, 122; institutional interdependence in, 182; Panathenaia of, 122, 123, 169; poleis of, 182; regional integration in, 126; united worship in, 182, 204. *See also* Ilion
Athenaios, on Lysippos, 90
Athenaios (naval commander), land grant to, 113
Athena Latmia, civic festival of, 178
Athenis (son of Apollodoros), financing of construction, 94
Athens: commercial eclipse of, 127; cults of, 146–47; under Demetrios Poliorketes, 56, 71n, 222–23; *eponymoi* of, 189; and Ionian decline, 130n; Macedonian power over, 31; mythology of synoikism, 173n; occupation of sanctuary of Apollo, 146; Pnyx of, 179; relationship of demes to, 172; synoikism of, 9n, 14; trade contacts of, 129
Athymbra, priestly families of, 209
Athymbros (founder of Nysa), 188
Attalid Apollonis, foundation of, 21
Attalids: military settlements of, 91n; urbanization under, 85
Attalos I, population transfer under, 114
Aurelios Teimasitheos (priest), Kentaurios title of, 218–19

Baba Kome, 115; sanctuary of Zeus at, 116, 169
Badoud, N., 212
Bakalakis, G., 164
Bakhuizen, S., 156n
Banabelos (estate manager): decree honoring, 116; sacrifice to, 170
Barjamovic, G., 15n
Belevi, mausoleum of, 186
Berkela, sanctuary of Pan, 174
Berlin, A., 168
Birytis, refoundation of, 64
Blegen, Carl: excavation of Ilion, 60n
Boibe, in Demetrias synoikism, 83
Boibe, heroön of, 194n
Boiotian League: dismantling of, 14; Thebes in, 207
Brasidas (founder of Amphipolis), 196

272 SUBJECT INDEX

Bresson, A., 112
Brocke, C. vom, 202n
Bronze Age, tombs of, 179
Brunel, J.: on *aphidruma*, 171n
Burkert, W., 217n
Buxton, R., 217n

calendars: eponymous names in, 205; of Kos, 189, 213; sacrificial, 208–14
Cassander: Aitolian conflict of, 47–48; and Akarnanian *koinon*, 47–48; alliance with Thebes, 50n; Athenian support for, 45; coinage of, 42n, 220; commercial aims of, 91; conflict with Antigonos, 47; conflict with Demetrios, 68; conflict with Polemaios, 50; conflict with Polyperchon, 44, 45; consolidation of Peloponnese, 67; consolidation of power, 35; control of Greece, 70; control of Macedonia, 35; control of Thessaly, 68; courtship of Kleopatra, 35n; death of, 71; dynastic legitimacy of, 46–47; following Alexander's death, 32, 33; foundation of Kassandreia, 35–36, 38; foundation of Thessalonike, 38–43; foundations of, 37, 38–51; independence from Successors, 45; kingship of, 35–36, 226; land policy of, 107–8; philhellenism of, 46; and poleis freedom, 44, 47; poleis' support for, 34; Ptolemy's abandonment of, 56n; reversal of Macedonian policy, 44; synoikisms of, 12; urbanization under, 34–51, 226–27
Chairemon of Nysa (landholder), 116
Chairephanes, *ateleia* grant to, 111
Chairephanes (son of Aischylos), 111
Chaironeia, lion monument at, 46n
Chalastre (Thracian polis), 39; in Thessalonike synoikism, 40
Chalketor, union of, 9, 10n, 20n
Chalkidian League, 36; dissolution of, 107
Chalkidians, synoikism into Olynthos, 14n
Chalkidike: agricultural estates of, 38; confiscated land of, 107; destruction of cities of, 78n; land status in, 111, 112; map of, 37; reorganization of, 43; synoikism of, 36, 38
Chankowski, V., 125n
Chares (Athenian general), 58n; control of Sigeion, 168
Cheiron: "descendants" of in Demetrias, 154, 218–19; healing arts of, 218, 219; mythology of, 157–58, 177; tutelage of heroes, 217; and Zeus Akraios, 154, 217–19
Chersonese, Thracian, 52–53, 54; agricultural wealth of, 53n; Lysimachos's urban centers on, 73
chōra, Hellenistic: collectivities of, 117; components of, 105n; connection to urban centers, 214; cult sites of, 179–80; landed estates of, 138; Thracian, 107; tribute from, 105. *See also* land
Chremonidean War, 115
Chrysa, in Alexandreia Troas synoikism, 65, 66
communitas, through cults, 166–67
communities: abandonment of, 19; centrifugal tendencies of, 4; consensus building in, 144, 189; *isopoliteia* of, 10; *politeuma of*, 10; power relations of, 31–32; state power in, 5
communities, cultic, 4, 144–45: politicization of, 223; royal intervention in, 166; unity in, 166–67. *See also* cults; religion; rituals
communities, synoikized: agency in, 144, 184–85, 228; alternative narratives for, 197; architectural traditionalism of, 178–80; boards of *oikistai*, 186; breakaway of, 144; civic cults of, 144–45; civic identity in, 7, 25, 214–21, 227; cultic identity of, 148–50, 181, 185, 192, 208, 214, 223; figure of king in, 185; founder cults of, 185–98; inorganic origins of, 4–5; institutions of, 25, 199, 201; myth in, 214–21; negotiation of rites, 192; priesthoods of, 208; reciprocity with kings, 24; religious identity of, 148–50, 223; reorganization of, 5; replication of sanctuaries, 171–80; ritual in, 214–21; role in Hellenistic imperialism, 25; sacred missions (*theōriai*) of, 180; size of, 139; social actors in, 23–24, 143; social fabric of, 88; and struggle for power, 31–32; under Successors, 31–34; traditional founders of, 171, 185–98; traditions of, 23, 199; of unequal sympolity, 9. *See also* poleis; synoikism
Constitution of the Athenians, settlement patterns in, 22
Cook, J., 64; on commerce, 130n; on Larisa, 65
Corinthian League, 31, 67
cults: abandoned sites of, 172, 182–83; adaptation under synoikism, 150–66; *aphidrymata*, 171; architectural conservatism of, 178–80; centralized rituals of, 166–71; *communitas* through, 166–67; defining of society, 184; discontinuity of, 144–45, 147, 150–66, 161; disruption of, 146–47, 183; diversity of, 167, 183; doubling of, 172–74, 214; epigraphic evidence for, 147–49, 150; indigenous, 145; maintenance of sites, 150–66, 171, 183; mitigation of disruption to, 183; monarchs' manipulation of, 182; mystery, 162–63; officials of, 208–14;

replication of, 171–80, 183; ruler, 51, 191–93, 196, 222; in *Shield of Heracles*, 151; symbolic power of, 169; in *sympoliteia* agreements, 150n; Thessalian, 151; ties to Panhellenism, 149; transfer to synoikized poleis, 154, 171–80. See also religion, Hellenistic; rituals
cults, civic: agency in, 144; belonging through, 144; change in, 161; competition among, 223; continuity in, 143–50, 161, 172, 208, 223; discontinuity of, 144–45, 147, 161; identity and, 143; poliadic, 171; political communities around, 183; sociopolitical reality of, 172; Sōter, 171; in sympoly agreements, 150n; under synoikisms, 7, 144–45
cults, founder, 185–98; choices in, 185–86, 197; of Demetrias, 190–94; descendants of founders in, 188; effect of synoikism on, 185; eponymous founders in, 189; evolution of, 197n; of heroes, 196; monarchs', 191–93, 196; multiple layers of, 197; of multiple synoikisms, 194; religious officials of, 192–93

Daskyleion: depopulation around, 119; eclipse of, 66; overland communication with, 134
Delian League, 4; political-religious intersection in, 146n
Delion, sanctuary of Apollo, 146
Delos: in Nesiotic League, 125; Oikos of the Naxians, 153; *panēgyris* of, 123n; regional economy of, 126
Delphi, road to Tempe, 156
Delphic-Anthelic amphiktyony, festival of Apollo, 156
Demeter, cult in Kos, 213
Demeter Eleusinia: cult of, 173; poliadic divinities of, 176
Demetrias: under Antigonas Gonatas, 80n, 84; Antigonid palace of, 128–29, 175, 176n; archaeology of, 128–29, 192–93; *astynomoi* (city wardens) of, 160; ceramics of, 128–29; *chōra* of, 202; coinage of, 204; commerce of, 128–29, 130n; connection with Phthiotic Thebes, 129; corporate religious life of, 191; cultic continuity/change in, 161; cultic life of, 151–61, 216–19, 220; cult of Aphrodite Neleia, 155–56; cult of *archēgetai*, 159, 161, 175–76, 191–94, 219; cult of Artemis Iolkia, 155–57, 175–76, 192, 217; cult of Asklepios, 154; cult of Herakles, 159, 160; cult of *ktistai*, 159, 161, 176, 191–94, 219; cult on Pelion, 157, 210, 216; cult of Zeus Akraios, 154–55, 157–58, 177, 210, 216–17, 219; development of, 128; domination of Magnesian League, 207, 210; elites of, 154–55, 160; as entrepôt, 160; ethnic identity of, 24, 202–3; *exēgētēs* (magistrate) of, 160; foundation of, 78, 80, 156; founder cults of, 190–94; founders' sanctuary, 192–93; grave stelai of, 130n; land of, 112; Mother of the Gods sanctuary, 160; movement away from, 217; multicultural milieu of, 158; populations of, 130n; population transfer to, 80–81; priesthood of Zeus in, 210–11; religious officials of, 192–94, 210–11; rites of, 82; ritual innovations at, 219, 220; social organization of, 80; strategic importance of, 72; synoikism of, 78, 80–84, 124, 180; territorial continuity of, 202; urban nucleus of, 81, 83; use of demotics in, 211n
Demetrios II, letter to *epistatēs* of Beroia, 159
Demetrios of Skepsis, 2, 3n; on Ilion, 60; *Trōikos diakosmos*, 61
Demetrios Poliorketes, 48; Achaia Phthiotis under, 78; Achaion *koinon* of, 69; alliance with Seleukos, 70n, 71; challenges to authority of, 222–23; coinage of, 176; conflict with Cassander, 68; control of Athens, 56, 71n; control of Greece, 67, 71; control of Macedon, 71; death of, 72; defeat at Ipsos, 70; founder cult of, 191; iconography of, 192; Magnesia under, 78, 203; negotiations with Athens, 222–23; and Nesiotic League, 182; Ptolemy's defeat of, 50; recovery of Kyklades, 125n; refoundations of, 68, 69, 77, 78; siege of Thebes, 46n; on Theban stele, 46; Thessaly under, 78; tomb-heroön of, 193
Derkylidas (Spartan general), liberation of Troad, 58n
Descat, R., 109, 113n
Diacoch Wars, 32, 33–34, 52. See also Successors, Alexander's
Diodoros Siculus: on Antigonos, 67n; on Antipater, 32n; on Argead dynasty, 51; on Cassander, 35, 36, 46; chronology of, 30n; on Demetrios's honors, 197; on kingship, 29; on Megalopolis, 173n, 175; on Nesiotic League, 124n; on Phthiotic Thebes, 68n; on Sybaris, 187
Dion (community), 68
Dionysios I, synoikisms of, 13
Dionysos: connection to water, 165n; Temple at Thessalonike, 164–65; Thracian rites of, 162–63
Dionysos Aisymnetes, cult of, 215–16
Dionysos Thermaios, sanctuary of, 164n
Dog Star, 216–17

Dokimeion: commerce of, 135; founding of, 68n
Dokimos (general), 68
Douris of Elaia, 74
Dunatis, dedication to Artemis of Pagasai, 155
dynasts. *See* monarchs; Successors

Egypt, Ptolemaic: private land in, 117
Elis, synoikism of, 13
elites, Hellenistic: of new poleis, 119–20; representation of cities, 120
empire, universal: Hellenistic claims to, 29
Endymion, 178; cult of, 197
Ennodia, cult of, 160–61
Epameinondas, and refoundation of Thebes, 45
Ephesos: amphorae of, 130, 131; Artemision of, 72n, 73, 186; city wall of, 93–94; commerce of, 130, 133; common road to, 135; community integration in, 201; cult of Artemis Soteria, 221; cults incorporated into, 147–48; "debt law" of, 72; *epiklētoi* of, 72n; flooding of, 73–74, 76; foundation celebration of, 186; foundation cult of, 186–87; *gerousia* of, 72n, 186, 220, 221; hinterland of, 76; institutions of, 201; Ionian foundation of, 186; lease of public land in, 93–94; Lebedioi at, 76; literary sources for, 73; Lysimachos's foundation of, 73–74, 76, 89, 94, 221; *neoi* of, 221; population transfer to, 74; religious innovation in, 220–21; strategic importance of, 72, 73; synoikism of, 73–74, 76, 89; Tetragonos Agora, 94; Tower of Paul, 94; transfer of Kolophon to, 93, 187; urban core of, 94
ethnicity: impact of empire on, 198n; in Macedonian policy, 203; macroethnic divisions of, 199; in synoikisms, 24, 198–208
Euaimon, union with Orchomenos, 8, 10
Euboian League, 203
euergetism, in synoikism, 20
Eumenes: Antigonos's defeat of, 34; conflict with Successors, 32n, 33
Eumenes II: foundations of, 21; land grant from, 117
Euphron (*archēgetēs*), 196
Euphronios of Akarnania, 72n
Eupolemos: coinage of, 220; rule of Karia, 49
Eurydikeia. *See* Smyrna
Eurypylos, cult of Dionysos Aisymnetes, 215–16

Fimbria (general), razing of Ilion, 61
foundation: processes of, 18–23; as religious act, 143. *See also* synoikisms
Furtwängler, A., 130n

Gabrielsen, V., 211
Gambreion (polis), land of, 109, 112
Gauthier, P., 17n, 91n
geographies, imperial, 3; deterministic, 127n; fragmented nature of, 29
Gergis: Homeric heritage of, 2n; land grants near, 113; population transfer from, 114; in synoikism of Ilion, 62
Getae, Lysimachos's struggle with, 71n
Glaphyrai: acropolis of, 194; in Demetrias synoikism, 83
Gomphoi, founding of, 16
Gordion: amphorae of, 135n; contact with Aegean, 134
Goritsa, depopulation of, 82
Goukowsky, P., 155n
Granikos valley: archaeology of, 66–67; depopulation in, 118–19; Persian domination of, 66; surface survey of, 118–19
Graninger, D., 194n
Great God, sanctuary at Theisoa, 174
Great Mother Kybele, cult of, 162

Hadaios (priest of Zeus Akraios), 210
Hadista (dedicator), 162
Hagnon (founder of Amphipolis), 196
Halasarna, cults of, 213
Halios (Rhodes): priesthood of, 200; tradition of, 170, 189, 212. *See also* Rhodes
Halos: coinage of, 69; commerce of, 129n; destruction of, 68–69, 78; earthquake (ca. 265), 152n; gates of, 69; refoundation of, 69
Hamaxitos (polis): in Alexandreia Troas synoikism, 65, 66, 166; sanctuary of Apollo Smintheus, 65–66, 166, 178, 204
Hansen, M., 11
Hatzopoulos, M., 155n, 159, 195n
Hegesias (*synoikistēr* of Syracuse), 8n
Hegesianax of Alexandreia Troas, 2n, 196n
Hegesippos of Mekyberna, 196n
Helios colossos (Rhodes), 67n. *See also* Halios
Helisson, sympoly with Mantineia, 150n
Hellenic League (302), 31, 67
Hellenistic period: chronological problems of, 30n; economic growth of, 138n; siege tactics of, 86; sovereignty of, 5n; spread of institutions in, 30; year of the king (306/5), 34. *See also* imperialism, Hellenistic; monarchs; Hellenistic
Hellespont, overland routes to, 134
Hellison, in polis of Mantineia, 180n
Helly, B., 68n

SUBJECT INDEX 275

Herakleia Latmos: under Asandros, 49; celebration of Endymion, 197; cults of, 178, 219; fortification of, 49; synoikism of, 49–50. *See also* Latmos
Herakleia Lynkestis, founding of, 16
Herakleides Kritikos, on Zeus Akraios, 216–17, 219
Herakleides Pontikos, *On Oracles*, 151n
Herakles: cult of (Demetrias), 159; temple on Thasos, 164n
Herakles (son of Alexander), 52
Heresianax (geographer), on Ilion, 61
Hermes Akakesios, cult of, 173, 174
Hermogenes (son of Hadymos), decree honoring, 210
Herodotos: on exiles from Kolophon, 181n; on Gergis, 2n; on Ionian *koinon*, 100n; language of synoikism, 9
Hesichios, use of *nebeusasa*, 155n
hestiatoria, of temples, 153, 155
Hetaireidia festival, 159n
hieromnēmones, Delphic, 207, 210
Hieron (landowner), 116
Hieronymos of Kardia, 51; bias against Lysimachos, 53; on empire, 29
Hippias (tyrant), 82n
Hippostratos (son of Hippodemos): *ateleia* of, 124; privileges of, 181
Homolion, in Demetrias synoikism, 83, 207
homonoia, cult in Kos, 213n
Hornblower, Simon, 11; on *synteleia*, 89n
Hydrela (Maeander valley), 85

Iatrokles (priest), 209
identity, civic: and disassociation from location, 199; under synoikism, 7, 25, 214–21, 227
identity, cultic, 208; around sanctuaries, 146; of Iolkos, 191; legitimization of monarchy, 222; of synoikized communities, 148–50, 181, 185, 192, 208, 214, 223
Ilion: amphorae of, 131; in Athena Ilias *koinon*, 182; Athenaion of, 122, 123, 124; commercial network of, 123, 131, 132; construction in, 121–22; excavation of, 60–61, 168; fortification of, 167; Homeric heritage of, 167, 168–69; honoring of Antiochos, 182n; land attached to, 113; under Lysimachos, 59–60, 62–63; material assemblages of, 168; Panhellenic sanctuary of, 132; political role of, 61, 123; prosperity of, 131–32; refoundation of, 59; symbolism of, 167, 168; synoikism of, 59–63, 123, 132; temple of Athena, 59, 60, 62, 131, 132, 167–68; West Sanctuary, 168. *See also* Athena Ilias *koinon*
imperialism, Achaemenid, 15–16
imperialism, Athenian, 36; impact on regional cults, 146n; resistance to, 14; *synteleiai* in, 14n
imperialism, Hellenistic: fiscal entities of, 137n; fragmentation of, 14; in polis society, 222; in religion, 184, 222; role of communities in, 25; synoikism in, 86; urbanization and, 12–18, 86. *See also* monarchs, Hellenistic
imperialism, Macedonian: Achaemenid land tenure in, 106; among Successors, 33; Cassander's reversal of, 44; forms of, 30; impact on religious life, 184; land system of, 105–10; manipulation of polis life, 222; siege tactics of, 86; urbanization in, 91, 137
imperialism, Spartan, 14–15; resistance to, 15
Intzesiloglou, B., 81n, 154n
Iolkos: association with *Argo*, 176; cultic identity of, 191; cults of, 156–57, 175–76; following foundation of Demetrias, 156; founder cult of, 190–91, 194; opisthographic stele of, 190–92; prehistoric, 82n; Pyliac *panēgyris* of, 156; transfer to Demetrias, 176
Ionia, 75; amphorae of, 130–31; Lysimachos's control of, 73; Persian control of, 130; Thucydides on, 58n; trade networks of, 131
Ionian *koinon*, 124, 203; communal identity in, 181; Herodotos on, 100n; religious identity in, 182
Ipsos, Battle of (301), 2, 70; aftermath of, 71, 219
Isis, *panēgyris* of, 123n

Kadmeia, Theban, 44n
Kaikos valley, Persian estates of, 118n
Kalindoia, 43; land of, 110; refoundation of, 107
Kalymnos, *homopoliteia* with Kos, 181n
Kappadokia, commerce of, 135
Kardakon Kome, royal land of, 117
Kardia, synoikism of, 53–54
Karia: amphorae of, 130–31; Antigonid control of, 50; Asandros's control of, 48, 49, 50; Eupolemos's rule over, 49; rural settlement in, 119; synoikism of, 21, 85
Karian League, Miletos in, 95n
Kassandreia, 43; under Antigonas Gonatas, 84; archaeology of, 36n; *archēgeteion of*, 194–95; civic territory of, 111; commerce of, 90, 130; Corinthians in, 202; eponymous priesthood of, 195n; estate holders of, 108; extent of, 38; founder's cult of, 194–95; *Hippolyteus* of, 201–2; *Hippotadeis* of, 201; Koan

Kassandreia *(continued)*
  theōroi at, 194; land status in, 111; residents of, 36, 38; resources of, 90; site of, 36; synoikism of, 35–36, 38, 111–12; territories comprising, 36; wine exports of, 90
Kastro Kallithea, refoundation of, 69
Kebren: in Antigoneia Troas synoikism, 63, 64; artifacts of, 64n; in Delphic *theōrodokoi* lists, 64n
Kelainai: commercial importance of, 103; common road to, 135; refoundation as Apameia Kelainai, 136
Keos, sanctuary of Zeus, 217
Kiddiou Kome, 115; sanctuary of Apollo at, 116, 169–70; synoikism with Neon Teichos, 116
Kindt, J., 222n
kingdom formation, Hellenistic, 226; agency in, 144; by Alexander's Successors, 1; authority in, 144, 185; local concerns in, 228; political ideology of, 226; processes of, 86; redrawing of political communities, 23; royal authority in, 228; synoikism in, 14; transformation of poleis, 4; urbanization in, 4–5, 7, 12, 86
kingdoms, Hellenistic: administration of communities, 12, 29, 86–87; and autonomy of poleis, 87; cities' status within, 23n; continuity with Persian Empire, 106; direct interventions of, 91; economic interests of, 87, 101–4; impact on settlement patterns, 16–17; infrastructure of, 31, 87; institutional complexity of, 104; interpolis rivalry among, 3; interregional trade among, 127–36; land systems of, 105–20, 119; legacy of, 227; local communities under, 29; Macedonian precedents for, 106; manpower of, 104; map of, 6; markets of, 101–4; monetized economy of, 104; mutual benefits in, 90; particularism of, 2, 184, 228; as predatory states, 90; reciprocity with communities, 24; resources in kind, 103; role of geography in, 3; shaping of economic activity, 91; symbolic orders of, 87. *See also* imperialism, Hellenistic
kingship, Hellenistic: administrative structures of, 30; among Alexander's Successors, 35, 226; Cassander's, 35–36, 226; cult of ruler in, 51, 191–93, 196, 222; improvisatory, 226; physical imprint of, 86. *See also* monarchs, Hellenistic
Kissos, in Thessalonike synoikism, 40
Kleisthenes, reforms of, 199
koina: administrative networks of, 101; of Athena Ilias, 120, 121–24; common coinages of, 92, 123n; community participation in, 180; councils *(synedria)* of, 121; economic interdependence of, 120–26; economic privileges of, 101; as extensions of synoikisms, 92; Hellenistic revival of, 120; interpolis theoric activity of, 182; Ionian, 124; patterns of exchange, 126; purpose of, 120–21, 126; regional consolidation in, 91, 120–26; religious roles of, 120; royal encouragement of, 126; shared infrastructure of, 137; shared institutions of, 92, 121, 137; shared markets of, 121; of The Troad, 2, 66; urbanization and, 121
koinonia, 9n
Kokkylion: site of, 62n; in synoikism of Ilion, 62
Kolonai, in Alexandreia Troas synoikism, 65, 66
Kolophon: construction commission of, 95; construction cost of, 93; decline of, 149; destruction of, 18n; excavation of, 74n; exiles from, 181n; fortification of, 57, 95; founder cult of, 187; mint of, 74n; *palaia polis* of, 149; population transfer from, 74; public revenues of, 95; rebellion of, 150, 187; religious identity of, 148–50; separation from Ephesos, 201; synoikism of, 19, 20, 150; transfer to Ephesos, 93, 187
Komaitho (priestess of Artemis Triklaria), love for Melanippos, 215
Korakai, depopulation of, 82
Korope (polis): classical, 83, 157; excavation of, 82–83; sanctuary of Apollo Koropaios, 157–58, 177
Kos: alliance with Maussollos, 15n; chiliasty of, 200; cults of, 173, 213–14; Dorian tribes of, 200, 214; *homopoliteia* with Kalymnos, 181n; laws of, 101; priesthoods of, 213; religious calendars of, 189, 213; religious life of, 212–14; sanctuary of Twelve Gods, 213; synoikism of, 173, 181n, 189, 200, 212; *theōroi* at, 194, 195n
Kosmin, P., 29n
Kouretes, rites of, 221
Krateros, siege of Thessaly, 31
Krateuas (landowner), estate of, 103n, 108–9, 110, 112
Kravaritou, S., 192n
Krinon (son of Parmenion), position in Demetrias, 208
Kromna, as birthplace of Homer, 205
ktistai: cult at Demetrias, 159, 161, 176, 177, 191–94, 219; Diodoros on, 187
kunēgoi (cultic officials), 159
Kydimos of Abydos (gymnasiarch), 122
Kyklades, in Nesiotic League, 124, 125–26, 182
Kyknos (mythical king), 152

Kyrbantes cult (at Trapeza Thessalonikis), 161–62
Kyrbissos, in Teos-Lebedos synoikism, 97

Lachares (estate manager): decree honoring, 116; sacrifice to, 170
Lamian War, 31, 67
Lampon (Athenian), 187
land, civic: of Gambreion, 109; private, 117n; versus royal land, 109, 117
land, royal: aggregates in, 29; versus civic land, 109, 117; devolution to cities, 106; indigenous populations on, 107; reconfigurations of, 143; relationship of cities to, 92; sale to cities, 114; synoikism of villages on, 116; in urban foundations, 116; urban markets and, 138
land grants: from Antigonos, 109; *en doreai*, 110n; *en patrikois*, 111; as *klerouchia*, 110n; to Miletos, 115; sources for, 106; urbanization and, 112–14; in usufruct, 107, 108, 109, 117
land tenure regimes: Achaemenid, 105, 106, 109, 118–19; Alexander's policy, 106–7, 108–9; destabilization of, 120n; evidence for, 117; fiscal status of, 105; in Hellenistic kingdoms, 105–20; inheritance, 117; patrimonial, 108; poleis', 105; under Successors, 108, 111; in synoikisms, 94, 110–11, 112; traditional patterns of, 120n. See also *chōra*
Laodike (wife of Antiochos II), divorce settlement of, 114
Laodike III, letter to Iasos, 8n
Laodikeia: foundation of, 115–16; Ionian settlers in, 116; synoikism of, 169–70; wool production at, 116n
Larichos (Seleukid), benefactions of, 114
Larisa, in Alexandreia Troas synoikism, 65
Latmos: sanctuary of Zeus Akraios, 219–20; *sympoliteia* with Pidasa, 48–49, 98–99, 150, 203, 219. See also Herakleia Latmos
law, divine origin of, 145, 146; in synoikism, 101, 200
Lawall, M., 90n
Lebedos (polis), 76; population transfer from, 74; synoikism with Teos, 20, 57–58, 74n; *synteleia* with Ephesos, 89–90. See also Teos-Lebedos synoikism
Lennatos (companion of Alexander), 107
Lentulus, Cnaeus Cornelius, 209
Lesbos, amphorae of, 131
Leventi, I., 154n
Levy, R., 215n
Lindos, cultic life of, 211–12

Livy: on Aineia, 195n; on Macedonian wars, 40; on Theoxena, 195; on Thessalonike, 202
Lydia, depopulation of, 119
Lykourgos: on Ilion, 59n; reforms of, 179
Lysandra (wife of Agathocles), 84
Lysias (priest of Zeus Akraios), 210
Lysias (son of Epiteles), benefactions of, 83
Lysimacheia: coinage of, 53; extent of, 53; site of, 52–53; strategic importance of, 55; synoikism of, 52–53, 55–57
Lysimacheion (heroön), 187n, 194
Lysimachos: burial site of, 187n; Chersonese foundations of, 73; commercial aims of, 91; conflict with Antigonos, 50, 55, 67; conflict with Seuthes, 55n; control of Ionia, 73; control of Macedonia, 50; death of, 55; development of Smyrna, 76–77; Ephesian cult and, 148; foundations of, 58; founding of Lysimacheia, 52–53, 55–56; intervention in Smyrna, 181; invasion of Asia Minor, 67–68, 70; mint of, 73n; murder of Agathocles, 84; neglect of Ilion, 167n; portrait at Ephesos, 186; and Priene, 99–100; refoundation of Alexandreia Troas, 64, 165; refoundation of Ephesos, 73–74, 76, 89, 94, 221; refoundation of Skepsis, 2, 3, 61; Seleukos's defeat of, 84; struggle with Getae, 71n; treatment of Ilion, 59–60, 62–63; war with Thracians, 55
Lysippos, ceramic vessel of, 90

Ma, J., 23n
Macedonia: archaic temples of, 164; Demetrios's control of, 71; divided ethnos of, 198; Gallic invasion of, 84; Lysimachos's control of, 50; relationship with Magnesia, 159n; Roman partitioning of, 198. See also imperialism, Macedonian; monarchs, Macedonian
Macedonian War, Third (168 BCE), 198
Maeander valley: synoikism of, 85; trade through, 136
Magie, D., 23, 99n
Magnesia, 79; cults of, 145, 151, 158, 176; in Demetrias, 78, 203, 204; under Demetrios Poliorketes, 78; as Macedonian dependency, 180; Plato's ideals for, 145; relationship with Macedonia, 159n; *sympoliteiai* with Smyrna, 93n; synoikism of, 77; Thessalian communities of, 180
Magnesian League, 151n; coinage of, 218; conflict in, 206–7; demotics of, 158; domination by Demetrias, 207, 210; ethnicities of, 202–3; stress in, 207–8

Malalas, on Seleukeia, 70n
Malousios (*synedrion* member): *ateleia* of, 122; economic contributions of, 121–22
Mantineia (polis): formation of, 13; Helisson in, 180n
Maussollos (Hekatomnid dynast), 49; centralization under, 50; synoikisms of, 11, 15, 227
McNichol, A., 49n
Megalopolis: Arkadian communities of, 175n; *chōra* of, 173n; cults of, 170–71, 174; foundation of, 45, 173n; *oikistai* of, 173; replication of cults in, 173–75; synoikism of, 11, 15, 173–75
Melanthios (royal officer), benefactions of, 147–48
Meleager: land grant from, 113; letter to the Ilians, 114
Melitaia, union with Pereia, 98n
Memnon, on Nikaia, 198n
Menandros (satrap), 109
Menandros (son of Nikon), ethnikon of *Demetrieus*, 202–3
Mende: amphorae of, 90n; under Cassander, 36, 38; tribute of, 38n; wealth of, 90n
Messene, foundation of, 45
Mētēr Antaiē sanctuary (Kolophon), 74n, 95, 149, 150
Meter Dindymene, agalma of, 174n
Methone: destruction of, 77, 127; reconstitution of, 128n
Metoikizein (to move a settlement), 9
Meyer, Ernst, 156
Mezières, M., 194
Migeotte, L., 125n
migration. *See* population transfer
Mikro Karabournaki, commercial links of, 43
Mileta, C., 24n
Miletos: absorption of Myous, 100n; *chōra* of, 119; in Karian League, 95n; royal land grand to, 115; *stephanēphoroi* of, 48n; union with Pidasa, 11, 98–99, 150n
military settlements, polis status of, 115
Miltiades the Elder, foundation of Agora/Chersonesos, 53
monarchs, Hellenistic: as city founders, 186; civic virtues of, 225; fostering of unity, 185; founders' cults of, 191–93, 196; identification with gods, 222n; legitimation through religion, 222; manipulation of cultic life, 182; naming of tribes after, 205; *philodoxia* of, 225; *philotimia* of, 225; in polis identity, 185; relationship with poleis, 3, 7, 30, 31–32, 91, 104, 185, 192, 222, 226, 228; restraints on, 184; rhetoric of benefaction, 20–22; role in civic norms, 205; role in religion, 158–60, 184; strategic aims of, 31; wealth of, 103. *See also* imperialism, Hellenistic; kingship, Hellenistic
monarchs, Macedonian: encounters with subject populations, 91; settlement policy of, 30
Mount Solmessos, Kouretes of, 221
Mygdonia, reorganization of, 43
Mykonos, cult of *archēgetēs*, 189n
Mylasa: land grant to, 115n; sympoliteia with Olymos, 212n
Myous, absorption of Miletos, 100n
Mytilene: dispute with Pitane, 114, 115; domination of Ilion, 131; revolt against Athens, 14n

Nakona, *genetores* of, 189n
Narthakion, fortification of, 69
Neandreia, 3n; abandonment of, 166; in Antigoneia Troas synoikism, 63; cultic continuity in, 166; cult of Apollo, 165, 177–78; Demeter sanctuary of, 166
Neapolis, Parthenos temple of, 164n
Neleia, absorption into Demetrias, 81
Neon Teichos, 170; synoikism with Kiddiou Kome, 116
Nesiotic League, 47, 71, 124–26; common cultic association of, 182; functions of, 125; sacred ambassadors of, 126; *synedrion* of, 125, 126
Nielsen, T., 11
Nikaia: coinage of, 198; refoundation of, 197, 198n
Nikephoros Gregoras, on Demetrias, 197n
Nikomedes of Kos, 65
Notion (Kolophon by the Sea), 76; population transfer to, 150
Nysa: foundation cult of, 188; priesthood of, 208–9; sanctuary of Pluto and Korē, 209

Old Oligarch, on synoikism, 14
Olymos, sympoliteia with Mylasa, 212n
Olympias: execution of, 34n; following Alexander's death, 32, 33; and Polyperchon, 34
Olynthos: Cassander's restitution of, 44; Philip's destruction of, 36; synoikism of, 9, 14n
Orchomenos, 68; union with Euaimon, 8, 10

Pagasai (polis): Argo myth of, 151, 152; cultic life of, 155; cult of Apollo, 151n, 152–54; elite of, 155; literary evidence for, 128; Macedonian control of, 77–78; in Magnesia, 151; myths of, 151–52; population transfer from, 80–81; site of, 152; temples of, 78

Pagasitic Gulf, 79; borders of, 151; commerce of, 128–30; consolidation under Demetrios, 128; cults of, 151–61; Macedonian domination of, 129n; synoikism of, 77
Pan, sanctuary at Berkela, 174
Panhellenic festivals, religious identity in, 180
Panhellenism, ties of cults to, 149
Panionia: choral performance in, 181n; location of, 182n; participation in, 181, 182; rituals of, 182
Papazoglou, F., 39
Parion: in Athena Ilias *koinon*, 122–23; ties to Skepsis, 122n
Parker, R., 146, 218n
Parmeniskos (son of Amyntas), in Delphic *hieromnēmones*, 207
Parmeniskos group, amphorae of, 129
Pasikrata (deity), 160–61
Patrai: festival of Dionysos, 215–16; formation of, 13; ritual in, 215; rural-urban link in, 216; sanctuary of Artemis, 215–16; synoikism of, 215
Pausanias: on Demeter Eleusinia, 173; on Epameinondas, 45n; on Kardia, 53n; on Kolophon, 150; on Lebedos, 89; on Lysimachos, 74; on Megalopolis, 173n; on *panēgyris* of Isis, 123n; on Thebes, 44; use of *synteleia*, 89n; on Zeus Lykaios, 174
peace of 311, 1, 51, 225
Peace of Antalkidas (387/86), 14
Peace of Apameia (188), 62
Peace of Nikias (412), 36
Peithon (satrap), 34n
Pelias (king of Iolkos), 156n
Pelion: cults of, 157, 210, 216, 217; mythology of, 210; temple of Zeus Akraios, 157, 177
Pella, expansion of, 127–28
Peloponnese: Cassander's consolidation of, 67; and refoundation of Thebes, 45
Perdikkas (general), conflicts with Successors, 32
Perdikkas (son of Koinos), land grant to, 108, 109, 111–12
Perdylos, in Thessalonike synoikism, 39
Pereia, union with Melitaia, 98n
Pergamon, control of Kaikos valley, 133
Persepolis Fortification Tablets, travel in, 133–34
Petra (*chorion*), land grant and, 113
Peuma, 69; coinage of, 69n; refoundation of, 68
Phaidimos (Olympic victor), 3n
Pharnabazos (Persian satrap), control of Skepsis, 58n

Pherai: Demetrios's seizure of, 179n; Doric temple at, 179n; under Philip II, 77; tyrants of, 81
Philetairos (ruler of Pergamon), land subsidy of, 114
Philip (brother of Cassander), assault on Anatolia, 48
Philip II of Macedon, 227; Aegean Thrace under, 39; Corinthian League of, 67; destruction of Halos, 68–69; land policies of, 106n, 107, 110; leadership of Thessalian *koinon*, 78; population transfer under, 16–17, 22n; razing of Methone, 77; urbanization under, 16–17
Philip III Arrhidaios, 33, 34; interment of, 36; land grant from, 109n
Philip V of Macedon, letter to Antipatros, 159
Philippoi: foundation of, 16; land of, 110
Philokles (king of Sidon), 125; on Theban stele, 46
Philokrates, dedication to Apollo, 154
Philotas (companion of Alexander), 107
Phoinix of Kolophon, lament of, 20
Phokion, exile of, 34n
Phrynichos, "Capture of Miletus," 20n
Phthiotic Thebes: connection with Demetrias, 129; Demetrios and, 68; grave stelai of, 129n
Phygela (polis), 74; incorporation into Ephesos, 147–48; minor cults of, 148; religious festivals of, 147–48; sanctuary of Artemis Mounychia, 148
Phylake, synoikism with Pyrasos, 68n
Pidasa: cults of, 150n; *sympoliteia* with Latmos, 48–49, 98–99, 150, 203; union with Miletos, 11, 98–99, 150n
Pindar, language of synoikism, 8n
Pitane, dispute with Mytilene, 114, 115
Pixodaros, heroön of, 186–87
Plato: on cult, 145–46; influence on naming, 205; *Laws*, 145, 205
Pleistarchos (brother of Cassander): coinage of, 220; rule of Karia, 49, 70
Plutarch: on Antigonas Gonatas, 191; on Demetrios, 72n; on Thracian Dionysos, 162n
Pluto and Korē, sanctuary at Nysa, 209
Plutonion (Nysa), priests of, 188n
poleis: agricultural hinterland of, 138; amnesty of 319, 33; autonomy for, 4, 19, 22, 51, 87, 92–104, 199–200, 208, 227; compromise in, 185; consumption of surpluses, 102; control of land, 92; disputes among, 100; diversity in, 228; dynastic names of, 197; and edict of Polyperchon, 33; egalitarian ideals of, 120; elimination of ethnicity, 199; essential mechanisms

poleis *(continued)*
of, 87–88; expansion of, 127; financing of public construction, 94–96; fiscal networks of, 101, 102; following Alexander's death, 33–34; fortification of, 5; freedom of, 44, 47, 51, 87, 198, 225; in Hellenistic economy, 101–4; Hellenistic political culture of, 119–20; impact of urbanization on, 7; indigenous deities of, 146; infrastructure of, 5; interregional trade among, 127; interstate relations between, 16; land systems of, 105; links to divine founders, 171; negotiations with kings, 20, 23, 222; new elites of, 119–20; particularism of, 228; political economy of, 91n; population decrease in, 137; pre-synoikism hegemons of, 196n; productive territory of, 226; relationship to royal land, 92; relationship with kings, 3, 7, 30, 31–32, 91, 104, 185, 192, 222, 226, 228; as royal allies, 23n; royal intervention in, 92; royal legitimacy in, 34n, 222, 226; sacred architecture of, 172; spatial reorganization of, 92; synoikized names of, 204; taxation of, 92; territories of, 13n; transfer of cults to, 154, 171–80; transformations to, 5; weakness in Hellenistic era, 23. *See also* communities; synoikisms
Polemaios: conflict with Cassander, 50; Peloponnese operations of, 125n; revolt of, 52, 56, 125n
politeuma, of communities, 10
Polybios: on Ilion, 60n; language of synoikism, 10–11
Polycharmos *(kunēgos)*, epitaph of, 160
Polyperchon, 32; conflict with Cassander, 44, 45; exiles under, 34n; proclamation of 319, 33, 44; propaganda of, 33; in Third Diadoch War, 52
population transfers, 30; Achaemenid, 22; archaeological evidence for, 19; Assyrian, 22; to Ephesos, 74; from Gergis, 114; hyperbole on, 17n; to Notion, 150; from Pagasai, 80–81; under Philip of Macedon, 16–17, 22n; and rhetoric of benefaction, 22; royal power over, 19; from Sindos, 41; of Skepsis, 3; in synoikism, 11; in The Troad, 57
Poris, flight from Thebes, 195
Poseidon, cult of, 202n
Poteidaia: Cassander's restitution of, 44; cult of Poseidon, 202n; elimination of, 128; site of, 36
power, imperial: consolidation of (311–301), 51–69; social reactions to, 5. *See also* imperialism

power relations, Hellenistic: local communities in, 31–32; in synoikism, 23, 31–32, 169
Prepelaion *(heroön)*, 74
Prepelaos (general), 48, 67–68; control of Ephesos, 72; founder cult of, 187
Priene, Alexander's letter to, 99, 105
Prokonessos, 175n
Ptolemaios (estate holder), 117; land grant to, 108
Ptolemais. *See* Lebedos (polis)
Ptolemies, control of Nesiotic League, 125
Ptolemy I: abandonment of Cassander, 56n; at Alexander's death, 32; conflict with Antigonos, 56; control of Alexandria, 34n; control of Cyprus, 52n; defeat of Demetrios, 50; freeing of Miletos, 52n; invasion of Peloponnese, 56; Nesiotic League of, 71
Ptolemy II, land grant to Miletos, 115
Ptolemy Keraunos, 84
Purcell, N., 18n, 127n
Pyrasos, synoikism with Phylake, 68n
Pyrrhos of Epeiros, 71

Reger, G., 125n, 126
Reinders, H., 69n
religion, Hellenistic: corporate expression of, 166–71; divisive role of, 215n; effect of synoikism on, 25, 143–45, 150, 180; imperialism in, 184, 222; military conquest and, 146; negotiation of authority in, 191; networks of, 180–82; as organizational resource, 215n; political aspects of, 143; promotion of unity, 218; resistance to authority in, 144; ritual innovation in, 216; role of Hellenistic monarchs in, 158–60, 184. *See also* cults; rituals
Rhodes: alliance with Antigonos, 67n; calendar of, 212; *chōra* of, 189; commerce of, 129; cult of Athana Lindia, 211; demes of, 199–200; elite competition in, 211; eponymous founders of, 189; religious life of, 211–12; synoikism of, 14n, 170, 189, 199–200; territorial *phylai* of, 199–200; traditionalism of, 211; war with Crete, 189n. *See also* Halios
Rhoiteion, in synoikism of Ilion, 62
Rhomaios, K., 42n, 43n
Rhoxane (widow of Alexander), 34, 45; execution of, 51
Rigsby, K., 56n
rituals: communities' negotiation of, 192; of girls, 155; innovation in, 216, 219, 220–21; integrative, 223; in maintenance of political body, 223–24; as methods of communication, 214; reflection of community tension in,

144; response to social pressure, 217; role in synoikism, 215; rural-urban links in, 216–18. *See also* cults; religion
roads: common, 134–35; Persian imperial, 118n, 134–35; royal, 133; sacred, 156; settlements along, 135–36
Robert, L., 55n, 62n; on *aphidruma*, 171n; on Kebren, 64; on Meander valley, 219n
Rogers, G., 186; on Soteria cult, 221n
Rome, economic history of, 91n
Rose, C. B., 60n, 167n

sacred places, pre-synoikism, 144. *See also* sanctuaries
Sacred War, Third (352), 78
sacrifice, guilt of, 217n
Salutaris, Gaius Vibius: benefaction for Ephesos, 186
sanctuaries: abandoned, 172, 182–83; common, 223; corporate religious expression in, 166–71; cultic identity around, 145; at depopulated communities, 173–75; preceding synoikisms, 166–71; replication in synoikized communities, 171–80; shared, 145; siting of, 214
Sardeis: 15, 110, 118, 133; royal road to, 133; temple of Artemis, 109
satrapies, Babylonian: division of, 32
Scheidel, W., 137n
Seleukeia, foundation of, 70n
Seleukid Empire: city building in, 103; coinage of, 103–4; economy of, 90n, 103–4; land alienation in, 112, 114; power in Asia Minor, 84–85, 114; royal road of, 133n; tribute to, 104
Seleukos: alliance with Demetrios, 70n, 71; conflict with Antigonos, 50, 52; control of Babylon, 32n; control of Syria, 70; death of, 84; defeat of Lysimachos, 84; foundations of, 70–71; invasion of Europe, 55n; treaty with Antigonos, 52n
Sepias, in Demetrias synoikism, 83
Seuthes III (Odrysian king), 55n
Shield of Heracles, Hesiodic: cults in, 151
Sicily, synoikisms of, 13–14
Sigeia, in Antigoneia Troas synoikism, 63
Sigeion: Athenian control of, 168; destruction of, 61n; Lysimachos's capture of, 62; in synoikism of Ilion, 62
Sikyon: founder cults of, 196; honoring of Demetrios, 190–91, 194, 196; refoundation of, 69
Sindos: abandonment of, 41; in Thessalonike synoikism, 39

Skamandra, *sympoliteia* with Ilion, 62
Skepsis: bronzes of, 3n; Homeric heritage of, 2; incorporation into Antigoneia Troas, 1–2, 3, 12, 63, 133; land grants near, 113; Lysimachos's refoundation of, 2, 3–4, 61; migration (*metoikisis*) of, 3; Persian domination of, 4; ties to Parion, 122n
Skopas of Paros, cult statuary of, 221
slaves, commerce in, 136
Smyrna: Antigonos's refoundation of, 77; coinage of, 77n; commerce of, 133; founders' cults of, 197; in Ionian koinon, 181; Lysimachos's refoundation of, 76–77; *sympoliteia* with Magnesia, 93n
Sopatos (Seleukid official), privileges of, 209
Soros, necropolis of, 153
Spalauthra, in Demetrias synoikism, 83–84
Sphodrias of Chios, 65
Stählin, E., 193, 194
Stephanos of Byzantium, 73–74
Strabo: on Achilleion, 61n; on Aigospotamoi, 53n; on Alexandreia, 64n; on Antigoneia Troas, 63n; on Artemis Soteria, 221; on Chrysa, 66n; on Demetrias, 80n, 81n; on Ephesos, 73; on Ilion, 59–61, 62; on Iolkos, 82n; on Nysa, 188; on Pagasai, 81; on *panēgyris* of Delos, 123n; on Pyliac *panēgyris*, 156; on Smyrna, 76n; on Thessalonike, 39, 40n, 41–42
Stratonikeia: foundation of, 169; multiple cults of, 169; Panamareis of, 209; religious identity of, 209; tribes of, 203
Successors, Alexander's: competition among, 18; conferral of *ateleia*, 112; conflict among, 4, 29–33, 47–48, 86; consolidation of power, 34; following Alexander's death, 32–33; ideal of empire, 29; intervention in autonomous poleis, 22; kingship of, 35, 226; land tenure under, 108, 111; local communities under, 31–34; normative influences on, 226; Persian imperial apparatus of, 17; reshaping of communities, 5; reshaping of political geography, 51; sources for, 30; urbanization under, 47, 52
sympoliteia (political union), 11n; Bundesstaat type of, 9n; citizenship in, 9, 10; civic finance in, 93; cults in, 150n; definition of, 9, 10, 11, 12; of Helisson and Mantineia, 150; of Iasos and Chalketor, 21; of Ilion and Skamandra, 62; of Karia, 12; of Kolophon and Notion, 76; of Kyrbissos and Teos, 93; of Latmos and Pidasa, 98, 150; of Lykia, 12; of Medea and Stiris, 93; of Melitaia and Pereia, 98,

sympoliteia (continued)
    100; of Miletos and Myous, 100; of Miletos and Pidasa, 93, 150; in modern scholarship, 8; Olymos and Mylasa, 212; of Phokis, 12; political connotations of, 11; of Smyrna and Magnesia under Sipylos, 93; of Stiris and Medeon, 150; *synoikismos* and, 11

sympolity: mutual agreement in, 12; unequal, 9

sympolizein (to unite), 8

Synnada (polis), 68

Synoikia festival (Athens), 172–73

synoikisis, Thucydides' use of, 8

synoikismos: definition of, 8, 9, 10, 11, 12; in marriage, 8; in modern scholarship, 8; physical connotations of, 11; *sympoliteia* and, 11

synoikisms, 1–2; administration of, 86–87; agricultural markets of, 102–3; alienation of land to, 110–11, 112; anxiety concerning, 216; archaeological evidence for, 19; archaic, 13; architecture of, 206; benefits for subordinate communities, 90; building projects of, 92, 94, 95–96, 121, 138, 168; central administrations of, 208; citizen groups in, 4; civic actors in, 88, 99; civic economy in, 92; civic identity under, 7, 25, 214–21, 227; civic infrastructure of, 96–97, 139; of classical world, 91n; coastal, 115, 127; coinages of, 204; common bonds in, 224; communal customs of, 198–208; community definition in, 214–21; compromise in, 214; concealed enfranchisement in, 25; in conception of polis, 13; consensus building in, 144, 189; as construct of historiography, 7; continuity in, 143–44, 201; continuity of cult in, 143–50, 161, 172, 208, 223; cost of, 99–101; cultic identities in, 148–50, 181, 185, 192, 208, 214, 223; cultic replication of, 171–80; cults' adaptations under, 150–66; debt management in, 102; depopulation under, 87; disintegration of, 223; disruptive, 223; durability of, 4, 5; of early Hellenic era, 36; economic aspects of, 90, 92–93, 99; economic interdependence of, 120–26; effect on founder cults, 185; effect on settlement patterns, 5, 7, 87; effect on territorial disputes, 99–100; epigraphic record of, 25, 228; eponymous names of, 205; ethnic groups in, 24, 198–208; euergetism in, 20; evolving, 24; in formation of Hellenistic kingdoms, 14; founders' descendants in, 188; frequency of, 5; grain supply for, 97; historical phenomenon of, 7; as ideological constructs, 7; institutions of, 25, 199, 201; internal city life under, 7; *koina* as extensions of, 92; landholders of, 105, 108, 116, 117–18; land systems of, 94, 110–11, 112; language of, 7–12; large-scale, 31; legal frameworks of, 99–101; literary sources for, 18, 19, 25; liturgical functions of, 97, 99; local autonomy in, 4, 19, 22, 51, 87, 92–104, 199–200, 208, 227; local dynamics of, 5, 18, 228; military aspects of, 226; monetized markets of, 101–4; negotiation in, 20, 23, 191, 192, 214, 222, 228; new citizens of, 92; phenomenon of, 7–12; physical migration in, 11; as physical processes, 7; political government following, 147; in power networks, 23, 31–32, 169; private property in, 94; as processes, 112n; processes of, 18–23, 24; public land in, 93–94; redistribution of property in, 92; religious effects of, 25, 143–45, 150, 180; religious prerogatives of, 208; reorganization of, 31; resistance to, 19–20, 227; response to fragmentation, 137; revival of poleis through, 181; role of individuals in, 214; role of ritual in, 215; royal ambitions in, 18; royal authority in, 205, 222, 225; royal/civic interests in, 103; royal financial support for, 93; royal initiatives in, 21; royal interventions in, 92–104; sanctuaries preceding, 166–71; seaborne trade among, 127–32; separatism in, 206, 208; social actors in, 23–24, 143; social organization of, 88, 198–208; social stresses of, 4, 7, 227–28; Spartan, 15; success of, 227; symbolic violence in, 227; taxation in, 102; territorial continuity of, 200–201; tribal reform in, 199; unequal, 11; unified communities of, 87; unity in, 206; urban forms of, 86, 88; urbanization through, 5, 85, 91, 136–37; willing participants in, 11

synoikisms, classical, 7; Old Oligarch on, 14

synoikisms, multipolis, 11, 12, 85; expenses of, 93; foundation cults of, 194; inclusive emphasis in, 188–89; scale of, 92–93

synoikizein: agency in, 9, 12; political meanings of, 9n

synteleia (joint distribution): in Athenian imperialism, 14n; economic priorities of, 89; elements comprising, 89

synthesis (agreement), of communities, 10

Syracuse, synoikism of, 13–14

Syrian War, Third (246–241), 76, 201

Tegea, formation of, 13
Teion, revolt from Amastris, 205
Telesphoros, revolt of, 52

SUBJECT INDEX   283

Teos-Lebedos synoikism, 20, 57–58, 74n, 93; Antigonos's administration of, 100–101, 102; arbitration of disputes in, 100–101; civic infrastructure of, 96–97; civic rights in, 97; civil law code of, 101; debts in, 100–101, 102; grain supply for, 97, 102; lawsuits in, 100; liturgies of, 97; raising of capital for, 97; religious aspects of, 180; stability of, 97; strategic importance of, 103. *See also* Lebedos
Thebagenes (priest of Zeus), 210
Thebes, 45; alliance with Cassander, 50n; *andrapodismos* at, 44; in Boiotian federation, 46, 207; destruction in 335, 46; donor stele of, 45–46; literary sources for, 45–46; refoundation of, 43–46; trade with Pagasai, 128n
Theisoa, sanctuary of Great God, 174
Theopompos, on Therme, 39n
theōrodokoi, and polis status, 180n
theōrodokoi lists, Delphic: Aineia in, 40, 181n; Kerben in, 64n; Larisa in, 65
Theoxena, flight from Thebes, 195
Thermaic Gulf, 38; cults of, 161–65; effect of synoikism on, 41; map of, 37; pre-Thessalonike sites of, 43; Thracian-Greek communities of, 40–41
Therme: site of, 41–42; in Thessalonike synoikism, 39
Thessalian *koinon*, Philip's leadership of, 78
Thessalonike: Aineia in, 202; Aineias cult of, 196n; archaeology of, 40–42; Cassander's foundation of, 38–43; commerce of, 130; commercial importance of, 38; consolidation of settlements at, 43; cultic life of, 161–65; cult of Aphrodite, 164n; cult of Asklepios, 202; environs of, 41; *ethnē* of, 39; extent of, 38–39; Hellenistic city of, 38–39, 41, 43; imperial Roman cult in, 163–64; Ionian temple of, 163; Iron Age assemblages of, 163; poleis of, 40–43; populations of, 43; religious life of, 196; settlements of, 39–40; settlements preceding, 42, 43; site of, 165; synoikism of, 39–43, 128; temple of Dionysos, 164–65; tribes of, 202; urban nucleus of, 163
Thessaly: Cassander's control of, 68; under Demetrios Poliorketes, 78
Thonemann, P., 91n, 118n; on traditional land tenure, 120n
Thourioi: Apollo's oracle for, 188; ethnic diversity of, 200; foundation of, 187–88; Sybarites of, 200

Thrace: indigenous cults of, 162–63; land status in, 111; Macedonian control of, 39, 55n
Thucydides: on cultic continuity, 146; on Ionia, 58n; language of synoikism, 8–9
Timoleon, synoikisms of, 13
Toriaion: commercial importance of, 103; common road to, 135
Torone: decline of, 38n; elimination of, 128; under synoikism of Kassandreia, 38
trade, interregional, 127–36; Achaemenid, 133–35; Aegean, 130; among poleis, 127; Antigonid policy on, 130n; common road of, 134–35; connectivity in, 133–36; overland, 133–36; realignment of, 127; seaborne, 127–32; urbanization of, 127
traditionalism, architectural, 178–80
traditionalism, Macedonian, 45, 49; reversal of, 35
Trapeza Lembet, necropolis of, 42
Trapeza Thessalonikis: necropolis of, 42; site of, 41; Kyrbantes cult of, 161–62; purification rites of, 162–63
Treaty of Apameia, 117
The Troad, 57; as Aegean/Asia Minor mediator, 131; Aiolian populations of, 204; Antigonos's reorganization of, 57–59; cults of, 165–66; grants to poleis of, 113; interpolis competition in, 2; Lysimachos's urban centers on, 73; Persian control of, 58, 131; poleis of, 58–59; political geography of, 59; population transfer in, 57; regional federation (*koinon*) of, 2, 66; strategic importance of, 58; unity of, 122; urbanization of, 113–14
Trophonios, and cult of Apollo, 151
Troy: competing traditions concerning, 2n; site of, 2
Twelve Gods, sanctuary of (Kos), 213

unification. *See* synoikism
urbanization: under Attalids, 85; under Cassander, 34–51, 226–27; civic economy in, 92–104; of coastal sites, 115; as construct of ancient history, 18n; corridors between, 86; demographic shifts in, 7; dynasts' investment in, 30; economic aspects of, 7, 91, 92, 94–95, 104, 137–39; forms of, 88; impact on poleis, 7; imperialism and, 12–18, 86; inland, 115; land grants and, 112–14; legal aspects of, 94; in Macedonian imperialism, 91, 137; of multiple communities, 7; nodal framework of, 18; in organization of Hellenistic states, 4–5, 7, 12;

urbanization *(continued)*
    under Philip of Macedon, 16–17; roads in, 133–36; Seleukid, 85; settlement hierarchy in, 86; social processes of, 18; socioeconomic flexibility in, 138; state-sponsored, 7; structural, 18; technological advancement in, 137; through synoikism, 5, 85, 91, 136–37; of trade routes, 127

Vlassopoulos, K., 18n
Voutiras, E., 164

water, divination through, 163n
Welles, C., 20; on land grants, 115

Xenokritos (Athenian), 187
Xenophon: language of synoikism, 10; on rule of tyrants, 22

Zeus: replication of sanctuaries of, 145; sanctuary on Keos, 217
Zeus, Idean: cave of, 145–46
Zeus Akraios, 82; Antigonid power and, 177; Cheiron and, 154, 217–19; cult at Demetrias, 154–55, 157–58, 177, 210, 216–17, 219; cult in Herakleia Latmos, 219; priests of, 210–11, 217, 218; sanctuary on Latmos, 219–20
Zeus Hetaireios, festival of, 159n
Zeus Karios, sanctuary at Panamara, 209
Zeus Lykaios, Parrhasian sanctuary of, 174
Zeus Philios, 170
Zeus Poleius, cult in Kos, 213–14
Zeus Sosipolis, temple of (Magnesia), 176
Zeus Sōtēr, 170–71
Zeus Thalios, 78
Zoilos (general), 210

INDEX LOCORUM

Acts of the Apostles		4.11.88	53
17.1	40	4.13.105	16
		Syriaca	
Aelius Aristides		1	53
Orationes		1.4	8, 55
20.5	197	28	55
20.7	76, 197	54	48, 56
20.20	76, 197	55	52
21.4	76, 197	62	55
21.20	197	63	194
		64	55, 187, 194
Aeschines			
2.27	38	Apollodorus mythographus	
2.162	17	*Bibliotheca Epitome*	
		2.7.7	152
Ager 1996			
no. 26	100	Apollonius Rhodius	
no. 30	69, 100	*Argonautica*	
no. 31	69	1.238	152
no. 32	100	1.359	152
no. 55	100	1.403	152
no. 56	98, 100	scholion to 1.407	152
no. 146	114	1.411–12	152
Anthologia Palatina		Aristophanes	
9.428	38	*Nubes*	
		332	187
Appian		*Plutus*	
Bella civilia		521	128

286 INDEX LOCORUM

Aristotle
Politica
1252b	13
1275b7–8	25
1311a14–15	22
1313b4–5	22

[Aristotle]
Athenaion Politeia
16.2–5	22
21.6	189

Arrian
Anabasis
1.7–9	44
1.9.9–10	44
1.12.1	58
1.13–14	66
1.16.5	106
1.18.1–2	17
7.9.2–3	16
7.10.4	106

Fragmente der griechischen Historiker 156
F1 1–8	32
F9 20–24	32
F9 25	32
F9 26	32
F9 28	32
F9 34–38	32
F10 1	32

Arvanitopoulos
1909b
no. 52	160
no. 80	130
no. 151	130

1929a
no. 420	160

1929b
no. 423	80, 81, 202

1929d
no. 425	190

1949
no. 257	130
no. 270	203

1952
no. 322	130
no. 347	130
no. 349	130

Athenaeus
Deipnosophistae
1.19b–c	46
1.29f–30a	4
3.54	35
4.155a	35
11.28	38, 90, 225
13.31	159
13.569	171

Athenian Tribute Lists
I 565	53

Batziou-Efstathiou and Pikoulas 2006	80, 112
Bencivenni 2003, 151–68	48, 58
Béquignon 1935, 74–77	190

Bielman 1994
no. 16	72
no. 51	148

Blümel
1997	48, 98, 150, 203
2000	10

Borza 1987	106

Brill's New Jacoby
369A
F2.8	155, 177, 210, 216, 217, 218
F2.12	155, 218, 219

Bringmann and Steuben 1995
130–33	45, 46

Buckler and Robinson
1912, no. 1	109
1932, no. 1	109

Buraselis 2014	35, 45

Callieri 1995
65–73	113
75–77	133

Callimachus
F18 (Pfeiffer)	152

INDEX LOCORUM 287

Callisthenes
Fragmente der griechischen Historiker 124
   F14   22

Certamen Homeri et Hesiodi
   l. 28   205

Chaniotis 2004
   381–83   188

Chaniotis 2009   188

Clemens Alexandrinus
Protrepticus
   2.19   162

Comicorum Graecorum fragmenta in papyris reperta
   238 9–10   156

Corpus des inscriptions de Delphes
   2 32, l. 48   207
   2 74, l. 40   207
   4 117, ll. 9–10   207
   4 119E   207

Curtius Rufus
   7.5.28–35   22
   10.1.44   55
   10.7–10.10   32

Demosthenes
   1.22   77, 78
   2.11   77, 78
   3.166   58
   6.20   36
   6.22   78
   7.10   36
   7.39   106
   9.22   17, 78
   9.22–27   78
   9.26   16, 40, 78
   9.34   78
   11.1   69, 78
   15.3   15
   15.27   15
   18.2   35
   18.36   17
   18.41   17
   18.302   175
   19.36   69
   19.39   69
   19.65   17
   19.81   17
   19.141   17
   19.163   17, 69
   20.60   36
   23.107–8   36
   23.154   58
   31.5   71
   50.5   174

Didyma. Vol. 2, Die Inschriften
   492 A–C   114, 118

Dilts 1971
   F20   22

Dinarchus
   1.24   44

Diodorus Siculus
   4.37.4   152
   5.56.3–6   170, 189
   11.54.1   13
   12.10.4   187
   12.10.7   200
   12.11   200
   12.11.1   187
   12.35.3   188
   13.75.1   9
   15.5.4   13
   15.38.4   89
   15.49   124, 172
   15.72.4   173
   15.76.2   15
   15.80.6   68
   15.94.1   9, 175
   16.3.7   16
   16.7.3   15
   16.8.3–5   36
   16.31.6   17, 77, 78
   16.34.4   17, 77
   16.59.4–60.2   78
   16.60.2   17, 78
   17.7.10   62
   17.8–14   44
   17.17.6   59, 169
   17.17.7   169
   17.18–21   66

Diodorus Siculus *(continued)*

17.22.1–4	58	19.52.4	35
17.119	22	19.52.2–4	36
18.1	169	19.52.3	225
18.2	32	19.52.5	35, 226
18.3.1	48	19.52.6–53.1	44
18.4.1–6	22, 169	19.54	225
18.4.8	32	19.54.1	46
18.7	32	19.54.2	35
18.8.2–7	47	19.55	34
18.11.1	68	19.56.5	34
18.17.6–8	31	19.57	47, 48
18.18	31	19.60.1	47
18.23	32	19.60.2–4.	48
18.25.3–4	32	19.61–62	35, 45, 47, 48
18.28.2–6	32	19.62.9	124
18.33–36.5	32	19.63.4	44, 47
18.38.3–6	47	19.67.3–4	48
18.39.5–6	32	19.68.1	48
18.48.4	32	19.68.5–7	48
18.49.1	32	19.69	48
18.49.2	29	19.73	71
18.50.1	32	19.74.3–6	48
18.51–52	33	19.75	48
18.52.7	33	19.75.6	46
18.54	32, 44	19.77.4–7	46, 50
18.55.2	33	19.77.5–7	55
18.55.4	33	19.77.2–78	50
18.56	33	19.80.3–85	50
18.57.1	34	19.86.4–5	50
18.57.2	33	19.90–92	50
18.57.3–4	33	19.94–100.3	51
18.64.3–5	33	19.100.5–7	51
18.65–69	34	19.105.1–2	51
18.66.2	33	19.105.4	29, 51
18.68–72	34	20.19.2	52
18.69.3–4	33	20.19.5	52
18.72.2–9	33	20.20	52
18.74–75	34, 45	20.21	52
19.11	34	20.27	52
19.12–35	34	20.27.3	52
19.17.6	134	20.28.1–3	52
19.35.2	44	20.29.1	52
19.35–36	34	20.37.4	35
19.37–44	34	20.45–46	56
19.46	34	20.46.5	67
19.48	34, 35	20.46.6	52
19.49–52	34	20.47–52	56
19.52.1	35	20.73–76	56
19.52.2	35	20.81–88	56
19.52.3	90	20.91–100.4	56
		20.99.3	67

20.100.2–4	67	Feyel 1940	123
20.102	67, 69, 197		
20.103	67, 191	Firmicus Maternus	
20.106.1–5	67	*De errore profanarum religionum*	
20.107	68	11	162
20.107.5	74		
20.108–11	68	*Fouilles de Delphes*	
20.110.6	179	III 1.275	3
20.111.3	72		
20.112.1	68	French 1997	133
21.1.5	70		
21F2	70	Frontinus	
21F4b	70	*Strategemata*	
21F7	71	3.3.7	72
21F12	71		
22.3–5	84	Gauthier	
		1989, no. 1	8
Dionysius of Halicarnassus		2001	98
Antiquitates Romanae			
1.49.1	196	Gawlinski 2012	123
1.49.4–5	18, 40, 164, 195		
		A Greek-English-Lexicon 9th ed.	
Diyllos		s.v. ἀφίδρυμα	171
Fragmente der griechischen Historiker 73			
F3	35	Habicht 1998b	48
Edson 1948		Harpocrates	
158–60	163, 165	s.v. "Aphrodite Pandēmos"	171
Ephippos			
R. Kassel and C. Austin, eds. *Poetae Comici Graeci*		Hasluck 1907, 65n8	64
F1	128	Hatzopoulos	
		1988	
Επιγραφές Κάτω Μακεδονίας, Τεύχος Α: Επιγραφές Βέροιας		17–54	38
		22–26	38, 108
3	159	26–28	195
		1990	
Ephorus		136–48	195
Fragmente der griechischen Historiker 70		1993	
F10	1	320–22	204
F15	199	1996, vol. 2	
F79	13	no. 4	39, 107
		no. 8	159
Euripides		no. 20	38, 108
Hercules furens		no. 21	205
389–93	152	no. 44	205
		no. 62	107
Eusebius		no. 72	165
Chronica		2006	
231–32	71	88–89	80

290   INDEX LOCORUM

Hatzopoulos and Loukopoulou 1992	107	5.94.1	58, 82
		5.122.2	2
Hekataios of Miletos		2.121.ζ.7	8
Fragmente der griechischen Historiker	1	6.3.1	22
F146	39	6.20.1	22
F147	41	6.21.2	20
		6.36.2	53
Hegesianax of Alexandreia Troas		6.42.1–2	100
Fragmente der griechischen Historiker 45	2	6.108.5	89
F7	196	6.119.1–4	22
		7.43	59
Hegesippos of Mekyberna		7.111	163
Fragmente der griechischen Historiker 391		7.123.3	41
F5	196	7.239.3	134
		8.98	134
Hellenica Oxyrhynchia		9.3.1	134
16.3	14		
17.3	14	Herrmann 1965	
		34–36, ll. 27–28	21
Helly			
1971	80, 157, 177	Herrmann and Malay 2007	
2006a	3	49–58, no. 32	117, 159
Heraclides Criticus		Hesiod	
Brill's New Jacoby		*Cat.* 73	196
369A		F7 West	159
F2.8	68, 177		
F3.2	68	[Hesiod]	
		Scutum	
Fragmenta Historicorum Graecorum		70	151
II 254–64		57–138	152
F2.8	155, 177, 210, 216, 217, 218	318–480	152
2.12	155, 218, 219	Hesychios	
		s.v. νέαι	155
Heraclides Pontikos			
F46a (Wehrli)	172	Holleaux 1938	
F137a (Wehrli)	151	1–40	45, 46, 62
Hermippos		Homer	
R. Kassel and C. Austin, eds. *Poetae*		*Iliad*	
Comici Graeci		1.37–39	166
F63.19	128	2.656	170
		2.662	170
Herodotus		2.816–77	5, 61
1.98.3	9		
1.142	89	Hommel, Kleiner, and Müller-Wiener 1967	
1.149.1–150.2	181	45–63	124, 181
5.15.3	22		
5.15.98	22	Humann et al. 1898	
5.94	62	no. 153	188

no. 255	188	63	62
no. 339a	188	64	62
		80, l. 9	62
Hyginus		125	166
Fabulae			
31	152	*Inschriften von Laodikeia am Lykos*	
Poetica astronomica		1	115, 169
2.37	152, 205	2, ll. 16–17	116
		85, ll. 16–17	116
Hyperides			
Fragmenta		*Inschriften von Magnesia am Maeander*	
76	16	53	
		ll. 75–79	76
Inschriften von Assos		2 ll. 79–81	76
4	64		
		Inschriften von Magnesia am Sipylos	
Inschriften von Ephesos		I	77, 93
Ia 3	73, 94		
Ia 4	72	*Inschriften von Mylasa*	
Ia 13 ii.18	136	21	109
Ia 26.1–6	186, 220, 221	22, ll. 2–4	115
Ia 27	186	861	212
Ia 29	186	ll. 3–4	9
IV 1381	94	913, ll. 2–6	21
IV 1408, ll. 1–9	147		
IV 1441	73, 94	*Inschriften von Pergamon* I	
V 1449	72	245 C	114
V 1450	72		
V 1452	72, 102	*Inschriften von Priene*	
V 1455	72, 102	1	99, 105
VII.1 3111	74	18	114
		139	124
Inschriften von Erythrai und Klazomenai		*Die Inschriften von Priene* (second edition)	
16	124	1	99, 105
504	124	29–31	114
		398	124
Inschriften von Iasos		*Inschriften von Smyrna*	
4	8	573	77, 93
		575.15–19	181
Inschriften von Ilion		577	73, 124, 181
1	59, 120	647	76
1–18	182	1004	203
2	122		
3	122	*Inschriften von Tralleis und Nysa*	
5	123	167	218, 219
10	123	134	218, 219
18	122		
25	167	*Inscriptiones Creticae*	
32, ll. 35–38	182	III.3. 3A, ll. 2–5	189
33	66, 112, 113		

INDEX LOCORUM

Inscriptiones Graecae

I³ 71.III.124	62, 65
I³ 71.III.126	62
I³ 71.III.130	65
I³ 71.III.137	62
I³ 244, face c1, ll. 16–20	173
I³ 259.iii.15	38, 90
I³ 260.vi.13, 267.V.17	89
I³ 260.viii.10	38
I³ 262.i.7	38, 90
I³ 265.ii.71, 101	38
I³ 266.ii.28	38
I³ 267.v.17	89
I³ 268.iii.5	38
I³ 279, col. 2, l. 29	63
I³ 281.ii.17	38
II² 646	71
II² 663	76
II² 1134, l. 14	207
IV 487–88	199
IV² 1 59, l. 12	10
IV² I 68	67
V 2 367	210
VII 2419	45, 46, 63
VII 7 506	125
IX 1 32	93, 150
IX 1² 1 188	98, 150
IX 1² 583	123
IX 1² 3 706	168
IX 2 205B	98
ll. 14–15	10
IX 2 358	161
IX 2 359a	159
IX 2 1098	152
IX 2 1099b	83, 158, 193, 194
IX 2 1100a	207
IX 2 1101	160
IX 2 1103,	
l. 7	210
l. 110	203
IX 2 1104, l. 36	203
IX 2 1105.I	175
IX 2 1105II, l. 2	210
IX 2 1105III, l. 3	
IX 2 1106	210
IX 2 1107b	160
IX 2 1108, l. 6	210
IX 2 1109	80, 81, 82, 83, 157, 202, 208, 210, 211
l. 4	81
IX 2 1110	176
IX 2 1111	80, 83, 158, 202, 210
IX 2 1112	80
IX 2 1122	82, 156
IX 2 1123	155
IX 2 1125	82, 155
IX 2 1128	218
IX 2 1133	160
X 2 1 61	164
X 2 1 278	202
X 2 1 299	164
X 2 1 625	164
X 2 1 965	164
X 2 1 185	165
X 2 1 259	39
X 2 1 503	163
XI 2 287B, l. 45	172
XI 4 1036	182
XI 4 1036.2	124, 125
XI 4 1038	125
XI 4 1040	125
XI 4 1235	209
XII 3 1286	148
XII 4.1 278	189
XII 4.1 280a–c	189
XII 5 1065	125
XII 5 1004	125
XII 7 13	125
XII 7 506	125, 126
XII 9 191	111
XII 9 210	63
XII supl. 169, l. 4	

Inscriptions of Alexandreia Troas

1–2	65, 95
4, l. 7	66

Inscriptions de Délos

1432, Bb, col. 2, ll. 9–10	181

Inscriptions grecques et latines de la Syrie

IV 4028, ll. 37–39	123

Intzesiloglou 2006	159

Iscrizioni di Cos

ED 71g B, ll. 6, 16	65

C. Jones 1999	48, 98, 203
Jonnes and Ricl 1997	117, 135
Judeich 1891, 291–95, no. 7	97

INDEX LOCORUM 293

Justin		33.40.6	53
Epitome of Pompeius Trogus		33.38.10–11	53
8.5.7	16	37.37.2	60
8.6.1–2	16	38.39	76
11.3	44	38.39.10	62, 114
13.3–4	32	40.4.4	195, 202
13.6.1	32	40.4.9	40, 161, 195
13.6.4–8	32	4.4.10	195
14.6.1–12	34	44.10.7	40, 195
14.6.3	35	44.11.2–3	36
15.2.1–3	52	44.32.8	195
15.2.5	51	45.27.4	40
15.2.6–9		45.28.8	40
15.4	70	45.29	198
15.4.23–24	71	45.30.4	195
16.1	71	45.30.5	40
16.1.19	71		
17.1.3–6	84	Lupu 2009	
17.2.2–4.	84	no. 26	189
24–25.1–2	84		

Lycophron
Alexandra

Kition-Bamboula V, Kition dans les textes:
Testimonia littéraires et épigraphiques
et Corpus des inscriptions
2015   159

scholion to l. 1236	196

Lycurgus
Against Leocrates

| Kizil et al. 2015 | 48 | 62 | 59, 167 |

Knoepfler 1989	205	Ma 2002	
		no. 5	10
Konon		no. 17	21

Fragmente der griechischen Historiker 26

F1 46	196	Maier 1959–61, 1	
		no. 69	58, 95, 148
Kontogiannis 2003	152	no. 70	95
		no. 71	94
LaBuff 2016		no. 72	94
81–84	48, 98, 150, 203		
93–103	98	Malalas	
108–12	212	8.199	70
124–29	10		

Marmor Parium
Fragmente der griechischen Historiker 239

Lefèvre 1998			
89	207	F B14	35
90	207	F B19	52

| Lindos: Fouilles et recherches | | | |
| 1 | 211 | Masson 1969 | 130, 160 |

		Mazarakis Ainian 2009, 273n33	154
Livy			
31.27.2	44	Meier 2012	
31.45.14	38	323–26	120

Meier 2012 *(continued)*
    362–68   95, 148
    369–73   95

Memnon
Fragmente der griechischen Historiker 434
    F4.9   70, 71
    F5.6   84
    F11   84
    F41   198

Meritt 1935
    no. 1   58, 95, 148, 187
    no. 2   95
    no. 6   74

Meyer, Ernst, 1936   80, 82, 157, 176, 190, 202

Migeotte 1984
    no. 69   95
    no. 87   95

Milet
    I.2, 10   73, 124, 181
    I.3, 33E   100
    I.3, 39   115
    I.3, 123   48, 115
    I.3, 142   74
    I.3, 146A, ll. 30–31   9
    I.3, 149   19, 93, 98, 150
        l. 49   9

Milojčić 1974, 74   154

Missitzis 1985   107

Moretti 1976
    no. 107, ll. 6–7   24, 203

Morricone 1949–51   212

Nicephorus Gregoras
Byzantina historia
    4.9   197

Nigdelis 2006
    147–49   39
    206–11, no. 15   196

Orientis Graeci Inscriptiones Selectae
    5   1, 63, 225
    6   2, 51
    10   71
    11   76
    13   100
    20   159
    219   182
    222   124
    229   77, 93
    225   118
    335   114

Oracula Sibyllina
    3.343   64

Özhan and Tombul 2003   123

Papaconstantinou-Diamantourou 1990   39

Papazoglou 1997
    T1   112, 113

Pausanias
    1.6.3   32
    1.9.6   71
    1.9.7   18, 19, 20, 74, 150
    1.9.8   18, 20, 53
    1.10.2   71
    1.10.3–4   84
    1.10.5   53
    1.22.3   171
    2.5.6   196
    2.6.5   196
    2.7.1   67
    2.9.4   196
    4.31.10   45
    4.32.1   45
    5.1.5   178, 197
    5.8.11   3
    7.2.11   100
    7.3.4   9, 18, 19, 20, 74
    7.3.5   9, 19, 74, 89, 150
    7.5.1   76
    7.5.1–2   58
    7.5.1–3   76, 197
    7.15.2–3   89
    7.18.2–6   13
    7.19.1–9   215
    7.20.1–2   216
    7.21.6   216
    8.3.2   171
    8.7.7   35
    8.27.1   13
    8.27.2   173

8.27.3–6	173, 175	9.1			17
8.29.5	173	11.6–12			44
8.30.2–3	174	15			17
8.31.4	171	15.3–4			106
8.36.10	173	15.7–8			169
8.38.8	174	16			66
8.45.1	13	49.14–15			47
8.46.4	174	*Aratus*			
9.7.1	44	53.2–4			196
9.7.2	44, 51	*Demetrius*			
9.7.3	35, 71	5.2			48
9.15.6	45	7.2			51
9.16.3	171	8–14			56
10.3.2	17	10.2–4			205
10.32.15	123	13			223
		15–16			56
Peek 1934		19.1–2			56
56–57, nos. 14–15	128	21–22			56
		25.1–2			67
Persepolis Fortification Tablets		25.2			67
a 30	134	25.3			67
1285	134	28–30.1			70
1363, 1409, 1572	134	28–29			70
		30			70
Peschlow-Bindokat 1996a, 224	219	31.2			71
		32.1–2			71
Pherecydes		31.4			70
Fragmente der griechischen Historiker 3		33.1			71
F103b	152	35			72
		35.3			71
Pindar		36–37			71
Olympian		40			46, 71
6	8	41			71
7.73–75	170	43–44			72
Pythian		44–46			71
4.185–88	152	46–52			72
F273	152	53.3			191
		Eumenes			
Plassart 1921		8.2			32
18, col. 3, l. 75	40, 181, 195	13			33
col. 1D, l. 19	65	13–19			34
		Moralia			
Pliny		193d–e			128
Naturalis historia		530c–d			52
4.48	53	557b			22
5.108	85, 188	647a1			218
5.118	76, 197	812d			187
5.122	62	814b			44
		Phocion			
Plutarch		27–28			31
Alexander		33–37			34
2.7–8	162	34.4			33

INDEX LOCORUM

Pyrrhus
6.2–7.1	71
11.4–5	71
11–12.6	71

Plato
Leges
5.745b–e	145
8.828	205
8.848c–d	145
2.947d–e	206

Symposium
180C–185C	171

Theaetetus
scholion to l. 153C	181

Polyainos
Strategemata
4.2.12	16
5.19	72, 73
6.1.6	77
7.23.2	49
8.53.4	49
8.57	73

Polybius
4.33.7	8
5.77.5	76
5.94.1	89
5.108.2	44
5.111.2–3	60
12.5.7	168
16.24.9	100
18.2.4	11
18.4.5–6	53
18.45.5–6	77
18.51.7–8	8, 55
28.14.3	11
30.31.6–7	116

Pomponius Mela
2.24.4–6.	52

Porphyry
Fragmente der griechischen Historiker 260
F46	76

Prozessrechtliche Inschriften der griechischen Poleis: Arkadien
15A1, ll. 2–6	8

Ptolemaeus mathematicus
3.12.2	53
3.12.22	40

Pugliese Carratelli 1967, 437	52

[Scylax]
64	68
66	39
67	53
99	49

Rhodes and Osborne 2003
no. 14	150
l. 2	10
no. 15, ll. 8–9	180
no. 16	100
no. 62	189, 213

Rigsby 2007	62

Robert, J., and Robert
1976	93
175–87	97
1989	
63, col. 1, l. 23	187
66, col. 3.21	74
63–64, col. 1, ll. 23, 36	74

Robert, L.
1936a, 25	3
1939	163
1946a, 15–33	67
1948a, 16–28	82, 157
1946b, 512	76
1955, plate 35	52
1960, 204–13	76
1962, 62	76
1966a, 19–23	120
1967b	147

Robinson 1938, 55–56, no.8	195

Royal Correspondence in the Hellenistic Period
1	1, 2, 63
3	20, 58, 96
ll. 2–4	180
l. 7	21
l. 60	20
l. 79	8
ll. 43–65	101

INDEX LOCORUM 297

ll. 58–66	101	9.5.14	68		
ll. 72–94	102	9.5.15	18, 80, 81, 82, 152, 155		
ll. 86–87	102	9.5.22	80		
ll. 94–101	102	10.5.4	123		
l. 103	8	11.11.4	22		
4	20, 58,	12.2.10	135		
96		12.3.10	19, 70		
l. 2	8	12.4.7	58		
9 l. 3	209	12.8.14	135		
10–13	66, 112, 113	12.8.15	136		
14	115	12.8.15	89		
ll. 5–6	52	12.8.16	116		
18	66, 113	13.1.26	2, 59, 60, 64, 165		
19–20	114	13.1.26–42	59		
29	10, 20	13.1.27	60		
64, l. 2	209	13.1.28	61		
		13.1.31			
Sayar		13.1.32	65, 66, 169		
2000, 291	52	13.1.33	1, 2, 61, 63, 100		
2001, 103	52	13.1.36	3		
2007, 271	52	13.1.38	58		
		13.1.39	58, 61, 62		
Segre 1938, 190–207	117	13.1.40	168		
		13.1.44	167		
[Sklyax]		13.1.47	65		
96	1	13.1.47–8	63		
		13.1.51	3		
Staatsverträge des Altertums		13.1.52	1, 2, 8, 63, 64		
II.445	197	13.1.59	9, 15		
III 446	67	13.1.70	114		
III 453	74	13.4.15	85		
III.492	10, 77	14.1.8	49, 178, 197		
III.545, ll. 15–16	10	14.1.10	100		
		14.1.20	148, 221		
Strabo		14.1.21	72, 73		
7aF20	40	14.1.37	76		
7aF21	18, 39, 40, 195	14.1.42	116		
7aF23	40	14.1.46	85, 188		
7aF24	39, 41, 195	14.2.6	170		
7aF25	36	14.2.19	15, 213		
7aF27	36	14.2.29	135		
7aF34	16	15.2.9	52		
7aF35	35	17.1.8	32		
7aF36	40	17.1.43	22		
7aF52	53				
7aF56	53	Sokolowski			
8.3.2	8, 13	1969			
8.6.25	67, 196	no. 65	123		
9.3.7	156	no. 83	82, 157		
9.4.15	77	no. 84	82, 157		
9.5.8	69, 78	no. 85	157, 177		

Sokolowski 1969 *(continued)*
no. 96	189
no. 151A	189, 213
no. 156B	173
no. 169	189, 213
1970, 114–15	181

Sophocles
Oedipus Coloneus
scholion to l. 10	171

Soueref 1990	162

Stamatopoulou 2008	160

Steinepigramme aus dem griechischen Osten
1.23.1, l. 6	178, 197

Stephanus Byzantinus
s.v. Αἴνεια	196
s.v. Ἀντιόχεια	188
s.v. Δασκύλειον (4)	58
s.v. Ἔφεσος	74
s.v. Θεσσαλονίκη	39
s.v. Νίκαια	58, 198
s.v. Πλειστάρχεια	49

Stronach 1978, 159–61	133

Suda
s.v. Ἀφροδίτη Πάνδημος	171
s.v. Δημήτριος	52, 56
s.v. Θυριομάντεις	187

Supplementum Epigraphicum Graecum
II 579	97
XI 293	199
XI 1054	3
XII 373, l. 15	191
ll. 14–15	194
XII 1 761	212
XII 4.1 276	213
XII 4.1 280a–c	213
XIII 488	109
XIX 698	58, 95, 148
XIX 699	95
XXIII 415–32	128
XXV 687	157
XXIX 600	202
XXX 119	189
XXX 355, l. 3	201
XXX 511	168
XXXIII 872	49
XXXIV 664	107
XXXV 570–71	152
XXXVI 626	17, 107
XXXVII 558	195
XXXVIII 619	38
XXXVIII 620	38, 108
XXXIX 595–96	195
XL 542	40, 107
XLI 1003	21
XLIII 379	159
XLIII 382	160
XLIV 456	155
XLV 1556	209
XLVII 686	159
XLVII 893	106
XLVII 940	38, 111, 195, 202
XLVII 1563	48, 98, 150, 203, 205
XLVII 1739	170
XLVII 1745	117, 135
LII 1038, l. 13	10
LIII 530–31	152
LIII 1373	123
LVI 766	196
LVI 999	181
LVII 1150	159
LVII 1264	62
LIX 1612	159

Sylloge Inscriptionum Graecarum[3]
134	100
136	77
302	103, 106, 108, 109
322	48, 115
332	38, 108, 191, 195
330	59, 120
337	35, 45, 46, 63
340, ll. 38–42	212
344	58, 96, 97
l. 7	21
348	62
354	72
364	72, 94
368	73, 124, 181
380, ll. 1–2	195
546 B, ll. 14–15	10, 98, 150
581	189
647	93, 150
688	100
736	123

741	116	Tziafalias 1984	152
781	209		
1024	189	Vatin 1984	107
1025	189		
		Verkinderen 1987, 247–69	59

Tacitus
Historiae

4.83.1	34

Vokotopoulou

1986	107
1997	38, 111, 195

Textbook of Syrian Semitic Inscriptions
Vol. III, no. 28 … 118

Walser 2008

11–24	72
87–104	72

Theophratus
De causis plantarum

5.14.5–6	107

Wiemer 2001 … 10

Theopompos
Fragmente der griechischen Historiker 115

Wilhelm

F27	17
F53	77, 128
F110	16
F140	39

1890	218
1909, 150–51	83, 193, 194
1939	
no. 1	95
no. 2	95

M. Tod. *A Selection of Greek Historical Inscriptions*

113	100

Wörrle

1975	115, 170
1977, 43	52
2003a, 121–22	48, 98, 150, 203
ll. 40–42.	10

Thonemann

2009	103, 106, 108, 109
2013a	99

Xenophon
Anabasis

Thucydides

1.10.2	13
1.58.2	9, 14, 20, 39
1.61.2	38
1.104.3	124
2.29.6	38
3.2.3	14
3.50.1–3	14
3.3.1	8
3.18–49	58
3.33.2	58
4.52	62
4.76.3	89
4.98.2	146
8.101	62

1.11.7–8	169
1.2.7–8	136
1.2.14	103
6.1.7–8	159
7.8.9–23	118

Hellenica

3.1.6	118
3.1.13	65
3.1.16	62
3.1.18–20	58
3.2.15	65
3.4.12–13	58
4.1.15–16	118
4.4.2	
4.4.6	10, 22
5.2.7	13
5.4.56	128
7.3.4–12	196

Thür and Taeuber 1994

no.9	150

Symposium

8.9	171

Tituli Asiae Minoris

V 2 1187, ll. 6–10	21

[Xenophon]
Athenaion Politeia
   2.2–3   14

Vita S. Pauli Iunioris in Monte Latro 18   220

Vitrivius
De architectura
   3.2.6   178
   4.1.4   181

Voutiras 1996   162

Zenon
Fragmente der griechischen Historiker 523
   F1   170

Zonoras
Historiae
   12.26   39

www.ingramcontent.com/pod-product-compliance
Lightning Source LLC
Chambersburg PA
CBHW030523230426
43665CB00010B/743